Connections with the Spirit World

Richard Gene, Ph.D.

Second Revised Edition
Including a Preview/Index

Connections with the Spirit World

Richard Gene, Ph.D.

Second Revised Edition
Including a Preview/Index

Alive Book Publishing

Connections with the Spirit World
Second Revised Edition
Copyright © 2019 by Richard Gene, Ph.D.

All rights reserved.
No part of this book may be reproduced or transmitted in any form or by any means without written permission from the publisher and author.

Additional copies may be ordered from the publisher for educational, business, promotional or premium use.
For information, contact ALIVE Book Publishing at: alivebookpublishing.com, or call (925) 837-7303.

Book Design by Alex Johnson

ISBN 13
978-1-63132-067-5

ISBN 10
1-63132-067-X

Library of Congress Control Number: 2019937490

Library of Congress Cataloging-in-Publication Data is available upon request.

Second Revised Edition

Published in the United States of America by
ALIVE Book Publishing and ALIVE Publishing Group,
imprints of Advanced Publishing LLC
3200 A Danville Blvd., Suite 204, Alamo, California 94507
alivebookpublishing.com

PRINTED IN THE UNITED STATES OF AMERICA

10 9 8 7 6 5 4 3 2 1

Table of Contents

Preface 13

Acknowledgements 17

Chapter One: Introduction 19
- Preview 19
- A Sample of Other Topics the Model Addresses 24

Chapter Two: Evidence of Life after Life 29
- Background 29
- Four Strange Events 31
  1. Interrupted Telephone Conversation 31
  2. Oily Streak 33
  3. White Aura 34
  4. At the Cemetery 36

Chapter Three: The Spirit World 39
- Opening Comments 39
- The Knowledge Base 39
- The Place Where Knowledge Resides 47
- Things in Universes and Their Connections with Spiritual Entities 55
  5. Defining Spiritual Entities and the Spirits and Souls of Living and Nonliving Things 55
  6. Universes Will Come and Go, and Each will be Different and Unique 60
  7. The Spirit World Creates Everything, But It Is All Imperfect 64

- 8 Evolutionary Processes Continue Over the Lifetimes of Multiple Universes..................70
- 9 Evolutionary Processes Will Retrace in a New Universe..72
- 10 Changes Could Also be Directly Made by the Spirit World 77
- 11 The More Advanced the Living Thing the Higher Its Rate of Advancement..................79
- 12 A Given Connection of the First Kind Can be Active for One Spiritual Entity and not for Another 87
- 13 Growth and Advancements Progress in Spurts..................90
- 14 Advancements Are Made When We Are not Using All Our Time and Energy to Simply Survive..................94
- 15 All Views of the Spirit World Are Valid and Correct but Incomplete 95
- 16 We Are Currently Not Aware of Other Existing Universes, But We Could Be..................99

- Spirits and Souls of Living and Nonliving Things..................101
  - 17 A Spiritual Expression Is Everything a Living Thing Was..................105
  - 18 Reincarnation for Humans Occurs with the Spiritual Entity, not with The Spirit 109
  - 19 Cross-Learning Among Members of the Same Species ..110
  - 20 Spirits and Souls of Nonliving Things..................112
  - 21 Thoughts Are Among the Most Powerful Spiritual Entities 113
  - 22 Science and Spirituality Already Go Together..................116
  - 23 Spirits and Souls of Elemental Things 122
  - 24 Quantum Superposition and Entanglement..................125

- The Number of Spiritual Entities More than Doubles with Every New Piece of Knowledge Generated 131
- A Living Thing's Role in a Universe 131
- Interactions among Spirit, Soul, and Body..................133
- Oneness in the Spirit World 141
- Wisdom 150
- Everlasting Desire to Learn and to Create..................155
- Personal Gods..................156

- A Partnership Relationship 157
- Fulfilling the Purpose 159
- Closing Comments for Chapter Three 166

Chapter Four: Attributes of the Spirit World 169
- What's in this Chapter and Chapters to Follow 169
- A Piece of Knowledge is Neither Good nor Bad 171
- Examples of Effects of Incomplete, and Therefore not Totally Accurate, Models 172
- Forgiveness in the Spirit World 178
- Issues and Tug-of-Wars 180
    25 New Issues Constantly Form and Existing Ones Change 180
    26 Mathematics, a Possible Commonality among Universes 182
- Ego and Excessive Enhancement of Personal Survivability ..186
- Intentions and Attitudes 187
- Thoughts 189
- Other Planets, Competition, Win-Win, Win-Lose, and Application of Wisdom 191

Chapter Five: Oneness and Other Workings in the Spirit World 197
- Oneness Comes About in Living Things Two Ways 197
- Effects of Inherited Oneness and Developed Oneness..........199
    27 Instincts, Intuition, and Gradations of Reliance on Instincts for Survival 201
    28 A Cursory Look at Healing Signals (More in Chapter Seven) 204
    29 Telepathy 205
    30 Different Living Things Have Different Sets of Spiritual Senses 210
    31 Cross-Learning Among Member of the Same Species 211
    32 Identical Twins 212
    33 Clones 213
    34 Transplants 213

- 35 Oneness Between Living Things and Formerly Living Things 215
- Various Ways Spirits of Living Things Can be Configured...215
  - 36 Human Spirits and Souls 219
  - 37 Spirits and Souls of Plants, Fungi, Algae, Lichens, Mosses, Single Cells, Viruses, Prions 222
  - 38 Spirits and Souls of Species of Creatures Other Than Humans...224
  - 39 Regenerative Powers of Living Things 225
  - 40 Spirits and Souls of Single Cells that Make Up Living Things 226
  - 41 Spirits and Souls of Monarch Butterflies, Salmon, Cicadas, etc...229
  - 42 Spirits and Souls of Colonies of Insects 232
  - 43 Spirits and Souls of Identical Twins and Conjoined Twins..234
  - 44 Spirits and Souls of "In Between" Living Things...........235
  - 45 Kids Could Work High-tech Devices Better Than Their Parents 237
  - 46 Spirits and Souls of Living Things that Harm Their Hosts 238
- Every Spirit Is a Mixture of Types...241
  - 47 Evolution Happens..244
  - 48 Different Roles Happen 248
  - 49 Tug-of-Wars Among Spirit Types 249
  - 50 Feeling More Alive..251
  - 51 Is Using A Jury the Best Way to Reach a Verdict?...........252
  - 52 Multiple Personalities 253
- Elemental Things Such a Electrons..255
- Handholds and Mentors 256
- Wisdom Is a Dynamic Thing that Pertains to the Future 257
- Reference 260

Chapter Six: Spiritual Senses and Consciousness 261
- No Limit to the Number of Spiritual Senses 261
- Various Natures of Consciousness 263

- Senses and Consciousness of Nonliving Things 265
- Leaning Takes Place in Our Spirit, not in Our Brain 268
- Body Intelligence and Body Consciousness........................274
- The Size of the Spirit and the Size of the Brain are not Proportional to Each Other 275
- Visitation to and/or from Other Universes.........................280
- Perceptions of Advancement, Improvement and Being Gifted 282
- Rhythms and Beauty 283

Chapter Seven: Spirit World and Physical World Interactions 285

- Supply vs. Demand for Spiritual Entities Capable of Serving as Spirits...285
- What is it Like in the Spirit World? Is it Crowded? 288
- Personal Gods in the Spirit World.....................................290
- Thoughts from the Spirit World..292
- Sleep, Dreams, Healing, Etc...298
  53 Why We Sleep and Dream, and Why Dreams are Surrealistic 298
  54 Do All Living things on Earth Need Sleep?...................308
  55 Why Our Brain Is Active During Sleep, but the Frontal Cortex Is Not..309
  56 Finding Things in, and Getting Messages from, the Spirit World during Sleep...313
  57 What are Near-Death Experiences? 316
  58 Why Short Term Memory Declines with Age................319
- Effect of Prayers and Wishes 322
- Stepping Out of Your Body and into Another Body 324
- Immune Systems, Issues, Intelligence, and Knowledge........325
  59 How the Spirit World Came Into Being........................329
  60 Implications of How the Spirit World Came Into Being.337
- Immune-System Discussion Continues..............................342
  Creation of New Features for Living Things and the "Use It or Lose It" Phenomenon..345
- Reincarnation 347

Chapter Eight: Extrasensory Effects..351
- Extrasensory Abilities..351
- Ghosts..354
- Out-of-Body Experiences 362
- Auras 365
- Remote Viewing 367
- Telepathy 368
- Telepathy and Brain Disabilities..370
- Time Travel Back to the Past 371
- Projections into Possible Futures...372
- Space Travel..374
- Travel to Other Universes 374
- Getting More in Touch with the Spirit World's Restoring and Healing Powers 375
- The Healing Powers of Statues and Other Physical Things ..380
- Karma 382
- Do We Formulate Models or Do Models Formulate Us, or Is It Both?..384

Chapter Nine: The Dominant Basis for How We Carry Out Our Lives 387
- Advancement and Increasing Complexity in the Spirit World...387
- The Dominant Basis for How We Carry Out Our Lives........389
- Leaders Do Not Exist in the Spirit World, But Humans on Earth Need Leaders...391
- Tapping Into the Oneness that Pervades the Spirit World 393
- Evolution Is a Part of Universes to Enable Them to Fulfills Their Purposes..394
- We Are Responsible for How Our Species Is Evolving.........404
- Can We Change Our Dominant Basis to "Empathy and Compassion for One Another?"..406
- A Disconnection Between the Intended and the Actual........410
- Issues Produced by the Spirit World while Caring About Every Living Thing It Creates..417
- Broadening Our View of the Spirit World 421
- We are Here for Two Purposes but are Doing Mostly the Less

- Important One 424
- Caring for Ourselves 432
  - 61 Be Inspired Instead of Judgmental 433
  - 62 Having Some Ups and Downs Could be More Fulfilling Than Not Having Any 436
- Be Ready to Give Care and to Receive Care 437

Chapter Ten: Possible Expectations Regarding Models 439

- Creativity is One of the Most Important Things We can Instill in Children 439
- Why Finding Our Personal Spiritual Model Could Make Us a Better Person 442
- Possible Way to Sense Spiritual Signals Indicating Life Exists after Life 443
- The Physical Part of Life Eventually Degrades, But the Spiritual Part Does Not 445
- Every Model We Use in Our Physical World Is a Spiritual Model of Some Kind 447
- The Level of Our Advancement Is Reflected in Our Models .. 451
- The Spiritual Part of Models Might Help Explain Some Unexplained Things 452
- Our Personal Spiritual Search Does Not Actually End 456
- The Mess We Made on Earth Got Us Sort of Trapped. But We Don't Have to Stay Trapped 457
- We Are Capable of Being More in Touch with Our Spiritual Senses 458
- Your Approach in Your Career Might be Best for Finding Your Personal Spiritual Model 460
- A Possible Role of Religions in a Personal Spiritual Search .. 461
- Old People, Young People; Being Interested vs. Being Excited 462
- Old People, Young People; Extrapolating the Past to the Present and Future 470
- Old People, Young People; A Personal Sketch 472
- Twenty Seven Years 477

Preview/Index 479

About the Author 501

The Spiritual Model Formulated in This Book Could Describe the Inner Workings of the Spirit World

Spirituality is revisited in a manner never done before. A measure of engineering logic is used instead of relying strictly on faith, which is the case for spiritual models that exist up to now. The new spiritual model describes the inner workings of the spirit world, defines our spirit and our soul, and describes the role of our spirit and soul in enabling our physical body to exist in our physical world. Thus, it shows how we are carrying out our lives simultaneously in the spirit world and our physical world. For example, our spirit resides in the spirit world while our body resides in our physical world. We form our thoughts and decisions in the spirit world, and we put them into action in our physical world. The model can plausibly spiritually explain common everyday observations and experiences. Examples are; why we need sleep, why dreams tend to be surrealistic, why evolution is spiritual first and physical second, how missing links can happen, how identical twins can communicate telepathically, how pets could understand their owners' thoughts telepathically, how some individuals can see and read auras, why our universe was brought into being, and how quantum superposition and entanglement can happen. Many other examples are also presented. Such extensive correlation with reality means the model is valid to a large degree. No other spiritual model that exists up to now could do similarly, and do it in the technical sense this model could. Thus, the model offers a new and very different perspective regarding spirituality. Ultimately, the model is capable of indicating why we are here and the purposes we are to fulfill.

Preface

This second edition of this book contains a **Preview/Index** at the end of the book. Feedback from readers of the first edition indicates this book is somewhat difficult to read, because it is dense with unconventional notions and concepts that require abstract thinking to follow. The **Preview/Index** was composed to help clarify these notions and concepts and to also serve as the Index. In addition, it provides a good summary of what is in the book. Therefore, a reader might consider taking a look at the **Preview/Index** to get a "preview" before reading this book.

My spiritual search began in my twenties as a casual search for evidence of life after life. Evidence came forth in my fifties. My search then turned serious, and I eventually found my personal spiritual model. I am a mechanical/civil engineer, so I began with an engineering-like notion that says "something somewhere somehow knows how to enable our universe and everything in it to exist." This grew over the next twenty-seven years. Along the way, my personal spiritual model emerged and grew, and continues to grow. The continued growth is not surprising since spirituality touches everything, and no model formulated by a human could ever be complete enough to capture all of what spirituality is. Therefore, more always exists for a model to grow and capture.

Chapter Two describes how evidence emerged to clearly indicate life exists after life. Being an engineer and used to figuring out how things work, I just had to figure out how life and life after life interrelate. Furthermore, since spirituality touches everything, I knew any spiritual model found would have to be one with the potential to touch everything.

As it turns out, the model I found certainly seems to have that potential. It correlates with all the common, everyday happenings I've been through. Therefore, it feels like a natural part of life, as a spiritual model should feel, in my opinion. For example, it explains why we sleep, why dreams tend to be surrealistic, how our body knows how to heal, how our instincts and intuition work, how we have a natural partnership with our creator and why we need to make it mutually beneficial for our creator and ourselves, and so on. Such attributes enable me to naturally remain tuned into the model and to sense its spiritual guidance every moment of every day. Its guidance is consistently gentle, caring, non-judgmental, undemanding, and very comfortable. It has helped me be a better person. I used to feel spiritual only at funerals, weddings, and various special religious events. Now I feel spiritual all the time, and it feels great.

Each individual is different and unique and has different and unique spiritual needs. This could explain why approximately 50,000 denominations of Christianity exist in the world, according to Brent Walters, the host of the "God Talk" radio program that up to January 2015 could be heard on the San Francisco station KGO Sunday mornings. About 22,000 are in the United States. Other religions also have large numbers of denominations. For example, Buddhism has about 2,000, according to a Buddhist friend. Such diversity indicates people in general are searching for their personal spiritual models and that, in general, each person needs something different from any of the basic models of the various religions.

My model contains unconventional concepts. It does not reject any religion and, in a sense, it is inclusive of all regions, traditions, customs, etc. Conventional spiritual concepts don't work for me, but various unconventional ones do, as described in this book. The reason for this book is not to convince others to accept my model as their own but to show by example how, if conventional concepts don't work, unconventional ones might. Because everyone is different and unique, with different and unique spiritual needs and spiritual models, each person needs to do his or her own personal spiritual search. For some, following a religion may work, as indicated in Chapter Ten. For others, starting from scratch on their own may work better, as it did for me.

This book also explains why my search took so long. If your search is progressing slowly or running into roadblocks, don't be discouraged. I found that going slowly and resolving roadblocks as they came up helped make my model better and more complete. It is worth the effort to stick with it.

Don't expect to find a model that will answer every possible question. We humans cannot formulate complete models. Our life contains models of all kinds and none are complete. But altogether they form a crazy-quilt patchwork that manages to cover things well enough to enable us to carry out our lives the way we do.

I concluded that there are no incorrect models, only incomplete ones, as explained in this book. Thus, don't declare models incorrect simply because they don't work for you. They work for somebody and that is why they exist. It's just that they don't cover parts of life important to you personally. By analogy, engineering models are unlikely to be of use to accountants because they don't cover the parts of life important to accountants. They are not incorrect, only incomplete.

Acknowledgements

My deepest love and acknowledgement are for my deceased parents who, after passing away, found a way to provide evidence of life after life. It is a gift more precious than anything physical. I am extremely grateful for the love, warmth, empathy, and compassion my sister Mabel, her late husband Bob, my brother Walter, his wife Eleanor, my sister Pauline, and her husband Bob have given me and sustained me. This similarly goes for my son Michael, daughter Catherine, and her husband Jon. My dearest love goes to my deceased wife Mae for her patience and support throughout my spiritual search. Even now her spiritual presence is evident and continues to be with me and to help me.

The many stimulating discussions with the Rev. Tommy E. Smith, Jr. during the early days of my search were inspiring and fascinating as both of us were searching. This was before my model was formulated. Health issues disrupted our contacts, but I look forward to reestablishing contact after this book is published.

My most special thanks go to my very special friend Rachel Burke whose ability to see auras enabled me to realize the meaning of the most significant of the four events described in Chapter Two. This then led me to understand the meanings of the other three events and to ultimately know that life exists after life. She considers her ability to see auras as a gift to be used to help others, and she does that most sincerely.

Michael, Catherine, and Jon enable me to better understand the issues and challenges of their generation and their generation's view of life. Michael is inspiring with his warm, thoughtful, and caring ways, and with his unconventional approach to life that works so well for him. Catherine and Jon make a wonderful and loving team as both are able, efficient, and effective in whatever they do.

Thanks to my friend Eldred Dance for giving me his old computer after he bought a new one. My 15 year old computer gave out, and for a while I thought my manuscript I worked on for 27 years was irretrievable since floppy disks are not compatible with today's computers. And, no one in any computer store seemed sure of being able to retrieve my manuscript. Eldred's computer was not as obsolete as mine, and I was able to find a way to have it serve as a bridge between floppy disks and flash drives and thus retrieve my manuscript.

I very much value the friendship of R. Ken Coit for his inspiring and caring approach to life. He has helped many individuals in many ways through the years, and he kept me informed on latest developments regarding bladder cancer treatment.

The fine editing by DeAnne Musolf and Eric Johnson is very much appreciated, especially for how they pointed out where further clarification and/or examples were needed and how they reworded here and there to help make the book easier to read.

And compliments go to Alex Johnson for his great job designing the book jacket. He is a talented and creative college student and the lead graphic designer at ALIVE Book Publishing.

Chapter One
Introduction

Preview

A group of friends, family members, and I attended church together as children. The church was good, especially for the very young. The pastor was dedicated, sincere, and charismatic. He and his wife lived very modestly and followed what they preached. He maintained two decommissioned military buses to transport parishioners to and from church, mostly the very young. Every Sunday after the main service, the congregation would seperate into study groups, one for adults, one for youth and one for children, all run by trained members. The church also held Wednesday evening sessions for those interested.

I started attending when I was a kid and found the church experience enjoyable, inspiring, and enriching. Many young members would leave when they reached high school age. The demands of school and for some, including me, part-time jobs left little time for church. Also, while the teachings connected well with the very young, they didn't necessarily connect as well with high school students. For example, we were not to watch movies, attend dances, wear lipstick in the case of girls, or do anything else considered worldly. Such restrictions tend to be at odds with typical teenage experiences.

As I approached my teens, I also reassessed other aspects of the teachings as well. For instance, if we committed a sin, we would go to hell upon death and eternally burn. However, while alive we could ask the

Lord to forgive our sins, and we would then go to heaven after we die. But then I figured out we would need to ask for forgiveness repeatedly since we are bound to sin repeatedly. After all, even a tiny lie is a sin, according to the teachings. A friend might ask "How do you like my new 'something'?" I might say, "It's great," even if I thought otherwise. Hence, I lied and therefore sinned. As a child, I worried about unknowingly sinning. I would pray each night before going to bed to ask the Lord to forgive whatever sin I might have committed that day. My brother, who is five years older, sometimes caught me doing this and laughed. I felt a bit silly, but I wanted to be sure I was safe from hell in case I died during the night. Also I wanted to start the next day safe, at least until I unwittingly sinned. I discovered many years later that a sister and some of my friends who attended the same church did the same thing each night when they were children.

I was a somewhat mischievous kid, so I asked the pastor some tricky questions. I asked what if we sin all our lives but ask the Lord for forgiveness just before we die. Would we go to heaven? He answered "yes." I then ask, what if we're so sick or injured we can't speak and therefore can't ask, then what? In essence, his reply was "Then you're sunk." I thought to myself, "Well, that's enough of that."

I reassessed more of the teachings and concluded something was missing. I eventually moved on. But I fondly acknowledged that the teachings had much that was good and that the fellowship among the members was warm and nurturing. The church experience definitely had a positive effect on me and on my eventual personal spiritual search.

I started posing other questions to myself, such as "Does life really exists after life?" The answer "yes" came forth in my fifties shortly after my mother passed away, three years after my father died. The evidence was in the form of the four events presented in Chapter Two.

Another question I asked myself regarding the church's teachings was if the creator created everything, then it must have created all the bad things as well as the good things. But why would the creator create bad things, such as diseases, floods, poison oak, earthquakes, mosquitoes, fleas, cancers, and so on? If the creator is God and God is said to love everybody, does God love such things as mosquitoes and fleas too? Do only people go to heaven or hell? Where do mosquitoes and fleas go after they die? How about poisonous spiders, poisonous snakes, scorpions, etc.? What if such things end up in heaven? Would I want to be there also? I guess they would make better company than eternal fire. And what about hell? Why would a God who is supposed to love everybody want to create a place like hell in which to put individuals who failed to have their sins forgiven? This didn't sound very loving to me. These were just some of my early questions.

As the result of such questions and a lack of satisfactory answers I decided to do my personal spiritual search essentially starting from scratch by putting aside to some degree the concepts of God, heaven, hell, etc. Therefore, in formulating my personal spiritual model, I chose not to say the creator is God. Each person is different and unique and therefore has a different and unique perception of God, even if the differences might be small. Hence, every person has a different and unique personal God. Then the question is: Which personal God did the creating? Or did they all share in the process? If so, then was our universe created by committee? Could this be why international relationships and various other conditions on Earth are such a mess? To avoid such complications, my personal spiritual model does not have the creator as God, although it does say personal Gods are real and exist.

By not saying the creator is God, I dropped all conventional notions I had about God as I worked on my model. Otherwise I might not have explored the various unconventional notions and concepts that eventually became a part of the model. Indeed, I might not have found my personal spiritual model at all if I kept the creator as God.

However, we will see in Chapter Three that as the model develops it becomes inclusive of all religions and all concepts of God. Thus, the model is not at odds with these, but is in a sense broader than any religion or concept of God.

I speculated on the nature of a creator who creates both good and bad things. The creator might not know ahead of time what would become good or bad. Or, it might simply create everything it could, regardless of outcome. This could explain why we have such a diversity of living things on Earth. Or, everything it creates could naturally possess both good and bad and thus nothing is purely good or purely bad. This seems to be the case for everything on Earth. Whatever the nature of the creator, there must be a reason why things on Earth are the way they are. For me to consider my search successful, such questions needed to be answered, and the answers needed to be consistent with common, everyday observations and happenings.

As it turns out, my model indicates all three possibilities are true. According to the model, the creator creates everything it could at any given point in time with the ingredients it has at that point in time. New ingredients are constantly being generated and added to the mix, and the creator has a lot of control over the kinds of new ingredients being generated, according to the model. Thus, the creator can determine what to create by controlling the ingredients. The new ingredients generated at any given point in time are the ones necessary to keep the creator healthy and viable at that moment. All this might sound mundane right now, like preparing food in the kitchen, but as the presentation unfolds, beginning in Chapter Three, it will become more interesting, namely because we humans play a large part in generating the ingredients, as so do other living things in our universe. Even nonliving things have a role.

In the model, the creator is a forever growing, forever changing spiritual entity referred to as the spirit world. Calling it the spirit world is reasonable. Besides creating everything, it is also the place where all smaller spiritual entities reside. We will also find that it creates more than just our universe and everything in it.

The model indicates we all participate positively and negatively in making the spirit world what it is through our intentions, choices, and actions. In this way, the spirit world is a vulnerable spiritual entity whose continued viability is partly in our hands. The existence of our physical world and everything in it depends on the spirit world remaining viable. Thus, the existence of our physical world and everything in it is partly in our hands as well. This means we need to give care to the spirit world as well as receive care from it. Each of us has a natural partnership with the spirit world, as explained as the presentation continues. According to the model, we are constantly receiving care from the spirit world whether or not we are aware of it. For example, the spirit world is caring for us every moment through our amazing immune system. How this comes about spiritually is also explained as the presentation continues.

According to the model, all personal Gods reside in the spirit world. We need to give care to our personal God as well as receive care from it. This is essentially the same thing as giving care to, as well as receiving care from, the spirit world, because in most cases our personal God is essentially our personal perception of the spirit world. Because each individual is different and unique, each personal God is a different and unique and is thus a different and unique part of the spirit world.

The model explains how the partner relationship forms naturally and is meant to be for the mutual benefit of the spirit world and us. If we prefer, the partnership can be perceived as between our personal God and us. Either way, it is the same idea. The model thus indicates one of our purposes for being here is to make the partnership as mutually beneficial as possible for the spirit world and for us.

As the presentation continues, we will see that the spirit world is naturally gentle, kind, caring, nonjudgmental, compassionate, empathic, and loving. It shouldn't be difficult for us to make the partnership we have with the spirit world mutually beneficial. But many of us don't realize we have this natural partnership and thus don't consciously do anything with it or for it. Consequently, we, as a whole, make a mess of things here on Earth.

The model indicates we are simultaneously carrying out our lives in the spirit world and in our physical world. Our physical body resides in our physical world and we have a spirit that resides in the spirit world. We have a soul that connects our body with our spirit and it resides partly in our physical world and partly in the spirit world while we are alive.

A lot of us think our life in our physical world is all that our life is. But our spirit knows there is more to life because it is a living thing and is aware of the existence of both our physical world and the spirit world. This may be why a lot of us are searching for our spirituality; i.e., to find out what it is that we could feel but have not been able to determine.

All this might seem abstract right now, but as the presentation unfolds it will become clearer. This brief preview sets the stage for more unconventional notions and concepts to come, especially starting with Chapter Three. I am a mechanical/civil engineer, therefore, the spiritual model likely to work best for me would be one based on engineering-like reasoning instead of one that mostly relies on faith for its acceptance. The model is definitely not a religious model, but it does not exclude any religion either.

A Sample of Other Topics the Model Addresses

According to the model, spiritual tug-of-wars are constantly and naturally being formed in the spirit world. Keeping them all reasonably balanced is vital to the viability of the spirit world, as we will see as the presentation continues. The physical counterparts of many of these spiritual tug-of-wars are nothing new in our physical world, and the need to keep them in reasonable balance is also nothing new in our physical world. For example, natural tug-of-wars go on in our bodies to keep our bodily systems functioning in a balanced manner, ecosystems work in a similar way, as do businesses, our economy, international relationships, family relationships and finances, factories, cars, and so on. Tug-of-wars being a natural part of the spirit world should not be a surprise since everything that exists in our physical world has its spiritual counterpart there. We have a role in keeping tug-of-wars in our physical world balanced; we also have a role in keeping tug-of-wars in the spirit world balanced, and how this works is discussed in the book.

The model also plausibly answers questions associated with common, everyday observations and happenings. For example, why we sleep, why we dream, how evolution works spiritually, how prayers and wishes work spiritually, etc. It also explains how a stem cell in our body knows what kind of tissue or bone it is to become, how we get our thoughts, how we find solutions to problems, and why we have intuition and instincts. Also explained are what comprises the spirit and soul of an individual, how oneness comes about among living things, and how oneness is pervasive throughout the spirit world and thus also pervasive throughout our physical world. It explains how real-life extrasensory abilities are possible, such as the ability to do telepathic communication and the ability to see auras.

These are among the many things the model, based on a lot of unconventional notions and concepts, is able to explain in an engineering-like, reasoning manner. If you happen to find yourself immediately rejecting some of these notions and concepts, stick with them for a while as you read on to see what they might bring forth. But keep in mind that this book is not to convince anyone to accept the model as his or her own but is to show by example that unconventional thinking might be able to accomplish what conventional thinking has been unable to for some individuals.

I did not start out thinking I would formulate a model that could provide plausible explanations for any of the topics mentioned, as well as other topics. I figured that once I found a reasonable description of how life and life after life interrelates, my spiritual search would be over. To my surprise, my model went much further. I started the formulation process with the simple notion that something somewhere somehow knows how to enable our universe and everything in it to exist. This notion grew and led me to an amazing place filled with wonders that are the spiritual counterparts of things commonplace in our physical world.

As discussed in the Preface, no model formulated by humans could be totally complete or absolutely accurate. This includes my personal spiritual model. Likewise, there are no incorrect models that are reasonably formulated, only incomplete ones. Every reasonable formulated model has some degree of correctness, thus some degree of usefulness. The more complete the model, the more accurate it will be and the more useful, depending on the requirements of the application. Another conclusion discussed in the Preface is that if everything that exists is created by the spirit world, then everything that exists is a part of spirituality. This means every model in every discipline is essentially a spiritual model, each capturing a different part of spirituality.

The Preface also talked about how our lives are filled with countless models of all kinds and how these models form a crazy-quilt patchwork that covers spirituality well enough to enable us to carry out our lives as we do. But our models so far have not captured the parts of spirituality that could have helped us avoid making the mess we've made on Earth. Wars and other kinds of conflicts are constant. Greed and corruption are commonplace. People in various places at various times are suppressed, mistreated, or starved, etc. The model presented in this book suggests that the ways we could clean up this mess are likely found in the spirit world rather in our physical world, and that a reason we have done little to clean up the mess is because we haven't been in tune enough with the spirit world to find the ways.

Scientists, including the late Albert Einstein, have been searching for the "model of everything." My personal spiritual model indicates if the model of everything as envisioned by scientists were to be found it would cover at best only our physical universe. It is unlikely to cover the entire spirit world or any other universe besides ours. My model indicates the spirit world has a need to periodically create new and difference universes, each to serve a new and different purpose. Also, according to my model, all universes have finite lifetimes so that some or all of the ones that came before ours might be gone by now. Those that may still exist are likely to be invisible to us because our major senses are unlikely to perceive their presence. As living things, they are bound to possess major senses different from ours, tuned into the attributes of their own universe. Thus, those living things are unlikely to sense our presence either.

My model indicates that evolution does not begin and end with our universe; it spans past and present universes. This is why Earth contains such a diversity of living things. Most or all of them evolved before our universe was created. This might also explain how we humans were able to emerge on Earth so quickly that we are perceived as being suddenly created on Earth. This might also explain how we humans are so much more advanced compared with other living things on Earth; i.e., our evolution might have spanned over the lifetimes of many more past universes than other living things have. There are likely other living things as intelligent, or more intelligent, than we are, that are suitable for other universes but not ours. Therefore, in the spirit world we humans would not be the only ones of very high intelligence.

In my search, I found that letting go of my ego and the desire to excessively enhance personal survivability was very helpful in finding my personal spiritual model. My letting go was my release from self-confinement. I became much more able to sense spiritual things, and this was how the model was able to lead me to an amazing place filled with wonders.

Excessive pursuit of enhanced personal survivability means the pursuit of things far beyond what is necessary for survival. Enhanced personal survivability is like a safety margin that is normal and reasonable for anyone to want to have, but an excessive pursuit of it can lead to greed and lack of empathy and compassion for others. Examples of things that can be pursued excessively include wealth, status, life style, career, possessions, control over people and events, etc.

Letting go of ego also enabled me to consider unconventional notions I otherwise might have rejected. For example, the model indicates our consciousness and intelligence do not reside in our brain but instead reside in our spirit in the spirit world. If I held onto my ego, I would have declared the notion nonsense, and that would have blocked further progress in my spiritual search. But accepting this and other unconventional notions enabled me to find plausible explanations for a lot of common, everyday observations and happenings. Could this mean some unconventional notions are more correct than some conventional ones in some situations? Could this mean our allowing some of our conventional notions to confine us would partly explain why we behave in ways that contribute to making the mess?

My model turns out to be gentle, nonjudgmental, and natural feeling. Because it provides plausible explanations for so many common, everyday observations and happenings, it feels like a natural part of life. Consequently, its spiritual guidance is easy to stay tuned into every moment. This helps to make me a better person. This is how I wanted my personal spiritual model to be and how I think personal spiritual models in general should be.

Each individual is different and unique and has different and unique spiritual needs. Thus, each individual needs a different and unique personal spiritual model. This means each individual's spiritual search will be different and unique as well. Therefore, while my search as described in this book works for me, but it might not work as well for anyone else, at least not in its exact form.

Some individuals might be having difficulty with their spiritual search, because they have been strictly told what they must do by somebody or something. I left the church I attended as a child because its teachings were too strict, leaving little room for personal spiritual needs outside the church's guidelines.

Chapter Three is where the fundamentals of model are presented. Some might find the chapter somewhat dry, but once you get into further chapters, you are likely to find them much more interesting. Various topics such as evolution, wisdom, reincarnation, etc. are discussed in multiple chapters. Each chapter provides a different view of such topics in accordance with the main subject of the chapter.

Chapter Two
Evidence of Life after Life

Background

Shortly after our mother passed away, following our father's passing three years earlier, strange events started happening as witnessed by my siblings, others, and me. Our parents left two matters they wanted to settle before their time ran out but couldn't. My oldest sister did the hard work of handling their estate and with some help from the rest of us completed the two unfinished tasks. It became clear to me afterwards that the strange events were brought about by the spirits of our deceased parents, and were intended to help us complete the tasks. At the same time, the events indicated life exists after life. Because the events are personal, in this book I cover only the four I had a part in experiencing. In all four events, someone besides me observed what happened or received the messages. This ruled out the possibility the events were something I imagined in my emotional state.

Our parents wanted their house to remain in the family but were unable to work it out before they died. At the time, all of us already owned homes, and some of us lived in other cities. The other unfinished task was deciding what to do about their beloved 1972 Cadillac, our father's golden anniversary gift to our mother. Looking back at the events, they were so well-timed and so relevant to the two tasks that it is hard not to conclude they were the work of the spirits of our parents.

I will point out that while four of us five children attended college and we are all financially secure now, the family was not always financially secure. In our early days, the seven of us commonly shared two eggs whipped up and extended with water and then steamed, accompanied by some vegetables and some other carbohydrate for dinner. And that was before there was welfare, food stamps, and food banks. Looking back, it was difficult, but the experience made our spirits more complete, for it is not uncommon even now for people to be in such conditions, or even worse. It gives us a better feel for how it is for them. It increases our empathy and compassion for others, and we didn't grow up with a sense of entitlement. The two eldest, especially my oldest sister, carried burdens that I, the youngest, did not carry. Her, my brother's and our parents' spirits would include knowledge of a kind mine would never have. But I could add to my spirit by honoring the four of them and be inspired by them.

Because our parents started out with essentially nothing, it is understandable one of their main goals was to get themselves financially secure and to have their children become financially secure as well. I often hear members of their generation say "you couldn't make too much money," which sounds to me disturbingly like saying "make money for the sake of making money." Today, our times and situation are different; that is, ours are more global. Our economy and businesses are more global. Consequently, our politics are not simply national anymore. Right now the nation's wealth is concentrating increasingly at the top while the middle class is shrinking and the number of poor people is on the rise. But a healthy democracy needs a large and healthy middle class to support it. Meanwhile, Congress is dysfunctional; getting re-elected seems a primary focus of many members. I had often wondered what would happen when some values of the Baby Boom generation increasingly effect how we run our government and businesses. The idea of making money for the sake of making money seems to continue to be a factor in creating the described unhealthy economic condition.

For our lives to be more in sync with the needs of our times, in the short run we need to look beyond our personal needs and wants and be more aware of those who need help and what the nation as a whole needs to remain healthy. In the long run, we need to become more knowledgeable about all the factors that have gone into making a mess in our nation and in the world in order to increase our effectiveness in doing something about it. In my mind, the idea of making money for the sake of making money is not in sync with the needs of our times and is not a pursuit that benefits our nation and the world in the long run. Making money is fine, but it needs to be for the sake of something more significant than simply making money.

Four Strange Events:

1. Interrupted Telephone Conversation

This subsection presents the first strange event. Virtually every family member took part in creating our parents' house. My oldest sister handled negotiations, contracts, accounting, and problems. My older brother designed and built the garage cabinets, finished the garage interior walls, built the furnace enclosure, designed and installed the sprinkler systems, designed the fishpond stone arrangement, tiled the basement floor, and added attic insulation. Our mother, the youngest of my sisters, and I worked out the site layout, floor plan, cabinetry, built-in desk, built-in dining room and family room cabinets, various architectural features, and landscaping design. I designed numerous brick flowerbeds, wavy shaped garden pathway circuit, carport, kitchen cook-top, basement staircase open enclosure, fireplace and side cabinets, covered patio with fishpond, and a brick bench.

The house was thus imprinted with the family's love and devotion for our parents, and our parents therefore wanted to keep the house in the family. After they passed away, my oldest sister handled their estate with great competence and wisdom. It took a year to complete as legal processes move slowly. Meanwhile, we all pitched in to maintain the house and grounds during that time. We felt as if, at any moment, we would find one or both of our parents somewhere in the house. While working in the garden, we felt as if one, or both, would soon come out of the house to join us as they usually would when they were alive. But we knew they would not anymore, no matter how much we longed for them to do so. We kept everything in place, neat, clean, and manicured. Our parents' essence and creations continued to surround us and we could feel their warmth still, now gently, silently, and preciously. We wanted to hold on to this as long as we could, knowing it would all evaporate once we let go of the house, and then only memories would remain.

For that entire year, we tried to figure out how to keep the house in the family but could not. Finally, we put it on the market. Soon afterwards, a retired couple came to look at it and told my oldest sister they liked it. Their lifestyle matched that of our parents'. They enjoyed gardening, their tastes matched our parents', the floor plan and site layout would work well for them, and they even liked the interior and exterior colors. They commented that if they were to buy the house, they could move in with very few changes. My sister was not going to tell us about the couple, until they showed further interest.

The first strange event took place that evening. My daughter was on the telephone, as teenagers often were in the 1980s before the advent of Facebook, Twitter, and other social media. The operator cut in to say a person named Bob was trying to get through with an urgent message. Two of my sisters have husbands named Bob. My daughter hung up and I called both sisters and found neither husband had been trying to reach us. But while on the telephone with my oldest sister, she decided to tell me about the couple because she knew I had a strong attachment to the house since I had designed a lot of its special features.

Or maybe our parents wanted all of us to know right away that they would be pleased if the couple bought the house. It's also possible our parents steered the couple to the house in the first place.

The next morning, the strange event continued. I am usually the first to be up; I would go through the family room, out the door leading to the garage, through the garage and onto the driveway to pick up the newspaper, and then retrace my steps back into the house. My son's bedroom shared a wall with the garage, and he would be aware of my actions each morning. Later that morning, he asked why I went out to retrieve the newspaper twice that morning. But I did it only once. What did he hear to make him think I did it twice?

The answer came when the third strange event happened a few weeks later as discussed in the subsection entitled "**3. White Aura**" presented two subsections later. This particular event convinced me life exists after life as explained in that subsection. After the third event occurred, in retrospect I concluded our parents had been in our house in order to initiate the operator's intrusion into my daughter's telephone conversation, which led to my oldest sister telling me and then the rest of the family about the couple. Our parents had then waited until morning before leaving our house so that they could do so in a way that wouldn't frighten us but would nevertheless make it clear they had been there.

A few weeks later, the couple bought the house, and they made very few changes upon moving in. The architectural features, landscaping design, colors, etc. all remain the same even to this day. Looking at the house now, more than two decades later, you could not tell that our parents no longer live there. We are happy to know our parents are bound to be pleased their house continues to be loved and well cared for.

2.   **Oily Streak**

This subsection describes the second strange event. The automatic garage door opener in our parents' garage would periodically drip oil onto the right rear fender of the Cadillac and leave a vertical oily streak. On one of my visits when our mother was still living, I saw such a streak and wiped it off.

After our mother passed away, the car remained in the garage an entire year while her estate was being settled. No one was interested in the car, not even me at the time. It's huge, gets poor gas mileage, is difficult to parallel park, wouldn't fit in some garages, is impractical for everyday use, and was incompatible with most young folks' lifestyle. My oldest sister was ready to put it on the market, but after thinking about it, I decided that since both of my cars were over ten years old, had about 140,000 miles on them, and our two children were starting to drive, we could use another car. I decided to take the car. It was fifteen years old, had only 28,000 miles, and was in showroom condition, inside and out. However, the handling and ride were mushy and sloppy. Driving the car was like driving a big marshmallow. Finally, I diagnosed the problem: all the rubber bushings and shock absorbers had deteriorated due to lack of use. I made repairs, then the car drove just fine, but for a while I thought, boy, I knew Cadillac made soft riding cars, but this was ridiculous.

It didn't take long for me to fall in love with the car. Nothing compares with the feeling you get driving a very old, showroom condition, and beautifully designed Cadillac with a long hood, long rear deck, and long rear overhang. And it is an expression of my parents' love and devotion for each other. I would often notice other drivers slowing down and hanging back a while before passing. Today, it is over four decades old and still in showroom condition. Onlookers often ask if I am interested in selling it. My response is always "It's my mom's." They would then say "Oh" with a disappointed chuckle. Funny, they never ask if she might be interested in selling it. Maybe they are too busy trying to figure out how many years beyond 100 she must be when they notice how old I appear to be.

The second strange event, the main topic of this subsection, occurred the day after I took possession of the car. Before I drove the car home, my children and I washed it on my parents' driveway. The next morning, at home, I walked around the car to make sure everything was fine. Then I drove it to work. Before leaving work, I walked around it again to ensure everything was still okay. Upon returning home, I parked it in our garage. Again, I walked around it to be sure it was still clean and everything is fine. The next morning, before getting in, I did that again. This time I was shocked to find an oily streak running down the right rear fender, exactly where I had seen such a streak on one of my visits with our mother. The streak was not there the previous day, and there's nothing in our garage that could produce a drop of oil that would make such a streak.

After the third strange event occurred as presented in the subsection entitled "**3. White Aura**," I came to realize in retrospect the oily streak must be my parents' way of saying they are happy their beloved car now has a loving and caring home.

3.   **White Aura**

This is the third strange event and is the one that convinced me life exists after life. It lead to my realizing the significance of the first two strange events and that they too were indications that life exists after life. A special friend and co-employee named Rachel was the recipient of this message and later conveyed it to me. She sees auras. She is special not only because she sees auras, she is also humble, exceptionally empathic and compassionate, and she considers her ability to see auras a gift to be used to help others. I sensed her wonderful nature the minute we met and we quickly became friends. Various individuals warned me not to get close to her because, I believe, they are afraid of her ability to see auras. But instead I was drawn to her wonderful nature and was fascinated by her special ability. Besides, I couldn't prevent her from seeing my aura anyway, so I didn't care.

In addition to my experience with Rachel, my wife and I had an experience with a woman who teaches others how to see and read auras. She had a booth at a women's health fair and was giving sample readings. She read our auras, and then described our strengths and weaknesses, our approach to life, and the nature of our influences on others. She was 95 percent accurate about us both. She was even able to identify something about my wife that only my wife and I know about, and furthermore she identified the source of that particular something. That was amazing! My experiences with her and Rachel convinced me auras are real and that they are immediate reflections of people's lives.

As it turns out, my model confirms that auras are real and that some individuals can see them. My model also confirms that an aura is reflective of a person's state of being. All this will become clear as the presentation unfolds.

Rachel could perceive my current state of health, emotion, and energy level by reading my aura, and she would be right-on every time. When Rachel is not feeling well, her ability to see auras could be a burden because an aura could indicate something is threatening the life of the person. What is she to do when she sees such an aura? Should she warn the person? If she did, and the person was unaware of a threat, he or she might consider Rachel some kind of nut. And if the person was already aware of it, he or she might become upset, considering it an invasion of his or her privacy. Thus, when Rachel is not up to dealing with such dilemmas, she wears sunglasses to block out people's auras. Unfortunately, she has a chronic illness that often makes her feel unwell, so she frequently wears sunglasses.

Rachel knew my mother had passed away and that I had inherited her car. She had not seen the car, didn't know the make, and didn't know I had started driving it to work. One morning, as she drove through the parking lot, out of the corner of her eyes she saw at a distance an extremely bright white aura. It was so intense, it penetrated her sunglasses and startled her to the point she almost lost control of her car. I had just parked and was putting a car cover over the car. What she saw was a bright white aura engulfing both the Cadillac and me. The only other such aura she has ever seen was one surrounding the casket of a recently deceased person.

Later that day, we happened to meet in a hallway. She asked if the car was my mother's. I said, "Yes." She described what had happened in the parking lot that morning. I was spellbound and speechless. Then she said, "Your mother must care a lot about you." I replied, "Yes, she does," as tears welled up in my eyes. We stood there holding each other in each other's arms for a long time.

I was on an emotional roller coaster the rest of day. Life does exist after life! The veil flung open wide; the meanings of the first two events were thus revealed, and their messages came through loud and clear. My interest in my spirituality intensified, and I became compelled to figure out how life and life after life could interrelate.

4.   At the Cemetery

This is the fourth and last strange event I experienced after our mother passed away. The cemetery where our parents are buried is midway between my home and ski resorts in the Sierra Nevada. I take the Caddy on ski trips, leaving our other two cars for the family, which they prefer. My skis fit inside the car's enormous trunk and its powerful engine takes the mountains like they weren't there. Unlike driving a smaller car, it feels as if it literally flies over the freeways. But can you imagine anyone nutty enough to take a beautiful, showroom condition, collectible car to ski resorts in the middle of winter? And it is a challenge finding a safe place to park it. On my way home, I would always drop by the cemetery to say hello to our parents and to show them their beloved car.

By the time I arrived, it would be dark and the cemetery about to close. While I am placing flowers on the gravesites, the guard would be making his final rounds in his car before locking up. I would almost always be the last visitor. He would come by and politely announce the cemetery was closed but that I could take my time and he would be waiting by the gate. I would thank him, quickly complete my visit, hop in the car, and proceed toward the gate.

On one particular occasion, upon reaching the gate, he asked, "Where is the other one?" I replied, "The other one what?" He answered, "There was another person with you at the gravesites." I responded, "No, there was just me." And then, I don't know what prompted me, but I added, "Maybe it was one of the souls from the graves."

He just stood there, as his eyes grew really big. I thought to myself, "Uh-oh! Now I did it!" So I quickly added, "Well, see you next time, and thanks for waiting," and I briskly drove off. I didn't look back to see what he did as I left. Then I thought to myself "Hey, maybe that was my dad or my mom he saw," and I became really happy with the thought. I was tempted to go back to ask him if the person he saw was male or female. Then I would know if it was my dad or my mom. But after recalling how he looked when I suggested he might have seen a ghost, I decided I better not.

It later dawned on me that this event was probably my parents saying goodbye. After all, their two unfinished tasks were now completed, and it seemed they would feel free to leave. And where would be a more appropriate place to say goodbye than at their gravesites? I experienced no more strange events after that. Now I kind of miss having them.

Chapter Three
The Spirit World

Opening Comments

The presentation of my personal spiritual model begins with this chapter. The model turned out to be significantly more complex than I envisioned when I began its formulation. It is a possible description of the spiritual counterpart to physical life in our universe, and if a model of physical life in our universe were formulated it too would be complex. Every part of physical life affects every other part of physical life. Which part is most important would change from moment to moment, depending on the situation at the moment. Therefore, if a model of physical life were formulated, it is not clear what would be the best approach to presenting it. This same dilemma applies to my personal spiritual model. Therefore, I chose to give an overview of major notions and concepts of the model in this chapter, followed by specifics and additional notions and concepts in the chapters to follow. For this reason, the phrase "as the presentation continues" appears often throughout the book. Also, the readers will find my right brain and left brain talking with each other once in a while.

Now how are readers going to know what you mean by that? Oh, they'll find out soon enough.

The Knowledge Base

I began the formulation with the first notion "something somewhere somehow knows how to enable our universe and everything in it to exist." Let's call this "something" the creator for now. Questions are then: Did the creator have a beginning? Did the creator come already equipped with its knowledge or did it acquire it through learning over time? Does time even matter to the creator? And, if it matters, what does the creator use to measure the passage of time?

To address the last two questions, the creator is bound to have something to measure the passage of time, to establish the chronological order of events, and to indicate the rate of growth of things. A parameter that is everlasting and general enough to serve this purpose is considered later in this section. We on Earth use Earth's rotation around its axis and its movement around the Sun to indicate the passage of time. But this wouldn't work for the creator because our solar system is not everlasting.

If the creator came equipped with its knowledge, it would not have acquired it through learning. It would simply be knowledgeable, and learning would not be something it has to do. This would be consistent with the commonly held impression that the creator simply knows everything. But in my mind this impression is questionable and tends to block any new ways of thinking about the creator. For example, we would tend see the creator as a fixed ultra-powerful entity, and it's not our place to question anything about it. This would be too confining for some individuals and would hinder their ability to find a personal spiritual model that meets their personal spiritual needs, as was the case for me.

I decided to see what happens if I assume the creator acquired its knowledge through learning. Well, lightning did not strike and I am still here. It turns out, this notion led to a spiritual model that is gentle, non-judgmental, and able to explain life's common, everyday observations and happenings. This feature is very important to me since it enabled the model to feel as naturally a part of everyday life as the air around us. In my mind, this is as a personal spiritual model should be. Staying tuned into its messages every moment of everyday thus becomes as automatic, easy, and natural as breathing. This makes the model extremely effective in making its messages heard and taken into consideration when I am making choices and taking action. Conversely, if I had a dominating, judgmental personal spiritual model, I might not want to listen to, or follow, its messages now and then because it would be too confining for me.

A consideration favoring the notion that the creator acquired its knowledge through learning is that if it is able to create living things then it must be a living thing itself. One of the attributes of a living thing is that it grows. As the presentation continues, we will see the creator is nonphysical; therefore physical growth wouldn't be a factor but nonphysical growth would. Learning is a form of nonphysical growth present in any physical or nonphysical thing that has consciousness and intelligence.

We might argue that learning can result in changes in the brain, and since the brain is physical, learning must be physical growth as well. On the contrary, as the presentation continues, we will see learning takes place in the knowledge base, not in the brain, and because that is where consciousness and intelligence reside. A given knowledge base consists of the collection of knowledge necessary for it to know how to enable a living or nonliving thing to exist. Each such individual knowledge base is a portion of the larger knowledge base the creator has that gives the creator the capability to enable our universe and everything in it to exist. In the case of a living thing, the collection of knowledge also includes the knowledge needed to form the consciousness and intelligence of the living thing in addition to enabling the living thing to physically exist. Thus, consciousness and intelligence reside in the knowledge base and therefore it is the knowledge base that has the capacity to learn. The brain does not do the learning, although changes might take place in it because of learning that occurred in the knowledge base. Learning results in knowledge gained, and the newly gained knowledge becomes part of the knowledge base. The brain and everything else about the living thing exist because the knowledge base enables the thing to exist. It follows, then, that any changes in the physical brain would come about because the knowledge added to the knowledge base enables those changes. Thus, any changes in the brain would be made by the knowledge base and not by the brain's learning and changing on its own. Changes in the brain would not take place every time the knowledge base learns something but only when necessary to maintain communication between the brain and the knowledge base.

According to the model, the brain is the body's main control center. It communicates with the knowledge base and controls body movements and bodily functions in accordance with the knowledge base's signals. It's like the computer control center we design into a satellite we send out into space. The computer communicates with us and it controls the satellite in accordance with our signals. We are like the knowledge base for the satellite in that consciousness and intelligence reside with us and not with the satellite's computer control center.

Incidentally, in mid-2014 some researchers were studying how the brain of a person emerging from a coma retains previous abilities. Well, the model in this book indicates a person's abilities reside in the spirit and not in the brain. The brain is like a computer that, once programmed to be the communications link between the spirit and the body, retains that program even after a coma.

Since the knowledge base is a nonphysical entity, any learning it does is nonphysical growth. The knowledge base grows and changes due to learning and it changes the brain accordingly as necessary in order to continue communicating with the brain. As we develop new technology, we change the design of the computer control center for the next new satellite to communicate with it using the new technology in much the same way. We learn and make the changes in the computer control center. The computer control center cannot change itself.

Research on the brain has established substantial correlation between an individual's activities and activity in the brain. This includes recalling things, mental activities, bodily functions, thinking, experiencing sensations and emotions, moods, attitudes, etc. The model accounts for such findings. In fact, the findings could be seen as confirmation that the brain is a communication link between the knowledge base and the body. One thing research does not address is the source of the will to do something when an individual is doing it; it addresses only what is going on with the brain and the body while the body is doing something. Apparently, the will to do something is assumed to simply exist somewhere within the body, most likely within the brain. However, according to the model, the will is not simply within our physical body; it comes instead from the knowledge base which resides in what we will call the spirit world.

Thus, the model suggests that researchers should account for the role of the knowledge base and its communications with the brain and body in their research. The model indicates an individual consists of a knowledge base, the communications between the knowledge base and the brain, and the communications between the brain and the body. Current research looks at only the physical parts (i.e., the brain and the body) but not the knowledge base.

Did the creator have a beginning or did it always exist? If it had a beginning, did it start out with zero knowledge or with some, but not all, of its current knowledge? Might there be a "parent" creator that created our creator? If so, then might there be a "grandparent" creator that created the "parent" creator and so on? Does the creator constantly grow or could it also shrink? We currently have no way to find definite answers to such questions. However, the notion that the creator has a beginning and is constantly growing is consistent with its being a living thing. As it turns out, the model does indicate that the creator has a beginning and is constantly growing. This indication was not a prescribed notion or concept for formulating the model. Instead, we will see how it naturally comes out of the model as the presentation continues.

Each living and nonliving thing that exists in our universe has its own knowledge base which knows how to enable it to exist. Except for elemental things such as subatomic particles, electrons, protons, neutrons, atoms, etc., each thing is different and unique and has a different and unique knowledge base. Because every individual knowledge base is a part of the larger knowledge base of the creator, each time the creator learns and grows, so do many or all of the knowledge bases within it learn and grow. As the presentation continues, we will see how this works.

We could understand how the knowledge base for a living thing could grow, but how could the knowledge base for a nonliving thing grow? When a living thing's knowledge base grows, the living thing changes and, in a sense, becomes a different living thing. A child grows and becomes an adult. Although the same individual, the adult is clearly different from the child and is thus in a sense a different living thing. The adult's knowledge base consists of the child's knowledge base plus the additional knowledge that enables the individual to now exist as the adult.

The first notion in the formulation is "something somewhere somehow knows how to enable our universe and everything in it to exist." The second notion is that new knowledge is generated by experiences and only by experiences and that living and nonliving things gain knowledge by going through experiences and only by going through experiences. New knowledge is knowledge that had not existed before. Knowledge is gained when existing knowledge is learned by a living or nonliving thing. When an experience of a living or nonliving thing generates new knowledge, the living or nonliving thing automatically gains the new knowledge. Experiences thus enable learning, either by generating new knowledge or by gaining existing knowledge. This correlates with how we learn something from every experience we go through. Taking lessons and attending classes are obvious examples of learning experiences. However, just about anything a living or nonliving thing goes through is a learning experience.

An obvious question is how could a nonliving thing learn anything and thus gain knowledge? Anything that happens to a nonliving thing is a learning experience in that the knowledge generated by the experience is added to its knowledge base. The difference between a living thing and a nonliving thing is that while a living thing can make experiences happen, a nonliving thing can only have experiences happen to it. A pair of shoes that is getting worn is an example of a nonliving thing having experiences happen to it. Other examples include a rock rolling down a hill and getting chipped, water being cooled to freezing, chemicals being induced to react, ball getting hit by a bat, raw materials being processed into useful forms, and so on. Such experiences generate new knowledge that then enables the nonliving thing to exist in a new configuration or state that could be perceived as a manifestation of learning. For example, a beautifully cut diamond tells us the knowledge it has gained from the experiences it has gone through by virtue of its appearance, and we could immediately understand what it is saying to us by virtue of its sparkle and beauty.

Because knowledge is added to the knowledge base of any living or nonliving thing that has gone through an experience, the knowledge base embodies a record of the experience, and in this sense it remembers the experience. A nonliving thing "non-mentally remembers" the experience. Examples include wear and tear and changes in configuration of the nonliving thing. A living thing has consciousness and intelligence and therefore "mentally remembers" as well as "non-mentally remembers" the experience.

We might ask; what about such things as plants? They are living things. Do they have consciousness and intelligence and thus mentally remember their experiences? Their consciousness and intelligence are not like ours, and their senses are not like ours. Their consciousness, intelligence, and senses enable them to know how to form stems, leafs, flowers, and seeds, and their seeds to know how and when to germinate and grow into plants. Plants in general know how to seek out the Sun. Some plants even know how to make insecticides and poisons to ward off living things that eat them. These are examples of plants mentally remembering experiences that go back thousands of years. We might argue plants don't have brains, so how could they mentally remember anything? The answer is consciousness and intelligence reside in the knowledge base and not in the brain, and thus memory resides in the knowledge base and not in the brain. Therefore, the fact that plants do not have brains doesn't mean they do not remember their experiences. Their knowledge bases remember their experiences. As the presentation continues, we will find that the model is saying the size of the brain depends on the range of things the body can do and the precision with which it can do them. Thus, the size of the brain is not a measure of level of intelligence, but a measure of the broadness and precision of things the body can do. For example, birds can be very intelligent but have small brains. This means their knowledge base is large relative to the size of their brains.

Also, scientific studies indicate some living things, especially tiny living things such as a bacterium that don't have typically recognizable brains, do have brain functions residing in their outer membranes. In my mind, this might apply to plants as well, in that brain functions might reside in the outer layer of their cells. Plants have such a limited range of things they can physically do that the amount of brain functions that reside in the outer membrane of their cells could provide all the brain power they need.

Nonliving things also have senses, albeit very elementary ones more like sensing switches, or automatic switches. So, in a sense, we could say they have very elementary consciousness and intelligence. For example, water can sense temperature and pressure. It freezes when these parameters fall below certain values and melts when they rise above certain values. Chemicals react under certain conditions. Living things are made of nonliving things and certain of their senses are made up of similar elementary senses. For example, a collection of nonliving atoms follows instructions on how to come together to form the DNA molecules that then follow instructions on how to make bacteria, plants, and creatures.

However, the knowledge base of a living thing consists of more than the sum of all the knowledge bases of the nonliving things that comprise it. Otherwise all animals would have more or less the same level of intelligence and consciousness since they are all made of pretty much the same kinds of nonliving things. Similarly, all living things within any other group would have almost the same level of intelligence and consciousness. The knowledge base of a living thing consists of additional knowledge that enables the living thing to be a member of a certain species and that gives the living thing a certain level of intelligence and consciousness within the typical range for members of that species.

The demarcation between something being either a living or nonliving thing is fuzzy. There is a gradation between the living and nonliving. Viruses, prions (which cause mad-cow disease), and possibly other microscopic things fall somewhere in the gradation between living and nonliving. Is a single DNA molecule living, nonliving, or in between? DNA molecules can reproduce and can make up complex living things, but they need instructions from something somewhere else telling them how to do so. So does this mean a DNA molecule is in between?

When a living thing dies it usually goes gradually from being living to nonliving. Therefore, it would exist for a while in that fuzzy state between living and nonliving. When the brain dies but the body is kept functioning, is the individual living or in between? When a living thing goes into an in-between state, would its knowledge base be reduced? According to the model, spiritually no, but physically yes. The knowledge base remains intact, but its connections with the body are reduced such that the body, including the brain, is communicating less with it.

This is further discussed as the presentation continues.

The Place Where Knowledge Resides

The third notion in the formulation is that knowledge comes in pieces. A typical experience generates many pieces of knowledge, some new and the rest duplicates of existing pieces. Multiple copies of any piece immediately merge into one; one is all that's needed. Duplicates don't increase the knowledge base since they don't add new knowledge. Once a piece of knowledge is generated, provided it isn't a duplicate, it exists forever. ("Forever" is qualified, as we will see at the end of this section.) This means that a knowledge base can only stay the same or become larger, which in turns means a living or nonliving thing can only stay the same or become more sophisticated and complex. This may be one reason evolution tends to produce increasingly sophisticated and complex organisms, as indicated by paleontological and paleozoological findings. By analogy we can see how our technological discoveries tend to result in our designing increasingly sophisticated and complex instruments, devices, equipment, and gadgets.

The fourth notion in the formulation is that all existing pieces of knowledge reside in the same place, and it's the only place in which they reside. This is the place we call the "spirit world" in the formulation of the model. Conversely we could also say the spirit world is made up of the totality of all existing pieces of knowledge. In this sense, the existing pieces of knowledge could be said to form the place in which they reside. It follows then that the spirit world and the totality of all existing pieces of knowledge are identical. Obviously, then, knowledge is the source of the spirit world's creative abilities. Our creator, the creator of our universe and everything in it, consists of a portion of all the pieces of knowledge that exist and is thus a portion of the spirit world; thus it resides in the spirit world. Therefore, the source of our creator's creative abilities is also pieces of knowledge. According to the model, the spirit world possesses significantly more pieces of knowledge than does our creator because it enabled countless other universes to exist besides ours. As the presentation continues, we will discover each universe is different and unique, and thus each has its own different and unique creator. We will also see how each universe is brought into being for a specific purpose as well as for a general purpose. For simplicity, from this point forward we will refer to the spirit world simply as the entity that creates everything, and will henceforth refer much less to individual creators of universes.

Now that the concept of the spirit world has been introduced, it's appropriate to call the knowledge base for a living or nonliving thing the "spirit" of that living or nonliving thing. Since the spirit world is made of all existing pieces of knowledge and all spirits are made of pieces of knowledge, each spirit is a portion of the spirit world and thus resides in the spirit world. The spirit of a living or nonliving thing consists of all the pieces of knowledge that, when combined, know how to enable the living or nonliving thing to exist. This includes all the nonphysical as well as physical attributes that the living or nonliving thing has. Nonphysical attributes include consciousness, intelligence, senses, emotions, feelings, reasoning ability, creativity, etc. A nonliving thing's attributes are also all its physical and nonphysical properties. Its nonphysical properties could consist of things such as elemental intelligence, elemental consciousness, elemental senses, etc. Such elemental properties could, for example, enable a nonliving thing that is a solid to know when to melt or to chemically react with something, etc.

The fifth notion in the formulation is that anything made of two or more existing pieces of knowledge is defined as a spiritual entity. The term "spiritual entity" has been around for quite a while, but the definition stated here is different from any of the past and applies only to my personal spiritual model. Obviously, the spirit world is the largest possible spiritual entity that exists at any given point in time.

Pieces of knowledge are analogous to words. A single piece of knowledge has very limited creative ability, and a single word has very limited expressive ability. The creative ability of multiple pieces of knowledge acting together far exceeds the sum of the individual creative ability of each piece of knowledge. This is because each combination of two or more pieces of knowledge has its additional creative ability. By analogy, the expressive ability of multiple words used together far exceeds the sum of the individual expressive ability of each word, because each combination of two or more words has its additional expressive ability.

Thus, the spirit world is analogous to a dictionary. It keeps only one copy of every existing piece of knowledge, just as a dictionary lists only one copy of every existing word. There is no limit to the new pieces of knowledge that can be generated, just as there is no limit to the new words that could be formed.

Extending the analogy further, words linked together form sentences that convey thoughts. Sentences linked together form paragraphs. Paragraphs linked together form articles and books. Pieces of knowledge connected together form spiritual entities. Smaller spiritual entities together form larger spiritual entities. All spiritual entities together form the spirit world. Smaller spiritual entities enable the materials and energies making up our universe to exist. Larger spiritual entities encompassing these smaller spiritual entities enable the materials and energies to form such things as planets, stars, galaxies, and so on. An even larger spiritual entity encompassing all the aforementioned spiritual entities enables our entire universe to exist.

While a sentence is a one-dimensional string of words, a spiritual entity has no dimensional limitations. The thought conveyed by a sentence requires time because a sentence must be read or orally expressed one word at a time. The thought carried by a spiritual entity can be conveyed instantaneously and without a spoken language. The unlimited dimensionality of a spiritual entity might be what enables its message to be conveyed instantaneously. Could this be similar to how a picture is worth a thousand words? A picture is, after all, multidimensional whereas words can form only one-dimensional sentences.

The creative ability of the spirit world exponentially increases as new pieces of knowledge are generated and added to its knowledge base. This suggests the spirit world could develop the ability to create something as complex as our universe rather quickly, starting from scratch, once its knowledge base commenced growth. Continued growth of its knowledge base would enable it to create new things at an accelerating rate. Thus, the number of different possible experiences all the things it created could go through would also increase at an accelerating rate. The rate of generation of new pieces of knowledge would then increase exponentially. This forms a vicious circle that would cause the creative ability of the spirit world to grow exponentially, therefore a natural attribute of the spirit world is that things happen at an ever-increasing rate.

We can see this attribute manifesting itself in various forms on Earth. Various things happen at accelerating rates at various times. Often such vicious circles lead to bubbles bursting. The recent burst of the housing market bubble is an example. The earlier burst of the so-called DOT.com speculation bubble is another fairly recent example. The tulip mania that occurred in Holland from 1633 to 1637 is a familiar historical example. Currently, the Internet, smart phones, and social media are resulting in significant and rapid changes in how we communicate and interact. However, these particular cases do not appear likely to lead to a bubble burst but could indirectly lead to the burst of other bubbles, by creating, for example, wild swings in the stock market.

New pieces of knowledge are constantly being generated because living and nonliving things are constantly going through experiences. Therefore, the spirit world is constantly growing and changing. The nature of the growth and changes would depend on the new pieces of knowledge generated. Consequently, the nature of the growth and changes will ultimately depend on the nature of the experiences the living and nonliving things are going through. Thus, the spirit world and our relationship with it are shaped by the experiences we, and other living and nonliving things, go through. We are responsible for our intentions, choices, and actions, and these shape our experiences. Therefore, we are responsible for our participation in shaping the growth of the spirit world. In other words, we need to do our part to take care of the spirit world in addition to receiving care from the spirit world. A natural partnership thus exists between the spirit world and each of us. As the presentation continues, the meaning of "taking care of the spirit world" and how that partnership is naturally formed will be further discussed.

When new pieces of knowledge are constantly generated and added to the spirit world, the size of spirit world constantly increases. This constant increase in size could be used to establish the chronologically order of things and events. In other words, it could serve as a means of measuring the passage of time for the spirit world. It is general enough to be useful to any spiritual entity within the spirit world and therefore could be applied in a consistent manner throughout the spirit world. And as long as the spirit world manages to keep itself viable, its growth would be everlasting. The topic of the spirit world's viability is further discussed later in this section.

While new pieces of knowledge are added to the spirit world, some become a part of our creator as well. This is the case particularly for new pieces of knowledge generated by the experiences of living and nonliving things in our universe. Therefore, our creator today has grown and is different from what it was long ago. So if our creator is creating things today, the things might not be similar to the things it created long ago. This could be yet another way of looking at how evolution works. Living things evolve because our creator is growing and changing and the changes are manifested on Earth as evolutionary changes in its living things. This is also consistent with the observation that the more a living thing partakes in a wide range of different experiences, the more it evolves. Conversely, living things whose experiences remain constant for thousands of years do not evolve; they remain unchanged for thousands of years. There are many examples of living things on Earth that have remained unchanged for thousands of years. The Latimeria Chalumnae species of fish, a member of the Coelacanthidae family of fish that lived in the latter part of the Palaeozoic era, were thought to have become extinct about 70,000,000 years ago, but they still exist today. One was caught off the South American coast. The Australian lungfish is another archaic living example. It is a member of the Ceratodus family that lived in the Triassic and Jurassic periods of the Mesozoic era beginning about 200,000,000 years ago. Two other genera of lungfish survive in the South America and African waters today. Xiphosurans, commonly called king crab, swordtail crab, and horseshoe crab, are another example of what are often referred to as "living fossils." However, they are not crabs at all but are related to scorpions, spiders, and other members of the class Arachnida. They are found on the east coasts of Asia and North America.

I often wondered how species get such interesting names. Well, maybe it is so that half-brain entities like us could have fun citing them. Hey, it is kind of fun as long as we don't have to remember them. Remember what?

What if changes in our creator are manifested in our universe in other ways besides evolutionary changes in living things and evidence of this could also be found in our universe? For example we can compare what we see happening billions of light-years ago in deep space with what we see close to home happening within our solar system. What is happening within our solar system reflects more of how our creator is today while what is happening out in deep space reflects more of how our creator was billions of years ago. Thus, while we learn how our universe has physically changed over billions of years, a lot might also be possible to learn about how our creator's portion of the spirit world has spiritually changed over that time span. For example, our creator started out by simply bringing into being subatomic particles. Since then, it learned how to make intelligent living things such as us humans out of such particles and how to form environments in which those humans would be viable. Is there anything about all this, spiritually, that could tell us what it was that made the spirit world decide to have our creator do this? In other words, there is bound to be a purpose for our universe being brought into being. What is it? As the presentation continues, we will find that the model gives a logical basis for a possible purpose for our particular universe.

A recent unexpected finding is that our universe is expanding at an accelerating rate. The previous thought was that our universe is either expanding at a decelerating rate or is contracting. Could our creator, with its knowledge base now much larger than what is was when it first created our universe, be applying its added knowledge and making our universe expand at an accelerating rate? Could it now be creating things it was unable to before, but we simply have not seen evidence of this because what we see in the telescope took place millions or billions of years ago? If we were able to look at a place in space to see an image of what happened, say, only thousands of years ago, would we see things that did not exist millions or billions of years ago? The creator might be expanding space to make room for its new creations. Some of the gas clouds we see here and there in our universe might be places where additional space is being brought into being to make room for new creations yet to come.

Earlier we speculated that our creator had a beginning. The same could be said about the spirit world. If the spirit world had a beginning, it would be when the first piece of knowledge was generated. But if the spirit world did not exist until after that happened, there would be nothing to go through any experience to generate any new pieces of knowledge. Therefore, it is unclear how the spirit world began, just as it is unclear what caused the Big Bang, assuming the Big Bang really happened. One possibility is that what we think of as being nothing is spiritually something. And that particular something is what generated the first piece of knowledge. For example, what if there is another level of spiritual existence and it consists of something more profound than pieces of knowledge? Since we can't conceive of such a thing, we might perceive such a thing as being nothing, when in fact it is actually something. What existed before our universe and the space in which it resides came into being? We tend to think there must have been nothing. But maybe that nothing was that spiritual something. More on this as the presentation continues. Also, we often wonder if there is an edge to space where space ends, and we tend to think that beyond that edge is nothing. But, again, maybe what is beyond that edge is instead that spiritual something.

Hey, whatever that particular nothing or something is, it's giving me, or us, a headache. So let's put it aside for now. OK. And besides, as said earlier, no model formulated by a human is going to be totally complete or absolutely accurate anyway. Well, that would be something that is nothing to laugh at, or cry about, or is it nothing that is something to do likewise about? Oh, well, where is the aspirin?

A follow up question regarding the spirit world's beginning and growth is when did the spirit world develop its consciousness? A plausible answer might be when it had enough pieces of knowledge to form its first thought. And just as its creative ability exponentially increased once its knowledge base began to grow, so did its consciousness also exponentially increased. With an increasing consciousness, the spirit world becomes increasingly able to formulate purposes behind what it does. And as the spirit world becomes increasingly large and complex, having purpose behind its actions becomes increasingly important for maintaining its ability to sustain its viability. It so happens that the spirit world's current state is viable. This implies two possibilities: One is that the spirit world has grown to the point it knows how to maintain its viability; the other is that it might not have reached that point and thus its existence could run into trouble. Therefore, the spirit world's growth goes through a vulnerable period before it is large enough to ward off hazards. This is analogous to how a newly born creature needs to survive its most vulnerable, early stage until it grows large enough and mature enough to fend off dangers. The fact that all complex creatures and plants on Earth start off vulnerable and need to survive that vulnerable period to become self-sustaining could be a sign they all inherited this attribute from the spirit world. It is a part of what the spirit world has gone through and is therefore simply a natural part of the complex living things it creates. It could then also be a reflection of the fact that living things on Earth all began with germination and an embryonic state to become first a vulnerable living thing. Each living thing then must survive through a vulnerable period to grow large enough and to learn how to maintain itself. This natural process all living things on Earth go through could be perceived as supporting evidence that the spirit world itself has gone through the same sequence of stages as well.

This could also mean it is possible a number of spirit worlds have come and gone in the past. Some of the past ones may have been unable to survive their early vulnerable periods and thus vanished along with everything they created. How the spirit world could become vulnerable will be explained as the presentation continues. But for now, keep in mind each of us has a role to play in keeping the spirit world viable. And if not enough of us are doing our part, the spirit world could run into trouble and its viability could fail. If that happens, the spirit and everything it created would vanish.

Incidentally, vulnerability encountered during the early period of growth is not limited to complex creatures and plants. It also applies to relationships, marriages, businesses, nations, etc. That this attribute is common to so many things means it's an attribute from a very basic source. And what could be more basic than the spirit world. Another perception is that such things as relationships, marriages, businesses, nations, etc., are in fact living things. They grow, change, and could die, lending further support to the concept that living things need to put forth a concerted effort to remain viable while growing through a vulnerable period before it could become more naturally able to ward off dangers.

Chapter 3

Things in Universes and Their Connections with Spiritual Entities

This broad topic is covered in several subsections. However, the subtopics are interrelated. Therefore, some amount of cross-talk will occur among the subsections.

1. **Defining Spiritual Entities and the Spirits and Souls of Living and Nonliving Things**

The spirit world consists of the totality of all existing pieces of knowledge interconnected together. Each existing piece of knowledge forms two kinds of connections. The first kind connects each piece of knowledge with every other piece of knowledge and carries signals from one piece of knowledge to and from every other piece of knowledge. Each piece of knowledge is different and unique and has a different and unique signal. The back-and-forth signals enable any assemblage of two or more pieces of knowledge to form a spiritual entity. Each spiritual entity consists of a different and unique combination of pieces of knowledge and therefore has a different and unique combination of signals differentiating itself from every other spiritual entity.

The second kind of connection gives a particular spiritual entity the ability to enable a particular thing to exist in a particular universe, and connections of the second kind are formed only when a spiritual entity is called upon to enable a thing to exist in a universe. Not every spiritual entity is capable of enabling a thing to exist in a universe or would necessarily be called upon to do so even if it could. It depends on many factors, as will be explained as the presentation continues. When a spiritual entity does enable a thing to exist in a universe, a connection of the second kind forms from each selected pieces of knowledge in the spiritual entity and goes into the world of the universe. Signals from those pieces of knowledge transmitted through the connections of the second kind into the world of the universe enable a certain thing to exist there. Feedback signals are transmitted from the thing to those pieces of knowledge through those same connections. The back-and-forth exchange of signals enable the thing to exist. As the thing goes through experiences it generates new pieces of knowledge or gains access to some already existing pieces of knowledge. These pieces of knowledge would become a part of the spiritual entity and they would also participate in enabling the thing to continue to exist. Accordingly, the thing would grow spiritually in the spirit world and also in the manner applicable to the world of the universe in which it resides. Thus, the thing would be ever-changing spiritually in the spirit world and in some manner in the world of the universe in which it resides as it continues to go through experiences. If the thing is a living thing, its ever-changing status reflects the fact that it is alive, thinking, moving, aging, healing, etc. If the thing is nonliving, its ever-changing status reflects such things as wear and tear, oxidation, corrosion, erosion, chemical reactions, breakage, melting, freezing, cracking, etc.

Usually only a portion of all the pieces of knowledge making up the spiritual entity would participate in enabling a living or nonliving thing to exist in a universe. Let's call this portion of the spiritual entity the spirit of the thing. Connections of the second kind go from the pieces of knowledge making up the spirit to the living or nonliving things existing in a universe. Let's call this collection of connections of the second kind the soul of the living or nonliving thing. Thus, according to the model, every living and nonliving thing existing in a universe has a spirit and a soul.

We might not be used to thinking of nonliving things as having spirits and souls. But as spirits and souls are defined in the model, nonliving things do have spirits and souls. In the model, having spirits and souls is how all living and nonliving things exist in a universe and how each one is ever-changing as it goes through experiences and generates new pieces of knowledge or gains access to existing pieces of knowledge.

The fact that in the model the same mechanism for existence in a universe applies to living and nonliving things makes sense because, as mentioned in the first section of this chapter, the demarcation between something being living or nonliving is fuzzy, not sharp. For example, viruses and prions are neither absolutely living nor absolutely nonliving. Likewise, many living things on Earth are an assemblage of components including arms, legs, hearts, brains, livers, etc. If any one component is separated from the body of a living thing, it doesn't remain living for long. Thus, the component is living and then slowly becomes nonliving, but it would retains a spirit and a soul that are portions of the spirit and soul of the living thing to which it was once attached. The part of the spirit and soul of the living thing that enabled the separated component to be alive have disconnected from the now nonliving component and only the part of the spirit and soul that enable the component to physically exist would remain connected to it. Eventually, the material and energy making up the component decomposes back into basic material and energy. At that time, the part of the spirit and soul of the living thing that had enabled the component to physically exist would also disconnect from the nonliving component. Then only the part of the spirit and soul of the living thing that enable the basic material and energy to exist remains connected to the basic material and energy. Because basic material and energy comprise every physical thing in our universe, all living and nonliving physical things in our universe share this part among all their spirits. This is one of many sources of oneness in the spirit world as we will see as the presentation continues.

We might ask; why only a portion and not the entire spiritual entity would participate in making up the spirit of a living or nonliving thing? This is because while the spiritual entity is serving as the spirit for the living or nonliving thing at this time it is not limited to only serving as spirit for that particular living or nonliving thing at some other time. At other times, the same spiritual entity could serve as the spirit of a different living or nonliving thing in the same or different universe. This is analogous to how a specific individual could be in different roles at different times. The individual might be the pilot of an airplane at one moment, a parent of children at another moment, and a real estate agent at yet another moment, etc. Thus the individual is more than any one of his or her roles. The same idea applies to a spiritual entity in the spirit world.

A spiritual entity, and the spirit it is serving as, could grow along with any growth of the spirit world. A manifestation of the growth would be evolutionary changes in the succession of spirits the spiritual entity could form and serve as. For example, before a bird was a bird it was a dinosaur that eventually evolved into a bird. A spiritual entity and its part that is the spirit that enabled a dinosaur to exist would grow over the lifetime of the dinosaur. Growth of the spiritual entity would continue with each new generation of dinosaurs, and eventually would have enough additional pieces of knowledge to form a spirit that could enable a bird to exist. When forming the spirit of a bird the spiritual entity would be employing new portions of itself while not employing some portions of itself that were employed to form the spirit of a dinosaur. Therefore, generation by generation, the dinosaur species would gradually evolve to become a bird species. Any portion of the spiritual entity not employed to form the spirit of a bird would still be a part of the spiritual entity. At some later time as evolution continues, some of the portions not employed to form the spirit of a bird could be employed to form the spirit for a member of a new species that evolved from birds. Also, if the spiritual entity is called upon to form a spirit for a living thing to reside in a different universe, the portion of the spiritual entity employed to form the spirit is bound to be different from the portion employed to form a spirit for a dinosaur, bird, or transitional creature that is between being a dinosaur and a bird.

Just as a spirit that enables a living thing to exist in a universe grows, a spirit that enables a nonliving thing to exist in a universe could also grow. Its growth would correspond to changes to the nonliving thing. For example, a piece of wood in our universe can be worked into becoming a part for a chair, but it remains the same piece of wood and therefore the same spirit still enables it to exist. The experience the piece of wood goes through to become a part for a chair generates pieces of knowledge that are added to its spirit. The grown spirit becomes able to enable the chair part to exist. While the chair part is physically smaller than the piece of wood, it requires more knowledge to enable it to exist because it is now more complex than when it was just a piece of wood. The spirit that enables the chair to exist would consist of all the spirits that enable all the parts of the chair to exist, plus additional knowledge that enable all the parts to come together to form the chair. The additional knowledge was generated by the experiences the parts went through while being assembled into a chair.

Meanwhile, the individual who shaped the chair parts and assembled them into a chair also went through a lot of experiences. These experiences generated a number of pieces of knowledge that became a part of the spirit of that individual. Thus the spirit and soul of that individual grew as well.

While the spirit of a living or nonliving thing grows as the living or nonliving thing goes through experiences, a difference is living things could make their own experiences in addition to going through experiences that are not in their control, whereas nonliving things could not make their own experiences. Their experiences are not in their control. Also the spirits of living things include parts that enable the living thing to be alive, whereas the spirits of nonliving things do not include such parts. However, as the presentation continues, we will see that the spirits of nonliving things have something similar, which enables nonliving things to have what is referred to in the model as elemental life.

The more complex is the thing, the larger is the spiritual entity that serves as its spirit and the larger is its spirit. As far as we know, humans are the most complex living things on Earth. Therefore, we would imagine a human spirit to be the largest among all living things on Earth. However, we would not know for sure until we return to the spirit world. The complexity of living things includes the degree and kinds of consciousness, intelligence, emotions, creativity, imagination, reasoning ability, etc., in addition to physical complexity. Many living things possess capabilities that are better or different than those we have. Therefore, their spirits contain parts our spirits don't have or have less of. So, who knows? The spirits of some nonhuman living things may be larger than the spirits of humans.

Oh, wouldn't that deflate our ego! Yep, it sure would, and that might even be a good thing.

Once a connection of either the first or second kind is formed, it exists forever, just as a piece of knowledge exists forever once it is generated and becomes part of the spirit world. However, "forever" applies as long as the spirit world remains viable and continues to exist, as mentioned earlier. This means nothing is absolutely assured of existing "forever," not even life after life. This could be why some individuals have the notion that there is nothing after life, because the possibility of "nothing" is real, according to the model, although hopefully slim. The knowledge of this possibility is a part of the spirit world and therefore signals from it could reach the spirits of individuals, causing some to conclude nothing exists after life, at least until they come across evidence that indicates otherwise.

The discussion so far indicates a living or nonliving thing residing in a universe consists of three parts. The first part, the spirit, resides in the spirit world. The second part, the soul, resides partly in the spirit world and partly in the world of a universe and is the connection between the other two parts. The third part resides in the world of a universe. In the case of our physical universe, this is the physical thing that exists in our universe. Since the spirit of the thing is made of pieces of knowledge, and all existing pieces of knowledge reside only in the spirit world, it follows then that all the knowledge a living or nonliving thing has at any given moment resides in its spirit. Thus, a living thing's consciousness, intelligence, senses, emotions, feelings, reasoning ability, imagination, creativity, etc. reside in its spirit and therefore in the spiritual entity serving as the spirit and not in its part that resides in the world of a universe. Consequently, for humans and other living things on Earth, consciousness, intelligence, etc. reside in the spirit and not in the brain. According to the model, the brain is the main control center for the body. The spirit sends spiritual signals to the brain through the soul, and the brain translates the spiritual signals into physical signals and then sends them to the body to control bodily actions. Physical signals are issued from the body as feedback to the brain and the brain translates them into spiritual signals and then sends them through the soul to the spirit. This constant exchange of signals is how the spirit "pilots" the body. By analogy, a constant exchange of mental, mechanical, electrical and other signals between a pilot and an airplane allows the pilot to fly an airplane. The implications of this are covered in more detail as the presentation continues, and it could explain various common, everyday observations and happenings. For example, it could explain where thoughts come from, why human possess fewer instincts than various other living things do, why we sleep, how the body knows how to heal, etc.

2. **Universes Will Come and Go, and Each Will be Different and Unique**

The model indicates that other universes exist, have existed, and will exist. A new universe is brought into being by the spirit world when the spirit world needs one to help restore balance in the spirit world's state of knowledge. Each new universe is different and unique because each is created to meet a different need. The need is different each time because the spirit world keeps growing and changing, and consequently the situation changes each time balance needs to be restored. The reason the spirit world must maintain reasonable balance in its state of knowledge will become clear when the topic of wisdom is covered as the presentation continues.

Our universe is physical; resides in its particular kind of space; is filled with countless galaxies, stars, planets, black holes, gas clouds, etc., all spread out over its kind of space. Other universes may be physical or nonphysical. Nonphysical ones may or may not need space in which to reside, whereas physical universes require space. The kind of space will be different and unique for each universe that needs it. Other universes might not be spread out over their kinds of space like our universe is in its space. Other universes may range from tiny to big, and might not be three-dimensional but feature a different number of dimensions. Each physical universe contains different and unique types of substances and energies. Each nonphysical universe is likely made only of energies, and each would be comprised of different and unique kinds of energies. The point is each universe is different and unique in ways we might not be able to imagine. Therefore, what is said in this paragraph is not likely to encompass the full range of possibilities.

A physical universe needs some kind of space in which to reside. In that case, the spiritual entity that enables the universe to exist might bring space into existence before bringing any physical thing into existence. If the universe were to have something akin to a Big Bang to bring physical things into existence, then space needs to be brought into existence first. Otherwise, the Big Bang would have nowhere to go bang and no space in which to blast the physical things into. Alternatively, space and physical things could be brought into existence simultaneously without a Big Bang. But we could argue that even in that case, couldn't both space and physical things still expand from a point in a manner of a Big Bang? The answer is no, because a Big Bang implies there must be existing space in which a Big Bang can blast physical things into. But space would not already exist if it were being brought into being at the same instant the physical things are being brought into being. If both space and physical things expanded together from a point, and if we were able to be within that point to witness the expansion, we would not experience the physical things blasting into the space. We would more likely witness space and physical things brought into being all together simultaneously without any kind of bang.

We might speculate that a universe could be created much like a balloon being inflated. Then couldn't the inflation happen very quickly like a Big Bang? The answer is no, because we are envisioning an inflating balloon as expanding into the space around it. In the case of space being brought into being, it is not expanding into any kind of space around it. There is nothingness there for space to expand into. We are so used to our three-dimensional physical universe that such a notion seems beyond our imagination even if we might conceptually understand it. Maybe a better analogy is how Brigadoon simply emerged gradually all over the place without pushing anything out of the way to make room for its emergence.

Hey, perhaps the Brigadoon story is so appealing because in the back of our minds it reminds us of how our universe came into being, and what a magical thing it is that we are here, living our lives in a Brigadoon-like universe. And in our old age it becomes increasingly clear that, like Brigadoon, we are here for only a moment. So then why is gaining absolute control over others so important for some people? Crazy, isn't it? And it certainly isn't making their partnerships with the spirit world mutually beneficial either. How do you know that? Oh, you will see as the presentation continues.

In the case of our universe, if the Big Bang did not occur, then our space, physical things, and its energies all could have been brought into being simultaneously, and it wouldn't have mattered if it took place quickly or slowly. In that case, the radiation we see far out in space might not be evidence of a Big Bang but of something else. The radiation might be where space ends and is produced when our kind of space meets the spiritual something that is the "nothingness" beyond. The radiation might consist of a kind of energy that forms a barrier keeping our kind of space separate from the nothingness beyond, sort of like how the skin of a spaceship keeps the air within the spaceship separate from the airless outer space beyond. The air in the spaceship would then be analogous to our universe's kind of space, and the airless space outside the spaceship would be analogous to the "nothingness" beyond our universe.

If this were the case, and if our universe were being brought into being slowly, then our universe might still be in the process of being brought into being. This could explain the recent determination that our universe is expanding at an accelerating rate. And the gas clouds seen in outer space could be places where our universe is still being brought into being. This could explain why new stars are being formed in these gas clouds. If such gas clouds came into being all at once the moment our universe came into being, and none have come into being since then, we would expect all the gases in those clouds to have condensed into stars by "now" and no such gas clouds would "currently" exist. The fact that such gas clouds exist now suggests more clouds were brought into being relatively recently, and this suggests our universe is still being brought into being. "Now" and "currently" are relative to the age of our universe.

Another possibility is that the physical materials and energies of our universe might not have been homogeneously spread out over space in the beginning. Therefore, there will be places with a heavier concentration of gases and places with a very thin concentration. Stars would form first in places with a heavier concentration of gases and much later where there's a very thin concentration. But then why would the gases in a thin concentration form gas clouds? Why wouldn't the gas be drawn by gravity to places with a heavier concentration instead and thus accumulate where stars have already formed? This tends to indicate gas clouds were brought into being much later, after our universe came into being. This could also be a sign that our universe is still being brought into being.

On July 4, 2012, scientists in Switzerland announced they had possibly found the Higgs boson, the elusive subatomic particle sometimes referred to as the "God particle," and in March 2013 it was confirmed. The Higgs boson is hailed as a key to understanding how life and diversity came into being in our universe; it is what gives elementary particles mass as predicted by the Standard Model that ruled physics for the past half-century. Scientists think the particle acts like molasses or snow. When other tiny basic building blocks pass through it, they stick together, slow down, and form atoms. Scientists think this is how the Big Bang created something out of nothing 13.7 billion years ago. But, in my opinion, their reasoning depends on there being space, "God particles," and basic building blocks already in existence in order for the process they described to take place. This leaves open the question as to what brought space, "God particles," and basic building blocks into being in the first place.

If each universe that needs space in which to reside has its own kind of space, what kind of space does our universe have? If space of any given kind is something created, then the space must be made of something. It would be different and unique for each kind of space. Could ours be made of the dark matter and dark energy (or zero-point energy) scientists say comprises approximately 80 percent of the matter of our universe? What makes up gravity is yet an unknown. Could gravity simply be an attribute of our kind of space? Thus, could gravity be an attribute of the dark matter and dark energy?

Some scientists might be looking for possible ways to tap into the dark energy as a potentially endless source of energy. But if dark matter and dark energy happens to make up our space and gravity, then consuming them would consume space and gravity. Our universe could become very crowded as the space separating the galaxies, stars, planets, gas clouds, black holes, and etc. becomes consumed. Gravity could decrease to the point that people weigh less leading some to think they no longer have a weight problem and thus would start pigging out on junk food. With little space remaining and less gravity to overcome, space travel to other planets and galaxies would be a cinch. On the other hand, with reduced gravity, those things would not hold together and continue being those things. The same would apply to Earth. So like it or not we might end up doing involuntary space travel, and without a spaceship at that.

Do you really think your ridiculous scenario could actually happen? No, but it is fun to speculate.

3. The Spirit World Creates Everything, But It Is All Imperfect

When a new piece of knowledge is generated, it immediately forms a connection of the first kind with every existing piece of knowledge. Therefore, every existing piece of knowledge has a connection of the first kind with every other existing piece of knowledge, even as new pieces of knowledge are continuously being generated and added to the spirit world. The constant communication among all pieces of knowledge by signals from every piece of knowledge to every other piece of knowledge carried through the network of connections of the first kind enables the entire assemblage to form the largest spiritual entity possible at any given point in time. As indicated earlier this entity is the spirit world.

The spirit world could be perceived as being all-knowing at any given point in time, since it possesses all the pieces of knowledge that exist at that moment. And since knowledge is the most powerful thing that exists, the spirit world could also be perceived as all-powerful at any given point in time. But because there is no limit to the new pieces of knowledge that can be generated, the spirit world would never possess every piece of knowledge possible to generate. This means perfection can never be achieved by the spirit world. Therefore, nothing it creates can ever be perfect either, and likewise perfection can never be achieved by any living thing created by the spirit world. Consequently, since every living or nonliving entity or thing, whether residing in the spirit world or in a universe, is created by the spirit world, perfection is only a concept and can never be reality anywhere. We can clearly see how perfection is only a concept and never a reality on Earth.

Perhaps it makes sense then that one-quarter to one-half of all the stuff I buy contain one or more defects. Hey if you bought it, I bought it too, and I say instead that 25 percent to 50 percent of the stuff we buy is defective. So who is being more accurate, you or me? Well, at least we agree to hang on to the boxes, so that we can more easily return all of that defective stuff. But then we end up with a house full of boxes.

But imperfection opens up interesting possibilities for evolution, because imperfections are variations. Environments can change and species that were once viable can become less viable in the changed environment if naturally occurring variations do not exist to enable them to evolve and to thus stay viable with the changing environment. This is one mechanism by which evolutionary changes can occur.

Survival of the fittest is often mentioned as a mechanism that drives evolutionary changes. This seems quite general and could have various specific meanings. For example, survival of the fittest could refer to the species most able to fight and win, escape and live, develop ways to repel predators such as how skunks and poisonous lizards could, etc. Sometimes it could be being the most beautiful, as in the case of the male peacock. Whatever is the mechanism, in general the mechanism has something to do with variations caused by imperfections.

Hey, when you point out such examples, we could conclude that being perfect would not be good, because that means no variations and therefore little or no possibility to evolve, and therefore such a living thing could not remain viable for long. Boy, you know, maybe we should be glad we and everything else are imperfect. Yeah, but then we end up with a house full of boxes.

Oh, and another thing. If the spirit world were perfect, meaning it would possess all pieces of knowledge possible to generate, then disaster would happen in two possible ways. One way is if its state of knowledge happens to be unbalanced, there would be no way to rebalance it since no new pieces of knowledge could be generated. Then things could go wrong all over the place and thus could lead to the spirit world vanishing. The second way is more likely whether its state of knowledge happens to be unbalanced or balanced. It is that with no new pieces of knowledge to generate, the spirit world could no longer grow. This means it would no longer be a living entity. This could lead to it vanishing for sure. Oh, you mean like dying of boredom? Well, maybe something like that.

Wow, am I glad the spirit world is imperfect and would stay imperfect forever. We should celebrate imperfection instead of striving for perfection. Perfection can't be achieved and mostly it would be a waste of time to pursue it. Since both of us are imperfect, lets hug. Yeah, each of us is only half a brain, and if that isn't being imperfect, what is?

In other words, variations are good. It follows then that diversity is good and should be valued and embraced, particularly diversity in mankind. Intuitively we tend to know that, regardless of how we react to diversity in mankind. As the presentation continues we will see how it is that intuitive messages are spiritual messages, guidance spiritual messages from the spirit world.

Our favorite things are often treasured for their uniqueness, such as some handmade things. Their uniqueness is in a sense a virtue of their imperfections. Our world is more interesting because nothing is exactly the same as any other thing. It is also nice that the person we fall in love with and marry is different from anyone else. Therefore, in general it is quite okay with us that the spirit world creates only imperfect things.

All the possible spiritual entities that could be formed from all the pieces of knowledge that exist at any given point in time have been formed at that point in time. This means everything that can be created with all the pieces of knowledge that exist at any given point in time have been created by the spirit world, and they reside in the spirit world in the form of spiritual entities. Some spiritual entities have the capability to enable things to exist in a universe and some do not. And not every spiritual entity that could enable something to exist in a universe has been called upon to do so. Therefore, there are a lot more creations residing in the spirit world than have ever been brought into being in any universe and new ones are being created constantly as new pieces of knowledge are generated constantly. This is great! As the presentation continues, we will see this enables us to use our imagination and creativity to always come up with new inventions and new things, at least new to us on Earth but not new to the spirit world.

Hey, you just gave a hint that could give away the rest of the story. Yeah, I know, but I wanna keep the readers interested.

The term "to create" traditionally means "to bring something into existence," usually physical existence. In this presentation, up until now, the term "to create" has been used in this traditional way with regard to creating our universe and living and nonliving things. But from this point forward, the term "to create" will also mean "to create spiritual entities" and that a spiritual entity might be capable of enabling something physical or nonphysical to exist in a universe. Therefore, when we say everything is created by the spirit world, we mean everything is created and exists in the form of a spiritual entity residing in the spirit world. New spiritual entities constantly being formed as new pieces of knowledge are constantly being generated and added to the spirit world. By this mechanism, the spirit world is constantly creating new things.

Each spiritual entity has two or more pieces of knowledge. Each has a different combination of pieces of knowledge, and is therefore different. Every piece of knowledge is a part of multiple spiritual entities. Smaller spiritual entities are a part of multiple larger spiritual entities. The result is that every spiritual entity shares one or more parts of itself with one or more other spiritual entities, or we could also say every spiritual entity is partially or totally part of one or more other spiritual entities. Ultimately, every spiritual entity is directly or indirectly partially or totally a part of every other spiritual entity. Larger spiritual entities could partially or totally encompass numerous smaller spiritual entities. This sharing of parts among all spiritual entities occurs throughout the spirit world and is the main source of the oneness that pervades the spirit world. This produces the feeling of love, empathy, and compassion that fills the spirit world to a degree we have never experienced on Earth. For one thing, everything on Earth is a separate physical thing such that one physical thing does not physically share a part of itself with any other physical thing. There are exceptions, such as conjoined twins and specially designed multi-tools, such as Swiss Army knives, but the latter are not living things and therefore love, empathy, and compassion are not likely to apply.

Individuals who have had near-death experiences describe the place they visited then as being filled with love, empathy, and compassion. They often say they preferred to stay there rather than return to Earth. The place they visited is likely a part of the spirit world. I say "a part" because as we will see as the presentation continues, our perception is so used to what we can perceive on Earth that if we visited the spirit world, we would recognize only the parts that have, or could potentially have, something to do with our universe. The rest of the spirit world would be unrecognizable to us and we would perceive it as simply unidentifiable background. For example, we are not likely to be able to make sense of a part that has to do with a universe with a dimensionality different from three, and in particular our specific kinds of three dimensions. Similarly, a real-life example on Earth is the case of a man who was blind all his life, but whose sight was restored in adulthood. He was unable to understand what he was seeing as being three-dimensional such that, for example, he perceives a staircase as a flat, two-dimensional stack of unrecognizable things.

Anything that exists in a universe exists because a spiritual entity exists in the spirit world that enables its existence. Since every spiritual entity is created by the spirit world, everything that exists in a universe is created by the spirit world. When an artist on Earth creates a piece of artwork, the artist did not really create it. It was already created by the spirit world in the form of a spiritual entity residing there. What the artist did was to spiritually go into the spirit world and, with his or her imagination and creativity, find that particular spiritual entity and then translate the spiritual entity, or artwork, into a form that could exist on Earth. Thus, the creativity of an artist is not the ability to create artwork but to spiritually go into the spirit world to find the spiritual form of it and then translate it. Artists do this by using their spiritual senses to make their way into the spirit world and find things there, much like they use their major senses to find things in our physical world on Earth. And then they use their spiritual senses and five major senses together to translate what they find into a form that could exist in our physical world on Earth.

While the model changes the perception of what artists do, it does not diminish the importance and value of it. To possess the extraordinary ability to find things in the spirit world and translate them into forms that can exist on Earth is highly admired, inspirational, and valued. It enables us to know more about what is in the spirit world. It also enables us to have a touch of how it would feel if we were to be back home in the spirit world. The same goes for other individuals with a high degree of creativity including inventors, scientists, authors, architects, choreographers, composers, etc. Longing to be back home in the spirit world touches all of us, and that's why we like works of art, inventions, new technologies, and so on. Have you ever heard someone describe a place that is peaceful and pleasing as being a piece of heaven? I have, and I know the feeling because I have experienced it. What that person is most likely referring to and spiritually feeling with his or her spiritual senses is the part of the spirit world that enables that place to exist on Earth.

Each spiritual entity is a different and unique combination of pieces of knowledge. Thus, each spiritual entity sends out a different and unique composite signal made up of the combination of single signals coming from each of the individual pieces of knowledge making up the spiritual entity. Therefore, each spiritual entity that could enable a living or nonliving thing to exist in a universe would enable a different and unique living or nonliving, physical or nonphysical thing to exist. A physical thing can exist only in a physical universe, but a nonphysical thing could exist or be expressed in either a physical or nonphysical universe. Such nonphysical things include thoughts, solutions, concepts, designs, stories, musical compositions, etc., and these can be translated and expressed on Earth.

When the spirit world is ready to create a new universe, it selects a group of spiritual entities that can bring into being a universe with the desired attributes. What determines the desired attributes depends on what the universe needs to accomplish to meet the needs of the spirit world at the time. The main purpose is to help the spirit world maintain its viability. As with any living and growing thing, some adjustments are needed now and then to maintain viability. How this applies to the spirit world is further discussed as the presentation continues.

4. Evolutionary Processes Continue Over the Lifetimes of Multiple Universes

We may have such an amazing diversity of living things on Earth because a number of species had already evolved over the lifetimes of multiple past universes. Therefore, their spirits already exist in the spirit world when our universe was brought into being, and they were ready to enable living things to emerge on Earth when the opportunity came. This same process applies to other planets in our universe, but the living things there could be different from those on Earth. This is because the environments on other planets differ from those on Earth, and therefore they would sustain different living things or the same living things but with different configurations. The creator of Superman long ago thought about this. Lucky for Earth, Superman happens to look human and is compatible with humans. This suggests he is likely to be a translation of a human spirit just as humans on Earth are translations of human spirits. But because he previously lived on another planet, the translation is different in that he has super powers. However, other living things on his planet might not look like any living thing on Earth.

Hey, I have question. Where did the idea of wearing a cape come from? Do humans on his planet wear capes? Well, a cape makes flying around look more stylish, and it keeps him from looking like a bird or an airplane. Oh, that's right. People were constantly yelling "It's not a bird. It's not an airplane. It's Soopperman!" And besides, his cape is easily imitated with a baby blanket, as I did as a kid. You? You mean we did? I was a part of doing it too, you know.

Evolution is not likely to start from scratch and end within the lifetime of any single universe, only to start from scratch again and end again within the lifetime of the next universe. Each such cycle is not likely to get too far, and highly advanced living things such as humans might not have a chance to evolve. To reach that level of advancement, evolution likely has to continue over the lifetimes of multiple subsequent universes. Likewise, to achieve such a diversity of living things as exist on Earth, evolution is likely to have to continue over the lifetimes of many universes.

Once the spirit of a living thing is formed, it remains in the spirit world and does not go away. Therefore, it only makes sense that it would continue to develop and grow whenever the opportunity to do so comes along, and this would include any opportunity that comes with each new universe. It thus follows that the process of evolution would naturally continue from the lifetime of one universe to that of the next and the next, and so on. And the process takes place in the spirit world, not in the world of any universe, although changes due to the process would be manifested in the world of the universe in which the evolved living thing resides.

Plausible physical evidence of this has been found. The recently invented X-ray microscope now enables us to see all at once in three-dimensions the fine details of the entire microstructure of a single living cell taken from an organism. Up to now, the electronic microscope enabled us to see only two-dimensional slices of a single cell. The amazingly complex microstructure of a single living cell and of the various bodily organs of creatures, including those of humans, suggests that they have evolved over the lifetimes of many universes. The lifetime of any single universe seems unlikely long enough for such complexity to evolve. Considering living things have existed on Earth for only a tiny fraction of the life of our universe so far, there really hasn't been much time for living things to have done much evolving here. And if the opportunities for evolving are also relatively short in other universes, it would take multiple subsequent universes to gain enough time to do the evolution necessary to achieve the complexity seen in living things on Earth.

What we see in the fossil evidence and interpret as true evolution might not be true evolution. Instead, it might simply be partial retracing of evolution that has already taken place in the spirit world. Partial retracing would be a relatively quick and convenient way of bringing certain living things into being in a universe, for example, on Earth. The rate of partial retracing revealed by fossil evidence might be more indicative of the rate of change of environments on Earth that are hospitable to the various stages of evolution of living things instead of the actual rate of evolution of those living things. This could explain how humans come into being on Earth extraordinarily quickly. The environments on Earth probably became hospitable to humans relatively suddenly at some point in the past. Thus, the retracing leading up to humans emerging on Earth took place so quickly that there was little time to leave behind fossils of "the missing link." This resulted in various individuals perceiving humans as being "suddenly created" on Earth.

If the model is correct about evolutionary processes continuing over multiple universes, this could explain why, for example, some living things on Earth are incompatible with various other living things. Couple this with the fact that nothing can be perfect and we get such things as allergies, bacterial and viral diseases, genetic diseases, cancers, tooth decay, food intolerance, clogged arteries, cataract, rashes, and so on. These could also indicate that some parts of the evolutionary processes that have taken place in some past universes may not fit well in our universe. After all, every universe is different and unique. What has "evolved to fit well" in one universe is not guaranteed to fit as well in another. The spirit world is likely to select species to reside in a new universe based partly on how workable the species would be in the new universe knowing the fit can never be perfect.

Conversely, a general lack of good fit could indicate the living thing did not do all of its evolving on Earth, and this supports the notion that evolution continues over multiple universes. Incidentally, if you have ever had a very severe hay fever attack, did you wonder at that moment if you really belong on the same planet with those allergy-producing plants? I did. And if you did too, well, maybe we were more on track than we realize.

5. Evolutionary Processes Will Retrace in a New Universe

An evolutionary process that has already taken place in the spirit world for a living thing will retrace itself in a new universe before moving forward in the new universe, if that living thing is brought into being in that universe. A retracing could look, and be perceived, as if evolution is happening. Once the retracing has reached where evolution left off, evolution can once more continue from that point on.

The question is how can we tell if what is observed from, say, fossil evidence is retracing or evolution? Sometimes we can tell it is retracing when what looks like evolution happened so quickly that little time was available to leave behind fossils. For example, the fact that we have not yet clearly found the "missing link" for humans suggests that humans emerged on Earth by retracing instead of by evolution. The retracing for humans might have happened so quickly that some people could perceive humans as being suddenly created. A number of other species seem to have "missing links" in their fossil records indicating they might have emerged on Earth through retracing as well. According to the model, retracing is natural and provides a logical and quick way of bringing living things into being in universes, as we will see as the presentation continues.

In the case of Earth, and probably elsewhere in our universe, the speed of retracing depends on the speed of change in the environments. For example, the first time an environment on Earth becomes hospitable to living things it might be hospitable only to primitive versions of only certain living things even if those living things have already evolved to more advanced versions in other universes. Therefore, only their primitive versions would first emerge on Earth. Thereafter, if that environment became hospitable to more advanced versions, the retracing could take place to enable the primitive versions to change to more advanced versions. The speed of the change would parallel the speed of change of the environment, fast or slow.

If the environment then becomes hospitable to even more advanced versions, but such versions have not yet evolved, then evolution could begin to move forward again for those living things. This means what is observed on Earth could start off as retracing that lasts for a while and then change to evolution from a certain point in time onward. The retracing part could happen so fast that there isn't time to leave behind fossils, whereas the evolution that follows could happen slowly enough to do so. This could explain why we find fossils of certain living things starting at some versions of those living things but not fossils of versions that came before those versions.

Such cases seem common on Earth, which indicates retracing could be real. And if it is real, then this indicates evolution does continue over the lifetimes of multiple universes and has taken place before our universe was brought into being. This then indicates universes have existed before our universe came into being.

Hey, you know some individuals are not going to buy this. I know, but like we said, no model formulated by a human is going to be totally complete or absolutely accurate. And besides, this book is not to convince readers to take our nutty personal spiritual model as their own anyway. You are correct, and in fact just because you and I are different sides of the same brain doesn't mean even we couldn't each have a different personal spiritual model. Hey, but we're still going to work on this book together anyway, aren't we? Yeah, I guess so, since it's kind of fun.

If the first living things to emerge on Earth are primitive, such as single cell things, slimes, etc., we might ask; how did such living things became more advanced living things, such as insects, reptiles, mammals, etc.? We have not yet found fossil evidence of such changes. A possible reason that those original primitive living things were selected by the spirit world to emerge on Earth first was because they would be viable in Earth's environments that exist at the time. But a more important reason might be that they could work on the existing environments to make them hospitable to other and more advanced living things. Therefore, after they had done their work, they would simply go extinct because they were not viable in the changed environments, in the same manner yeast turns sugar into alcohol in wine- and beer-making, and when all the sugar is consumed the yeast is no longer viable in the changed environment. After Earth's environment changed, other more advanced living things emerged, like worms, which left no fossil record either. Thus, there would be no fossil evidence linking the early living things to the living things that emerged later.

Suppose those worms had already evolved in the spirit world to become snakes, lizards, frogs, etc. Then if the environments on Earth were to quickly become hospitable to such more advanced versions, retracing could quickly accompany the environmental changes to enable the worms to quickly, generation by generation, change into their more advanced versions. Again, the retracing could have happened so quickly there wasn't enough time to leave behind fossils to indicate the changes.

This may be the case with humans. If this lack of fossil evidence has led some individuals to perceive humans to be suddenly created on Earth, then other creatures with missing links could also be perceived as being suddenly created on Earth. I suppose, in a way, perceiving quick retracing as being sudden creation is okay since what is considered "sudden" is relative. After all, we could say a copier suddenly created a copy of a painting because the time taken to make the copy is a lot shorter than the time taken by the artist to create the original version, even if making the copy was not truly instantaneous.

We might ask; why the spirit world doesn't bring new universes into being already with environments hospitable to the most advanced versions of the living things it selected to reside in that universe? The answer is if the spirit world were able to do that, the spirit world would already have to have most or all of the pieces of knowledge the new universe could generate. Thus, there would be little or no need to bring such a new universe into being. In the usual case, while the spirit world has the knowledge to bring a new universe into being it would not know how to work competently with the new universe without going through some learning experiences with the new universe first. Similarly, we might know enough to buy a certain piece of equipment for a certain purpose, but we still need to go through some learning experiences with that equipment to know how to use it competently.

In the case of our universe, the spirit world needs to go through experiences such as forming gas clouds and galaxies, and observing what happens in those things, including the birth and death of stars, the formation of black holes, finding out that larger stars are brighter but burn out faster, seeing what kinds of radiation are released from different phenomena, etc. With Earth, the spirit world needed to see what could be accomplished with volcanoes, storms and erosions, lightning, plate tectonics, magnetic fields, chemical reactions, etc. The knowledge generated or gained enabled the spirit world to then know how to form environments on Earth that would be hospitable to the kinds of living things it had selected to reside on Earth.

This could explain why Earth is such a rare planet in our universe. If the spirit world didn't have to do the learning from such experiences, it would have to already know from the start how to form planets like Earth that could support life. Then such planets would be common instead of rare in our universe. But then, as said earlier, the spirit world would have little or no need to bring our universe into being, since it would already possess most or all the pieces of knowledge that can be generated by our universe. A very similar universe would have already existed and with living things similar to the those in our universe.

Look at what we had to learn to enable us to develop the ability to build a space station hospitable to humans. Look at all the technology, equipment, and facilities we developed and used to gain the knowledge. And consider the vast infrastructure that must exist in order to make the components for the space station and to assemble them out in space. And notice space stations are rare compared with other things we built. Thus, we could say Earth is littered with all the things we built that led up to our building the space station. By analogy, our universe is littered with all the things the spirit world built throughout space that led up to the spirit world building planets that could support life. And such planets are rare compared with other things the spirit world built in our universe.

As mentioned earlier, the kinds of living things that can be sustained are likely to be different on each planet of our universe. For example, living things on Earth are carbon-based. It is possible living things on some other planet would be other than carbon-based. Even on Earth, a certain species of clams living beneath the sea near volcanic vents are sustained differently from how all other living things on Earth are sustained. They derive their energies from the hydrogen-sulfur gas emitted from volcanic vents where groups of such clams would live next to. We might ask; how were these clams brought into being on Earth? Since they survive so differently from how all other living things survive on Earth, could they have emerged by actual evolution on Earth? Or did they emerge by retracing? If no fossils can be found regarding their origin, then retracing is probably more likely.

6. Changes Could Also be Directly Made by the Spirit World

Changes in living things could be brought about directly by the spirit world instead of by evolutionary processes. For example, the spirit world might know of a pending environmental change and would initiate changes in a species ahead of time rather than wait for the environmental change to occur that would initiate the evolutionary changes. A certain species of fish developed the ability to crawl out of the water onto land before the environment changed to the point requiring the members to do so for survival. The spirit world may have wanted to ensure that that particular species of fish survived, rather than leaving its survival to chance. Another kind of direct action by the spirit world could look like experimentation. It's sometimes referred to as "tinkering by Mother Nature." A certain species of clam has an appendage that mimics a tiny fish to lure larger fish to come near enough to be caught. The clam's appendage varies in color, color pattern, and physical action from one member of the species to another. Some combinations of these attributes work better than others and some not at all. The spirit world must have a reason to experiment with this species of clams. The spirit world might be trying out new versions of a feature it has created. It might be similar to how, for example, after we humans develop ways of doing genetic engineering, we experiment to see what we can do with it.

The spirit of a living thing is a part of a spiritual entity able to serve as the spirit for a living thing, and, at some other time, it can serve as a spirit for any one of a variety of living things. Each such spiritual entity is composed of a whole bunch of smaller spiritual entities. For example, a smaller spiritual entity would be one that enables an arm to exist in a universe and be a part of a living thing, or a leg, ear, wing, heart, lung, kidney, brain, skin, tooth, feather, scale, fin, leaf, seed, flower, etc. Each of such smaller entities represents a feature that could be a part of a member of a variety of species. The spirit world has an enormous collection of features for living things, and it could assemble various features into any combination that would form viable living things.

In addition to assembling features into living things, the spirit world can also add one or more features to members of an existing species. Certain species of dinosaurs developed feathers, for example and these species eventually evolved into birds. Researchers have yet to figure out for sure why feathers were originally added to the dinosaurs. Some thought it might be to provide insulation to help keep the dinosaurs warm. But what if dinosaurs were cold blooded as some lizards are today? Then why would they need feathers for insulation? Perhaps the spirit world saw a need for birds on Earth and that having dinosaurs evolve into birds was a convenient way to quickly meet the need. The fact that very few fossils are found showing feathers on dinosaurs, suggests the emergence process for birds must have been quick. Evolution from dinosaurs to birds might just have happened quickly, or the emergence process for birds might have been a retracing. If it is retracing that took place, then the reason to have feathers added to dinosaurs must have existed in some past universe where adding feathers made sense. Therefore, the observation that feathers appeared on dinosaurs on Earth without a clear reason could be additional evidence that past universes existed and that evolution continuously takes place over the lifetimes of multiple universes.

When one of the smaller spiritual entities is called upon to enable a feature to exist in a universe, the form it takes in that universe depends on the attributes of the universe. Some universes are physical, some are nonphysical, and what each universe is made of is different and unique. A smaller spiritual entity that enables an arm to exist on Earth in our universe would enable something different to exist in another universe. But in either case, it would still spiritually be an arm. Therefore, whatever form it takes in a given universe would simply be a translation that could exist in that universe

It thus follows that if the same human spirit that enables a human to exist on Earth were to enable a human to exist in another universe, that human is not likely to look like the human on Earth. Therefore, if humans in that other universe were to visit Earth, or we to visit them, we would all spiritually be humans, but we might not recognize each other as humans. And we might look as strange to them as they might look to us. But if we were able to realize that we are all humans spiritually, and therefore a part of each other, we might have no trouble getting along.

Hmm, the same idea might even have a chance of working among us humans on Earth. Yeah, it's certainly worth a try, but unfortunately the idea of oneness among all humans has not had much luck so far. Well, maybe a model that could reveal more clearly how the oneness comes about might have a better chance of working. Wow, that sounds like our model.

7. **The More Advanced the Living Thing the Higher Its Rate of Advancement**

Aside from changes brought about by direct action of the spirit world, such as those discussed in the preceding subsection, there are at least three possible ways evolutionary changes could happen. Two are well-known. The model reveals a third as the one accompanied with increased advancement for the species. A given species could undergo evolutionary changes by any one of the three ways or any combination of them. Usually, it's a combination of the third way plus the first and/or second ways.

The first way is as follows. Within members of a species are variations in attributes such as abilities and configurations. If the environment changes such that the abilities and configurations that work best for survival change, then those members with these abilities and configurations that now work best would survive best and reproduce best. These abilities and configurations would then become increasingly predominant in subsequent generations. Since these abilities and configurations were already a part of the members' spirits, the change wouldn't be the direct result of any pieces of knowledge added to their spirits. Therefore, this way of bringing about evolutionary change would not be directly accompanied by advancement of the species.

An example would be Darwin's finches, a group of about fifteen related species. Some have short bills if their available food requires short bills to eat, others long bills if their food requires long bills, but they are essentially alike in every other respect. Somewhere along the way, evolutionary change happened; either the variation with short bills formed from the long-billed, or vice versa. Or both the long- and short-billed finches formed from finches with medium-size bills. Regardless, the change did not seem to make any significant difference in advancement between the two variations.

Hey, I know why. Oh really, why? It's because the brains of the two variations do not reside in their bills. Well, you are partly correct anyway.

If the environment changes substantially and remains changed a very long time, evolution can result in the formation of a new variation of similar species, as with Darwin's finches, or a new entirely new species, as with birds having evolved from dinosaurs. Another possibility is species could go extinct. Many dinosaur species are believed to have gone extinct due to a variety of possible environmental changes, one of which is that sunlight was obscured by heavy dust in the atmosphere after a massive meteor impacted Earth.

The second possible way evolutionary changes can occur is when members of a species migrate to another region. Abilities and configurations that work best for survival in the new region would likely be different from those that work best for survival in the old region. Resulting evolutionary changes can then come about in a manner similar to the first possible way evolutionary changes can occur. Again, since the abilities and configurations required for survival in the new region are already a part of the spirits of the members, the changes would not be the direct result of any added pieces of knowledge to their spirits. Therefore, this way of bringing about evolutionary change would also not be directly accompanied by advancement of the species.

A major difference between the first and second ways is that in the first way the terrain, elevation, latitudinal and longitudinal location, climate, available food and water, natural resources, proximity to the sea, predators, and so on remain mostly the same, whereas in the second way most of these factors are different. Therefore, abilities and configurations that work best for survival in the second way could change more drastically, and thus resulting in more noticeable evolutionary changes. This could explain how the various races of humans came about in the various regions on Earth since humans appeared to have migrated quite a lot in the distant past.

The third possible way evolutionary changes might occur is when members of a species go through experiences and generate new pieces of knowledge or gain access to existing pieces of knowledge. All such pieces of knowledge get added to the members' spirits if they are not already a part of their spirits. The spirits and the spiritual entities serving as the spirits would thus grow and change. Growth and change are more noticeable when the experience is very different from any the members have gone through before. Manifestations of any growth and change on the bodies of subsequent generations are usually not noticeable after a single such experience. But if essentially the same experience is regularly repeated throughout the members' lifetimes and continues for many generations, the resulting evolutionary changes would become increasingly predominate with each subsequent generation. This is because when pieces of knowledge are repeatedly used, the influence of their signals in configuring the body increases with each use. Because the evolutionary changes are direct results of growth of the spirits and spiritual entities serving as the spirits, the evolutionary changes are directly accompanied by advancements of the species.

If members of the species stop repeating the experience, they stop repeated use of those pieces of knowledge. The influence of the signals of those pieces of knowledge would gradually decline, and the advancements would gradually fade over many generations. It is the "use it or lose it" phenomenon. But the pieces of knowledge involved would remain a part of the spiritual entity. We humans work around the "use it or lose it" phenomenon by having various individuals become experts and specialists, each maintaining one or more areas of advancements such that our species as a whole would keep its advancements active. We also document our advancements with records and publications so that they can be recalled and be reenergized with relative ease as necessary. Thus, we do not have to "reinvent the wheel."

This suggests advancements are fragile for living things in our universe and perhaps for living things in other universes as well. If something were to destroy our documents and equipment, and keepers of advancements were silenced, we could revert back to a lower level of advancement. This would particularly be the case if survivors were forced to spend all of their time and effort over many generations simply surviving. It seems such events might have happened in some regions on Earth in the past. Various ancient ruins indicate occupants of the region achieved impressive advancements at one time, only to lose the advancements by allowing them to fade to where they become inactive in their descendants. However, pieces of knowledge once generated remain forever a part of the spiritual entities involved. Thus, the descendants could reactivate the pieces of knowledge and therefore regain the advancements with greater ease than re-developing the advancements from scratch.

We might ask; would the pieces of knowledge associated with advancements automatically become a part of a descendant's spirit since they are a part of the spiritual entities that had served as spirits for past members of the species such that a descendant could automatically possess all advancements? Obviously a newly born descendant doesn't automatically possess any advancement. The descendant has to go through learning experiences to gain them. The question is why advancements are not automatically possessed by descendants? Three possibilities that could explain this are:

A) The first possibility is that the pieces of knowledge associated with advancements would automatically become a part of a descendant's spirit. For simplicity for our present discussion, let's call such pieces of knowledge "inherited" ones, although there are many other kinds of pieces of knowledge in a descendant's spirit that came from their parents as well. An example of this can be seen in how children tend to physically resemble their parents in various ways. The inherited pieces of knowledge have connections of the first kind with every other existing piece of knowledge making up the spirit. In the first possibility, the connections are inactive when the descendant is born. Therefore, the pieces of knowledge aren't actively participating in the descendant's spirit until the connections are activated. When the descendant go through experiences, some of the connections get activated and thus the individual learns things. Which connections get activate depends on the experience. Certain pieces of inherited knowledge would then become actively participating in the descendant's spirit. As the descendant continues to go through experiences, he or she would continue to gain access to more of the advancements made of those who came before. The first possibility is plausible because it is consistent with the "use it or lose it" phenomenon. In this case it is different in that it is the "use it and regain it" phenomenon.

B) The second possibility is also that the pieces of knowledge associated with advancements would automatically become a part of a descendant's spirit. The difference is that it is the pieces of knowledge and not the connections of the first kind that are inactive and need to be activated. With both the first and second possibilities, activation of connections of the first kind or pieces of knowledge that are already a part of the spirit is easier than if they were not. Consequently, for example, a child could master certain skills and abilities easier and more fearlessly than their parents did. The second possibility is plausible since it is also consistent with the "use it or lose it" phenomenon. However, it is less plausible than is the first possibility, because connections of the first kind seem more likely to fade and become inactive than pieces of knowledge would.

C) The third possibility is the most likely one of the three and is the one most consistent with what has been discussed, or will be discussed, regarding the relation between the spirit and the spiritual entity that is serving as the spirit in the case of humans. It is that humans are designed purposely to not remember the lives of members that came before. This is so that the descendant could generate a greater number of new pieces of knowledge than they would otherwise. More specifically, they would not be swayed by the experiences of members who came before. For example this could explain why the fears some members of the previous generation have about using high technology devices are not automatically inherited by their children. Thus, their children are more able to master the use of such device than the parents were able to. This means the third possibility is that the spirit of a newly born descendant includes only those pieces of knowledge necessary to enable the descendant to physically exist and be alive. All other pieces of knowledge that are a part of the spiritual entity serving as the spirit remains with the spiritual entity, including those associated with intellectual and other nonphysical advancements. However, those pieces of knowledge being a part of the spiritual entity would be much more easily gained access to by the spirit of the descendant than if they were not a part of the spiritual entity. But the descendant would still need to go through learning experiences in order to gain access to such pieces of knowledge. Because gaining access to pieces of knowledge that are already a part of the spiritual entity is easier than if they were not a part of the spiritual entity, again this could explain why a descendant could master certain skills and abilities easier and more fearlessly than their parents could.

As discussed earlier, no two experiences can be exactly identical. Therefore, a descendant can never have a learning experience identical to the original experience that generated or gained access to those pieces of knowledge. The more similar the learning experience is to the original experience, the higher the number of the pieces of knowledge gained access to. This means a descendant would need to go through several different learning experiences to more completely gain access to a given advancement. This is why students, in order to gain all the pieces of knowledge on a particular subject, usually need to do homework and sometimes also hands-on laboratory sessions in addition to class lessons. Nevertheless, gaining an existing advancement is easier than developing it from scratch.

As mentioned above, the relative ease of gaining an existing advancement could explain why children could develop certain skills and abilities more easily than their parents did. An example is their ease at developing the skills and abilities to use high-technology devices. This could also explain why children can easily master common, everyday tasks such as brushing their teeth, putting on clothes, speaking a language, reading, drawing, and so on.

Research on animal behavior indicates animals can be trained to perform various activities. For certain animals and certain activities, they seem to gain the ability to do the activity by learning. Some other animals seem to simply mimic but not actually learn. Could it be that the activities they are able to learn are the ones for which they already have the pieces of knowledge in the spiritual entity that is serving as their spirit and are relatively easy to gain access to them? And could it be that the activities they simply mimic are ones whose pieces of knowledge are not a part the spiritual entity serving as their spirit? Mimicking is an experience but not one that produces the intended learning. For example, a student copying another student's test answers is going through an experience but not one that gains access to the intended pieces of knowledge. The pieces of knowledge generated or accessed would instead develop, or strengthen, the student's ability to copy test answers. It follows then that an animal that performs an activity by simply copying another animal would not necessarily learn how to do the activity but would instead learn better how to copy activities.

Experiences that gain access to pieces of knowledge in the spiritual entity would also generate new pieces of knowledge and/or gain access to pieces of knowledge already existing in the spirit world. Thus, the experience would also further the ability to become more advanced and/or to achieve new advancements.

I suspect today's children are more able to develop an ability to use high-technology devices than older adults could because their parents were exposed to precursors of these devices, including computers and computer programs; early calculators and cell phones; programmable remote-controlled TVs, VCRs, and other appliances; digital cameras; electronic typewriters with memory; cordless phones; etc. The parents' spirits grew from their experiences and that growth got passed on to their children. The children gained access to the growth by playing with, and using, current high-technology devices. Because the growth is the direct result of pieces of knowledge added to the parents' spirits and passed on to the children, it is directly accompanied by advancement of the human species. Children working with current high-technology devices will further the advancements achieved by their parents and/or cause the advancements to branch off into new advancements. Companies that design high-technology devices could sense potentially new branches and develop new devices to match them.

Among the three ways evolutionary changes could occur, the third is the one directly accompanied by advancement of the species. Some form of mechanism that works similarly to that described for the third way is likely to be speculated to exist by other individuals. However, to my knowledge, a model that describes such a mechanism and how it may work has not been available until now.

Every significant evolutionary change in a species would likely be accompanied by advancements of the species. For example, a major change in the environment in which a species lives would cause a major change in the living thing's behavior and thus some major changes in the living thing's experiences. Major changes in experiences are likely to generate more new pieces of knowledge and/or access more existing pieces of knowledge than would minor changes in experiences. This means major changes in experiences would generally result in greater advancements for the species. Therefore, any significant evolutionary change in a species would be the result of a combination of the third way plus the first and/or second ways discussed above.

For most living things on Earth, changes in their environment are not within their control, and for most of them their environments usually change very slowly, if at all, or only temporarily. We humans are different in that we induce changes in our environments through our discoveries, innovations, creations, constructions, manufacturing, extractions, urbanization, energy consumption, cultivation, migration, wars, greed, and so on. Every new discovery, innovation, and creation expands the diversity of our experiences. The more diverse our experiences, the more chances we have to generate new pieces of knowledge and/or to gain access to existing ones. The more chances we have to do this, the more frequently we can make advancements, and therefore the more rapidly we can advance. And the more advanced we become, the more diverse our experiences. Consequently, the more advanced we become the faster we become more advanced.

Therefore, once we humans got ahead of the pack, we increased our lead more quickly. Once we hastened our advancement, then within a relatively short time span we could become much more advanced than any other species on Earth. This vicious circle mirrors the nature of growth of the spirit world. I.e., the more the spirit world grows, the faster it grows. It only makes sense the living things the spirit world creates embody some of the vicious circles naturally embodied in the spirit world.

It follows then that the more recent segment of our evolutionary path must have been traversed very rapidly. If this segment were traversed rapidly, then retracing it would happen even more rapidly. Thus, the chances of having enough time to leave fossils behind during the retracing would be very low. The fact that we have yet to find a single definitive fossil of the human missing link tends to support the notion that we humans emerged on Earth through very rapid retracing. It would be interesting to see if the phenomenon of the missing link also applies to other highly intelligent living things such as dolphins, elephants, whales, octopi, etc. since they might have also emerged on Earth through rapid retracing.

If we humans did emerge on Earth very rapidly, it's understandable why some individuals would believe humans were instantaneously created. On the other hand, considering how long our universe has been in existence, by comparison the short time the human species took to emerge on Earth could be perceived as instantaneous. Therefore, there might be some validity to saying we humans were instantaneously created. It would then be similarly valid to say various other living things on Earth were also instantaneously created, and I guess the same individuals would believe that is the case as well.

At the other end of the spectrum, some species on Earth have not changed much, if at all, over thousands of years. This is because their experiences don't differ much from day to day, year to year, century to century, etc. and not a whole lot of growth happens to their spirits even over thousands of years.

8. **A Given Connection of the First Kind Can be Active for One Spiritual Entity and not for Another**

Oh, by the way, I've been waiting to ask a question. No kidding, you were willing to wait to ask? Yeah, it's because I was confused. No kidding, you, confused? Well, yeah, if a piece of knowledge has connections of the first kind with every other existing piece of knowledge, and every piece of knowledge is shared among multiple spiritual entities, how come some connections are active for some spirits and some are inactive for other spirits until activated? Oh, brother, I knew you were going to ask that. Well, get ready for a long but interesting answer.

When a spirit of an individual gain access to a piece of knowledge that already exists in the spirit world or is a part of the spiritual entity serving as the spirit, the spirit could be perceived as activating the connections of the first kind that are between that piece of knowledge and all the pieces of knowledge making up the spirit. This is how that piece of knowledge becomes a part of the spirit. Now, the following discussion is to answer the question asked.

A) The way things work in the spirit world is different from how things work in our physical world, and sometimes it is mysterious to us, because we are accustomed to our physical world. For one thing, the spirit world is nonphysical and not restricted to three dimensions, and certainly not restricted to our particular three dimensions. Therefore, it is unlikely any human would know for sure how things work in the spirit world.

B) A similar question to the one asked is how could a given spiritual entity be a separate entity in the spirit world when every piece of knowledge is connected with every other existing piece of knowledge by connections of the first kind? The fact that each spiritual entity could be a separate entity means there must be a way for a given connection of the first kind to be active in some manner for some spiritual entities but be inactive, less active, or more active in some manner for other spiritual entities. How this works might have something to do with the spirit world having no limitations on dimensionality or kinds of dimensions. For example, what if each spiritual entity has a different combination of dimensions? Another thing is the kinds of spiritual energies are bound to be more numerous than the kinds of energies we are use to in our physical universe. There may be no limit to the kinds of spiritual energies, and more could be created as more new pieces of knowledge are generated and added to the spirit world. Thus each spiritual entity might be active with a different kind of spiritual energy.

C) Each spiritual entity being different and unique might be more easily illustrated by looking at their spiritual signals. A specific spiritual entity would encompass a specific set of pieces of knowledge. That spiritual entity would thus issue a signal consisting of a specific combination of signals, each signal being issued by a different piece of knowledge in the set. Therefore, each spiritual entity would be distinguished by its different and unique signal. There is no limit to how many different spiritual entities could be formed as long as new pieces of knowledge continue to be generated, in a manner similar to how each sentence is distinguished by its word set and sequence, with no limit to the number of possible different sentences as long as new words are being formed.

D) Regarding spirits of living things, at the start of a living thing's lifetime the inherited pieces of knowledge are encompassed in the spiritual entity serving as the spirit and are not yet an active part of the spirit. As the spirit goes through learning experiences, for example, by piloting the living thing through experiences, it may gain access to specific inherited pieces of knowledge, which ones would depend on the experiences. These then become an active part of the spirit. The experiences would also generate new pieces of knowledge and/or gain access to pieces of knowledge already existing in the spirit world that are not already encompassed in the spiritual entity serving as the spirit. These added pieces of knowledge would make the spirit and the spiritual entity more advanced than they were before, and the newly generated pieces of knowledge would also make the spirit world more advanced than it was before. All the pieces of knowledge added to the spirit would change the spirit and its signal, and its changed signal would enable the spirit to do things it was unable to do before.

E) Not every piece of knowledge encompassed in the spiritual entity can be accessed via the learning experiences available in our physical world. However, such pieces of knowledge might be accessible to spirits of living things residing in some other universe if the learning experiences available there are able to gain access to such pieces of knowledge. This could be the case if the same spiritual entity at a different occasion were to serve as the spirit for a living thing residing in such a universe. Thus, only those pieces of knowledge accessible to a spirit would be considered "inherited" for that spirit, while other pieces of knowledge would not be considered inherited for that spirit, even though they are all a part of the spiritual entity serving as the spirit.

F) The spirit of a living thing is a portion of a larger spiritual entity and is not a stand-alone spiritual entity because the spiritual entity serving as the spirit holds the advancements made by predecessors and makes the advancements accessible to the spirit.

G) Conversely, if the inherited pieces of knowledge were inherent in a spirit, the spirit would not need to learn to access them and wouldn't generate new pieces of knowledge for the spirit world and for the spirit itself. Consequently, an effective means of furthering advancements and/or achieving new ones would not be put into action for the spirit world or the spirit. This would not be wise or consistent with the spirit world's need to maintain wisdom to remain viable. The conclusion then is that the spirit world purposely made everything work the way they now work in order to continue its own growth and viability and therefore also the growth and viability of everything it creates.

H) This also explains why a newborn human baby doesn't know what its predecessors have learned. This is not necessarily the case for some other species, according to the model, as explained in Chapter Five.

The response to the question asked continues with the discussion presented in the following subsection.

9. Growth and Advancements Progress in Spurts

The discussion in this subsection is a continuation of the response to the question asked in the beginning of the immediately preceding subsection. The question is "If a piece of knowledge has connections of the first kind with every other existing piece of knowledge, and every piece of knowledge is shared among multiple spiritual entities, how come some connections are active for some spirits and some are inactive for other spirits until activated?"

A) Growth and advancements seem to naturally progress in spurts rather than in smooth, continuous progressions. For example, the first automobile built is not like today's automobiles. Designers arrived at today's design by learning from past designs, and the advancements were made in spurts. More specifically, approximately every five years completely new and more advanced models are designed and produced after learning how well the previous models performed. The same kind of spurts in progression has been true for airplanes, boats, light bulbs, refrigerators, wine production, medical procedures, high-technology devices, etc. The same goes for advancements in any field of research; i.e., advancements are achieved by reviewing what has been achieved to help gain insight on what is possible to achieve next. Thus, it is by design that the spirit world purposely makes learning a part of life in universes. What is learned in universes would be part of how the spirit world grows and how it maintains its viability by using what is learned to help determine what advancements to achieve next and thus how to design the next universe. This suggests that because advancements are naturally achieved in spurts in the spirit world and in our universe, it is likely also be the case for all universes.

B) This also indicates that advancements are not done randomly but instead follow some logical progression. For example, they are done with some goal in mind, and the goal is bound to vary with time. Notice how this is the case for how humans made advancements. For example in the case of automobiles, some advancements are to make cars safer, some are to make cars easier to drive, some are to make cars more fuel efficient, etc. Ultimately, the purpose is to make automobiles more attractive to buyers for the situation, concerns, and resources that exist at the time. This is how the automobile industry maintains its growth and viability.

C) The formulation of my model also progressed in spurts. The process of reviewing each draft for typos and grammatical errors also enabled me to find more things the model could explain, and thus the formulation spurts forward with each review.

D) The consciousness of the spirit of a living thing focuses mainly but not totally on the world of the universe in which the living thing resides. The other part of its consciousness focuses on the spirit world in order for the spirit to find thoughts, solutions, concepts, inventions, etc. in the spirit world. Meanwhile, the consciousness of the spiritual entity serving as the spirit remains focused on the spirit world. All this is part of how every living thing carries out life simultaneously in the spirit world and in the world of the universe in which the living thing resides.

E) The concept that every individual has a "guardian angel" could be real, and the guardian angel entity would essentially be the spiritual entity serving as the spirit for that individual. It would encompass all the knowledge, wisdom, advancements, etc. achieved by predecessors of the individual. Being equipped with all these qualities, it would be able to, in a sense, watch over the individual in a manner similar to what we might imagine a guardian angel would do.

F) The process of making advancements in spurts by first reviewing advancements already achieved and then figuring out the next advancement could explain why all living things on Earth have finite lifetimes. Finite lifetimes might apply to living things in other universes as well. The spirit of a living thing and the spiritual entity serving as the spirit grow as the living thing goes through experiences and generates new pieces of knowledge and/or gains access to already existing pieces of knowledge over its lifetime. This spurt in growth for the spirit and the spiritual entity ends when its lifetime ends. Another spurt in growth would begin for the spiritual entity when another occasion comes up for it to serve as spirit for a living thing. To maximize the next spurt in growth, all the advancements achieved during the lifetime of the preceding living thing would be employed by the spirit world to design the next living thing whose spirit the spiritual entity would serve. This would enable the new living thing to go through the kinds of experiences that could best further the advancements achieved and/or best branch them off to form new advancements. Thus, periodic updating of living things to take advantage of advancements achieved is a possible reason living things in our universe, and perhaps in other universes as well, have finite lifetimes. One generation of living things would live for a while and then die off, because after they have achieved a certain level of advancements, their advancements could be better continued by the next, more advanced generation of living things.

G) This is analogous to how spurts in advancement of high-technology devices are made by device designers and makers. The current generation of devices goes through experiences that generate the knowledge designers need to design the next, more advanced, generation of devices. The next generation of devices being more advanced, are able to have experiences that maximize advancements that could be achieved in the next spurt of advancements. This process continues as long as advances continue. Each subsequent generation of devices renders current devices obsolete and their useful lives finite, as users go for the newer devices. This enables the device industry to continue growing and to remain viable.

H) All the attributes, workings, and advancements that are discussed in response to the question asked, are able to exist because each spiritual entity is a separately identifiable entity. Each spiritual entity could be separately identifiable because each connection of the first kind could be active for one spiritual entity and not for another. Therefore, the answer to the question asked is that the spirit world simply purposely made the connections of the first kind this way in order for the spirit world to maintain its own growth and viability.

Oh my! After that long answer to my question I am kind of dizzy. I think I will take a nap. Hey, the answer could have been simply the very last sentence in the preceding paragraph. But, the question gave an opportunity to explain things about the spirit world that might not have an opportunity later to be explained. Therefore, your asking the question was a good thing.
    Hey, talk about sleep, why we sleep and how sleep works will be explained later, in Chapter Seven. Oh no, not another long and complicated explanation! Well sort of, but it will be very interesting and fascinating. Well, then I better—zzzz. While the other half brain sleeps, let's go on.

10. Advancements Are Made When We Are not Using All Our Time and Energy to Simply Survive

An interesting observation worth thinking about regarding living things on Earth is that when they are spending all their time and effort on basic survival, not much, if any, advancement happens to their species since the skills required for basic survival are already a part of every living thing's spirit. This could explain why most creatures on Earth are not advancing very fast, if at all. This is because most of them are primarily consumed with simply surviving. Thus, if a population of humans is forced into a situation in which the individuals are putting all their time and effort into simply surviving, they are not likely to contribute much, if anything, to the advancement of our species. Essentially, all the advancements our species have made were accomplished when we were researching, experimenting, innovating, exploring, brainstorming, constructing, inventing, problem solving, renovating, etc., and not while we were simply trying to survive. Our species could be losing out on what some individuals could contribute if they were put into situations in which they are simply trying to survive. Therefore, nations in which their leaders put their own people and/or people of other nations in situations in which they are simply surviving are hindering the advancement of our species, not to mention of the leaders themselves and their own descendants. Thus, it is to the benefit of our species that all of us do our best to ensure all able-bodied able-minded individuals are not placed in situations that force them to simply survive.

The phenomenon that more advanced living things advance faster applies throughout our universe, thus there are likely to be living things elsewhere in our universe that are considerably more advanced than we are. We might ask; how we would know they are more advanced when we meet them someday? The answer is likely to be that they would have figured out how to either avoid making a mess on their planet or how to overcome any mess they might have made. By comparison we humans are still mired in the mess we have made on Earth.

I have another question for you. Awake already? Can't sleep; you think too loudly. Anyway, here's my question. Why do you say "when we meet them someday?" Well, of course we will. Even if we never get advanced enough to travel to other planets, they might be advanced enough to travel to Earth. And if neither they nor we can travel to other planets, then when their lives and our lives are over, our spirits would meet in the spirit world. Them and us dying? OMG, your response turned out to be less interesting and less exciting than I expected.

We will also see, as the presentation continues, that an increase in advancement in one segment of a species could result in the same increase in another segment due to "cross-learning," even though the second segment did not go through the experience that produced the increase in the first segment. Cross-learning is an actual observable phenomenon, as described later in Chapter Five. The model explains how it might work, that it takes place in the spirit world, and that its effects could be observed in our physical world. This is further discussed later in this chapter and in greater detail in Chapter Five. In humans, when children in one segment of our species become, say, more able to develop the ability to use high-technology devices, children in other segments are likely also more able to do so as well. This is the case even if their parents have never used such devices or their precursors.

Hey, this means we can let our kids play all day, not go to school, and let cross-learning do all their learning for them. No, no, no! Being able to develop ability does not mean automatically having ability. You need to have an opportunity to develop it and you need to put in some effort. Oh, so, children who never get to see or touch a high-technology device would never develop the ability to use it even though they might be able to do so easily because of cross-learning? Yeah, that's more like it, and the phenomenon applies to all kinds of abilities, not just the ability to work high-technology devices. Gee whiz, you sure have a way of putting a damper on what looked like might be the neat idea of letting cross-learning do all the learning for kids.

11. All Views of the Spirit World Are Valid and Correct But Incomplete

Our body has five major senses, and they are tuned into our physical world. As the presentation continues, we will see, according to the model, we also have an undetermined number of spiritual senses, and they are tuned to the spirit world. We use our spiritual senses to find things in the spirit world such as thoughts, solutions, answers, concepts, ideas, designs, story lines, etc. We use our spiritual senses and our five major senses to translate what we find into forms that can be expressed or exist in our physical world.

I suspect we humans in general do not consider the idea that we have spiritual senses or that we carry out our lives simultaneously in the spirit world and our physical world. Consequently, we interpret what we sense in the spirit world as being in our physical world. This might be contributing to the mess we humans make on Earth.

The spirit world is so large that each of us could sense only a tiny part of it. Since each individual is different and unique, each would sense a different part of the spirit world, although the difference may be small among members within a given group. What this means is that what each of us sense of the spirit is valid and correct, but incomplete.

As far as I can tell, the notion of "valid and correct, but incomplete" is generally not considered. This could be among the reasons why various groups of individuals form various religions, and the various religions are not acknowledged to reflect the various different parts of the same thing, the spirit world. Therefore, disagreements could come up between different religions. Add egos and desires to enhance survivability into the mix and we could have wars and other conflicts over religious differences. Disagreements, wars, and other conflicts are unnecessary if members of different religions would realize that different religions simply reflect different parts of the spirit world. It thus follows that instead of wars and conflicts, it would be better to combine the various religions and thus come up with a more complete understanding of the spirit world.

What is keeping us from doing this is our response to our egos. Sometimes our desires to enhance survivability could also get in the way. Thus, while religions are beneficial to humans in many ways, they could also hinder the advancement of our overall world population by, for example, diverting our time, resources, and energies into wars and various conflicts when they could be used for more constructive purposes.

Another factor that comes with not realizing we simultaneously carry out our lives in the spirit world and our physical world is we tend to consider everything we find in the spirit world as belonging in our physical world. This is understandable if we do not realize the spirit world exists or if we do not understand what the spirit world is even when we realize it exists. The things we find in the spirit world belong in the spirit world, and it is our translations of those things in forms that could be expressed or exist in our physical world that belongs in our physical world. The translations are not quite the same as the real thing in the spirit world. In general we can see on Earth that the translation of anything is not quite the same as the original.

Since oneness pervades the spirit world, empathy and compassion also pervades the spirit world. Therefore, everything in the spirit world embodies qualities of empathy and compassion. When we find something in the spirit world and translate it into a form that could be expressed or exist in our physical world, the translation tends to have less, or none, of the qualities of empathy and compassion. This is because every living or nonliving physical thing in our physical world is separate. Physical oneness does not exist among living or nonliving physical things and therefore the qualities of empathy and compassion tend to range from being less to almost none among them as compared to how it is for their spiritual counterparts in the spirit world.

This could explain how it is that an individual is able to allow himself or herself to kill another individual. Not enough empathy and compassion exist between them to block the act of killing partly because they are not physically a part of each other. If they realize they have spiritual counterparts in the spirit world and that they are a part of each other there, they might have enough empathy and compassion for each other to block the act.

We might ask; how could the translated form of something that is in the spirit world end up with a lower quantity of empathy and compassion than that something has in the spirit world? Let's consider a thought as an example. A thought existing in the spirit world is in pure thought form. The translated form that could be expressed in our physical world would be in terms of a spoken language, a symbol, or a body language. If the spoken language were French it is likely to embody a higher quantity of empathy and compassion than if the spoken language were English. This is because French is one of the "romantic" languages whereas

English is not. A "romantic" language embodies a higher quantity of empathy and compassion than a "nonromantic" language does, and that is why it feels romantic. We can feel the difference when we hear it, and it could influence our mood. We do not know the quantity of empathy and compassion the thought has in the spirit world, but the fact that its translated form could have different quantities depending on the spoken language indicates that the translated form must have less quantity than the thought has in the spirit world.

This would similarly be the case if the thought were translated into a body language. The body language of a woman in general tends to be softer than that of a man. Therefore, in general a higher quantity of empathy and compassion would be conveyed by the body language of a woman than that of a man for the same thought expressed. This is partly why in general women are seen as more nurturing than men, although the difference is narrowing with the younger generations.

A similar phenomenon applies to something that translates into a physical thing to exist in our physical world. For example, it is well known that certain colors look appealing on a given model of an automobile and certain other colors look unappealing on the same model. The more appealing an automobile is to us, the more we are likely to cherish it if we own it. In other words, the more appealing the automobile the higher the quantity of empathy and compassion it has for our taste in automobiles, and we in turn would have a higher quantity of empathy and compassion for it and would take good care of it.

These examples illustrate how it is that quantity of empathy and compassion is less in our physical world than the quantity is in the spirit world. The quantity of empathy and compassion we have for each other influences how we carry out our lives on Earth, especially if we think life on Earth is all that life is. But, if we were to realize we have a spiritual part of life as well, and to understand how that part is naturally rich with empathy and compassion, our actions in our physical world are bound to embody more empathy and compassion for each other.

We might ask; what about things that would be bad to begin with in the spirit world, such as the thought that is a decision to murder someone? The answer is; every universe is different and unique and has a different and unique purpose. What is perceived as being bad in our universe could be perceived as good or neutral in another universe, and vice versa. Therefore, something we consider bad to begin with in the spirit world might not be bad but that only its translated form that could be expressed or exist in our universe is perceived as bad by us. However, there are some things that are bad to begin with in the spirit world. The thought that is a decision to murder someone is an example. No spiritual entity in the spirit could be murdered. That is because a piece of knowledge once generated would exist forever in the spirit world. Therefore, the thought that is a decision to murder someone is only a concept and not a practice in the spirit world. However, concepts in the spirit world are among things that could be found by humans and be translated into a form that could exist and acted out in our physical world. This is one of the ways universes could provide opportunities for the kinds of experiences not possible to have in the spirit world, and that is partly the reason why universes are periodically designed and brought into being.

12. We Are Currently Not Aware of Other Existing Universes, But We Could Be

Living things in different universes have major senses tuned to the attributes of their own universe. This means living things in one universe are not likely to sense the presence of other universes. Consequently, living things could think their universe is the only one that exists, whether or not that is the case.

Every living thing in every universe has a spirit in the spirit world, and the spirit has spiritual senses in the spirit world. Therefore, the spirit of one living thing could sense the spirit of another living thing regardless of the universe in which each resides. However, the spirit doing the sensing is designed to be the spirit of a living thing residing in a certain universe and therefore generally cannot make sense of what is sensed if it pertains to a different universe. One spirit might regard the other as simply one of many undefined things in the background, similar to how we could recognize what is said in our native language but not what is said in an unfamiliar language. We are likely to perceive what is said in that language to be a part of background sounds if it were not spoken specifically to us.

The consciousness of the spirit of a living thing is designed to be mainly, but not totally, tuned to the attributes of the universe in which the living thing resides in order to pilot the living thing within that universe. The other part of its consciousness is tuned to the spirit world enough to enable the spirit to find things there but not enough to make sense of everything there. Generally, the spirit is able to make sense of things that can be translated into forms that can be expressed or exist in the universe in which the living thing resides. But it also depends on the level and kind of advancements the spirit has made. For example, a spirit advanced in medicine might not be able to make sense of a complex mathematical expression, but a spirit advanced in mathematics could. Conversely, a spirit advanced in mathematics might not be able to make sense of a sick patient's diagnostic data, but a spirit advanced in medicine could. However, when either individual go through more diverse experiences and thus gain more diverse knowledge, then either individual could become able to make sense of the subject matter of the other.

This indicates that the more advanced the spirit and the more diverse its advancements, the more things in the spirit world the spirit is able to make sense of. Thus, it is theoretically possible for a spirit to make sense of a spirit of a living thing residing in a different universe. Researchers are making discoveries today because their advancements have progressed enough to enable them to make sense of the things they find. Predecessors of the researchers might have run across these same things but were unable to make sense of them.

With every discovery we make, we learn more about the workings of the spirit world. While the workings we learn about are the ones that pertain directly to our universe, they could also indirectly pertain to other universes. This could be the case because of the oneness that pervades the spirit world, in the same way every spiritual entity is directly or indirectly a part of every other spiritual entity. This means that as our level and kinds of advancements progress we could eventually become aware of the presence of other existing universes and be able to correctly interpret what we are sensing.

This also means there might be very advanced living things "out there" from a different universe that can sense us and understand what they are sensing. They could be watching but leaving us alone because we are too primitive and not peaceful enough to interact with them constructively. For example, we might mistakenly think they want to invade Earth and take it over especially since such invasions are commonly depicted in our science fiction stories and movies. According to the model, if the advancements of such living things have progressed to the point they can sense our presence and understand what they are sensing, then they are likely to have progressed to a way of life different from ours. They are likely to understand that a way life based on empathy and compassion for one another is far better than one based on ego and enhancement of survivability, such as the dominant basis we chose as our way of life. Also, perhaps it is because they are empathic and compassionate that they are patiently waiting for us to progress to a way of life comparable with theirs before they attempt interaction. After all, they might have tried in the past a little more than 2,000 years ago and it didn't work well because a representative they sent was eventually killed. If this is the case, then according to the model there are living things "out there" that love us and care about us. Interestingly, many of our religions say a similar thing.

The workings of an awareness of other universes take place in the spirit world, not in the world of any universe, including ours. This means that if we want someday to develop this awareness, we need to be more aware we are carrying out our lives simultaneously in the spirit world and our physical world. We have been focused on trying out all kinds of activities we can do in our physical world but have not focused much on the kinds of activities we can do in the spirit world, for example, having more empathy and compassion for all other living things, especially other humans. However, it is never too late to start.

Spirits and Souls of Living and Nonliving Things

As discussed earlier, the spirit of a living or nonliving thing is only a portion of the spiritual entity serving as the spirit for the living or nonliving thing. On a different occasion the same spiritual entity could serve as the spirit for a different living or nonliving thing residing in a different universe. Thus, a different portion of the spiritual entity would be employed serving as the spirit at that time.

The spiritual entity serving as a spirit encompasses all the pieces of knowledge it has acquired from all the experiences it has gone through in addition to anything the spirit world decides is a part of the spiritual entity. The sum total of such factors means that on any given occasion the unemployed part of it is quite complex and extensive. Some things in it can be translated into forms that can be expressed or exist in the universe involved at that moment while other things in it may not. On another occasion, a different set of things are compatible with the universe involved at that moment and other things in it are not. This means the spiritual entity is likely to include pieces of knowledge that could enable certain features to appear on a living thing that resides in one universe but not on a living thing that resides in another universe. For example, this could be the case if the dimensionality is different for each universe, and certain features could be made to exist only in certain dimensionalities. Differences in the substance making up the different universes could also play a role. Other possibilities include physical universes versus nonphysical universes, universes with gravity versus universes with no gravity, various kinds of spaces for universes that require space to exist, etc.

The unemployed part of the spiritual entity would include features that were once a part of living or nonliving things and could be a part of living or nonliving things again on a future occasion. Evolutionary changes can bring some of these features into being on a species of living or nonliving things, and can also make features on a species of living or nonliving things go away and be "stored" in the unemployed part of the spiritual entity for future use.

Evolutionary changes of living things are usually responses to changes in the environment, such as climate changes, and other changes living things make, such as migrating to another region on Earth, discovering new ways to do things, discovering new kinds of food, etc. Evolutionary changes to nonliving things are all due to changes that happen to them, either by "Mother Nature" or by living things. Once the spirit of a living thing is formed it can only grow as the living thing goes through experiences and generates new pieces of knowledge and/or gains access to existing pieces of knowledge. All such pieces of knowledge are added to the spirit and thus the spirit grows, and growth will continue as long as the living thing is alive.

The spirit of a nonliving thing can grow or come apart. For example, the spirit of a plain piece of wood being worked into a fancy leg for a chair grows and becomes more complex in order to enable the more complex chair leg to exist. When the chair is discarded, all of its parts eventually decompose back into the basic materials and energies that make up Earth. Accordingly, the spirit of the chair leg breaks down into parts, some of which become inactive in enabling the chair leg to exist, while some remain active to enable the basic materials and energies to exist that once made up the chair leg.

When a living thing dies, it becomes a nonliving thing. Its spirit immediately separates into two parts. One part enabled all the body's basic materials and energies to exist and to formerly come together to form the living thing's body while it was alive. This part eventually decomposes in a manner similar to that of the spirit of any nonliving thing. The other part of the spirit detaches from the body upon death and remains intact and exists in the spirit world forever. This is the part that is everything the living thing is, minus the physical body.

What eventually evolved into humans were apparently sea dwelling creatures with gills. Remnants of gills can still be seen in the very early stage of the human embryo, but disappear as the embryo continues to develop. The pieces of knowledge associated with gills used to be a prominent part of the spirit that evolved into a human spirit but are no longer prominent. But they remain a part of the human spirit enough to enable remnants of gills to show up in the very early stage of the human embryo. Pieces of knowledge once a part of a spiritual entity will always be a part of the spiritual entity. Therefore, if someday humans were to become sea-dwelling creatures again, the part of the spiritual entity having to do with gills could once more become prominent in the human spirit.

This brings up an interesting feature of spirits and souls, and of spiritual entities that could serve as spirits. As the presentation continues, we will see how the spirit and soul of a living thing together embody a record of every experience the living thing has gone through in its lifetime up to the present. Similarly, in terms of what has been presented, the spiritual entity, together with all the spirits it has served as, embodies a record of all the evolutionary changes that the spiritual entity has been a part of since it was creation by the spirit world. With all such records being a part of the spirit world, it is possible to see the entire history of the spirit world up to the present once our lifetime is over and our consciousness becomes completely tuned to the spirit world.

While alive, we could see a portion of the entire history of the spirit world up to the present if we were able to identify and recognize everything in the spirit world that is possible for us to find using our spiritual senses. But right now our consciousness is not tuned enough to the spirit world to enable us to develop enough proficiency in the use of our spiritual senses to be able to find everything there that is possible for us to find, let alone to identify and recognize them.

We might ask; why only a portion? The answer is because living things, including humans, in our physical world would have only a portion of all the spiritual senses that exist in the spirit world at any point in time. The portion includes only those spiritual senses that are needed for the spirits of the living things to be able to sense things in the spirit world that could be translated into forms that could be expressed or exist in our physical world. This is because living things in our universe are to go through experiments that could take place in our physical world. Therefore, any additional spiritual senses would enable the living things to sense bits and pieces of things in the spirit world that pertain to, for example, other universes. That would make the experiences confusing and thus the living things would be unable to make sense of what they are experiencing. Consequently, the kind of pieces of knowledge that are supposed to be generated would not be generated.

The confusion would be similar to how our dreams tend to be surrealistic. The topics of sleep and dreams are among the topics in Chapter Seven. The discussion there indicates the surreal nature of dreams is due to pieces of knowledge generated not on Earth getting mixed in with pieces of knowledge generated on Earth. The surreal nature can be confusing, but our spirit seems okay with it probably because it is okay with the spiritual entity serving as the spirit. The spiritual entity most likely understands why it happens and that it is a natural result of how the spirit world functions, as explained in Chapter Seven. However, if the same kind of confusion were to happen with our experiences while we are awake, it would not be okay with our spirit. That is because it would have to deal with it, whereas in a dream it doesn't.

Yeah. If all our experiences were surrealistic everyone would end up in the nut-house. But, on the other hand maybe we would then not make the mess we made on Earth. Well, maybe not the same kind of mess anyway.

The notion that living things in our physical world have only a portion of the spiritual senses that exist in the spirit world at any point in time could be confirmed by the fact that different species of living things on Earth have different sets of abilities. This could happen only if living things have only a portion of the spiritual senses that exist at any point in time, and different species have different positions.

Everything a living thing does, mentally or physically, involves the use of its spiritual senses. For example, our spirit pilots our body by sensing the feedback signals from our body. We use our spiritual senses to find solutions to problems. We interact with others by using our spiritual senses to find thoughts and to sense the thoughts expressed by others. Our other mental and physical activities work the same or similarly. This indicates spiritual senses play a major role in enabling our abilities to exist and to function.

After a living thing's life in our physical world is over and its consciousness becomes completely tuned to the spirit world it would be logical that its spirit would then have access to every spiritual sense that exists in the spirit world at any point in time. This is because the spirit thereafter and forever will participate with every other entity in the spirit world to help maintain the spirit world's viability. The only way it could do that is to have access to every spiritual sense that exists at any point in time.

1.   **A Spiritual Expression Is Everything a Living Thing Was**

Pieces of knowledge once generated will exist forever in the spirit world, and connections of both the first and second kinds once formed will also exist forever. Therefore, spirits and souls once formed will exist forever. While a living thing is alive, its soul is partly in the spirit world and partly in the world of the universe in which the living thing resides. After the living thing dies, the main part of the soul immediately, or eventually, becomes completely in the spirit world, depending on what the spirits wants it to do. The main part of the soul makes the living thing what it is while the living thing is alive.

The rest of the soul consists of the souls of the materials and energies that make up the living thing. This part of the soul is essentially on loan to the living thing just as the materials and energies that make up the living thing are essentially on loan to the living thing. After the living thing dies, the materials and energies go on to make up new living and nonliving things. The connections of the second kind comprising this part of the soul of the formerly living thing separate from the spirit of the now deceased living thing and become a part of the souls of new living or nonliving things. Thus, this part of the soul in reality is a part of the soul of the universe in which the living thing resided, just as the materials and energies in reality are a part of the universe. The spiritual entities that enable the materials and energies to exist are thus a part of the spirit of the universe.

For any universe at any point in time, its soul is made up of every connection of the second kind that has ever been formed and that has to do with that universe up to that point in time. This includes connections of the second kind having to do with the materials and energies it is made of and connections of the second kind having to do with every living and nonliving thing that ever resided in that universe up to that point in time. Each universe is different and unique and thus its particular connections of the second kind are different and unique. This means we could identify the universe in which a living, nonliving, or formerly living thing reside or resided via the particular connections of the second kind making up its soul. It follows then that every piece of knowledge that has anything to do with a universe at that point in time is a part of the spirit of that universe at that moment. Thus, the spirit of every living and nonliving thing that has ever resided in that universe is a part of the spirit of that universe. Unlike its soul, which is unique to that universe, every part of its spirit is shared with the spirits of countless other things in the spirit world. Again, this is because of the oneness that pervades the spirit world. Once the lifetime of a universe is over, its materials and energies vanish, but its spirit and soul exist in the spirit world forever.

A spirit always has its associated main part of the soul connected to it. The spirit and the main part of the soul form the spiritual expression of the living thing. While the living thing is alive, its spiritual expression has the main part of the soul partly in the spirit world and partly in the world of the universe in which the living thing resides. After the living thing dies, the main part of the soul is "normally" completely within the spirit world and the spiritual expression is a living entity in the spirit world forever. It is everything the formerly living thing was, minus the part that used to reside in a universe. The spirit's consciousness is then fully tuned to the spirit world. Thus, the spiritual expression is then able to interact fully with spiritual expressions of other formerly living things.

The reason we say the main part of the soul is "normally" completely within the spirit world is because the spirit of the spiritual expression might want to keep a presence for a while after death in the world of the universe in which the living thing had resided. This was apparently the case for my parents after both of them died, and apparently also the case for my wife after she died. The spirit of the spiritual expression might also want to return to the world of the universe for visits occasionally. That would be possible as long as the lifetime of the universe is not over.

We might wonder about spiritual expressions of living things that are still living. Wouldn't spiritual expressions of formerly living things notice them in the spirit world and interact with them? The answer is yes to both parts of the question. But the consciousness of the spirit of a living thing is mainly tuned to the world of the universe in which the living thing resides and less tuned to the spirit world. Whatever interactions a living thing's spiritual expression has with spiritual expressions of formerly living things could be manifested in the living thing's dreams, daydreams, intuitions, instincts, and various other subconscious signals, etc.

We might ask; are there various other kinds of subconscious signals besides those mentioned? I did not used to think so, but evidence arose recently that indicated otherwise, which made me think back to many past occasions involving others and myself that also indicated otherwise.

Some of these are mentioned in passing later in the book. A very recent occasion happened on my late wife's sister's birthday. I would call my late wife's siblings on their birthdays to wish them happy birthday. But on this occasion I was too tired to do it early in the day, and thought that if I waited, her sister usually had more time to talk in the evening anyway. So I decided to take a nap and call her afterwards, but I was especially tired and napped longer than usual. While asleep, I heard my neighbor call my name. Because I kind of look after her and always respond quickly if she needs me, I woke up with a start, but then immediately realized that, with closed double-pane windows, I would not hear her voice from outside so loudly. Besides, whenever she needed me, she normally called me on the telephone. One glance at the clock and I decided I better call my wife's sister before she goes to bed. I caught her just in time to say happy birthday. The voice that woke me up must have been my late wife's; she knew I needed to wake up right then in order to catch her sister before it was too late. She made her voice sound like my neighbor's because she knew my neighbor's voice would wake me up right away.

Getting back to interactions among spiritual expressions, if a spiritual expression of a formerly living thing tries to interact with that of a living thing, it would be like a living thing trying to interact on Earth with another living thing that is asleep. The spiritual expression of a formerly living thing is likely to get only low-level response from that of a living thing. This means that in the spirit world there are a whole bunch of spiritual expressions of living things, all seemingly asleep. That is because the spirit of each is mainly focused on the world of the universe in which each reside. But since things in the spirit world do not sleep, spiritual expressions that look as if they are asleep can be easily identified as belonging to living things residing in various universes.

Thus, according to the model, if we are alone in our physical world, it is possible not to feel lonely if we realize we also live in the spirit world. All our deceased loved ones are there with us and are caring about us in a place where oneness and love pervade throughout.

So you are saying the spirit world is full of dreamers being watched over by the rest of the spiritual expressions? Yep, it is sort of like that. *How fascinating. I guess we better not say "Boo" when we are there or we might wake them up.* Well, at least don't say it loudly. We often say our deceased loved ones love us and are watching over us, and I guess this is one way how that works. *You know, in a way it is sort of comforting if all this is true.* Yeah, and it is kind of emotional too. Yeah, it kind of makes you want to be as good a person as possible as a way *of saying back to them, "I love you too." In fact, this might be yet another source of the notion regarding guardian angels watching over us. It would touch us even more deeply if we were to think about living things, especially highly intelligent ones such as humans, as spiritual expressions who are willing to go into the risky state of being a living thing in a universe. And they are doing it for the sake of helping the spirit world maintain its viability and the viability of everything else in the spirit world. Yeah, and our making an effort to help keep them viable is like saying, "I love you too." That makes sense. It's similar to the way various individuals on Earth are willing to go into the risky state of being members of the military to help their nation maintain its viability and its population's viability. Wow! So, members of the military are in sense saying to us, "I love you?" So, we who are residing in a universe have agreed to tackle some really important risky tasks? It looks that way. Well, somebody has to do it, just as somebody has to be in the military. So, it is very possible we are here on Earth for a noble cause, and we really need to look at it that way and be careful not to make a mess of it? Sigh. It would sure be nice if we hadn't made a mess on Earth already.*

2. Reincarnation for Humans Occurs with The Spiritual Entity, not with The Spirit

The spirit of a deceased highly intelligent living thing does not become the spirit of a new living thing. The spiritual expression, consisting of the spirit and soul of the deceased living thing, has other responsibilities as a part of the spirit world and all the things the spirit world does to stay viable and growing. Therefore, when reincarnation takes place, it is not the spirit that reincarnates, it is the spiritual entity that served as the spirit that reincarnates, and it forms a different and unique spirit each time it does.

If the reincarnation stays with the same species, then the evolutionary changes that occurred during the lifetime of the previous living thing are incorporated into the new spirit. Thus, the new living thing is more advanced than the previous one. However, at least in the case of living things on Earth, the advancements happening over one generation are usually slight and likely not perceptible. But over many generations, they could be.

Up to this point in this section, the topics of spiritual expressions and reincarnation have been discussed in a manner that pertains to humans even if they were not always referred to as pertaining to humans. We will see as the presentation continues into Chapter Five that, according to the model, for certain other species on Earth, it is possible that both the spirit and the spiritual entity could reincarnate together. There are also species whose spiritual entities reincarnate piecemeal, not all at once.

3. Cross-Learning Among Members of The Same Species

Highly intelligent living things such as humans mainly do their own thinking. More specifically, it is their spirits that mainly do their own thinking. By contrast, living things that primarily rely on instincts for survival rely on the spirit world and/or their spiritual entities serving as their spirits to do a lot of their thinking.

Because the spirit is only a portion of the spiritual entity serving as the spirit, cross-learning in general can occur among members of the same species of any living thing but especially among living things that primarily rely on instincts for survival. Spiritual entities serving as spirits for members of the same species are all very similar, sharing a large portion of themselves with one another. Therefore, when one member goes through an experience and generates pieces of knowledge and/or gains access to existing pieces of knowledge, those pieces of knowledge become a part of its spirit and its spiritual entity. The part of its spiritual entity that grew might be a part shared among the spiritual entities of essentially all other members of the species. When this happens, all these pieces of knowledge also become a part of the spiritual entities of essentially all the other members. This is how cross-learning works.

Each member of any species is different and unique. Therefore, in most cases there are bound to be a few that did not benefit from the cross-learning, because their spiritual entities do not happen to be sharing in that particular part of the spiritual entity of the member that did the learning. This may be yet another way new branches on an evolutionary tree could form, albeit probably not a very strong way compared with the ways discussed earlier in this chapter.

If the species is one in which members primarily rely on their spiritual entities to do a lot of their thinking for them, then essentially all members immediately know what the member that did the learning knows. These are the species whose members rely heavily on instincts for survival, but this does not mean all members behave in unison. Each member still behaves independently. Cross-learning is a proven phenomenon that has been observed in the behavior of certain species of animal, as discussed further in Chapter Five.

Species whose members mainly do their own thinking also share large parts of their spiritual entities, but it is their spirits and not their spiritual entities that mainly do the thinking. Therefore, while cross-learning could add pieces of knowledge to their spiritual entities, their spirits still need to gain access to those pieces of knowledge before their spirits know what the member that did the learning knows. It is easier for a spirit to gain access to pieces of knowledge already a part of the spiritual entity than if the pieces of knowledge were not. Thus, cross-learning benefits such species by making it easier to learn what one or many other members of the species already know. For example, as described earlier in this chapter, children can develop the ability to work with high-technology devices more easily than their parents could because of cross-learning, but they do not automatically have the ability. They still have to go through some learning process, but the learning process is made easier because the living things have intuition and weak instincts. The signals from the cross-learned pieces of knowledge come through weakly as intuition and instincts.

It is often said the best business people are those with good intuition and who follow it. This could be an example of cross-learning at work for humans. This suggests we could benefit by tuning into our intuition more, because it helps us tap into what has been learned by others. This is assuming what has been learned by others is beneficial in the first place. Humans being how we are, this might not always be the case. This might explain why we sometimes do not trust our intuition. We might have had a bad experience doing so. For example, a good experience for someone could be a bad one for someone else. Intuition could get us to try an experience because it was a good one for someone, but it might not be able to indicate whether the experience will be a good or bad one for us if we do not think thoroughly enough about it first.

4.   **Spirits and Souls of Nonliving Things**

Conventional thinking does not indicate a nonliving thing has a spirit or soul. But the model indicates a nonliving thing, as well as a living thing, has to have a spirit and a soul in order to exist in a universe. Also, as discussed earlier, nonliving things are alive in an elemental sense, and living things are made of nonliving things. Accordingly, the spirit and soul of a living thing are made of the spirits and souls of the nonliving things plus additional pieces of knowledge to enable the living thing to be alive, functioning, and a member of a species.

When a living thing dies, its soul partially detaches from the body. The part that detaches is what enables the living thing to be alive, functioning, and a member of a species. The part remaining attached enables the materials and energies making up the body to remain in existence.

Likewise when a nonliving thing is destroyed, its soul also partially detaches from what was the thing. The part that detaches is what enables the nonliving thing to be what it was. The part remaining attached enables the materials and energies making up the nonliving thing to remain in existence.

In both cases, the spirits and souls of the materials and energies later become parts of the spirit and soul of the next living or nonliving thing to be made of those same materials and energies. Thus, the materials and energies along with their spirits and souls are repeatedly recycled. In a sense, we could say in general that the materials and energies along with their spirits and souls are always temporarily on loan to some living or nonliving thing.

At least in the case of a human and various other creatures on Earth, even while alive the materials and energies making up the body are constantly being recycled. Old cells die and are cast off, and new cells replace them. The cells of a donor organ in an organ recipient's body are gradually replaced by the recipient's own cells. In due time, the organ is composed entirely of the recipient's own cells, and rejection of the organ by the recipient's body is no longer a problem. This is a fairly recent speculation, and it could only happen if the organ recipient managed to live long enough for it to happen. Generally, in the past not many organ recipients manage to live a very long time so that such a speculation has not been made. However, as organ transplants become more common and as procedures improve, more organ recipients are living longer, and thus the speculation is recent. However, very likely not enough cases are available to indicate for sure if the speculation would be true or if the phenomenon would be completely enough with every kind of organ and with every organ recipient who managed to live a very long time. Consequently, organ recipients are still instructed to continue taking anti-rejection medication the rest of their lives even if they were to live a long time.

Joe, my best friend since childhood, is a truly wonderful and caring person, and he is one of the longest surviving kidney-transplant recipients. He has had the transplant for more than twenty years, and by now the kidney is very likely to be composed entirely of his own cells. That is wonderful, pal, and you certainly deserve to be so lucky!

5.   **Thoughts Are Among the Most Powerful Spiritual Entities**

Everything residing in the spirit world is in the form of a spiritual entity, and every spiritual entity is made of pieces of knowledge all interconnected by connections of the first kind. Thoughts are also spiritual entities, and it is logical that thoughts would be made of interconnecting pieces of knowledge. As discussed earlier in this chapter, pieces of knowledge are analogous to words. Spiritual entities being made up of pieces of knowledge interconnected together are analogous to sentences made up of words connected together. Sentences convey thoughts. It is interesting that thoughts are spiritual entities, and spiritual entities are analogous to sentences.

Everything is created by the spirit world, including thoughts. We humans do not create thoughts. We find them in the spirit world by using our spiritual senses and then we translate them into forms that can be orally expressed or exist in writing in our physical world. The notion that we do not create thoughts, but instead we find thoughts, is counter to conventional thinking, but according to the model this is how the process of thinking works. And it is consistent with the notion that the spirit world creates everything. Sometimes we even say things like "I can't find words to express my feelings," which suggests, subconsciously, we know we look for thoughts rather than create them.

Since all spiritual entities are made of interconnecting pieces of knowledge, they can all be perceived as various forms of thoughts. Thus, spiritual entities that can enable things to exist in a universe can be perceived as essentially very complex thoughts. Therefore, by this perception, when a spiritual entity enables something to exist in a universe, it can be perceived as essentially its thought that is enabling that thing into exist in that universe. Accordingly, we are all here in our universe because it is the thoughts of various spiritual entities in the spirit world that are enabling us to exist in our universe. The same goes for everything else that exists in our universe. Thus, our entire universe exists because the thoughts of a whole lot of spiritual entities in the spirit world are enabling our universe to exist.

This means while living and nonliving things residing in a universe might seem real to each other, they are all essentially only figments of the spirit world's thoughts. For this reason, thoughts can be perceived as being among the most powerful spiritual entities in the spirit world. Interestingly, scientists working to identify the smallest possible subatomic particle once said that when we get down to a level of existence that small, the particles seem to take on qualities of a thought.

Oh, wow! The spiritual entities enabling our universe to exist better not get a headache so severe they can't think. Yes, and they better not get drunk either. Hey, you know, some individuals say that when a natural disaster happens, it is because a certain God got angry. Such individuals must have a notion in mind similar to how our model says things exist in our universe because the thoughts of spiritual entities are enabling things to exist. Therefore, what if we say such spiritual entities are like their Gods, and that the spiritual entities could get angry sometimes? OMG, don't imagine they could get angry. Some spiritual entity might then get angry, because recall earlier we said that anything we could imagine could be imagined because it already exists in the spirit world in the first place. Oh, well, then I could remedy that by simply imagining that spiritual entities simply do not get angry even though they could. Hey, I like that. So keep imagining that. Yeah, let's both imagine it together. A whole brain doing it is better than just half a brain. Hey wait a minute, I thought we said it is our spirit that does the thinking, thus also the imagining, not the two halves of our brain. Oh, details. The readers know what we mean.

As an aside, an interesting analogy could be drawn between the discussion of this subsection and what might be happening when an author composes a story. The setting, things, and people in the story are all figments of the author's thoughts. But within the world of the story, all these are perceived to be real to each other. Could it be that a universe is formed inside that story by the author's thoughts, and the things residing in the universe of the story are brought into being in that universe by the author's thoughts? And could it be that an individual reading that story could detect that universe and the things in it using only his or her sense of sight? His or her other five major senses need not be tuned into any of the attributes of that universe in order for him or her to sense that universe and what is going on in it?

Perhaps this is how it will be for us humans when someday we achieve inter-universe travel. When we are visiting another universe, we might be lucky if even just one of our five major senses could tune into the attributes of that universe. Living things residing there are bound to have multiple major senses tuned into attributes of their own universe, and we are not likely to have any of their major senses. Therefore, what we would sense of their universe could be very different from what they sense of their own universe. This is analogous to how we sense the universe of a story by sensing the words the author composed. Thus, what we see in our mind while reading the words may be very different from what the people in the story would actual see in their own universe. In other words, the people in the story are bound to have major senses tuned into attributes of their universe, and we are not likely to have any of their major senses. Thus, it also follows that what a reader sees in his or her mind while reading the story is never identical to what the author sees in his or her mind while composing the story, or what another reader sees. We are each different and unique.

This is something to think about when someday we do inter-universe travel, i.e., how to communicate with living things there if, for example, only one of our major senses can tune into attributes of their universe. If we can form a picture of what is going on in a story by using only one of our major senses, we might be able to form a picture of what is going on in another universe by doing the same. But could we communicate with living things there if what we sense of their universe is different from what they sense of their universe? We will have to figure out how to handle that possibility before we visit other universes. In fact, such a communication hurdle may be why we keep thinking visitors from outside of Earth are likely to be hostile when in fact may not be.

One thing we might do is to learn to communicate telepathically. We will see as the presentation continues that telepathic communication is universal among all universes because it functions by going through the spirit world and not by going through any universe.

Incidentally, according to the model, in order for an author to compose a story, the story has to already exist in the spirit world. The spirit world creates everything, including stories, and an author uses his or her spiritual senses to find the story in the spirit world and then translates it into the form of a book that can exist in our physical world. The author does not create the story but instead his or her creativity is a reflection of how proficient he or she is in using the spiritual senses to find stories in the spirit world.

Oh, so then you are saying our model already exists in the spirit world, and we are only finding it, not formulating it. Well, I guess you are right about that, according to our model. Well, then good thing there are two of us doing the finding instead of just one of us. Yep, a whole brain is better than half a brain for doing that. Also we could bounce ideas and thoughts back and forth between the two of us without bothering anyone else. And, as long as we do not talk out loud while doing that, other folks will not think we are crazy. Well, even if they do, they'll think only your half of our brain is crazy, not my half. No, no, they would think it is your half.

6. Science and Spirituality Already Go Together

We often hear people say science and spirituality do not go together. But as discussed in the Preface, according to the model, every model in our life is essentially a spiritual model. Things such as concepts, definitions, mathematics, formulas, assumptions, and approximations that make up any model reside in the spirit world. However, the things to which we apply any of our models reside in our physical world. Thus, right away there is a connection between the spirit world and our physical world, and it is embodied in our various models. There is more.

Everything in our universe has connections of the second kind with a spiritual entity in the spirit world in order to exist in our universe. How everything functions in our universe is governed by how the spiritual entity to which it is connected functions in the spirit world. Thus, how everything functions is embodied in the connections of the second kind that connect a thing in our universe with its spiritual entity in the spirit world. This means how everything functions in our universe is embodied in the soul of our universe, which at any given point in time consists of the souls of all the living and nonliving things that exist in our universe at that point in time.

Thus, as living things evolve in our universe, our universe also evolves. This means that while our universe physically changes, it also spiritually changes. The changes usually mean advancements. For this reason we cannot rule out the possibility that living things in our universe, currently or in the future, will be able to do things such as travel to other existing universes. Likewise, living things in other existing universes may be able to travel to our universe. More on this as the presentation continues.

What is embodied in the soul of our universe is what we humans are trying to capture with our countless models. Each model can capture only a tiny portion of what is in the soul of our universe and only in an approximate manner. Science can thus be perceived as an ongoing effort to continue formulating models so we can continue to capture more of what is in the soul of our universe. Therefore, from this point of view, science and spirituality inherently go together and thus have always gone together.

More than one model can approximate the essence of a given portion of the soul of our universe. For example, one model might be in the form of mathematical expressions. Another might be in the form of curves drawn on grids. Another might consist of a set of procedures, such as in the finite element method of structural analyses. A model can be theoretically based or empirically based. And so on. Thus, each model could be perceived as being based on what could be seen in the soul of our universe from a specific vantage point in our physical world. Every model is associated with a different and unique vantage point. All reasonably formulated models are correct because they all come from looking at the same thing. However, all are also incomplete because none come from looking at the totality of the soul of our universe. Not even Einstein, who tried to formulate the model of everything, was able to do so.

If we were able to see what is in the soul of our universe from vantage points in the spirit world, we are likely to come up with very different models. The models are likely to have very strong spiritual qualities just as how our current models have very strong physical qualities. Perhaps it is in this sense that some people might say science and spirituality do not go together. For one thing, the models with very strong spiritual qualities are likely to be so foreign to us that we not likely to be able to apply them in a practical manner since our consciousness is mainly tuned to our physical world and not so much to the spirit world.

However, according to the model, some of our models could be more complete if spirituality were taken into greater consideration in their formulation. These would include, for example, models to do with human relations, behavior of living things, biological processes, medical diagnostics and treatments, ecological issues, etc. But, for example, structural design and analysis models usually do not need to take spirituality much into consideration since they deal heavily with attributes of our physical world and not much with attributes of the spirit world. On the other hand such model might still be more complete if spirituality were taken into consideration in their formulation.

For example, we might wonder why something fails, not function well or as intended, or is not liked by users. Three possibilities come to mind. One possibility is; the model or models used to design the item was too incomplete and therefore the design was inadequate and thus the item failed in use. The second possibility is; if the design involved the use of multiple models, the models were not mutually compatible. This could be perceived as a kind of human error, for example, in the choice of models. Thus flaws were unintentionally built into the item. The third possibility is; the model or models used did not have enough of a spiritual component in them, and their use was thus incompatible with how humans would typically use such models. Consequently, the item got designed poorly. This could be perceived as human error because experience could have enabled the user of the models to compensate for such an incompatibility. Or an insufficient component of spirituality in the model or models could product an item that turns out to be incompatible with how a user would typically use such items. Consequently, users do not like the item.

If more spirituality were formulated into the models and formulated appropriately for the specific models, possibilities two and three could be avoided. This is because possibilities two and three have to do with how humans would typically go about using a model of a certain kind or an item of a certain kind.

I bought an emergency radio with built-in light and built-in flashing red light a few years ago to be used in case of power outage. The item has a crank I could turn to operate a built-in charger to charge up a rechargeable battery. The outside surface of the item was coated with a rubbery coating that made the item comfortable to hold and not slip in my hand as I crank the charger. The item worked well and was nice to use. However, years later the rubbery coating became icky sticky, and handling the item leaves my hands icky sticky with some unknown, possibly toxic substance. I couldn't remove the rubbery coating or its icky stickiness. Therefore, the item became very undesirable and more or less unusable, unless I am willing to put up with icky sticky hands while poking around the house in the dark if the power happens to go out when it is dark.

Oh, that reminds me I once had a pair of shoes with a rubber-like sole that soon got icky sticky. Yeah, and you walked around the house wearing those shoes leaving icky sticky shoe prints all over the floor, and I had to clean them up. Yeah, I know. I felt so bad for you that I tossed the shoes. Hey, you didn't ask me first before you tossed them. They were my shoes too. But then if you wear them later, you would leave icky sticky shoe prints all over the floor too. Yeah, and then YOU would have to clean the floor instead of me. That's why I wished you didn't toss them.

The spirit world obviously has some pretty complete and pretty accurate models in order to be able to design and bring universes into being. But even its models are not totally complete or absolutely accurate. That is because the spirit world can never possess every single piece of knowledge that can be generated, and thus the spirit world can never be perfect. Perfection is only a concept, not a reality, even for the spirit world, and this is also the case for everything it creates.

Nevertheless, the spirit world's models are far better than any model we humans have formulated. The spirit world knows how to design and build amazing living and nonliving things. We humans formulate models to help us understand how to do what the spirit world does, if only in an approximate manner. There are many examples of amazing things the spirit world can do. Spiders, for example, spin web strands with a tensile strength higher than that of steel but flexible. Certain carnivorous plants have non-stick surfaces slipperier than any non-stick coating made by humans so far. Researchers are discovering ways of growing components for batteries while producing far less polluting wastes than are produced by current methods. Antibiotics and various other medical compounds could only be extracted from plants and various other living things. Geckos have toes that can cling to any surface, including windows, well enough to support the weight of the gecko, though their toes are not icky-sticky or equipped with suction cups.

The extraordinary consciousness and intelligence of the spirit world is demonstrated by its ability to design and bring into being an amazingly variety of complex living and nonliving things using the same simple basic building materials and energies. Every living and nonliving thing in our universe is made of simple electrons, protons, neutrons, and sometimes also various other basic subatomic particles. It takes a lot of knowledge and cleverness to design and bring into being the enormous variety of living and nonliving things that exist, or have existed, in our universe from these few simple basic elements. Additional evidence of the spirit world's genius is how it uses very simple principles in complex ways to enable complex living things to live and function.

The fact that our universe was brought into being using just these few particular simple basic elements as building blocks means that something somewhere somehow has a purpose in mind for our universe that it needed to fulfill before our universe was brought into being. It already knew the kinds of living and nonliving things these basic elements could be assembled into which would make our universe the specific kind of universe it needed. However, as with any new tools and building materials, it has to play around and experiment with them before it becomes highly proficient at using them. After all, although few in variety and simple, these basic elements are sophisticated and complex in terms of what they can become and/or do once assembled.

Because such evidence strongly indicates our universe was brought into being to fulfill a purpose, past universes must have existed, and they too must have had purposes. After all, the amount of knowledge and cleverness employed to design and bring into being our universe has to have come from a lot experience at doing such things. It also follows that the evolutionary process for living and nonliving things must have spanned the lifetimes of these past universes. Thus, it stands to reason that our universe is simply a part of the current segment of the ongoing process of growth for the spirit world and that other universes exist and are part of the current segment as well.

All the models we humans formulate are only approximations; i.e., correct but not totally complete or absolutely accurate. Each model has a limited range of applicability. But with enough models covering enough of the important areas in our lives we are able to carry out our lives the way we do. The entire collection of models in our lives could be envisioned as if they make up a crazy quilt consisting of countless pieces of fabric, each piece with a different pattern, color, texture, size, and so on. There are holes here and there in the quilt, where no models have yet been formulated to cover. There are gaps between pieces we must learn to work around, and where now and then we make an error and things fail. But overall, the crazy quilt is complete enough to enable us to generally do okay carrying out our lives. But there are still a lot of problems in the world that our models are not addressing adequately. Our crazy quilt needs to be more complete and more accurate. The model indicates it could also benefit by including more spirituality in its fabric.

In terms of the model presented in this book, such particles as the Higgs boson discussed earlier are likely to be manifestations of how the spirit world figured out how to make the enormous variety of things that exist on Earth, starting with elemental things such as subatomic particles, electrons, protons, neutrons, elemental atoms, etc. Thus, if what the scientists say about Higgs-like particles is true, then the model they eventually come up with that characterizes Higgs-like particles should be very interesting. They might need to include in their formulation spiritual considerations beyond the usual concepts, definitions, mathematics, assumptions, and approximations, and so on found in our current typical models.

7. Spirits and Souls of Elemental Things

While everything visible to the naked eye in our universe looks different and unique, this is not the case for elemental things such as subatomic particles, electrons, protons, neutrons, elemental atoms, etc. For example, all electrons are identical, all protons are identical, all neutrons are identical, all atoms of the same kind and isotope are identical, etc. Such particles are sometimes called quantum particles.

At a level of existence that small, the range of possible experiences such things could go through is quite limited and can be quickly gone through. Once all the possible experiences are gone through, no additional new pieces of knowledge can be generated and thus added to their spirits. This means the spirit of each elemental thing grows quickly, then reaches its growth limit and remains unchanged for the rest of the lifetime of our universe.

Spirits of molecules are like this as well especially small ones such as molecules of water, hydrogen, nitrogen, carbon dioxide, etc. The range of possible experiences for such molecules is also limited. Therefore, their corresponding spirits also grow quickly, then reach their growth limit and remain unchanged the rest of the lifetime of our universe.

In the case of physical things large enough to be visible to the naked eye, the range of experiences becomes unlimited. Thus, the spirit of such things continues to grow over the lifetime of our universe, provided the opportunities to do so exist. Since such things always have new experiences they can go through, the spirit of each enables just one in that exact form to exist. It is sort of like, why bother with identical copies of the same thing when just one can go through new experiences just as easily as multiple identical ones could. Besides, there is no rush in the spirit world to go through as many experiences as quickly as possible, and it is simpler to enable just one thing in that exact same form to exist.

Accordingly, then, for example, the spirit of one grain of sand would not enable another identical grain of sand to exist at the same time. Every grain is naturally different in physical shape and in the way its various atoms are arranged. A different spirit for each grain enables each to be different in ways consistent with the natural processes in our physical universe. As time goes by, a grain's physical shape changes through natural abrasions and erosion. Such experiences generate pieces of knowledge that change its spirit, and this enables changes in the shape of the grain. A whole bunch of grains can become covered with layers of sediment and be compressed into rock. The spirit of each grain then becomes a part of the spirit of the rock. The rock can remain buried for millions of years, and its spirit might hardly change over that period. However, its range of possible experiences remains unlimited. For example, someday the rock could be extracted and used for building things, could be heated and melted by volcanic action, could be broken up by tectonic movement, etc. But if such opportunities do not come along, the spirit and rock could remain essentially unchanged for the rest of the lifetime of our universe. However, the spirit world would not call upon the spirit to enable any other identical thing to exist as long as new experiences are possible for that rock.

This is different for the spirits of elemental things. Such spirits do not have any more new experiences to go through. Therefore, they cannot generate any more new pieces of knowledge. Consequently, they remain unchanged for the rest of the lifetime of our universe. Accordingly, it makes no difference whether they enable just one member in that exact form to exist or an unlimited number of identical members to exist as far as going through new experiences and generating new pieces of knowledge are concerned. This is why the electron spirit is called upon to enable every electron in our universe to exist, the proton spirit to enable every proton to exist, the spirit for one kind of water molecule (there are three kinds; one has ordinary hydrogen atoms, the other two have one of two rare isotopes of hydrogen atoms, deuterium and tritium) enables every water molecule of that kind to exist, etc.

Ugh! I thought water was supposed to be good for us. Don't worry. The other two kinds are rare. Rare? You mean if we cook them they would be okay? Hey, maybe your side of the brain absorbed too much of the uncooked, I mean rare, kinds. Now you got me doing it.

Spirits of elemental things exist by design by the spirit world. In order to design and bring universes into being, the spirit world needs building materials, physical ones and nonphysical ones, for all varieties of substances. Spirits of elemental things are the spirit world's building materials. The spirit world would have a collection of spiritual entities capable of serving as "building material" spirits, and new ones would constantly be formed as new piece of knowledge are constantly being generated and added to the spirit world. By analogy, living things on Earth always need building materials of all kinds to build all kinds of things. Birds need materials to build nests, beavers need materials to build dams, termites to build hills and tubes, bees to build combs, and we humans to build all kinds of things.

Spirits not of the "building material" kind would be large enough and complex enough to have an unlimited range of experiences. Even the spirit of as simple a thing as a grain of sand would always have possible new experiences.

Although not an elemental thing, DNA molecules are building materials for building living things. A particular living thing is made of multiple copies of a particular DNA molecule. Because the DNA molecule is a building material its spirit can enable multiple copies of it to exist for the purpose of building that particular living thing.

Since the spirit of an elemental thing can enable an unlimited number of the same elemental thing to exist, it is possible that the spirit world is calling upon such spirits to continuously bring into being additional members of elemental things into our universe. Thus, our universe can continue to grow. This could explain why we still see gas clouds in outer space, as mentioned earlier, and why our universe appears to be expanding at an increasing rate. The gas clouds could be where additional space and members of elemental things are continuously being brought into being, and that could be why new stars are continuing to form there. Otherwise, as discussed earlier, you would think all such gas clouds would have condensed and all new stars would have already been formed.

However, there is always a chance the gas clouds could be the result of old big stars dying and exploding. This would produce the heavy elements that make up such things as the living and nonliving things on Earth, as well as the planet Earth itself along with various other planets. But to form such huge localized gas clouds would require an awful lot of old big stars to die and explode within a limited region in space. Therefore, I think a more likely possibility is that the gas clouds are where our universe is continuously being brought into being.

Thus, it might be that as long as our universe continues to grow and expand, its lifetime will not be over anytime soon. After all, as older planets become unable to sustain life, as long as new stars and planets continue to form, there will always be some new planets that can sustain life. But don't forget that the gas clouds could be millions and billions of light years away; what we see may have happened millions and billions of years ago. Therefore, for all we know, new gas clouds might no longer be coming into being anymore and our universe might not be growing and expanding anymore.

Oh, my, that could be bad. We might as well pig out on junk food while we can.

8. Quantum Superposition and Entanglement

The model provides a plausible explanation for why quantum superposition and entanglement happen. The Institute for Quantum Computing stated the following in its article "Quantum Computing 101," available online January 6, 2014:

> **A)** Quantum superposition and entanglement can be seen only when looking at the tiniest quantum particles, such as atoms, electrons, protons, etc.
>
> **B)** Superposition is essentially the ability of a quantum system to be in multiple states at the same time. Something can be "here" and "there," or "up" and "down" at the same time.
>
> **C)** Entanglement is an extremely strong correlation that exists between quantum particles, so strong, in fact, that two or more quantum particles can be inextricably linked in perfect unison, even if separated by great distances. The particles remain perfectly correlated even if separated by great distances. The particles are so intrinsically connected they can be said to "dance" in instantaneous, perfect unison, even when placed at opposite ends of the universe. The seemingly impossible connection inspired Einstein to describe entanglement as "spooky action at a distance."

The preceding subsection of this chapter explained that all members of the same kind of elemental thing share the same spirit. For example, all electrons share the same electron spirit, all protons share the same proton spirit, all atoms of the same element and isotope share the same elemental spirit, etc. This is why all electrons are identical, all protons are identical, all atoms of the same element and isotope are identical, etc. However, according to the model, the states of existence of members of the same kind of quantum particle would generally vary from member to member and would be associated with the situation they are in. The model also indicates that under certain situations some quantum particles of the same kind could have the same state of existence, and this is when quantum superposition and entanglement would occur.

Every quantum particle is a separate particle. That means, for example, the electron spirit has a separate electron soul connecting it to each electron that exists. While the set of connections of the second kind making up an electron soul is the same for every electron soul, none of the electron souls share parts of themselves among each other or with the soul of any other thing. However, an electron is usually a part of a larger thing, and thus the electron spirit is a part of the spirit of that larger thing, and the electron soul of that electron is a part of the soul of that larger thing.

Because every quantum particle of the same kind is separate, though identical, each has a degree of autonomy regarding its state of existence. For example, one electron could be a part of a human body, and another could be a part of a piece of granite. The state of existence would be different for each. However, under certain situations, the states of existence of two or more electrons could be identical. For example, they could be at essentially the same location in the same living or nonliving thing. They would also need to have certain other commonalities, such as being a part of the same atom or molecule, or be the same kind of atom or molecule, for their states of existence to be identical. When their states of existence are identical, the two or more electrons would be essentially "one" and behave as "one," and then quantum superposition and entanglement would occur.

I suppose when two or more quantum particles of the same kind are being observed by a researcher using special equipment, they would all be put in the same situation and would thus have identical states of existence. Therefore, the model indicates it is possible that the process of observing quantum particles for quantum superposition and entanglement behavior could contribute to bringing about quantum superposition and entanglement behavior. This could be confirmed if such behavior is consistently seen when looking for such behavior. If this is the case, then quantum superposition and entanglement might not always exist when quantum particles are in common natural everyday situations. The Institute for Quantum Computing article did not say whether the phenomena always, or only sometimes, exist for quantum particles.

The model indicates the state of existence of a living or nonliving thing depends on the signals coming from its spirit. The signals are enabling the thing to exist in the situation it's in and are thus giving it its state of existence for that situation. The same process applies to quantum particles.

Each piece of knowledge in the spirit that has a connection of the second kind with a quantum particle sends through this connection its particular signal at a particular strength to enable part of the particle to exist in the situation it's in. Every other such piece of knowledge sends its particular signal at a particular strength through its connection to the particle as well. Recall that in the early part of this chapter each piece of knowledge issues a specific signal, and that a spiritual entity being made of pieces of knowledge would issue a signal consisting of a combination of signals issued by each piece of knowledge. This is how each spiritual entity can be sensed by its signal as being different and unique. The totality of all such signals to the particle thus has a particular pattern of strengths among the collection of signals. The collection of signals, regardless of their pattern of strengths, enables the particle to exist. It is the pattern of strengths that gives the particle its state of existence. Therefore, while every quantum particle of the same kind is identical, each can have a different state of existence.

This means, for example, the electron spirit is capable of issuing a different pattern of strengths to each electron that exists. Thus, the electron spirit consists of more pieces of knowledge than just those that have a connection of the second kind to each electron that exists. It is these extra pieces of knowledge that enable the electron spirit to give each electron its own state of existence. Thus, while an electron is tiny, the electron spirit is larger than we might expect. However, because quantum particles are elemental, the variety of situations any quantum particle, such as an electron, could be in is relatively limited. This means their range of states of existence is relatively limited and it's relatively easy for the states of existence for two or more quantum particles to be identical.

The model indicates the reason quantum superposition and entanglement have been observed only with the tiniest of particles is that any elemental thing larger has too many possible situations it could be in for two members to easily achieve identical states of existence. There would be too many pieces of knowledge in the spirit to have to match up their patterns of strengths for two or more members to easily achieve identical states of existence.

Thus, as indicated in the article by the Institute for Quantum Computing, the largest quantum particles are atoms, not molecules or anything larger, even if they are elemental things such that every member shares the same spirit. Consequently, we are unlikely to see, for example, water molecules behaving in a quantum superposition and entanglement manner.

According to the model, the spirit of something needs a spiritual entity to serve as its spirit. The spiritual entity embodies (1) the pieces of knowledge necessary to build the spirit, (2) the pieces of knowledge on how to build the spirit and form the various states of existence, (3) the pieces of knowledge necessary to enable the spirit to form different states of existence for different situations, and (4) whatever else the spiritual entity needs to enable part of the spirit to be translated into a physical form that can exist in a physical universe. Keep in mind, not everything could be translated into a physical form, but some can still be expressed in a physical world. Therefore, there can be more to a spirit of a living or nonliving thing in a physical world than what is required to enable the living or nonliving thing to physically exist there. For example, in the case of a human individual, his or her spirit includes pieces of knowledge that give him or her intelligence, consciousness, emotions, feelings, etc. All such pieces of knowledge are a part of (1) and (3), but they don't play a role in enabling anything to physically exist in our physical world but only to be expressed in our physical world.

The spirit of something in our physical world consists of (1), (3), and (4). The physical thing and its state of existence in our physical world involve (1), (2), (3), and (4). This means in order for the states of existence of two or more physical things to be identical, the states of (1), (2), (3) and (4) of each thing must be identical to those of the others. For quantum particles, the range of possible states of existence is relatively limited so that achieving identical states of existence for two or more particles is relatively easy. But as we get into molecules, which are made of two or more atoms, there is involved another layer of the (1), (2), (3), and (4) kinds of pieces of knowledge in addition to those for each of the atoms involved. Therefore, the range of possible states of existence is exponentially greater, even for elemental kinds of molecules, whose members which all share the same spirit. Water molecules are an example of this. Consequently, achieving identical states of existence for two or more of the same kind of elemental molecules becomes exponentially harder, and thus quantum superposition and entanglement are not likely to happen.

When we get to a spirit as complex as that of a living thing on Earth, the model indicates anything similar to quantum superposition and entanglement are not going to happen at all. In order for anything similar to that to happen, a spirit of a living thing must first be able to enable multiple identical living things to exist at the same time, and no spirit of any living thing on Earth can do that. Some plant spirits enable multiple plants to exist when humans start new plants from the plant's cuttings. But the plants are not identical and the spirit for each such plant becomes different right away anyway, because each plant immediately goes through a different set of experiences and generates different pieces of knowledge that are added to each spirit.

This notion that the pattern of strengths could be an indicator of state of existence applies to any living or nonliving thing, and not just to quantum particles. For example, the state of existence of a sick individual is different from the state of existence of the same individual when he or she is well. The signals from the individual's spirit are different in the two situations. The signals of the sick individual would include stronger ones of the kind that instruct the body on how to heal. Examples of other different states of existence include an individual being happy versus sad, satiated versus hungry, excited versus bored, awake versus sleeping, working versus playing, etc.

When the states of existence of two or more quantum particles of the same kind are identical, the particles are essentially "one" and behave as one. Consequently, the "same" quantum particle is both "here" and "there" or "up" and "down" at the same time. They can also be "dancing" in perfect unison even when separated by great distances, and even if one is moved to one end of our universe opposite the other. Thus, quantum superposition and entanglement occur.

Keep in mind that separation distance exists in our physical world but not in the spirit world, especially when quantum particles such as electrons are spread out throughout our universe but only one electron spirit exists in the spirit world. Therefore, when quantum superposition and entanglement occur, the distance separating the quantum particles involved doesn't matter.

The possible patterns of strengths of signals are not limited to just one for any quantum particle. Therefore, the state of existence for quantum particles is not limited to just one, even when quantum superposition and entanglement occur. This suggests that the "dancing" in quantum entanglement could be different for different states of existence. For example, the "dancing" could be circular, oval, a figure-eight shape, linear, steady versus wiggling, going up and down, going left and right, and so on, depending on the state of existence. Therefore, the dancing could be different for quantum particles depending on their composition, temperature, whether they are a living or a nonliving thing, etc. It would be interesting to see if such differences exist since the model suggests they could.

Quantum computing is being further studied and is currently being used in many applications, including encrypting messages and passwords. If what the model says is true, quantum computing would be an example of how we are tapping into the attributes of the spirit world to achieve our technological advances. As mentioned earlier in this chapter, everything we could find in the spirit world is meant for us to find and to explore. The fact that we are exploring what could be done with quantum computers could be an example of this. Much of the phenomena behind the workings of our technological advances are associated with various attributes of the spirit world, particularly those workings that tap into the natural electronic properties of natural material

The Number of Spiritual Entities More than Doubles with Every New Piece of Knowledge Generated

Every new piece of knowledge generated and added to the spirit world results in countless new spiritual entities created. Each new piece of knowledge immediately forms a connection of the first kind with every existing piece of knowledge. Therefore, every spiritual entity that exists gets a new piece of knowledge added to it. This creates "x" number of new spiritual entities from the "x" number of existing ones, and meanwhile the original "x" number of spiritual entities is still there. Thus, the number of spiritual entities doubled. But in addition, the new piece of knowledge also creates "y" number of new spiritual entities consisting of two pieces of knowledge connected together from the "y" number of existing pieces of knowledge. Therefore, number of spiritual entities in the spirit world more than doubles by the addition of just one new piece of knowledge. This means the spirit world grows at a fantastic rate. This could explain why we have such a wide variety of living things on Earth, why there is a seemingly endless variety of thoughts we can find, why the number of things we could bring into being on Earth with our creativity seems limitless, etc.

Since there are bound to be universes that came before ours, all the new pieces of knowledge generated by living things that resided in them already enabled the spirit world to create countless other living and nonliving things before our universe came into being. This could be why there seems no limit to the things we can find in the spirit world and translate into forms that can be expressed or exist in our physical world. The fact that there is no limit to things we can find in the spirit world and that we have such an amazing variety of living things residing, or that have resided, on Earth tend to support the notion that past universes have existed before our universe came into being.

A Living Thing's Role in a Universe

Any living or nonliving entity or thing can go through experiences and generate new pieces of knowledge. This applies to spiritual entities residing in the spirit world and things residing in a physical or nonphysical universe. Spiritual entities capable of serving as spirits for highly intelligent living things able to reside in universes have higher-than-average influence in shaping the spirit world. This is because highly intelligent living things can do more to shape their experiences than others and thus have more control over the kinds of new pieces of knowledge generated. This places a lot of responsibility on highly intelligent living things, such as us humans on Earth, although in the case of us humans, some of us don't seem to realize our responsibility. Nevertheless, we probably sense we have a purpose to fulfill, even though we might not know quite what it is. This could be why a lot of us are searching for our spirituality, perhaps as a part of trying to discover our purpose.

We might wonder why the spirit world doesn't simply tell us what our purpose is. The answer is the spirit world never tells highly intelligent living things such as humans on Earth what to do. It also wants us to generate as many new pieces of knowledge as possible. And since it does not know the new pieces of knowledge possible to generate (otherwise it would already have them), it does not restrict what highly intelligent living things do. However, it provides guidance subtly in an attempt to keep highly intelligent living things from wandering too far off course. But if highly intelligent living things do so anyway, the spirit world accepts that as part of the risk it takes, and it forgives. After all, it could always design and bring into being another universe to restore balance as long as itself remains viable. Thus, one of its own responsibilities is to be sure it keeps itself viable. And here is where wisdom comes into play as further discussed later in this chapter.

The spirit world knows the kinds of experiences that generate the kinds of new pieces of knowledge that will help restore its state of knowledge to within reasonable balance. So the spirit world designs a new universe where the kinds of experiences it needs living things to go through are possible. But the spirit world doesn't know the exact experiences, only the kinds of experiences. By analogy, let's say we know we need to go to a hardware store to buy some house maintenance tools, but we don't know exactly what tools are there and what each tool can do. Therefore, we do not go with specific tools in mind; we allow ourselves the freedom to look, try out some tools, and make choices. The spirit world gives living things, especially highly intelligent living things, freedom of choice because it doesn't know ahead of time exactly what experiences are possible in a universe, only the kinds of experiences. Just as the various tools can be used constructively or destructively, various experiences can be also. And what is perceived as constructive or destructive depends on the intent of the living thing and the situation it is in.

This likely applies in any universe. Highly intelligent living things in any universe are likely to also sense that they have a purpose in their universe and are likely to feel a need to search for their spirituality, similar to the way we humans do on Earth. We might keep this in mind when someday we do inter-universe travel. Understanding that this commonality likely exists among other highly intelligent living things including us could ease our making a positive connection with them. In fact, this might even help us humans get along better with each other here on Earth.

As the presentation continues, additional notions and concepts will be introduced that may help us figure out our purpose while residing on Earth more specifically. But for now we can always tune into our intuition for a greater sense of our purpose. My intuition says, in the simplest terms, we need to have more empathy and compassion for one another.

Interactions among Spirit, Soul, and Body

The spirit of an individual encompasses a multitude of smaller spiritual entities. Each one enables a part of the individual, be it brain, eyes, ears, heart, lungs, kidneys, head, arms, legs, hair, blood, etc., to exist on Earth. Some enable the individual's intangibles to exist in the spirit world. These include the spiritual senses: consciousness, intelligence, reasoning ability, creativity, feelings, ego, etc. The spirit also includes spiritual entities that instruct these spiritual entities on how to come together to form a living, functioning, and viable individual. A similar assemblage of spiritual entities makes up the spirit of other creatures. This also applies to non-creature living things, such as plants, fungi, alga, etc. The spirits of nonliving things ranges from simple to very complex depending on what it is. For example, the spirit of a toy automobile would be simpler than that of an actual automobile.

According to the model, our spirit is where our spiritual senses, consciousness, intelligence, etc., reside. Feelings, emotions, empathy, compassion, ego, etc. also reside in our spirit. They are neither good nor bad, right nor wrong. But our actions in response to them can be perceived as good, bad, or neutral, depending on the situation.

Intuition and instincts are not a part of our spirit but are instead signals from elsewhere in the spirit world and are sensed by our spirit. Instincts are signals issued by the spiritual entity serving as our spirit, and intuitions are signals issued by various other entities in the rest of the spirit world. Our spirit senses both kinds of signals with its spiritual senses. The issuers of intuition signals could be spiritual expressions of deceased individuals or by the spirit world in general.

More discussions on intuition and instincts will come later in the book as we talk about living things that rely heavily on the spirit world to do their thinking for them for their survival as opposed to highly intelligent living things such as us humans that do most of their own thinking.

When we are thinking, our spirit uses its spiritual senses to search through the various spiritual entities that are thoughts to find one that fits our purpose. It does this proficiently and quickly. Then it uses its spiritual senses, including the five extended into our body to give us our five major senses, to translate the thoughts into forms that can be expressed in our physical world. Thus, we do our thinking in the spirit world and we act out our thoughts in our physical world. Similarly, our intentions, attitudes, etc. are also in the form of spiritual entities in the spirit world, and our spirit searches through them to find the ones that fit our situation, and then translates them into expressions we carry out in our physical world.

As a common example, when our body gets tired, injured, or ill, our body's constant communication with our spirit through our soul reveals this to our spirit. Our spirit then issues signals to our body through our soul to help our body recover. The signals can include feelings of tiredness and sleepiness. These feelings reside with our spirit in the spirit world, and our bodily expressions are carried out in our physical world by, for example, going to bed. The signals could induce sleep or, if our condition is severe enough, coma. As the presentation continues, we will see how putting our body to sleep or into a coma increases our body's ability to physically respond to our spirit's healing signals and thus heal faster and more effectively. Among our spirit's highest priorities is keeping our body as viable as possible. Incidentally, as the presentation continues, we will see the spirit itself never tires, suffers injury, or becomes ill. It is the body, being a physical living thing, that suffers wear, tear, injury, illness, and requires regular refueling. And as with any physical thing in our universe, our body ages and eventually wears out.

Oh, gee, you would have to point that out. Well, it's only reality. Oh, but what if it is because the spirit world is imperfect? Maybe, but then even universes have finite lifetimes, so we are not alone in this. Yes, and even the spirit world itself could vanish, as we will see later in the chapter, if we don't do our part to help it maintain balance in its state of knowledge. Oh, gee, now you would have to bring that out.

Conventional thinking would have our senses, consciousness, intelligence, ego, etc. residing in our brain, and our feelings, emotions, intuition, instincts, etc. triggered in our brain. The concepts of spirit world and spiritual senses as expressed in this book are new ways of perceiving the roles of the spirit, soul, and body. But with conventional thinking, all the mentioned intangibles are perceived to pertain to our physical world instead of pertaining to the spirit world. When we mix the two worlds together and attribute it all to our physical world, we get unanswered questions such as the following. How could our brain do all the amazing things we assume it does? How could some birds, which have very small brains, possess such intelligence? A dead person's brain is dead, so how could ghosts have consciousness and intelligence and be real, as indicated in Chapter Two, if consciousness and intelligence are supposed to reside in the brain? And so on.

I think most of us believe we have a spirit and/or a soul but are not sure what they are. We might wonder if they are separate things or the same thing, and what roles they have in our lives. Such vagueness is clarified in the model. The model defines the spirit and soul of living and nonliving things, and their roles in the thing's existence in a universe. The definitions are likely to be at odds with dictionary definitions and conventional thinking. Therefore, while reading this book, the reader is recommended not to follow conventional thinking regarding the spirits and souls of living things, and regarding nonliving things as not having spirits or souls.

To suggest to a typical person, say a man, that his senses, consciousness, intelligence, ego, feelings, emotions, intuition, instincts, etc. do not reside or occur in the brain but instead reside or occur in some intangible entity located elsewhere might be an affront. That man is likely to think anyone with such notions should be immediately transported to where that entity is. To him, such notions might imply his brain is less than what he thinks it is and therefore he would be less than what he thought he was. Our ego often keeps us from being more open-minded and thus tends to keep us stuck in our ways and beliefs. This could hinder our ability to find our personal spiritual model. Regardless of the spiritual model we would eventually find, letting go of the ego and being more humble would help greatly in our search. Having our senses, consciousness, intelligence, ego, feelings, emotions, intuition, instincts, etc. residing in our spirit or sensed by our spirit instead of residing in our brain does not reduce us. According to the model, our spirit is everything we are, and our body is simply the living physical thing that gives us the ability to express our self in our physical world. So we do need to take good care of our body in order to maximize how well we can perform the expressions we choose to perform and to thus work toward fulfilling our purpose for being here.

As mentioned earlier, our brain is the main control center for our body, the main "computer" that handles the constant communication our body has with our spirit. It receives signals from our spirit through connections of the second kind in our soul, translates the spiritual signals into physical signals, and sends the physical signals through nerve fibers to the rest of our body. Our body responds to the physical signals and sends feedback physical signals through nerve fibers to our brain. Our brain translates the physical signals into spiritual signals, and sends the spiritual signals to our spirit through connections of the second kind in our soul. This back-and-forth transmission of signals is how our spirit pilots our body, in much the same way a pilot flies an airliner or a driver drives a car.

Have you ever started doing something but then suddenly realized it wasn't really what you intended to do, but your body went ahead and did it anyway before you could stop it? I have. Didn't it feel as if you sent a signal to your body to do something, but before you could send a revised signal, the first signal got through anyway? It sure felt like that to me, and it sure seems to support the idea that the first spiritual signal was sent from our spirit to our brain. While our brain was translating the spiritual signal into a physical signal, our spirit suddenly realized the wrong spiritual signal had been sent to our brain. But before our spirit could send a revised spiritual signal to our brain, our brain sent the physical signal to our body and, voila, our body did what we first instructed it to do.

Likewise, do you ever have the sensation that you are inside your body and are piloting it? I do, all the time, and I have wondered since childhood what the sensation means. The sensation also seems to support the notion that our consciousness, intelligence, senses, etc. reside in our spirit and not in our body.

So what happens when we consume alcohol or take drugs? Alcohol and drugs interfere with the spirit-body communication by degrading the brain's performance as the main control center for our body. After all, the brain is still only a physical thing in our physical world. It needs the right kinds of nutrients to function well, much like a car's engine needs the right kind of fuel, the transmission the right kind of fluid, etc. in order for the car to function correctly. The spirit cannot be drugged but the body can, including the brain. When the body is drugged, communication from spirit to brain remains intact, but the brain's translation of spiritual signals into physical signals gets distorted. The body receives distorted signals, and because the body is drugged it sends distorted feedback to the brain. The brain's translation of physical signals into spiritual signals is also distorted and the doubly distorted spiritual signals are sent to the spirit. The doubly distorted spiritual signals give our spirit a woozy perception of what is going on and thus it gets a woozy feeling. When the distortion becomes severe enough, the spirit is unable to pilot the body properly, and the body behaves erratically. If the condition gets bad enough, the spirit might put the body to sleep to maximize the body's ability to receive the spirit's healing signals in order to get over the drug effects.

The reason we humans have a relatively large brain is because our body can do a very wide variety of things and with a high degree of precision. Our body can build skyscrapers, fly airplanes, thread a needle, do brain surgery, perform amazing snowboarding tricks, write books, invent, win Olympic Gold medals, cook gourmet meals, play the piano, etc. Therefore, our body needs a large brain to house all the complex control systems necessary for doing such things and to handle the high volume of signals generated by such complex, imaginative, and diverse experiences. It is interesting to note that this is the case even though our major senses are not necessarily greater in number and/or higher in acuity than those of other living things on Earth. It is instead our larger spirit and larger brain that enable us to do form and go through such complex, imaginative, and diverse experiences.

In contrast, the body of a bird can do a relatively limited variety of things. A bird needs only a small brain to house only a relatively small number of control systems. A bird's consciousness and intelligence are not in its brain but in its spirit. Therefore, its spirit might be much larger than we might think. This could explain why some birds exhibit a surprisingly high level of intelligence even though they have small brains. For example, some birds figured out how to drop nuts on the road so that cars would run them over and crack them open. Some birds figured out how to trigger a sensor to automatically open the door of a store so that it could fly in or out of the store. Thus, according to the model, the size of the brain is reflective of the living thing's body's range of physical abilities, while the spirit is reflective of the living thing's level of consciousness and intelligence. We cannot determine the size and complexity of a spirit; however, we can get a rough estimate, based on its level of intelligence.

While the brain is the main control center for the body, the rest of the body has some degree of direct communication with the spirit as well. This gives the body a certain level of "body intelligence" in addition to "brain intelligence." Body intelligence is nothing profound. Any living thing without the usual recognizable brain but still with intelligent behavior possesses body intelligence. A bacterium is an example. Plants and jellyfishes are other examples. Consequently, the notion that our body has body intelligence as well as brain intelligence is not surprising.

In the case of a bacterium, its skin appears to play the role of a brain. It could be that its brain is composed of the same tissue that makes up the skin of a bacterium but is all clumped together to form a brain. If a bacterium's skin cells also have brainpower capacity, then there is no doubt that "body intelligence" is a real thing since the human body is made completely of cells. That is why I say the brain is the main control center for the body, implying that the body also has its own control and communication links with the spirit.

We might then ask why our body even needs a brain. It is because our body is complex and everything has to work together to keep all bodily systems functioning and coordinated, for the entire body to move together to perform specific activities, and to keep us alive. Thus, it needs a control center to coordinate the activity of every cell in the body.

It has been determined that the more dense and complex the brain's folds in a certain region, the more brainpower that region has and the more "skin" that region has. This seems to support the notion that in living things that have no conventional brain the skin may contain the brainpower. This could apply particularly to plants. It is sometimes said that plants seem to react to nearby activities and even to the thoughts of nearby individuals. Plants have lots of leaves, leaves have a lot of cells, and cells have skins. Therefore, the consciousness and intelligence of plants might mainly reside in their leaves. Deciduous plants go dormant in the winter, and this might be why they drop their leaves then, so they can shut down their consciousness and go to sleep.

When we were first learning to ride a bicycle, we had to consciously think about keeping the bicycle from falling over. We were applying brain intelligence. Once we became proficient, the bicycle seemed to stay upright without our thinking about it. In fact, if we try to disrupt the bicycle's tendency to stay upright, it's difficult to do so. Our body intelligence has taken over keeping the bicycle upright. This also happens with a lot of other routine tasks our body performs. When we first learn to hammer a nail, chances are we end up with a lot of bent nails. Once we're proficient, the nails seem to stay straight automatically. These examples could indicate that the cells of our body are able to coordinate their actions without help from the brain once we have had enough practice at new activities.

I would assume body intelligence and brain intelligence would usually work together, but they could also work independently. For some individuals, doing certain activities, the body and brain seem to work independently. For example, some individuals are expert at doing something but are unable to teach it to others. Others can teach an activity but are not good at performing it.

A study was conducted on the response of living cells separated from the body and the findings, in my opinion, could be interpreted as confirming the body receives signals from the spirit without involving the brain. In the study, some living cells were removed from an individual and taken to a different room. The individual was then subjected to a stimulus and the response of cells in his body and the response of the cells in the other room were monitored. The cells in his body and the cells in the other room responded the same way simultaneously. The separated cells had no physical connection with the brain, but they still had spiritual connection with the spirit. Therefore, their response seems to strongly support the notion that they, and the body in the other room, were simultaneously corresponding with the spirit. This also tends to support the notion that we have body intelligence as well as brain intelligence, and that we have a spirit and a soul in addition to a body. To go even further, this tends to support the notion that a spirit world exists besides our physical world.

The results of this study could also explain how an organ-transplant recipient can sometimes take on attributes of the organ donor, such as developing a craving for certain foods the donor liked. The donor's brain may be dead, but the donor's spirit remains alive and is issuing signals to the still-living donated organ to keep it in existence and alive. There was a case in which a young girl who received an organ donated was able to help detectives find and identify the murderer of the girl whose organ she received. She had never met the girl.

The growing human population on Earth raises concerns regarding adequate food supply and adverse environmental impact. I have known individuals who wonder where all the spirits for all these people come from, and whether we could run out of spirits for humans someday. The answer to the latter is no. Remember how adding just one new piece of knowledge to the spirit world more than doubles the number of spiritual entities in the spirit world? This suggests the number of spiritual entities that could serve as human spirits also more than doubles each time. As the human population grows, there will be more individuals to go through experiences to generate new pieces of knowledge. Thus, the rate of increase in available human spirits will exceed the rate of growth of the human population. Consequently, the chances of running out of human spirits are zero. But the question of the food supply and environmental impact remains. We will see as the presentation continues that these are very likely among the tasks we are here on Earth to address.

A question we might ask related to spirit, soul, and body interactions is could the model explain why we tend to remember some things better than some others? An attribute of the connections of both the first and second kinds is that the more often they transmit a specific signal, the better they become at transmitting it. And the less often they transmit a specific signal, the worse they are at transmitting it. This is the "use it or lose it" phenomenon. Thus, we tend to recall something better when it is regularly repeated. The connections also transmit a specific signal better right after it was already transmitted. Thus, we more easily recall something that happened recently. An extraordinarily big event has such strong signals that the transmissibility of the connections of them remains high longer than usual. Therefore, we can recall a big event long after it is over.

Oneness in the Spirit World

Because only one copy of each existing piece of knowledge is kept, certain characteristics come about in the spirit world, and various kinds of certain ones manifest in various ways in various universes. For example, every spiritual entity in the spirit world is automatically different and unique, and in general this results in everything residing in a universe being different and unique, even if only minutely so in many cases. However, exceptions are possible, as we've discussed, in our universe there are the basic elemental things such as subatomic particles, electrons, protons, neutrons, elemental atoms, and various relatively simple molecules.

Another characteristic is that oneness pervades the sprint world. Every spiritual entity shares one or more pieces of knowledge with one or more other spiritual entities. Every larger spiritual entity encompassing multiple smaller spiritual entities shares one or more smaller spiritual entities with one or more other larger ones. Both situations produce direct forms of oneness. Indirect forms would be when, for example, two spiritual entities share one or more of their smaller spiritual entities with a third, but do not share any with each other. This produces indirect forms of oneness in which oneness goes through a third-party spiritual entity. This is analogous to a friend of a friend indirectly being a friend.

We might ask; if both forms of oneness can be manifested in our universe? The answer is yes, in a manner similar to the way both forms exist in the spirit world. For example; the direct form applies to everything in our universe in that everything is made of the same basic elemental things. Aside from this, we also have indirect oneness similar to the way the spirit world has indirect oneness. For example, a metal spoon and a plastic spoon have direct oneness because they both have the same general shape and use. A frying pan and a metal spoon have direct oneness because both are made of metal. Thus, a frying pan and a plastic spoon have indirect oneness because each has direct but different oneness with a metal spoon, but has no such direct oneness with each other. And accordingly we could go to an extreme and also say a massive, heavily armed armored military tank has indirect oneness with a plastic spoon.

Oh, brother! If you start saying things like that, then the oneness in your half of the brain must be coming apart. No, no, your half must be coming apart to ask the question in the first place, because it leads to this kind of conclusion.

Getting back to oneness in general, aside from oneness associated with basic elemental things, members of the same species obviously have direct oneness with one another. Members of the same family have a greater degree of direct oneness with one another. Identical twins have an even greater degree of direct oneness with each other. Members of all animal species have a greater degree of direct oneness with one another than they do with members of non-animal species such as insects and fishes. But members of all species, including plants, have some form of direct and/or indirect oneness with one another in that each could be sharing one or more of its genes with various others. All varieties of oneness in our universe stem from the varieties of oneness in the spirit world. This indicates oneness in various forms and degrees is bound to be a part of every other universe as well, and oneness could even bridge universes. Thus, someday when we do inter-universe travel and/or when living things from other universes visit us, it would be helpful to know we all may possess oneness with one another and that we could tap into it to help make a positive connection.

Following this same idea, we could tap more into the oneness among all humans to help us get along better on an international level. We are using oneness to enhance international relationships through the arts, academics, tourism, sports, business, humanitarian aid, etc. These tend to be more on the personal level where oneness has greater influence. Oneness is more remote, and thus has less influence, on a governmental level. Consequently, governmental activities tend to be driven more by ego and the desire to enhance survivability, and this does not improve international relations. The relations would improve if we increased the influence of oneness in the government of every nation. The increasingly global economy is indirectly doing this between certain nations through business and is thus improving their international relations.

However, the economic effects on the ego and survivability of the people within each nation could be undesirably uneven. This goes to show how oneness and the combined effects of ego and the desire to enhance survivability can occupy opposing sides of a lot of issues. This suggests that, among our tasks on Earth, is the necessity to seek a balance of knowledge on both sides so that the issues involved can be addressed with wisdom. This would be consistent with the model's indication that we are here to help the spirit world restore balance and that the spirit world gave us the freedom to choose so that we could generate as many new pieces of knowledge as possible. The net result is to help the spirit world maintain its ability to form wisdom to assure its own viability and the viability of everything it has created.

Spiritual entities that share almost all of themselves with one another are very much alike, and thus could serve as spirits for living things of the same species. Spiritual entities only need to differ by one piece of knowledge to be different and unique. Therefore, a group of such spiritual entities, each consisting of "x" number of pieces of knowledge, could have "x" number of members. I would imagine that a spiritual entity capable of serving as the spirit of a living thing would need billions of pieces of knowledge. This could be why there seems no limit to the number of members of certain species, because there are always more spiritual entities capable of serving as spirits for that species than there are living members of that species at any one time.

Conversely, we could get a very rough idea of the number of pieces of knowledge a spiritual entity needs to possess to enable it to serve as the spirit of a living thing by determining the largest number of simultaneously living members in any given species that ever existed. Let's not consider insects for now because, as the presentation continues, we will see how the model indicates the nature of the spirits of some insects is different from the nature of the spirits of most other creatures. The human species currently might have one of the largest numbers of living members (the world population is now approximately seven billion). This means a spiritual entity capable of serving as the spirit of a human individual needs to have several billion or more pieces of knowledge. The portion that forms the human spirit alone would take up several billion or more pieces of knowledge. The rest of the spiritual entity would need to match and, thus likely to also consist of, several billion or more, pieces of knowledge.

Another example of a species that once had a very large number of living members is the passenger pigeon. They once numbered about five billion in our country alone, enough it is said to have darkened the sky for fourteen hours as flocks that extended for 300 miles flew by overhead. They went extinct after foreigners arrived on the North American continent and hunted them to extinction. It just goes to show that even though we humans are members of a more advanced species, we do not necessarily have more wisdom.

Generally, the higher the degree of oneness that exists among individuals, the higher the degree of empathy and compassion the individuals would have for one another. Family members have more oneness among them than with others, and thus generally have more empathy and compassion for one another than for others. Identical twins have such a high degree of oneness that in some cases one twin feels the emotions and pains of the other even when they are not together. This indicates there has to be something besides our physical world connecting the twins, and it is the spirit world where their high degree of oneness resides. We humans have more oneness with mammals than with fish, reptiles, insects, etc.; therefore, we tend to have more empathy and compassion for mammals than for fish, reptiles, insects, etc. For example, we usually have no bad feelings about swatting a mosquito or a fly, or spraying termites and ants, or catching fish with nets and hooks, etc. This indicates that under certain circumstances we humans are capable of setting aside certain influences of oneness.

So, what is it that could cause us to set aside certain influences of oneness? Hunger, ego, physical threat, the desire to enhance survivability, etc. could do it. In the last section of this chapter, the model indicates these factors constitute the main obstacles we humans need to work on if we are to help our universe fulfill its purpose of helping the spirit world restore balance. Any obstacles to our fulfilling this purpose stems from things that cause us to set aside certain influences of oneness.

So, when we say "we are just being human," does it mean we are influenced by oneness, or does it mean we are likely to set aside certain influences of oneness, or both? It seems to be both. It means we must have tug-of-wars going on in our spirit. This would be natural since the spirit world is full of tug-of-wars, and our spirit is a tiny portion of the spirit world. This supports the notion that we are here to help the spirit world restore balance in its knowledge and thus in its tug-of-wars. Later in this chapter we will see how restoring balance relates to the spirit world's ability to form wisdom and thus its ability to maintain its viability and the viability of everything it creates.

The oneness discussed so far is inherited. Oneness can also be developed through shared experiences. Developed oneness carries as much influence in the spirit world as inherited oneness does. Couples, friends, classmates, teammates, coworkers, competitors, opponents, and roommates, etc. often develop oneness. Developed oneness can come about in additional to inherited oneness to strengthen an inherited relationship. Developed oneness can become a part of inherited oneness for members of subsequent generations. For example, children of close friends are likely to be considered friends.

We humans perceive the concept of an opponent as being real because we are physically separate in our physical world. In the spirit world, an opponent is only a concept and not a reality, because spiritual entities are all directly or indirectly a part of one another. A spiritual entity cannot be an opponent to any other spiritual entity when they directly or indirectly share parts among each other. Any form of oneness is basically good. However, while our actions in response to oneness are usually constructive, but because the concept of opponent is real to us, our actions in response to oneness can sometimes be destructive. Some examples are given as the discussion continues in this section.

No matter whether oneness is inherited or developed, it becomes a part of the spiritual entities serving as the spirits of the individuals involved. Whatever becomes a part of any spiritual entity also becomes a part of the spirit world and thus has an influence on its future. Inherited oneness automatically comes about and is beyond our control. But the control we have over our developed oneness is part of how we help or don't help the spirit world restore balance. Also, by being physically separate, we humans are able to bring into being various kinds of developed oneness impossible to bring about in the spirit world where all living entities are a part of each other. Conversely, living entities in the spirit world, and living things in universes in which they are a part of one another, could bring about various kinds of developed oneness we humans cannot bring about. And since each universe is different and unique, this means our universe must be designed for a purpose unique to our universe. Thus, it would be a shame if we mess up because no other universe is going to be able to do what our universe was created to do.

If the spirit world cannot form certain kinds of developed oneness by itself, then how can the kinds of developed oneness that we humans form become a part of the spirit world? And since we are physically separate, wouldn't the developed oneness we form be spiritually separate and thus be incompatible with the spirit world? The developed oneness we humans form isn't spiritually separate. We share our developed oneness with whomever we formed it, and thus the developed oneness starts out being shared in our physical world. Ultimately, all types of oneness ends up in the spirit world, and all consist of pieces of knowledge connected together by connections of the first kind. Thus, they are all spiritual entities.

This relates to the concept of opponent, in that a possible reason our universe was designed so that the concept of opponent could be perceived as real is to have living things here generate new pieces of knowledge by responding to this perception. Such pieces of knowledge are apparently partly what the spirit world needs to restore balance at the time when our universe was designed and brought into being. What the spirit world also needs in particular from us humans, being the most conscious and intelligent living things on Earth, is to generate new pieces of knowledge by going through experiences in which the perception of opponent is handled constructively. In my mind, we humans have found some, and they take the forms of various friendly competitions performed for the sake of promoting excellence.

But we have also found destructive ways, and they take the form of hostile competitions, wars, corruption, crime, etc., all for the sake of control, ego, and personal material enrichment. Our technical advances across many fields are wonderful, for example, but their application is not always in response to our oneness in the spirit world. Some are more in response to our separateness and perception of opponent in our physical world. For example, advances that include the development of more advanced weaponry and other potential war-related capabilities could then cause the escalation of global conflict. This is not very constructive, although the threat of mutual total destruction among major nations seems to help prevent world wars. This is yet another example of how nothing is totally bad or totally good in our universe.

The model indicates we need to do away with destructive ways and focus on coming up with additional constructive ways. And how we go about responding to oneness is an important part of such an effort.

In general, the applications of advanced technologies have primarily been for monetary profit. However, the technologies enable us to do things we otherwise could not do and to do some things better and more quickly, which makes the pace of life faster. This is usually considered desirable, even if it does not necessarily improve the quality of life. Whatever amount of time we save from moment to moment can sometimes be overtaken by the time needed to deal with technological malicious intents, system malfunctions, and addictive use of devices. While the applications are in response to our separateness in our physical world, the devices produced open up new opportunities to respond to both our oneness in the spirit world and our separateness in our physical world in both constructive and not so constructive ways. Thus, within our purpose for being here is making advances in physical technologies. But, what are needed to go along with it are advances in spiritual technologies, and this is lagging far behind. This could be at least partly why we made a mess on Earth.

We might ask; why I would think someday we could do inter-universe travel when it would seem incompatible with each universe being different and unique and having its own different and unique purpose? There are at least two possible reasons. One is that all universes have a commonality, and it is the spirit world. I think inter-universe travel through the spirit world is possible, but not in the manner usually imagined or depicted in fictional stories and motion pictures. As we learn more about the spirit world, our imagination will expand and we could come up with ways we have not thought of. The second reason is that so far we have talked about each universe being designed from scratch and brought into being by the spirit world. But what if another way is to have two or more universes advance to the point living things in each could become conscious enough to be aware of the existence of other universes besides their own. At that point, two or more universes could communicate, interact, and thus essentially form one or more new universes. How well this could work could all depend on how constructively living things in each universe respond to oneness, especially any oneness that bridges across universes. Another universe might be such that living things share parts of themselves with one another, and/or the universe is nonphysical, and/or the universe is other than three-dimensional, etc. The model indicates these are possibilities. Getting more in touch with the spirit world and the various ways of oneness in it could enable us to develop the consciousness to be aware of other universes, if they exist along with ours.

Because everything in the spirit world is directly or indirectly a part of everything else, the oneness produced in the spirit world makes the spirit world naturally a gentle, kind, caring, nonjudgmental, compassionate, empathic, and loving place. However because each universe is different and unique, the oneness would manifest differently in each universe. Since no spiritual entity could be as complete as the spirit world, and because a spiritual entity enables a universe to exist, every universe can also not be as complete as the spirit world. Consequently, the oneness in each universe is not as complete as the oneness in the spirit world.

However, the oneness in the spirit world is not totally complete either, because the spirit world is never going to be totally complete. Therefore, there is always room for growth. Consequently, it is possible for the spirit world to design universes such that living things residing in them are able to develop oneness that is different from the oneness the spirit world could form on its own, in the same way we humans are able to design machines to do things we personally cannot do, even though any machine we design is not going to be as complete as we are.

Any oneness newly developed in a universe is immediately added to the spirit world as part of its natural process of growth. Therefore, the manifested oneness in a universe plus any newly developed oneness in that universe will never add up to being as complete as the oneness in the spirit world. Consequently, no universe can ever be as gentle, kind, caring, nonjudgmental, compassionate, empathic, and loving a place as the spirit world. This could explain why, while our intuition or conscience (signals from the spirit world) tell us that our intentions and actions ought to embody qualities such as those in the spirit world, we do not always choose to follow them. It is because our oneness is less than the oneness in the spirit world, and thus we are not driven to behave with all the good qualities of the spirit world.

Because things are physically separate in our universe, oneness takes on attributes not always found in the spirit world. For example, oneness on Earth brings members of a group closer together. But the closeness does not necessarily bridge across groups. Thus, competition is always possible between groups. The notion of one group winning and the other losing can take hold. Consequently, win-lose concepts come in countless forms in all kinds of activities and all fields of pursuit on Earth. Competition is good, if it drives self-improvement and the pursuit of excellence, but not necessarily good if for personal gain and enrichment. The former is win-win, whereas the latter is usually win-lose. It can even be lose-lose if competition is carried out foolishly.

Because everything in the spirit world is directly or indirectly a part of everything else, competition does not exist there. Therefore, the fact that competition exists on Earth makes a lot of the experiences possible here that are not possible in the spirit world. Thus, such experiences generate new pieces of knowledge that cannot be generated by experiences in the spirit world. This indicates that the existence of competition must have been purposely designed into our universe. This is another way of saying the concept of opponent is perceived to be real in our universe because of the design our universe. It thus follows that part of what we need to do to fulfill our purpose is to find ways to constructively work with or around our perceptions of opponent. We are not doing very well in this regard as indicated by the way we often treat those we perceive as our opponents, especially those we call enemies or, rightly or wrongly, want to have control over.

While all of this is true, as the presentation continues, we will see how it is we are here to make all such things somehow produce constructive results. Three main obstacles are identified later in this chapter as part of what is designed into our universe. According to the model, we are to find ways to work with or around the obstacles designed into our universe, especially the three main obstacles, and to then make our universe as gentle, kind, caring, nonjudgmental, compassionate, empathic, and loving as possible. In other words, we are to make our universe as much like the spirit world as possible with respect to these qualities. The opposite would be to make our universe a place where disputes, jealousy, greed, dishonesty, status-seeking, fights, wars, mistreatment and lack of care of others, etc. are commonplace. Right now, too much of the opposite of what we are here to accomplish is a part of what we are doing on Earth.

Holy cow! I used to hear people say everything has oneness with everything else, and I would simple think "Yeah, that's probably true, but so what?" But now it is clear that how we respond to our oneness in the spirit world and our separateness in our physical world are important. Yeah, and it is good to keep in mind that you and I are simply different halves of the same brain and therefore have a common spirit. So you are saying you and I have this oneness in the spirit world even though we are separate halves in our physical world, and the caring and respectful manner in which we communicate is a constructive way to respond? Yes, and we could tell the constructive response is working well when we feel like hugging each other. Yeah, let's hug.

Wisdom

model indicates the spirit world's most important task is to keep itself in good shape in order to be able to form wisdom. This is in the same way one of our most important tasks is to keep ourselves in good shape mentally and physically so that we could function well. "Good shape" to the spirit world means keeping its knowledge on all sides of all the issues in reasonably good balance so that wisdom can be formed. As it turns out, wisdom plays a vital role in maintaining the viability of the spirit world and everything it has created in ways we are not likely to imagine with conventional thinking. It also reveals the importance of our task as living things on Earth of helping the spirit world stay in good shape. Otherwise, the spirit world could become no longer viable and thus vanish, and we would all vanish as well.

As discussed earlier, the spirit world can never possess every possible piece of knowledge, because there is no limit to the new pieces of knowledge that can be generated. Thus, the spirit world can never be perfect. On the other hand, because there is no limit to the new pieces of knowledge that can be generated, there is a future as well as a past to the growth of the spirit world and thus for our growth as well. If no more new pieces of knowledge were left to generate, we would become similar to elemental things in that our experiences would not generate any more new pieces of knowledge and therefore our future experiences would simply be repeats of past experiences. Consequently, we would have a past but essentially not a future, because our future would simply be exactly like our past. So, thank goodness there is no limit to the new pieces of knowledge that can be generated, and thank goodness the spirit world and everything it creates are imperfect, including us.

However, because the spirit world is imperfect, it has to be able to form wisdom to compensate for its imperfection. Similarly, because we are imperfect and the living and nonliving things we live with are imperfect, we also have to form wisdom to deal with all the imperfections in our lives. As we can see, the mess we humans have made on Earth is largely because we humans as a whole have not been very wise. As with the spirit world, we too need balance in our knowledge of our issues in order to form wisdom.

We need wisdom to handle our issues well. And by handling our issues well we would be able to continue to form wisdom. Conversely, if we allow our wisdom to degrade we would not handle issues well and our ability to continue to form wisdom would also degrade. This then is a vicious circle that could go unstable very quickly and thus needs our concerted effort to keep it going in a stable manner. The possibility of instability exists in the spirit world in the first place and that is why it exists in our physical world. If wisdom degrades in the spirit world it would not be able to create new things in a wise or appropriate manner. Things not created wisely or appropriately would not function well in helping the spirit world restore balance. The spirit world would then go more unbalanced. Eventually, viability would be lost and it could happen very quickly once it starts. That is the nature of instability situations. In our physical world, this could explain how we easily fell into situations that produced the mess we made on Earth because in general we have not been very wise.

Therefore, one of our tasks on Earth is to achieve balance in our issues and thus be more able to form wisdom. I think one source of our imbalance is that we pay significantly more attention to the physical-world part of our lives than to the spirit-world part.

In my mind, wisdom is the ability to make credible extrapolations sideways and forward, based on knowledge of the present and the past, and to then take action to ensure the future will be good. Otherwise, the future could be bad. "Extrapolation sideways and forward" is to take knowledge from one area and see what it could tell us about another area, such that the knowledge gets expanded sideways, and thus maximizes its value while extrapolating forward. Analogies, looking for commonality among areas, applying creativity, etc. are examples of the concept of extrapolating sideways. The next step would be to then extrapolate all of it forward into the future in an attempt to make the best future we can. "Extrapolating sideways" is not necessarily a skill everyone is able to exercise well. But all of us can make extrapolations forward into the future, to make the best future we can with or without making extrapolations sideways.

The past is fixed, but the future is fluid. If the spirit world extrapolates into the future based on its knowledge of the present and past finds what it sees is bad, it could do something in the present to make the future better. It would have to have a balanced state of knowledge in order to know how to do that; i.e., the process works well only if the extrapolations are credible. The more credible the extrapolations, the better the process works. This means that the better the wisdom the spirit world can form, the more effective its actions in the present will be when attempting to improve the future, when necessary to do so. Wisdom can be formed by the spirit world at any given point in time only if knowledge is balanced on all sides of every issue existing in the spirit world at that point in time.

As explained earlier, just one added new piece of knowledge more than doubles the number of spiritual entities in the spirit world. This means if action to make an otherwise bad future a good one were ineffective, subsequent futures could become increasingly bad very rapidly and in an unstable manner. The viability of the spirit world could then degrade in an unstable manner to the point that the spirit world and everything it has created could vanish, possibly very quickly once degradation passes beyond the point of no return.

It is possible that the collapse of the spirit world happened many times in the past, and its initiation happened many times. As with any living thing, it would be the most vulnerable during its early life. In the case of the spirit world in early life, its ability to form wisdom is limited, because the number of pieces of knowledge and the number of spiritual entities it has to work with are relatively few. The longer the spirit world survives, the more able it is to survive. We might ask; where the spirit world is now in terms of its ability to survive? We cannot tell. But according to the model, we need to do our part to help it remain viable regardless of where it is in terms of its ability to survive, because no matter what, its ability to survive depends on it.

Wisdom can be formed regarding any given issue when knowledge on all sides of the issue is reasonably balanced. There are a countless number of issues in the spirit world, and more are constantly formed as new pieces of knowledge are constantly generated and added to it. Issues are essentially tug-of-wars, and when they are manifested in our physical world, they take the form of physical and/or nonphysical tug-of-wars. For example, tug-of-wars maintain the health of our ecosystems by keeping all the forces involved in balance. They occur in our bodies to keep all bodily functions in balance so that we can remain healthy and alive. We designed them into our machines so that the machines can operate without overheating or malfunctioning in other ways. They are part of our marriages, families, and friendships. They are part of the means by which businesses, local and national governments, and international relationships are able to function, and galaxies and our solar system to remain together, and our Earth to support life, etc.

In the spirit world, newly formed issues might need to be balanced, and a constant need exists to re-balance various old issues that are now out of balance in light of new pieces of knowledge. The spirit world needs to keep track of all issues. Periodically, the spirit world needs to design and bring into being a new universe to help restore balance. This occurs when the kinds of experiences that could generate the kinds of new pieces of knowledge needed to restore balance are not possible within the spirit world itself. Recall we earlier indicated that spiritual entities could go through experiences and thus generate new pieces of knowledge within the spirit world. Those kinds of experiences could take place only in the spirit world because that is the only place pieces of knowledge, and therefore spiritual entities, reside. An example is when they serve as a spirit for something to reside in a universe. Other examples are when they participate with all other spiritual entities to help the spirit world form wisdom, make extrapolations into possible futures, design and bring into being new universes, issue intuition messages to living things residing in universes, etc. But they cannot generate the kinds of pieces of knowledge to help restore balance if the kinds of experiences that could generate such pieces of knowledge are not possible in the spirit world. For example the kinds of experiences needed could be those that could only exist in a physical world whereas the spirit world is nonphysical. Therefore, the spirit world would design a universe in which the necessary kinds of experiences to generate that kind of pieces of knowledge are possible. As said before, the spirit world would not know exactly what the possible experiences would be; it would only know the kinds of experiences possible. Another way to look at it is that it would not know exactly the new pieces of knowledge that can be generated; it would only know the kinds of new pieces of knowledge that can be generated. Otherwise, if the spirit world already knew what new pieces of knowledge could be generated, it would already have those pieces of knowledge. Then it would not need to design the new universe to generate them.

We might ask; why there is no limit to the new pieces of knowledge possible to generate? As mentioned earlier, a piece of knowledge is analogous to a word. There is also no limit to the new words that can be formed. As new pieces of knowledge are generated and added to the spirit world, the spirit world grows and more spiritual entities are formed. New pieces of knowledge and new spiritual entities bring with them new possible experiences, similar to the way more and new varieties of building blocks enable us to build things we hadn't been able to build before. Or the way new words allow for more kinds of sentences can be composed. Therefore, the more the spirit world grows, the more new experiences are possible. And more new experiences bring forth more new pieces of knowledge and more new spiritual entities. It is a vicious circle. Consequently, there is no limit to the new pieces of knowledge that can be generated.

Good thing the spirit world has this vicious circle going on. Otherwise the spirit world would not grow, would not have a future, and we would not have a future either. More specifically, all our futures would simply be our past. Then even if we don't vanish, we would simply die of boredom.

Oh, wait, we can't die of boredom if there is no future in which we could do that. Oh, man, why do you have to bring up such a thought? Well, that's what our model indicates. *Oh, my. Good thing the spirit world has its vicious circle going on so that such a situation would never happen, we hope. Why do you say "we hope?"* Well, you know, no model formulated by a human could ever be totally complete or absolutely accurate. *Ugh, that's right!*

Everlasting Desire to Learn and to Create

A newly generated piece of knowledge immediately forms a connection of the first kind with every other existing piece of knowledge. Conversely, every existing piece of knowledge constantly looks for new pieces of knowledge with which to form a connection of the first kind.

This elemental energy that every piece of knowledge has is the elemental form of life that makes up the higher forms of life in the spirit world, in the various forms of spiritual entities. The highest form of life at any point in time is the spirit world itself.

Another way to look at it is that this elemental energy gives every piece of knowledge an everlasting desire to learn (to connect with more pieces of knowledge) and to create (to form more spiritual entities). This means every spiritual entity, including the spirit world, also has an everlasting desire to learn and to create. The larger and more complex the spiritual entity, the more ways it is able to learn and to create (i.e., it has more pieces of knowledge and includes a larger number of smaller spiritual entities).

Spiritual entities can form thoughts, concepts, solutions, designs, stories, and serve as spirits for living or nonliving things, etc. They can combine with other spiritual entities to form larger spiritual entities and the larger the spiritual entity, the more complex the thing it can form. When they all combine to form the spirit world, the spirit world is able to design and bring universes into being.

The elemental energies the pieces of knowledge and smaller spiritual entities have are analogous to the elemental energies that subatomic particles, electrons, protons, neutrons, and atoms have. Subatomic particles can form electrons, protons, and neutrons. Electrons, protons, and neutrons can form atoms. Atoms can form molecules. And so on. When we get to highly intelligent living things such as humans, humans can invent and build things.

Personal Gods

Each individual is different and unique and has a different and unique perception of God, even if the differences in the perceptions among some individuals might be small. Therefore, it is appropriate to say each perception of God is a personal one, and therefore each perceived God is a personal God. According to the model, in order for a personal God to be perceived, that personal God has to already exist in the spirit world in the form of a spiritual entity. As said earlier, everything is created by the spirit world. Consequently, if something has not been created, it does not exist and cannot be perceived. For this reason, every personal God is real and is just as valid as any other personal God. Since the model does not exclude any personal God, it does not exclude any religion either. Every religion is a part of the spirit world and therefore each religion is just as real and valid as any other religion.

Also, because each individual is different and unique, each individual has a different and unique perception of the religion he or she chooses to follow, if any. Consequently, each such individual in essence actually has a different and unique denomination of a religion. This could explain why there are about 50,000 known denominations of just Christianity alone. Other religions also have a lot of denominations. This has to be the result of efforts to accommodate the diversity of personal spiritual needs and perceptions within the various religions.

We might ask; whether any personal God could be the entire spirit world? The answer is no. The spirit world is so large no living thing in any universe could have a complete view of it. This is a natural outcome of each universe being designed to be different and unique and to provide experiences not possible in the spirit world. This automatically limits the view of the spirit world possible from each universe. Therefore, since living things in a universe cannot sense the entire spirit world, they cannot perceive what makes up the entire spirit world. Therefore, a personal God cannot be the entire spirit world.

A Partnership Relationship

As with anything that grows, the total knowledge in the spirit world needs adjustment now and then. In the case of the spirit world, the adjustment is to restore balance in the knowledge on all sides of each issue. When necessary, the spirit world designs and brings into being a new universe to help make the adjustment. Each new universe addresses the issues needing attention at the time. This suggests that if we could identify the issues that are a part of our lives and our universe, we could get an idea of how we could go about helping our universe fulfill its purpose of helping the spirit world restore balance. This topic is discussed in greater detail in the next section of this chapter.

For each living or nonliving thing that exists in a universe, a spiritual entity in the spirit world is enabling it to exist. The spiritual entity thus contains the spirit of the living or nonliving thing. Therefore, the living or nonliving thing consists of its spirit in the spirit world, its body or thing in our physical, and its soul that connects the two parts together and carries the signals between the two parts. If it is a living thing, the spirit world gives the spirit the freedom to choose. This means a spirit has a certain degree of autonomy and independence from the spiritual entity of which it is a part. Thus, a natural partnership is formed between the spirit and the spiritual entity. This partnership accommodates the autonomy and independence while maintaining a relationship between the spirit and the spiritual entity. Since the spiritual entity is a part of the spirit world, the partnership is also with the spirit world. The spirit world, including the spiritual entity, could thus provide guidance to the spirit, but would not control the spirit. Although depending on the role of the living thing in the universe in which it resides, they could do the thinking for the living thing to varying degrees from essentially none for us humans to essentially completely for certain others. Various cases are discussed in later chapters of this book.

All this is part of the plan. For highly intelligent living things, at least for humans as far as we can tell, any awareness of the plan or any memory of their spiritual entities' past is hidden from the spirits of the living things once the living things are brought into being in a universe. This is so that the spirits of the living things will not be "contaminated"' by such awareness that might alter or constrain how their spirits might have the living things go through experiences, and thus how they would go about generating more new pieces of knowledge. This is because, as said before, while the spirit world knows the kinds of pieces of knowledge that the universe could produce, it does not know exactly the new pieces of knowledge that can be produced. Therefore, the spirit world allows the spirits the freedom to discover on their own the exact pieces of knowledge that can be produced in order to maximize what is produced. This is analogous to how we send a rover to Mars. We know we want information about Mars, but we don't know exactly what information could be obtained. Therefore, we designed into the rover a certain degree of freedom to explore Mars. This forms a partnership between it and us, and is part of the communication between it and us. Through this partnership and our guidance of the rover, we attempt to maximize what can be discovered about Mars. By analogy, we on Earth serve as the spirit for the rover, the rover serves as the body on Mars, and the partnership and communications equipment are part of the rover's soul. The rest of the soul is nonphysical and consists of all the effort that went into designing and building the rover and then launching it to Mars to enable it to exist there.

As the presentation continues, we will see that the degree of autonomy and independence the spirit world gives a living thing's spirit depends on the level of consciousness and intelligence embodied in the spirit of the living thing. The higher the level of consciousness and intelligence a living thing has, the greater its autonomy and independence. Living things with lower levels of consciousness and intelligence also have freedom to choose and also produce new pieces of knowledge, but their purposes are different in nature from those of highly intelligent living things. Their range of choices, possible experiences, and possible new pieces of knowledge are more limited. For example, in the case of our universe, particularly on Earth, some of them might be here to help produce and/or maintain the various ecosystems so that the various environments become and/or remain hospitable to a variety of other living things. Typically, the first such living things are slimes and single-celled things that turn toxic gases into life-sustaining gases such as oxygen and carbon dioxide. The limited purpose of these slimes are a part their natural partnership with the spirit world.

This discussion leads naturally into the topic of the next section of this chapter.

Fulfilling the Purpose

Continuing from where the preceding section left off, an example of living things with a limited range of possible experiences is honeybees. Their range of choices and experiences mostly have to do with keeping themselves alive, keeping their hive viable, and incidentally pollinating plants. Their third purpose is their most important to the overall workings on Earth, but the bees probably don't even know they have the third purpose, since it is incidental. They also incidentally provide honey for various other creatures, including us humans, and the bees probably don't know they have this purpose either since it is also incidental. Living things in general, not just bees are probably not aware of their incidental purposes. Earthworms are not likely to know that the way they aerate the earth and recycle dead plant material benefits living plants. And plants are one of the most important kinds of living things on Earth.

Oh, and earthworms also help fishermen catch fish. Oh yeah, don't forget that.

Some of the most important purposes of many living things are incidental. For example, plants incidentally serve as, and/or provide, food for a wide variety of creatures. Creatures in general incidentally serve as food for various other creatures. If plants and creatures did not have such incidental purposes, the workings on Earth would be very different, perhaps even unable to support many of its existing species of highly intelligent living things, including us humans.

Accordingly, when some individuals say in essence that all living things are here for the benefit of us humans, they could be sort of correct because in a way this could be a possible interpretation of the way things currently work on Earth. But it is a very egotistic interpretation, and therefore not helpful to have in mind in any personal spiritual search. I think a more humble approach would open one's mind much more and thus enable one's search to go much better. For one thing, how do we know these other living things are not doing a much better job of helping the spirit world restore balance than we humans are doing? After all, they are not making the mess we are making.

So what about us humans, do we have incidental purposes? I think in one sense we might and in another sense we don't. Other creatures simply go about doing what they need to do to stay alive and to keep their species going, and they automatically fulfill their incidental purposes. Humans are different in that we are more conscious and more intelligent, and we do more than simply go about doing what we need to do to stay alive and to keep our species going. For example, although we humans can also become food for other creatures, we are aware of that possibility and can usually successfully prevent it from happening. We could interpret this as meaning we were not meant to become food for other creatures and therefore such a possibility is not an incidental purpose for us.

We are capable of being aware of a wide variety of other possible incidental purposes, and we have been successful to varying degrees in all cases to do something about them. Therefore, we could conclude that none of the possible incidental purposes we have become aware of were meant to be incidental purposes for us.

For example we have been incidental participants in discovering the hazards of eating trans fats, a formerly common ingredient in many processed packaged food products. We eventually became aware of their bad effects and eliminated or greatly reduced them in most processed packaged food products. Thus, we are essentially no longer incidental participants, and we were not meant to be that for the purpose of making the discovery. Another example, we were not meant to be incidental indictors of the presence of scams, hackers, identity thief, and the like for the purpose of finding them and counteracting them. But we are by sometimes being incidental victims of them, and we have been successful to varying degrees in counteracting them. Unfortunately, in this case, we are likely to continue to be incidental indicators since such malicious activities are wide spread and increasingly sophisticated.

We could then ask what about things such as when we hunted passenger pigeons to extinction? How come we did not become aware that we could incidentally cause them to go extinct? The answer is that we have the capacity to become aware of this, but we made a mistake and didn't think about it at the time.

So you say being stupid is not an incidental purpose? Well, if you put it that way, gee, I dunno. We seem to have a habit of making mistakes. But, making mistakes is a part of learning, and learning usually leads to greater awareness. Therefore, I would say being stupid is curable through learning and thus it is not an incidental purpose. Whew, now I feel better. Why, because you make a lot of mistakes?

Continuing on, then the next question is what possible incidental purpose could we humans have since it seems we have the capacity to become aware of just about anything that goes on in our physical world? The answer could be that our possible incidental purposes are less likely to do with things that could happen in our physical world but are more likely to do with things that could happen in the spirit world. And in this sense, we humans are different from other creatures on Earth again. Other creatures could also have some incidental purposes in the spirit world, but mostly their incidental purposes are in our physical world. Incidentally serving as food for various other creatures, as mentioned, is an example.

An example of an incidental purpose humans have in the spirit world is we are generating as many new pieces of knowledge as we can to help the spirit world continue to grow while we are pursuing our main purpose of helping the spirit world restore balance. Some of the other creatures, such as animals that have a significant amount of intelligence and are thus designed to do a lot of their thinking for themselves, are likely to also have such an incidental purpose. But theirs is to a much lesser degree than humans have since the range of their experiences is much more limited. Creatures such as various species of insects that relies heavily on instincts for survival and thus the spirit world does all or most of their thinking for them probably do not have much or any of such an incidental purpose.

Therefore, when some individuals say we humans are apart from other creatures on Earth, in this sense they might have a point. But it doesn't necessarily mean we are doing better at fulfilling our purpose than other creatures are at fulfilling theirs. For one thing, other creatures do not do the kinds of horrible things to other members of their own species that we do to other humans. Accordingly, in this terrible sense we could say we humans are also unfortunately apart from other creatures on Earth. Therefore, we should not let the notion of our being apart from other creatures go to our head and inflate our ego.

Earlier in this section I said that in one sense we have incidental purposes, regarding what could happen in our physical world, and in another sense we do not. If we do not have the capacity to figure out the issues designed into our universe, and if we unknowingly address them anyway, then they would be our incidental purposes. However, if we have the capacity to figure out the issues designed into our universe and are able to purposely do something about them, then they would not be our incidental purposes. In my mind, we humans have this capacity, and the effort to figure out the issues designed into our universe could begin as follows.

The model indicates that the spirit world is gentle, kind, caring, nonjudgmental, compassionate, empathic, and loving. Therefore, I could not imagine the spirit world meant our partnership with it to be as traumatic and messy as we have made it to be on Earth. In my mind, to be consistent with the loving nature of the spirit world, the partnership was meant to be such that we would make Earth a gentle, kind, caring, nonjudgmental, compassionate, empathic, and loving place for all humans. However, to maximize the amount of knowledge our universe could produce intelligent living things are given the freedom to choose. Also, the spirit of each of us is only a tiny part of the spirit world. Consequently, we might not be expected to make the loving qualities to be present on Earth to be as good as they are in the spirit world. On the other hand, we were not likely expected to make Earth as messy as it is either.

The model indicates our universe is designed to have a bunch of obstacles that each of us is to work with or around to make our partnership with the spirit world to be as indicated. Given that the spirit world is gentle, kind, caring, nonjudgmental, compassionate, empathic, and loving, our task must not have been intended to be really difficult or traumatic. In my mind, it was likely meant to be such that in essence we simply need to have a lot of empathy and compassion for other living things, especially other humans. Although the details of carrying out the task are much more involved, it is still unlikely to be really difficult or traumatic. What it really takes is a lot of wisdom to avoid tripping over the obstacles designed into our universe and thus making the mess we have made. I think we might have found every obstacle, and we did it by tripping over them instead of by identifying them first and then working with or around them.

Oh, well, at least we found them. Yeah, but have we really identified them to the degree that we can figure out how to work with or around them? Hmm, not sure about that since we continue making messes here on Earth. Yep, it looks like we need to do more figuring out and thinking about this. Hey, how about us humans first lowering our egos and our desire to enhance our personal survivability? Wouldn't that help us do better figuring out how to work with or around the obstacles we face? Wow, for being only half a brain, you have a great idea! And, wow, for being only the other half of a brain, you are able to see what I suggest as a great idea! Let's hug!

If we look at what we need to do now to make Earth a gentle, kind, caring, nonjudgmental, compassionate, empathic, and loving place for all humans, the task looks impossibly difficult. That is because, ideally, we need to first clean up the mess here. As a possible place to start, let's see if we can identify the most important obstacles. In my mind, they are the following:

> **Obstacle (1):** Our universe is made of materials and energies that can be posessed, controlled, and/or consumed.
>
> **Obstacle (2):** Highly intelligent living things such as us humans on Earth have egos and a desire to enhance survivability.
>
> **Obstacle (3):** Mobile intelligent living things (those that can walk, swim, and/or fly) need to eat other living things to survive.

An important characteristic of Obstacle (1) is that any growth that requires the consumption of resources that are limited often results in opposing, though equally valid, short-term vs. long-term needs. This is an example of where wisdom comes in really handy in helping find a resolution. And, wisdom can be formed only if we have sufficient and balanced knowledge on all sides of the issues involved.

Living things grow physically and/or spiritually regardless of their age. An example of spiritual growth is when a living thing is gaining knowledge by learning things, and this can happen at any age. Living things reside in universes and are a part of how each universe works. Therefore, universes are living things too. Living things will grow with or without guidance or control. The spirit world forms wisdom and uses it to guide its own growth. In the case of Earth, it is clear that in essence we humans are currently carrying the main responsibility for how Earth spiritually grows, and the model says this is part of our partnership with the spirit world. The model also says we are supposed to make Earth a gentle, kind, caring, nonjudgmental, compassionate, empathic, and loving place for all humans while working with or around the obstacles designed into our universe. The model thus indicates that this is a major part of Earth's spiritual growth we humans are suppose make happen. The experiences we may go through to make this happen are therefore the kind of experiences that would generate the kinds of new pieces of knowledge the spirit world needs to restore balance. If we do otherwise, then the new pieces of knowledge our experiences generate will not be the kind needed to restore balance but are still potentially useful to the spirit world in the future. But nevertheless, our higher priority is to help the spirit world restore balance.

We might ask; why the spirit world doesn't simply tell us what to do instead of letting us make a mess? One reason, as we discussed earlier, is that the spirit world doesn't know exactly the experiences that are possible on Earth; therefore it cannot really tell us what to do. Another is that in order to form wisdom at some unspecified time in the future, the spirit can, in due time, use just about any new pieces of knowledge that can be generated, and besides, the mess we made is a valuable learning situation for the spirit world, even if it doesn't help restore balance. Thus, our making the mess is a risk the spirit world was willing to take. In my mind, this is partly because the spirit world is wise enough to allow for the possibility that living things in general can go off-course such as in the manner we humans have done. The spirit world is likely to have something akin to safety margins or compensating factors ready to accommodate any mess we make. For example, our universe is bound to have lots of other planets with living things on them so that if we mess up on Earth, living things on other planets can still enable our universe to fulfill its purpose. But do we want to be the ones in our universe to fail, especially when there is a natural "freedom of information" policy in the spirit world? Every spiritual entity has connections of the first kind directly or indirectly with every other spiritual entity. Therefore, every spiritual entity is in communication with every other spiritual entity at all times.

The makers of the mess on Earth do not include everyone on Earth. If enough of us are doing our part on a personal basis to help Earth fulfill its purpose, Earth might still make a "passing grade," such as at least a "D" on an averaged basis.

OMG, a "D!" Good thing the spirit world is a gentle, kind, caring, non-judgmental, compassionate, empathic, and loving place. Well, maybe some other planet might get an "F" so that at least we would not be "last" if that happens.

Even if we fail, when we die and our consciousness is then completely tuned to the spirit world, we will find that no spiritual expression of any deceased living thing will judge us. After all, every spiritual entity is directly or indirectly a part of every other spiritual entity. Therefore, no spiritual entity is going to judge any direct or indirect part of itself. Our results will be a part of every other spiritual entity's results. We will be the only ones to assess how well we have done. What we learn will become a part of what every other spiritual expression learns. Every spiritual entity will welcome that, given how everything in the spirit world is made of pieces of knowledge and does not mind receiving additional pieces of knowledge.

Closing Comments for Chapter Three

Based on the model, I believe deep down that we know we should make Earth a gentle, kind, caring, nonjudgmental, compassionate, empathic, and loving place, because subconsciously we know that the spirit world, the permanent home we came from, is like that. We receive guidance messages from the spirit world, but spiritual signals are soft and easily drowned out by the loud physical signals of our physical world. This could be why we find being in a quiet, peaceful wilderness so liberating, nurturing, and regenerating. It is where we can sense more clearly the signals from the spirit world, and thus we feel more like we are there, in our permanent home. I remember the first time I camped in Yosemite. It was in 1963, before campsites needed to be reserved way ahead of time, and before there were huge crowds and shuttle buses. As I climbed the Yosemite Falls Trail the very first time, it felt like "this is home; this is where I belong."

Even in a busy city, if we can find a quiet peaceful place, we can still get this kind of feeling. As a working graduate student, I could only afford a unit of an old four-unit rental located in a somewhat rundown business section of a town between where I worked and the university. I slept on a mattress on the floor, and cardboard grocery boxes made up my bookcase. My desk was a 3-foot-by-4-foot piece of plywood on removable legs. The unit I rented was the farthest from the street, and therefore quiet and peaceful. On weekends, I would study in complete silence. Not even the radio was on. I could just feel the "garbage" that had accumulated in my head floating out, clearing my mind. During such moments, that unit was a piece of heaven. Incidentally, the freedom that comes with not possessing a lot of stuff was at that time very liberating.

A lot of parallels have been drawn between what the model indicates about the spirit world and what experiences and observations are common in our physical world. In my mind, a spiritual model needs to have a lot of such parallels in order to be as complete as possible. This is because spirituality is a part of everything at every moment. To capture that, a spiritual model needs to be as much a part of natural, everyday life as possible.

Since our universe is designed and brought into being by the spirit world, our universe is bound to have a lot of the attributes of the spirit world. The main difference is that some of the attributes manifested on Earth are physical translations as determined by the materials and energies that make up our universe.

The fact that the model can provide plausible spiritual explanations for virtually all the experiences and observations common on Earth makes the model feel a part of everyday life as natural as the air around us. This makes staying constantly tuned into its spiritual messages as natural as breathing. This is how a spiritual model ought to be in order help us be better people every moment of everyday.

If you are searching for your personal spiritual model, try to find one that provides such qualities for you. You will know you have found the model that fits you best if it does. The model might not do that for anyone else, but that doesn't matter as long as it does that for you. Everyone is different and unique and has different and unique spiritual needs. Therefore, do not accept anyone else's model, including mine, without doing your own personal search first. Your personal search is likely to lead you to a different model, one that fits you better than any that already exists.

I more or less followed principles of my profession as an engineer in doing my search. I believe following the principles of your profession or career would work best for you as well since those are the principles you are most proficient at applying. Accordingly, those are the principles most likely to be helpful to you in your search.

Chapter Four
Attributes of the Spirit World

What's in this Chapter and the Chapters to Follow

This chapter and the chapters to follow address topics that further illustrate how the model correlates with common, everyday observations and experiences. The model also indicates that various configurations are possible for spirits of living things, and this could explain why various species carry out their lives in the manner they do.

For example, monarch butterflies go through four generations during their annual migration, covering thousands of miles and lasting many months, and yet the returning fourth generation is able to find and settle into the same grove of trees from which the first generation began the migration. How are the members of the fourth generation able to identify the grove the members of the first generation started from? Conventional thinking says it is instinct. But how could their instincts be so precise? Why would they not simply go to any other similar grove in the same region? Could they have something else guiding them in addition to their instincts? The model provides a plausible explanation. The model also shows how instincts can function differently for different spirit configurations.

Another example is that members of colonies, such as ants and honey bees, seem to automatically know their roles in the colony, and their bodies are even configured differently to match their roles. The model indicates how their spirits' configuration differs from that of, for example, monarch butterflies, and thus their instincts work differently from those of monarch butterflies.

A third example is how the spirits of living things that rely heavily on instincts for their species' survival have yet another spirit configuration, and thus their instincts work in yet another way. All the various possible spirit configurations I can think of, based on observed creature behavior, are covered in more detail as the presentation continues.

We might ask about human instincts. Our instincts appear to be weaker than those of other creatures. According to the model, this is because we rely much less on instincts for survival of our species than do other creatures. Otherwise our instincts appear to function in essentially the same manner as those of other species of animals, not other creatures, but animals. Our spirit configuration is very similar to those of other animals. The major difference is that our spirit configuration is such that we do not rely on instincts as much as they do. However, like humans, other animals generally also teach survival skills to their young. Therefore, while other animals rely on instincts more than we humans do, they do not rely on instincts as much as some other creatures, such as insects.

Other phenomena the model plausibly explains are also discussed as the presentation continues, including telepathic communication, ability to see auras, extrasensory ability, out-of-body experiences, remote viewing, ghosts, etc. and body intelligence vs. brain intelligence.

Uh, we didn't say our model can explain vampires and werewolves. Well, we did say that anything that could be imagined has to already exist in the spirit world. Therefore, since we can imagine vampires and werewolves, they already exist in the spirit world. It is just that we can grab them and translate them into existence on Earth only as fictional characters. The spirit world apparently did not include them as living things residing in our universe, at least not on Earth, and the same goes for monsters that live in closets and under beds. Whew, now I feel better. Oh, but then wouldn't we find them in the spirit world after we die and our consciousness is fully tuned to the spirit world? Yeah-h-h…. Heh-heh-heh! But remember, while they are scary in our universe, they might not be scary in another universe and certainly not scary in the spirit world. Oh, phooey.

A Piece of Knowledge is Neither Good nor Bad

The analogy mentioned in Chapter Three between pieces of knowledge and words goes further. Every piece of knowledge is useful to the spirit world no matter the experience that generated it. Analogously, every word is useful to us no matter its origin. Any piece of knowledge by itself is neither good nor bad. With few exceptions, any word by itself is neither good nor bad. When pieces of knowledge are combined to form a spiritual entity in the spirit world, any spiritual entity by itself is neither good nor bad. But when translated into a form that can exist in a universe, the translated form can be perceived as good, bad, or neutral depending on the design of the universe and the situation in the universe. For example, if the translation of a spiritual entity into a form that can be expressed on Earth is "I'm leaving now," the expression could be perceived as good or neutral if by a person leaving for work, and bad if by a person going to rob a bank.

Because every piece of knowledge is useful to the spirit world, every new piece of knowledge generated is accepted and becomes a part of the spirit world. Every newly created or existing spiritual entity is useful to the spirit world and can play many different roles. All pieces of knowledge and all spiritual entities participate in the spirit world's constant task of forming wisdom.

By analogy, every new word is useful to us and is accepted to be part of our vocabulary. Every newly formed or already formed sentence is useful to us and has many different purposes. All words and sentences become part of our constant task of communicating with one another such that, ideally, we could all do things wisely.

We might ask; what is a piece of knowledge? Would it be really as analogous to a word as described? We can see and/or hear a word, but we cannot sense a piece of knowledge with any of our five major senses. The answer is that a piece of knowledge resides in the spirit world, and we sense it with our spiritual senses. Via our spiritual senses, we know we have a piece of knowledge when we have it even though we cannot sense it with our five major senses. Thus, a piece of knowledge cannot be defined in terms of attributes of our physical world. A word or a sentence is a translation of a spiritual entity in the spirit world into a form that can be expressed or exist in our physical world. The same spiritual entity can be translated into different forms in different countries, cultures, traditions, etc. For example, a word or sentence can be different in different languages and may have a somewhat different meaning in each. A word or a sentence is a product of translation, and no translation of anything is exact, not even from one language to another. Therefore, we could also ask what a word is and what a sentence is. Are they symbols, sounds, gestures (using our vocal cords, tongue, and mouth), signals, or what? The answer is just about as vague as the answer for what is a piece of knowledge. Nevertheless, a piece of knowledge is real. Otherwise we would not know anything.

Oh, and according to the model, if pieces of knowledge were not real, we would not exist. Yeah, then it would not matter if we didn't know anything. Yeah, so then when we say "I dunno," we would really mean it. Wow, that's brilliant, especially for half a brain!

Examples of Effects of Incomplete, not Completely Accurate, Models

We use incomplete models all the time in our lives. They are the only kind available. They work well enough to meet most of our needs most of the time. In technical areas, such as in engineering, we use safety factors and margins, limits on range of applicability, etc., to compensate for the incompleteness of models. For common, everyday non-technical models, compensation for incompleteness is generally left to the user to handle, based on the user's own experiences.

In my mind, we have made a mess on Earth partly because our models are incomplete, and in many situations we do not, or cannot, compensate well enough for the models' incompleteness. We arrive at incomplete and inaccurate conclusions, and our actions then add to the mess. I think this particularly applies to models directly or indirectly dealing with human behavior. Human behavior has so many variables and so many ways the variables can interrelate that it is difficult to formulate very good human behavior models and to compensate for their incompleteness.

For example, we would think that by now we would have a reliable handbook on how to bring up children. But ideas and concepts on what constitutes the best methods keep changing, partly because the way we live keeps changing and the world keeps changing.

To illustrate how incomplete models can actually result in incorrect and/or non-helpful actions, I chose a real life situation and real life actions by real individuals. The situation in the illustration is neither common nor everyday in nature. Therefore, a typical individual is not experienced at grabbing the best models or at compensating for the incompleteness of the models. Consequently, the result of his or her action has an above-average chance of being not quite what he or she intended.

Keeping a good sense of humor can help things go more smoothly, especially when this happens. This could be why the spirit world designed us humans to have a sense of humor, because it knows we will sometimes trip over our models. It is not clear if any other species on Earth has a sense of humor. For one thing, they do not deal with the enormous variety of models we humans do, and therefore they might not need a sense of humor.

In the following, the situation is serious and the actions by loved ones are attempts to be helpful but sometimes are instead humorous. Seeing the humorous side makes it easier to appreciate the love and care. Having empathy and compassion for the loved one trying to help is also helpful. When my mom was dying of cancer, she was empathic and compassionate of her loved ones and their efforts to be helpful. It was a precious gift from her to us.

A terminally ill cancer patient is being cared for by her spouse 24/7. Neither of them is getting much rest or sleep, and they barely have time to even eat. She needs to go to the hospital weekly for chemotherapy injections. She also needs to be tube fed almost around the clock. It is complicated to leave the house for the injections that take hours to perform. Side effects get worse with each treatment. The cancer is not responding, and she is slowly dying. Although she is being tube fed, she is encouraged to eat a little if she can, to help her feel psychologically better. It is tricky to prepare something she can eat, and she is able to eat only very little. The tremendous stress of helplessly watching her slowly die over seven months gives him terrible panic attacks. He is running on adrenaline nonstop, his nerves are shot, he feels like he can't breathe, and nothing looks or feels real. He desperately goes out to the garden and jumps, trying to jump out of his panic attack and get some relief, but it doesn't work. He feels as though he is an alien not of this universe. His limbs won't quite move as instructed by his spirit. He can't drink from a cup because a cup in front of his nose would feel suffocating. He can't write in a straight line, and writing a check is almost impossible.

The following are examples of actions by loved ones:

Example (1): The situation leaves hardly any time for neither patient nor spouse to rest or sleep. A loved one, doesn't know the patient requires 24/7 care and thinks the spouse is not getting enough sleep because he is having difficulty sleeping. Thus, the loved one tries to help by suggesting the spouse take sleeping pills, when in fact the spouse is so tired he falls asleep immediately when he has the chance. The loved one is using a model for normal circumstances, not for 24/7 care-giving.

Example (2): A loved one wants the spouse to buy a new computer, get on the Internet, and learn to use both right away. The spouse hardly has time to eat and sleep, let alone to learn two new systems. He is surprised the loved one suggests this, especially at such a time. The loved one never explains why. Later, the spouse concludes that he must have wanted to help the spouse pay bills more easily, and apparently did not know about automatic bill pay and pay by phone, which are either effortless or require no more effort than pay by computer.

These first two examples illustrate how attempts to be helpful might not be helpful.

Example (3): Sometimes a loved one suggests care-taking procedures that he or she thinks are better than those instructed by the nurses and doctors. Often this is because the loved one doesn't understand the medical reasons for doing the procedure as instructed. Having to deal with such actions makes care-giving more stressful, because the caregiver then also has to take care of the loved one when he or she feels hurt and becomes argumentative when the suggestion is not followed. Publications are available at hospitals to indicate what loved ones can do and not do to be helpful. The list of suggestions is fairly long and therefore not listed here. However, the examples given here provide an idea of what some of the suggestions are.

Example (4): A loved one who is a great example of someone with lots of kindness, care, empathy, and compassion pushes the spouse hard to get hospice help to give him a chance for more rest and sleep. The spouse thus asks the doctor if the family should go for hospice care, and he says no. As it turns out, neither the loved one nor the spouse realize that entering hospice care requires giving up hope of defeating the cancer. Thus, the doctor says no, because he is not ready to give up yet, and thinks the spouse knows about the choice between treatment and hospice. The spouse does not insist on hospice help because he assumes the doctor thinks the spouse is doing a fine job of care-giving, which he is, and therefore hospice help is unnecessary. Thus, there are incomplete models going all around.

Out of the most loving, caring, empathic, and compassionate intentions, the loved one wrote to the doctor, asking to provide hospice care for the patient in the hope of getting some help for the spouse. Meanwhile, before receiving the letter, the doctor was ready to start a round of a different kind of chemotherapy. To help convince the doctor to follow her request, the loved one pointed out her own credentials in the medical community, and this might have helped made the doctor decide to go with her request. It is also possible the letter prompted the doctor to reassess the condition of the patient and decided further treatment is not likely to help. In either case, the way a nurse informed the spouse of the letter indicated the letter strongly influenced the doctor's decision. Consequently, the doctor abruptly stopped the process to start the second chemotherapy, and entered the patient into hospice. Both the patient and spouse were extremely disappointed because the new chemotherapy was their last hope. Knowing the letter was a sincere attempt to be helpful in a most empathic and compassionate manner, the spouse did not mention the letter to anyone, not even the loved one who wrote it.

Utter chaos followed, with even less time for rest and sleep for patient and spouse. Hospital-owned bed and feeding-tube equipment had to be replaced with hospice-owned ones. Hospice equipment arrived, and hospital equipment was moved to the living room and dining room where they got in the way for over a week before being picked up. Interviews with a different hospice person each day dragged on for a week, begging the question: Why can't they all come at once, in one day? After all, they were all seeking essentially the same information. Thus, the family experienced a week of total disruption on top of all the tasks that had to continue nonstop.

Therefore, a word of caution for future patients and caregivers who are ready to enter hospice: Be ready for a possible week of utter chaos and disruption before any hospice help can provide relief. Hopefully, hospices have streamlined their initiation processes by now.

About a week later, the patient had to go to the ER, and she died shortly afterwards. Thus, in this case, hospice did not have a chance to provide much help. When the patient was back in the hospital and still alive, hospice wanted their equipment at the home replaced with hospital ones since the patient had essentially resumed treatment and was thus no longer in hospice care. But the spouse was constantly with the patient at the hospital and was never home to enable them to take back their equipment until after the patient died.

After the turmoil was over, the spouse couldn't help treasuring the love, kindness, care, empathy, and compassion shown by the loved one. It was a beautiful thing to behold and to receive. It came from a truly beautiful heart. She was following the guidance of a beautiful model, and the model was beautiful even though it was incomplete and inaccurate. Realizing this, the spouse chose to not tell the loved one that the nurse showed him the letter. The loved one did not know that if the patient entered hospice that all medical procedures would stop. She was only trying to get some help for the spouse.

Example (5): The spouse had his cancer before the patient had hers, but his seemed under control after two years of treatment. Then his spouse came down with terminal cancer. The stress and lack of rest during the seven months of care-giving brought back his cancer. He was aware of it but ignored it to care for her for as long as he could. After she died, he discovered his cancer was twice as bad as before. He needed surgery again, the third time, followed by three and half years of chemotherapy. After the first year of chemotherapy, he was physically spent. A loved one suggested he consider stopping the chemotherapy since the cancer seemed again under control (for that moment with chemotherapy). The loved one apparently did not realize the treatment had to continue for three and a half years to maximize its effectiveness, and was looking for ways to relieve the spouse of its side effects.

Example (6): Because of the surgeries, chemotherapy, and an enlarged prostate, the spouse had to void every 30 to 120 minutes day and night. A good night's sleep was impossible. A loved one suggested wearing a diaper at night. Oh, my gosh! Was the loved one suggesting he learn to void in bed and then try to fall back asleep with a wet diaper, and to repeat this four to 16 times a night without worrying about possible leakage onto the bed? Yikes! This was supposed to improve the quality of sleep? He thought not. The suggestion might apply if he had lost bladder control and/or couldn't make it to the bathroom on time, but he was not that bad yet. But he very much appreciated the loved one's care and concern.

The following examples illustrate three cases in which the model used by a loved one matched the situation well, and thus the actions were very helpful.

Example (7): A loved one became aware of the difficulty the spouse was having handling all the well-meaning telephone calls from people wanting to know how things were going as he was caring for the patient 24/7. All that the spouse could do was to say "I can't talk right now, I'll call you back," but he never had time to call back. The loved one thus very thoughtfully set her self up as the information center for all calls and she thus relieved the spouse of a big burden. The spouse very much appreciated what the loved one did and was very impressed by how quickly and how well she sized up the situation and came up with an action that really helped. It is little wonder that this loved one is doing extremely well in her career.

Example (8): Realizing how difficult it was for the spouse to find time to prepare food while doing care giving 24/7, a loved one prepared a bunch of soups and froze them so that they could be used at any time. Even though the patient was unable to eat some of the soups because she could eat only very soft and bland food, they were tremendously helpful for the spouse.

Example (9): A loved one very thoughtfully brought over some medical supplies that might come in handy and a couple of pairs of very soft slippers for the patient to wear even in bed to help keep her feet warm. This loved one has a history of being very aware of what is going on in just about any situation.

If in case you are thinking the last three examples seem to have a common thread, you are correct. They are by the same loved one, the patient's and spouse's very able and efficient daughter Catherine.

In a situation such as this, be prepared for all kinds of actions by loved ones beyond those described here. Some actions may even border on being shocking and/or hurtful, but be assured that the loved one is only trying to be helpful to someone and that someone may be other than the patient or the caregiver.

This section indicates the effects of incomplete models can be wide-ranging. Multiply this by all the past and present situations on Earth, many of which are more serious than the situation discussed and not necessarily accompanied with love and care, and we can see how incomplete models can contribute to making messes here on Earth. But the examples also indicate that if enough thought, awareness, empathy, and compassion went into selecting or formulating the models and into compensating for the incompleteness of the models, conditions could be less messy or possibly prevented altogether.

Forgiveness in the Spirit World

Because of the loving nature of the spirit world, everything the spirit world or a spiritual entity does is done with empathy and compassion. But a spirit of a living thing is only a portion of a spiritual entity; therefore it might not always act with as much empathy and compassion as the spiritual entity would and even less likely as much as the spirit world would. The spirit is also given the freedom to choose. Therefore, while the spirit world sends guidance messages to the spirit, the spirit does not always follow them.

In my mind, because living things on Earth have the freedom to choose and are separate individuals, as opposed to sharing parts of themselves with one another, they naturally have egos and the desire to enhance survivability, especially the highly intelligent living things such as us humans. Among the traits living things can have, these would most easily match the most obvious way to survive on Earth where materials and energy can be possessed and controlled and consumed for survival. This is what we might call a "no-brainer." And unfortunately they can also decrease the tendency of living things to express empathy and compassion for one another.

For living things to function in our physical world, certain ones of their spiritual senses have to be tuned to a greater degree to our physical world than into the spirit world. Consequently, signals from our physical world can easily drown out signals from the spirit world. This further decreases the tendency of living things to express empathy and compassion for one another.

One of the results is that living things do bad things to one another, even among members of the same species. For example, a male lion taking control of a pride of lions kills off all the young ones fathered by the previous male lion in charge. Some primates do similarly. And we humans, with our superior creativity and imagination, are capable of doing some very horrible things to one another. Thus, we have shown in lots of ways that we are more capable than are other living things, positively and negatively.

But whether or not a living thing acted with empathy and compassion, the new pieces of knowledge generated by an experience are automatically added to the spirit world. Each new piece of knowledge forms a connection of the first kind with every already existing piece of knowledge, and new spiritual entities are created as a result. Therefore, the new pieces of knowledge immediately participate in continuing the oneness that pervades the spirit world and also the loving nature of the spirit world. In this sense, the spirit world automatically forgives a living thing for acting without much or any empathy and compassion if it happens to do so. The spirit world does not have to make a concerted effort to forgive. Forgiveness is simply an automatic part of how it grows. This is another reason why, after we die and our consciousness becomes completely tuned to the spirit world, we will find that no spiritual expression there judges what we did on Earth. Only we will assess the value of our contributions to the spirit world and determine what can be learned from having been a living human on Earth.

Issues and Tug-of-Wars

This section is about issues and tug-of-wars in the spirit world, how they manifest themselves in the world of a universe, and how they influence the design of a universe.

1. New Issues Constantly Form and Existing Ones Change

New pieces of knowledge are constantly being generated and added to the spirit world. New issues are thus constantly being formed, and existing ones constantly change as new pieces of knowledge are added to them. By analogy, we can see how new technology brings on new issues and changes old ones. For example, the Internet, social media, and smart phones bring on new ways of doing things, including some criminal ways, and are changing how we deal with privacy issues. We are unlikely to permanently resolve all issues, because new ones keep coming up and old ones keep changing as technology continues to advance.

This means that while a universe may have been designed to address a certain collection of issues, it was also designed to address a certain kind of new issues that will come up and a certain kind of existing ones that can become unbalanced. Because the spirit world does not know exactly what new pieces of knowledge will be generated, but only the kind, likewise it only knows the kind of new issues that will come up and the kind of existing issues that can become unbalanced. It does not know exactly what new issues will come up or exactly which existing issues will become unbalanced. As said before, otherwise, the spirit world would already have the new pieces of knowledge the universe was designed to generate and would not need to bring the universe into being in the first place.

One way the spirit world handles changing demands brought on by new issues and changes in existing issues is to design the universe to continuously evolve to match the changing demands. It appears to be doing this in two ways. One is by having living things residing in the universe evolve so that their ability to address the issues keeps up with the changing demands of the issues. This could be the spiritual reason why evolution occurs with living things, while what we see on Earth are physical causes and effects of evolution; i.e., the physical manifestations of spiritual reasons. Changing demands mean increasingly complex demands since they are brought on by increases in knowledge. Therefore, the evolution of living things would essentially always bring about increasingly advanced living things in order to match increasingly complex demands. And we can see that evolution does bring about increasingly advanced living things.

Another way to handle changing demands brought on by new issues and changes in existing issues is to bring the universe into being slowly and continuously, as opposed to all at once or suddenly. This enables continuous adjustments to the design of the universe so that the universe can be continuously matched to the changing demands. This only makes sense because what is needed to restore balance at the time the universe is designed continues to change once the universe is designed such the initial design will not remain effective unless it is continuously adjusted. This means we might want to look for indications that our universe is being brought into being slowly and continuously, and I think there is such evidence.

For example, we are discovering that our universe is expanding at an accelerating rate. As discussed already, gas clouds seen in outer space could be locations where our universe is continuously being brought into being. To test this theory, we could see if these gas clouds contain things not found in very old stars and planets, or even on Earth or on other planets in our solar system. The gas clouds could also be growing in number, and additional space would need to be brought into being to house them. This could explain why our universe is expanding. We could show that if the number of gas clouds (expansion sites) per cubic volume of space were constant and if each expansion site were expanding at a constant volume per elapsed time, then the number of expansion sites coming into being would be increasing at an accelerating rate. This would mean our universe would be increasing in size at an accelerating rate.

This would also mean that while the distances separating things that currently exist in space are increasing at an accelerating rate, each thing should eventually not have anything close to it. However, new things would be constantly come into being to fill the increasing distances between those things that currently exist. Therefore, an accelerating expansion of our universe by itself would not lead to the end of our universe's lifetime as some individual speculate.

2. Mathematics, a Possible Commonality among Universes

The model indicates that anything within our ability to find in the spirit world is meant for us to grab and make a part of our experiences. Each universe is different and unique, and thus the living things residing in each universe are different. Therefore, the number and kinds of spiritual senses living things have in each universe are different. Consequently, what the living things are able to find in the spirit world are different for each universe, and thus the kind of experiences living things can have are different in each universe. This is consistent with the notion that each universe is designed to fulfill a different purpose, as the model indicates. For example, the kind of experiences in a nonphysical universe will be different from the kind in a physical universe. The same goes for a universe with dimensionality different from a three-dimensional universe or different from a universe with gravity, and so on.

However, there is bound to be some commonality among universes. The passage of time is one commonality. As discussed in Chapter Three, the model indicates the passage of time is a natural part of growth, growth is a natural part of being alive, and universes are living things and as is the spirit world a living thing. Therefore, the passage of time is a reality for all universes, just as it is for the spirit world, also discussed in Chapter Three. However, each universe has its own way of monitoring the passage of time. For example, we use the Earth's rotation on its own axis and its orbiting the Sun as measures. Living things in other universes have other ways, especially in universes that do not have planets and/or suns.

Growth is an obvious commonality. It is the constant increase in knowledge that happens with the spirits of all universes, just as it does with the spirit world. Increasing knowledge leads to evolution in the design of living things, including universes. As we said, universes are living things and are thus subject to evolutionary changes. We mentioned earlier that the existence of gas clouds in outer space in our universe might be an indication that our universe is undergoing continuous evolutionary change.

This means evolution happens with living things in every universe and with the universes themselves, and thus evolution is a commonality among universes. This lends support to the notion that the evolution of spiritual entities serving as spirits for living things naturally continues over the lifetime of one universe, and then carries over to continue into the lifetime of the next universe, and then the next universe and the next, and so on. When the lifetime of one universe ends and a new universe is designed and brought into being, some or many of the spiritual entities serving as spirits for living thing residing in the new universe could be among those that served as spirits for living things that resided in a past universe. Some newly formed spiritual entities that are capable of serving as spirits for the living things could also be in the mix. They would be like something akin to "new blood" in the evolutionary process and thus bring new ways of designing and bringing living things into being in a universe. This might be how clams and other species of living things came about on Earth, living near hot gas vents on an ocean floor and surviving with the help of the hydrogen sulfide gas coming out of the vents. Therefore, their lives are supported by a mechanism different from that of all other living things on Earth (which require oxygen).

As the evolutionary process passes through a universe, that universe leaves its imprint on the process. This could explain why, for example, we humans are allergic to various plant pollens. You would think that if all plant species and the human species evolved together from scratch strictly on Earth that humans would be more compatible with plant pollens and not be allergic to any. The fact that humans have such allergies suggests that some plant species and the human species did not evolve together.

This also means the evolutionary process does not follow just one path. The path can split off into multiple paths, some of which may later merge together, and this splitting and merging in countless ways are constantly going on. This could bring about other phenomena besides allergies such as genetic diseases, albinism, the elusive evolution of feathers, and why there are things happening that we call "tinkering by Mother Nature."

It is also possible that human evolution and plants evolution could repeatedly stop and start. Human evolution could progress for a while in one universe and stops when the lifetime of that universe ends. Meanwhile plants might not exist in that universe and therefore plants evolution was on hold during that time. When a new universe is brought into being at some later time, plants might exist there but humans might not. Then plant evolution would progress while human evolution would be on hold. This would be another mechanism by which incompatibilities could develop between humans and plants.

In either case, the fact that plant allergies exist for humans could support the notion that other universes could exist beside ours, and / or existed in the past, and that evolution could span over the lifetimes of multiple universes.

To monitor the passage of time, some form of mathematics is the most obvious to be involved and is likely to be the case in all universes as with the spirit world. This suggests mathematics in its various forms is another commonality among all universes. Notice that mathematics is not limited in dimensionality, and its applications are not limited to physical things. The design of universes by the spirit world is bound to involve some use of mathematics in its various forms. Therefore, the fact that mathematics is not limited in dimensionality or to physical things suggests that universes are also not limited in such ways.

All the models we use in our lives involve some amount of some form of mathematics. This is obvious for models in physics, engineering, chemistry and other scientific and technology fields. Models in the medical fields involve statistics, determining rates and duration of reactions, deciding the time lapses between taking medications, measuring blood counts, monitoring blood pressure and pulse rates, etc. Mathematics are also obvious a part of financial and economics models. They are also in models used by nutrition consultants, as a part of food recipes, and in making food labels. Etc.

Highly intelligent living things in any universe are likely the ones to use mathematics the most, just as we humans are on Earth. This suggests that highly intelligent beings in different universes can potentially figure out how to use mathematics to communicate across universes, sort of as a universal language since they are all likely to be using mathematics.

Mathematics could, in that case, help living things in one universe understand the models used by living things in another. We might or might not be able to do actual inter-universe travel, but we might be able to get an idea of what other universes are like just by seeing the models used by their highly intelligent living things. For example, if they use models similar to ones we use to design and construct high-rise buildings, this means their universe is likely physical, has gravity, and is made of materials that can be used to build tall structures. If their models are similar what we use to design airplanes, then they must have a gaseous atmosphere but not necessarily gravity since they might use aerodynamics simply to change directions in flight with or without gravity. Their space might be such that it is completely filled with some kind of atmosphere, particularly if their universe does not have gravity to cause their atmosphere to concentrate around certain objects. Therefore, it is possible space travel could be common and a regular part of their lives in their universe.

The next question is how can we determine what models highly intelligent living things in another universe are using? We have made amazing technological progress in many areas and might someday find a way to do this. A likely option is to learn how to telepathically communicate with highly intelligent living things in other universes. Telepathic communication takes place in the spirit world without the use of spoken language. Therefore, theoretically, telepathic communication among existing universes is possible. We would need to learn how to do telepathic communication and how to do it across universes. This would require our being able to recognize that a thought is coming from another universe when it is. Such thoughts might come through when physical signals from our physical world are least likely to drown out spiritual signals. This would include moments when we are sleeping. Therefore, such signals could come to us as our dreams, and that might be why dreams tend to be surrealistic. And if living things in other universes happen to sleep too, then our thoughts would come through to them in their dreams, cause their dreams to be surrealistic to them. These are just ideas—fun to toss around.

Some humans on Earth already can communicate telepathically. For example, some identical twins do so with each other. More discussions on this and related topics will follow as the presentation continues.

Ego and Excessive Enhancement of Personal Survivability

As explained earlier, having the freedom to choose and being separate individuals can naturally bring out the traits of ego and a desire to enhance survivability in living things, especially in highly intelligent living things such as us humans. It is possible that these traits are meant to help us survive as separate individuals with the freedom to choose while residing in a world that has the three main obstacles identified in Chapter Three. These obstacles are listed again below.

For example, having enhanced personal survivability is like having a safety margin to help ensure survival. We all naturally want some degree of safety margin, but some individuals pursue enhancement of personal survivability way beyond ensuring survival. Such individuals appear to be pursuing it for status, ego, control, power, greed, materialism, etc. since their safety margin is already so large that ensuring survival is no longer an issue.

But there are also individuals who happen to have the right skills, at the right time, and in the right place. Some such individuals do what they enjoy doing, and significant enhancement of personal survivability simply happens. Such individuals are likely to become philanthropic when very financially secure, and many of them are well known for it.

In my mind, when the pursuit of enhancement of person survivability is for status, ego, control, power, greed, materialism, etc., then the individuals who are doing that are the ones likely trapped by the following obstacles:

> **Obstacle (1):** Our universe is made of materials and energies that can be posessed, controlled, and/or consumed.
>
> **Obstacle (2):** Highly intelligent living things such as us humans on Earth have egos and a desire to enhance survivability.
>
> **Obstacle (3):** Mobile intelligent living things (those that can walk, swim, and/or fly) need to eat other living things to survive.

The more an individual possesses and/or controls materials and energies, the more access that individual has to food and other amenities, and thus the greater the individual's safety margin. The greater the safety margin an individual has, the more the individual tends to be admired by others, and this boosts the individual's ego, status, power, and control. This can also inspire others to seek to boost their own egos, status, power, and control in an addictive ego trip. These three obstacles of our physical world have essentially trapped such individuals. I think this is more likely to happen to those who think there is no life after life.

Following the logic expressed, I think the three obstacles are the main ones of our physical world that can trap us. I also think they are designed into our universe not to trap us but to have us go through the kind of experiences that will enable us to work with or around them so as to not get trapped. And I think these are the kind of experiences that generate the kind of new pieces of knowledge that would help the spirit world restore balance. While these three obstacles might be the main ones, there are many other important ones as well; including the inability of spoken languages to always express thoughts precisely, and thus by finding ways to work with or around this would help prevent misunderstandings.

Intentions and Attitudes

In general, any given spiritual entity when translated into a form that could exist in a universe would have a different form in different universes. For example, the translated form that could exist in a nonphysical universe would be different from the translated form that could exist in a physical universe. And, if two physical universes differ in dimensionality, the translated form that could exist in one would also be different from the translated form that could exist in the other. Also, the translated form in one universe could be perceived as good by living things in that universe, while the translated form in another universe could be perceived as bad by living things in that universe.

However, there are some spiritual entities whose translated forms are bound to be perceived the same way by living things regardless of the universe in which they reside. For example, according to an earlier discussion, spiritual entities that are mathematics concepts and theories are likely to be among these. This is bound to be the case because mathematics has no restrictions as to dimensionality or as to whether the things they are applied to are physical or nonphysical.

Other spiritual entities whose translated forms can be perceived the same way regardless of the universe in which their translated forms could be expressed include those that are thoughts, feelings, emotions, attitudes, intentions, etc. This is because these spiritual entities and those of mathematics concepts and theories, when translated into forms that can be expressed in a universe, do not have to take on attributes of that particular universe in order to be expressed there. Whereas, for example, in the case of our physical universe, translated forms that could exist as things in our universe have to take on the physical attributes of our universe.

Spiritual entities that are thoughts, feelings, emotions, attitudes, intentions, etc. whose translated forms are perceived the same way in any universe generally have the greatest influence on how highly intelligent living things in universes shape their experiences and thus the new pieces of knowledge they generate. This is because such spiritual entities do not get translated into forms that could exist in a universe but only into forms that can be expressed in a universe. This means the activities of such spiritual entities are spiritual and thus can take place only in the spirit world and not simultaneously in the spirit world and the world of a universe. This is consistent with how we do our thinking, feeling, choosing of attitudes and intentions, etc. in the spirit world, but carry out our actions in our physical world. This is how things work for living things in any other universe.

It should be pointed out that while thoughts, feelings, attitudes, and intentions are perceived the same way regardless of which universe they are expressed in, how a living thing in any universe respond to them by its actions could be perceived differently in different universes and different situations in the universes. For example, the thought that indicates "I am not going to let that thing stay here" if acted upon in our universe could be perceived as good if "here" is our residence and that "thing" were dangerous, but bad if that "thing" lives in our residence. In another universe and/or another situation "here" could be a dangerous location and acting in response to the thought would be perceived as good regardless of what that "thing" is. Such differences in perception would apply also to actions in response to feelings, attitudes, and intentions.

Thoughts

While sentences convey thoughts, thoughts don't have to be expressed in the form of a sentence to be conveyed. For example, we can beckon someone to come to us using a gesture, and the desire for that person to come to us is clear without our saying a word. Sentences are sometimes a clumsy and imprecise way of expressing thoughts. Thoughts in their pure form devoid of spoken language are concise, compact, and can be instantly telepathically transmitted and received regardless of their complexity. Any individual, regardless of his or her spoken language, can understand pure thoughts received telepathically, provided the individual is able to do telepathic communication. Some non-human living things are able to understand unspoken thoughts in pure form. For example, some pets are able to sense their owner's thoughts even when the thoughts aren't spoken or directed at them, and even when the owner is far away. This is discussed in greater detail as the presentation continues.

Oral and written communication takes place in our physical world using our major senses. Telepathic communication takes place in the spirit world by our using our spiritual senses. Thoughts are spiritual entities in the spirit world, just as everything else is a spiritual entity there. In telepathic communications, the spirit of an individual finds a thought in the spirit world and directs the thought's signals to the spirit of a second individual. The spirit of the second individual senses the signals and thus receives the thought. The entire process takes place essentially instantaneously. Telepathic communication works just as well between individuals on opposite sides of Earth as between individuals in the same room. Some examples of this independence on separation distance are given as the presentation continues.

Some individuals who are very tuned into certain telepathic signals are able to sense such signals even when the signals are not directed at them, similar to the way some pets sense their owner's thoughts even when the thoughts are not directed at them. For some identical twins, one twin can sense what is going on with the other twin even when they are not together. The model explains that, in their case, such telepathic ability is a natural part of being identical twins and is not something they have to learn. However, understanding the mechanism by which they do it, as explained by the model, can point the way for the rest of us to develop telepathic ability. More on how some identical twins are able to telepathically communication as the presentation continues.

Instinctive and intuitive messages issued by the spirit world come to living things as pure thought telepathically. This is why we and various other creatures have instincts and intuition, and why instinctive and intuitive messages are not expressed in any spoken language. Various other creatures rely heavily on instincts for their survival and that of their species, whereas we humans do not. Therefore, their roles in helping our universe fulfill its purpose are different from ours. This is further explained as the presentation continues.

We might ask; could we humans learn how to do telepathic communication? The answer is; yes, according to the model. The model says telepathic communication is just one of many phenomena whose workings take place in the spirit world, including the ability to see and read auras, to do remote viewing, and to have out-of-body experiences. Some individuals have a natural proclivity for these abilities, and others are able to learn to do some of them.

Other Planets, Competition, Win-Win, Win-Lose, and the Application of Wisdom

Chapter Three explains how each living thing residing in a universe has a natural partnership with the spirit world. The partnership can be perceived as having two parts. The first functions in the spirit world and is between the spirit of the living thing and the spirit world. The second part functions in a universe and is between the living thing and every other living thing in that universe.

The second part is like a representative residing in that universe to represent the first part which is residing in the spirit world. This is analogous to an individual sending someone else to a gathering as a representative. Accordingly, a living thing residing in that universe is a representative for a small portion of the spirit world, and the entire collection of living things residing in that universe is like the representative for the part of the spirit world associated with that particular universe.

Each living thing provides for the spirit world a set of major senses that are tuned to the attributes of that universe so that the spirit world can experience that universe through the living thing. Each living thing is different and unique and therefore each provides a different and unique set of experiences for the spirit world over its lifetime.

Let's now consider Earth specifically. Each species has unique abilities within its major senses and a different kind and level of consciousness and intelligence. Each member of a given species is also different and unique. Therefore, all living things on Earth combined at any given moment enable the spirit world to experience Earth as broadly and deeply as possible at that moment. One of the reasons why Earth is inhabited by such a diversity of living things may be to enable the spirit world to experience it in every possible manner at any given point in time as it changes with time.

The following examples illustrate how each species on Earth has unique abilities within its major senses and a different kind and level of consciousness and intelligence. The eyes of each species tend to be different. Platypuses can sense electrical charges under water to find food. Sharks can sense magnets nearby and swim away from them for reasons yet unknown. Pigeons and dogs apparently can sense Earth's magnetic field perhaps giving them their ability to find their way home even when hundreds of miles from home. Bats use echolocation to navigate and to find food. Rattlesnakes sense heat to locate prey. Some creatures seem able to sense precursors to earthquakes. Birds were recently discovered to be able to sense an arriving storm and fly away from the area before the storm arrives. Researchers think the birds are sensing perhaps some very low frequency sound waves that arrive ahead of time produced by an arriving storm. And so on. We can see how the combination of such diverse senses could provide the spirit world with a broader and deeper experience of Earth than any single species could.

Now, let's consider our universe specifically. Earth is likely to be one of a small percentage of planets hospitable to highly intelligent living things. The human species is the only one on Earth able to explore our universe to some extent. This enables the spirit world to experience our universe to the extent we humans are able to experience it. But the spirit world is not likely to limit itself only to what we could experience.

For the spirit world to experience more of our universe, it is likely to design numerous planets to be hospitable to a variety of highly intelligent living things capable of exploring our universe. To avoid a lot of overlap among what the various kinds of highly intelligent living things can do, each such planet would be different and as would be the collection of living things residing in each. This indicates that someday, when we are able to do inter-planetary travel, we could expect to find each such planet to be different from Earth and from one another, and the highly intelligent living things residing in each to be different from humans and from one another.

The spirit world is likely to want all the highly intelligent living things in our universe to eventually get together, directly or indirectly, to combine what's been learned into a cohesive body of knowledge about our universe. It would be done simultaneously in our universe and the spirit world. More specifically, it has to be done before the lifetime of our universe ends, because the living things are bound to want to run experiments to fill in any gaps in the body of knowledge that are revealed, in the same manner that designers of cars, airplanes, high-technology devices, and so on run tests and make any necessary adjustments before releasing a final product.

If this is true, then we need not worry about our universe coming to its end until the spirit world calls for this get-together. However, if we on Earth cannot eventually clean up our mess, we might not be included. If so, it may be because we simply don't have a whole lot of knowledge to contribute beyond what the others could. Besides, our usual mindset is to do battle with the living things of other planets, as commonly depicted in our stories and movies.

H-m-m, hey, left brain, do you suppose some individuals on Earth might intuitively feel something of a get-together will eventually happen, and that it could be in the form of what some call the second coming of Christ? Yeah, I suppose, and also some individuals might be left behind by being excluded from the get-together. Do you suppose such individuals could be us humans on Earth if we cannot clean up our mess? Golly, we need to get going with the cleanup right away, because I suspect it might take generations and require new ways of thinking that mainly members of newer generations could come up with. You mean something like having "empathy and compassion for one another" as our dominant basis for carrying out our lives as opposed to our current "ego and the desire to enhance survivability?" Well, that could be a good first step. Hey, right brain, but you know we would still get to return to the spirit world regardless. After all, where else is there for us to go, at least according to our model? Whew! Thank goodness for that.

Any partnership would be for the mutual benefit of the entities involved. This means any interaction among the entities in a partnership is supposed to produce a win-win outcome. For example, this should be the case for a partnership in a marriage, business, and between parents and teachers, citizens and government, nations on Earth, the spirit of a living thing and the spirit world, etc.

However, since the spirits of living things on Earth are given the freedom to choose, the partnerships between the spirits and the spirit world might not always function in a win-win manner. This then could make essentially all other partnerships on Earth, such as those mentioned above, not always function in a win-win manner either. The spirit of a living thing makes choices in the spirit world, and the living thing carries out actions in our physical world that correspond with the choices. Therefore, when a part of the partnership between a spirit and the spirit world is not functioning in a win-win manner, then neither would the corresponding part of the partnership between the living thing and other living things in our physical world.

We tend to perceive the combination of spirit and living thing as a unit. But according to the model they are separable; e.g., the spirit exists forever in the spirit world while the living thing exists only for a while on Earth. They are connected to each other by the soul while the living thing is alive. The spirit and soul combination embodies a record of the living thing's lifetime from its beginning to its present or to its end. The spirit and soul combination forms the spiritual expression of the living thing and continues to be a living entity in the spirit world after the living thing dies on Earth. Accordingly, if the partnership is mutually beneficial for the spirit and the spirit world during the lifetime of the living thing on Earth, then the beneficial evidence is forever embodied in the spiritual expression. Conversely, if the partnership is not mutually beneficial, the lack of beneficial evidence is also forever embodied in the spiritual expression. Thus, it would seem logical we would want to carry out our life on Earth in a manner that would make the partnership we have with the spirit world mutually beneficial. This means we would want to make our interactions with other living things on Earth produce win-win outcomes as much as possible.

We might then ask why some individuals seem unconcerned about making their partnership mutually beneficial. One possibility is the notion of a partnership is not a part of their personal spiritual model. Another possibility is the notion of life after life is not of part of their beliefs. Regardless of what their personal spiritual model and/or beliefs encompass, it does not necessarily mean their model is not as good as any other. It might have other notions that could also provide good spiritual guidance. Whatever model works best for an individual is the appropriate one for that individual. However, if his or her model includes the notion that life exists after life, it would seem logical that the model's guidance would be aimed at making life after life as meaningful as possible. It would also seem that this would mean making life on Earth as meaningful as possible. However, what is meaningful for one individual might not be meaningful for another, and it might even be perceived as bad by most other individuals.

For the model in this book, the notion that a natural partnership exists between a living thing and the spirit world gives spiritual meaning to the concepts of win-win and win-lose by putting them in terms of a partnership that is mutually beneficial or not. Competition in various forms and in varying degrees is a part of almost everything we do on Earth. Anything we do that has the possibility of a win-lose outcome is some form of competition. After all, something has to win and something has to lose; therefore, competition in some form exists between the two things involved.

We humans tend to think winning is a "must" in just about anything we do, whether it is a win-win or win-lose situation. This is understandable if we are in a win-lose situation in which the short-term short-range objective is far more important than any long-term long-range objective, say, a life-or-death struggle. Battles during wars are such cases. But, for situations in which the long-term long-range objective is more important, then a win-win outcome is usually better and could help form a better future. That is why negotiation is preferred, if possible, over battle.

Competition has its good side when it promotes improvement, and thus a win-win is the outcome in a spiritual sense even if the score says win-lose in our physical world. It has its bad side when it promotes a win-lose mentality and thus a win-lose is the outcome in a spiritual sense. Therefore, the score in our physical world might indicate win-lose, but spiritually it can be win-win or win-lose, depending on the mentality of the individuals involved, including possible observers. For example, in Little League Baseball, the score in our physical world is not supposed to matter, and everyone involved is supposed to spiritually choose to have a win-win mindset. I say "supposed to" because not every parent does, and we have seen cases in which some parents do not.

It is more likely that such parents cannot do so rather than will not. We humans seem to require some effort to spiritually maintain a win-win mindset while dealing with some of the competitions that are a part of almost everything we do. It seems easier to spiritually fall into a win-lose mindset. If we consistently focus on short-term short-range objectives for our everyday competitions, then we risk developing a habit of spiritually maintaining a win-lose mindset. We are likely to vent or do battle whenever we think we are losing. A highly respected mental health therapist once said that getting angry is an easy and mindless way to react to anything we don't like, and that it takes more mindfulness to react in a more constructive manner.

There are couples who bicker over just about everything big or small, and it's hard on their kids to have to live with it and understandable if the kids would want to move out the first chance they get. Sometimes their kids even dislike the family car not because of the car but because of the bickering that goes on inside of it.

If such discontent can develop within a family because of spiritual win-lose mindset habits, similar discontent can develop within a community, state, nation, or the world because of such habits. This is the bad side of competitions being a part of almost everything we do. It is not only because competitions exist. A lot of it has to do with how humans in general tend to develop a win-lose mentality, and in my mind it is because we take "ego and the desire to enhance survivability" as the dominant basis for how we carry out our lives.

Chapter Three explained that the spirit world is full of tug-of-wars and that they all need to be kept reasonably balanced so that the spirit world can form wisdom. Competitions in our physical world are translated forms of some of those tug-of-wars, forms that can be expressed or exist in our physical world. We can handle any competition in our physical world better if we find, grab, and apply the wisdom available to us in the spirit world.

A win-lose mentality in most cases indicates we are not applying the wisdom available in the spirit world. For example, some major events have been followed by zero-wisdom actions such as fights among attendees, battles with police, overturning and burning of cars, breakage of store windows, etc., all because of the win-lose mentality among some attendees.

Chapter Five
Oneness and Other Workings in the Spirit World

Oneness Comes About in Living Things Two Ways

The spirit world keeps just one copy of every existing piece of knowledge. This brings about oneness in the spirit world, makes every spiritual entity different and unique, and results in their sharing parts of themselves with one another. And because spiritual entities are all directly or indirectly a part of one another, oneness pervades the spirit world and makes it a gentle, kind, caring, nonjudgmental, compassionate, empathic, and loving place.

The spirit world designs living things residing on Earth to be separate individuals, but their spirits share parts of themselves directly or indirectly among each other. Oneness between any two spirits comes about in two ways. It can be inherited and is manifested in the case of creatures on Earth in their genetic commonalities, physical similarities, personality similarities, and other shared characteristics. Thus, two members of the same species have the same body design, bodily systems, major senses, level of intelligence, degree of consciousness, etc. Members of different species within the same biological kingdom, such as members of every species of the animal kingdom, could have a lot of similarities that span across species.

Oneness could be developed through shared experiences. Thus, two members of the same family, community, school class, sports team, orchestra, place of work, club, jail cell, etc. would develop oneness through shared experiences. Both inherited and developed oneness are a part of the spirit of an individual. However, because each kind of oneness comes from a different source, each kind has a different likelihood of fading.

Recall that the conductivity of a connection of the first kind increases for a given signal with increased frequency of transmission of that signal, and conversely the conductivity decreases with decreased frequency of transmission. Signals having to do with inherited oneness are naturally more frequently transmitted than are signals having to do with developed oneness. This is because we are constantly reminded we are members of our species simply by our doing the things members of our species are able to do. But we are not constantly reminded of shared experiences.

The familiar "use it or lose it" phenomenon works in a similar manner in the spirit world. But as with this phenomenon or with the fading of any developed oneness, nothing in the spirit world ever fades to zero. A piece of knowledge exists forever, and a connection of the first kind between any two pieces of knowledge exists forever. Thus, anything that has faded can always be revitalized, but the will to make it happen must be there.

Developed oneness can stand alone or be in addition to inherited oneness. For example, family members who do things together have developed oneness in addition to inherited oneness. A living thing of one species can share more developed oneness than inherited oneness with a living thing of another species. An example is the start of a symbiotic relationship between members of different species. Once the symbiotic relationship is well established, the resulting developed oneness would become part of the inherited oneness for members of subsequent generations. This would explain why members of subsequent generations of the two species automatically form the same symbiotic relationship as formed by members of previous generations.

Oneness is a positive thing in the spirit world besides making the spirit world a gentle, kind, caring, nonjudgmental, compassionate, empathic, and loving place. For example, all spiritual entities participate cooperatively in the constant effort of the spirit world to form wisdom. However, spirits of living things in a universe have to be designed such that their consciousness is more tuned to the world of that universe than to the spirit world. Because universes are purposely designed to be different from the spirit world, oneness there can bring about negative behavior as well as positive behavior.

Living things on Earth are separate individuals and highly intelligent ones have egos and the desire to enhance survivability. Combine this with the fact that materials and energies making up Earth could be possessed and controlled and the fact that we humans need to eat other living things to survive, then oneness has the potential to promote negative, as well as positive, behavior. For example, oneness within each of two rival groups could intensify their rivalry. In a similar manner, wars could start between nations. Competitions based on a win-lose mindset could become more commonplace in how we humans carry out our lives.

As the presentation continues, we'll see that better mindsets are possible and that we might be able to eventually assume them as our evolution continues. But to do that we need to find ways to work with or around the obstacles designed into our universe instead getting trapped by them.

Effects of Inherited Oneness and Developed Oneness

Inherited oneness is pretty much alike for all members of a given species, and that is why they are members of the same species. If all members go through pretty much the same experiences over their entire lifetimes, then the developed oneness is also pretty similar for all members by the end of their lifetimes. Their developed oneness is added to their inherited oneness, and the sum total is the next generation's inherited oneness. Because the inherited oneness for the new generation is different from that of the previous generation, members of the new generation are different from them. They are more advanced since their spirits have more pieces of knowledge. An incremental advancement is thus be made as part of the species' evolutionary process.

Now what if, for example, half of the members go through one set of experiences over their entire lifetimes and the other half goes through a different set? Then the developed oneness is different for the two groups and their total oneness is different at the end of their lifetimes. Consequently, the inherited oneness for members of the next generation is different for the two groups. This makes the descendants of the two groups different, and the difference could initiate the formation of two separate species from the original. Subsequent generations of the two species are likely to continue going through experiences that are different for each one. This causes the two species to become progressively more different.

Thus, we can see two possible effects of inherited oneness and developed oneness on the evolutionary process. One is the continued evolutionary advancement of a species. The other is the possible formation of multiple species from an original single species.

A third possibility is that an evolutionary change in one species can carry over to another, not necessarily related, species. The spirit world keeps a collection of features for living things from which it selects certain ones to be assembled into the kinds of living things it wants to reside in a new or existing universe. The collection includes such things as legs, arms, eyes, hearts, lungs, stomachs, gills, teeth, fangs, feathers, hair, fins, stingers, antennae, shells, stamens, flagellum, alveoli, melanocytes, maculae, temporomandibular joints, hooves, claws, antlers, toes, etc. New features are constantly being added to the collection as living things advance through the evolutionary process, and existing features change and/or branch off into new features. Such new features could then be used by the spirit world to design the latest forms of living things to reside in a new or existing universe.

Included in the collection of features are features that appear on living things in other universes or other planets in our universe that we have not seen. Unfortunately, I was unable to find the names of such features in medical publications, biological publications, or any other informational sources on Earth. Google and other high-technology informational media could not provide the names either. We will just have to wait until we do inter-universe and/or planetary travel to find out the names of such features. They will probably have impressive sounding names such as temporomandibular joints.

1. Instincts, Intuition, and Gradations of Reliance on Instincts for Survival

The spirit of a living thing constantly receives guidance signals from the spiritual entity serving as the spirit and from the spirit world. The signals range from being very strong and not necessarily easily drowned out by signals from our physical world to being very soft and easily drowned out. They also range from being quite simple and direct to being quite complex and either direct or indirect. They would also range from being instructions for survival to being simply information for consideration. We might ask; how is it that spiritual guidance messages could be so diverse in so many ways? The answer is as follows;

Spiritual guidance signals include those referred to as instincts and intuition. The model views instincts and intuition basically as the same kinds of signals but from different sources, and differing mainly in their functions and directness. This is further covered in the second subsection to follow where telepathy is discussed.

The spirit of a living thing is a portion of the spiritual entity serving as the spirit. The larger the spiritual entity, the larger would be the spirit and the higher would be its level of intelligence and consciousness. Conversely, the smaller the spiritual entity, the smaller would be the spirit and the lower would be its level of intelligence and consciousness.

Therefore, something like an insect has a small spiritual entity serving as the spirit, and the spiritual entity is mainly capable of issuing relatively simple spiritual guidance signals directly to the spirit. The signals being simple would mainly consist of instructions for survival. A small spiritual entity shares parts of itself with relatively few other spiritual entities. Therefore, relatively few signals come indirectly from the other spiritual entities to the spirit. Being indirect, such signals are few and soft and are easily drowned out by signals from our physical world. Consequently, they have little effect on the living thing's behavior. It is therefore logical that living things such as insects would be designed not so much to think for them selves but mainly to follow the guidance signals coming directly from their spiritual entity, and such signals would be mainly instructions for survival, which we call instincts.

A human, on the other hand, has a very large spiritual entity serving as its spirit. It is capable of very complex spiritual guidance signals, almost all of which serve to enhance the spirit's capacity to think for itself rather than direct instructions on what to do. Because these signals are coming directly from the spiritual entity, they are strong and not necessarily easily drowned out by signals from our physical world.

Such signals would include, for example, what preceding living things the spiritual entity served as spirits for has done and therefore might be worth considering by the current living thing. The spiritual entity becomes more advanced each time it serves as the spirit for a living thing. Thus, each subsequent living thing the spiritual entity serves as the spirit for becomes more advance and more able the think for itself.

The spirit of any living thing in our physical world is designed to do certain things regardless of its size and the species of the living thing. One is to enable the body to exist and be healthy. The spiritual signals it issues to enable the body to exist are also the ones that enable the body to be healthy. This only makes sense. As with any spiritual signal, these signals can be slightly, moderately, or highly drowned out by the louder and more demanding signals coming from our physical world. A living thing's consciousness being naturally more tuned to our physical world than to the spirit world (in order for the spirit to pilot the body in our physical world) is a natural contributing factor. The louder and more demanding are the physical signals, the more they would drown out spiritual signals, including those that enable the body to exist and be healthy. This could explain why when physical signals get very severe we want to get away from them, probably partly because they severely drown out the spiritual signals that enable our body to exist and be healthy.

All physical signals will drown out spiritual signals to some degree, and it depends on their severity. Therefore, while we are awake and are going about with our activities in our physical world the spiritual signals that enable our body to exist and be healthy get drowned out in varying degrees, not enough to cause our body to not exist but enough to not keep our body as healthy as it would otherwise. Thus, our body gets wear and tear while awake. However, our body is designed to sleep, and we naturally want to sleep in a quiet and peaceful place so that the spiritual signals that enable our body to exist and be healthy could come through without being partially drowned out. The signals thus heal our body each night, and we are able to live, on average, into our eighties. Living things such as insects, on the other hand, do not sleep, as far as we know. Therefore, one of the possible reasons their lifespan is short compared with that of living things that sleep is that they do not heal from their wear and tear.

A very large spiritual entity, such as one that serves as our spirit, shares a lot of parts of itself with a large number of other spiritual entities. Therefore, a lot of spiritual guidance signals come from a lot of other spiritual entities to our spiritual entity and then to our spirit; i.e., indirectly from them to our spirit. In essence, these signals are coming from the rest of the spirit world. Being indirect, they are naturally soft and thus easily drowned out by signals from our physical world. Since our spirit is designed to think for itself, some signals coming directly from its own spiritual entity, those telling us what to do, are purposely made soft so as to not normally have much influence on how we think. Thus, they are also easily drowned out but less easily than are signals coming from other spiritual entities.

Soft signals coming directly to our spirit from its own spiritual entity are referred to as instincts. Soft signals coming indirectly to our spirit from other spiritual entities are referred to as intuition. Instincts usually tell us what to do, and intuition usually conveys wisdom. And wisdom comes from the spirit world.

Examples of instincts of living things are the following. Birds know how to build nests of the kind members of their species build; newly hatched baby giant sea turtles know they must go immediately to the sea; each member of an insect colony knows its role in the colony and has the body configuration to match, etc.

Nothing in the spirit world is completely one way or another. They are always located somewhere on a gradation. For example, ants are not strictly guided by instincts. They seem to have a bit of ability to think for themselves as they know when to scramble to get away from danger in some situations. Plants, on the other hand, cannot scramble from danger, but some can form chemicals to counter certain attacks. We humans do not always act only in response to thoughts. We can act instinctively too. For example, we keep a bicycle upright as we ride without thinking about it once we've learned, as discussed before.

Instincts could be how the cells making up our body know how to stay together to do so and to function in a way that enables us to be healthy and alive.

A researcher discovered in late 2013 that a fear a father mouse has can be passed on to his offspring. Mice most likely rely a lot on instincts for survival, and this kind of knowledge transfer is one of the ways instincts work. In terms of the model, this knowledge transfer comes from the spiritual entities serving as spirits for the father and the offspring sharing that part of them selves that contains this knowledge with one another. The report on this research did not mention any such knowledge transfer from the mother mouse.

We might also ask; why some individuals have stronger instincts and/or intuition than others? It is similar to the way some individuals are more in touch with their feelings than others. Being in touch with feelings is being in touch with spiritual senses. Spiritual senses are what sense signals in the spirit world. Therefore, individuals more in touch with their spiritual senses are better at sensing instinctive and/or intuitive signals.

Different species also have different sets of spiritual senses. This could partly explain why they possess different instincts. For example, some animals can tell ahead of time when an earthquake will occur whereas humans cannot. Birds are recently discovered to possibly able to sense when a storm is approaching whereas not every other species of living things could.

2. A Cursory Look at Healing Signals (More in Chapter Seven)

Since healing was mentioned in the preceding subsection, it would be appropriate to discuss it in a cursory manner here to put aside for the moment any questions we might have about it. More about healing is presented in Chapter Seven.

The spirit of a living thing in a universe has all the pieces of knowledge to know how to enable the living thing to exist in that universe. Therefore, the spirit also knows how to enable the living thing to heal from any injury or disease by employing those same pieces of knowledge needed to restore the body to its original healthy configuration. Accordingly, the spirit performs healing by issuing signals from these pieces of knowledge to the body through the soul of the living thing. This would be the case whether the living thing is physical or nonphysical and works the same way regardless of the universe in which the living thing resides.

If an injury, disease, or medical procedure alters the configuration of the body of living thing, such as losing a body part, the experience would generate pieces of knowledge that would alter the spirit accordingly. The altered spirit would be able to then enable the altered living thing to heal and to exist and be healthy in that altered configuration after healing is completed. The healing signals would heal the living thing in accordance with the altered configuration instead of restoring the original configuration.

The original spiritual configuration would still be a part of the spirit. Therefore, when the lifetime of the living thing is over, its spiritual expression to reside in the spirit world forever thereafter would reveal both the original and the altered configurations. The spirit expression can chose at any time to be at any age the living thing has been at while alive because it embodies an entire record of the living thing's life. The age chosen would be accompanied with the configuration the living thing had at that age. Thus, the spiritual expression would have that configuration until it chooses to be at a different age the living thing has been at while alive.

3. Telepathy

All spiritual entities are constantly communicating with one another in the spirit world. Each piece of knowledge has its unique signal, each spiritual entity has its unique set of pieces of knowledge, and therefore each spiritual entity has its unique signature in its signals. Every spiritual entity can thus tell which signal comes from which spiritual entity. We humans refer to such spiritual communications as telepathic communications. All telepathic communications function in the spirit world, not in our physical world or the world of any other universe, and we sense telepathic messages with our spiritual senses, not with our five major senses. Instinctive and intuitive messages are telepathically issued by spiritual entities and telepathically received with our spiritual senses.

All of us have instincts and intuition; therefore all of us have had experiences with the telepathic phenomenon. Telepathic communication takes place between some identical twins, between some pets and their owners, and among members of certain groups of individuals. Author Robert Sheldrake[1] (reference given at the end of this chapter) gives examples of the last two situations. I have met identical twins in which one of the twins could telepathically receive signals from the other twin, but not necessarily the other way around. This shows that the spirits of identical twins are not exactly identical, just as the model indicates they could not be, and thus each twin could exist as separate individuals. Otherwise, if their spirits were identical, the spirits would merge and only one would remain, and thus only one of the twins would exist.

We might ask; if all spiritual entities could telepathically communicate with one another, why all human spirits cannot do so, since a spirit is a portion of a spiritual entity? The answer is; our purpose on Earth is such that our spirits cannot do general telepathic communications with one another. Otherwise we would also sense very clearly instinctive messages that would instruct us on what to do, and this would be counter to our being designed to think for ourselves. However, our spirits can still receive instinctive messages clearly when necessary to save us from immediate danger. This means our spirits include certain spiritual senses for certain kinds of instincts, but our total set of spiritual senses does not include the ones needed for general telepathic communication. The spiritual senses of various other creatures include certain spiritual senses necessary for certain kinds of telepathic communication, as in some animals being able to sense earthquakes ahead of time. Robert Sheldrake's book gives other examples of telepathic communication among various creatures, such as cross-learning among members of the same species. More details on the various topics of this paragraph are given as the presentation continues.

We might then ask; how it is that some twins and certain groups of individuals can telepathically communicate? The model suggests there is more than one mechanism for telepathic communication in the spirit world. One mechanism is described above; another mechanism is that messages from one spiritual entity get through to another spiritual entity by means of the oneness between them. If the level of oneness is high enough, and if the receiving spiritual entity is serving as a spirit, and if the spirit has the spiritual senses that are tuned to the oneness, then the spirit is able to sense the message clearly enough to be understood. A low level of oneness might not be enough, and not having the right spiritual senses does not work.

This oneness mechanism does not enable instinctive message to come through, but it can enable some intuitive messages to come through. This is because instinctive messages come from the spirit's own spiritual entity while intuitive messages come from other spiritual entities. It is the spirit's own spiritual entity that enables the living thing to exist, and therefore it is the spiritual entity that issues instinctive instructions to the spirit on what to do and how to do it. Intuitive messages, on the other hand, come from other spiritual entities, thus essentially from the spirit world, and that is why intuitive messages tend to carry a lot of wisdom, because wisdom comes from the spirit world. The oneness mechanism lets signals from the spirit world come through to the spiritual entity serving as the spirit, and thus also to the spirit, but the oneness mechanism does not apply to the spirit's relationship with its own spiritual entity. This is why the oneness mechanism does not work for instinctive messages.

Spirits of identical twins automatically have a high level of oneness between them and thus some identical twins are able to telepathically communicate by means of the oneness mechanism alone. A pet can develop a high level of oneness with its owner, and the oneness mechanism can add to the other telepathic mechanism to enhance the pet's ability to telepathically receive its owner's signals. We might then ask; why sometimes only one twin can telepathically receive signals from the other twin but not the other way around? Also, why can't the owner of a pet telepathically receive the pet's signals through the oneness mechanism? The answer is one twin might be more in touch with his or her spiritual senses than the other is, and the pet might be more in touch with its spiritual senses than the owner is with his or hers. Also, the pet has two telepathic mechanisms working for it; i.e., an ability resulting from the need to sense messages from its own spiritual entity clearly so that the pet could have strong instincts and the ability to sense messages by means of the developed oneness it has with its owner. Whereas the owner has at best only the developed oneness mechanism working for him or her.

The human species is the only one on Earth whose members can choose among a wide variety of careers for survival. Part of this is because we humans are designed to think for ourselves; i.e., we are not tuned to the instinctive messages from our own spiritual entity instructing us on what to do and how to do it. On the other hand, this means we humans need to go through a lot of learning in order to do a good job of thinking for ourselves and to find good ways of assuring survival for ourselves. Consequently, we are the only living things on Earth that attend school, college, university, etc. Our lack of ability to telepathically communicate is part of the package. On the other hand, lacking this ability enables us to develop the habit of learning. This is part of what the spirit world wants us to do. This enables us to go beyond just surviving, for better or for worse. For worse includes greed and lust for power, for better includes that we are able to invent things and to constantly push forward the forefronts of technology. If we can keep advancing constructively, for example making physical and spiritual advancements, the model suggests someday we will be able to figure out how to telepathically communicate with one another with the spiritual senses we have. For example, by enhancing our present rather weak ability to tune to intuitive messages, we could use it to very clearly telepathically send and receive messages with one another. Because intuitive messages tend to convey a lot of wisdom, we could even pick up a lot of wisdom along the way. We would then be telepathically communicating not for survival but for becoming more conscious of the part of our lives that goes on in the spirit world and therefore become more able to combine spiritual technology with physical technology and advance both. We would then be able to get a more complete picture of why we are here and thus start cleaning up the mess we made on Earth and move forward with helping our universe fulfills its purpose.

Hey, left brain, that sounds great, but you know all this might be just a pipe dream. Oh, but, right brain, pipe dreams stimulate creativity, and more creativity is what we need to help find better ways to do things. Yeah, that sounds right because right brains are good at being creative, and also if we could pick up a lot of wisdom along the way that would help too. Yeah, and then calling someone a wise guy would become a compliment. Oh, you think so, huh? You wise guy.

There are some rare individuals who seem automatically able to do extraordinary things such as quickly name the day of the week for any given date, or to play the piano expertly by simply listening to an expert play. There are always variations and diversities in living things. Such individuals happen to have the spiritual senses that enable them to do these things, whereas a typical individual does not. Therefore, they are extraordinarily able to find certain things in the spirit world, such as the day of week for a given date, or to telepathically sense spirit world instructions on piano playing. In all such cases, the knowledge for doing such extraordinary things already exists in the spirit world otherwise they would not be able to do them.

The following are examples of various telepathic communications I was a part of or that I personally know about, in addition to the case of the identical twins mentioned earlier. (1): One of my sisters knew one of her daughters was badly injured the very moment it occurred even though the daughter was hundreds of miles away. (2): When I was about ten years old, I heard my mother call me while we were working in the garden late in the evening at widely separate locations, and it was getting dark. I went to her. She was surprised I heard her, because she did not call out to me but was only thinking she would like me to come to her. That was a sweet moment, even to recall it now many decades later. (3): One night I dreamed my oldest sister called me on the telephone sounding very distraught. She is usually so level-headed; I never recalled her ever getting so distraught over anything. The following day she called me on the telephone, and she was as distraught as she was in my dream as she described how she found our closest uncle dead of a heart attack alone in his apartment. (4): A new roof with a 50 year warranty was installed on my house four years ago and therefore I expected no problems will occur for quite a while. Two days before the heavy rain that came in December 2014 I dreamt a roof-leak occurred and water was coming down from a door frame. I dismissed the dream, and besides roof-leaks normally would have water coming down from places other than a door frame. When the rain arrived, guess what, a roof-leak occurred and water was coming down from a door frame.

In his book, Robert Sheldrake describes many examples of telepathic communication that fit the model. Mentioned are pets that know when their owners are coming home the moment the owners initiate preparations to head home, irrespective of the distance between them or the time of day. The owners could be overseas on the other side of world. The owners might be returning from work, shopping, or visiting with friends and the pets go to the door or sit on the windowsill and wait.

Apparently humans very long ago had an ability to telepathically communicate, at least among members of close-knit groups. In his book, Sheldrake also describes how certain groups can still do so. For example, a group of men go out to hunt for food, and before they return home the people at home would already know whether or not the hunt was successful.

We humans might have once had higher levels of developed oneness and were thus more able to telepathically communicate by the oneness mechanism. Perhaps we are feeling the loss and that could yet be another reason why we are generally searching for our spirituality.

4. Different Living Things Have Different Sets of Spiritual Senses

As mentioned above, Sheldrake describes in his book several cases in which pets read their owner's mind, even when the owner's thoughts were not directed at them. We might ask; why can't animals read everyone's mind? The more obvious answer is that they have not developed a level of oneness with everyone that they have developed with their owners. A more off-the-wall answer would be that if they could read everyone's mind, the jumbled mess of signals would be so distracting the pet might not be able to think straight.

On the other hand, animals consistently seem more in touch with their set of spiritual senses than we humans are with ours. Some animals can sense earthquakes before they happen, can find their way home from distant places, can sense when a person with epilepsy is about to have a seizure, can sense the presence of cancer in a person, can even seem to sense something invisible in a room, etc. Dogs were recently discovered to be able to sense Earth's magnetic field, and this could be part of their ability to find their way home from distant places. Some cats are said to also be able to find their way home too; therefore, they might also be able to sense Earth's magnetic field.

We might ask; if animals are more in touch with their spiritual senses than we are with ours, why is it that they can't find things in the spirit world better than we can? The answer is that they have a different set of spiritual senses than we do. This supports the notion that there are a wide variety of spiritual senses in the spirit world. Only the spirit world has all of them, and each spiritual entity has only some. Another supporting observation is that each of us is good at doing a different set of things. That is why some of us are business people, some are researchers, some are artists, and some are engineers, and so on.

5. **Cross-Learning Among Members of the Same Species**

Cross-learning takes place when knowledge gained by members of a species going through an experience is automatically gained by other members of the species, even though they have not gone through the same experience. Sheldrake describes the following two such cases in his book. Cross-learning is a term I use, and was not used by him.

When cattle guards were first used to prevent cattle from wandering off, cattle attempting to cross them would get their legs caught and suffer injuries. They eventually learned to avoid the guards. Later, when other cattle were introduced to cattle guards, they instinctively avoided them even though they had never experienced cattle guards before nor had come in contact with cattle that had.

In a second case, when barbed wire was first used for fencing to keep horses within an area, the horses would run into the wires and get badly injured. They eventually learned to keep a safe distance from them. Later, when other horses were introduced to barbed-wire fences, they instinctively avoided them even though they had never experienced them before nor had had any contact with horses that had.

According to the model, such cross-learning is made possible by the high level of inherited oneness among members of the same species combined with the fact that the species involved rely to some moderately high level on instincts to survive. Therefore, the members are able to telepathically exchange messages with one another, perhaps especially messages having to do with dangers, similar to the way we humans seem more able to sense instinctive messages having to do with dangers than we are able to sense other kinds of instinctive messages.

6. Identical Twins

Identical twins probably have the highest level of inherited and developed oneness found between two individuals. They have identical genes and they shared the same experiences in the womb. Identical twins are also likely to continue sharing a lot of experiences and would thus continue to form a lot of developed oneness. Therefore, their total oneness could be extraordinarily high, enabling some twins to telepathically communicate between each other. For example, some identical twins feel the other twin's feelings, and finish the other twin's sentences. In some cases, only one twin can do such things while the other cannot.

These examples indicate that some identical twins are able to receive signals telepathically from the other twin. But it is unclear if any have ever intentionally telepathically sent thoughts to the other twin and have the thoughts clearly understood. Such communications would seem possible if their level of oneness were high enough.

On the other hand, if it were possible it would likely have already happened, but I am not aware of any evidence of this. In the case of some pets and their owners, all it takes is for the owner to have thoughts and the thoughts don't even have to be aimed at the pets. But some pets might just happen to have the spiritual senses needed to tune to their owner's thoughts, whereas identical twins might not have the spiritual senses needed to tune to the other twin's thoughts.

However, in some of the earlier examples in this section, some individuals who are not twins are able to telepathically send thoughts to those who could telepathically receive them. This means those receiving individuals must have spiritual senses tuned to the thoughts of others. Therefore, it is possible that some identical twins could also have such spiritual senses.

We might ask; what if one twin were to intentionally aim a thought specifically at the other twin? Would that increase the chances that the other twin would telepathically receive the thought? It would be interesting to try it, and it would be best to try it with twins who are already able to telepathically receive other kinds of signals from each other.

7. Clones

We might ask; whether a cloned individual and the clone itself would have a higher level of inherited oneness between them than identical twins? A clone and the cloned individual would be genetically identical, just as identical twins are. We might then ask; wouldn't the developed oneness that the cloned individual has before being cloned become a part of the clone's inherited oneness? The answer is no. Inherited oneness comes from the parents. A clone and the cloned individual have the same parents because a clone is essentially a replica of the cloned individual. Therefore, they would have the same level of inherited oneness as identical twins have.

Regarding developed oneness, for the clone to be an individual separate from the cloned individual, he or she has to have a spirit that is different from the spirit of the cloned individual, even if the difference is slight. Each identical twin also has a different spirit, even if the difference is slight. This means the clone begins with a brand new spirit, and a brand new spirit has to develop its own developed oneness with others. Therefore, the developed oneness the cloned individual has would not carry over to the clone or become a part of the clone's inherited oneness.

8. Transplants

The oneness between the organ donor and the recipient as a result of a transplant procedure is neither inherited nor developed, but is loaned from the donor and borrowed by the recipient. The donor is usually deceased, except for the organ that is donated. That means the donor's soul has usually detached from his or her body, except the part pertaining to the donated organ, keeping it existing, alive, and functioning. The recipient's soul has detached from the replaced organ but otherwise remains attached to the rest of the recipient's body, keeping it existing, alive, and functioning. The spirits of the donor and the recipient are thus sharing between them the part of the donor's spirit pertaining to the donated organ. Therefore, the composite body of the recipient is kept existing, alive, and functioning by a part of each spirit. Meanwhile, the part of the recipient's spirit that used to keep the original organ existing, alive, and functioning is essentially taking a break while remaining a part of the recipient's spirit.

After the recipient dies the borrowed part of the donor's spirit returns to the donor's spirit. In fact, if the recipient lives long enough, the cells of the transplanted organ are gradually replaced by the recipient's own cells, and eventually the organ consists entirely of the recipient's own cells. The borrowed part of the donor's spirit is thus gradually returned to the donor's spirit, and the part of the recipient's spirit on break gradually resumes its role of keeping the organ existing, alive, and functioning.

This gradual restoration works the same way restoration of our body occurs while we sleep. The spirit of a living thing simply has this power to restore the body to its intended shape. Otherwise, what else would be bringing about the new recipient organ cells to replace any donor organ cells that age and die?

While the oneness is only loaned and borrowed, it still has interesting effects. Some attributes of the donor can be manifested in the recipient, such as a new affinity for certain foods or activities. This could be perceived as a form of telepathic communication from the donor's spirit to the recipient's spirit, telling the recipient's spirit what the donor's spirit likes. The fact that this happens tends to confirm that life exists after life. After all, such infusion of information to the recipient has to come from something still alive, and it has to be some intelligent and conscious part of the donor's spirit. Therefore, that indicates that the donor's spirit remains alive and is now residing in the spirit world even through the donor's lifetime on Earth has ended.

We might ask; since a part of the donor's spirit is shared with the recipient's spirit, does this mean telepathic communication tends to go more from the donor's spirit to the recipient's spirit then the other way around? The answer is; it seems that could be the case, but unless we know what is going on with the donor's spirit, we don't know for sure whether it is sensing any messages from the recipient's spirit.

We might ask some living donors, such as those who donate a kidney.

These would be interesting cases to look at. Right now, I am not aware of any widely available information about what a living donor or a recipient might have experienced regarding telepathic communications between them. I would imagine the experiences of the recipients would be similar to those of other recipients, particularly if they do not know the identity of the donor. But the interesting part would be the experiences of the donors.

9. Oneness Between Living Things and Formerly Living Things

All living things have oneness with formerly living things, and telepathic and other kinds of communication can take place through such oneness. Intuitive messages are examples, since they come from spiritual entities that served as spirits of formerly living things. Instinctive messages, on the other hand, come from the spirit's own spiritual entity and therefore are not from spiritual entities that served as spirits of formerly living things.

Other examples of messages from formerly living individuals are presented in Chapter Two. Another possible way is that the spirit of a formerly living individual might make something in our physical world move for no apparent reason. For example, a painting by my wife that has been standing on a chest of drawers and leaning against the wall for years suddenly fell over a few days after she died. Thereafter, time and again things happened that would be helpful to me, indicating she was watching over me and helping me.

Various Ways Spirits of Living Things Can Be Configured

This section pertains only to living things on Earth. Since I have not yet taken the time to visit other planets and universes, I have no everyday observations or experiences about how things work in those places. Therefore, I hope the living things there don't mind not being included in the following discussion.

The following subsections discuss the various possible configurations of spirits of living things as designed by the spirit world. Each configuration enables a different lifestyle to be possible for the various kinds of living things on Earth. Up to now, I suspect we assumed the spirit of every living thing has the same configuration as that of a human spirit: i.e., perhaps a sort of un-definable ghostly blob. But the model indicates there are no restrictions on spirit configurations. Observations of the various lifestyles of living things indicate that the configuration of that of human spirits alone could not bring about lifestyles that are different from that of humans. Therefore, the fact that other lifestyles exist for the various living things indicates that other spirit configurations must exist, and the model points out some possible configurations for living things on Earth.

This also suggests other spirit configurations exist in the spirit world that are not used to design living things on Earth. Such configurations could be used to design living things in other universes. For example, a universe with a dimensionality greater than three would accommodate a wider or different variety of spirit configurations than our three-dimensional universe could, and a universe in which living things are not separate individuals would accommodate spirit configurations different from those of living things on Earth.

We humans, through our inventions and creativity, find spiritual configurations in the spirit world that apply to the spirits of, for example, the increasingly advanced high-technology devices we build. The spirit configurations and lifestyles of such devices might, or might not, be like those of living things on Earth. But for sure the spirit configurations are somewhere on one or more gradations between those of spirits of elemental things and those of spirits of living things.

We design increasingly more life into increasingly advanced devices by incorporating increasingly more intelligence into each generation of the devices. For example, we are now building "smart" devices with chips that can learn the habits of the user so as to adjust its functions to fit the user better. This suggests the chip has intelligence and is of a form that falls somewhere on the gradation between elemental intelligence and intelligence we perceive living things have. Likewise, we have the technology now to build self-driving cars. Such cars have a form of intelligence that falls on the gradation as well.

O-o-o, wow, I can hardly wait for that, so I can sleep while the car drives. Yeah, but it will cost you a bundle of dough. You mean cost us a bundle of dough.

So, which do you, I mean we, prefer, sleep or dough? Hey, the next thing will be cars with beds inside instead of seats. That is, beds with safety belts and air bags, of course. Bucket beds would be even better.

The fact that we can build devices that have life and intelligence that fall on various locations of various gradations is natural, because gradations are a natural part of the spirit world. Very early versions of such human-built devices include automatic control systems of all kinds. Similar devices are increasingly sophisticated and miniaturized and are now a part of just about everything we now build. The greater the number of such devices designed into a complex device, the more alive that device generally is.

When a living thing dies, it usually does so gradually. Therefore, its location on some gradation gradually changes too. We can thus see that there exists varying levels of being alive and therefore gradations between being alive and not being alive are real and a natural part of the spirit world.

Some living things are more alive than are others. Being alive has different meaning in different ways and likely also in different universes. Thus, countless gradations are possible with different ones applying to different universes. For our physical universe, in which living things are separate and physical individuals, parameters that define the aliveness of a living thing include consciousness, physical wellness, and the capacity to grow mentally and/or physically regardless of whether or not growth actually takes place. With respect to these parameters, we could say, for example, animals are more alive than plants. And in some ways, some animals are more alive than humans and, in other ways, humans are more alive than animals. Therefore, there are multiple ways of being alive and thus multiple gradations for living things to be on.

There are some things the spirit world brought into being on Earth, such as prions and viruses, that fall somewhere on a gradation between being living things and nonliving things. Every spirit in the spirit world is located on one or more gradations, and so would the spirit of a living or nonliving thing that resides in a universe. Nothing more complex than elemental things would be located on any extreme limit of a gradation, and if they are located on an extreme they would not remain there for long. The reason is as more things are constantly being created by the spirit world, the gradations in the spirit world would constantly grow and expand. Therefore, old extremes would sooner or later be overtaken by new and further out extremes. Consequently, things located on the old extreme would become located on a place on the expanded gradation away from the new extreme.

This phenomenon manifests itself in our physical world in many ways, particularly regarding our human perceptions as we humans continue to gain knowledge. For example, we did not realize so many galaxies exist in outer space until we developed our current ways of looking out there. Some of what we thought were stars turned out to be galaxies, and what we thought was empty space between "stars" turned out to be filled with more galaxies. And within just our own galaxy, we are discovering thousands of planets exist, some of which are in the Goldilocks zone (not too hot or too cold but just right) in which life similar to what's on Earth might exist.

Thus, we came to realize that Earth is not likely to be on an extreme limit, such that life could exist only on Earth, but that Earth is more likely to be on some gradation along with countless other planets on which life could also exist. In this case, a gradation could refer to the various kinds of life that could exist on the various planets and another gradation could refer to the varying degree of aliveness of the various planets. Another example is that we used to think electrons, protons, and neutrons were the most elemental things on Earth until we discovered the existence of subatomic particles. Since then, we've continued to look for things more elemental than subatomic particles already found, and we are finding them. Thus, while electrons, protons, and neutrons were once perceived as the most elemental things, they are now perceived to be on a gradation regarding how elemental they really are compared with subatomic particles.

It is therefore possible that whatever is the most elemental thing in our universe might have had the most elemental spirit configuration in the spirit world at one time. But with all the new pieces of knowledge generated and added to the spirit world since then, some other even more elemental spirit configurations are likely to exist in the spirit world by now. Spirits with those spirit configurations could be enabling what's currently the most elemental things to exist and they could be making up a universe being brought into being right now. This means such a universe would have things that are more elemental than anything in our universe.

Gradations have to be commonplace in the spirit world. Many examples of gradations that could be observed on Earth associated with living things are presented in Chapter Three and in this chapter. Every attribute and parameter associated with living and nonliving things are on one or more gradations. For example, the size and configuration of things, the intensity and variety of colors, the frequencies and volume of sounds, the intensity and variety of flavors, etc. Evolution proceeds gradually and therefore evolving living things are on one or more gradation. So are natural things such as plants, eco systems, rocks, etc.

All gradations we can observe on Earth have their spiritual counterparts in the spirit world, and so would gradations that are bound to exist on other planets of our universe and in other universes. As new pieces of knowledge are constantly generated and added to the spirit world, new kinds of living and nonliving entities with new kinds of attributes and parameters would define new and additional gradations in the spirit world. Therefore, gradations are commonplace in the spirit world and are increasing in numbers.

What the discussion so far in this chapter means is that when we try to figure out what the spirit world is like, understanding that gradations are a natural attribute of the spirit world is bound to help. By keeping this in mind we might be able to make better sense of what we can see on Earth and perhaps help us find better ways to do things and eventually find ways to clean up the mess we humans made on Earth. In my mind, being able to help us do this is among the most important things a spiritual model should be able to do.

Some examples of how the concepts covered here might work are found in the discussion on the spirits of living things as the presentation in this chapter continues.

1.   **Human Spirits and Souls**

Human spirits and souls are among those that go through only one lifetime on Earth. Based on the model, this seems to be the case in general for spirits and souls of living things that do not rely heavily on instincts for the survival of the individual and species. The spirits and souls of the more intelligent animal species are among these. But this is not necessarily the case for the spirits and souls of living things that rely heavily on instincts for survival of the individual and species. Spirits and souls of insects are among these, as explained in greater detail later in this chapter.

Each human spirit enables only one individual to exist. After the individual dies, the spirit does not enable another individual to exist. A human spirit therefore does not reincarnate, but the spiritual entity serving as the spirit can reincarnate by serving as a brand new spirit for a brand new individual. The spiritual entity grows over the lifetime of an individual and thus becomes more advanced and more able to form a more complex and more advanced subsequent spirit. This is one of the ways the evolutionary process for living things in general moves forward.

After an individual's life is over, the spirit and soul remain together to form the spiritual expression of the deceased individual. The spiritual expression is then a living entity that exists forever in the spirit world. The spiritual expression is everything the individual is, minus the physical body, and embodies a complete record of the individual's lifetime on Earth and the continuing life of the spiritual expression in the spirit world. This is automatically the case because every experience the individual goes through on Earth and that the spiritual expression goes through in the spirit world generates new pieces of knowledge, and/or gains access to existing pieces of knowledge. All such pieces of knowledge become part of the spirit and its spiritual entity, and thus naturally form a record of all the experiences. The soul on the other hand embodies a complete record only of the individual's lifetime on Earth.

The spiritual entity has as many spiritual expressions attached to it as the number of spirits it has served as. A spiritual expression is able to find in the spirit world the spiritual expression of every deceased loved one and of every other deceased individual and formerly living thing, regardless of the universe they had resided in. Spiritual expressions of living and nonliving things are also in the spirit world, enabling living and nonliving things to currently exist in existing universes. The spirit world could be perceived as resembling an Earthly environment if a spiritual expression chooses to perceive it that way. Each spiritual expression can have any available perception it wants, and it can change it at any time and in any manner it desires.

When a spiritual expression initially tunes completely to the spirit world, it is still used to the environments of the universe in which its living thing resides or used to reside. This could explain why some human individuals who have had a near-death experience describe what they saw of the spirit world as resembling an Earthly environment, but filled with empathy, compassion, and love. Earthly environments are the only kinds of environment a human has known up to his or her near-death experience and thus tends to naturally perceive the spirit world as resembling an Earthly environment. The same goes for the spiritual expression of an individual who has just died. The spiritual expression of a deceased living thing that used to reside in any other universe is likely also to initially perceive the spirit world as resembling an environment of that universe until the spiritual expression becomes more used to being completely tuned to the spirit world.

A spiritual expression continues to grow, and because the growth takes place in the spirit world, the spiritual expression increasingly gains wisdom. Therefore, when our life is over on Earth and our consciousness becomes completely tuned to the spirit world, we are going to find all our deceased loved ones there to be much wiser than they were when they were living individuals on Earth. Ego and the desire to enhance survivability will be gone though they remain part of the record embodied in their spiritual expressions.

The lifetime of a human individual on Earth begins at conception. The spiritual entity serving as spirit has already formed a basic human spirit that works with any human genes. Thus, the spirit begins putting together a viable baby as soon as gestation begins. Whatever experiences the embryo or fetus, goes through during gestation generate pieces of knowledge that get added to its spirit, and thus the spirit grows beyond what is needed to know how to put together a viable baby. Some of the generated pieces of knowledge are new to the spirit world and are added to the spirit world and the spirit. Some of the generated pieces of knowledge will already exist and will thus be added only to the spirit. Any piece of knowledge added to the spirit can influence the continued development of the baby. Thus, it has been said that if the mother, for example, talks or sings to the fetus, the influence can be beneficial to the development of the baby. The model indicates how this is likely to be true, because the fetus sensing the voice and/or the music would have experiences that generate pieces of knowledge that become a part of the spirit of the developing baby.

A human soul starts forming at conception and continues to form over the entire lifetime of the individual. Every new piece of knowledge generated and every existing piece of knowledge gained access to would form a connection of the second kind between the body and the spirit and becomes part of the soul. An experience can never be repeated exactly, thus every experience is different, unique, and new even if it is perceived to be a repeated one. This is as explained in Chapter Three. Therefore, every experience generates new pieces of knowledge and/or gains access to existing pieces of knowledge. This means every spirit and soul is different and unique and thus every individual is different and unique, even those of clones and identical twins.

While a human spirit and its spiritual entity share parts of themselves with other spirits and their spiritual entities, a human soul does not share any part of itself with any other soul, human or otherwise. That is why humans are separate individuals. The same applies to any other living things that are separate. Exceptions might be conjoined twins. But even for them their souls are not necessarily sharing parts between each other even though their bodies are connected, and that is why some can be surgically separated and become two viable separate individuals.

2. Spirits and Souls of Plants, Fungi, Algae, Molds, Lichens, Mosses, Single Cells, Viruses, Prions

Near one end of a gradation specifically for living things on Earth are spirits of humans in that they rely heavily on their own thinking for survival of the individual and species. Near the other end are the spirits of plants, fungi, algae, molds, lichens, mosses, single cells, viruses, prions, etc. in that they rely heavily on instincts for survival of the individual and species. In between are all other living things on Earth.

Spirits of plants and various plant-like living things are unique in several ways. They are initially active for a while to enable seeds or spores to form, and then they become more or less dormant until the seeds or spores sprout. Then the spirits are active again to enable the plants or plant-like things to grow. There seems to be very loose limits as to how they grow or the size to which they grow. The wait for the sprouting phase ranges from brief spans to years. The life span of plant and plant-like living thing ranges from months to thousands of years depending on the species and the environment. Some species of plants go dormant in the winter and while dormant can be dug up, trimmed way back, and still remain viable. Some plants can be grown from cuttings or certain parts taken from an original plant. This indicates the entire spirit is involved with enabling each and every part of the plant to exist such that any part removed from the plant can potentially grow into another complete plant.

By contrast, the entire human spirit does not get involved with enabling any one part of the human body to exist. I.e., we cannot regenerate another entire human individual from any one part of the body such as an arm, leg, ear, toe, etc. It seems that the simpler the living thing, the more the entire spirit gets involved with enabling each and every part of the living thing to exist. The subsection two subsections following this subsection covers this further.

Once a cutting or a part of a plant forms a new plant, the spirit of the new plant quickly becomes different from the spirit of the original plant. The new plant goes through experiences different from the experiences the original plant and, therefore, the pieces of knowledge being added to its spirit are different from those being added to the original spirit. However, the differences are usually slight such that any differences between the new and original plants are not generally noticeable until generations later after differences have accumulated.

A plant has a certain level of intelligence and consciousness. That is why it sends roots to places where nutrients and water exist and why its foliage and branches grow toward light. However, its ability to think and thus to give it its intelligence and consciousness was already done by the spirit world and was built into the spirit of the plant by the spirit world. By analogy, any ability a Mars rover has to think and thus to give it its intelligence and consciousness to roam around Mars was already done by humans, and was built into the rover by humans. Therefore, humans did the thinking ahead of time for the rover so that any thinking it appears to be doing was done by humans. Similarly, any thinking a plant appears to do was done by the spirit world. This is how a plant relies entirely on instincts for survival of the individual and species.

When in danger, a plant would not be able to figure out what to do to save itself if the needed thinking was not built into it. This is like how one of the rovers humans sent to Mars was unable to avoid getting trapped in a spot where the Sun would not shine on its solar panels to the degree necessary for the rover to gain the power to get out of the trap. The ability to detect and avoid such traps was not built into the rover.

3. Spirits and Souls of Species of Creatures Other Than Humans

Animals in general appear to rely more on instincts to survive than humans do. But, most animals still do not rely heavily on instincts to survive. Therefore, everything said about human spirits and souls more or less applies to most animals. However, different species of animals have different sets of spiritual senses and different strengths among their spiritual senses. This means a lot of different kinds of gradations must exist in the spirit world in order for animals to have such variations. The spirit of a given animal would therefore fall somewhere on each of many gradations.

Some non-animal creatures that rely heavily on instincts for survival also have some capacity to think for themselves. Bird species and some reptile species are among these. Their spirits are designed by the spirit world to have a certain capacity to make choices and to think for themselves. But in general, the spirit world still does a good part of the thinking for them, and this comes across as instincts that are built into the spiritual entities serving as their spirits, similar to the way humans designed the Mars rover mentioned above to have a certain capacity to make choices and to think for it self. But in general, humans still did most of the thinking ahead of time for it, and this comes across as certain automatic behaviors built into the rover. I.e., the rover has a spiritual entity serving as its spirit. We built certain knowledge into the spiritual entity, and the automatic controls tap into this knowledge in order to know when to do what.

4. **Regenerative Powers of Living Things**

The simpler the spirit of a living thing, the simpler the living thing, and the more the living thing relies on instincts for its survival and the survival of its species. One other correlation is that the simpler the spirit and living thing, the greater the ability of the living thing to regenerate certain lost parts.

Not counting single-celled living things, plants probably have some of the simplest spirits of living things, and they rely essentially totally on instincts to survive. One or more new side branches can form near where a branch is pruned or removed. This could be perceived as the plant essentially regenerating a lost part. And, as discussed earlier, some parts of some plants can regenerate an entire plant.

The spirits of creatures are more complex than spirits of plants. Creatures have things such as eyes, mouths, and bodies that are mobile. Nevertheless, some creatures can regenerate certain lost parts such as an arm, leg, or tail. Examples are salamanders, tadpoles, lizards, fresh-water polyphydras, starfish, planarian flatworms, sea squirts, etc. A planarian flatworm can be divided into several parts and each part can regenerate an entire flatworm. Removing the head can result in two heads regenerated in its place. A head can form at both ends of a removed middle segment. Thus, the regenerative power of flatworms also makes mistakes. This might be because the spirit is too simple to be able to be very precise and thus a regenerated form might not be viable. An arm removed from a starfish can regenerate a complete starfish. All such creatures mentioned in this paragraph happen to rely heavily on instincts for survival of the individual and species.

It seems that the simpler the spirit and the living thing, the more the entire spirit is involved in enabling each and every part of those living things to exist. The spirits of starfishes and planarian flatworms are "almost" as involved with enabling each and every part of the living thing to exist as the spirits of plants are involved with enabling each and every part of them to exist. The reason it is only "almost" is because the regenerated parts are not exactly like the original in terms of, for example, skin texture and size. Thus, we can tell what is original and what is regenerated. But for plants, we would not be able to tell. Other living things such as salamanders, tadpoles, and lizards, can regenerate only lost arms, legs, and tails. Therefore, not as much of their entire spirits are involved with enabling each and every part of those living things to exist.

When we come to complex spirits and complex living things, such as the spirits and bodies of animals, their bodies cannot regenerate any lost parts. Animals in general do not rely heavily on instincts for survival of the individual or species. They rely heavily instead on their own thinking. The entire spirit of an animal does not get involved with enabling each and every part of the body to exist.

A human spirit and body, probably the most complex spirit and body among living things on Earth, have a certain amount of regenerative power. A human spirit knows how to regenerate all varieties of body cells, tissues, bone, etc. to enable the body to heal from injuries and illnesses and to remain healthy. Every living thing on Earth from the simplest to the most complex is vulnerable to injury or illness, and their spirits all have the capacity to heal. This means every living thing on Earth has to have some ability to regenerate in order to remain viable.

A tadpole developing into a frog is an interesting case of a living thing's regenerative powers declining from its young form to its mature form. A tadpole can regenerate just about any part of its body that is lost. But a frog cannot. It appears that the tadpole stage is a very generative stage. The generative power stops after the tadpole becomes a frog. Decline in generative and regenerative powers with maturity is true of all or most living things on Earth. For example, a very old human heals more slowly than a very young human. And the continued decline in regenerative power eventually leads to death.

5. Spirits and Souls of Single Cells that Make Up Living Things

Cells that make up the body of a living thing all start out as stem cells and are all genetically the same. This means a single "stem cell spirit" enables all of the stem cells that make up the body of the living thing to exist. Endless varieties of stem cells exist in our physical world, which means an endless number of stem cell spirits exists in the spirit world to enable countless living things to exist in our universe. A stem cell spirit is part of the spirit of a living thing. And, it is purposely designed to enable multiple stem cells to exist and be viable only within the body of the living thing. Another part of the spirit of the living thing instructs the stem cell spirit on what kind of specialized cell each stem cell is to become and where in the body of the living thing it is to be located. Another part of the spirit instructs every specialized cell on how to cooperatively come together and interact with one another to enable the body to be function as a healthy living thing. The spirit includes other parts such as those that give the spirit its intelligence, consciousness, spiritual senses, creativity, feelings, etc.

The more we learn about stem cells, the more we understand their ability to repair injury and heal disease. This ability is partly the flexibility built into stem cells to become any kind of specialized cell that make up the body, and it is partly the work of the spirit of the living thing. Place a stem cell at a location where a certain kind of specialized cells reside in the body, and that stem cell becomes that kind of specialized cell. This indicates there is a "field" of spiritual signals "occupying" exactly the same volume of space the body of the living thing is occupying. The signals are transmitted from the spirit of the living thing through the soul of the living thing to the location of the living thing in our physical world. This field of spiritual signals has exactly the configuration of the physical body, down to the minutest of details, tracing blood vessels, nerve fibers, individual body cells, complex construction of the inner ear and of the eyes, etc. The spirit of the living thing puts this field in place, and it is the specialized signals at specific locations in the body that instruct a stem cell to become a certain specialized body cell.

Many years ago, some research was done on images of human auras captured on photographic development paper. In one study, an image of the missing limb was captured shortly after the limb was lost. The image very likely captured the spiritual energy embodied in the spiritual signals that were still present where the missing limb had been.

This also indicates that there are spiritual energies in the spirit world that are not the kinds of energies we are used to dealing with in our physical world. Like anything else in the spirit world, there are likely to be endless kinds of spiritual energies in the spirit world, and some are likely to be extended into our physical world to give our universe its kinds of energies. Others kinds would be extended into the worlds of other universes and give them their kinds of energies, different from the kinds in our universe. This would be consistent with how every universe is different and unique. This also means when we eventually visit other universes, do not expect to find the energies there to be like the energies we are used to on Earth. Also, again as with anything in the spirit world, the kinds of spiritual energy that exist there will continue to increase as new pieces of knowledge continue to be generated and added to the spirit world.

We might ask; what happens when a body cell becomes a cancer cell? Does that mean the stem cell spirit contains a portion that can somehow get activated and thus enable a normal specialized cell to become a cancer cell? The answer is; this could be the case for cancers that are genetically based. However, this would not be the case for cancers caused by exposure to certain chemicals or radiation. The experience of the exposure generates pieces of knowledge that get added to the spirit of the living thing. If some of the added pieces of knowledge got added to the stem cell spirit part the spirit of the living thing, then a cancer stem cell spirit can form and exist along with the original stem cell spirit. This has to be the case since something in the spirit of the living thing is enabling cancer cells to exist and grow in the body. And we are now discovering that cancer stem cells can remain in the body even after the cancer is brought under control. This further indicates there is a cancer stem cell spirit residing in the spirit of the living thing. This means the cancer can recur at some future time, as it sometimes does.

This also means that the battle against cancer needs to be fought in the spirit world as well as in our physical world. Training the immune system of the living thing to fight the cancer is one way to fight the cancer in the spirit world. In the training, the living thing goes through experiences that generate pieces of knowledge that get added to the part of the spirit involved with the immune system and thus alter the immune system to counter balance the actions of the cancer stem cell spirit.

Another possible way to fight the cancer in the spirit world is to develop experiences that generate pieces of knowledge that get added to the cancer stem cell spirit and render it either inactive or non-cancerous. The trick is to find out how to develop such experiences. This could be part of a research effort to understand more about the spirit world.

We might ask; what about diseases? Bad bacteria and viruses sometimes get into our bodies. Aren't they there because something in our spirit enables them to be there? The answer is that they invaded our body and are there because their own spirits enable them to do so. Bad bacteria cell spirits and virus spirits are not part of our spirit. When a disease is cured, there are no residual bad bacteria cells or viruses left in our body, in the manner cancer stem cells are left in our body.

6. Spirits and Souls of Monarch Butterflies, Salmon, Cicadas, etc.

As discussed before, monarch butterflies go through four generations during their annual migration. The fourth generation somehow knows how to return to the same grove of trees from which the first generation took off. In order for members of the fourth generation to do this, their spirits have to have the knowledge. If it is instinctual, this means the spirit world built this knowledge into the spiritual entities serving as the butterflies' spirits. But why would the instincts apply to only one specific grove of trees? Why would it not apply to other groves of the same species of trees when there are multiple such groves in the same area? Instincts are not so specific in this manner when alternatives are equally workable. Therefore, it must be something other than instincts.

A more probable explanation is that the same spirits go from one generation of members to the next generation, and the next and the next, etc. This means the lives of subsequent generations are continuations of the lives of the current and previous generations. The reason the spirit world does not simply have the same physical individuals continue to live on and on is because in our physical world physical living and nonliving things wear out. Also, in the case of living things, some members get captured and eaten. Therefore, the spirit world enables generations of living things to exist with limited lifetimes so as to regenerate the population of various species on a regular basis.

The model indicates that spirit world generally chooses the simplest way to get a job done if more than one way exists. Having the same spirits go from generation to generation in this particular case is simpler than forming new spirits for each generation. Therefore, this and the physical evidence indicate having the spirits continue from one generation to the next is the most likely way the spirit world would choose to get this particular job done.

The physical evidence that supports this notion is that monarch butterflies die immediately after mating. This means the spirits of the members that mated immediately become available to be spirits for members of the next generation formed via the mating or for members of some later generation. There are always more eggs fertilized than there are members that succeed in living out their entire lifetimes. Therefore, there are always a lot of spirits available and waiting in the spirit world to become spirits for some future monarch butterflies. Thus, the life of members of one generation is a continuation of the life of members of previous generations. Therefore, the members of the fourth generation know exactly which grove of trees from which members of the first generation began their migration.

Actually, the continuation is not one specific spirit of a member of the current generation continuing as the same specific spirit for a member of the next or some future generation. During mating, the genes of the pair get mixed together. Therefore, the spiritual entities/spirits of members of the next or some future generation are a mixture of parts of the spiritual entities/spirits of the current or some previous generation. Consequently, the lives of members of the next or some future generation are a mixture of the lives of the current or some previous generation. But since every spirit entity/spirit has the knowledge to migrate and return to the same grove of trees, a next spirit being a mixture of previous spirits still has all this knowledge.

We might ask; what happens to the spirits when lots of members exist in some years and only a few members exist in other years? The answer is; the excess spirits during lean years simply wait in the spirit world for the next opportunity to be spirits for future members.

We would say the ability of monarch butterflies to know how to do what they do is due to instinct. The model says instincts come from the knowledge the spirit world has built into the spiritual entity serving as the spirit of the living thing. Therefore, it would be the spirit world that has done the thinking ahead of time for the spirit of the living thing. But in the case of monarch butterflies, the knowledge is in their spiritual entities/spirits because the spiritual entities/spirits in essence continue from one generation to the next. However, the knowledge is in the spiritual entities/spirits anyway, so we can still call it instinct. But it would be more descriptive and more accurate to say it is simply due essentially to the continuation of life from one generation to the next.

Accordingly, now we have not only instincts and intuition as ways current living things receive knowledge from previous living things, we also have continuation of life from one generation to the next as a third possible way for current living things to receive knowledge from previous living things. This third way is not available to all species but only to certain species, particularly those whose members die immediately after mating.

We might ask; then if animal spirits are spirits for only one generation of individuals, why would monarch butterfly spirits not be the same way? The answer is; each species has a different purpose. For example, the purpose of the first species to emerge on Earth was likely to help make Earth's environments more hospitable for the more advanced species to come. Monarch butterflies have their purpose. They need to migrate in order for their species to remain viable so they can perform their purpose, and what they do during their migration can also be part of performing their purpose. The spirit world must have decided that the simplest way to enable them to do what they do is to have their spirits in essence continue from one generation to the next.

In their case, instead of each spiritual entity having multiple spiritual expressions attached to it, as is the case with spiritual entities serving as spirits for humans, a monarch butterfly's spiritual entity is a mixture of numerous monarch butterfly spiritual entities. This means a monarch butterfly's spiritual expression must be a mixture of numerous monarch butterfly spiritual expressions. This might result in a whole group of their spiritual expressions being as spectacularly beautiful in the spirit world as a whole group of their physical individuals is in our physical world.

Various other species of living things also have lives that are essentially continuations of the lives of previous generations. Examples include salmon and cicadas. They too die immediately after mating, which again means the spiritual entities/spirits of the members that mated mix and form the spiritual entities/spirits for members that result from the mating or for members of some future generation. The spiritual entities/spirits of subsequent generations have the knowledge of the spiritual entities/spirits of previous generations such that the new members know how to repeat over their lifetimes what the members of the previous generations have gone through over their lifetimes.

This would explain how wild salmon are able to know how to return to a specific river or steam, swim up the river or stream, and find the place to mate where members of the previous generation mated. This is very similar to how members of the present generation of monarch butterflies are able to know how to return to the same grove of trees members of the first generation took off from to start their migration.

We might ask; what happens to spirits of members that happen to die prematurely before mating? For example, a lot of monarch butterflies and salmon get captured and eaten by members of other species. The answer is that their spirits become inactive and wait in the spirit world for the next opportunity to be spirits for future members. Notice how the number of fertilized eggs produced during mating always far exceeds the number of members mating. A lot of spirits exist in the spirit world that are waiting to be spirits for future members, and enable a lot of fertilized eggs to exist even if not all of them successfully live out their entire lifetimes.

7. Spirits and Souls of Colonies of Insects

Honeybees are among the species of insects that form colonies. Others include ants, wasps, termites, and other bees. Jellyfish are sometimes considered colonies of cells. But then the bodies of all living things are also made up of individual cells, even bodies of humans. Therefore, the bodies of all large living things can be perceived as colonies of cells. But then colonies of cells are not the same as colonies of insects. There is just one stem cell spirit for a human body. There is no such thing as a "stem member" for a colony of honeybees, and therefore no "stem member spirit" exists either.

A colony of honeybees has three kinds of members: workers, drones, and a queen. Each is assigned a different task by the spirit world and their body configurations are designed to match their tasks. Workers do most of the work of caring for the young, keeping the hive clean and cool, building combs, gathering food, and incidentally pollinating plants. Drones have only the function of being potential mates for the queen. The queen's only function is to produce both fertilized and unfertilized eggs. Unfertilized eggs develop into drones, and fertilized eggs develop into females that can become workers or a queen, depending on how much they are fed and on the needs of the colony.

I guess a fertilized egg is as close to being a kind of "stem member" as we can get in a honeybee colony. But, a fertilized egg cannot become a drone. And, it takes actions by worker bees to make a fertilized egg become either a worker bee or a queen bee.

In a sense, the colony is the main living thing, and the spirit of the colony is the main spirit for the honeybees. All the members of the same kind together constitute a vital "bodily" organ for the colony. Therefore, all the worker bees together constitute the health maintenance organ of the colony. All the drones together constitute the fertilizing organ of the colony. The queen bee is the egg-producing organ of the colony. Each organ has a smaller spirit as part of the colony spirit, and each bee has an even smaller spirit as part of an organ spirit. The exception is the queen bee in that her spirit is the egg-producing organ's spirit.

The colony spirit instructs the organ spirits on how to function to enable the colony to remain viable. Each organ spirit instructs each of its bee spirits on what it is to do to make the organ function properly. All this determines how many of each kind of bee to produce, when the colony needs to form a second colony, when to clean and/or to cool the hive, how much honey needs to be produced, how to build the comb, how to care for the young, etc.

The concept of a large living thing being made up of a colony of smaller living things applies even to the spirit world. The spirit world is simply the largest possible spiritual entity and is made up of smaller spiritual entities. A difference between the spirit world and living things in our physical universe is that the spiritual entities making up the spirit world are all directly or indirectly a part of one another. In our physical universe, living things are all physically separate or meant to be physically separate.

A colony of honeybees would swarm in late spring after the population has grown during the spring. A new queen bee develops and the old queen along with various members leaves the colony to find a place to start a new colony. Based on the model, this means the spirit of the original colony formed a second spirit for the new colony. This is similar to how it is in the formation of identical twins. The original human spiritual entity/spirit forms a second human spiritual entity/spirit, and this enables the original embryo to split into two embryos. The two spiritual entities/spirits immediately become different, as each embryo immediately goes through different experiences and thus generates different pieces of knowledge. Thus, one spirit gets pieces of knowledge that are different from the pieces of knowledge the other spirit gets, and the two immediately become different. This same thing goes on when a bee colony spirit forms a second bee colony spirit.

8. Spirits and Souls of Identical Twins and Conjoined Twins

Right after conception, only one spirit, one soul, and one embryo exist. As the embryo grows, it goes through experiences, pieces of knowledge get added to the spirit, and new connections of the second kind get added to the soul. In the case of identical twins, the spirit probably has a built-in mechanism to form a second spirit when a certain set of criteria is met. The criteria could be genetically related since identical twins sometimes run in families. It is likely to be something similar to the way a colony of honeybees would split into two colonies when a certain set of criteria for their case is met. After all, something has to instruct the original single human spiritual entity/spirit when to form a second human spiritual entity/spirit. Otherwise if forming multiple human spiritual entities/spirits were automatic, we would have a lot of identical multiple births.

As discussed above, once there are two embryos, each immediately goes through different experiences, even if simply by being in different locations of the womb. Thus, the two spirits immediately become different as well. The two spirits become increasingly different as the fetuses continue to develop. After birth, the two babies still look essentially alike, but minor physical differences exist. Intangible differences also exist.

In the case of conjoined twins, a second spiritual entity/spirit also forms. In both cases, the two spirits share major portions of themselves with each other. Part of the shared portion of the spirits, for some reason do not form two separate parts of the soul, as happens for identical twins. Therefore, a part of the two embryos remains as one so that the total embryo consists of two separate parts and a shared part. As a result, conjoined twins are produced.

Recall the spirit world is not perfect. Therefore, imperfections are natural and can be found in everything on Earth. Therefore, the fact that conjoined twins are produced is simply a possible, but rare, natural occurrence.

9. Spirits and Souls of "In Between" Living Things

Living things that rely partly on instincts and partly on their own thinking to survive are what I refer to as being "in between." I.e., their spirits are located within the middle portion of the gradation between relying heavily on instincts to survive and relying heavily on their own thinking. Birds are an example. They have enough instincts to automatically know how to build nests of the kind that their species build, raise their young, find food, etc., and many species seem to have quite a lot of intelligence as well.

For example, a group of birds learned to fly in front of a motion sensor that opens the automatic door of a store so that they could fly in. They also learned to do the same inside of the store to open the door so they could fly out. Automatic doors with motion sensors are a fairly recent invention. Therefore, the knowledge to operate such doors did not come from ancient instincts or ancient intuitions. This knowledge has to come from their ability to think for themselves. After a few generations, such knowledge could become instincts or intuition for members of subsequent generations.

According to the model, "in between" species should be able to develop instincts the fastest. They can think for themselves so that they are able to come up with new ways of doing things, as in the case of the birds. This knowledge becomes a part of their spirits and the spiritual entities serving as their spirits. Therefore, when the spiritual entities reincarnate to serve as new spirits for new members of the same species, the knowledge becomes part of the reincarnated spiritual entities and issues instinctive signals to the new spirits. Species that are good at sensing instinctive signals can easily pick up the signals and, in the case of the birds, will instinctively know how to work motion sensing automatic doors. In this case, one reincarnation could be enough to develop this instinct.

If members of each subsequent generation continue to work motion sensing automatic doors, the instinct will become increasingly strong with each generation. Otherwise, the instinct will fade with each generation. Possible fading of an instinct is a concern with laboratory-born salmon. If they continue to be laboratory-born over many generations, will they retain the instincts to do what wild salmon would instinctively do? What wild salmon instinctively do is an important part of maintaining the ecosystem of the region surrounding the place where they mate. Some serve as food for bears and various other creatures. After they die following mating, their decomposed bodies provide fertilizer for the forests in the surrounding region. Thus, maintaining the ecosystem in such regions involves maintaining the spiritual part as well as the physical part of the various salmon species. Again, this shows how it is that each living thing on Earth lives simultaneously in the spirit world and our physical world.

If a second species of birds happens to have spiritual entities/spirits that share a lot of themselves with the spiritual entities/spirits of the species of birds that work the automatic doors, then the knowledge to do that could be picked up by the second species as intuitive signals. The intelligence of the second species would have to be comparable with the intelligence of the first species in order for this to work well. A high degree of sharing of spiritual entities/spirits between the two species could automatically mean a comparable level of intelligence exists between the two species.

Knowledge transfer through instincts does not work very quickly for humans, because humans cannot sense instinctive signals very well. It also does not work very quickly for species such as insects that do not think for themselves very much, because it takes thinking for oneself to come up with knowledge to transfer in the first place.

The fact that the process works quickly for "in between" species could be why we are most often impressed and amazed by what members of such species can do. For example, they can learn how to make good choices, perform tricks, understand commands, etc. It might be that their skills for doing such things are the result of all the instincts they have picked through their many generations of interacting with humans. The phenomenon of cross-learning discussed earlier in this chapter probably helps as well. Cross-learning is likely to work most effectively for "in between" species for the same reason instincts develop most quickly for them. Certain "in between" species such as dogs, cats, some birds, etc. make the best pets, because they are "in between." And all domesticated animals were able to be domesticated because they are "in between" species.

10. Kids Can Work High-tech Devices Better Than Their Parents

An ability to work computers, smart phones, and other high-technology devices comes more naturally to kids than to their parents. It is possible the kids got this ability through instinctive and intuitive signals stemming from experiences of members of previous generations. Instincts are likely involved in addition to intuition, as explained later, even though, as discussed, we humans generally do not sense instinctive signals very well.

According to the model, instincts and intuition could theoretically develop quickly depending on the species and the situation, as discussed above. For intuitions regarding high-tech devices to be developed quickly, the spirit needs to be sharing a part of itself with a spirit that is good at working them. The second spirit can then easily transmit intuitive signals to the first spirit on how to work such devices. Human spirits commonly share parts with one another and thus a typical kid very likely receives a variety of intuitive signals. A typical kid is likely to be better than adults at sensing intuitive signals, since they tend to be quite open-mind and not set in their ways. Therefore, they are likely to sense intuitive signals very well on how to work high-technology devices.

Incidentally, kids being able to sense a variety of intuitive signals well could be why they are mischievous. They are too inexperienced to know what is good or bad, appropriate of not, etc., while all these intuitive signals are saying this or that might work this way or that way if they do this or that. Therefore, it is possible that what is perceived as being mischief could also be perceived as being experimentation and an indication of intelligence. Notice only those species with very high intelligence are mischievous, never those species that rely heavy on instincts for survival.

Instincts could also play an "indirect" role in enabling kids to work high-technology devices better than their parents. It is "indirect" because we humans cannot sense most instinctive signals very well, but we can sense instinctive signals having to do with fear very well. A possible hurdle for older folks learning to work high-technology devices is that their fear that the devices could "blow up" if they do something "wrong." Very early models of computers "blew up" easily. But today's devices are a lot better and the older folks' experiences with them have improved a lot. Therefore, while they might still have some fear brought on from the past, the fear has decreased. Having fear is instinctive, and therefore a decrease in fear is also instinctive. Thus, the decreased in fear could be transmitted to the kids as instinctive signals of a kind that humans in general sense very well. Therefore, the kids have less fear of experimenting with the devices. Consequently, this could help enable them master the workings of the devices better than their parents.

Hey, you know, as Churchill once said, "The only thing we have to fear is fear itself." OMG! That's right! And he never knew his words would someday be relevant to the use of high-technology devices. Yeah, can't you just imagine him smiling now? Yeah, and probably wishing he has some high-technology devices to play with.

11. Spirits and Souls of Living Things that Harm Their Hosts

Living things that harm their hosts include viruses, parasites, cancers, and some bacteria. They remain alive as long as the host is alive. If the host dies, they soon die. Viruses, parasites, and bacteria invade one's body from the outside, whereas cancers generally originate within the body.

We might ask; why the spirit world would design our universe to include such diseases? The model indicates the issues in the spirit world need periodic rebalancing at various times. Our universe is designed to address those needing attention at the time. As with everything in the spirit world, issues have to do with spiritual entities. Certain spiritual entities when translated into forms that can exist in our particular physical universe could be diseases such as the ones mentioned. They just happen to be associated with some of the issues our universe is designed to address.

Hey, left brain, so this implies living things in future universes will not have these diseases, at least not in the near future? Well, that is if our universe fulfills its purpose. On the other hand, while our universe addresses these issues in its particular physical manner, the same issues might also need, for example, a nonphysical universe to address them in its particular nonphysical manner. *Uh-oh, so living things in future universes could have some of the same diseases plus some others as well?* Yep, so don't complain. *Ugh, talk about the spirit world being imperfect.* Well, the spirit world just cares about every living thing it creates that's all. And besides, when one species on Earth needs to eat another species, isn't that sort of like a disease for the species getting eaten? *OMG, now you are saying the human species is sort of like a disease to the species we eat.* Yep! Well, at least you and I are each only a half of a disease instead of a whole disease. *Whew, now I feel only half as bad.*

Incidentally, spiritual entities that translate into diseases in our universe might translate into things in another universe that are perceived as good things there. *Hey, that wouldn't be fair.*

Other similar physical and/or nonphysical things that exist on Earth could be a part of the same or similar issues. Examples are hackers who invade the lives of others like a disease, dishonest individuals who enrich themselves at public expense like parasites, corrupt entities inspiring and/or funding other entities to practice and/or participate in corrupt behaviors so that the behaviors spread like a cancer, etc.

While our universe is designed to provide opportunities for experiences that can generate the kinds of knowledge the spirit world needs to restore balance, not all experiences that are possible in our universe generate that kind of knowledge. For example, we can build prisons and arrest criminals or we can do things that build self-respect so that criminal behavior is less likely. Both kinds of experiences address the same issue. But according to the model, we are here to also have empathy and compassion for other living things. This means the second kind of experiences are more likely to help the spirit world restore balance. Incidentally, self-respect is different from self-esteem. Self-respect is good to achieve, while self-esteem is not necessarily good to have. A lot of people who behave badly have high self-esteem and probably low self-respect, and that's how they have the nerve to behave badly. Sometimes people say someone gained self-esteem by doing something good when I think they really mean that the person gained self-respect.

What viruses, parasites, cancers, and some bacteria do is consistent with living things generally needing to eat other living things for survival of the individual and/or species. But when the mentioned living things that make diseases are left to die if their host dies, their spirits must be more interested in the survival of the species than the survival of the individual. Therefore, how are we to have empathy and compassion for such living things when their spirits do not seem to care much about them individually?

On their microscopic elemental level of existence I doubt if our having empathy and compassion for them individually means anything to them. However, our empathy and compassion can be directed at the disease victims. This means our effort to find a cure or prevention for these diseases are experiences that help the spirit world restore balance, and it also incidentally lowers the occurrence of disease that leaves living things to die if the host dies.

Viruses and disease-causing bacteria invade our body from the outside. Their spirits coexist with our spirit but are not a part of our spirit. Therefore, our immune system will recognize them as not belonging to our body and will try to get rid of them.

Cancer spirits originate within our spirit and cause cancers to originate within our body. As we go through experiences and generate pieces of knowledge that get added to our spirit, sometimes a cancer spirit will form within our spirit. Smoking and exposure to radiation or certain chemicals can cause this. Recall researchers have discovered stem cancer cells exist and remain in our body after the cancer is controlled and can then cause the cancer to recur. The existence of stem cancer cells confirms that cancer spirits exist in the spirit world. Any one of them could merge with one that happens to form within an individual's spirit if the one that is formed happens to be identical with it, and thus it becomes a part of that individual's spirit. Or if the cancer spirit that is formed is a new strain of cancer, then it simply remains a part of the individual's spirit but it also remains in the spirit world forever.

A cancer spirit can be a part of an individual's spirit in just the same way the spirits of bodily organs and bodily systems are parts of an individual's spirit. Consequently, the immune system of the individual might not always effectively rid the body of the cancer cells. Cancer cells can come across so much like legitimate cells that some of them get the body to form blood vessels by angiogenesis specifically to nourish the cancer and thus enable the cancer to grow and spread.

If our immune system cannot rid the body of cancer cells, then we need to fight the cancer in the spirit world as well as in the physical, as discussed above. The treatment needs to include the individual going through experiences that generate pieces of knowledge that counteract the actions of the cancer spirit. Training the immune system to fight the cancer is one such way. As with anything formed in the spirit world, the cancer spirit remains in the spirit world forever, and can be shared among multiple spirits of living things. This could explain in a spiritual manner why some cancers tend to run in families.

The model can plausibly explain the mechanisms behind how various diseases work in the spirit world. Therefore, the model sometimes suggests possible ways to spiritually counteract diseases. And it can also stimulate our imagination and creativity to come up with spiritual ways that we have not thought of before.

As said earlier, we carry out our lives in both the spirit world and in our physical world. Therefore, anything we do physically automatically has a spiritual component. For example, our intentions are part of the spiritual component. According to the model, everything that happens in our physical world has its origin in the spirit world, whether it originates from the spirit world doing the thinking or from a highly intelligent spirit doing its own thinking, or a mixture of the two.

Every Spirit Is a Mixture of Types

Discussed so far are spirits of various types, such as ones that go through just one lifetime, continue from one generation to the next, are of colonies, rely on instincts, rely on thinking for themselves, etc. However, nothing in the spirit world is purely one way or the other, including spirits. A spirit of any living thing is a mixture of a variety of types. A given spirit is located somewhere on a variety of gradations corresponding to a variety of spirit types, and is hardly ever at an extreme location of any gradation.

This has to be the case in order for new species to evolve from existing species, as indicated before and explained in greater detail later. This also has to be the case in order for individuals to be able to take on different roles in different situations. This is how great actors and actresses are able to do what they do so well.

What this means is that within the combination of spirit types a given spirit has are types that are stronger and types that are weaker. Another spirit with the same combination can have a different distribution of strengths. Another spirit can have a different combination of types and with its own distribute of strengths. Every spirit is different and unique just as every living and nonliving thing is different and unique.

A common, everyday example is how we behave differently away from work than at work. We are more independent individuals when away from work, and we are members of an organization when at work. Our spirit is more the type that thinks for it self when we are away from work, and it is more the colony spirit type when we are at work. A person is essentially a different person in each role.

The well-being of the organization (colony) can sometimes be more important to us than our own well-being, depending on the situation. For example, we are more willing to work harder for the organization if it needs us to do so for its survival than we do for our own well being, especially if we have a stake in its survival. Likewise, if a nation is attacked, its citizens are more willing to risk their lives for the survival of their nation than they would if not attacked.

The model indicates if we are a different person in each role, it is possible that we could be at a disadvantage in the long run if we cram too many roles into our lives. Being a different person in each role, we are bound to perceive things differently in each. A large number of roles mean we are in each role only briefly. Thus, we only have a short time to do what we need to do in each role. Consequently, we don't have time to develop a very complete perception of longer-term longer-range things in each role, because we are too busy to think about anything but our immediate objective in each role. A saying often heard is "I'm too busy fighting off the alligators."

This means we are not likely to have adequate knowledge on which to base certain important decisions, ones that have long-term long-range consequences and are often not well addressed. We thus become more vulnerable to being manipulated in our decision-making. An example of this is our voting decisions. When this occurs, our government that is supposed to be for the people and by the people turns into one that is for the manipulators and by the manipulators.

This also means that we can be lured into taking on too many roles by the enticing things that, for example, high-technology devices can do. High technology is wonderful in the way it can greatly leverage our research efforts and enable us to make amazing progress in our understanding of things, in accessing information, in automating operations, etc. But some of the ways we are using high-technology smart devices are not necessarily improving how we manage our time and energy. They are so enticing, so immediate in action, and so much fun that they keep us occupied with mostly short-term short-range activities. The manipulators know that as long as we are preoccupied with mostly such activities, we are unlikely to have much time to develop a very complete understanding of things that have long-term long-range consequences. Thus, they learned how to give us sound bites to manipulate decisions we make that have long-term long-range benefits for the manipulators and that could be at our expense. They know sound bites can resonate with us if they make them brief, clever, and sort of fun. Therefore, we are more likely to grab and run with them during the brief moments we have in each of our roles.

A reason why what manipulators say could sway us is because no model formulated by humans is incorrect but only incomplete. Therefore, what a manipulator says is based on a model that is correct but incomplete in a manner that favors what the manipulator wants us to believe. We can be swayed because what is said is correct. But we must also seek out additional information because what is said is also incomplete. As an example, what a manipulator says could be correct short-term short-range information while leaving out correct long-term long-range information, or vice versa. Short-term short-range information tends to grab us more because it is associated with things we are dealing with right now. Long-term long-range information tends to grab us less because it pertains to things more distant in time and therefore is less visible and takes more effort to think about. Another example, what is said can be correct facts but will not include all correct facts.

Manipulators rely on the correctness but incompleteness of what they say to sway us and often they succeed, because the correctness is persuasive while the incompleteness is not obvious. This means we need to be careful about accepting anything said especially by those and things that have reasons to sway us, such as candidates at election time, politicians in general and from any nation, advertisements, infomercials, etc. This is not to say these are bad, but we need to seek out additional information so as to respond to them more wisely.

1.   Evolution Happens

Numerous gradations exist in the spirit world including those corresponding to the numerous spirit types that exist at any given point in time. The gradations in the case of spirit types would be the strength of each spirit type; i.e., the strength of each can range from weak to strong.

The spirits of members of a given species have the same combination of spirit types. The strength of any one of the types for each member will vary but will be located within a certain region on the gradation for that spirit type. Every spirit type in the combination will be located within its own region in its own gradation. The combination of spirit types together with the combination of different locations on gradations will be an attribute of the species and explain why all the members are similar physically and intellectually and in their abilities and behavior. No two members can have spirits identical regarding this attribute; i.e., their spirits cannot be exactly identical. Otherwise the spirits would merge and only one would remain and only one of the two members would exist.

The strength locations on each of the gradations are likely distributed on a bell-shaped curve. Members whose spirit type strengths are located within a close neighborhood of the peak for each distribution are likely the most viable members and will produce more off springs that are viable than the other members will. Thus, the location of the peak for each distribution is likely to stay the same until something happens to cause a change. If this happens then, an evolutionary change will occur.

As members go through new experiences and more pieces of knowledge get added to their spirits, their species would not necessarily become a different species but would become increasingly advanced. This is probably the most common way all living things evolve, although possibly relatively slowly for most species compared with some other possible ways. For some species hardly any or no change would take place for thousands of years, which suggests their experiences do not generate new pieces of knowledge at a very fast rate at all. This then indicates their experiences are not much different from year to year, decade to decade, etc. Dinosaurs are examples of living things that remain more or less the same for thousands of years. The various "living fossils" mentioned in Chapter Three are also examples.

The more diverse the new experiences, the greater the number of pieces of knowledge generated, and therefore evolution by advancement goes faster. This way of evolving probably applies particularly to humans on Earth based on the fact that humans are the most intellectually advanced species on Earth. The model indicates intellectual advancement has a technical component and a spiritual component, and that for us humans our spiritual advancement is laggings behind our technical advancement. This is made evident by the horrible things some humans do to others of their own species.

Another way evolution happens is when something changes in the environment such that some members of a species whose spirits have strengths that are located far from the peaks of the distributions of locations for their species will now become the most viable members. Such members will now produce the most viable offsprings. Thus, the species will gradually change. If the change is significant enough, the species has evolved into a different species. Then their branch on the evolutionary tree is perceived to have progressed to a next stage.

When members whose spirits have strengths that are located far from the peaks of the distributions for their species migrate to a region on Earth where their viability is significantly better, they will produce a lot of viable off springs there. After many generations the members can define a new species. Meanwhile, other members of the original species that continue to stay where they are can eventually evolve in the manner described in the preceding paragraph. In this case, their branch of the evolutionary tree progresses to a next stage and it also forms a new branch for the new species formed by the members that migrated.

Other possible ways evolution could occur include the following. (1) The spirit world could purposely change the spirits of the members of a species and thus form a new species. The spirit world might be aware of impending change in the environment and want members of a particular species to remain viable afterward. Therefore, the spirit world would change members accordingly ahead of time. There is evidence something like this has happened; e.g., a species of fish developed strong fins and other bodily organs that enabled members to go in and out of the water before they were eventually forced to do so to remain viable. (2) The spirit world could be experimenting with a new feature and is trying out various configurations and/or color patterns to see what works best. Evidence could be found to indicate this could happen, and is sometimes referred to as "Tinkering by Mother Nature," as mentioned before. (3) The model indicates that cross-learning could be another way the spirits of members of a species could be changed and, therefore, another means of evolution. The discussions on the evolved behavior of cattle and horses are examples of this.

Members of the human species are said to be very adaptable to a wide variety of environments. Thus, humans can live almost anywhere in any environment on Earth without evolving into new species. This is because we are intelligent and creative enough to develop ways to make the environment right next to our body fit our physical needs regardless of where we are on Earth. For example, we build houses and other structures, invent clothing, make fire as needed, develop ways to travel quickly such that we can move from one environment to another easily, etc. We also invent furnaces and air conditioners that some of us are fortunate enough to take advantage of. Therefore, while members of our species live in a variety of environments on Earth, we actually live in essentially the same environment next to our bodies. Consequently, our species does not need to physically evolve in order to remain viable, but we could intellectually evolve as mentioned earlier.

Incidentally, according to the model, while we are increasing our knowledge of our universe, we are also increasing our knowledge of the spirit world whether we think of it this way or not. We tend to attribute everything we learn as pertaining to our physical world when in fact it pertains to both the spirit world and our physical world. If we would recognize this we could become more able to tap into the powers of the spirit world and this could help us become better people by becoming more spiritually advanced.

This indicates that our usual way of charting evolution in terms of physical changes is incomplete. Not accounted for are evolutionary changes regarding intangible attributes such as intelligence, consciousness, creativity, senses, etc. Each of such attributes could be charted on a separate evolutionary tree, and this could provide a multidimensional picture of evolutionary changes among species. This could indicate, for example, the human species might have physically evolved from apes, but we intellectually evolved from dolphins or living things that do not reside in our universe but resided in past universes. One possible result of this is that we would then realize that the process of evolution takes place in the spirit world over the lifetimes of many universes, and that only certain parts of the process can be translated into forms that can physically exist in our physical world. Other parts exist in the spirit world and thus could only be expressed in our physical world.

A possible indication that human intelligence did not evolve from ape intelligence is that recent studies indicate humans can follow lessons whereas though apes might sometimes imitate what is taught to them, they seem unable to follow lessons. This suggests that while apes can figure out many things on their own, the range of situations they can deal with are limited to only what they can figure out on their own. Humans, on the other hand, can extend the range of situations they can deal with by learning from lessons. This enables humans to advance ahead of apes in terms of what we are capable of doing intellectually and otherwise.

Some individuals do not believe in evolution. One possible reason is because the process of evolution takes place in the spirit world over the lifetimes of multiple universes, and only certain parts of it can be translated in forms that can exist on Earth. Therefore, because such individuals cannot see the entire process of evolution, they do not believe in it. On the other hand, individuals who believe evolution is solely based on evidence found on Earth are unable to explain why there are missing links here and there for a variety of living things onEarth. Missing links are actually there in the spirit world, but for various reasons they apparently cannot be, or are purposely not, translated into forms that can exist on Earth. For example, fast retracing of evolutionary paths can result in missing links.

2.   Different Roles Happen

An individual can take on a variety of different roles, each role in a different situation. An individual's spirit is a mixture of a variety of spirit types with each type having a different strength. The individual's identity is determined by the mixture of spirit types, and by the strengths of the various spirit types that make up his or her spirit. This is how all of us are different physically and each of us would have different personalities, characters, values, skills, abilities, likes and dislikes, etc.

An individual can, by choice or by circumstance, be any one of the spirit types making up his or her spirit and thus behave accordingly. This is how he or she can be in a different role in each different situation. How well he or she functions in a role depends on his or her strength of the spirit type required to play that role. Some individuals are uncomfortable when forced to play a role in which his or her required spirit type has low strength. For example, some group leaders are simply not good at doing annual reviews for the people he or she supervises. Great actors and actresses have a wide variety of spirit types making up their spirits and most or all of their spirit types have substantial strength.

An important implication of this is that a candidate running for office is not going to be the same person after he or she is elected. The two situations are different and a different spirit type governs how the same individual behaves in each. This means we need to base our voting decisions on how a candidate will behave if elected into office instead of on how the candidate behaves as a candidate. This could explain why we are often disappointed with a candidate's behavior once elected. This means our campaign process needs to be modified such that we can assess how a candidate will behave if elected. Our current campaign process does very little of that, even though candidates say they will do this or that once in office. But they don't say how he or she will do this or that given the environment he or she will have to deal with in office.

A similar thing applies regarding the person we date vs. who that person becomes as a spouse and as a parent. This could explain why the divorce rate is approximately 50 percent. Even if two individuals live together for a while before getting married, everything about each person as a spouse and as a parent is not revealed. The two situations might be physically similar but spiritually different; i.e., the commitment is different.

Spirits of nonliving things are also mixtures of a variety of spirit types, and thus nonliving things can also be in a variety of roles. How well it plays a role depends on the strength of its spirit type required to be in that role. Take a spoon for example. A spoon can be used for eating food, serving food, measuring ingredients, taking medications, etc. It can also be a cooking utensil, gift, prop in a magic trick, hand on a clock, vessel for heating drugs, gardening tool, scrapper, chopper, masher, launcher, etc. Spoons come in various shapes and sizes and can be made of various materials. How well a spoon performs in each role depend on such attributes, and such attributes correspond with the strengths of the various spirit types making up the spirit of the spoon.

3. **Tug-of-Wars Among Spirit Types**

Much of the kinds of issues, or tug-of-wars, our universe is designed to address are the kinds that take place among the spirit types that make up our spirit. For example, one of the spirit types might want to spend money now to have a vacation abroad, and another spirit type might want to save money for retirement. One spirit type thinks short-term and another spirit type thinks long-term. A tug-of-war thus takes place within the spirit of the individual, and the stronger spirit type more often has its way. Thus, when an individual tends to think one way in one situation, he or she can be more likely to think the same way in other situations; e.g., more consistently short-term or more consistently long-term. This can happen when the strength of the stronger spirit type is significantly higher than those of the other spirit types comprising the individual's spirit. It is like while the weaker spirit type is in charge of a meeting, the stronger spirit type attending the meeting could dominate in the decisions made in the meeting.

When an individual makes a decision or carry out an action, what we see is perceived as a reflection of individual's values, personality, character, and etc. But what is going within the individual are tug-of-wars among his or her spirit types. Each spirit type has its own values, personality, character, and etc. Therefore, the values, personality, character, and etc. that we perceive at a given moment are not likely to be the same for every other moment for that individual. That is why it is commonly said we do not know a person until we live with him or her. But even then we might not get a chance to be with that person in every possible situation such that we could ascertain every one of that person's spirit types.

The lives of us humans in general have lots of issues and each commonly has more than two opposing sides. We are given such issues and we are designed to think for ourselves. This indicates that addressing such issues are part of the purpose we are to fulfill, and that we are to address them wisely and constructively and certainly not destructively.

Our experiences in dealing with such issues generate the kinds of pieces of knowledge the spirit world intended for us to generate. We would be fulfilling our purpose if the pieces of knowledge help the spirit world restore balance. And if they don't do that, they will at least contribute to the growth of the spirit world by increasing its amount of knowledge.

Conversely, a living thing that relies heavily on instincts to survive has few or no issues to worry about since the spirit world has already dealt with them for them. Their purpose is simple compared with that of humans, and likewise their effort to fulfill their purpose is simple and essentially automatic since the spirit world is doing, or have done, the thinking for them.

Assuming nearly every universe has some highly intelligent living things residing in it, nearly every universe then is designed to address complex issues. Any universe that would never have highly intelligent living things is not likely to be designed to address complex issues. Their purposes might be, for example, to generate new pieces of knowledge to enable the spirit world to know how to create addition elemental living and nonliving things so as to be able to design universes that can have new kinds of highly intelligent living things residing in them.

4. Feeling More Alive

Ever wished you could feel more alive? I have, especially in my advancing age. It also seems now to require more effort and more creativity to do the things that can make me feel more alive, as the kinds of things I can do become more limited with age. Bone joints wear out, tendons get tendonitis, arms and legs don't quite move as instructed, and bodily systems don't work as well, etc. Now sometimes when I look at something, it doesn't seem quite real anymore. It is a strange feeling. When my mom was dying of cancer she once said that it seems as if her entire life is now like one big dream; in other words, it seems not totally real anymore.

I am not near death yet, but already things are starting to sometimes seem not totally real anymore. On the other hand, the model indicates that our universe and everything in it exists because the spirit world is thinking all of it to exist. And it is interesting that, when I look at physical things now, they come across to me as if they are indeed more a thought I am sensing than something physically real I am seeing.

Nevertheless, one sure way to feel more alive is to be a contributory part of life; i.e., to be like a living branch of a living tree and to be contributing to the life of that tree. Thus, one way to feel more alive is to do something that is contributory to something important and worthwhile that is bigger than what we could be on our own. It is exciting, interesting, and stimulating to do something that benefits mankind, and to leave behind something worthwhile. Being excited, interested, and stimulated makes anyone feel more alive.

There is no end to the things we could do to become more excited, interested, and stimulated. It is a personal thing as to what works best for each individual. Some such things are shorter-term shorter-range, some are longer-term longer-range, some we are able to do, some we are unable to do, some are perceived to be good for us, some are perceived to be bad for us, etc. Examples are learning something new, developing new skills, making new friends, visiting new places, doing extreme sports, mastering the use of a new high-technology device, watching certain movies especially ones with lots of things getting blown up, playing certain video games, trying out different foods, volunteering, etc.

But again, not all these things are perceived to be good for us personally. Some could make feel more alive in the short-term and some in the long-term. Some could help us be contributory to something larger that is good, and some would not. I think it is good to always have one or more things among the things we do that are long-term and contributory. That way we will feel more alive continuously and will tend to not feel less alive occasionally.

Hey, you left out an important way. What's that? It is to have your left and right brains talk with each other. Gee, who in his or her right mind would want to do that? No one, except those who are able to be in his or her left mind as well as be in his or her right mind.

5.   Is Using A Jury the Best Way to Reach a Verdict?

As explained earlier, our spirit is made up of many spirit types. This means each of us essentially consists of many different persons. Which one of our persons is present at any given moment depends on the situation at that moment. Therefore, our perception of any given thing can differ from one moment to another depending on the situation from one moment to another.

We discussed earlier that in elections and in marriage we need a lot more information about someone than we usually get before we make the important decision. An example of another such issue is one we face while being a juror. We might get a lot of information about someone else, but in being a juror we might need to know more about ourselves than we know before making the decision. Which one of our spirit types would serve the jury system best and how could we be sure we are in that spirit type while serving? And even then, how do we know that particular spirit type of ours has enough strength to do a good job? Or would that particular spirit type of ours easily give in to the positions of others? Some jurors regret their decisions after a trial is over. That's a bad sign about our jury system, but at least it is good that a bad sign can be revealed so that we might try to improve the system.

We apparently realize the possible shortcomings of the jury system in that we allow for appeals and declarations of mistrials. But if we were to have a reliable and universally acceptable model of how things work in the spirit world, would it be possible to come up with something better than our jury system? This might be something worth exploring, when and if we ever come up with such a spiritual model.

6. Multiple Personalities

The model indicates each individual has multiple spirit types and therefore theoretically each individual is naturally capable of having multiple personalities. An individual would be perceived as normal if his or her behavior were within a range perceived as normal by others. The locations on the gradations corresponding with the spirit types making up the spirit of a normal individual are generally within a region where most other individuals are located. Upbringing and general interactions with others influence the locations on the various gradations such that an individual would understand what constitutes acceptable normal behavior there.

The model also indicates that a normal individual who usually behaves normally can behave abnormally part of the time, naturally, although it might not necessarily be desirable. For example, an individual might have been mistreated badly and unjustly when very young but for various reasons was never able to address it with the people involved. That person could harbor much unresolved anger. Thus, that person could constantly look for opportunities to vent that anger even if the person or object receiving the venting is not its source. It would be analogous to a terrible itch that must be scratched regardless of when and where the scratching could be done, even though scratching would not resolve the cause of the itch. And, when we have to scratch, our rational reasoning tends to be pushed aside while our emotions tend to take over. In the case of the anger, the individual may have a normal personality part of the time and an angry personality part of the time. And because the person vents whenever an opportunity to do so comes along, the venting distorts and mixes up the way he or she applies his or her values and principles such that the result could be counter to those values and principles. It is like venting must come first before upholding any values and principles, in the same way that putting scratching the itch first could result in actions that are counterproductive to what the person would normally want to accomplish. This could leave an observer confused as to exactly what the person is trying to accomplish. If the observer is that person's child, the child could become confused well into adulthood.

I personally know an individual who has a very bad "itch," and felt stuck in a situation in which that individual would not seek help to resolve the "itch." This example shows how essentially a dual personality can come about and that the process by which it comes about is natural, although not desirable. It is because of how the spirit of an individual is made up.

The same process could result in an individual having more than two personalities. I.e., something has caused more than one spirit type to develop a very bad "itch," and those spirit types simply have to "scratch" whenever and wherever the opportunity to do so comes up. There could thus be a battle for opportunities to scratch among all those spirit types, and this could produce behaviors that would come across as that of several personalities.

I often wonder why we humans keep repeating the same kinds of bad behaviors generation after generation. You would think that with our superior intelligence we would learn from the past and know better than to repeat bad behaviors. But the fact that bad behaviors repeat suggests something is re-germinating the bad behaviors generation after germination. I conclude that one of probably many re-germination mechanisms is the formation of hang-ups. Anger as discussed above is an example of such a hang-up. Any hang-up can be like a very bad itch that causes an individual to be preoccupied, and could result in behaviors that are counterproductive. As discussed above, this could cause confusion in an observer. If the observer happens to be that person's child, the child could become confused well into adulthood. This would be a possible re-germination mechanism for bad behaviors, as the child could behave badly well into adulthood because of a confusing upbringing. Thus, whatever was learned by members of past generations tend to get pushed aside by hang-ups, and members of the current generation would need to do the learning all over again. This could explain why we humans often repeat some mistakes over and over again for hundred of years.

This could also explain why conflicts among nations could go on endlessly. Each nation in effect has a nation spirit, and the spirit could embody many spirit types and each spirit type could have hang-ups that the nation spirit has not found a way to resolve. We can see examples of unresolved hang-up in just about every nation. We can see examples of hang-ups within a nation that cause conflicts within the nation. Our nation certainly has hang-ups as made evident by unsolved conflicts.

Therefore, a conclusion is that if we have a hang-up that causes us to be preoccupied with scratching it, we need to get the hang-up resolved as soon as possible. We would be doing both mankind and ourselves a favor.

Elemental Things Such as Electrons

As explained in Chapter Three, every member of the same kind of elemental thing shares the same spirit with every other member. Thus, only one spirit exists for all the electrons that exist in our universe. Only one spirit exists for all the protons. The same goes for every other kind of elemental thing that exists in our universe. Each such spirit consists of just one spirit type. Therefore, every member of any one kind of elemental thing behaves within the same spectrum of ways, although within the spectrum would include various states of being as indicated in Chapter Three where quantum superposition and entanglement are discussed for certain elemental things. This is the reason the various theories and models of physics, chemistry, electronics, etc. work so reliably regardless of the kinds of material and/or forms of energy to which they are applied.

While elemental things are spread out all over our universe, each kind has only one spirit in the spirit world. This makes the spirit world very compact compared with our physical universe. This is how the spirit world can be everywhere in our physical universe, and yet be nowhere in our physical universe. We will run into such dichotomies a lot when we attempt to describe the workings of the spirit world in terms of attributes of our physical world. The oneness produced by elemental things connects every living and nonliving thing with every other living and nonliving thing. Intuitively, we can sense we are a part of everything in our universe and everything in our universe is a part of us. The feeling of oneness comes through especially well when we are in a quiet place such as unspoiled wilderness. As mentioned earlier, the first time I visited Yosemite in the early 1960s, before there were shuttle buses and the need to reserve camping sites, as I was on the trail to the top of Yosemite Falls it felt like, "This is home, this is where I belong."

Handholds and Mentors

It is common knowledge that an individual can benefit greatly by having one or more mentors. I have mentors, but I find I use them more as handholds. Mentors are counselors or guides that teach us how we can apply our abilities. Handholds are entities that we hold onto much the same as handholds in mountain climbing, and they give us the confidence and courage to move onward via our own abilities and in whatever direction we see appropriate for ourselves.

In general I think mentors are particularly important for an individual who is conventional and wants to carry out life in a conventional manner. In general, I think handholds are particularly important for an individual who is unconventional and who tends to not worry too much about what others might think. They like to custom-design things to fit their own tastes. Such individuals are artists or are artists at heart. I am an artist at heart. My wife and I live in a house we designed ourselves. I designed and shaped the topography of our hillside lot to give the garden three elevations. I designed and planted the landscaping and installed all the patios, walkways, and stairs myself, brick by brick and stone by stone.

The garden has four areas each with a different mood. I love driving my three mid 1970s cars, and they are the only cars I own. One is the golden anniversary gift from my dad to my mom. One belonged to my late spouse. The third belongs to me. It is small, nimble, and the most versatile of the three. Family members and friends periodically ask when I am going to buy a new car. But why should I when what I have are all spiritually beautiful as well as each being physically "one of a kind" left. Onlookers regularly ask if I want to sell the car I happen to be driving at the time.

Conventional thinking so far has not been able to come up with ways to fix the mess we made here on Earth. Perhaps we need some new ways of thinking. High technology has made communications around the world much easier and more open. This could open up new ways of doing things since good communications can do amazing things. Unconventional ways of thinking could also help us tap into this new capability to help fix the mess.

The model indicates we need to be more aware we are carrying out our lives in the spirit world as well as in our physical world. We need a better balance in our awareness of the two worlds and that we are living in both. Unconventional thinking could help us achieve this. A better balance here would mean a better balance in our knowledge of what life is about and could thus enable us to carry out our lives in a wiser manner. The topic of wisdom is further discussed in the next section of this chapter.

Both of the two notions mentioned above indicate that unconventional thinking could help. This means we need to have available to us handholds as well as mentors. Literature exists on how to be mentors and how to use mentors in constructive ways. We need similar literature regarding handholds to encourage those who are inclined to think unconventionally to do so, and to do so in constructive ways.

Wisdom Is a Dynamic Thing that Pertains to the Future

Wisdom is a changing thing that needs to be constantly updated as new pieces of knowledge are constantly generated. With each new piece of knowledge, new issues are formed and could need balancing, and various existing issues may need re-balancing. This is analogous to how our position on a subject can change as we gain more knowledge about the subject, and this could entice us to seek out additional knowledge about the subject before taking any action; i.e., to be sure we know as much as we can so that we could act more wisely.

This means, in the spirit world's case, wisdom could quickly become irrelevant if not constantly updated. Even so, wisdom can never be totally complete or perfect since the spirit world can never be totally complete or perfect. Wisdom can only be kept as good and up to date as possible. One of the spirit world's most important tasks is to maintain balance in its state of knowledge so that it can form good, up-to-date wisdom at all times. Perfect balance would be ideal, but it can be rarely achieved, and if achieved it lasts for only an instant until the next new piece of knowledge is generated.

The spirit world's viability depends on how well it manages its own growth. This requires wisdom, which in turn requires reasonably balanced knowledge of all issues. Conversely, maintaining reasonable balance requires wisdom to know how to do so. If wisdom cannot be formed, reasonable balance cannot be maintained. Without reasonable balance, wisdom cannot be formed. Therefore, it is a vicious circle. If the vicious circle ever runs badly, it could become unstable and go extremely bad at an accelerating rate. Then the viability of the spirit world and everything it created would go bad. Then everything including the spirit world would vanish. Such a disaster might have happened in the past, and possibly multiple times. Regardless, the possibility of it happening at any time is real, if enough universes fail to fulfill their purposes of helping the spirit world restore balance.

In a forever incomplete and imperfect spirit world, wisdom provides the ability to make multiple reasonable extrapolations into possible futures based on knowledge of the past and present. Therefore, wisdom brings to light multiple options for actions, and the pros and cons of the options. Sometimes none of the options are desirable. Then the spirit world must figure out which option offers the best chance for restoring balance. This too requires wisdom.

If restoring balance is not possible to achieve in one step, then it might be wiser to think in terms of multiple smaller steps. Weighing long-term long-range actions versus short-term short-range actions is always a consideration. If both are of equal value, then long-term long-range actions are given higher priority, because the spirit world must plan as far forward as it can into the future it wants in order to get it.

We might ask; what about humans regarding wisdom? In general, the older an individual becomes the better his or her ability to form wisdom should be, because the knowledge he or she accumulates increases with age. Then how come some older individuals do not seem to have a lot of wisdom? Two possible reasons come to mind. Perhaps the most common one is that older individuals often are not up to date with the times. Consequently, while their wisdom was relevant in the past, it might not be now. And if they insist on pushing their outdated wisdom onto others, then they come across as not being very wise.

Another reason I have seen is that individuals of all ages are sometimes unable to shed some big hang-ups, and big hang-ups distort how the individual forms wisdom. As discussed earlier, a big hang-up can be like a terrible itch, and the individual is preoccupied with looking for opportunities to scratch. The preoccupation distorts how the individual forms wisdom. The hang-up might be unresolved anger, as discussed earlier. Another one I have seen is a forever-ongoing competition in where one individual forces his family into participating against another family. Almost everything he does has something to do with making his family get ahead of or catch up with the other family. This caused some members of his family to have resentments and/or anger that lasted their entire lives because they were forced into being not what they preferred to be. This then created hang-ups in these members. Such strange ways of carrying on life probably happen often, since we all have hang-ups and some are big and unsolved. I once had a big hang-up, and I was fortunate to resolve it fairly early. Incidentally, if we were to ask someone what his big hang-up is, he might not know he has one. Or if he knows he has one, he might not want to say he has one or give more details about it, especially if he has not, or could not for various reasons, resolve the hang-up.

Not everyone gets a big hang-up under the same conditions. It is a personal thing and thus it depends on one's personality, ability to soul search and to forgive, resourcefulness, self-sufficiency, ego, empathy and compassion for others, objectivity in thinking, etc.

The wise young individual can still extract wisdom from out-of-date wisdom of the old by gaining an understanding of what the old have gone through to form the wisdom. This puts the wisdom in proper perspective and thus the wise young individual is more able to extrapolate it to the present. Unfortunately, in today's ultra-busy way of life, young individuals usually have more pressing things to do. After all, it does take a lot of effort to extrapolate an old individual's out-of-date wisdom to the present, and it's often not clear to the young whether it is worth the effort. Therefore, it would better if an old individual who wants his or her wisdom to be used by the young to put in the effort to update that wisdom to make it relevant to the present. This would be a win-win effort since it would help bring the old more into the present and the updated wisdom would be more useful for the young.

Reference:

[1] Rupert Sheldrake, "Dogs That Know When Their Owners Are Coming Home;" Three Rivers Press, New York, New York, 1999.

Chapter Six
Spiritual Senses and Consciousness

No Limit to the Number of Spiritual Senses

Living things in our universe have major senses that are tuned to our physical world and spiritual senses that are tuned to the spirit world. Our major senses are certain spiritual senses extended into our physical world to give us our major senses. Each species has its particular set of major senses, and the set can be different for each species in terms of particular senses making up the set and of the acuity of each of the senses.

Examples mentioned earlier of major senses and/or acuity that other living things on Earth have that we humans do not have include the major senses of platypuses, which can sense electrical charges under water to find food; of pigeons and dogs, which can sense Earth's magnetic field; of bats, which use echolocation to find food; of snakes that sense heat to locate prey; of sharks that can sense magnets nearby; and of eagles and vultures whose visions are sharper than human's, etc. The model indicates that consciousness depends on the spiritual senses and their acuity. This means each of such creatures has a different kind of consciousness that are also different from human's. This explains why in general different creatures, including humans, can be aware of different things and/or can be more aware or less aware of certain things.

No living thing in any universe can have every spiritual sense that exists in the spirit world since the spirit of any given living thing is only a small portion of the spirit world. Additional spiritual senses in the spirit world are constantly being created as new pieces of knowledge are constantly being generated and added to the spirit world. Some of the new spiritual senses are no more complex and advanced than existing ones, and some are more complex and advanced than existing ones. The increasing number of pieces of knowledge in the spirit world enables the spirit world to design and bring into being increasingly complex and advanced universes. The living things to reside in them will be more complex and advanced to match, and their major senses and spiritual senses will need to include at least some that are more complex and advanced. Therefore, such living things will have consciousness's that are different from, and more complex and advanced than, those of living things that came before.

Hey, does that mean they might be able to understand what is happening on other planets without space traveling to them? Maybe, but only if their universe has space and planets. Oh that's right, and planets could mean something different in their universe anyway. Gee, the spirit world could sure makes thing complicated, Yeah, especially for us with only half a brain.

In addition to what these half-brained guys are talking about, since every universe is different and unique, living things in each universe will have sets of spiritual and major senses that are different and unique. For example, living things in a nonphysical universe will have sets of senses different from those of living things in a physical universe. Living things in a physical universe made of substances different from those making up our physical universe are likely to have sets of senses different from those of living thing in our universe. The same goes for universes with dimensionalities different from one another. Etc. Therefore, it follows that a given universe will be inhabited with living things with consciousness's that are different from those of living things inhabiting another universe. It then also follows that since there is no limit to the kinds of universes the spirit world can design and bring into being, there has to be no limit to the number of spiritual senses that can be created by the spirit world. The fact that various species of living things on Earth can have different sets of major senses could be because of that.

Various Natures of Consciousness

Some of the forthcoming chapters will cover some phenomena that take place in the spirit world but are perceived by us humans as taking place in our physical world. This seems to be the way human consciousness works. But according to the model, the consciousness of other living things might, or might not, work this way. Some living things might perceive things that happen in the spirit world as happening in the spirit world, and things that happen in our physical world as happening in our physical world. This is the case if a living thing's consciousness is tuned comparably to both the spirit world and our physical world. Human consciousness is tuned to the spirit world as well, since that is where we find thoughts, ideas, solutions, etc. and get our intuition and instincts, etc. But it is apparently not comparable to the degree our consciousness is tuned to our physical world.

Evidence exists that indicates some creatures seem to be able to sense some nonphysical things we cannot sense. For example, cats and dogs, especially cats, are sometimes observed behaving as if sensing something invisible to us. Could it be that they are so in touch with their spiritual senses that they are sensing such things in the spirit world? The possibility cannot be ruled out since various animals appear to be more in touch with their spiritual senses than we humans are with ours. Some examples are as follows.

As mentioned before, some pets telepathically sense the thoughts of their owners. Cross-learning among members of the same species of animals occur because members can sense what was learned by other members. Examples pertaining to nonliving things are given in the section following this section.

If some animals are in touch with their spiritual senses enough to sense things in the spirit world that we cannot, can they tell the difference between something in the spirit world versus something in our physical world? If the nature of their consciousness is difference from that of human consciousness, then they possibly can. On the other hand, since they are designed to reside in our universe they are likely to still superimpose their spiritual images onto our physical world and will see what is happening in the spirit world as happening in our physical world. A difference might be they might still be able to differentiate what is happening in the spirit world from what is happening in our physical world.

Based on the model, all our senses are spiritual senses. Five of our spiritual senses are extended into our physical world and into our body to give it its five major senses. Other living things have different sets of spiritual senses and different subsets of their spiritual sense extended into their bodies to give them their major senses. Usually their major senses are different in kind, number, and/or acuity from human major senses and they are also different from one species to another. This indicates their spiritual senses are likely to be different in kind, number, and acuity from one species to another as well.

A living thing's consciousness comes from its spiritual senses. The more spiritual senses it has, the more conscious it is. The more in touch it is with its spiritual senses, the more conscious it is. This means it is possible that some living things can be overall more conscious than humans, and some are certainly more conscious in certain ways than humans are in those ways.

Each living thing on Earth has multiple roles on Earth. One or more roles are the major one or ones at any given point in time. Which ones become major and which ones become minor depends on Earth's environmental and evolutionary changes. Right now, we humans are the major explorers and shapers on Earth, and this particular role of ours could be a major one at the moment. This could be a reason our consciousness is more tuned to our physical world than to the spirit world. Other living things do not knowingly do anything purposely to shape Earth in any major way. Thus, their consciousness does not need to be tuned to our physical world to the degree human consciousness is. Their consciousness is thus freer to be tuned to the spirit world than we choose to have our consciousness be. I say "we choose" because I believe we could have our consciousness become more tuned to the spirit world than it is right now if we want it to. I think once we are convinced that the spirit world exists and that we are simultaneously living in it and our physical world that we will seek out ways to have our consciousness become at least more tuned to the spirit world than it is right now. However, I also don't think our consciousness could ever be made to be more tuned to the spirit world than it is turned to our physical world, because we are here to go through experiences that could take place in our physical world but not in the spirit world.

The net result is various non-human living things are more able to sense things in the spirit world than we can, they can communicate telepathically better than we can, and they are likely to understand the spirit world better as well. This means we humans might be able to learn a lot about the spirit world through them. Such notions could be perceived as a challenge to our self-perceived superiority over other living things. But according to the model, each living thing has major roles. From a spiritual stand point for why our universe is created, they are here for a reason, and in their major roles they are superior. Therefore, what superiority is most important at any given moment in time depends on what it is that Earth needs at that moment. One of the things that Earth needs right now is for us to use our superiorities to clean up the mess we made with our superiorities.

Got a question, if our superiorities got us to make the mess on Earth that we made, are our superiorities really superior? Well, our superiorities are from being more advanced; therefore they are superior. Yeah, that makes sense. Then it must be the messy ways we are applying our superiorities. Yeah, that makes sense too. But how come we can't seem to understand our applications are messy? It is because we chose "ego and the desire to enhance survivability" as our dominant bases for carrying out our lives, and that makes our applications messy. And then our ego makes us think our applications are superior because they satisfy our ego and therefore we think they are OK as well. Thus, we continue to make the mess. So, that means our ego is keeping us from being more wise. Yeah, I think so, and that is why both you and I consider "ego and the desire to enhance survivability" one of the three major obstacles you and I identified that humans are here to work with and/or around. Yeah, I couldn't have done it without you. Yeah, and I couldn't have done it without you either. So, like they say, two half brains are better than one. I thing they say two heads are better than one. Really? Why would anyone want to have two heads?

Senses and Consciousness of Nonliving Things

According to the model, nonliving things as well as living things have senses, but their senses are not like those of living things. Their senses are elemental, more like automatic switches that respond when certain parameters reach certain values. For example, ice senses its temperature and responds by melting when its temperature rises to a certain level. Some chemicals sense the conditions they are in and react when the conditions are such that they can do so. Some crystals change phase when certain parameters reach certain values. Elemental senses of various kinds are the basis for some of the workings of our high-technology systems, devices, appliances, gadgets, etc. This is especially true as computer chips become smaller and smaller. The intelligence, and therefore the consciousness, of such things as smart phones and other smart devices come from the intelligence of elemental senses and their interactions.

If consciousness comes from being in touch with spiritual senses, then because nonliving things have senses, they have spiritual senses that extended into them to give them their senses, and if they have spiritual senses they have consciousness. However, their senses, spiritual senses, and consciousness are elemental. If life is perceived to exist when consciousness and senses exist, then nonliving things have life; i.e., elemental life. However, for convenience and simplicity we will continue to use the term "nonliving" for things we are accustomed to consider as such.

While elemental senses and elemental life exist in our physical world, elemental spiritual senses and elemental spiritual life exist in the spirit world. However, such elemental components in the spirit world are not spiritual counterparts of such elemental components in our physical world. It takes a lot of knowledge to enable anything to exist in any universe. Therefore, such elemental components exist in our physical world because spiritual entities in the spirit world enable them to exist, not because some specific elemental components by themselves in the spirit world enable them to exist.

The most basic spiritual thing, a piece of knowledge, has elemental spiritual sense and therefore elemental spiritual consciousness. These would not be like the spiritual senses and consciousness of the spirit of a living thing. Again, the elemental spiritual sense of a piece of knowledge is sort of like an automatic switch. An existing piece of knowledge can sense when a new piece of knowledge is generated and will consciously form a connection of the first kind with it. Conversely, a newly generated piece of knowledge can sense the presence of every existing piece of knowledge and will consciously form a connection of the first kind with each of them. Either way, only one connection of the first kind will exist; i.e., when each of two pieces of knowledge forms a connection with the other, the two connections will merge and only one will remain.

Elemental spiritual senses and elemental spiritual consciousness of pieces of knowledge enable the spirit world to create spiritual entities with pieces of knowledge. Everything created by the spirit world is in the form of a spiritual entity. Spiritual senses are among the things created by the spirit world; therefore spiritual senses are in the form of spiritual entities. This means elemental spiritual senses and elemental spiritual consciousness are among the ingredients that go into making up spiritual senses. Therefore, spiritual senses can be perceived as composed at least "partly" of elemental spiritual senses. Also since every spiritual entity embodies elemental spiritual senses and elemental spiritual consciousness, every spiritual entity, even nonliving ones, embodies elemental spiritual life.

The reason we say "partly" is because when we combine "x" number of pieces of knowledge together to form a spiritual entity, the spiritual entity can do more than the sum of what each piece of knowledge can do individually. This is true for anything made of many parts; e.g., an automobile can do more than the sum of what each of its parts can do individually. Therefore, a spiritual entity that is a spiritual sense can sense more than the sum of what each piece of knowledge can sense individually with their elemental spiritual senses. This means the interactions among the individual pieces of knowledge making up the spiritual entity give the spiritual entity added capabilities. By analogy the interactions among the parts making up an automobile give the automobile added capabilities and thus the automobile becomes a motor vehicle.

The added capabilities in both cases also come from signals issued by various other spiritual entities included in the spirit of the thing, whether the thing is a living or nonliving thing, automobile, or something else. In the case of a living or nonliving thing brought into being by the spirit world, it is the spirit world that instructed those other spiritual entities to go into action. In the case of an automobile, it is the actions of humans and/or machinery built by humans who found these other spiritual entities in the spirit world and translated them into actions that could be expressed in our physical world.

Another way to look at it is as follows. The specific set of major senses a specific living thing has is the extension of a specific set of spiritual senses into our physical world and into the body of the living thing. Each species has a different set of spiritual senses extended into our physical world and into their bodies. The set involved for each species is not entirely dependent on the physical materials and energies making up the body. For example, the bodies of all animals on Earth are made of more or less the same kinds of materials and energies, yet the different species have different sets of major senses. This indicates that major senses are not associated with only the elemental senses embodied in the body. The "other spiritual entities" mentioned in the preceding paragraph are a part of what enables major senses to exist.

Learning Takes Place in Our Spirit, not in Our Brain

When we get educated and/or trained, the model indicates it is our spirit that gets educated and/or trained, and not our brain or our body although our brain and body participate in the process by going through the experiences of getting educated and/or trained in our physical world. Some exceptions are presented in the next section where the topic of body intelligence and body consciousness, as opposed to brain intelligence and brain consciousness, are discussed. I.e., our spirit issues spiritual signals directly to our body without going through our brain and then to our body.

However, in either case, the spirit is where we do our thinking and where our intelligence and consciousness reside. Everything about us and everything we are able to do are embodied in our spirit. Our spirit uses its spiritual senses to sense what is going on in the spirit world and in our physical world. Other than the exceptions discussed in the next section, it then sends spiritual signals to our brain. Our brain translates the spiritual signals into electrical physical signals and sends them to the rest of our body. Our body responds accordingly and sends feedback electrical physical signals to our brain. Our brain translates the feedback electrical physical signals into feedback spiritual signals and then sends them to our spirit. The spirit senses the signals and uses them to get an update on what is going on in the spirit world and in our physical world. The cycle thus repeats constantly as we carry out our life. The cycle repeats extremely rapidly such that our thinking process and our actions take place smoothly, similar to the manner in which the image on a television screen is updated so rapidly that the motions shown are perceived as progressing smoothly.

Consider an entity consisting of a driver and a car. By analogy, the driver is the spirit of the entity, the computers and controls in the car make up the brain of the entity, and the rest of the car is the body of the entity. The driver (spirit) is the part of the entity where intelligence and consciousness reside and is the part that learns how to drive the car, not the computers and controls (brain) and not the rest of car (body). The driver (spirit) senses what is going on in the environment and what is going on with the car. The driver (spirit) issues instructions to the computers and controls (brain). The computers and controls (brain) sense the driver's instructions and translate them to signals understood by the rest of the car (body). The car responses accordingly, and sends feedback signals to the computers and controls. The computers and controls translate the feedback signals into signals understood by the driver. The driver senses the signals and gets an update on what is going on in the environment and what is going on with the car. The driver then issues new instructions to the computers and controls. The cycle thus repeats constantly as long as the driver is driving the car.

With robotics and other high-technology innovations, experimental cars have been designed that drive themselves. Therefore, does this mean the brain of the entity has sufficient intelligence and consciousness to drive the car without involving the driver, the spirit of the entity? The answer is a qualified yes. The intelligence and consciousness needed to drive the car are designed and built into the brain of the car by humans. Therefore, the designers and builders have carried out all the thinking regarding all the possible situations the car can encounter. Thus, the car (body) is relying on the designers and builders (spirit world) to do all the thinking for it so that it can negotiate traffic safely without the driver (spirit) being involved. Consequently, the designers and builders are actually doing the driving, not the car itself. This is analogous to living things, such as plants, that rely totally on instincts to survive. Such a living thing relies totally on the spirit world to do all the thinking for it.

Even modern cars, which still require drivers, are increasingly equipped with sensing and control systems that do some of the driving for them. Examples are systems to prevent skidding during braking, to automatically parallel park, to maintain the speed while on cruise control, to warn the driver of objects in blind spots, etc. Thus, the driver (spirit) is doing part of the driving and the designers and builders (spirit world) of such systems are doing part of the driving of a lot of the modern cars. This is analogous to how some living things rely moderately on instincts to survive. Such living things do part of their own thinking and rely on the spirit world to do the rest of their thinking to survive.

When we interact with another individual, it is our spirit and the other individual's spirit that are interacting. Our brain and body and the other individual's brain and body are participating in the interaction by voicing or writing thoughts, drawing pictures, conveying body language, producing tone of voice, etc. While pictures, body language, and tone of voice are not spoken or written expressions of thoughts, they are nevertheless expressions of thoughts. Thoughts are actually very compact and can be expressed by something as concise as a picture, body language, or tone of voice. Speaking and writing are slower and less concise but are usually more precise ways of expressing thoughts.

Before there were spoken/written languages, there were thoughts. Exchanges of thoughts by other means such as gestures, sounds, lights, colors, patterns, etc. were carried out before complex spoken languages developed. Could the use of complex spoken/written languages be the beginning of abstract thinking? Other creatures have spoken languages as well, although not as complex as the spoken/written languages of humans. Does this mean other creatures are capable of abstract thinking too, albeit not as complex as human capabilities'?

When I started to learn calculus, trying to comprehend what calculus was about in terms of mathematical concepts I was familiar with at the time was extremely difficult. After struggling for two weeks, I came up with a new and more abstract way of thinking that turned out to be my key for understanding calculus. With the new way of thinking came a new mathematical language that enabled me to have the kinds of communications and interactions with the teacher and textbook necessary for learning calculus. Similar things happened when I started to learn other advanced mathematics such as complex numbers, transformations, matrices, tensors, etc. Each case required me to come up with a new and abstract way of thinking, and an accompanying new mathematical language.

At the time, I wondered when I would use such complex mathematics in my common daily activities. As it turns out, I didn't use them very much after college, although I am sure some individuals use them a lot, depending on the profession they are in. However, I use abstract thinking a lot. In my mind, abstract thinking is the ability to extrapolate knowledge we already have and thus to come up with reasonable ways to address unfamiliar situations. This enables us to take knowledge from one area and apply it to unfamiliar and unrelated areas. Sometimes a new way of thinking is part of the process. It is essentially leveraging our knowledge to cover more than the lessons we have had. Abstract thinking is thus part of our ability to form wisdom. Thus, a very wise leader is able to successfully guide an organization through uncertain and unfamiliar situations.

A common use of abstract thinking is in the formation of analogies to help clarify unfamiliar situations. All of us have come up with analogies. Therefore, all of us have the ability to do abstract thinking. Studying technical subjects such as mathematics, engineering, physics, and chemistry strengthens the ability. Being observant of everyday happenings and of any commonality among them also helps.

Since we reside in a physical universe our consciousness is more in tune with the physical part of our lives than with the spiritual part. Thus, the spiritual part will always be abstract to us even though we are carrying out our lives in both our physical world and the spirit world. This means in order to be more conscious of the spiritual part of life it helps to be more able to think abstractly. Some of the more important things in the spiritual part of life are feelings, intentions, attitudes, emotions, intuition, instincts, creativity, imagination, empathy, compassion, etc. If we find we are losing touch with such things, it might mean we are overly immersed in the physical part of our life.

The model indicates that anything in the spirit world within our ability to find and explore is meant for us to find and explore. Accordingly, it would be appropriate, and perhaps even expected, for us to try out new and unconventional ways of thinking, and thus also new and unconventional ways of finding things in the spirit world so as to broaden the range of things we could find there. It is possible that by being overly confined to thinking conventionally we are unable to find things that might have prevented our making the mess we made on Earth, particularly if those things we are unable to find are spiritual in nature.

Are we therefore saying that unconventional thinking could produce things that would counteract certain things we get from conventional thinking? In my mind, one of the most confining features of conventional thinking is the importance given to upholding ego. Just about everything we do has something to do directly or indirectly with upholding ego, strongly or mildly. If ego were upheld in my search for my personal spiritual model, I would not have considered the model presented in this book. If ego were not upheld we might have avoided a lot of wars. If ego were not upheld Congress would behave in a more bipartisan manner and get more things done. Ego tends to lead us to do things that have manmade, Earth-bound values, but likely to have little value in the spirit world since ego is only a concept and not a practice in the spirit world. This is because everything in the spirit world is directly or indirectly a part of everything else.

Animals cater to ego probably because they cannot handle situations more creatively. Thus, a male lion taking over a pride of lions and killing all the infants of the previous dominant male lion, as mentioned before, is establishing his own line of descendants. Some primates do the same. Fights to establish a dominant male member are common. These are examples of ego-driven, noncreative ways of handling situations. So, here we humans come with our far superior intelligence, creativity, imagination, reasoning ability, and ability to gain wisdom. While we generally handle situations creatively, imaginatively, and wisely, we still cater to ego. Thus, while other animals keep their bad behaviors confined to their own groups, we use our superior abilities to make a mess that covers the entire Earth.

Catering to ego happens easily, naturally, and insidiously when we are overly stimulated and are then provoked by something. For example, when we are driving an automobile, especially in heavy traffic, we are more likely to cater to ego when provoked than we normally would. So many things are demanding our attention and our quick responses that not much attention remains to help us stay levelheaded. Afterwards, in quieter moments, we are likely to regret the way we behaved. The bad behavior seemed to simply creep in insidiously, and we sort of did not mean for it to happen.

What this says is that we are basically still animals. Catering to ego plays a role in self-preservation for animals. When we are overly stimulated and when even a touch of self-preservation is involved, our animal nature often takes over. Unfortunately, contemporary life is increasingly overly stimulating and competitive, and threats to our enhancement of survivability from the competition are often interpreted as threats to our self-preservation. The ways we are applying high technology are accelerating our over-stimulation. Global competition and economics are also factors. Our increasing addiction to over-stimulation doesn't help. Special effects in movies and video games are increasingly spectacular and violent, theme park rides are increasingly thrilling, rock concerts are loud and increasingly packed with pulsating light effects, food is increasingly spicy and overly flavored, extreme sports are increasingly perilous, etc.

It is natural to think about self-preservation first. Thus, when we are overly stimulated, there is little time left to think beyond ourselves and be empathic and compassionate of others. Consequently, ego tends to take control of our behavior. Very quick and short-term results tend to be what we choose. This tends to leave behind a mess. Continued over-stimulation provides an excuse to not look back at the mess. Thus, an addiction to over-stimulation ensues. I suspect business individuals know people become addicted to over-stimulation, and I suspect they are taking advantage of this to make a profit.

We might ask; what are we to do in today's fast-paced way of life, when so many situations come our way in which we could, and sometimes do, mess up? In a way, messing up once in a while is only human. If we have a conscience and have regrets afterwards, it reminds us to be humble and that we are no better than anyone else is. This can turn a "mess up" into something more positive; e.g., forgiving ourselves as well as forgiving those who provoked us, and realizing again how important it is to slow down and take the time to be more empathic and compassionate of others.

Body Intelligence and Body Consciousness

Some exceptions to the discussions in the preceding section are physical activities that when we become proficient at doing, our body gets trained and can do them essentially automatically such as keeping a bicycle up right while we ride it, keeping a nail straight while we hammer it, and making certain moves essentially automatically while skiing.

Our spirit has a degree of direct connection with our body via our soul for such proficiencies to exist without going through our brain since our soul carries spiritual signals that enable to our body to exist in the first place. Therefore, for the sake of efficiency, it is logical our spirit would issues such proficiency associated spiritual signals directly to our body so as to lessen the load on our brain. In addition I suspect based the sizes of brains in other creatures that the spirit of a living thing would enable only as big a brain as necessary to exist to enable the living thing's body to perform the activities the living thing is designed to perform. Therefore, any activities not necessary to go through the brain to pilot the body, such as the examples given, the spirit would handle these directly with the body without going through the brain. As discussed in more detail in the next section, where the topics include the size of the brain relative to the size of the spirit, the skin of a living single cell is capable of being the "brain" for the cell. Since our body is made of living cells, this can be the mechanism by which body intelligence and body consciousness work.

This could also be how our body respond instinctively and immediately to dangers without waiting for our brain to first receive spiritual signals from our spirit, translate the signals to physical signals, and then issue them to our body. To save our body in dangerous situations our spirit directly instructs our body to respond without going through our brain. Thus, our body will respond more immediately than it will if our spirit goes through our brain instead. However, the spirit is bound to use this mechanism only for simple actions our body performs and can perform without thinking about it such as the examples given and the initial response to danger.

This could also be the mechanism by which our bodily systems can function automatically without instructions from our brain such as in the case of a brain-dead body. A brain-dead body can remain living with the help of life sustaining equipment. Very long ago a gruesome news item revealed how a beheaded chicken's body was kept alive by being fed with an eyedropper through its now open neck. The news item even included a photo of the beheaded chicken standing up straight on its legs looking otherwise quite normal. Its body intelligence and body consciousness must be keeping its bodily systems functioning in order for it to stay alive without its head and thus without its brain.

However, in the case of a human, being a more complex living thing, a brain-body might need some part of the brain to remain functioning when the rest of it is dead in order for bodily systems to remain functioning. That part of the brain might be the most primitive part located at the lower part of the brain.

The Size of the Spirit and the Size of the Brain are not Proportional to Each Other

The spirit is everything a living thing is, if we don't count the brain and the rest of the body. For example, after we die, we are still everything we are, even without our brain or body. The spirit is where intelligence, spiritual senses, consciousness, creativity, reasoning ability, memories, etc. reside. The more intelligent the living thing, the more spiritual senses it has, and the more consciousness it has, the larger its spirit is.

The spirit pilots the body. The brain is the computer center for the body and is the main communication link between the spirit and the rest of the body. It receives spiritual signals from the spirit, translates them into electrical signals, and sends the electrical signals to the rest of the body. The body then responds accordingly and sends feedback signals to the brain. The brain translates these into spiritual signals and sends them to the spirit. Thus, the cycle constantly repeats very quickly, and this is how the spirit pilots the body.

The physical attributes of the brain have more to do with what the body is designed to do and less to do with the intelligence and consciousness of the spirit. The complexity and size of the brain depends on the range and precision of activities the body is designed by the spirit world to do. A body designed to be capable of doing a very wide range of things and to do them precisely, such as a human body is designed to do, needs a large, complex brain; i.e., a large, complex computer control center. Conversely, a body designed to be capable of doing a very narrow range of things not necessarily precisely needs a much smaller, simpler brain. A very large creature needs a larger brain than a very small creature simply because it has more of a body to whose health needs to be monitored and larger bodily functions and associated physical activities to control. This is true even if both creatures have equal intelligence and consciousness.

A human individual thus has a large spirit and a large brain. Intelligent creatures such as dolphins and whales have a large spirit. However, their bodies are designed to be capable of doing far fewer things, and less precisely, than a human body is designed to be capable of doing. Therefore, their brains are smaller relative to the size of their bodies than a human brain is relative to the size of a human body. Some birds exhibit a high level of intelligence but have very small brains. This means some birds have a much larger spirit than the size of their brain would suggest. Their body is typically small, and the range of things their body can do is relatively small; thus, they simply have a small brain even though some of them are quite intelligent.

In late 2013, alligators were found to be cleverer than might be expected for their pea-size brains. Multiple alligators were observed acting cooperatively to better capture prey. Again, according to the model, their intelligence resides in their spirit, not in their brain. Their brains are pea-size because that is all the brain they need to control all the things their bodies can do, the range of which is extremely limited compared with the range of things a human body can do. For example, the human body threads needles, cooks food, builds complex equipment and structures, performs surgery, operates smart phones, speaks languages, produces paintings, pivots airplanes, rides bicycles, writes sentences, hand feeds babies, puts on clothes, etc. An alligator doesn't do any of such things. Therefore, an alligator's body gets by just fine with a pea-size brain, because all its body needs to do basically is to swim, craw, and catch prey. But its intelligence, which resides in its spirit, enables it to swim and catch food in clever ways rather than just in simple-minded ways.

Some living things seem to have no brain at all, at least not one with the usual physical attributes of a typical brain. For example, a bacterium does not have a recognizable brain, yet it exhibits intelligence and consciousness in its behavior. For example, each species has an intricate way of propelling itself. Some species wave bundles of threadlike flagella to swim, some throw out "lassos" to grab onto other objects including other bacteria to pull themselves forward, and some have tiny nozzles on their bodies through which they emit jets of slime and thus move by jet propulsion. Their ability to use their propulsion systems indicates they have intelligence and consciousness. Since they have spirits, they naturally have some level of intelligence and consciousness. But where are the computer centers for the bodies of bacteria? The current thinking is that their computer center is their outer membrane or their skin. Studies indicate that their skin can sense what is going on in their immediate surroundings and thus serve as the brain or computer center for the body. While the skin is physically simple, the part of the spirit that enables the skin to exist must be a lot more complex than we might expect in order to give each bacterium the intelligence and consciousness it exhibits.

Since we are now able to map brain activities and monitor brain waves, it will be interesting to see if what is discussed in this section makes sense relative to such measurements. For example, does a brain appear to be communicating with something other than the rest of the body, such as an unseen spirit? Does a brain translate electrical signals from the body into some other yet-unknown form of signals that are referred to as spiritual signals in the model? If such phenomena could be monitored, then this could be further confirmation the spirit world exists.

A certain kind of brain cells is determined to be associated with having the capacity to be empathic. This kind of brain cell is found in human brains, and was once thought to exist only in human brains. They have since been found also in the brains of elephants, dolphins, and various other animals. They were also found fairly recently in the brains of certain whales such as gray whales. The capacity for such empathic behavior must exist first in the spirit, according to the model, in order for it to appear in the behavior of such living things. However, the brain must also have the physical capacity to communicate empathic signals between the spirit and the body, and apparently this requires this certain kind of brain cell to be present in the brain. This suggests there might be other kinds of brain cells required to handle other kinds of mental states as well. If humans are capable of a larger variety of mental states than are other creatures, this could further explain why humans have a proportionally larger brain than other creatures have.

Whales may have something else to tell us. Humpback whales sing at a certain time of year and their songs can travel miles through the Pacific Ocean. All the humpback whales in the Pacific Ocean sing at the same time. Scientists have yet to determine why they sing and why they do so simultaneously. Could it be something to do with communicating with the spirit world?

What has been ignored in scientific investigations in general is the spiritual part of whatever phenomenon is being investigated. This could be why our findings sometimes cannot be explained. Some important factor in the phenomenon seems to be unidentified or ignored.

Whales, dolphins, and porpoises are amazing creatures with high levels of intelligence and consciousness. Many species interact very intelligently with humans. One species of whales has worked with human fishermen for more than a century, helping each other capture fish. And it looks like the whales know exactly what they are doing as they time their various actions to first help the fishermen capture fish and then themselves to capture fish right afterwards. The video of their actions is impressive in terms of the intelligence and consciousness the whales show. At a certain time of the year, there are whales in the waters of Baja California that come close to boats carrying human whale-watchers and interact by letting the humans touch them, and even hug and kiss them. They seem to be people-watching to the same degree the humans are whale-watching.

The physical body of a living thing exists and is the way it is because the spirit of the living thing enables the body to exist and be the way it is. This includes the make-up of the brain and how it is wired. The brain is the main communications center between the spirit and the body. The spirit can thus make adjustments in the brain if it needs to do so to maintain good communication with the body.

A recent study found that when mice are kept in total darkness, their sense of hearing increased to compensate for the loss of their sense of sight. Additional connections grew in the brain that would correlate with an increase sense of hearing. The brain eventually returned to normal when the mice were removed from total darkness. It was implied that the brain made the changes on its own. But according to the model, it is instead the spirit that instructed the brain to make the changes. This could be so that the brain would be better able to sense feedback signals from the body in the dark that are different from feedback signal the body sends when not in the dark.

Recently, changes are observed to occur in the brain when an individual is learning something and mastering something. The model indicates that it is not the brain that does the learning by making the changes. Instead it is the spirit that does the learning and gaining new pieces of knowledge. These new pieces of knowledge will then issue new signals to the brain. Therefore, it is the spirit that instructs the brain on how to change so as to be able to sense the new signals from the new pieces of knowledge.

In my mind, this is analogous to the way the spirit knows how to heal the body when the body is injured, and it issues instructions to the body on how to heal. In the case of mice being in total darkness, the spirit knows how to have the body compensate for the loss of sight and thus issues instructions to the brain on how to change to compensate. This is also consistent with how evolutionary changes come about. For example, if a group of mice were to live in total darkness generation after generation, then the changes seen would likely become permanent after many generations have passed. Other changes are likely to occur permanently as well. Thus, a new species of mice would be formed. Because the brain is the main communication center between the spirit and the body, any changes that help the living thing to adapt to changes in the environment can be expected to occur in the brain before changes occur anywhere else in the body.

Visitation to and/or from Other Universes

Actual inter-universe travel is less likely or unlikely since every universe is different and unique such that living things from one might not be able to enter another. For example a living thing from a four-dimensional universe might not be able to fit into a three-dimensional universe. But perhaps a living thing from a nonphysical universe might be able to enter a physical universe. Alternatively, virtual inter-universe travel by going through the spirit world is theoretically possible. We might also perceive manifestations of visitors from other universes doing virtual travel to our universe, but we are less likely or unlikely to understand what we perceive. For example, we might see an unidentified flying object (UFO), but we would not fully understand how they could change direction instantaneously or accelerate at infinite rate. The model explains how such maneuvers are possible for certain UFOs.

Since every universe is different and unique, the spiritual senses and the major senses of living things in them are tuned to the attributes of the universe the living things reside in, and would not likely be tuned to some or all of the attributes of any other universe. Our universe is physical and three-dimensional and is made of certain kinds of energy and physical substances. Other universes could have different dimensionality, be nonphysical, be made of different kinds of energy and physical substances if physical; they might not have gravity and/or inertia, or need space in which to reside, might need a different kind of space than our space if space is needed, etc. These are examples of why senses of living things tuned to attributes of their own universe would be less likely or unlikely to be able to tuned to the attributes of another universe. Therefore, this is another reason actual inter-universe travel is possibly less likely or unlikely.

Even if we were able to actually travel to another universe, because our senses are not tuned into the attributes of that universe we are not likely to fully understand any signals we might encounter in that universe. For all we know, other universes might be intermingled with our universe, and we would not even know their inhabitants are here, nor they know we are here.

How things work in the spirit world is different from how things work in a universe. The spiritual senses of a living thing can sense anything in the spirit world relevant to the universe in which the living thing resides; i.e., anything that can be translated into a form that can be expressed or exist in that universe. However, everything in the spirit world is directly or indirectly a part of everything else in the spirit world. Therefore, anything we could sense in the spirit world directly or indirectly embodies a part, or is a part, of things that living things in another universe could sense. Therefore, theoretically we are directly or indirectly sensing parts of things in the spirit world that are relevant to other universes.

The trick is to distinguish those parts. We need to also figure out which other universe or universes are involved. This could require a lot of innovation and a lot of advancement in our abilities. However, if we were someday to have it all figured out, we would then be much more aware that we are carrying out our lives in both the spirit world and our physical world. We would then know how to do virtual inter-universe travel by going through the spirit world.

Currently, when we sense something in the spirit world we tend to perceive the process of sensing it as taking place in our physical world, because our consciousness is so used to being focused on our physical world. Therefore, for example, when we see UFOs we think we are seeing them in our physical world when, according to the model, we are actually sensing them in the spirit world and perceiving them as being in our physical world.

When we sense something in the spirit world relevant to another universe but not to ours, we are not likely to fully understand it. Thus, we could see UFOs as if they are in our universe, and we would call them UFOs because we do not fully understand them. They could indicate living things in another universe have figured out how to do virtual inter-universe travel to our universe. Another possibility is that living things on another planet in our universe have figured out how to do virtual space travel to our planet, Earth.

Virtual travel by living things from another universe to our universe is a matter of the spirit of their universe finding a way of issuing signals directly to the spirit of our universe. Thus, it is possible for all living things in our universe to sense such signals and perceive the signals as manifestations in our universe. But we are sensing the signals in the spirit world, and we perceive them as manifestations in our universe. Because they are not really physical things in our universe, they do not have mass and therefore do not have inertia. Therefore, they can change their direction of motion instantaneously and can accelerate at infinite rate. UFOs are known to be capable of such maneuvers.

This also applies to virtual travel by living things from another planet in our universe to Earth; it is a matter of the spirit of that planet finding a way of issuing signals directly to the spirit of Earth. Thus, it is possible for all living things on Earth to sense such signals in the spirit world and perceive the signals as manifestations on Earth.

Perceptions of Advancements, Improvements, and Being Gifted

As new pieces of knowledge are constantly being generated and added to the spirit world, the spirit world constantly creates new spiritual entities, some of which are new spiritual senses. This means each time the spirit world creates a new living thing, the new living thing could have more spiritual senses than past living things, and, thus, could be more complex and have higher intelligence and consciousness. This could explain why evolution tends to produce increasingly complex and advanced living things. By analogy, almost anything we humans design and build tends to become increasingly complex and advanced with each new design because of the knowledge we gain from using previous versions of the same, similar, or associated things.

Although in our case, advancement does not necessarily mean improvement if a very incomplete model was used to design the new and more advanced thing. For example, using new and more advanced touch-screen controls on car dashboards is more distracting and unsafe while driving than using the previously designed, less-advanced knob controls. The model used to design touch-screen controls did not account for the increased attention needed to locate the control spots on the touch screen and the safety problems that could arise while driving.

Within each species, each member has more or less the same set of abilities, but each member has a unique subset of abilities that are better than average and a unique subset that are worse. Each member also has different physical proportions, physical strengths, distribution of acuity among its spiritual senses, kinds of intelligence and consciousness, etc. This is why within the human species some members make good scientists, some good artists, some good athletes, some good business people, etc.

For most of us, our better-than-average attributes do not always work together in a cohesive manner. Our interests might not match our strongest abilities. Life's circumstances might have us doing other than that which we could do best, what we could do best might not be marketable, etc. We might have hang-ups (bad itches) that cause us to be preoccupied with reacting to the hang-ups (scratching the itches) instead of doing what we could do best because we have to "scratch," etc.

However, there are individuals in which all, or most, of their better-than-average attributes manage to come together and function in a cohesive manner. Those individuals can thus be perceived as being gifted. The model indicates all, or most, of us have this potential. However, not everyone wants to carry out life in the manner of a gifted individual. But it is nice to know all, or most, of us have that potential.

Rhythms and Beauty

From observations, one of the many bases for our perception of beauty is the way life is sustained in our universe. This notion is likely to be valid for other universes as well. Thus, we could use it to help us better understand what is, and is not, considered beautiful there, so that someday when we do inter-universe travel or virtual inter-universe travel we will be better able to make a positive connection with living things elsewhere. For the present, we can use the notion on Earth to help individuals make more positive connections with individuals of other nations. This is already often done through the arts.

Rhythms are the topic of this section as an example of how life is sustained on Earth and likely also elsewhere in our universe. Other attributes are also a part of how life is sustained. For example, each nation has different attributes as part of their culture, traditions, religion, environment, history, etc. Therefore, the arts, architecture, and patterns of things take on different forms corresponding to the different attributes that help sustain life in each nation. However, rhythms are a common attribute for every nation.

Rhythms naturally come about because our universe is physical, three-dimensional, and is made of its particular kinds of materials, energies, and space. Something other than rhythms could sustain life in other universes. Nonphysical universes and ones with no gravity or other attraction forces could be among such universes. Therefore, for example, while music and dance are perceived as beautiful and universal languages on Earth, they might not be perceived the same way in other universes.

Natural rhythms in our universe include the orbiting of moons, planets, and stars around other planets and stars, the rotation of such objects around their own axes, the rotation of galaxies, the orbiting of elemental things around other elemental things such as electrons around nuclei, etc. Rhythms in living things include heart beats, breathing, walking and running, flying, the cycles of deciduous plants, seasons, ocean waves, undersea currents, air streams, etc. Rhythms in the things we produce to make our lives easier (and sometimes more complicated) include alternating electric currents, engines, motors, generators, clocks, refrigerators, washing machines and dryers, annual events, high-technology devices, etc.

Things that capture the rhythms that sustain life are perceived as beautiful. They include music, dance, sports, flying, fruits and vegetables, waterfalls and streams, clouds, eclipses, Earth viewed from outer space, sunrises and sunsets, lightning, flags moving in a breeze, symmetry and repetition in patterns, the shapes of living and nonliving things, etc. They are also the sculptures and paintings and photos of living things, hand-made things embodying more of life than do manufactured things, floral arrangements, dwellings and nests of living things, architectural and landscape designs with patterns and shapes in harmony with the nature, etc. They are things we rhythmically use every day such as musical instruments, organs, harps, pianos, furniture, lamps and light fixtures, eating utensils and dishes, clothing, drapes, windows, doors, staircases, etc. Thus, as the song goes "There is Beauty Everywhere" as life's rhythms are everywhere.

Chapter Seven
Spirit World and Physical World Interactions

Supply vs. Demand for Spiritual Entities Capable of Serving as Spirits

Because the spirit world has an everlasting desire to learn and to create, it is forever growing and thus forever a changing and an interesting place. New things are constantly being created, and some of them are beyond our imagination. As explained in Chapter Three, even the addition of one new piece of knowledge to the spirit world more than doubles the number of spiritual entities in the spirit world. Since new pieces of knowledge are constantly being generated and added, the number of spiritual entities is constantly more than doubling. Consequently, the spirit world is not likely to run out of new and interesting creations to look for, find, and explore as long as the spirit world remains a viable living entity.

As we've already discussed, we might ask; as the human population continues to grow on Earth, can the spirit world ever run out of available spirits for humans? And, what about enough spirits for all the other living things on Earth, all the living things on other planets in our universe, and all the living things in other universes that happen to also exist at this time? The answer is; it is unlikely the spirit world will run of spirits. And if it does, all it has to do is to wait for another new piece of knowledge to be generated and the number of available spiritual entities capable of serving as spirits for living things will double.

To illustrate how rapidly the number of spiritual entities can increase, suppose the spirit world starts out with just one spiritual entity capable of serving as a spirit for a living thing. If the number of spiritual entities doubles with each added new piece of knowledge, then the number of spiritual entities capable of serving as a spirit will increase to 1,073,741,824 after only 30 new pieces of knowledge are added to the spirit world. After adding another 30 new pieces of knowledge, the number grows to approximately 1,152,921,000,000,000,000. Thus, it seems unlikely the spirit world would ever run out of spiritual entities that can serve as spirits for living things.

On the other hand, look at how many living things are on Earth alone. Every grass plant in a lawn is a living thing. Every bacterium is a living thing. Every tree in a forest is a living thing. Living things are everywhere in the oceans, on land, and in the air around us. Add to that the number of living things existing elsewhere in our universe and in other existing universes, and a number like 1,152,921,000,000,000,000 might not be way beyond the number of existing living things.

Also, as explained earlier in the book, our universe might be growing, not just expanding, at an increasing rate so that the number of planets hospitable for living things could be increasing at an increasing rate. Therefore, a very fast rate of increase in the number of spiritual entities capable of serving as spirits for living things could be part of what is driving the growth of our universe, and maybe other existing universes as well. This may seem bizarre to us on Earth, but it may be just how it is in the spirit world.

It is also possible that the reason we have so many living things on Earth is because there are so many spiritual entities available and willing to serve as spirits for them. Therefore, to accommodate them, the spirit world might have decided to bring into being all the living things we have on Earth. Accordingly, it might not be a question of whether or not there are enough spirits to enable all the living things that can come into being to come into being. Rather it might be more a question of whether or not enough living things can come into being to satisfy all the spiritual entities that want to serve as spirits for living things.

A similar discussion applies to spiritual entities that can serve as spirits for nonliving things. While we humans produce a lot of nonliving things, nonliving things were naturally on Earth before any living thing emerged here. Once living things, especially humans, emerged on Earth, additional nonliving things are produced at an increasingly rapid rate.

A typical physical nonliving thing made by humans and sold in stores or online is wrapped in plastic or paper and put in a box that has a label stuck on it. Thus, a total of four nonliving things are involved; i.e., they are the nonliving thing, wrapper, box, and label. A typical edible thing sold in grocery stores comes in a glass, plastic, or paper container with a cover, a seal to secure the cover, and a label on the container. A total of five nonliving things are involved. Each physical thing and each edible thing serve more than one person, and each person uses up a portion of several physical things and a portion of several edible things. If this averages out to be one physical thing and one edible thing per person per day, a family of four uses 252 things a week, 56 consumed or used up and 196 that become trash. In a year, the total number of things used by a family of four is then 13,104 of which 2,912 that are consumed or used up and 10,192 that become trash. Therefore, there has to be a lot of spiritual entities in the spirit world capable of serving as spirits for nonliving things as well.

As mentioned earlier, each time a new piece of knowledge is added to the spirit world, a new generation of spiritual entities is created. Each new spiritual entity has one piece of knowledge more than the original one from which it was created, and meanwhile, the original one also continues to exist in the spirit world. Thus, the average spiritual entity becomes increasingly advanced as the number of pieces of knowledge making up the average spiritual entity continues to increase. This means that the new creations made by the spirit world are on average more advanced than creations that preceded it. And as mentioned earlier, this is partly why the process of evolution leads to increasingly advanced living things. This is also part of how and why every new generation of things humans invent and/or design are more advanced than that of the generation before. We can see how this is the case for just about everything in our lives, particularly high-technology things and transportation vehicles.

What is it Like in the Spirit World? Is it Crowded?

There must be what seems like an infinite number of spirits in the spirit world, given that there is what seems like an infinite number of living and nonliving things on Earth alone. Therefore, isn't it extremely crowded in the spirit world, especially considering space is not a part of the spirit world? Also, some of the living things on Earth are kind of yucky such as tapeworms, brown recluse spiders, scorpions, flesh-eating bacteria, etc. Their spirits are there too. Are we sure the spirit world is a nice place to return to?

The answer is this: Something yucky to us humans on Earth might be nice to other living things on Earth (for example, vultures like to eat yucky raw, spoiled meat) or in other universes (are there vultures there too?). Also, spiritual entities that serve as the spirits for yucky things are not yucky themselves. In fact, we share some of the genes with some such yucky things. This means their spirits and ours are sharing parts of themselves with one another. In the spirit world, we are a part of yucky things, and yucky things are a part of us.

Ugh, suddenly I feel kind of sick. Oh, but then again the spiritual entities serving as spirits of yucky things are not yucky themselves. Uh, do you hear me? Are you OK? You look kind of green, like some of those yucky things that are a part of you. Well, maybe you will feel better if we change the subject.

Let's talk about whether or not the spirit world is extremely crowded. For one thing, everything is directly or indirectly a part of everything else in the spirit world instead of being separate as in our physical world. We can imagine this makes things take up less space and thus reduces the congestion. But actually it makes no difference. Being crowded implies a lot of things crammed in a limited space. But the spirit world does not reside in any kind of space or need any kind of space in which to reside. Therefore, the notion of being crowded doesn't apply. When we die and our consciousness is completely tuned to the spirit world, we don't have to feel like we are crammed into a place with no space. If we want to feel like we are in a place where space exists, we can simply tune into the signals of the spiritual entity that enables the kind of space to exist for our universe and we will feel like we are in open space.

This brings up another question. When our consciousness is fully tuned into the spirit world, what kinds of environments are we going to find there, especially when the spirit world doesn't need any kind of space in which to reside? The answer is, just realize that the environments we are used to on Earth exist because some spiritual entities in the spirit world enables them to exist. These same spiritual entities will be in the spirit world and we will be able to tune into their signals at any time in the spirit world. Therefore, if we feel more comfortable thinking we are in an environment similar to Earth's, these spiritual entities can issue signals to us so that our spiritual senses will have us feeling as if we are in that environment.

Spiritual expressions of formerly living things from other planets or universes can do similarly to enable themselves to feel as if they are in an environment like that on their planet or in their universe. They can also choose to enable themselves to feel as if they are in an environment like that on another planet or universe. This is one way to sort of visit other planets and universes. There are also ways to visit other planets and universes by doing so in the form similar, or analogous, to the way ghosts could visit Earth. Aside from all such concerns and questions, just remember as stated at the very beginning of this chapter, the spirit world is an ever-growing, changing, and interesting place to explore, and we will never run out of things to explore since new things are constantly being created.

Every spiritual entity in the spirit world is thought-like. This means the perceptions any spiritual entity provides is by means of thought-like signals. Therefore, in essence thoughts make perceptions in the spirit world. This is the opposite of the way it is in our physical world in that here physical things provoke perceptions that invoke thoughts. Therefore, whether the spirit world can be perceived as crowded or not depends on which spiritual entity's signals we chose to tune into. While reality to us residing in our physical universe involves physical things, reality in the spirit world involves what are essentially thoughts, and thoughts can be about anything.

Similarly, it is possible for us upon returning to the spirit world to choose to tune into a spiritual entity whose signals give a perception of heaven or one whose signals give a perception of hell. As mentioned earlier, anything we can imagine already exists in the spirit world in order for us to imagine it. Therefore, if we ever wonder if heaven or hell exists, in a sense they do. But they are not places that we will be forced into after we die. However, we could take a peek into them if we want to satisfy our curiosity. While alive, we might find that the concept of hell is horrible, but when we are spiritual expressions in the spirit world we might find it's not. Remember, what is a bad place to us in our universe can be neutral or good place in another universe, and it certainly is so in the spirit world since there is no bad place in the spirit world. In addition, we are likely to find a lot of other things in the spirit world more interesting to explore than hell, or even heaven.

Oh, incidentally, if we were to visit hell, remember to grab some hot dogs and marshmallows, and some fireproof insulated air-conditioned hermetically sealed suits with a built-in self-contained breathable air supply. Oh, there are no such suits. Sure there are. If we can imagine them, than they already exist in the spirit world.

Personal Gods in the Spirit World

Can we meet our personal God when we return to the spirit world? Anything we can imagine already exists in the spirit world, and that is why we are able to imagine it in the first place. The process of imagining or envisioning something is to find it in the spirit world by using our spiritual senses. Our personal God is whatever we envision God to be, and we will be able to find and meet our personal God when we return to the spirit world.

If the model is correct about the oneness that pervades the spirit world, then those who pushed for wars and other bad behaviors to handle conflicts, including religious conflicts, might be surprised to find their personal Gods are sharing parts of themselves with various other individuals' personal Gods. And these various individuals are of various different religions. Because of the oneness, essentially all personal Gods are unlikely to favor using wars or other bad behaviors to handle conflicts. In keeping with the nature of the spirit world, the personal Gods are more likely to favor individuals having empathy and compassion for other individuals as a way to handle conflicts. Wars and other bad behaviors exist in the spirit world only as concepts, not as practices, and the spirit world prefers not to have them translated into destructive forms that can be expressed or exist in any universe. The concepts are there mainly to provide balance in the knowledge of the spirit world so that wisdom can be formed. Therefore, the concepts and the wisdom are all available for us to grab. If we are going to grab the concepts, we should also grab the wisdom, but it seems we tend to grab the concepts more than we grab the wisdom.

This goes to show that just about anything has a good side and a bad side. The good side in this case is that the concepts provide balance in the state of knowledge, and the bad side is that the concepts are available for living things such as humans to find and to translate into destructive forms that can be expressed or exist in our physical world. Thus, the spirit world is not a place filled with only good, pleasant, and nice things. It is filled with knowledge in a reasonably balanced state, and therefore also wisdom. Thus, just about anything in the spirit world can be used for good or for bad. This means whenever we look for things in the spirit world, we really ought to also look for the appropriate accompanying wisdom. We often overlook the wisdom, especially when we are overstimulated and take little time to do so in our fast-paced way of life.

Because of the oneness that pervades the spirit world, every spiritual entity is directly or indirectly a part of every other spiritual entity. Therefore, no spiritual entity has an ego, and ego exists in the spirit world only as a concept and not as a practice. Individual survivability is not a concern for any spiritual entity, although survival of the spirit world as a whole is a concern as discussed earlier. Possession and control of anything by any spiritual entity does not happen in the spirit world. After all, everything is already directly or indirectly a part of everything else. Therefore, the enhancement of personal survivability is also only a concept and not a practice in the spirit world. This means if an individual perceives his or her personal God as having an ego and a desire to excessively enhance personal survivability, as some individuals apparently do, that individual will be surprised upon returning to the spirit world. His or her personal God is likely instead to be holding these only as concepts and not as practices, and only for the purpose of forming wisdom. Therefore, personal Gods have wisdom not always grasped by individuals who have them as their personal Gods.

By analogy, because we know a certain concept is available, it does not mean we should practice it. For example, by analogy, the concept of cooking food until it is burned to a crisp kills bad germs, but this does not mean we should cook food until it is burned to a crisp. Thus, if an available concept, such as killing bad germs by burning to a crisp, when practiced would defeat a more relevant concept, such as cooking food so that we can eat it, then we should not practice the first concept.

Once we return to the spirit world, another finding is that each of the various human attributes exists because a spiritual entity enables it to exist. A spiritual entity enables love to exist in a universe, another enables music to exit, another for dance, another for life, another for death, and etc. Therefore, the notion that there are the Gods and Goddesses for things, such as a Goddess of love, Goddess of music and dance, Angel of life, Angel of death, etc. might not be so far-fetched. It simply means some of us chose to give these spiritual entities fanciful names. Often we find certain concepts of ancient folks turn out to have merit. This might be because they get such concepts through intuitive and/or instinctive messages. And according to the model such messages come from the spirit world and thus often carry certain timelessly valid information regarding the spirit world.

Thoughts from the Spirit World

Thought-like signals from the spirit world are what enable things in our universe to be perceived by us as existing and real, and are what enables things in other universes to be perceived as existing and real by living things in those universes, whether the universe is physical or nonphysical and regardless of its dimensionality and other attributes. Thus, the spirit world is essentially thinking our universe and everything in it to be perceived as existing and real by our spiritual senses and therefore our consciousness. But our spiritual senses themselves exist because thought-like signals from various spiritual entities enable them to exist. Therefore, the spirit world is also thinking our spiritual senses to exist. Since we sense things, find things, translate things, etc. with our spiritual senses, in essence various thoughts of the spirit world are interacting with various other thoughts of the spirit world. Each new thing the spirit world's thought-like signals enable to exist is a new invention, and the interactions of spiritual senses with it enable the spirit world to learn more about how well the invention works, what it can do, and how it can be used. Such interactions are experiences and thus generate new pieces of knowledge that get added to the spirit world.

This process is a vicious circle in which knowledge enables more knowledge to be generated, similar to the way the more we learn in the high-technology industry, the more things we can invent. The more things we invent, the more opportunities there are to learn. The experiences we are going through in the high-technology industry, and in every other forefront industry, are generating new pieces of knowledge for the spirit world and also enabling us to gain pieces of knowledge existing in the spirit world. This process that goes on in industry is thus similar to the vicious circles that go on in the spirit world.

Among all living things on Earth, we humans search the most for inventions of the spirit world, and we do the most explorations on what the inventions can do. Therefore, on Earth in our universe we are the main physical means by which the spirit world applies spiritual senses to learn more about its inventions as they exist in forms that can be expressed or exist in our physical universe. Similarly, other universes provide their means by which the spirit world can learn more about its inventions as they exist similarly there. Thus, each universe provides opportunities for the spirit world to learn different things about its inventions. To achieve balance in the knowledge on all sides, it is likely all inventions undergo explorations in multiple universes. Thus, someday when we return to the spirit world, it will be interesting to see how all the three-dimensional versions of things on Earth look like in, for example, a universe with dimensionality different from three and/or with dimensions that are different from the dimensions making up our three dimensions.

Hmmm, can we imagine for example, a car in four dimensions? Would it then need six wheels to provide the same stability? Yeah, and then would it need two steering wheels? Sounds like getting a driver's license can be more complicated. Could be, but sounds like it can be more fun to drive there. And, we can go to more places since there are more dimensions and thus more directions we can go in.

How the thoughts of the spirit world enable a universe and everything in it to exist is, in a limited sense, analogous to how an author composes a story. The author's thoughts enable the storyline, setting, characters, etc. to exist in the world of the story. The story unfolds as various thoughts of the author interact with other ones. Within the world of the story, everything that is a part of it is perceived as existing and real in that world, but in the world of the author they are all in the form of thoughts. A reader mentally goes into the world of the story and thus mentally perceives everything in the story as existing and real in the world of the story. Before the story was composed, the thoughts the author grabbed would have already existed in the spirit world in order for the author to do so. The author guides the reader by means of the story to find the thoughts in the spirit world and to string them together in proper sequence so as to form the story in the reader's mind.

The analogy does not necessarily stop here, although the purposes are not necessarily analogous. The spirit world brings new universes into being to generate new knowledge to help restore balance. An author composes stories mainly to present information, or for entertainment, or for documentation, etc. But sometimes by composing a story, the author gains more insight into how things work in our universe and thus also in the spirit world. When this happens, the purposes become analogous in that in both situations additional knowledge is either generated or gained.

How the author strings various thoughts together can trigger various emotions in the reader. Emotions are among all the smaller spiritual entities that make up the spirit of the reader. Different readers have different sets of smaller spiritual entities making up in their spirits, depending on their backgrounds and experiences, and thus different readers have different emotions and experience different intensities of emotions while reading a story.

Whenever something brings about an emotional connection of any kind, the spirit world is always where the connection is made. That is because it is a spiritual interaction. The same goes for emotional connections brought about in any other universe. Because an emotional connection takes place in the spirit world, it momentarily makes us feel as if we are home again in the spirit world. This sometimes brings tears to our eyes because very likely deep down we want to be back home again in the spirit world. Very likely we are a bit homesick, and spiritually we can sense home is very near but yet very far. What we are likely to be homesick about are the empathy, compassion, gentleness, caring, non-judgmental environment, and love that pervade the spirit world. A story can bring about such emotions because a reader can mentally observe such connections being made in the spirit world and, for a brief moment, the reader is engulfed in all the wonderful attributes of the spirit world. Then, like mist carried on a breeze, it leaves again when the reader takes a break from reading.

This brings up an interesting point. Spiritual entities that are emotions are not things we can find in the spirit world in the same way a spiritual entity that is a thought or object can be found. Spiritual entities that are emotions are already a part of our spirit. Thus, they can only be triggered. A skilled actor or actress can trigger his or her own emotions at will. That may be why some actors and actresses are famous and admired.

Love is an example of an emotion that can only be triggered. Our spirit cannot go forth to find the spirit entity that is love, because the spiritual entities that are the various forms of love are already a part of our spirit. Then we might ask; how we can choose to love or not to love, or to hate or not hate? The answer is; the signals we receive while going through an experience can trigger multiple emotions in our spirit, including various forms of love and hate. While some emotions are more strongly triggered than others, it is up to us to choose which, if any, to tune into. For example, it is common for someone to love and hate his or her spouse, and to choose one or the other in different situations. Or we might choose to have some kind of hate for a person considered to be some kind of enemy because we are expected to, but because that person is also a fellow human we might feel some kind of love for him or her as well. Thus, a soldier who shoots an enemy soldier is changed forever because of the emotions that are triggered and that might never calm down. War is really between the governments involved and not necessarily between the soldiers in the field.

Getting back to how a universe and everything in it can be perceived to exist and be real, another possible way we might choose to look at it is that it is all a daydream by the spirit world. For example, an author doesn't always write down the first version of a story on paper. Often an author first daydreams various versions of the story and reshapes them many times before selecting a version and writing it down. Yet every version is still a story and are still thoughts of the author interacting with other thoughts. Likewise, our universe and everything in it can be perceived to exist and be real because the spirit world is having a daydream. And the fact that we humans made a mess on Earth could simply be the current version being daydreamed by the spirit world. It is thus possible the spirit world will not like this version and could start daydreaming about a new version. Then, poof, we could all vanish and our universe could start all over again.

However, according to the model this is not going to happen. According to the model, the spirit world daydreaming is not how a universe and everything in it are brought into being. Daydreaming is how an author tries out various versions of a story and determines a beginning and ending for each. By contrast, the spirit world designs a universe and everything in it to serve a specific purpose and to generate new pieces of knowledge. The spirit world brings the universe into being, and then essentially lets the universe take its own course over its lifetime.

Whew, wow, now I feel better! I just hate it when I vanish by going poof. Oh, come on, you have never vanished by going poof before. So how would you know you will hate it? Hey, wouldn't that be an experience too and thus generate new pieces of knowledge too. Yeah it would, and the pieces of knowledge are bound to remind the spirit world not to create such a universe again. Oh, and that would help the spirit world form wisdom alright.

Ever wondered whether or not we are awake or dreaming? I used to wonder, especially when I was very young. After all, whether awake or dreaming, whatever we perceive is the result of thoughts of the spirit world interacting with other thoughts of the spirit world. However, as I aged I become more aware of the difference. For one thing, dreams tend to be more surrealistic.

Hey, are you saying reality is also kind of surrealistic? Yes, actual reality is what is in the spirit world. Our translation of what's in the spirit world into forms that can be expressed or exist in our physical world is not really reality. After all, the translation of the same spiritual entities into forms that can be expressed or exist in another universe are bound to be different. Therefore, neither translation is going to be completely what the spiritual entities really are. It is like a given thought translated into a sentence in one language will not come out exactly the same as when translated in another language. Therefore, neither translation is going to be exactly what the thought is. I guess you are right. The lack of actual reality in our perceptions while awake or dreaming might be why a young child sometimes wonders if he or she is awake or dreaming. Also, you and I being two different sides of the same brain and talking with each other like two separate individuals is sort of surreal. Yes, even more so when we are disagreeing about something. I disagree with you about that. I don't remember us disagreeing about anything.

The discussion so far indicates thoughts are powerful. But our ability to find and grab them is malleable and fragile. Thoughts can be accessed only when the spirit of a living thing has the intelligence and consciousness to access them. Intelligence and consciousness exist only when enough knowledge has been generated by experiences to enable them to exist. Experiences involve thoughts. If intelligence and consciousness is low, then the level of thoughts being accessed while going through an experience will be low and relatively few new pieces of knowledge will be generated. The same experience by a living thing with a higher level of intelligence and consciousness will result in higher levels of thoughts being accessed and thus a lot more new pieces of knowledge being generated.

This is similar to two individuals reading the same book. Each individual is different and has a unique level of intelligence and consciousness. Each also comes from a different background. Therefore, each individual is going to get something different out of reading the same book.

Likewise, when we watch a movie a second time we see things we did not see the first time. It is the same movie, but our level of intelligence and consciousness has broadened, increased, etc. regarding the movie after seeing it the first time. Thus, we are more in tune with the movie. Consequently, the level of thoughts that we access are also higher the second time, and we get more out of the movie.

Notice in both examples how the level and kinds of thoughts we access while going through an experience are strongly influenced by our previous experiences. In my mind, this indicates our ability to find and grab thoughts is malleable and fragile.

Because thoughts are powerful but our ability to access them is malleable and fragile, we could conclude our intelligence and consciousness can be powerful but also malleable and fragile. In this regard, our intelligence, consciousness, and the thoughts we access can be manipulated and shaped positively or negatively and thus also be rationalized in positive or negative ways. This is how some individuals go forth to do great things and others do horrible things. And in each case, it can all be rationalized. Therefore, being malleable and fragile has both good and bad sides, just as everything else.

This means we can be manipulated for good and/or for bad without our knowing it. And because the things we do are influenced by the experiences we previous go through, especially the more recent ones, in a sense we are constantly being influenced by something to some degree. Thus, we need to be more aware of this when the influences are done on purpose by those who have something to gain by our being influenced and thus manipulated. Examples include candidates during elections, politicians, and even corporations with their enticing products and money to buy influences.

Sleep, Dreams, Healing, Etc.

Sleeping, dreaming, healing, unconsciousness, near-death experiences, memories, etc. are among experiences that can help us understand the spirit world better. This is explained in this section in terms of the model. Other kinds of experiences such as finding thoughts, receiving intuitive or instinctive messages, having feelings, having emotions, etc. can also help us understand the spirit world better, and these are covered elsewhere in the book.

1.   Why We Sleep and Dream, and Why Dreams are Surrealistic

Our body and health exist because our spirit has the knowledge to enable them to exist, and it is our spirit's thought-like signals that produced our body and health and enable them to be perceived as real in our physical universe. If we get ill or injured, our spirit employs the appropriate portions of its collection of pieces of knowledge to restore our body and health. Since the signals from a certain portion of the pieces of knowledge in our spirit are what produced our body and health in the first place, they can also restore our body and health. However, the effort will not be successful if the illness or injury is severe enough to cause death.

The spirits of some fairly simple living things include the knowledge to regenerate certain lost body parts. This is probably because the amount of knowledge required is relatively small for fairly simple parts of fairly simple living things. We humans are very complex living things so that our spirit does not include the knowledge to regenerate lost body parts. This is probably because a very large amount of knowledge is required, and our evolutionary process has not included the experiences that can generate the required pieces of knowledge.

However, our spirit includes the knowledge to regenerate tissues, bone, skin, blood vessels, nerve fibers, etc. This is probably because a relatively small amount of knowledge is required to regenerate these relatively simple bodily components. Such knowledge plays an important role in restoring our body and health.

As a kid, I wondered how our body knows how to heal, form new tissue, bone, and skin, and to do it in just the right way at just the right locations. However, sometimes the original configuration is not perfectly restored, and a deformation or scar remains. The experience of getting ill or injured generates or gains pieces of knowledge that become a part of our spirit, and they can enable a deformation or a scar to form. In any case, the model explains that the knowledge to restore our body and health is the same knowledge that enables our body and health to exist in the first place. Therefore, the ability to heal our body is a natural part of our spirit. The workings of this knowledge are physically manifested in our genes, DNA, body cells, stem cells, etc., and our spirit issues signals via our brain to these bodily entities on what to do to regenerate tissue, bone, skin, and etc. in just the right way at just the right locations.

We might ask; why we do not always regain our full health after a serious illness or injury when our spirit has the knowledge to have us do so? The answer is; as indicated earlier the experience of getting ill or injured generates or gains pieces of knowledge that become a part of our spirit. This changes our spirit such that our restored body will not perfectly match the original. Often the difference is minor such as a small interior or exterior scar. But if the difference is large, we might not completely regain our original configuration and/or our full health.

The model indicates the restoration process is working constantly whether we are awake or asleep. Our spirit is constantly issuing the signals that enable our body and health to exist, and at the same time these signals are constantly doing restoration as necessary. But it works more effectively when we are asleep so that the time we spend sleeping is the time when serious restoration is performed.

The model explains this in a spiritual manner, why we need sleep, and why the following happens. We feel refreshed after a good night's sleep, we get drowsy when we are tired, and our spirit puts our body in a coma when we get badly injured. A doctor sometimes induces a coma in a patient to promote healing, although the practice is most likely developed from observations rather than from spiritual considerations. It has been shown that if deprived of sleep long enough, our health will decline to the point at which our body is no longer viable.

When we are awake, signals from our physical world are very loud and demanding and produce wear and tear on our body. They will also drown out most, or all, of the restoring spiritual signals from our spirit so that the constant natural restoration process is partially or totally disrupted. Consequently the wear and tear process overtakes the natural restoration process, and wear and tear thus accumulates over the course of a day. We then need to sleep to enable the constant natural restoration process to work undisrupted so that our body and health can be restored.

The spiritual signals are soft and gentle and are easily drowned out by the louder and more demanding physical signals of our physical world. The spirit world purposely made spiritual signals soft and gentle. Otherwise the process of restoring our body and health from illness or injury can be as traumatic as the process of getting ill or injured, and that will be inconsistent with the caring, gentle, empathic, compassionate, and loving nature of the spirit world.

Our consciousness resides in our spirit. Our spirit issues spiritual signals to our brain (the main control center for our body), which translates them into physical (electrical) signals and sends them to our body to instruct it on what to do and how to do it. Our body sends feedback physical signals to our brain, which translates them into spiritual signals and sends them to our spirit. The entire process gives us the impression that our consciousness resides in our brain and body instead of in our spirit.

This is because while our spirit indirectly instructs our body on what to do and how to do it, our brain directly gives those instructions to our body. The mechanism by which our brain does this resides in our physical world, and because our consciousness is tuned mostly to our physical world we get the impression that our consciousness resides in our brain. Therefore, in this sense we can say our spirit sort of extended its consciousness into our physical world and into our brain.

This is somewhat similar to how our spirit extends five of its spiritual senses into our physical world and into our body to give our body its five major senses. However, the difference is our spirit only sort of extends its consciousness into our brain by sending spiritual signals to our brain and relying on our brain to send translated signals to our body. By contrast, our spirit actually extends five spiritual senses into our body by enabling nerve cells and nerve fibers to exist in our body to give our body five major senses that will function in our physical world.

All this is to enable our body to go through experiences in our physical world and generate pieces of knowledge. The portion of our spirit's consciousness not extended into our body stays in the spirit world where it does all its thinking, reasoning, sensing, decision-making, problem-solving, inventing, feeling, emoting, etc. Our spirit is who we are, and we pilot our body from the spirit world so that our body can go through experiences in our physical world.

As mentioned earlier, since childhood I always have the sensation I am piloting my body from somewhere inside my body. The model indicates the sensation is real and that the "somewhere inside my body" is the spirit world, where my spirit resides and from which I am doing the piloting.

Now, what goes on when we are asleep or unconscious? In order for our spirit to adequately restore our body and health, the physical signals must be reduced to the point they do not drown out our spirit's restoring signals. Our spirit makes this happen by putting our body to sleep, and the intent is to take the time daily to focus on restoration.

Our spirit puts us to sleep gradually by gradually reducing its spiritual signals that are specifically for piloting our body. Meanwhile the signals for keeping our bodily systems functioning are not reduced. The reduction makes us feel drowsy, and our drowsiness increases with increased reduction. It is like dimming the light by reducing the electricity via a dimmer. It is only a feeling but a feeling that we perceive as real and should be taken as real even though our spirit remains fully alert and active. Our spirit never gets tired or needs restoration since pieces of knowledge never get tired or need restoration, and our spirit is made of pieces of knowledge.

The acuity of our major senses is reduced but is kept at some minimum level so that we can wake up if something strange happens around us or when the alarm clock goes off. This reduction is so that we will not sense the signals from our physical world as much as we would while awake. Also, we will naturally choose if we can to sleep where physical signals such as light, sound, motion, odor, uncomfortable temperatures, etc. are zero or at least nearly zero.

Our spirit will apply its energy saved by doing all the reductions to enhance its restoration process. This is why serious restoration is done when we sleep. This is even more so when we are unconscious, because while unconscious the signals sensed by our five major senses are either blocked or are ignored by our spirit so as to save even more of its energy for restoration. Thus, our spirit puts our body in a coma if we are very ill or badly injured so as to intensify its restoration process.

The model indicates our brain must remain active while we sleep or are in a coma in order for the restoration process to work. Brain activity measurements indeed indicate our brain remains active while we sleep. I am not aware of any study to confirm that our brain remains active when we are in coma, but the model says it must be. Our spirit issues spiritual signals to our brain on what our body needs to do to restore itself such as what kinds of new bodily cells to form and where to form them. Our brain has to remain active to receive and translate the spiritual signals and send them to our body. Our body sends feedback physical signals to our brain, and again our brain has to remain active to receive and translate those signals and send them to our spirit. This back and forth exchange of signals is a part of the restoration process and our brain must remain active throughout the process.

This exchange of signals induces dreams, and the dreams are usually surrealistic because the signals that restore our body include signals from pieces of knowledge not generated in our universe. The model indicates our evolutionary process spans the lifetimes of many past universes and is continuing over the lifetime of our universe. Therefore, our spirit's restoration signals include those derived from knowledge generated in past universes, and this makes our dream images surrealistic. This is because no past universe is going to be like our universe. Therefore, any dream images induced by signals from knowledge generated in past universes are not going to be like images in our universe or reflect how things work in our universe.

For example, we might dream about our house, but the house in our dream will not look like our house and it will have features not found on houses on Earth. Yet we will know it is supposed to our house. The surrealistic nature of our dreams is more than just visual. It can also be about how things work. For example, we might move around in our house in our dream. As we move from place to place, things in our house can change in shape, size, functionality, etc. Yet it doesn't bother us. Our spirit resides and functions in the spirit world and knows all this strangeness will happen in our dreams. Therefore, it accepts them, never questions them, and is not bothered by them.

From a spiritual standpoint, according to the model, the surrealistic nature of dreams can provide an entertaining glimpse of other universes and therefore also of the spirit world. This means we should be able to learn something about the spirit world through our dreams. But, first we need to remember our dreams, and this is something we commonly do not do well. In my case, I can remember I dreamt, but I might not remember what the dream was about. However, sometimes I do remember dreams. Examples are presented elsewhere in the book.

Hey, right brain. Yes, left brain? Do you remember when our kids were really young, we used to tell them we are from Mars? Oh, yeah, and they would ask how come we don't all have antennae. Hee-hee, and we would say they come out at night when we sleep. Ha-ha, and we found out much later our daughter would wake up in the middle of the night and feel her head for antennae. But you know, right brain, we were correct in concept, because our model says when we sleep, we, the brain, get a lot of restoring signals from our spirit. Yeah, and part of those signals are from knowledge generated by living things in past universes, and some of those living things are likely to have antennae. Therefore, the concept is likely correct. Wow, it is nice to know that now, forty or so years later.

We might ask; what is going on when we are half-asleep or drowsy? The answer is; when our body accumulates wear and tear, the feedback signals it sends to our spirit via our brain will be degraded. Our spirit will correspondingly reduce the signals to our body via our brain that are specifically for piloting our body. The greater is the amount of accumulated wear and tear, the greater will be the degree of reduction, and thus the greater will be the degree of drowsiness. Initially the degree of drowsiness is minor and not felt. Eventually it will reach a level that cannot be ignored, and we will become quite drowsy and even half-asleep. All this is our spirit signaling that the need for restoration has increased to where it has to be done in order for us to continuing functioning.

But our spirit is given free choice, and it sometimes chooses to stay awake even when restoration is really needed. This is an example of the countless tug-of-wars that goes on in the spirit world. The tug-of-war in this case is in our spirit. While our spirit knows restoration is really needed, it also really wants to do some other things as well. And since restoration can be delayed for a while, our spirit would sometimes delay it. Other examples of tug-of-wars in our spirit are the following. We have difficulty making up our mind about something, we will sometimes love and hate our spouse at the same time, and we will sometimes drive over the speed limit even though we know we shouldn't.

Really? Only sometimes? Well, it's your fault. No, it's your fault. You should get the speeding ticket. No, you should. Is this another one of those tug-of-wars? It's in your side of our brain. No, it's in your side.

Notice that when we are drowsy we tend to be wobbly, make mistakes, move imprecisely, etc. Wobbliness happens when our tired body is sending degraded feedback signals to our spirit via our brain. Our tired brain's ability to translate signals to and from our spirit and to and from our body also degrades. Our spirit thus gets doubly degraded signals and consequently its ability to pilot our body degrades, and our body gets wobbly, makes mistakes, and moves imprecisely.

We might ask; what about our brain? It is a part of our body and it gets wear and tear and needs restoration just like the rest of our body. As indicated, our brain has to stay active while we sleep to participate in the restoration process. Our brain indeed stays active while we sleep as mentioned earlier. Apparently our brain is designed to be able to participate in the restoration process even when it has wear and tear. It might be that the effort required of the brain during restoration is not as demanding as the effort required when our spirit is piloting our body.

During restoration, the brain has to do some restoration on itself first in order to participate more effectively in restoring other parts of our body. This may be why we go through the various stages of sleep. The early stages are when our brain is doing some restoration on itself, and the later stages are when it is participating in restoring other parts of our body.

Notice that we go through the various stages of sleep several times each night. It is possible that restoration of our body follows some order of priority. For example, aside from our brain itself, the first priority could be our heart, then our immune system, then our various other vital organs, etc. Each cycle of the various stages of sleep focuses on a specific part of our body. This could explain why we need seven to eight hours of sleep a night, to cover all parts of our body. If we do not get enough sleep, then the parts of our body with lower priority do not get the restoration they need, but the higher-priority parts do. Thus, we would still be able to function the next day, although not necessarily at our best.

If we do not sleep for enough days, it has been shown that our body becomes nonviable. It may be that our brain eventually gets so much wear and tear that it is unable to participate in doing even the initial restoration on itself, let alone to participate in restoring the rest of our body. Therefore, the communication link between our spirit and our body degrades to the point it no longer works, rendering our body nonviable. Under such a condition, it might be possible for medical personal to do resuscitation to keep our body alive and, hopefully, allow our brain to slowly restore itself to the point it can resume participation in restoring the rest of our body.

Likewise, panic attacks can occur when we are persistently highly stressed and restoration is inadequate. Being persistently highly stressed and without adequate rest is like driving our car with the accelerator floored continuously. Something somewhere in the mechanical workings is bound to get overheated, distorted, broken, etc. and the car will not function correctly. Feedback signals from our car are bound to become erratic. In the case of panic attacks, we get erratic sensations such as feeling like we cannot breathe and thus are afraid to fall asleep, looking at something but feeling like we are not really looking at it, being unable to write in a straight line, etc. All such erratic sensations are manifestations of our brain not functioning accurately, our body not providing feedback signals accurately, and thus our body is not piloted accurately. All this can happen when although our body has accumulated lots of wear and tear, the adrenaline produced by our body under high stress is keeping our body going, although erratically.

Great success can be achieved if restoration is more fully allowed. The San Francisco Giants won the World Series in 2010, 2012, and 2014. The managers modified the team's travel schedule to allow the team to get a full night's sleep before a game. Normally, teams immediately hop on an airplane to the next city right after a game and try to sleep on the airplane. After a game, the Giants now stay overnight and then fly out the next day. This enables the team to get a better night's sleep, and it apparently makes a difference in their performance. The players had a higher level of restoration.

The spirit world needs restoration too. Balancing of new issues and re-balancing of existing issues must be done constantly in the spirit world in order to maintain wisdom while new pieces of knowledge are constantly generated. In many ways, wisdom is to the spirit world as health is to our body. While our body's health needs to be restored by counterbalancing the wear and tear, the spirit world's wisdom needs to be restored by balancing new issues and re-balancing existing issues. While our physical body gets wear and tear that disrupts it, the spirit world gets new pieces of knowledge and associated unbalance that disrupt it. The parallel between spirit world wisdom and physical body health just goes to show how the attributes of the spirit world are manifested in various ways and forms in the things the spirit world creates, including universes and living things residing in universes. Issues, tug-of-wars, and wisdom are thus obviously very important for the spirit world and are addressed further later in this chapter.

The discussion indicates, according to the model, the reason we need sleep is because the spirit world purposely made spiritual signals soft and gentle. This is because the spirit world cares about every living and nonliving thing it created, and this is because of the oneness that pervades the spirit world. And oneness pervades the spirit world because the spirit world is made up of pieces of knowledge and the connections of the first kind that connect every piece of knowledge with every other piece of knowledge. Therefore, the need for sleep for certain living things residing in our universe is a manifestation in our universe of a fundamental feature of how things work in the spirit world.

Some living things in some other universes might not need sleep. That might also be the case for living things that do not get wear and tear, say, in nonphysical universes, assuming it is mainly physical things that get wear and tear. After all, a nonphysical place such as the spirit world is unlikely a place where living things need sleep. As indicated in the discussion, our spirit is always active whether our body is awake or asleep. Therefore, our spirit doesn't sleep. And since our spirit is a portion of the spirit world, this suggests that living things in general in the spirit world might not need sleep.

We humans wondered for a long time why we sleep. Researchers suggested perhaps sleep is involved with processing what is learned and storing it into long-term memory in our brain. According to the model, these are by-products of what goes on while we sleep, since they are incidental products and not sleep's main purpose. The model indicates the main purpose of sleep is to restore our body and health. In the process of restoration, the spirit revisits the pieces of knowledge generated or gained while the body is getting wear and tear. The revisiting is to determine what needs to be done to accomplish restoration. For example, restoration for wear and tear from mental labor is different from restoration for wear and tear from physical labor. The process of restoration thus incidentally puts what was learned into perspective and stores it into long-term memory. This is discussed further later in this chapter.

The revisiting of knowledge generated or gained naturally improves our understanding of the knowledge and our ability to recall it. Students who get a good night's sleep before a test, for example, usually do better than students who stayed up all night cramming for the test. The model indicates that getting rested and developing better understanding and recall during sleep are not separate processes. Instead, they are products of the same process, that of restoring our body and health.

Keep in mind, the spirit world cares about every living and nonliving thing it creates. Therefore, maintaining viability is what it wants for the things it creates. The spirit world already has the pieces of knowledge generated or gained; thus, it does not need to revisit them for the purpose of understanding or recalling them better. But it does need to revisit them to determine how to maintain the viability of the living things it creates. Our spirit, on the other hand, is only a portion of the spirit world and thus does not have all the abilities the spirit world has. Therefore, the process of revisiting knowledge does incidentally help our spirit understand and recall the knowledge better.

2. Do All Living Things on Earth Need Sleep?

All animals, birds, and reptiles apparently need sleep. Some animals even need to hibernate. Do fishes, insects, snails, worms, plants, algae, bacteria, etc. need sleep? Some of them apparently do not. Some might not get wear and tear of the kind that needs sleep to restore. Or they might be designed to have a very short life span such that restoration from wear and tear is not part of their lives. Some plants go dormant during winter. Is this sleeping and is restoration taking place? Some plants that go dormant in the winter don't go dormant when grown in places where the climate remains mild the year round, such as in Hawaii. But the plants will thrive there anyway. This seems to indicate going dormant is not the same as going to sleep and that restoration doesn't happen during dormancy. Plants going dormant might be similar to hibernation in certain animals. Dormancy and hibernation are perhaps simply means of surviving winter rather than enhancing restoration. For example, I would imagine animals that hibernate also need daily sleep.

It seems the more intelligent and conscious the living thing, the more likely it needs sleep. Also, it seems the more structurally complex the body of the living thing, the more likely it needs sleep. Both of these factors seem to suggest that for the spirit to pilot the body well, the body needs to be maintained in good shape. Thus, the body needs sleep to enable restoration, or maintenance, to take place, similar to the way we maintain our complex car so that we can pilot it well, but we do not bother to do maintenance work on something like a simple manual can opener. If it gets worn out, we simply replace it. Thus, a complex car needs to "go to sleep" periodically for restoration while a simple manual can opener does not.

But you know, a simple manual can opener can have a lifespan longer than that of a complex car. Yeah, that's true especially if the complex car is not well maintained. Also, having life for a nonliving thing such as a can opener or a complex car is not the same as having life for a living thing. That's right. So what you said in the first sentence can only come from half a brain.

3. Why Our Brain is Active During Sleep, but the Frontal Cortex is Not

Our spirit is always active whether we are awake or asleep. While we are awake our spirit is primarily piloting our body and processing the pieces of knowledge we are generating by our experiences. While we are asleep or unconscious, our spirit is primarily restoring our body and health.

To restore our body from the wear and tear of an experience, our spirit revisits the pieces of knowledge we generated or gained during that experience. This is to determine how the wear and tear came about and to evaluate the nature and extent of the wear and tear. Each individual is different and thus the wear and tear varies in magnitude and in nature from one individual to another even if the individuals go through the same experience. Our spirit then identifies the pieces of knowledge it already has that will counterbalance the pieces of knowledge associated with the wear and tear. Combined signals from both sets of pieces of knowledge are then issued to our brain to tell our brain what it needs to have our body do to restore itself and its health.

Our brain might have our body form new cells to replace those damaged or dead, repair a strained tendon, mend a fracture, restore chemical balance in our bodily systems, fight viruses, etc. Every experience we have gone through while awake is addressed in this manner during restoration, at least to the extent they can be, given the quality and quantity of sleep we get. If we do not get enough sleep, restoration is incomplete. If restoration is incomplete day after day, then in due time, the accumulated wear and tear eventually takes its toll on our well-being.

Having a mechanic restore our car is an apt analogy. The mechanic assesses the nature and extent of the wear and tear, revisits the activities that caused it, and then decides what replacement parts and tools are necessary to restore the car. Every car part the mechanic gets and every tool the mechanic has available are looked at to decide what to use to perform the restoration. All these things will come from the various sources that manufacture such things to enable the car to be built in the first place. Therefore, they can also be effectively used for restoring the car. In other words the knowledge that went into building the car can now also be used to restore the car.

If not periodically restored, the accumulated wear and tear can render the car unreliable, and it would no longer be able to do what it was designed to do. By analogy, the same applies to our body if we do not get enough daily sleep.

As discussed earlier, studies on brain activities during sleep indicate we go through multiple repeated cycles. Each cycle progresses through four stages of non-REM sleep and one stage of REM sleep, with each succeeding cycle shorter than the one before. Recall, this suggests our spirit restores our body in steps, perhaps in order of priority. Because humans perhaps tend to not get adequate sleep, our spirit evolved to the point where it can do the restoration in several smaller steps instead of one big step. This way at least our spirit will restore some parts of our body; i.e., the more important parts first, and the rest within the quantity and quality of sleep we get that is capable of restoring more.

For each cycle, our spirit revisits the pieces of knowledge produced by some past experience or several past experiences, and figures out how to counterbalance those pieces of knowledge. Then our spirit issues restoration spiritual signals to our brain. Our brain then translates the spiritual signals into physical signals to instruct our body on what to do to carry out the restoration. As said before, early cycles may restore the more important parts of our body first such as our brain, heart, and various other vital organs. If the quality and quantity of sleep are low then complete restoration is not achieved, and we wake up still feeling tired.

The ability that the spirits of certain living things have to bring about sleep or unconsciousness is created by the spirit world to enable these spirits to make the time to focus on restoration. Humans and various other creatures on Earth are among those that need regular restoration and therefore regular sleep. We can achieve some degree of restoration without being asleep or unconscious by quieting our mind and body. Quiet enough moments can be achieved by meditating, creating artwork, working on a hobby, doing mindless repetitive work such as hoeing weeds, etc.

When we are not feeling well, we naturally want to be in a quiet peaceful place. We seem to intuitively know being quiet and peaceful will enhance the restoration process. This lends support to what the model is saying about how the restoration process works.

Each individual is different and the situation leading to the need for restoration is different. In some cases, the need to be in quiet peaceful place can last for years and can even be never-ending. This can happen after a prolonged, highly stressful period. An example of this is described in Chapter Four in which an individual has gone without rest for seven months caring 24/7 for his terminally ill spouse and helplessly watching her slowly die. After that he had to undergo surgery and chemotherapy treatment for three and a half years for his own cancer. The individual might look fine and even feel fine for short moments, but in his case the need for quiet, peace, and rest dominated endlessly afterwards. Loved ones are all different. Some, younger and in good health, don't seem able to relate to such a condition, having never experienced it to know what it is like. The individual with the condition furiously wants to stay independent and not depend on others, finds himself unwilling to completely explain what he is going through that might suggest he could be losing his ability to stay independent. And this doesn't help the loved ones to better understand, especially when the individual makes an effort to look fine for the moments he is with loved ones.

Insufficient understanding and therefore insufficient empathy and compassion by loved ones can induce further stress and thus hinder the restoration. This is especially so when they seem to think the individual should be able to do the things they do. Loved ones also sometimes seem to forget that the loss of a spouse means the individual must now do the tasks the spouse used to do in addition to the tasks he has been doing, all of which he must handle with his degraded condition. Consequently, the individual now has significantly less free time than he had before.

Researchers studying sleep processes found that our brain remains active while we sleep. The model explains why this is has to be the case, as discussed earlier. Researcher also found that the frontal cortex of our brain is essentially inactive while we sleep. They interpret this as the frontal cortex shutting down. But the model says otherwise. The model says the frontal cortex must be just as ready for action as the rest of our brain is while we sleep. The frontal cortex is the part of our brain that handles spiritual signals having to do with thinking, reasoning, decision-making, creating, etc. But when we are asleep, we are not thinking, reasoning, making decision or creating. Therefore, our spirit is not issuing much, if any, spiritual signals having to do with those activities to our brain and specifically to its frontal cortex. This is why activity in the frontal cortex significantly decreases while we sleep, not because the frontal cortex shuts down. The frontal cortex is ready to spring into action when it needs to. This is why we can wake up in response to unusual disturbances, to go to the bathroom if necessary, when the alarm clock goes off, or even shortly before it goes off. Also, our body shifts position while we sleep. These are among the things our spirit needs to be ready to consider and decide whether or not our body needs to do while we sleep. Accordingly, the frontal cortex of our brain needs to be ready to receive such spiritual signals while we sleep. Therefore, it has to remain active even if measurements of our brain activities do not indicate it is.

Being unconscious is different from being asleep. Our spirit can render our body unconscious in response to severe illness, injury, or medication so that it can focus more on restoring our body and health than it could by simply putting our body to sleep. When our body is asleep, it can still change position periodically and it can still wake up if something strange is happen around us or when an alarm clock goes off. But when unconscious our body does not move, although it might respond to deep pain with involuntary movements. According to the model, this means our spirit might be choosing not to respond to feedback signals from our body via our brain unless the signals indicate deep pain. By significantly decreasing its response to feedback signals from our brain in this manner, our spirit is able to more fully dedicate its efforts to restoring our body and health as demanded by the severity of the injury or illness.

In the case of medically induced unconsciousness, the medication is a physical thing and works in our physical world physically on our body, and not spiritually on our soul or spirit, although its action has a spiritual counterpart in the spirit world. This suggests the possible effects of the medication include making the sensitivity of nerves having to do with body movements and pain sensations be significantly decreased as are corresponding feedback signals from our body to our spirit via our brain. This then again enables our spirit to dedicate more of its efforts to restoring our body and health. Doctors medically induce unconsciousness for various reasons including surgery and to help promote healing from a severe illness or injury. Doctors obviously know medically induced unconsciousness promotes healing, but I suspect they are not aware of the spiritual mechanism by which it works.

As indicated earlier in this chapter, we have body intelligence in addition to brain intelligence, in which our spirit can communicate directly with our body, without going through our brain, and thus directly have our body move in certain ways under certain circumstances. Therefore, we might ask whether or not our body can still move under body intelligence even when our body is unconscious. The answer is; when our spirit puts our body into unconsciousness, the whole idea is to dedicate more of its effort into restoring our body and health. Therefore, our spirit is not about to put any effort into body movement under body intelligence.

4.   Finding Things in, and Getting Messages from, the Spirit World During Sleep

We sometimes find a solution for something while asleep that we could not find while awake. Anything that can be found while we are awake or asleep already exists in the spirit world in order to be found.

The more our spiritual senses are tuned to the spirit world, the more likely we are to find what we are looking for there. Recall that while we are awake, signals from our physical world are loud and demanding and thus can interfere with or drown out signals from the spirit world. We sometimes hear people say they can't think with all that noise or a student say I need it quiet to study. Consequently, our spiritual senses are less able to sense signals from the spirit world, and we are less able to find something there, especially if it is something difficult to find in the first place.

While we sleep, our consciousness is more tuned to the spirit world. Signals from our physical world are nearly zero or much softer and less demanding. Thus, our spirit and spiritual senses do not need to deal with what is going on in our physical world. Our spiritual senses can then sense signals from the spirit world more clearly, and we will more easily notice things there, even if we are not purposely looking for anything.

Another possible factor is by consciously looking for a specific thing in the spirit world while awake sensitizes our spiritual senses to the signals issued by that specific thing. Thus, we will be more able to notice that thing while asleep. Consequently, it is possible for us to find something in the spirit world while asleep that we were unable to find there while awake.

We sometimes get spiritual messages in our sleep. Spiritual messages of all kinds are constantly being transmitted throughout the spirit world, and at any given moment, some of them might be relevant to us. While awake, we might not notice them because we are more tuned to our physical world. But while asleep we are more tuned to the spirit world, and therefore we have a better chance of noticing spiritual messages that are relevant to us.

Here is a real life example. I dreamed I went shopping and found two empty wallets. I found the first one on the front passenger seat of the car, although I had been the only one in the car lately. I arrived at the store and found the second one on the cashier's counter. Two days later, I went shopping, found what I needed, and was going to pay with my credit card. I discovered my credit card was missing from my wallet, and I did not have enough cash to make the purchase. I essentially had an empty wallet. Then I remembered I had used the credit card to pay for work a contractor did in the house, and forgot to put the card back in my wallet. The spirit world was trying to tell me in my dream that my credit card was not in my wallet. The spirit world must have been issuing the message for days, but I did not notice while awake and only finally noticed in the form of a dream while asleep.

We might ask; if the spirit world bothered to tell me something not extremely important, how come it does not tell people in general about everything else equally or more important? The answer is; the spirit world probably does, but we usually simply do not notice. For some reason, I just happened to notice the messaged described above. There are bound to be relevant spiritual messages I do not notice every day. Certain other living things are better able to notice certain spiritual messages than we humans. This could be a possible reason why some animals and birds seem to know ahead of time that an earthquake, flood, storm, or some other destructive thing is about to happen, and would move or fly to a safer location ahead of time.

I wonder why the spirit world did not simply show in my dream that I forgot to put the credit card back in my wallet instead of showing me two empty wallets. I am going to have to remember to ask that when I return to the spirit world. Now you watch. I am likely to forget. I better bring along a copy of this book to remind me.

What? You can't do that! We can't bring anything physical into the spirit world. OMG, you are correct. So, that's how the spirit world gets itself off the hook. That spirit world is such a wise guy. Yeah, now we know the real reason the spirit world puts so much effort into forming wisdom. It is to have you forget to ask your question.

No, no, the real reason is that dreams are produced partly by signals from knowledge from past universes. The ways things work in other universes are different from the way things work in ours. Therefore, in my dream I might have gotten a glimpse of a past universe in which messages work better indirectly than directly. Even on Earth, sometimes conveying a message indirectly through someone else is better than conveying it directly ourselves. This indicates that when we do inter-universe travel someday we might want to leave open the possibility that communications there might be better if done indirectly than directly.

For example, what if telepathy is their main way of communicating, and spoken messages are purposely short, simple, and often indirect mainly as needed to point to the more detailed and more direct relevant telepathic message? Then we would look completely "not with it" if we give them direct messages. But then we would most likely not be with it anyway since we humans in general cannot communicate telepathically.

Incidentally, while we cannot bring anything physical, such as a copy of this book, into the spirit world, there is a spiritual entity in the spirit world that enables this book to exist. Therefore, we don't have to bring a physical copy anyway. There is a spiritual copy there. Now you watch, I am going to forget to find that spiritual entity and therefore forget to use it to remind me to ask the question.

Huh, what question?

5. What are Near-Death Experiences?

Sometimes an individual upon awakening from momentary death says he or she had a near-death experience. One obvious explanation is that the individual's consciousness was momentarily tuned almost completely to the spirit world. After all, our consciousness would be tuned to the spirit world permanently if we were to die.

Another possible explanation is as follows. Since with near-death experiences our body is brought back to life, our spirit must have performed restoration. The restoration effort required would be so great that it would need the resuscitation effort of individuals in the medical field. Dream images will form during our spirit's restoration effort just as they do during our spirit's usual restoration efforts while we are sleeping.

The amount of knowledge our spirit needs to use for the restoration depends on the severity of our injury or illness. If our injury or illness is so severe that we could die, our spirit would need so much of the knowledge it already has that the total amount used could include knowledge from just about every past universe that was part of our personal evolutionary process. The larger the number of past universes included, the larger the portion of the spirit world is used in the restoration process. Consequently, the dream images would not only be surrealistic but would embody quite of lot of the attributes of the spirit world. Since oneness pervades the spirit world, attributes formed by the oneness would be very apparent in the dream images. Therefore, when we have a near-death experience we are likely to get powerful feelings of love, empathy, compassion, care, gentleness, etc. The total effect would feel so much like we are back in our permanent home that we would want to stay. But the spiritual entity serving as our spirit would say to our spirit that it is not time for our body to die and therefore we (our consciousness) must go back to (get back to being mostly in tune with) our physical world. The spiritual entity serving as our spirit will know at that moment whether the restoration will be successful or not, and, if so, our spirit will get the message informing us to go back to our physical world.

The discussion above generally correlates with typical descriptions given by individuals who had near-death experiences. Deceased loved ones can also be a part of the dream image. This is because our past experiences with those loved ones generate pieces of knowledge that are a part of our spirit. These pieces of knowledge are likely to be included in the restoration process especially if a very large amount of knowledge must be employed to perform the restoration. Therefore, deceased loved ones can appear in our dream.

The environments in the dream images, while surrealistic, still resemble environments on Earth; e.g., they are three-dimensional and can be perceived to reside in a kind of space like the kind in which our universe resides. This is because we are used to only the attributes of our universe. Attributes of other universes are bound to be included in our dream images, but we are able to make sense of only the parts that resemble attributes of our own, and the rest is perceived as background.

When my mom was terminally ill, she once momentarily died and was revived with the help of medical personal. She described her near-death experience as being in a room with a lot of other people. The environment thus resembled environments on Earth. One by one the others were called to leave the room to go to another place. Eventually, she was the only one left in the room and was never called. It must have been her spirit entity essentially saying it is not time for her to leave our physical world, even as she was momentarily with those whose time had come to leave.

We might ask; if it is possible that a near-death experience might not be filled with pleasant feelings? Since anything we can imagine must already exist in the spirit world in order to be imagined, if we can imagine a near-death experience not filled with pleasant feelings, it must be possible. For example, my mom's near-death experience was apparently filled with neutral feelings rather than with obviously pleasant feelings.

We might then ask; what determines the kinds of feelings that come about in a near-death experience? The answer is that it might have something to do with the state of mind of the individual at that moment. For example, when we know we are near death with illness, as my mom was, we are likely to give into death so that a near-death experience could be filled with neither pleasant nor unpleasant feelings.

If our mental state is such that there is no reason to give into death, and there is every reason to continue with life, then I suppose the near-death dream images would be filled with pleasant feelings. Conversely, if we are in a very angry or negative state of mind, then I suppose the dream images might include some unpleasant feelings.

We might then ask; if a very angry or negative individual were to permanently die, would that individual perceive the spirit world as being filled with unpleasant feelings? The answer is no. Permanent death is not the same as momentary death. With permanent death, the individual is completely in the spirit world and thus feels all of it, and all of it is filled with pleasant feelings. With momentary death, the individual is only partially in the spirit world; i.e., only the part touched upon by the personal evolutionary path of the individual. All personal evolutionary paths are bound to include some unpleasant experiences, and the associated pieces of knowledge could potentially form dream images with unpleasant feelings. For example, sometimes even our normal dreams include unpleasant feelings, especially if we go to sleep angry or upset. I imagine a similar thing could happen with near-death dream images.

We might then further ask; if unpleasant feelings have to be a part of the spirit world in order for us to have unpleasant feelings? So, if feelings of love, empathy, compassion, care, and etc. pervade the spirit world, how could unpleasant feelings be in the spirit world? The answer is that while feelings of love, empathy, compassion, care, and etc. pervade the spirit world, they are not the only feelings in the spirit world. When we are in the spirit world, we can seek out unpleasant feelings and choose to feel them if we want to. They are a part of the oneness that pervades the spirit world, and thus they help provide balance in the spirit world such that wisdom can be formed. But also keep in mind that what we perceive as being good or bad in our universe can be perceived as being bad or good in another universe. The way things work in each universe is different, and the way things work in the spirit world is different from the way things work in any universe. This is why universes are created in the first place, to provide opportunities for experiences not possible to have in the spirit world or in past universes.

6. Why Short Term Memory Declines with Age

The concept of short-term and long-term memory storage in the brain is well-known. However, according to the model, the knowledge we generate or gain access to by going through experiences exists forever in the spirit world and is a part of our spirit forever. Therefore, it is possible to recall any piece of knowledge and thus also any experience. Consequently, short-term and long-term storage of knowledge is only a concept and not a reality in the spirit world. The model indicates knowledge and spiritual entities are not stored; they simple exist forever.

We might then ask; why some old individuals have poor short-term memory and better long-term memory? Memories of experiences are spiritual entities made of pieces of knowledge generated or gained from experiences. Being able to find such a spiritual entity is being able to recall an experience. But in order to find such a spiritual entity, it has to be recognizable in the first place. Some old individuals have problems making such spiritual entities recognizable, and this causes their short-term memory to be poor. Old individuals have better long-term memory because the experiences involved were gone through when the individuals were young and better able to make spiritual entities that are memories recognizable and thus easier to recall.

How all this works according to the model is that it is not as much a matter of knowledge storage but more a matter of how well knowledge is assembled when generated or gained. Well-assembled knowledge forms a clear spiritual expression of an experience and is thus easily recognized and recalled. The spiritual expression consists of the signals issued by the spiritual entity that is the memory of the experience. Poorly assembled knowledge forms an unclear spiritual expression of an experience and is difficult to recognize and therefore difficult to recall.

The model indicates four factors of aging that can contribute to poor short-term memory. Any one or combination of these factors can bring about the condition, depending on their severity. If all factors are severe and exist all at once, then for sure poor short-term memory will result.

In general, the brain and everything else about the body functions well when the individual is young. Therefore, the knowledge generated or gained from an experience then is well-assembled. The spiritual expression of the experience is clear and easily recognized. Thus, the experience can be easily recalled, even when the individual becomes old. Therefore, an old individual will have relatively good long-term memory.

The first factor giving rise to poor short-term memory is that, as with all living things in our physical universe, our body declines with age. Joints stiffen, muscles weaken and become less flexible, pain develops here and there especially in joints and tendons, and the overall effect is that our body simply does not move with the ease and precision it once did. It is almost like needing to learn how to walk, run, climb stairs, and so on all over again. I used to fly up and down stairs when young. Now I have to concentrate and do it slowly to be sure my feet land where they need to land. In general, in old age our spirit uses more of its consciousness to safely pilot our body. Consequently, less consciousness goes into going through an intended experience. Therefore, the intended experience is not experienced fully. This means fewer pieces of knowledge are generated or gained, and this, in turn, means a less complete and a less clear spiritual expression of the intended experience is formed. To further complicate things, the pieces of knowledge generated or gained by our experience of needing to be more careful while piloting our body get mixed in with the pieces of knowledge generated or gained by going through the intended experience, and the knowledge from the intended experience gets blended with other pieces of knowledge. This makes the spiritual expression of the intended experience further unclear and unrecognizable. Therefore, the intended experience becomes difficult to recall.

Another factor is that older individuals have a lot more things to do, and to remember to do, in order to keep their health and lives going. Multiple medications need to be taken, each at possibly a different time interval. Moisturizer needs to be applied after each washing to keep thinner and dryer skin from cracking and developing sores. Dental care becomes more complicated as gums recede and dentures and/or implants need special attention. Diet becomes more restricted. Quality of sleep declines, leaving the individual generally tired. Regular doctor visits take up time and energy. Declined eyesight and hearing makes doing certain things more difficult and time consuming. Overall, the net result is less time, energy, and consciousness are available for going through intended experiences, and thus the pieces of knowledge generated or gain from an intended experience are likely to be poorly assembled.

A third factor is that as our body declines, so do our five major senses. Therefore, when we go through an intended experience, we are not experiencing it fully and thus fewer pieces of knowledge are generated or gained. Consequently, the spiritual expression formed of the intended experience is less complete and less accurate, and thus less clear.

A fourth factor is that our brain is the main computer for our body, and if it declines with age it does not function well. It does not properly translate our spirit's piloting signals for our body, nor properly translate our body's feedback signals for our spirit. Consequently, our spirit is not able to pilot our body well, and thus our body can behave as being somewhat not with it. Therefore, the pieces of knowledge generated or gained by going through the experience of dealing with our faulty brain can get mixed in with the pieces of knowledge generated or gained by going through an intended experience. The result is a garbled, confusing, and unclear spiritual expression of the intended experience.

In summary, according to the model, our spirit does not age and therefore does not decline. But when our body ages and declines, we might not be able to form clear spiritual expressions of intended experiences. This then leads to poor short-term memory. A decline in our brain's function leads to a decline in our spirit's channel of communication with our body. This can lead to our body behaving as if somewhat not with it.

Because our spirit does not age or decline, its consciousness remains high as ever. When we return to the spirit world we can choose to have our spiritual expression take the form of whatever age we choose, and we can change our choice at will. Therefore, when we see deceased loved ones there, they may appear as young and sharp as ever, or appear old and be old, or at any age in between. Keep in mind, the way things work in the spirit world is not the same as the way things work in our physical universe. This is one of many reasons why we will never be bored in the spirit world even though our spirit and therefore our consciousness will exist there forever.

Effects of Prayers and Wishes

The effects of prayers and wishes are real, according to the model. The effects take place in the spirit world and manifest in our physical world if the prayers and wishes were made for living or nonliving things in our physical world. It follows then that it is also true that prayers and wishes can be made in one universe for things in another universe and will work the same way. This is because the effects take place in the spirit world and not in a universe.

Hey, then we can pray or wish that someday, when living things from another universe visit Earth, that they are peaceful. Yeah, we can do that, and theoretically it will have an effect. Oh, but what if being peaceful means to them something different from what peaceful means to us? After all, something perceived as good to us can be perceived as bad to living things from another universe. Uh, oh, uh, I think I will wish that you would stop asking questions like that. Oh, gee, I was wishing you had the answer.

Forming a prayer, wish, rejoice, appreciation, regret, and etc. constitutes an experience, which generates new pieces of knowledge that get added to the spirit world. And that has an effect on the spirit world in a variety of ways. In a sense, this supports the notion often expressed as "God listens to our prayers."

Studies have suggested that a sick or injured individual's recovery is improved when a large number of people pray for it. The discussion earlier in this chapter indicates that healing takes place in the spirit world and manifests in our physical world; i.e., spiritual signals that can restore our body and health are first formed in the spirit world before they are issued into our physical world to heal our body and health. Therefore, it follows that prayers can promote healing by generating pieces of knowledge that form thoughts that could do so. After all, the model indicates that all spiritual entities are thought-like, and that includes the one serving as our spirit. Since our spirit enables our body and health to exist on Earth in the first place, it can also enable our body to recover from illness or injury. Therefore, any additional spiritual entities, such as thoughts, formed by prayers to promote our recovery from illness or injury would improve our recovery.

It also helps if the ill or injured individual believes in the powers of prayers and wishes. The individual's spirit then becomes more aware of the thoughts of the prayers and wishes and more likely to grab them and add the healing powers of such thoughts to its own healing powers. It is often said that something can affect us only if we believe that it can. This indicates a positive outlook can help us as well, and that it is better to avoid a negative outlook.

A group at a university got individuals, likely numbering in the thousands, throughout the country to concentrate all at once to make a certain event happen. I believe it was to have a certain random number generator at the university stop behaving randomly in its generation of numbers during the time period when every participant was concentrating. Apparently, the study worked. Theoretically, according to the model, if enough individuals are concentrating on such a thing to happen, then there would be enough spiritual entities formed such that their combined signals could have enough total strength to make it happen. The effect takes place in the spirit world and manifests in our physical world.

We might ask whether or not we could make something bad happen through prayers and wishes too. The answer is that it is unlikely. The spirit world being a place filled with empathy, compassion, care, love, and etc. is naturally inclined to make good things happen. Therefore, prayers and wishes for good things to happen simply add to this inclination, and thus the good things are more likely to happen. Conversely, prayers and wishes for bad things to happen go against the natural flow in the spirit world, and therefore the bad things have a much lower chance of happening. However, I suppose they could slow down the natural flow of things if the individual the prayers are aimed at believes they could. And if the effected individuals deeply believe they could, then it might not be so much the prayers and wishes alone making bad things happen, but something going on with the effected individual that causes it.

We might ask; if we humans can make miracles happen? Theoretically it is possible. The model indicates it would work best if we could first identify something that the spirit world is strongly inclined to do anyway. And then we would need to find some way of generating new pieces of knowledge that would add significantly to that inclination. Such inclinations could vary with time, situation, location, etc. The trick is figuring out how to identify a strong inclination in the spirit world, when and where it is strongest, how to add to that inclination, and then to do it at the right moment.

It might be that Jesus had all these skills and was thus able to make miracles happen. For example, he might have known how to tap into the spirit world's gentle, kind, caring, nonjudgmental, compassionate, empathic, and loving nature, and figured out how to add to it at the right moment. The nature of his miracles did match the nature of the spirit world.

In my Acknowledgements, I mentioned the Reverend Tommy Smith Jr. In one of our discussions, he wondered how we might be able to make miracles happen. He said it would have to be for something good to order to happen. As it turns out, the model now indicates he has the right idea, and that was way before the model existed.

Stepping Out of Your Body and into Another Body

As a kid I always felt like I was inside my body, and therefore it seemed I should be able to step out my body and into another body if there was one available I liked better. Chapter Three described how the feeling of being inside our body and piloting it turns out to be real, based on the model.

So as a kid I would imagine how neat it would be if I could be in a different body each day. I could be a genius scientist one day, an Olympic champion the next day, a Nobel Prize winner another day, a movie star yet another day, etc. Boy, wouldn't that be fun. But now, because I have the model, it has become clear it is not worth the bother.

My spirit is really who I am. For me to step out of my body and into another would mean my spirit would have to disconnect my soul from my body and connect it with another. But my body is what it is because my spirit enables it to exist and be as it is. Therefore, when it disconnects my soul from my body and connects it with another body, that body can exist only if my spirit can enable it to exist. But my spirit can enable it to exist only if that body is exactly the same as my original body. This means as soon that as I step into that body, voila, it would have to immediately change and be exactly like my original body in order to exist. Consequently, I decided it is not worth the bother, and thus I decided not to try doing it. Besides, all the bodies I would like to try stepping into are already occupied anyway.

Immune Systems, Issues, Intelligence, and Knowledge

All spiritual entities that are living entities in the spirit world are usually a part of multiple issues in the spirit world. All issues in the spirit world need constant monitoring and re-balancing. These two attributes form the spiritual basis by which immune systems work on Earth in our physical universe, according to the model. The translation of the spiritual basis and associated living spiritual entities into forms that can exist in a universe takes on a variety of possible forms or configurations. On Earth, some are very much like tug-of-wars. Immune systems in living things are an example. Examples of others are given as the presentation continues. They too are more or less like tug-of-wars, and thus can be perceived as essentially variations of immune systems.

Once a piece of knowledge is generated, it exists in the spirit world forever. The spiritual entities they naturally form also exist in the spirit world forever. The entire collection of pieces of knowledge that exists at any given point in time constitutes the spirit world at that point in time. Therefore, when pieces of knowledge form a spiritual entity, it is appropriate to say the spirit world created it.

Some spiritual entities are living entities and some are nonliving. As indicated earlier, those considered nonliving have at least some form of elemental life. Examples found on Earth are given earlier in the book. The forms of elemental life manifested in a universe depend on the universe. Larger, more complex spiritual entities tend to be living. Smaller, simpler ones tend to be considered nonliving. For example, a spiritual entity capable of serving as the spirit for a living thing is large, complex, and grows by going through experiences on its own while serving or not serving as the spirit for a living thing. On the other hand, for example, a spiritual entity that is a word is small, simple, and does not go through experiences on its own and is thus considered nonliving.

We humans assign a symbol and a sound to a word. These and the meaning of the word do not change with time. We sometimes give multiple meanings to a certain symbol and sound. In such cases, we actually have multiple words and each will be a different spiritual entity that carries a different meaning. An example is the word "head." Its symbol and sound can mean an anatomy of a living or nonliving thing, to go toward somewhere, or a position in an organization.

A nonphysical thing, such as a word, can only be expressed in the case of our physical world while a physical thing can exist in our physical world. Multiple copies of a nonphysical thing, such as a word expressed with the same meaning multiple times, need only one spiritual entity to enable all of the expressions to be made. This is because multiple copies of such a nonphysical thing are all identical. On the other hand, each of multiple copies of a physical thing has its own different and unique spirit in order for each to exist as a separate thing. This is because no two physical things are identical. There are always differences, even if only minute. Therefore, each copy is different and unique, even though all copies might look alike to the naked eye. Exceptions are elemental things such as electrons, protons, neutrons, atoms, etc. as discussed earlier in the book. I.e., all electrons are identical and thus need only one spirit for all copies to exist in our universe.

Every spiritual entity is a portion of the spirit world. Therefore, the spirit world cares about everything it creates. Because living spiritual entities grow and evolve, they have a larger effect on the future of the spirit world than do nonliving spiritual entities. This means that issues involving living spiritual entities become unbalanced faster, need closer monitoring, and require re-balancing more frequently.

Every spiritual entity in the spirit world is neither good nor bad. Issues in the spirit world can manifest in a universe in a variety of forms or configurations depending on the universe, the living or nonliving things translated to be expressed or to exist in that universe, and the situation. In the case of living things and our physical universe, when issues manifest as essentially tug-of-wars as they do on Earth, then some living things involved can be perceived as good and some bad. For example, our immune system helps to prevent certain bad things from happening to our body and/or helps our body recover when certain bad things happen to it. Consequently, we may perceive as bad the living or semi-living things that can enter our body and do bad things, while other living things in our body that help rid them from our body are perceived as good. Such tug-of-wars are going on constantly in our body and the bodies of other living things on Earth.

Some physical tug-of-wars in our physical universe involve living or nonliving things perceived as neither good nor bad. Examples are the livings things in the tug-of-wars going on in the ecological systems on Earth, gravitational and centrifugal forces that keep our solar system together and stable, power generation and cooling systems in cars that keep engine temperature in an optimum range, etc. A more controversial example is powers involved in the arms race remaining reasonably balanced during the former Cold War to prevent the two nations from annihilating each other and possibly starting another world war.

Hey, wait a minute. Those guys with their arms are bad, and we with our arms are good. Yeah, but who are "those guys" and who are "we" would depend on which side we are on. Well, we are on our side and those guys are on their side. Then who would be calling themselves "we?" Well, we would call ourselves "we." But so would those guys. No, they would not be us. I'm getting a headache; where's the aspirin?

In the case of us humans, we use our intelligence and creativity to participate in some natural tug-of-wars. However, because we have only incomplete models to guide us, we can produce some desirable short-term effects, but also some undesirable long-term effects. In such cases, in a sense a tug-of-war between short-term and long-term effects exists within the natural tug-of-wars in which we are participating. This illustrates the complexity of some natural tug-of-wars and of how our models tend not to account for all the factors involved.

For example, we develop antibiotics and/or other medications that can help cure a disease. The bacteria causing the disease can mutate and become resistant to the antibiotics and/or medications. We then develop more powerful antibiotics and/or medications. The disease then mutates again and becomes resistant to these antibiotics and/or medications. We eventually run out of ways to develop more powerful antibiotics and/or medications, and some diseases become resistant to any available medication interventions.

We might ask; what about more drastic interventions such as surgery in the case of some cancers? Can cancers become resistant to surgery? A recent discovery suggests that the answer might be yes, at least in my mind. As discussed before, researchers discovered that some, and possibly all, cancers have cancer stem cells. Therefore, even if the cancer is surgically removed, cancer stem cells can remain undetected and later regenerate the cancer. As with any living thing on Earth, cancer stem cells are bound to have variations. Some variations would be more difficult to detect than others. If we develop a way to detect and remove some of them, undetectable ones could remain and regenerate the cancer. We could improve our detection techniques, but cancer stem cells that are extremely difficult to detect could then be missed, remain and regenerate the cancer. So similar to the way we end up with antibiotic-resistant bacteria, we could end up with surgery-resistant cancer.

We have manmade tug-of-wars on Earth. They exist in businesses, national and global economies, energy production and use, environmental protection, water supply and use, food production, waste management, education, health care, technological advances and applications, sports, arms races, etc. While such tug-of-wars can be perceived as manmade, in a sense they are spirit-world-made. This is because our universe was designed to provide opportunities to have experiences not possible to have in the spirit world or weren't possible in past universes. Anything we can find in the spirit world is meant for us to find and explore. This includes the various issues, or tug-of-wars.

1.   **How the Spirit World Came Into Being**

We might then ask; why the spirit world creates such things as issues, or tug-of-wars, like those mentioned? The model indicates issues are a natural part of the spirit world. In a sense, the spirit world can be perceived as being brought into being by issues, and thus it needs issues to maintain growth and viability. When all issues that exist at any given time are within reasonable balance, the spirit world is able to form wisdom at that point in time.

Wisdom enables the spirit world to maintain its own viability and the viability of everything it creates. New pieces of knowledge are generated constantly, and are thus changing the state of balance in the spirit world constantly. Therefore, the spirit world must keep track of its state of balance and be ready to take action to restore balance when necessary. Among the possible actions is to design and bring into being new universes to help with the process.

We might ask; what is meant by "the spirit world can be perceived as being brought into being by issues?" Answering the question involves several steps. According to the model, before the spirit world existed, there was a particular nothingness. Other kinds of nothingness possibly also existed, but this particular one could produce the particular spirit world that pertains to us.

Notice how we can say nothing is in a box, nothing is said in a document about a particular subject, nothing is done on a project, etc. These are just three examples of the kinds of nothingness we can find in the spirit world and translate to be expressed in our physical world. Since a variety of nothingness can be found in the spirit world, a variety of nothingness likely existed outside the spirit world and before the spirit world came into being. After all, there always is a specific nothing before there is a specific something, especially when it comes to creating and inventing things. Therefore, all kinds of specific nothings exist. For example, there is a specific nothing that pertains to air travel before airplanes were invented. There is a specific nothing that pertains to mass-production manufacturing until the concept was created and put into practice.

The particular nothingness that brought the spirit world into being is the kind that can generate two opposing things that balance each other. Two opposing things can remain in existence as long as they reasonably balance each other such that the particular nothingness remains essentially nothing. This is similar to if we have "x" amount assets and "x" amount of debits, we have essentially nothing, but the assets and debits can still exist and be used.

If it becomes unbalanced, the existence of the particular nothingness becomes violated. Then the opposing things vanish, and only the particular nothingness remains, at least until it generates opposing things once more. This indicates that if the spirit world becomes nonviable and vanishes, the particular nothingness can start another spirit world again, and again, etc.

The way our physical universe can exist is similar to how the spirit world can exist. Our physical universe exists because the spirit world brings both physical matter and physical antimatter into existence. Our universe cannot exist if only matter or only antimatter exists, because the matter or antimatter would simply dissipate without the other to balance it, similar to pulling on a spring at only one end. The force simply dissipates into nothing, and the spring does not stretch and store energy. Thus, analogously, by having matter and antimatter being brought into being together and "pulling" against each other, our physical world is therefore made of various kinds of energies in addition to matter and antimatter. This could also explain why when a piece of antimatter meets a piece of matter, they annihilate each other and energy is released.

Yeah, it is like if the opposing forces pulling on a spring go away, the spring releases its energy and goes "boing." Really? I thought it would go "doing." Well, we both could be "wroing."

Since matter, antimatter, and the energies in our universe all came into being by the same spiritual mechanism, matter and antimatter can be converted into various forms of energy and vice versa. This could explain why researchers are able to produce antimatter in a laboratory by applying certain kinds of energies in certain ways. They have produced electrons with the same mass as ordinary electrons but with a positive charge (positrons), protons with the same mass as ordinary protons but with a negative charge, and neutrons identical to ordinary neutrons but with magnetic properties reversed in sign.

In the case of the particular nothingness that brought the spirit world into being, the opposing things it brings into being are pieces of knowledge which thus form the spirit world. With enough pieces of knowledge brought into being, the spirit world grows to the point it can enable elemental things to exist of the kinds that can make up universes. Eventually, the spirit world grows to the point it can design and bring into being various kinds of universes.

We might ask; how this particular nothingness was able to bring opposing pieces of knowledge into being? The answer is; this particular nothingness is the kind that can generate pieces of knowledge by going through experiences. So how can this nothingness go through an experience, and what kind of experience would that be? The model indicates there must be intelligence before there is anything else, including knowledge. After all, something has to have the intelligence to figure out how to bring something into existence, i.e., to create something or invent something.

Therefore, the model indicates this particular nothingness must be made of intelligence of the kind that can figure out how to bring pieces of knowledge into being. It figures out how to have experiences, although not necessarily the kinds of experiences we humans are used to. And its experiences are such that they always generate opposing pieces of knowledge, which is a difference between its kinds of experiences and our kinds of experiences. Ours generate pieces of knowledge but not necessarily opposing pieces.

Recall that in Chapter Three we said the following regarding what might have been there before the spirit world came into being.

> **A)** "What if there is another level of spiritual existence and it consists of something more profound than pieces of knowledge? Since we can't conceive of such a thing, we might perceive it as being nothing, when in fact it is actually something."

This "actually something" is this particular nothingness and it is made of intelligence. Intelligence can be perceived as being "more profound" than knowledge, as explained as the presentation continues.

So, when this particular nothingness generates pieces of knowledge, the pieces of knowledge form the spirit world. The intelligence of the spirit world is the intelligence of this particular nothingness. More accurately, the spirit world is made up of all the existing pieces of knowledge plus this particular nothingness.

Now, if we think a piece of knowledge is intangible, intelligence is even more intangible. For example, when we learn something, we can approximately quantify how much knowledge we gained. But how can we approximately quantify our intelligence? We can take an IQ test, but the meaningfulness of that test is increasingly questioned because the score can be affected by a number of factors. And we are now increasingly recognizing there are other kinds of intelligence not measured by IQ tests that are also important or even more important. For example, there is what I would refer to as "streets smarts." Individuals with lots of "streets smarts" but earn average grades in college can do better in life than individuals who earn the highest grades.

In the early stages of the spirit world's formation, the pieces of knowledge are generated only by this particular nothingness, and thus they are all opposing pieces. Being opposing pieces, they form issues. More complex issues are formed later that have multiple opposing sides. One way this happens is when newly generated pieces of knowledge pertain to an existing issue and thus form new opposing sides for that issue in addition to its existing opposing sides. Another way is that some issues simply come with multiple opposing sides. The net result is that we can say:

B) "The spirit world could be perceived as being brought into being by issues."

Every piece of knowledge generated either by this particular nothingness going through an experience, or by living or nonliving things going through an experience, exists because of the intelligence that is involved in figuring out how to go through the experience in either case. Therefore, a specific bit of the intelligence of this particular nothingness is enabling a specific piece of knowledge to exist. Among the things this bit of intelligence does is to enable a piece of knowledge to figure out how to form a connection of the first kind with every other existing piece of knowledge. This enables pieces of knowledge to form spiritual entities. The more pieces of knowledge constituting a spiritual entity, the larger would be the spiritual entity. Because each piece of knowledge comes with its specific bit of intelligence, the larger the spiritual entity the higher its level of intelligence.

This means that among all the living things on Earth, we humans, being the most intelligent living things among them, must have the largest spirits among them. This also means all spiritual entities, no matter how small, have some amount of intelligence. This is why we are able to explain in Chapter Three how elemental things in our universe have elemental intelligence.

We might ask; with no limit to the number of pieces of knowledge that can be generated, would some eventually end up the same bit of intelligence even if each piece of knowledge is different and unique? The answer is; no. Intelligence has no limit. This is why the number of pieces of knowledge that can be generated has no limit. This is also why, for example, the number of things we humans can invent on Earth has no limit. Besides, if two pieces of knowledge happen to have the same bit of intelligence, the pieces will be identical, since it is the bit of intelligence that enables a piece of knowledge to exist. The two identical pieces of knowledge would merge and only one would remain.

Eventually the spirit world grows to the point some of the spiritual entities are large enough to become living entities and thus are able to go through experiences on their own. The knowledge they generate does not necessarily come in opposing pieces, as explained as the presentation continues. Up to that point, the spirit world would not have been concerned about its state of knowledge going out of balance, but now it has to be concerned. The spirit world must now keep track of its state of balance and figure out how to restore balance when necessary. One way is to design and bring into being universes to help with the process.

We can perceive the two, and possibly more, stages of growth of the spirit world as being similar to the way we humans grow from childhood to adulthood. In childhood we are generally not concerned about staying viable on our own, but in adulthood we are. Because the spirit world's growth encompasses such stages, in general the living and nonliving things it creates also do. This is the case in our physical universe on Earth. It would be interesting to see if this is also the case in other universes.

Oh, you mean, would there be baby, kid, adult, and geriatric aliens in other universes? Yes, most likely, and there would also be brat aliens.

Regarding the particular nothingness under discussion, one of the differences between intelligence and knowledge is that intelligence, for example, figures out how to do things while knowledge knows how to do things. The knowledge required to do things has to be generated by intelligence going through the experiences of figuring out how to do them. The experience generates pieces of knowledge and the experience is such that the knowledge comes in opposing pieces. The opposing pieces would be the "knowledge to know how to do things" vs. the "knowledge to know how not to do things." This is similar to the way we have lots of knowledge on how to drive safely, and we also have lots of knowledge on how not to drive safely, including driving too fast, driving under the influence, texting while driving, etc.

The spirit world, with its unlimited intelligence, can automatically generate such opposing knowledge as it generates the knowledge on how to do things. Ideally, we humans can also generate opposing pieces of knowledge as we go through experiences. However, we cannot do a complete job of it because our intelligence is limited, whereas the spirit world with its unlimited intelligence can. Other living things on Earth have lower levels of intelligence; therefore they can do an even less complete job of it. For example, a bird knows how to build a nest, but it does not know how not to build a nest. This explains why birds cannot refuse to build nests and why the nests they build cannot be different from the specific kind each specific species builds. Also, various human individuals have various kinds and levels of intelligence; therefore, various individuals produce various degrees of completeness. The same goes for the various spiritual entities in the spirit world. All this explains why the knowledge in the spirit world can go out of balance.

It follows then that intelligence is more profound than knowledge in that knowledge needs intelligence to bring it into being. This is the case whether knowledge is generated by the spirit world going through an experience or by a living or nonliving thing residing in a universe going through an experience.

Intelligence is the ability to think, reason, figure out things, realize the need for wisdom, etc. But intelligence needs something that knows how to carry out what it figures out. When the spirit world goes through the experience of figuring out how to do something, the experience generates pieces of knowledge that know how to figure out how to do something, but it does not generate the knowledge on how to do it. It needs a living thing with the ability to do it to go through the experience of doing it in order to generate those pieces of knowledge. This is one of the reasons why the spirit world needs to design universes and bring them into being, to have living things with the ability necessary to reside in a universe that provides opportunities for them to go through the necessary kinds of experiences.

This is analogous to the way we learn to ski. We can read up on how to ski, and the experience of reading enables us to gain the knowledge on how to figure out how to ski. So we put on a pair of skis and get on the slope, and, OMG, we find that gaining the knowledge to figure out how to ski is not enough. We have to go through the experience of learning to ski to gain the knowledge necessary to know how to ski. The same goes for learning a new language, or how to ride a bicycle, how to drive a car, how to make a pie, etc.

When balance needs to be restored in the spirit world, the spirit world can figure out what to do to restore balance. The spirit world can then design and bring into being a universe that can in general generate at least most, but not all, the pieces of knowledge that help restore balance. We might ask; why "most, but not all?" The answer is; while the spirit world can figure out what to do, because it has all the intelligence of the particular nothingness that brought it into being, what it has figured out to do generally cannot be done perfectly. This is because the knowledge necessary to carry out what it has figured out to do is always incomplete. Keep in mind that the spirit world can never possess every possible piece of knowledge that can be generated, because there is no limit to the pieces of knowledge that can be generated. Therefore, the spirit world is always imperfect in terms of knowing how to do things, even though with the intelligence of the particular nothingness it could figure out how to do things.

Using the ski analogy again, this is similar to what happens after we learn how to ski. There is still more to learn to get better at it. And we never get to the point we ski perfectly, because not all the knowledge to enable us to know how to do so has been generated. Ski designs are varied and keep changing, which means even skis are never perfect.

A larger spiritual entity encompasses more pieces of knowledge and therefore has a higher level of intelligence. This enables it to be able to figure out more things and thus go through more experiences of figuring things out and of doing things. This enables the spiritual entity to generate more pieces of knowledge faster. This means a larger spiritual entity is able to become more advanced and more intelligent faster. We humans, being the most intelligent living things on Earth, can thus become more advanced and more intelligent fastest and could explain how we humans became so advanced and intelligent compared with other living things on Earth.

Accordingly, the following conditions are possible:

A) A highly intelligent individual who did not attend college can still be more intelligent than an average individual that attended college and who might be more knowledgeable.

B) Sometimes it is difficult to tell the difference between a more intelligent individual and a more knowledgeable individual because both can come across similarly. The difference can show up when they try to figure out something. The more intelligent individual will likely be more creative and do it better.

C) Gaining more knowledge can also increasingly activate intelligence, which then strengthens the ability to gain more knowledge.

D) It's possible for individuals to possess different kinds of intelligence and different kinds of knowledge and to prefer to do different kinds of things. Preferences also change with situation and age. Thus, it is good to form wisdom first so as to be able to extrapolate into possible futures and to then choose wisely which future to strive for.

A conclusion I reached from this is that one of the most valuable things we can encourage individuals to do is to exercise their creativity. This is because, according to the model, creativity is directly associated with intelligence. I have heard others emphasize the importance of promoting creativity. They arrived at the same conclusion from a different direction, and this helps to confirm the validity of my conclusion.

Gee, whiz, why didn't we explain all this back in Chapter Three? Hey, formulating this model is tricky, as you know. After all, you are a part of it. We would have liked to blast out the concepts of the model all at once in the beginning, but that would be overwhelming and confusing to the reader. Why do you suppose we went through more than ten drafts trying to form a mental path on which the reader could travel to gradually gain a clearer picture of how the model is put together and what it can do? Yeah, it took more than ten drafts and like 27 years to get to here. Well, you and I are each only half a brain, so what do you expect? Oh, is that why we keep reminding the reader that our model works for us but not necessarily for anyone else, and that each individual needs to find his or her own person spiritual model? Yep. But hopefully we can also encourage others to try unconventional thinking when looking for their personal spiritual models if conventional thinking has not worked for them.

2. Implications of How the Spirit World Came Into Being

Regarding universes, while the knowledge that makes up the spirit world must stay reasonably balanced, the opposing substances making up a universe need not be in equal amounts. What this means for our physical universe is that opposing physical substances making up our universe need not be in equal amounts as long as the knowledge in the spirit world stays reasonably balanced.

This also means individual issues making up an overall issue need not be balanced immediately as long as the overall issue stays reasonably balanced. However, as long as the individual issues remain unbalanced, wisdom cannot be formed to resolve the overall issue.

For example, during the Cold War, the arms of the two nations involved were not exactly equal in number or destructive power, but yet neither nation used them to attack the other. This is because the overall knowledge encompassing the totality of all factors of the Cold War was kept reasonably balanced and that prevented attacks from happening. The amount of arms on both sides was just one factor. Others included each nation's economy, political climate, and diplomatic activities, as well as developments in other nations, the global economy, and in technological advancements such as in space exploration, etc. While the overall knowledge stayed reasonably balanced, the knowledge associated with each of the factors eventually achieved reasonable balance individually, thus allowing wisdom to be formed, and the Cold War to come to a peaceful end.

Regarding opposing physical substances making up our universe not needing to be of equal amounts, it is likely that the amount of antimatter in our physical universe is far less than the amount of matter in our universe. The knowledge that enables our physical universe to exist has to do with other factors besides the amounts of matter and antimatter. And it is the overall knowledge in the spirit world that needs to be kept reasonably balanced and not the amounts of matter and antimatter.

How this can work is, for example, suppose some of the galaxies in our universe are made of antimatter. And living things residing there are generating a lot more pieces of knowledge of the kind the spirit world needs than are living things residing in galaxies made of matter. In that case, our physical universe can get by with a lot lesser amount of antimatter than matter.

Since the amount of antimatter is actually less than the amount of matter, this could mean that while we humans residing in our "matter" part of our physical world are making a mess on Earth, highly intelligent living things residing in their "antimatter" part of our physical world are not making a mess. This seems likely since having no mess is the opposite of having a mess. And, according to the model, the way we were intended to help our universe fulfill its purpose is to do it without making a mess. If the antimatter living things are doing just that, it would mean they are way ahead of us in helping our universe fulfill its purpose. Therefore, our universe can indeed get by with a lesser amount of antimatter than the amount of matter. And, conversely, since the amount of antimatter is less than the amount of matter, this means the antimatter living things must be way ahead of us also in other ways besides helping our universe fulfill its purpose. For example, they can be much more spiritually and physically advanced than we are and are thus wiser than we are.

They could be the ones in the UFOs that visit Earth, and are wise enough to only observe us but not directly interact with us knowing how behind we are compared with them. Also they would know that if they physically interact with us, they and some of us would go "poof" and a lot of destruction would occur. Now if we were to visit their part of our universe we are likely to try grabbing a whole lot of antimatter, and then bring it back here to interact with matter to produce a lot of energy. And then, given the amount of wisdom we have exhibited throughout our history, we would include the use of this new source of energy to invent new kinds of weapons so that we could make the mess we made on Earth worse. The antimatter living things are likely to know that too, since that is what we seem to always do with the sources of energies we have. Therefore, they have yet another reason to not directly physically interact with us in case they could be captured, their spaceship used for experiments, and their advanced intelligence and technologies tapped for finding ways to get antimatter from their galaxy to develop a new source of energy on Earth.

OMG! You think we humans would really do that to those antimatter living things? Well, since we humans have proven capable of doing unthinkable things to other humans, some might. Also, some of us would do just about anything to gain access to sources of energy. Yeah, but this source works by making antimatter and matter go "poof." So wouldn't we be consuming our universe? Yes, we would. But humans in general tend not to think long-term long-range. Look how we are destroying our rainforests, polluting Earth's atmosphere, emptying our underground aquifers, producing super-bugs by using antibiotics too much and needlessly, ruining agricultural land by over using fertilizers, etc. Yeah, and we hunted and/or consumed some species of living things to extinction or near extinction; for example, the passenger pigeon. Therefore, by allowing ourselves to make antimatter and matter go "poof" as an energy source, eventually we might not need to be concerned about space exploration because there would be nothing left to explore. Oh, but that is such a long ways off. See! That is the kind of thinking that keeps us from thinking long-term long-range.

Incidentally, researchers expected matter and antimatter to exist in equal amounts based on relativistic quantum theory and therefore many decades ago they expected antimatter galaxies to exist in our physical universe. However, attempts to find antimatter galaxies have so far turned up no clear evidence they exist. But, according to the model presented in this book, the fact that no such evidence has been found could mean the amount of antimatter in our universe is simply much less than the amount of matter such that antimatter galaxies are few and thus difficult to find. How this possibility could come about is inferred above and is further discussed as follows.

Our physical universe might have begun with equal amounts of matter and antimatter, with or without the Big Bang. But if our universe is continuously being brought into being, as the model indicates as a possibility with or without an initial Big Bang, then as time goes by, the rate of antimatter being brought into being could become much lower than the rate of matter being brought into being. This could be a natural result of living things residing in antimatter galaxies generating much more pieces of knowledge the spirit world needs than are living things residing in matter galaxies. Over time, the amount of antimatter could become much less than the amount of matter. If what is say here is correct, then the fact that the amount of antimatter is much less than the amount of matter would support the notion that our universe continues to be brought into being rather than all of it having been brought into being at once.

Since matter can be converted to energy, then antimatter can also be converted to energy, and we might call it anti-energy to distinguish it from the other energy. This means there must exist anti-energy. We are familiar with the kinds of energies associated with matter, but we have not identified anything we might call anti-energy. This means if we were to run across anti-energy, we might not know what it is. Therefore, it could be that the dark energy in outer space is what antimatter would be when converted into some form of energy. If the combination of dark matter and dark energy is what our kind of space is made of, as speculated earlier in the book, then our universe's kind of outer space is actually a physical thing.

This could then help explain how we can have less antimatter than matter in our universe and yet the knowledge in the spirit world remains reasonably balanced. The knowledge that enables all the antimatter to exist plus the knowledge that enables all the dark energy to exist might reasonably balance the knowledge that enables all the matter to exist plus the knowledge that enables all the familiar kinds of energy to exist. The knowledge enabling dark matter and dark energy to exist in outer space might by itself already be balanced in order for outer space to be able to house both matter and antimatter without annihilating either matter or antimatter.

We might ask; how could those "antimatter kind of" living things be doing better than we "matter kind of" living things are doing, if they are? The answer is; they might be carrying out their lives based largely on empathy and compassion, whereas we are carrying out our lives based largely on ego and enhancement of survivability. After all, "empathy and compassion" and "ego and enhancement of survivability" are sort of opposing. We are carrying out our lives based on empathy and compassion as well, but to a lesser extent.

According to the model, both the "antimatter kind of" living things and we are supposed to carry out our lives based on empathy and compassion. But since they and we are given the freedom to choose, they are probably not doing it completely, and we certainly are not. However, it might be that they simply have a greater tendency to do it than we do, because they are made of antimatter and we of matter.

We might then ask; is it possible that those "antimatter kind of" living things include what we might envision as angels. Well, like we say, whatever we can imagine has to already exist in the spirit world in order for us to imagine it. It is possible that some things we can imagine already exist somewhere in our physical world as well, such as in antimatter galaxies. Based on the discussion so far, living things in such galaxies could come across as being angel-like to us.

We might then also ask whether or not they can communicate telepathically and do space travel, etc. in the manner we might imagine angels do. That is interesting to speculate about, because chances are they would not make a mess on their antimatter planet like the mess we made on Earth, and thus they would not have wasted time and personal and physical energy making, and being mired in, a mess as we have done. Consequently, they could evolve faster and become advanced enough to be able to do things such as telepathic communication and space travel before we could. This could mean, as suggested earlier, UFOs might originate from antimatter galaxies. And if they carry out their lives based on empathy and compassion, they would be friendly visitors instead of hostile invaders.

Explained earlier in this section was how highly advanced living things become more advanced faster. Therefore, if living things made of antimatter are not mired in a mess like we are, they could very well become significantly more advanced than we are.

The model indicates space travel by them or by us would likely be done virtually. If they visit a matter plant, virtual space travel would work better. Otherwise, if they were to do actual space travel and enter the atmosphere of, or land on, a matter planet such as Earth, they and a part of the matter planet would be annihilated and cause a release of energy that could cause further destruction on the matter planet. Virtual space travel could also explain something we have already touched on: why UFOs have been described as capable of instantaneous velocity changes and instantaneous ninety-degree turns as if they have zero mass. This is because virtual travel does not involve the transport of mass.

Immune-System Discussion Continues

Just about every living thing on Earth needs to eat other living things in order to survive. But the spirit world cares about every living thing it creates. This brings about various tug-of-wars, and some could be perceived as variations of immune systems. Certain tug-of-wars can be within other tug-of-wars, just as in the spirit world smaller spiritual entities can be within larger spiritual entities such that certain issues can be within other issues.

An example of a tug-of-war that could be perceived as a variation of immune systems is the following. Some lizards evolved to excrete poison through their skin to discourage other creatures from eating them. Creatures that prey on them evolved to become resistant to the poison so they could eat the lizards. The lizards then evolved to become more poisonous, and the creatures that prey on them evolved to have greater resistance. Thus, a tug-of-war ensues that could be perceived as being a variation of immune systems.

Other examples are the following. Some plants evolved to produce chemicals to prevent attacks by insects. Others quickly alter their biological make up to make them selves less tasty after insects attacked them. Skunks developed a spray to ward off attackers, and porcupines, sharp bristles. Hawks fly faster than pigeons and can catch and eat them. But pigeons last longer in flight than hawks, and can escape.

The fact that certain issues can be within other issues can also be seen on Earth. In the case of the lizards and the creatures that prey on them, for example, a tug-of-war is going on. Meanwhile, an immune system, or tug-of-war, exists in each of their bodies enabling each lizard and each creature to be viable and participate in the tug-of-war going on between them.

All such physical issues or tug-of-wars are manifestations of spiritual issues or tug-of-wars in the spirit world. This suggests that issues or tug-of-wars in the spirit world can also manifest as issues or tug-of wars in other universes. But the forms they take are bound to be different in different universes. Someday when we do inter-universe travel it would be interesting to see if issues or tug-of-wars exist in other universes and what forms they take.

The following are examples of some interesting features of issues or tug-of-wars:

Example (1): Viruses developed tricky ways to prevent being attacked by immune systems of certain creatures. For example, some viruses can trick healthy living cells into hiding them and keeping them viable until they have a chance infect other creatures.

Example (2): Some bacteria similarly developed a way to invade certain creatures without making them ill so that those creatures can be carriers and spread the bacteria over a wider region, infecting other creatures.

Example (3): Some individuals are naturally immune to the HIV virus. Unlike most other individuals, their body cells lack the kind of receptor sites that the HIV viruses attach themselves. In fact, this may be an example of the phenomenon of cross-learning, discussed in Chapter Three, playing a role in the continued updating of immune systems. Individuals born after the AIDS disease first emerged exhibit immunity to the disease even though they, their parents, and their grandparents were never exposed to the disease. In the spirit world, all spiritual entities share parts of themselves directly or indirectly with every other spiritual entity. Thus the individuals may have gotten their immunity from there. This may be the mechanism by which cross-leaning takes place and by which immunity might have developed in those individuals.

Example (4): In a sort of perverse way, when financial institutions are perceived as too big to fail, this gives them some immunity to being broken into smaller entities. Otherwise they would have been broken into smaller entities by now. We might ask; whether such financial institutions are like living things? The answer is; yes, and they need "food" to survive. We might want to be more aware of how they get their food, what they eat, and how they got so big.

Example (5): It takes a lot of pieces of knowledge to form a spiritual entity that is a living thing in the spirit world. We can see evidence of this in the minute detail of just about any living thing on Earth. Even the tiny pollens of plants are intricately detailed when seen under a high-powered microscope. The structures of our eyes, inner ear, brain, etc. are almost unimaginably complex microscopically. In order for such complexity to be formed within nine months of gestation, something must have a lot of knowledge about how to do it so quickly. That something is our spirit. It follows then that it takes a lot of knowledge to form our immune system for the same reason. It takes a lot of experiences to generate that knowledge. This knowledge needs constant updating because everything changes with time in our physical world. The rate of change might be too slow for us to notice from day to day, but every change is important to the spirit world in its continuing effort to keep our immune system up to date. Therefore, while experiences such as brushing our teeth daily seem the same each day to us, each is a new and different experience to the spirit world, and each generates new pieces of knowledge for it.

The model in this book could enable us to be more aware of the workings in the spirit world and could thus point to things we might use our spiritual senses to look for in the spirit world. This is similar to the way various scientific theories point to certain things that ought to exist and, sure enough, researchers eventually find them in our physical world. For example, relativistic quantum theory predicted the existence of antimatter and, sure enough, antimatter was found to exist and could be produced in a laboratory. If we can use physical theories to help us do such things in our physical world, we should be able use spiritual theories to help us do similar things in the spirit world. And if we succeed, it could help us formulate models that include spiritual factors in addition to physical factors to make our models more complete, more accurate, and more effective in guiding us.

Incidentally, if we were to visualize all existing pieces of knowledge and the connections of the first kind connecting each piece with every other piece as if they reside in three-dimensional space, we would perceive a structure that resembles the microscopic structure in the interior of our brain. This similarity might have something do with how our brain is able to be the main communications link between our spirit and our body. If spiritual signals are issued from such a spiritual structural configuration, then the receiver might sense the signals best if it has a physical structural configuration that more or less matches that of the sender. Remember how the old TV roof antennas needed to have a certain configuration in order to receive TV signals well?

The rest of our body, aside from our brain, directly receives spiritual signals from our spirit to thus give our body its body intelligence. But since the microscopic structure in the rest of our body is not like that inside our brain, our body cannot serve as a major communication link with our spirit, but it can serve as the minor link to give our body its body intelligence.

Creation of New Features for Living Things and the "Use It or Lose It" Phenomenon

The spiritual entity serving as the spirit for a living thing grows in size and complexity as the living thing goes through experiences and generates new pieces of knowledge that get added to the spirit and the spiritual entity. New smaller spiritual entities form within the spiritual entity. Some of these can be new features that can be used for designing future living things. This is one way the spirit world can create new features that get added to the collection of features it maintains for designing living things. Also, one or more of the new features might emerge in future members of the species that helped form the features because the experiences that formed the features indicate the features could contribute to the viability of the species.

The spirit world might bring a new feature into being on members of an existing species to purposely initiate a new branch on the evolutionary tree as part of its plan for the future. For example, feathers emerged on some species of dinosaurs for reasons that are not obvious, and these dinosaurs eventually evolved into birds. The spirit world apparently needed birds to be a part of Earth's future at that time.

Other evidence exists that indicate features emerging on living things before they were necessary for survival, including the species of fish mentioned before that developed fins that enabled it to crawl onto land before it needed to. When it eventually faced a threat that forced its members to crawl onto land for safety, the fish was ready. The spirit world must have had a plan for the future that included that species of fish as living things on land.

A feature is prominent on a living thing as long as that feature is regularly used. Regular use makes the signals that enable the feature to exist remain strong, and thus the feature stays prominent. Conversely, disuse causes the signals to become weak and the feature to diminish in size and can eventually physically vanish on the living thing, although the spiritual entity that enabled the feature to have existed will remain as part of the spirit of the living thing.

All this works because the transmissibility of connections of the first and second kinds for a given signal increases for that signal with high frequency of transmission of that signal. Conversely, the transmissibility decreases for low frequency of transmission. This is how the "use it or lose it" phenomenon works in the spirit world. It is designed by the spirit world to help enhance the viability of a species by making more prominent a feature that contributes to the viability and helps eliminate a feature that has become an unnecessary burden.

An example of a diminished feature can be seen in some species of whales that have rudimentary legs, indicating the species was once land-dwelling. Another example can be seen in a human embryo because it would initially show remnants of gills. These eventually disappear as the embryo continues to develop, but they indicate humans were once sea-dwelling creatures.

Reincarnation

Spirits of living things on Earth come in a variety of constructions as described in Chapter Five. Some reincarnate and some do not. For those that do not, it is the spiritual entity serving as the spirit that reincarnates.

According to the model, a human spirit goes through just one lifetime and then it and the soul form the spiritual expression of the individual that exists in the spirit world thereafter forever. Therefore, a human spirit does not reincarnate. The spiritual entity that served as the spirit, however, can reincarnate in that it can serve as a spirit again but for a new human individual. A brand new spirit is then formed for the new individual.

The spirit world designed the process so that the new human spirit does not know what any preceding human spirits have been through. This is so that the new individual can generate new pieces of knowledge that are relevant to the present instead of being influenced by what was relevant in the past. This enables the spirit world to stay better up to date with the present and thus can form wisdom more relevant to the present and can also make more credible extrapolations into possible futures. The spirit world does this mainly for human spirits because we humans are the living things on Earth that have the most influence in shaping the state of knowledge in the spirit world. We will see as the presentation continues how this is not done for spirits of some of the other living things.

A spiritual entity that serves as spirit for a human individual does not necessarily serve as spirit for a future human individual. It can reincarnate and serve as a spirit for a member of a different species. The living thing can even reside on a different planet in our universe or reside in a different universe. This is how, for example, the evolution of the human species can span the lifetimes of multiple past universes.

We might ask; why some individuals seem to "remember" events that took place in a "past lifetime?" As we said before, the spirit world is not perfect. Therefore, sometimes bits and pieces of lifetimes of past human individuals leak through and reach a presently living individual. Notice that when an individual "remembers" something from a past lifetime, it is never more than bits and pieces.

When that happens, the "past lifetime" is not a past lifetime of the present individual. Instead, the bits and pieces may be from when the spiritual entity served as the spirit of a different individual. Alternatively, because every spiritual entity shares parts of itself directly or indirectly with every other spiritual entity, the bits and pieces could also come from a different spiritual entity that served as the spirit for a different individual. In any case, the model indicates a present individual cannot be the reincarnation of him- or herself from a past lifetime.

The spirits of some of the other living things on Earth could work the same way the human spirit works as far as reincarnation is concerned. Generally, this is likely to apply to living things that rely a lot on their own thinking for the survival of the individual and the species. Such living things include other animals, as could be inferred from the discussion in Chapter Five.

A spirit that could be perceived as one that reincarnates is a spirit that goes through the lifetime of a member of a species and then through the lifetime of the next generation of that species and so on without end. As discussed in Chapter Five, the spirits of monarch butterflies, salmon, cicadas, etc. would be among such spirits. These are living things that live, mature, and then mate one time and immediately die. This suggests that their spirits disconnects from their bodies right after mating and then immediately become spirits for the next generation brought forth by the mating.

These are living things that remember very clearly what members of previous generations have gone through in their lifetimes. This indicates that spiritually each member is continuously living through one generation to the next and the next and thus has clear memories of what members of past generations have gone through.

If a member of such a species happens to die prematurely by being eaten before it reaches maturity and mates, its spirit returns to the spirit world and waits for the next opportunity to live through another generation. A similar thing happens when a member dies after mating, and an opportunity to live through the next generation is unavailable. Its spirit waits in the spirit world for the next opportunity to live through another generation.

Spirits of living things that live as members of a colony most likely do reincarnate, because members of such species automatically know what to do to carry out their lives, i.e., they clearly remember what members of past generations did. As discussed in Chapter Five, the more encompassing spirit in the case of colonies is the one that is the spirit of the colony. The spirits of individual members are each a part of the colony spirit. Therefore, if the individual spirits reincarnate, then the colony spirit also reincarnates, but in a piecemeal manner. This is because the members of the colony die and their spirits reincarnate not all at once but in a piecemeal manner.

Some creatures such as giant sea turtles do not die right after mating, but live for many decades and mate many times before dying. Newly born sea turtles immediately know what to do to prevent being eaten, i.e., they clearly remember what members of past generations had to go through to survive. This indicates that the spirits of giant sea turtles reincarnate. Because members do not normally die right after mating, their spirits do not immediately reincarnate after the members die, because an opportunity to do so is unlikely available. A spirit of a deceased member thus waits in the spirit world for a next opportunity to live through another generation. Meanwhile while the spirit is waiting in the spirit world, the spirit can continue to be the spirit for a living giant sea turtle if that turtle has not died.

Chapter Eight
Extrasensory Effects

Extrasensory Abilities

According to the model, if we have an extrasensory ability, it comes from our being extraordinarily in touch with certain spiritual senses such that we can sense certain things in the spirit world much better than usual. All of us are likely to have one or more extrasensory abilities, especially when we are very young. The abilities usually go dormant when we become adults. The model indicates it is natural to have extrasensory abilities, and that they can go dormant if their use is discouraged. But, they still exist and can be revitalized. This is why in general we can learn to see auras, do remote viewing, have out-of-body experiences, and so on.

What we sense with our extrasensory ability is sensed in the spirit world with our spiritual senses, but our consciousness (the consciousness of our spirit) perceives it as sensed in our physical world. While we are alive, our consciousness is so used to being tuned to our physical world that it superimposes what is sensed in the spirit world onto our physical world. It is like placing a transparency with an image on it over a photo such that the image appears as if it is part of the photo.

For example, if we sense an aura in the spirit world surrounding the spiritual expression of a living individual, our consciousness superimposes the image of the aura onto the body of that individual in our physical world, and the aura appears surrounding the body of that individual. It is easy for our consciousness to combine the spiritual image and the physical image it senses simultaneously, because both images are sensed with the same set of spiritual senses.

We might ask; whether or not a living individual has a spiritual expression in the spirit world like how a deceased individual would? The answer is; yes. A spiritual expression consists of the spirit and the soul of an individual, living or deceased. The spirit is always in the spirit world. The soul is partly in the spirit world and partly in our physical world if the individual is living, and completely in the spirit world if the individual is deceased. The difference shows up in the spirit world. The behavior is also different since the consciousness of a living individual is mainly tuned to our physical world while that of a deceased individual is tuned to the spirit world.

Our mental activities could also be perceived as taking place in our physical world. For example, when we are searching for a thought or a solution, it is our spirit doing the searching in the spirit world. But it feels like we are doing it in our physical world. This suggests that if we want to strengthen our sense of how it feels to be in the spirit world we can try getting more in touch with the sensations we are experiencing when we are searching for thoughts, solutions, concepts, etc. in the spirit world.

Acquiring an extrasensory ability through training is likely to be easier if the ability has to do with an object that is right before us, which we can see. When we sense the object simultaneously in the spirit world and our physical world, our consciousness naturally combines the two images together, as explained earlier regarding seeing auras.

This means acquiring the ability to do remote viewing is more difficult, because remote viewing is normally performed on an object far away, such as in another country, and we cannot see that object. If we are very familiar with the distant object, then remotely viewing it is easier than if we are not. Having a photo and/or a motion picture of that object should also help.

Adults with an extrasensory ability often have a parent with an extrasensory ability. We might say it is in the genes. The model suggests it might also be that a parent with an extrasensory ability is more accepting of the child's and therefore would not discourage its use. The ability could then remain active into adulthood. Conversely, I know an individual who as a child had an extrasensory ability, and it led to his being punished because of it. The ability consequently went dormant.

From observations, it seems extrasensory abilities are fragile things. It is because they require being very in touch with spiritual senses. Because our consciousness is mainly tuned to our physical world, it tends to be in touch with its spiritual senses mainly in a manner that has to do with our physical world. Any tendency of our consciousness to be in touch with our spiritual senses in a manner that has to do with the spirit world is generally ignored. An apt analogy is shopping specifically for socks in a department store. We would focus on finding socks and everything else would be ignored. It is natural in our busy life to focus only on what is important to the task at hand.

Could it be that in ancient times, life was less busy so that the people could take time to pay more attention to their extrasensory abilities? Based on their arts and other objects they produced, it seems their lives were less busy. It is possible that while our busy lives might make us feel as if we are more productive, but we may be missing out on things that are more important.

According to the model, the ability to think, reason, find solutions, find thoughts, etc. are in the same category as extrasensory abilities. They remain active and strong because we nurture them and encourage their use. And, we do this in a manner that pertains mainly to our physical world.

In my mind, what this means is that intentionally or unintentionally suppressing extrasensory abilities is shutting down a natural ability that could enhance our communications and our understanding of things. Enhancing communications and understanding is always a good thing and could lead to improvement and advancement of our species. Therefore, when we see someone with a genuine extrasensory ability, we ought to value it, be inspired by it, and not be frightened by it, as some individuals seem to be. When we see a child with an extrasensory ability, we ought to nurture it and encourage the child to use it in constructive ways.

Ghosts

When a deceased individual was alive, the soul was partly in the spirit world and partly in our physical world and thus forever embodies certain attributes of our physical world. This means the spirit of a deceased indiidual can have the soul partly reenter our physical world at any time if it wants it to. According to the model, the same kind of thing can take place in other universes.

If the soul partly reenters, or partly stays, in our physical world it can manifest as a ghost and/or cause ghostly things to happen by interacting with physical things. Examples of such happenings after my parents died are presented in Chapter Two. Similar happenings also occurred after my wife died, although less dramatically because no third-party observers witnessed the happenings, whereas many third-party observers witnessed the happenings after my parents died.

It was interesting that while I was caring for my wife during her final days I wondered who might care for me if my cancer recurred. (It turned out it was already recurring, and I felt it but chose to ignore it to devote all my time and energy to caring for my wife.) She said, "I will be there" with a definite tone of voice, and she has kept her word even though she was dead by the time the recurrence was diagnosed. It was as if as she was nearing death she was becoming increasingly in touch with the spirit world and thus knew her soul could partly stay in our physical world if it wanted to.

Many times, decades ago, I thought about asking individuals near death what they were thinking about. I had many opportunities, but I never did it. It just did not seem appropriate at such a time. But on her last few days, my wife said to me on her own, "I love you more and more." It was as if she was able to drop the hang-up that had always kept her from being fully who she was and her true self finally fully emerged.

We all have hang-ups, and they can hinder our finding ourselves if we let them. When an individual is near death it seems he or she becomes more able to put things in better perspective and thus hold onto what's important and let go of what's not. By doing this, the individual is able to find him or her true self, if only for a moment, before dying.

Even now, as I approach closer and closer to the end of my days, I find myself no longer caring about what others think should be my priorities. Their opinions do not create hang-ups for me like they might have in the past. I have projects I want to finish, such as this book, and just about everything else is lower priority to me, at least at the moment.

In a survey, dying individuals were asked, is there anything they wished they had done in their lives? The most common response was they wished they had been nicer to others. No one said they wished they made more money or possessed more things. In my mind, the fact that so many individuals near death feel this way confirms that when we are near death we become more able to put things in better perspective. Consequently, if there are any advantages to dying slowly, as opposed to dying suddenly, perhaps it is to have that chance to find our true selves before dying.

I experienced what my own hang-up could do. I was fortunate enough to get out from under it fairly early in my life, and I could actually feel myself spiritually break out of confinement and spiritually growing after that. It wasn't until then that I realized how powerful and confining hang-ups could be. As I described earlier, a hang-up is like a bad itch. Our consciousness is constantly aware of the itch and takes every opportunity to scratch it, even if the result of do so will impact the wrong individual(s) for the wrong reasons and at the wrong time in the wrong situation. It is almost as if we are constantly looking for whatever reason there is as an excuse to scratch. This is because when we have to scratch, our rational reasoning tends to be pushed aside while our emotions tend to take over. This colors almost every thought we have and almost everything we do, whether or not we are aware of it. I know, because I have experienced it, and I have seen it happen with many other individuals.

In my wife's case she knew her hang-up and its source before we met. She told me about it a few years after we were married. It was so powerful and confining that it prevented her from seeking help. She told our son about it shortly before she died. The relief that must have brought and the fact that she was dying enabled her to finally drop it. Based on her experiences, my experiences, and my observations of others, if we have a hang-up, we must not underestimate its power, nor wait until near death before doing anything about it to resolve it. If we find we cannot confront its source, then at least try to forgive the source. And if we are unable to do that, then when worse come to worse we might have to simply exclude the source from continuing to be a part of our life.

Some might say sensing ghosts is just our imagination. In my parents' case, as described in Chapter Two, it was definitely not my imagination as many third parties were involved in the events described in Chapter Two. In my wife's case, it was unlikely my imagination either. Simply too many things happened that helped me a lot or gave me what I wanted or needed for such things to be coincidences. The most plausible explanation is that she had a part in making these things happen. Such things continue to happen even now, more than eight years afer her death.

Based on what my parents did after they died and what my wife has been doing since she died, I am beginning to think that an indication of true love is how it continues to be expressed even after death. And then there is me. What does it mean about me when I find I simply cannot get rid of her stuff? I washed all her clothes, sorted them, and was preparing to give them away. But I could go no further. Everyone else I know had gotten rid of his or her spouse's stuff after the spouse died. But I couldn't do it. To walk into the bedroom and see all her clothes there is comforting. To open drawers to see all her lipsticks, powders, combs, manicure set, watches, accessories, and etc. is comforting. I can't let go of her ashes, so I keep them in the house. We designed the house together. This is the only house we ever owned and lived in together. She is a part of it; this is where her ashes and all her things belong, here with me. So I have yet to figure out what it is about me that makes me feel this way. You would think true love wouldn't be so tormenting, but maybe it is, for some people in some situations.

Getting back to ghosts in general, we perceive a ghost as being in our physical world whether we sense it in the spirit world or in our physical world for the same reason presented in the preceding section regarding images sensed with extrasensory abilities. If the soul of a deceased individual reenters or stays partly in our physical world, it can be sensed as a ghost in our physical world and/or ghostly things can happen. In this case, the spirit has a reason to want the soul to be partly in our physical world. It likely has something to do with sending a message to a loved one or to help a loved one. If the spirit wants to only spiritually interact with a living individual, it would not need to have the soul be partly in our physical world. It could simply interact with the spirit of the living individual in the spirit world. The living individual could then sense a ghost and perceive it as being in our physical world.

What this indicates is that if we sense a ghost, we might be sensing it either in the spirit world or in our physical world. So, we might ask; how can we tell which way it is that we are sensing it? If others also sense the ghost, or if ghostly happenings physically occur, then we are sensing it in our physical world. If we are the only one sensing a ghost, even though others are present, then we are likely sensing it in the spirit world. But, we might be sensing it in our physical world and the spirit of the deceased individual wants only us to sense it. In this case, we would not be able to tell if we are sensing it in the spirit world or in our physical world.

In the cases of my deceased parents and my deceased wife, their souls apparently stayed partly in our physical world probably to interact with physical things as they see necessary. The oily streak appearing on the rear fender of my mom's car as described in Chapter Two is an example. My parents stayed to help my siblings and me finish tasks that they tried to finish before they died, but time ran out before they could. And either incidentally or purposely, they indicated that life exists after life. It seems likely that it was purposeful, because they got my very special friend Rachel, who can see auras, involved, and it was she who conveyed the message to me as described in Chapter Two.

As described before, right after my wife died, the largest of the paintings she had created, which had been leaning against a wall for years, suddenly tilted forward and fell over. She was apparently letting me know that she knew my cancer had recurred, even though I never told her, and she will be staying here to help me as she said she would if my cancer recurred. She might or might not be able to directly help rid me of my cancer, but a lot of things started happening that helped make life easier for me. For example, my upcoming surgery was scheduled to be performed 35 miles away at a new facility that, among other things, specializes in surgery for my kind of cancer. But, it was suddenly rescheduled to be performed at the facility seven miles away where my first two surgeries were performed. Things like that keep happening. If only a few happened, it could be coincidence, but not when they continue to happen now for more than eight years.

An event occurring as recently as August 13, 2014, indicates my deceased wife is still around and watching over me, now more than six years after she died. Photos in heavy frames and ceramic figurines on top of a bookcase were located above where I usually slept. They have been there as is for two years. On August 13 while I was up and around during the day, those items fell off the bookcase and landed on where I usually sleep. I put away the heaviest item and rearranged the rest more securely. On August 17, 2014, at 3:20 a.m. in the morning the Napa Valley magnitude 6.0 earthquake struck. The items all stayed in place, but had they not fallen on August 13, they would have fallen on top of me during the earthquake while I was asleep. It might have been my wife knocking them down four days earlier so that they would not fall on me during the earthquake, or there might have been a small precursor earthquake four days earlier that knocked them down. However, I live so far away from the Napa Valley that a precursor strong enough to knock down the items would have been noticed in the Napa Valley and be reported. But no such precursor were ever mentioned in the news before or after the quake. In addition, nothing anywhere else in the house fell on August 13. Therefore, I conclude it was my wife that made the items fall ahead of time.

The model indicates the mechanisms by which ghosts can be sensed would function in other universes as well, which means living things in other universes can sense ghosts as well. We might then ask if we could sense in our universe the ghosts of deceased living things that resided in another universe. The answer is yes, if we sense them in the spirit world, but not in our physical world, because their souls cannot enter our physical world. However, we are not likely to recognize what we sense while alive and our consciousness is mainly tuned to our physical world. We are more likely to perceive them as undefined background things.

Unfortunately, this tends to make us think our universe is the only one that exists. Likewise, living things in other universes might tend to also think their universe is the only one that exists. But the model indicates other universes could exist besides ours, because the spirit world is so large and its issues are so numerous and varied that it might at times need more than one universe to help restore balance at the same time.

We might then ask what about ghosts of deceased living things that resided on other planets in our universe. Is it possible for us to see them? The model indicates we could, theoretically, and living things on other planets could theoretically see ghosts of deceased living things that resided on Earth. However, the model indicates that deceased people who want to be sensed as ghosts do so mostly for some purpose having to do with helping living things, such as loved ones. Therefore, they are not likely to want to be sensed by living things on other planets. If they simply want to visit other planets out of curiosity, they do not have to enable themselves to be sensed as ghosts there. Similarly, I would think deceased living things that resided on other planets are not likely to want to be seen as ghosts by us humans on Earth.

I would imagine a ghost would be able to decide who could sense it and who could not. Therefore, it could be in the presence of multiple individuals and not all would sense it. It would be like if we could communicate telepathically we could telepathically issue a message to a specific individual such that only that individual would receive it. However, an individual who is very in touch with his or her spiritual senses would be able to sense the ghost whether or not the ghost wanted that individual to sense it. All this would be the case whether the ghost is sensed in the spirit world or in our physical world.

Then we might ask; whether a human individual very in touch with his or her spiritual senses could realize he or she is sensing ghosts from other planets when he or she is? Again, theoretically this could happen. But if living things on another planet are not anything like living things on Earth, the consciousness of the human individual might sense the ghost but not recognize it and might thus perceive it as background things. Because no two planets are identical, living things on one planet are not likely to be like living things on another. Different gravitation forces, atmospheric make up, elemental materials, evolutionary paths, etc. are among the factors that can make living things in one planet different from those on another. Even on Earth, we are finding out that life could exist where oxygen is not available. As mentioned earlier in the book, clams living on the ocean floor next to hot hydrogen sulfide gas vents where two tectonic plates meet are thriving and are supported by the hydrogen sulfide gas instead of by oxygen. Therefore, this suggests that the bases for life other than those found on Earth can be possible on other planets.

Yeah, but Superman looks like a human and acts like a human, that is if you sort of ignore that he has super powers and can fly without wings. I know, and it is really too bad his planet blew up. It would have been good to see what his planet was like compared with Earth. Yes and when I was a kid, I always wondered if he ever needed to eat, what he eats, and if he ever needed to go to the bathroom, because they never show him doing any of these things.

There are supposedly cases in which a deceased individual doesn't realize he or she is deceased. The soul would thus remain partly in our physical world and the spirit would continue to carry on as if the individual were still alive. We might ask; how the spirit could not know the individual died? The answer is; it would be similar to how it is possible for an individual who almost died and was temporarily in a coma to not remember what happened to cause his or her near-death. This seems more likely to happen when coma or death comes about suddenly, while the body is in good health such in a bad accident. The spirit knows what is happening to the body by means of the feedback signals the body sends to the brain for the brain to translate and send to the spirit. If the body and brain are suddenly unable to function, then the spirit does not get any signals about what has happened and thus does not know, or remember, what happened. This could also explain why some ghosts seem to stay around forever, such as those regularly seen in haunted houses.

We might ask; why ghosts are often depicted in movies and stories as scary? The answer is; in my opinion, ghosts are like ordinary individuals in how they feel when they think they are still alive and are still living in their houses. When strangers move into their houses, what do you expect them to do? Wouldn't you expect them to want to do something to get the strangers out? Then what about ghosts that seems to be OK with strangers living in their houses? Well, those ghosts might simply enjoy having the company. Some individuals like to entertain a lot.

Hmm, I wonder if I would like being entertained by a ghost. Well, it would be interesting. Yeah, and besides, you might not even know it is a ghost that is entertaining you. Well, a ghost would say "Boo," wouldn't it? Theoretically, it could, but according to our model, not necessarily. For example, it could express it telepathically instead of saying it.

The fact that ghosts have consciousness and intelligence would lend support to the notion that consciousness and intelligence reside in the spirit, not in the brain. After all, the brain of a deceased individual no longer functions.

Brain waves and other measurable brain signals must therefore be manifestations of what the brain does in its communications role, not manifestations of the brain doing the thinking. This unconventional interpretation of the brain's role and its activities could open the possibility that what is measured as brain waves and various brain activities could enable us to look into the spirit of the individual and perhaps also into the spirit world. In this regard, a brain could be a portal between our physical world and the spirit world.

Ghosts of individuals in a coma have allegedly been seen. This is theoretically possible. A portion of the soul could temporarily detach from the body and roam around our physical world and be sensed as a ghost. We might then ask; what about a sleeping individual's soul partly detaching from the body and appearing as a ghost? The answer is that being asleep is not the same as being in a coma. We can instantly awaken a sleeping individual at any time, but not so an individual in a coma. This means the soul of a sleeping individual remains completely attached to the body at all times and is not partly free to roam around.

Very traumatic events that happen at a specific location on Earth can later be seen replaying repeatedly at that location and be perceived by those who can sense the replay involving one or more "ghosts" in action. According to the model, such occurrences are ghost-like, but they do not involve actual ghosts. Nearby nonliving things such as furniture, walls, clocks, vases, etc. have spirits and souls, according to the model. When such nonliving things go through experiences, they generate new pieces of knowledge that get added to their spirits, and connections of the second kind get added to their souls. A nearby traumatic event can involve such high emotions among the individuals involved that the experience can get strongly "imprinted" onto the spirits and souls of nonliving things and would thus become an unusually prominent part of their spirits and souls. Thus, the pieces of knowledge that got into the spirits of the nearby nonliving things could cause an image of the event to be replayed repeatedly in the spirit world. An observer with a certain extrasensory ability could sense the replays in the spirit world, superimpose them onto the location of the traumatic event, and perceive them as occurring at that location in our physical world. Thus, while what is sensed can be perceived as ghosts in action, real ghosts are not involved. The ghost-like figures are not able to interact with the observer as they would if they were real ghosts. Instead, they simply go about their business of replaying the event without showing any awareness of the observer's presence.

There are stories of ghost ships, ghost cars, ghost horse riders in the sky, etc. How such images come about could be similar to how the images discussed in the preceding paragraph come about. Or they could be real ghosts. After all, according to the model, ships, cars, horses, etc. have spirits and souls and therefore their spiritual expressions can be sensed in the spirit world by individuals with extrasensory ability and be perceived as ghosts in our physical world.

In the case of a ghost ship full of people, we might ask; why a whole load of spiritual expressions of dead individuals on a ship would decide to stay on the spiritual expression of the ship in the spirit world? Wouldn't they rather go exploring the rest of the spirit world instead? The answer is that if such an image is seen and keeps repeating, then all the people appearing on the ship are not real ghosts. Again, the image is produced by a very traumatic event imprinting onto the nonliving things making up the ship, and the image is thus being repeatedly replayed in the spirit world.

Out-of-Body Experiences

Some patients say that while under general anesthesia they had an out-of-body experience. They say they left their bodies and floated up to the ceiling and elsewhere. They looked down and observed what the medical staff was doing. Upon awakening, they describe what they saw, and it matched what actually took place while they were unconscious. In one case, the patient said he floated to the roof of the hospital and saw a pair of shoes there. He described in detail the shoes' design and location. Staff members later found shoes there that matched the patient's description.

General anesthetic works by depressing the function of nerves. Certain physical signals that are normally transmitted between the brain and the body are blocked so that the body becomes unconscious and feels no pain. Spiritual and physical signals keeping the body existing and alive are not blocked. Certain parts of the spirit and the soul that normally handle the spiritual signals associated with now-blocked physical signals are now free to take a break. This part of the soul would thus temporarily disconnect from the body. During the break, an out-of-body experience happens if the spirit wants it to. The spirit has two possible ways to make it happen. A third and totally different way is to do it at will without general anesthesia, but most individuals would need to learn how to do it first.

> **First Way:** During the break, the spirit could decide to roam around the spirit world. Its consciousness would still be mainly tuned into our physical world. Therefore, it would recognize mainly spiritual expressions of currently existing living and nonliving things, and it would perceive what it senses as happening in our physical world.
>
> **Second Way:** Alternatively, the spirit could decide to have the part of the soul on break to temporarily disconnect from the body and roam around our physical world. In this case, other individuals might see a ghost of that individual. I have heard of only one case in which a ghost was seen. The second way might be rare.
>
> **Third Way:** A third way is to have out-of-body experiences at will, but this needs to be learned. One such individual said he (or she) floated to the moon. Theoretically, we could float any where in our universe, and this could be a way to explore our universe. Some individuals would notice they are tethered to their body by an infinitely stretch able silvery cord as they

floated around.

An individual having an out-of-body experience the third way could be "awakened" from the experience by physical stimulation. This is similar to how a sleeping individual could be awakened by physical stimulation. This means one hundred percent of the soul stays connected to the body in the third way, like it would be when the individual is sleeping. An individual having an out-of-body experience the first or second ways could not be awakened by physical stimulation, because physical signals giving the body its consciousness are blocked.

Since one hundred percent of the soul stays connected to the body in the third way, it must be the spirit doing the roaming in the spirit world, and it perceives it as being done in our physical world.

Since the spirit is roaming the spirit world in the first and third ways, ways, if an infinitely stretchable silvery cord is visible in the third way, it should also be visible in the first way. The cord would be one hundred percent of the soul in the third way, and only part of the soul in the first way; i.e., the part that carries the spiritual signals to enable the body to exist and be alive while the rest of the soul is temporarily disconnected from the body and therefore is not a part of the silvery cord. The soul is a spiritual thing such that the distance separating it and the spirit has no meaning since the connection between the two resides in the spirit world. The cord is perceived to be stretchable because the roaming is perceived to be in our physical world though it is actually in the spirit world.

Can we tell which of the three ways is functioning when we have an out-of-body experience? The answer is yes. We would obviously know when the third way is functioning. The first way would be functioning if an infinitely stretchable silvery cord connecting us to our body were visible. The second way would be functioning if no such cord were visible.

We might ask; if an individual who is brain dead could have out-of-body experiences, and if so, which of the three ways would be functioning? The part of the brain that has to do with giving the body its consciousness is dead. Therefore, theoretically either the first or second way could be functioning. If we happen to see a ghost of the individual, then the second way is functioning. Otherwise, the only way we could tell is if we could telepathically communicate with the spirit of the individual and ask.

Auras

As signals are transmitted back and forth between the spirit and body, they produce an aura as they go through the soul. The signals are a form of spiritual energy, and can be sensed by spiritual senses. The aura surrounds the spiritual expression of the individual in the spirit world, but it is perceived to exist in our physical world and be surrounding the individual's body in our physical world.

Since the spirit world is nonphysical and requires no space in which to reside, it is difficult for us being used to our three-dimensional physical world to visualize how the aura looks in the spirit world. However, the fact that an aura appears to surround the body of an individual in our physical world could mean the aura appears to surround the spiritual expression of an individual in the spirit world, since the spiritual expression is really who the individual is. This then could mean the way the soul is connected with the spirit is akin to the way wearing clothes covers the body in our physical world. The soul transmits the signal between the spirit and the body and therefore the aura formed by the spiritual energy of the signals surrounds the spiritual expression much like clothes surround the body.

If this were true, then a record of an individual's entire lifetime would surround the spiritual expression much like clothing surrounds the body. This means if we want what we are wearing to look good after we return to the spirit world, we need to do what we can to be sure that's the case while we are still alive on Earth.

Hmm, I wonder if that is what is meant when people say we could be in heaven or hell after we die, depending on what we do while alive. Yep, it is all about the "clothes" we are wearing after we return to the spirit world. Yep, and after we die we are stuck forever in what we are wearing. And, worse, even if we wish we could die because we are so embarrassed by what we are wearing, we cannot die anymore. OMG! That does sound like hell. Well, only if you are a fashion freak.

The spirit and soul of the individual embody a record of the individual's lifetime up to the present. The signals going back and forth between the spirit and body reveal this record. Thus, so does the aura produced by the signals. Those able to read auras thus gain knowledge about the individual including state of health, emotions, fatigue, approach to life, hang-ups, ability to stay on track, etc. Some real life examples are presented in Chapter Two.

The nature and intensity of an aura are different depending on whether the individual is alive or recently deceased. When the individual is alive, an aura is formed as described earlier and has various colors, combinations of colors, patterns of colors, etc. When the individual is recently deceased, the aura is high intensity and so bright it appears white as all the colors and patterns are washed out.

Most of the soul disconnects from the body right after the individual is deceased. The remaining part enables the body to exist for a very short while. During this time, the body can be brought back to life, depending on the cause of death. If the body is not brought back to life, then the remaining part of the soul disconnects, and the body begins decomposing back into the basic materials making up Earth. And then only the part of the soul that enables the basic materials to exist remain connected to the basic materials. This is a borrowed part also borrowed by the souls of all living and nonliving things on Earth. Therefore, by this time the soul of the individual is considered totally disconnected from the body.

The recently disconnected part of the soul no longer has the body to which to transmit spiritual signals. However, spiritual signals continue to be issued by the spirit for a while. The signals thus spew out freely into the spirit world, producing a high intensity aura. The spirit apparently lets this happen for a while before turning off the spiritual signals. The spirit might simply need time to adjust to the major change. This is likely to be especially true for highly intelligent living things. When we humans are alive, we need time to adjust to a major change in our lives. Since our spiritual expression is really who we are, our spiritual expression likewise needs time to adjust after a major change.

After the soul has disconnected from the body, the white aura may not necessarily be seen surrounding the deceased body. But it can roam around the spirit world and be perceived surrounding other objects in our physical world. My friend Rachel saw a white aura on two occasions, as described in Chapter Two. One such aura surrounded the casket holding the body of a recently deceased individual. The other surrounded my mother's car and me as I was covering the car with a car cover.

In the early days, after I took possession of the car, I noticed other drivers noticing the car more than expected. It was 15 years old at the time and was beginning to be rare, but not rare enough to be very special yet. Drivers would slow down very suddenly alongside and slightly behind me and stay there for quite a while before moving on. At that time, I was unaware that a white aura could be surrounding the car, or that such an aura could even exist. Maybe a bright white aura was what caught the attention of some of the other drivers, i.e., those who could see auras. Drivers today still tend to slow down a bit to look at the car but not as drastically as before. The car is now over 40 years old, still in showroom condition, and is now truly rare. I therefore conclude that a white aura more than likely had been surrounding the car in the early days. It must have been there when an oil streak was formed on the right rear fender, as described in Chapter Two, because my deceased parents must have been there to produce the oily streak.

Remote Viewing

In terms of the model, remote viewing is done using spiritual senses to sense in the spirit world the spiritual counterpart of what is going on at a specified location in our physical world. The specified location is usually far away, sometimes in another country, such that we could not directly see it. What is sensed can be perceived as taking place in our physical world. It exactly matches what is going on in our physical world because everything that goes on in our physical world has a spiritual counterpart going on in the spirit world.

As indicated in the first section of this chapter, unless the remote viewer is very familiar with the location to be remotely viewed it is difficult to be sure the location being remotely viewed is the specified one. I would imagine trying to find a specific location in the spirit world would be as difficult as trying to find a specific location in our physical world if we are unfamiliar with the area and don't have a map or a high-technology locating device.

In our physical world we have maps, landmarks, high-technology systems, etc. to help us. I don't know what is available to help us in the spirit world. I suppose we could learn to use the spiritual counterparts of maps, landmarks, high-technology systems, etc. if that is possible. On the other hand, in the spirit world we would have lot of additional spiritual senses to help us besides just our five major senses. Therefore, perhaps trying to find a specific location in the spirit world is like trying to find a specific thought, solution, concept, etc. in the spirit world: The more we practice the better we would become at doing it.

In this sense, doing remote viewing might be similar to having an out-of-body experience at will, at least according to the model. It would be interesting to see if those who can do remote viewing are also able to have out-of-body experiences at will, and vice versa.

Telepathy

All kinds of signals are constantly being issued and received among spiritual entities in the spirit world. Telepathic communication is when the signals are thoughts, feelings, solutions, concepts, etc. being issued and received among spirits of living things. Looking at it this way, it has to be a natural part of how the spirit world functions. Consequently, the fact that some living things on Earth are able to communicate telepathically is more a natural ability than an extrasensory ability. Then is it possible that at one time we humans had the ability to communicate telepathically? If so, why and how did we lose it?

As mentioned earlier, in his book Robert Sheldrake indicates certain groups of humans today have this ability. Did these groups always have the ability or did they develop it? As we will see later in this section, there could be reasons why humans in general might have started out with this ability, then lost it, and those who now have it could be a step ahead of the rest.

Telepathic communication is most efficient when thoughts are communicated in pure thought form, i.e., not expressed in any kind of spoken language. Pure thought forms can be telepathically communicated instantly and can be understood instantly and precisely. Therefore, telepathic communication can be done among individuals who speak different languages by using pure thought forms. It works independent of the distances separating the individuals, because it takes place in the spirit world and not in our physical world.

Thoughts expressed in a spoken language can also be telepathically communicated, but it takes much longer and can be less accurate. A spoken language acts like a filter that can distort an intended thought.

Telepathic communication between different species has to be done in pure thought forms. Recall, Robert Sheldrake's book gives examples of pets telepathically sensing and understanding the thoughts of their owners, even though the thoughts are not directed at them, and great distances separate them from their owners.

Since telepathic communication takes place in the spirit world, and it involves spirits sending thoughts, and spiritual senses sensing the thoughts. This means we need to be more in touch with certain of our spiritual senses in order to telepathically communicate. The level at which living things are in touch with their spiritual senses does not appear necessarily related to their level of intelligence, but it might be associated with their level of consciousness.

The model indicates that the more in touch we are with our spiritual senses, the more conscious we are. It also indicates that the more spiritual senses we have the more conscious we would be. Since living things that can telepathically communicate are less intelligent than we are, this suggests they are either more in touch with their spiritual senses than we are with ours, and/or they have more spiritual senses than we have. Therefore, while we are more intelligent, some of them appear to be more conscious than we are. This could also explain how some creatures can predict earthquakes, floods, big storms, or other natural disaster, while we humans cannot do that without sophisticated instruments.

The model indicates evolution continues over the lifetimes of multiple universes. Thus, the human species being the most advanced living things on Earth did not do all its evolution on Earth. Humans began as some less intelligent species in some past universe, and very likely relied heavily on the spirit world to do most, or all, of its thinking to survive at that time. At that time members of the species would have had to be very in touch with their spiritual senses in order to sense the spirit world's instructions for survival. Being very in touch with spiritual senses means the members of our species at that time were likely able to communicate telepathically with one another as well.

As the human species continued to evolve, it eventually reached a stage at which the members of our species were intelligent enough to think for themselves for survival. Members thus no longer needed to rely on the spirit world to do their thinking for them in order to survive. Accordingly, the members started to become less in touch with the spiritual senses necessary to sense survival instructions from the spirit world. These included the spiritual senses that enabled telepathic communication to take place, and instinctive and intuitive messages to be sensed, etc. Thus, the human species eventually lost its ability to communicate telepathically, although some members are able to retain the ability to some degree.

At some point in time, the knowledge in the spirit world became unbalanced in a manner that required a universe with living things that have all the attributes of our species to help the spirit world restore balance. Thus, our physical universe was designed and brought into being, and our species was selected to be the most advanced living things on one of the planets, Earth, at least for the current era. In order for the human species to most effectively fulfill its purpose, it is obvious its members needed to very effectively communicate with one another. Our current way of communication is clearly not working well. The most effective, precise, and accurate way to communicate is by telepathy, with thoughts in pure thought form. It thus seems very likely that humans are meant to redevelop the ability to communicate telepathically. It would be a significant step toward improving our relationships with one another.

We know we can develop this ability because we very likely once had it and because various groups of humans and various other species on Earth still have it, as do some identical twins with each other, as discussed. Because the human species likely had the ability before, those groups of humans who can communicate telepathically now were either very wise to retain the ability or they have evolved to the point they now have redeveloped it. Either way, they could be a step ahead of the rest of us.

Telepathy and Brain Disabilities

An individual experiencing brain disability due to stroke, disease, cancer, trauma, drugs, etc. has impaired communications between the spirit and the body. Because the brain is disabled, it is unable to translate the spiritual signal from the spirit properly to send to the body or the feedback signals from the body properly to send to the spirit. Therefore, symptoms such as poor sense of balance, speech difficulties, weak or paralyzed limps, confusion, etc. can result. But the spirit remains in good condition. Therefore, if others could telepathically communicate with the spirit of the individual, life for the disabled individual could be more manageable.

Living things have a way of compensating for disabilities. For example, if one of our five major senses is disabled, the other four can become more acute to compensate. A similar compensation might be possible for an individual with permanent brain disability who has difficulty communicating in the usual manner. Such an individual might more easily develop the ability to communicate telepathically than could a typical individual. This possibility has probably never been explored. For one thing, someone able to communicate telepathically would need to know how to work with disabled individuals. But I suspect that individuals unable to communicate in the usual manner wish others could read their minds and understand the thoughts they are unable to articulate clearly. Thus, they are bound to be motivated to learn, if the opportunity to do so ever arose.

This is what the model suggests might be true. Therefore, if we want to explore the possibilities of doing telepathic communication among human individuals in general, this might be one of the ways to start, and it could be a win-win situation for the disabled individuals and for our species.

Time Travel Back to the Past

The spirit world has a complete record of the past, and it can thus reproduce an expression of any segment of time in the past. However, according to the model, if an expression were reproduced and if we were to go into it for the purpose of interacting with it and thus changing it, we would find we would not be able to do so. We could only be observers, in much the same way we can only be observers while watching a movie. Therefore, if time travel back into the past is defined as doing so to interact with it and thus change it, then the conclusion is we could not do it. No matter what we do, we are always moving forward into the future. Thus, if we were to observe an expression of the past, we would be going through a new experience and thus moving into the future. The new experience would be our observing an expression of the past, and the new experience would generate new pieces of knowledge that would get added to the spirit world just as any other new experience would.

Projections into Possible Futures

The spirit world is constantly making projections into possible futures based on all the pieces of knowledge and all the spiritual entities that exist at the time each projection is made. The spirit world is thus constantly extrapolating the past and the present into possible futures. This is an important part of the spirit world's process of forming wisdom, i.e., to be prepared for all possible futures and to know what actions are necessary now to prevent as much as possible an undesirable future, and/or to help assure a desired future is the one most likely to happen.

We might ask; if this means the spirit world does not know what the future holds? The answer is that it does not know. In order to continue to grow and be a living thing, the spirit world must always have a future that it does not know. This could explain why we humans must also always have a future that we do not know, and that is why we too should be putting effort into forming wisdom to prepare for possible futures. The following paragraph may help clarify.

At any point in time, countless futures are possible. Each has a different likelihood of coming true, and none can be assured of being the one to come true. If the spirit world knows which will be the one to come true, then the spirit world already knows the future, and that means it already possesses whatever new pieces of knowledge that would be generated by experiences yet to come. Then those experiences must have essentially already taken place and thus the "assured future" would actually be part of the past. Therefore, the conclusion is that none of the projected possible futures can be assured of being the one to come true. For the spirit world to know the future would thus mean it has no future, and that would be a bad situation for anything that needs to grow in order to continue being a living thing.

We might ask then; what would determine which projected possible future would be the one to come true? The answer is; the "what" is all living and nonliving things that exist in the spirit world and the existing universes at that instant in time. Here is how it works.

As new pieces of knowledge are constantly generated and added to the spirit world, the projected possible futures are constantly changing as the spirit world is constantly changing. The entire collection of projected possible futures is constantly being updated. One of the projected possible futures comes true for an instant and the rest become irrelevant. In the next instant, one of the updated projected possible future comes true for that instant, and it might, or might not, be different from the one that came true for the preceding instant. The process progresses continuously in this manner. It thus follows that the wisdom that was formed during the preceding instant and that was relevant for that instant would also be updated, and modification would be made as necessary to make it relevant for the current instant.

Since only one projected possible future would come true at any one instant, we might ask; when we make a decision to do something and actually do it, would we be in a sense selecting the projected possible future to come true by our action? This is a great question. Based on the existing knowledge and spiritual entities, the spirit world would know there is a possibility we would do what we would actually do. Therefore, a group of projected possible futures would include the possibility that we would do what we did. Thus, in a sense, our doing something is selecting a certain group of projected possible futures to come true. The same thing applies to every living and nonliving thing that exists. The action each living and nonliving thing takes is in a sense selecting a certain group of projected possible futures to come true for it. When all the selections are combined, there would be only one projected possible future that would be common to all the selections, and that would be the one to come true. Therefore, in this manner all living and nonliving things that exist at that instant in time together determine which projected possible future will come true for that instant.

This highlights the fact that every living and nonliving thing has a role in shaping the future. Some of us might tend to dismiss the importance of our individual role probably because the magnitude of the effects of our actions is usually not immediately apparent. But it is analogous to launching a projectile. A slight change in the angle of launch might seem minor, and it probably is minor in the short term. However, it makes a big different in the long term as to how far the projectile goes and where it goes. This then says that in order for our universe to fulfill its purpose, each of us needs to do our part and to realize that in the long term what we do at every moment really does matter. We are shaping the future at every moment, and the effect of our actions is felt most strongly in the long term while it may not necessarily be apparent in the short term.

We have many examples of how we humans tend to think short term only to have long-term consequences hit us in the future. Examples include our water and energy use, our financial planning, our voting decisions, our diets, etc. A hazard is that, when we make decisions based on a short enough time-frame, anything can look okay. It is like an individual falling off a four-story building saying to someone on the second floor "I'm still okay for this instant."

Space Travel

Long-distant space travel for humans beyond our moon with our current technology is impractical. Someday when we develop other ways to travel, perhaps something like teleportation, long-distant space travel could become more doable. Also if we were to consider unconventional forms of space travel, such as by means of the spirit world as discussed already, this might open up new ways to think about what space travel could entail including virtual space travel. As mentioned earlier in this chapter, remote viewing and out-of-body experiences might be possible ways to do virtual space travel. We might not be able to do all the things we could if we were physically there. But we would still be able to do a lot and learn a lot.

Travel to Other Universes

Travel to another universe is very likely made impossible by the spirit world since it is likely to be in conflict with each universe having a different and unique purpose to fulfill. On the other hand, we cannot rule out the possibility that some universes are designed so that certain visits to certain other universes are part of the purpose they need to fulfill. We might ask; could this explain UFOs? And could some UFOs come from nonphysical universes such that they could make instantaneous changes in speed and direction of travel because they have zero mass? And being nonphysical, would they take up space or displace the air or another other physical material where they are? If they do not, then this could also explain why they do not get heated up by air friction when moving at high velocity and burn up as meteors do.

We might also ask; if our universe is one of those whose purpose involves certain visits to certain other universes or is our universe one of those whose purpose does not include visits to other universes? And if our universe is the former, would humans be among the ones in our universe to eventually visit another universe? Perhaps we humans need to learn how to clean up the mess we made on Earth first, i.e., we need to learn how to interact with one another without making a mess before we are ready to interact with living things residing in other universes.

However, if we were to interact with highly intelligent living things residing in other universes or residing on other planets in our universe, we are most likely going to find they have abilities we humans do not have. Therefore, we are likely to perceive them as being more advanced than we. However, we are likely to have abilities they do not have and therefore they might perceive us as being more advanced than they. I think it is best if we do not assume they are more advanced than we are, or that we are more advanced than they are. We need to expect differences, look for ways to mutually complement one another's abilities as in a partnership, and treat them as equals and therefore with care, empathy, and compassion. After all, the model indicates that we all share parts of one another in the spirit world.

Getting More in Touch with the Spirit World's Restoring and Healing Powers

Chapter Seven explained that we sleep so that our spirit can restore our body from the wear and tear of the day, and we go into a coma so that our spirit can heal our body from severe disease and injury. But our spirit alone cannot restore or heal everything that happens. For example, the spirit world cares about every living thing it created, including things that cause diseases and infections. Consequently, spirits of such things can sometimes have their way over our spirit. Likewise, under some situations our spirit cannot rid our body of normal cells that became cancer cells. As a third example, while we sleep, the spirit restores our body, but it does not restore it to the exact state it was in the day before. Our spirit and body grow with time, and the experiences producing the growth can leave behind scars, losses, and age-related physical degradations. Our spirit alone cannot rid such things once they form, and thus their disabling effects accumulate with time. Consequently, our body will age and degrade.

While our spirit alone cannot heal everything or do a one-hundred-percent restoration, the spirit world can. After all, it designed and created everything in the first place. The spirit world can apply the pieces of knowledge it has that can enable a human body to do one-hundred percent regeneration of body parts badly diseased, badly injured, or lost. Such pieces of knowledge are not a part of a human spirit.

Such pieces of knowledge are not a part of Earth's spirit either. I.e., no living thing on Earth that can regenerate lost parts can regenerate parts that are exactly the same as the original. Examples are given in Chapter Five. The spirit world would have to change Earth's spirit to include those pieces of knowledge to enable regenerated parts be the same as originals. The spirit world is unlikely to do this, because Earth would then not be addressing the issues it was originally designed to address, and this goes similarly for human spirits. Consequently, a human spirit cannot heal everything or do a one-hundred percent restoration of a human body.

However, we can get more in touch with the spirit world's restoring and healing powers to enhance our spirit's restoring and healing abilities.

We can do this in three possible ways; i.e., (1) by going through our physical world, (2) by simultaneously going through both our physical world and the spiritual world, and (3) by going through the spirit world. Some examples are the following.

> **Example (1):** We continue to developed diagnostic procedures, medications, treatment procedures, parts replacement technologies, transplant procedures, ways to train our immune systems to fight various diseases, better understanding of foods and their effects on our health, better understanding of the various exercises and their effects, etc. These are examples of how we are going through our physical world to get more in touch with the spirit world's restoring and healing powers.
>
> **Example (2):** Practitioners often rely on placebo effects to help enhance their treatments, and they can do this by enhancing the patient's faith in the practitioner's skills and the effectiveness of the treatment. The patients can maintain a positive attitude. The patient can assume the treatment will be successful and thus plan for a good future. Family and friends of the patient can send prayers and good wishes to the patient, and it has been show in some studies that a group of individuals doing this simultaneously can enhance the effectiveness of the treatment. These are examples of how we are going through both our physical world and the spirit world to get more in touch with the spirit world's restoring and healing powers.
>
> **Example (3):** Treatments designed to help patients resolve personal problems are relying on the patient going through the spirit world to get more touch with the spirit world's restoring and healing powers. Practitioners such as those in India referred to as medicine men or medicine women who gives the individuals who come to them the ability to heal themselves are also relying on those individual to go through the spirit world to tap into the spirit world's powers. Such practitioners are very much in tune with the beliefs, faiths, and hopes of the people. Thus,

they giving the individuals empathy, compassion, love and hope, and they might combine this with materials, herbs, and movements.

Going through both worlds simultaneously is consistent with how we are carrying out our lives simultaneously in both worlds. This suggests we can generally heal more effectively by going through both worlds instead of just one. We could do, and most likely have done, this in a variety of other ways besides the ways mentioned in Example (2).

The variety of medications, vaccines, antibiotics, medical procedures, treatments, etc. continues to expand and improve as research continues. Researchers are the ones who find the restoring and healing powers in the spirit world and translate them into forms that can be expressed or exist in our physical world. Thus, more specifically, when a doctor is applying a medical procedure in our physical world, he or she is going through the researcher(s) who found and translated a certain restoring and healing ability of the spirit world. Therefore, in essence today's doctors are going through both our physical world and the spirit world when they apply modern day treatments.

Modern medical practices rely heavily on patients willing to go through with the treatments in our physical world. But the patients need to also go through the spirit world; i.e., they need to have faith the medical procedure will work. Otherwise, they will prefer not to go through with the treatment.

A real life example of a patient who was not willing to go through with a treatment is as follows. My mom went through surgery and chemotherapy the first time and had terrible side effects. Today's chemotherapies are said to produce less severe side effects. When the cancer recurred five years later, it had spread throughout her body and into her bones. This time, she turned down all medical procedures, because she did not believe they could help her now. In her case, her lack of faith in the medical procedures available was probably justified, given how serious her cancer had become.

A patient can experience a placebo effect when the patient goes through only the spirit world but thinks he or she is also going through our physical world. An example of this is when a patient takes a sugar pill but thinks it is medication, and gets better. A lot of modern medical practitioners rely on placebo effects to help with their treatments. However, the spirit world is complex and thus a lot of factors are involved such that placebo effects do not always happen. The dictionary definition of placebo effect is "improvement in the condition of a sick person that occurs in response to treatment but cannot be considered due to the specific treatment used." It says placebo effect is "improvement;" it didn't say "heal" or "cure." Nevertheless, any improvement is helpful with a medical treatment, because it encourages the patient and therefore a more positive attitude in the patient. A more positive attitude enhances the effectiveness of the treatment. An increase in effectiveness further encourages the patient. This then forms a vicious circle such that while a placebo effect might not directly heal or cure, it indirectly does so.

Some practitioners in certain fields of medicine rely heavily on the patient going through the spirit world to make their treatments work. Treatments designed to help patients resolve personal problems are among these since it is ultimately the patient who must resolve the problem him- or herself. The treatment only helps the patient find a possible way but the treatment itself is not the resolution.

We might ask; what about individuals such as those in India referred to as medicine men or medicine women? They also rely heavily on the individuals who come to them for help going through the spirit world to make their treatments work. While the practitioners discussed previously connect with their patients mainly through our physical world, it appears medicine men and women connect with the individuals mainly through the spirit world. Therefore, their approach is very different. They essentially inspire the individuals to go through the spirit world to find the bit of the spirit world's restoring and healing powers that applies to their individual medical condition. The medicine people do this by giving the individuals empathy, compassion, love and hope, and they might combine this with materials, herbs, and movements. Thus, they are using the powers of both worlds to maximize their effectiveness. We might ask; are they producing restoration/healing or a cure? Or are they producing placebo effects? The answer has to be that if restoration/healing or a cure happens, then they produced restoration/healing or a cure. If only improvement happens, then they produced perhaps a placebo effect. And if neither happens, then just as with any other treatment, effectiveness in favor of humans is not a sure thing for the three reasons given at the start of this section.

The preceding discussion could also explain why when we have a positive attitude about a modern medical treatment it enhances the effectiveness of the treatment. A positive attitude enables the patient to find on his or her own additional bits of the spirit world's restoring and healing powers that apply to his or her individual medical condition. Thus, by adding this to the bit of the spirit world's restoring and healing powers that come with the treatment, healing is enhanced.

This could also explain how a positive attitude is a good thing in general, because it enables us to be more likely to find things in the spirit world that could help us in general. It is like a positive attitude finds open doors while a poor attitude doesn't bother to even look. It is often said one of the most important things we can encourage in our kids is to be creative. Creativity to me is the ability to find open doors, to find new ways of thinking and of doing things and making things work, etc. Being able to be this way enables an individual to never feel enclosed, confined, restricted, limited, etc. and thus the individual is naturally going to be positive.

One thing brought out by this discussion is that while we tend to think modern medical practices lack spirituality, they in fact involve a lot of spirituality. It is only our perception of the practices that might lead us to think they are lacking in spirituality. Thus, this discussion explains how our attitude in dealing with our medical problems can have a powerful effect on how well we restore and/or heal. The attitude we choose is something we get in touch with in the spirit world, because it is only in the spirit world that all spiritual entities reside, and attitudes are spiritual entities. Therefore, looking for them and finding the ones that help us is going through the spirit world to be more in touch with its restoring and healing powers. This is case for any restoring and healing we need to do, including the daily restoring we do when we sleep.

The Healing Powers of Statues and Other Physical Things

My mom had a bunch of figurines and statues inside her house and around her garden. Some are historical, some are cute, some pretty, some whimsical, and all are interesting. It never dawned on me, when I was very young, that they had any powers. They were just pieces of material shaped like living things. But now I realize they must have had spiritual powers that touched her, and that it is a personal thing.

Losing my wife followed by three and a half years of treatment for my recurred cancer made going places and having visitors difficult because of permanent side effects that came with my immune system being permanently trained and changed by the chemotherapy to fight the cancer. These include persistent tiredness, frequent headaches with nausea; unpredictable sensitivities to foods and medications, and frequent urgency that happens dozens of times day and night. By restricting what I eat to only bland things like plain white bread, drinking hardly any liquids, and taking a long nap, I am able to be with others without frequent urgent visits to the bathroom or needing a nap for the time I am with them. But this tends to make them think I am just fine and can do all the things they can do, when in fact what I need is plenty of rest, peace, and quiet. Thus, I spend a lot of my time quietly and slowly cleaning up, reorganizing, and renewing the house and garden. After more than forty years since the house was built, they need a lot of work and attention.

In the process, I realized how beautiful the garden has become as the landscaping has matured over the years. The garden had been mainly a source of work in the past when my main focus was on career and the family. Meanwhile, the garden's beauty developed unnoticed. Today, with my changed outlook, suddenly the garden has become a wonderland with healing powers. Now I enjoy finding ways to enhance its beauty and healing powers, and thus I am healing myself through these powers.

When the house was built, as I mentioned before, I configured the garden to have three elevations and several regions, each region with a different mood. The plants and trees on each level have now matured and the moods are now fully developed; they only needed chairs or benches to make them more inviting. I also added various statues such as ones of St. Francis, Primavera, angels, Buddha meditating, children playing, etc. To my surprise, the statues significantly enhance the moods and healing powers of the garden. The model explains how the statues are able to do this.

As discussed earlier in the book, nonliving things have spirits and souls just as living things do. They have physical shapes because their spirits contain the knowledge that enables them to do so. When their shapes resemble living things, especially humans and spiritual beings such as saints and angels, the statues' spirits include parts that resemble the spirits of such individuals and spiritual beings. Therefore, each statue captures a bit of the living spirit of a saint, individual, or spiritual being and brings an actual bit of that saint, individual, or spiritual being into the garden. Each statue thus has a certain oneness with human individuals, and this gives the statue its healing powers. It follows then that the statues can decrease loneliness and enhance the peacefulness and comforting nature of the garden.

Fortunately, the garden is fairly large and quite private. I was able to design it such that it is possible to enjoy it via brisk walking or sitting and relaxing. The various regions lead from one to the next in an irregularly shaped continuous loop that includes steps and slopes going to and from each of the three levels. I enjoy the garden most when I am walking the circuit, passing through each region and passing by each statue. I try to do this every day for at least 30 minutes when the ground is not muddy from rain. This enables me to do my daily walk most of the time while staying close to home where I need to be when frequent urgencies come on.

Part of the loop is paved with bricks or paving stones I put in myself through the years. The rest is simply bare earth. There are no concrete slabs. I thought about paving the entire loop so that I could do the walk even when it's wet. But there is something very healing about walking on unpaved earth. It is more in touch with nature and thus the spirit world. Even the areas paved with bricks or paving stones feel more spiritually alive than would slabs of concrete. They embody the personal effort and dedication that went into putting in each brick and stone by hand and the carving of each edge piece so as to form smooth wavy curving borders for the paths and the irregularly shaped sitting areas.

Karma

The dictionary definition says "it is the force generated by a person's actions held in Hinduism and Buddhism to perpetrate transmigration and in it ethical consequences to determine his destiny in his next existence." The model is compatible with this definition; i.e., knowledge in the spirit world must be kept reasonably balanced. Therefore, if an individual goes through an experience that generated a certain amount of knowledge that caused a certain degree of imbalance in the spirit world, then sooner or later another experience needs to take place that will generate knowledge that restores the balance. This is compatible with the concept in the dictionary definition for karma.

The main difference is that the dictionary definition says the counterbalancing experience is to take place in the individual's next lifetime whereas the model says it can take place at any time, perhaps the sooner the better. It might not be karma, as karma is strictly defined, but a lot of people think certain things can happen to them in the present because of something they did earlier in their life. I.e., they believe they do not have to wait until their next lifetime to do something to counterbalance something they did in this lifetime. Once in a while, restoring balance appears to happen within the same lifetime, or perhaps it's simply coincidence, or our imagination going along with our expectations, etc.

One example might be a couple who does not particularly support each other. One day the wife fell off a ladder and cut her leg badly on some rose bushes, and she pretty much had to tend to her injury by herself. Years later, soon after she passed away, he fell trimming the same rose blushes and cut his arm badly, and he had to tend to his injury by himself. This sort of seems like karma is doing its thing within the same lifetime.

At one period in my life, I faced a no-win situation. No matter the path I chose I would hurt someone. I chose what I perceived as the more honorable path, and it hurt my parents a lot. I always regretted the hurt I caused, but if I had to choose again, I would do the same, not because it turned out to be necessarily the better choice, but because it still seems the more honorable choice, for better or worse. My mom came down with cancer a few years afterwards. I always wondered if I might have contributed to the cause. When I reached the same age my mom was when she got her cancer, I got my cancer. I always wondered if karma had anything to do with it or was it simply coincidence, or was it just in the genes.

Whichever it was, I accepted it and dealt with my cancer as a natural part of my particular life. Thus, rather than letting it get me down I decided to take advantage of the freedom the cancer gave me from having to tend to a lot of things I might be expected to tend to if I were in good health. Although, I have wondered if I had chosen the other path and ended up hurting people but not my parents, what would karma have done then? What I could imagine happening would be different but just as bad. Therefore, I might as well not have any regrets. Besides, it is up to me to use the knowledge gained from the experience positively or negatively and it's better to use it positively.

This does not mean pretending the experience was good. Pretending only means hanging on to it. If the truth is that it was bad, it has to be recognized as such in order to let it go, so that the knowledge gained can be released from confinement and denial and be free and recognized to be used positively.

Do We Formulate Models or Do Models Formulate Us or Is It Both?

We might think that when we formulate a model, any kind of model, that we have complete command in shaping the model. But no, this is not the case. I am sure anyone who has formulated a model knows that the model takes us by the hand and leads us through fascinating places. For example, time and time again, models predict certain phenomena should be possible, and sure enough, sooner or later, some researcher discovers the existence of the phenomena. Upon making the discovery, we then move forward to further develop the model or formulate the next model for the next phase. The model is in essence shaping us while we are shaping the model.

Some common evidence of this is how our lives are filled with models of all kinds, and how the models shape the way we go about our daily lives. Models enable us to realize we can design and build high-rise structures, space ships, sophisticated medical equipment, high-technology devices, self-driving cars, etc. After we have succeeded in building such things, as the models predicted we could, we then move forward to form models for the next level of advancement. Three-dimensional printing technology and computers miniaturized to the scale of atoms are examples.

We might ask; why models are able to lead us through places that are fascinating? As mention early in the book, every model is a spiritual model in that every model is an approximation of a small part of spirituality. Spirituality is so expansive and enormous that no one single model formulated by a human can capture all of it. Thus, we can only formulate models that are essentially fairly simple, and each can capture only a small part of spirituality and only in an approximate manner. Thus, no model formulated by a human is going to be totally complete or absolutely accurate. However, wherever the part of spirituality a model captures, the places it takes us through are still fascinating because the places are the various parts of the spirit world that we have not been to before while as a human on Earth.

Therefore, this means that if we want to discover more about the spirit world for the sake of understanding the spirit world more, as opposed to doing so for the sake of understanding our physical world more, we need to formulate more models that are more about the spirit world. The models we now have are mostly more about our physical world. We have fewer models that are about the spirit world, although we do not normally think about them as such. Models about the spirit world would directly or indirectly touch on the behavior of living things, particular the behavior of humans. They would naturally include the various religious models and models to do with beliefs, traditions, customs, ways of life, etc. We could have thousands of denominations of various religions, and thousands of versions of various beliefs, traditions, customs, etc. Each denomination and/or version would be a personal thing in that each individual would follow it in a manner that works best for that individual.

Chapter Nine
The Dominant Basis for How We Carry Out Our Lives

Advancement and Increasing Complexity in the Spirit World

Chapter Three explained that each universe is designed to help the spirit world restore balance so that it can continue to form wisdom. Wisdom is vital to the viability of the spirit world and everything it creates. The spirit world keeps growing as new pieces of knowledge are constantly generated and added to it. Thus, it keeps getting more advanced and complex. Tasks necessary to restore balance keep getting more complex as well. Consequently, besides needing to stay balanced, the spirit world also needs its advancement to keep up with what is needed to handle its increasingly complex tasks.

We might ask; if the spirit world's advancement could ever fall behind the complexity of the tasks? The answer is; it is unlikely in an overall sense, since continued advancement and continued increase in complexity are due to the same continued increase in knowledge. This is assuming balance is maintained so that the universes or other entities generating the new knowledge are designed by the spirit world with its wisdom in good shape.

While overall balance is maintained within a reasonable level in the spirit world, balances in local portions can vary but are still within acceptable limits. The local variations result from the spirit world keeping only one copy of each piece of knowledge. Thus, the spirit world is naturally not perfectly homogeneous on a local level while appearing homogeneous on a global level, similar to the way something in our physical world can appear homogenous from a distance, but has local variations when looking at it up close. Earth appears beautiful, harmonious, and peaceful when viewed from outer space, but up close that is not the case everywhere.

While the overall advancement of the spirit world keeps up with its overall complexity, the advancements in various portions can be "ahead of," "on par with," or "behind" their complexities. This doesn't mean things always go well for an "ahead of" portion of the spirit world and always go badly for a "behind" portion. Everything in the spirit world has a certain probability of being at certain level of near-perfection. Notice how everything in our physical world is like this, and it is because the spirit world is like this. It follows that things in the "ahead of" portion of the spirit world have a higher probability of going well while things in the "behind" portion have a lower probability. Likewise, in our physical world an expensive version of an item is usually better than an inexpensive version, but not always.

In the spirit world, which portions are "ahead of," "on par with," or "behind" is very clear. But at times things in a "behind" portion can go better than things in an "ahead of" portion. Nevertheless, to restore balance in each portion, those that are "ahead of" present a less-than-average challenge while portions that are "behind" present a greater-than-average challenge. But this doesn't mean portions that are "behind" are less valuable than portions that are "ahead of." In fact, all portions directly or indirectly share parts of themselves with one another. Consequently, there are no differences in value among the portions.

Interestingly enough, restoring balances for some portions that are "behind," can be more challenging than average and require going through more experiences. This means they can generate more new pieces of knowledge than average to restore balance, and in this sense they can do more than average to help the spirit world grow, while not necessarily helping the spirit world restore balance as much as an "ahead" portion can.

The Dominant Basis for How We Carry Out Our Lives

We might wonder whether our universe, and particularly Earth, was enabled to exist by a portion of the spirit world "ahead of," "on par with," or "behind." The answer is we are not likely to know while we are alive on Earth but will find out after our life is over and our consciousness returns to being fully tuned to the spirit world. Besides, according to the preceding section, the way things are happening on Earth can still occur whether or not the advancement on Earth has kept up with the complexity of the portion of the spirit world that enables Earth to exist. In other words an "ahead of" Earth can be doing just the same as a "behind" Earth during any given period.

Regardless, if we are supposed to make Earth resemble the spirit world as closely as possible (i.e., make it gentle, kind, caring, nonjudgmental, compassionate, empathic, and loving), we are likely to be at a low level of near-perfection anyway, considering what we humans as a species do to one another. Other species on Earth behave much better in how the way they treat members of their own species, and yet we consider ourselves to be more advanced.

It turns out that, as we will see later in the next section, according to the model, it is theoretically reasonable that other species are more advanced spiritually while we are more advanced physically. We might then ask if they are doing more to help the spirit world restore balance than we are? The answer is that they could be, and that they are saving Earth from being an utter failure in helping the spirit world restore balance. I suppose this could mean that their role is to have Earth fulfill its purpose of helping the spirit world restore balance, while our role as humans is to help the spirit world grow as much as possible.

That doesn't sound very good. As indicated above, our being at a low level of near-perfection means we have an opportunity to contribute more than average to the growth of the spirit world. But I doubt that the spirit world meant for us to contribute to its growth in some of the ways we do. We have been doing some of the same spiritually awful things for thousands of years but with progressively more advanced physical methods. Are these all the kinds of advancements we choose to make as the most intelligent species on Earth? Yikes!

This is likely because generally we are not very aware we are carrying out our lives simultaneously in the spirit world and our physical world. Consequently, the dominant basis we chose for how we carry out our lives has been "ego and the desire to enhance survivability" for thousands of years. Right away this is not similar to the way it is in the spirit world. This means that if we keep this as our dominant basis, the model and our history indicate we have very little chance of making Earth resemble the spirit world as closely as possible in terms of the qualities mentioned.

We would all like to always be treated with such qualities. And, we are intelligent enough to know everyone needs to always act with such qualities in order for everyone to always be treated with such qualities. So, why doesn't everyone always act with such qualities? I think it is because we all have hang-ups. Some are significant enough to be like severe itches that we scratch whenever the opportunity to do so comes up. And, when we have to scratch, our rational reasoning tends to be pushed aside and our emotions tend to take over. Consequently, our hang-ups, particularly the severe ones, color everything we do, how we look at things, how we express ourselves, etc.

Because our physical universe is made of materials and energies that can be possessed and controlled, and natural resources are limited, hang-ups can easily and naturally develop in us if we let them. They are like bacteria and viruses that are all around us and could easily and naturally infect us if we let them. Most or all of our severe hang-ups come from our "ego and the desire to enhance survivability," that we choose as the dominant basis for how we carry out our lives. This means if we change our dominant basis to "empathy and compassion for one another," we are likely to drop most or all of our severe hang-ups. We would not be as self-focused and thus not be as vulnerable to being infected by hang-ups.

However, just like everything else in our physical world, most hang-ups have their good sides and their bad sides. Everyone is different and unique and has a different and unique set of hang-ups. Some hang-ups are minor and some are major. The way we choose to respond to them can also be good or bad.

For example, we have different ways of boosting ego and of enhancing survivability. Some individuals work hard and become recognized experts in what they do. Some individuals repeatedly do criminal acts and become notorious criminals.

Most of us try to lead the life of a good person, but having "ego and the desire to enhance survivability" as our dominant basis causes some of us to do bad things. This can then cause some of the rest of us to be a part of doing bad things, sometimes unintentionally. For example, we can have corrupt leaders who manage to hide their corruption so that we support what they do because they are able to make what they do sound good. Then the victims of the bad things do bad things back to us, and we do not fully understand why and thus consider them bad people. We then tend to support doing something back at them. They might also have leaders who are corrupt, unbeknownst to their people. Meanwhile, most of us, including most of those "bad" people try to lead the lives of good people. By this scenario, the main problem appears to be our species choosing "ego and the desire to enhance survivability" as the dominant basis for how we carry out our lives.

Leaders Do Not Exist in the Spirit World, But Humans on Earth Need Leaders

The spirit world is made of all the pieces of knowledge that exist up to that given point in time. It is also made of all the spiritual entities that can be formed from all the pieces of knowledge that exist at that point in time. Because of the oneness that pervades the spirit world, every spiritual entity is directly or indirectly a part of every other spiritual entity. Therefore, communication throughout the spirit world is complete and instantaneous within the spirit world. Consequently, there is no need for leaders in the spirit world. The entire spirit world functions as a single unified entity. The spirit world determines what kinds of new pieces of knowledge need to be generated to maintain reasonable balance. It forms every possible spiritual entity that can be formed at any given point in time with the pieces of knowledge that exist then. Therefore, we could say the spirit world has one leader, and it is the spirit world itself. On the other hand, the spirit world is made of all the pieces of knowledge that exist and all the spiritual entities that exist at any given point in time.

Therefore, it is a question of who is leading who. Is the spirit world leading the pieces of knowledge and spiritual entities, or vice versa? The answer is both, because all the pieces of knowledge and all the spiritual entities that exist at any point in time comprise the spirit world at that point in time. In other words, the spirit world leads itself, no matter how we look at it, and therefore the spirit world has only one leader and it is itself.

On Earth in our physical universe, living things are separate entities. Some living things rely heavily on the spirit world to do their thinking for them, and thus they can get by without having leaders. This is because communications among all members of a species take place automatically in the spirit world.

A gradation exists between such living things and humans in that we humans rely very little on the spirit world to think for us; i.e., we mainly think for ourselves. The less a species consists of living things that rely on the spirit world to think for them, the less of the automatic communication that exists in the spirit world is translated to exist for such living things. Consequently, the more such living things need leaders to hold any group of them together and to behave in a mutually supportive manner.

We humans, being the living things on Earth that rely least on the spirit world to do our thinking for us, are thus the ones that most need leaders to hold groups of us together and behave in a mutually supportive manner. This also means we humans are the most vulnerable to being led by bad leaders. Living things that rely a lot more on the spirit world to do their thinking for them might also need leaders, but their leaders are less likely to be bad, since their leaders are more guided by the spirit world than human leaders are. This could explain why we humans are capable of doing horrible things to other humans while living things of other species would never do such things to members of their own species. Such observations further support the notion that the spirit world has all the positive attributes that come with the oneness that pervades it.

The fact that we humans and living things of various other species need leaders explains why ego is included in the design of our universe, or at least on Earth. In order for any individual to want to be a leader, that individual needs a certain amount of ego. A positive amount is enough for the individual to want to be a leader for the sake of making a positive contribution to the species. This seems usually the case for most species that need leaders. The exception seems to be us humans. Sometimes we are fortunate enough to have leaders with this positive amount of ego. Nelson Mandela is a good example. Some human leaders would have too much ego such that they want to be a leader for the sake of having power and control more than for the sake of making a positive contribution to mankind. Throughout history we have seen leaders who are obviously this way.

What this says is that having ego is not a bad thing. In fact, ego and the desire to enhance survivability are necessary for maintaining the viability of individuals and groups, provided "ego and the desire to enhance survivability" exist in a positive amount. The model indicates that a positive amount is such that "ego and the desire to enhance survivability" is not the dominant basis for carrying out our lives. This means we must give it a lower priority than the priority we give to "empathy and compassion for one another" such that "empathy and compassion for one another" becomes our dominant basis for how we carry out our lives.

Tapping Into the Oneness that Pervades the Spirit World

The oneness that pervades the spirit world enables communications to be complete and instantaneous throughout the spirit world. This is part of what gives the spirit world its positive attributes. This indicates that if we humans could tap into the oneness that pervades the spirit world, we as a species could develop at least some of the positive attributes of the spirit world.

Communications appear to be the key, specifically communications that are as complete as possible and as quick as possible. Poor communications can be misleading, manipulative, and lead to bad behavior based on inaccurate information. Therefore, we need to think of ways to enhance communication to make it as complete as possible and as quick as possible. Our advancements in electronic high technology could be a part of enabling us to achieve this.

It is obviously unconventional, but if we could learn how to communicate telepathically, that would be a very good way to accomplish this. Telepathic communication functions by going through the spirit world and would thus automatically embody at least some of the positive attributes of communications there. The model indicates telepathic communication is possible for us humans, as discussed earlier, including that observed between identical twins. Various other individuals who see and read auras, do remote viewing, and have various other extrasensory abilities are other examples, because these also function by going through the spirit world.

The main idea is for us to think of ways to tap into the oneness that pervades the spirit world. Enhancing communications that function in as complete a manner as possible and as quickly as possible is one way. Being as complete as possible is important, because then the various sides of issues can be better communicated and both the good and bad intentions of leaders would also be more apparent. Therefore, for highly intelligent living things such as us humans who think for ourselves, we as a species ought to behave better than we have throughout our history.

With our advancements in electronic high technology and the evidence that we have the ability to do things that function by going through the spirit world, we might finally be able to make a significant and positive change in the way we behave as a species. Thus, when we finally elect a leader who tends to do things in an unconventional but kinder and more caring way, let's not say that the leader is a bad leader just because he is not as ego-driven as leaders we are used to. Let's instead explore how such unconventional ways can help us. After all, look what Nelson Mandela was able to accomplish in spite of all that had happened to him in his past. Conventional thinking would have had him behaving in the opposite manner, and events could have been very bad.

Evolution Is a Part of Universes to Enable Them to Fulfill Their Purposes

Spiritual advancements take place in the spirit world, and advancements relevant to the world of a universe take place in that world as life is being carried out simultaneously in both worlds. For example, spiritual advancements we humans made enabled us to better understand human behavior, be more accepting of human differences, be more creative and inventive, and be more able to solve problems and develop concepts, etc. These are examples of how our spiritual advancements enable us better able to find things in the spirit world and translate them into forms that can be expressed, but not physically exist, in our physical world. We might refer to such advancements as being better able to do abstract thinking, be creativity, be imaginative, handle problems, sense intuitive and instinctive spiritual signals, make extrapolations and interpolations, etc.

Physical advancements we make are those that enable us to (1) better able to find increasingly complex things in the spirit world and translate them into physical things that can exist in our physical world, and (2) better able to go through experiences that generate knowledge that enable us to better understand physical things that already exist in our physical world. Examples include scientific discoveries; inventions; the construction of complex structures; the design and making of mechanical, electrical, high-technology things; new and better ways to treat or cure diseases; ways to land a satellite on a comet; etc.

For a nonphysical universe, the advancements living things there will make are ones relevant to the world of their universe and that are different from spiritual advancements they would also make. Both kinds will be nonphysical in nature. The difference is the former will take place in the world of their universe, and the later will take place in the spirit world.

Our spiritual advancements are directly useful in the spirit world such that we can "bring" them with us when we return to the spirit world. This is because spiritual advancements are made in the spirit world in the first place. The spiritual parts of our physical advancements such as concepts, designs, and pieces of knowledge we generated are also directly useful in the spirit world such that we can also "bring" those with us when we return to the spirit world. But we cannot "bring" the physical parts of the accomplishments with us. This is because the spirit world is nonphysical. Also, our universe is only three-dimensional and has a particular set of three dimensions out of all the dimensions that exist in the spirit world. Such reasons would render the physical parts of our accomplishments to be compatible only with our universe. And, they will vanish when the lifetime of our universe is over. So, even if we can "bring" them with us into the spirit world, why bother. All other universes, including nonphysical ones, would have similar situations.

Advancement in the spirit world does not mean advancing ahead of others. All spiritual entities are directly or indirectly a part of one another in the spirit world. Therefore, one spiritual entity advancing ahead of another is only a concept and not a practice in the spirit world. However, in our physical world where living things are physically separate, one living thing advancing ahead of another has meaning. This is an example of how universes, in this case our physical universe, can provide opportunities for experiences not possible in the spirit world and therefore generate knowledge the spirit world cannot generate on its own.

Advancement in the spirit world means simply moving forward in knowledge and complexity, and thus being able to play an increasingly knowledgeable and complex role in an increasingly knowledgeable and complex spirit world. The spirit world consists of all possible sizes and varieties of spiritual entities, ranging from ones consisting of only two pieces of knowledge to ones approaching the size of the spirit world. Every spiritual entity is important and has a role in the spirit world, similar to how in our physical world every component, no matter how big or small, has an important role in making a physical things such as a space station, bridge, skyscraper, jumbo jet, car, smart phone, can opener, mechanical pencil, etc. function properly.

Every new universe is different from any that came before. Therefore, a spiritual entity serving as the spirit for a living thing residing in a new universe will be dealing with attributes, environments, how life is sustained, natural resources, etc. that are different from any it dealt with before. Consequently, it has to first get acquainted with the new universe. After that, it can start making advancements relevant to the spirit world and/or the world of the new universe. Getting acquainted takes time. The spiritual entity serving as the spirit for a living thing must first have the living thing be in a primitive form such that it can to go through "primitive" experiences that are possible in the new universe. The spiritual entity will progressively gain the proficiency to pilot progressively more advanced living things that it is within its capacity to enable to exist in the new universe. Therefore, when it is ready to enable the next, and more advanced, kind of living thing to exist, it will let go of the current kind and begin to enable the next kind to exist.

During the process, the spiritual entity will grow and its capacity will expand and be capable of enabling living things that are more advanced than the kinds it had been able to exist up to now. This progression will continue for as long as the universe's lifespan has not ended and for as long as the conditions in the universe become progressively more hospitable to more advanced kinds of living things. Eventually, the spiritual entity will be able to enable to exist the kinds of very advanced living things that are capable of making the most significant spiritual advancements and advancements of the kind that are relevant in that universe. Up to that point in time, all or most activities are to prepare the universe to accept such living things and to prepare the spiritual entity to be able to enable such living things to exist there.

This indicates every new universe naturally starts off with living things that can be perceived as primitive, and that evolution and the retracing of already existing evolutionary paths are important parts of every universe. This is how a typical universe would grow and "mature" to where it eventually can do the most significant things that help fulfill its purpose. The meaning of "retracing of already existing evolutionary paths" is covered in Chapter Three.

Hey, that makes sense. So, is our universe doing OK, and where is it in its progression? Well, lets see. Lets look at where it has been up to now. Yeah, frankly I'm worried because it looks like we are not doing so well right now.

In the case of our physical universe, what the concept of progression can mean is that a spiritual entity capable of serving as spirit of, for example, a human on Earth will first serve as the spirit for some primitive living thing on Earth for a while. As the spiritual entity becomes more acquainted with our universe, it will start serving as the spirit for a more advanced but still relatively primitive living thing. Eventually, as it works its way up the chain of progressively more advanced living things, it will learn enough to be ready to serve as the spirit of a living thing as advanced as a human such that it can pilot the human proficiently on Earth. This is analogous to how a pilot of the most advanced jumbo jet begins by first learning how to pilot very simple airplanes and then gradually increasingly advanced airplanes until he or she becomes proficient enough to pilot the most advanced jumbo jet. It takes time to progress to that level, just as it takes time for the spirit world to be ready to bring humans into being on Earth.

This means that the notion that we humans and other living things on Earth all originated from the first primitive living things that came into being on Earth is likely to be true in both the spirit world and our physical world.

The consciousness of the spirit of a living thing residing in a new universe will be partly tuned to the spirit world and partly tuned to the world of the new universe. The living thing finds thoughts, solutions, concepts, ideas, intentions, etc. in the spirit world and it receives guidance signals such as intuition, instincts, etc. in the spirit world. At the same time, it goes through experiences in the world of its universe to generate new pieces of knowledge or gain access to existing pieces of knowledge. The ratio between the degree of being tuned to the spirit world and the degree of being tuned to the world of the universe will be different for different living things and for different universes.

We can see on Earth that different living things have different ratios. Living things that rely heavily on the spirit world to do their thinking for them have ratios heavily biased toward the spirit world. We humans do almost all of our own thinking, and we have a much greater range of abilities. Therefore, our ratio is heavily biased toward our physical world. Animals in general do a lot of their own thinking as well, but not as much as humans, and their range of abilities is more limited. Therefore, their ratios are biased toward our physical world as well, but not as much as ours is.

The ratios might generally be more biased toward the spirit world for living things in nonphysical universes than are ratios of living things in physical universes. This is because nonphysical universes are more like the spirit world in that both are nonphysical. Consequently, the consciousness of the spirits of nonphysical living things are used to dealing with a nonphysical world and thus might more easily tune to the spirit world than can the consciousness of spirits of physical living things.

The ratio influences the manner in which a species' advancements can progress. On Earth, for example, living things with ratios biased toward the spirit world make more spiritual advancements than physical advancements. And, living things with ratios biased toward our physical world make more physical advancements than spiritual advancements. This could explain why, for example, monarch butterflies with their ratio heavily biased toward the spirit world never do awful things to one another, and why some of us humans with our ratio heavily biased toward our physical world do awful things to one another. But monarch butterflies never invent smart phones, discover ways to treat diseases, drive cars, etc. In other words, monarch butterflies can make spiritual advancements but cannot make many physical advancements. We humans, on the other hand, are able to make great discoveries, invent amazing things, produce great works of art, etc., but we can't seem to avoid making a mess on Earth or find a way to clean it up. Thus, we can make a lot of physical advancements but not as much spiritual advancement.

This suggests that we might be able to tell what the ratio for a living thing is, in a relative sense, by observing its behavior. For example, animals fight with members of their own species but don't do anything close to some of the awful things some humans do to other humans. This indicates again that the ratios of animals are not as biased toward our physical world as much as our ratio is.

It is interesting that most of the living things on Earth are smaller and simpler than most animals, and essentially all of them generally do not purposely harm members of their own species. Black widow spiders and praying mantises are among the exceptions in that a female sometimes eats the male after mating. But in general their ratios must all be heavily biased toward the spirit world. In a sense, we could perceive such living things as being here to keep ecosystems and environments hospitable to the more advanced living things on Earth, because that is more or less what most of them have a part in doing. Therefore, in a sense they are representatives of the parts of the spirit world whose main purposes are to enable Earth to be hospitable to living things in general. Consequently, the ratios of such living things would naturally be heavily biased toward the spirit world, and their behavior supports this possibility.

The model says each universe is designed and brought into being mainly of help the spirit world restore its balance. Therefore, once balance is restored to reasonable balance, keeping the universe existing will be counterproductive. This means every universe is designed to have a finite lifetime, unless it continues to emerge. But even then, the continued emergence could end and the existence of the universe will eventually end.

Every universe must have life-supporting ingredients in order for living things to thrive in it. On Earth, examples of such ingredients include natural resources, hospitable environments, food such as plants and various other living things, water, and organisms that recycle various spent ingredients to make them life-supporting again. However, since every universe has a finite lifespan and living things in it must progressively evolve to become progressively more advanced living things, the life-supporting ingredients in it have to be finite from the standpoint of any given living thing that exist at any given moment in time. In other words, for example on Earth, the ingredients that supported a bunch of early living things will gradually change such that they can no longer support those living things, but they would then become able to support the next, and more advanced, bunch of living things. This goes on continuously such that from the standpoint of any given living thing that exists at any given moment in time, the life-supporting ingredients is finite and can gradually be exhausted. On Earth right now, we can see how this applies to humans as the supply of ingredients that supports our lives is gradually decreasing. Examples are crude oil, clean air, clean water including water in underground aquifers, rain forests (one of the "lungs" of the Earth), fertile land for food production, various salt water and fresh water creatures that we consume, rare earth materials needed to make high technology things, etc.

We might ask; would finite lifespan apply to living things in the spirit world? The answer is, yes, if the spirit world becomes nonviable and vanishes. Otherwise, no. A piece of knowledge once generated exists forever, provided the spirit world remains viable. And, living things there are made of pieces of knowledge. Thus, life in the spirit world is spiritual life and is different from life in a universe. A universe is designed and brought into being by the spirit world mainly to fulfill a certain purpose, and when that purpose is fulfilled, keeping the universe in existence will be counterproductive. Therefore, the universe has a finite lifetime. The spirit world does not have a finite lifetime as long as it remains viable. To better understand how a piece of knowledge once generate will exist forever, we will have to wait for a model to be formulated that describes the workings of the world consisting of the intelligences that initiated the spirit world. We might have to wait until we return to the spirit world before we can formulate such a model, because we are unlikely able to formulate such as model while we are alive on Earth.

Hey, maybe the spiritual expression of someone like Albert Einstein has already done it there. Yeah, maybe. Then maybe you and I ought to try finding it there. Oh no, not another 27 years project!

What the discussion so far implies is that a universe with an extremely large amount of life-supporting ingredients for a given species of living things would enable that species to thrive for an extremely long time. The species would then be able to make advancements of both kinds for an extremely long time and thus become extremely advanced in both ways.

Conversely, a universe with an extremely small amount of life-supporting ingredients for a given species will mean that species will be able to advance relatively little in both ways and therefore will not be particularly advanced in both ways. And, as the life-supporting ingredients dwindle to where they cannot satisfy the number of existing members, over-population can be perceived to have taken place. The members will then be fighting each other to gain control over the dwindling ingredients. They would thus waste their time and personal energy as well as waste the dwindling ingredients by making fighting equipment and by fighting. A good part of the species remaining lifespan would be spend destructively instead of making advances of either or both kinds. Consequently, the species will unlikely make much progress in their advancements of either way for the rest of its lifespan.

OMG! All this sounds familiar. Could it be that Earth is a planet with a low amount of life-supporting ingredients. Well, that is a good question. Read the next paragraph.

This same phenomenon applies to the various life-supporting planets in our physical universe. The planets with an extremely large amount of life-supporting ingredients are likely to produce living things that are extremely advanced spiritually and physically. Conversely, a planet with a small amount of life-supporting ingredients are likely to produce living things that are significantly less advanced in both ways.

Under the best of circumstances in our physical universe, advancement can reach a level high enough for living things to find ways to continue making advancements over the remaining lifetime of the universe without exhausting the life-supporting ingredients of their planet. For example, they can become advance enough in both ways to thus choose "empathy and compassion for one another" as the dominant basis for how they carry out their lives. They will have gained enough wisdom to realize this is the better choice from a long-term long-range standpoint. They will understand this will allow them to apply their time and personal energy to develop ways to make renewable what they need to consume to remain viable. (Otherwise they are likely instead to be wasting time, personal energy, and life-supporting ingredients doing things such as developing equipment for battle, doing battle, doing corrupt things, seeking power for the sake of having power, and other destructive activities.) And, they will also be wise enough to keep their population in balance with their capacity for renewing and producing life-supporting ingredients. Therefore, they will continue to become more advanced over the remaining lifetime of our universe without exhausting the life-supporting ingredients of their planet.

In addition, they will understand that good communication is important such that everyone can be well informed when significant decisions arise that need everyone's participation to address, such as those that come up during elections, if things like elections exist on their planet. To find ways to make good communications possible, and being highly advanced, they are likely to develop the ability to communicate telepathically. The sum total of how they are carrying out their lives will become close to how life is carried out in the spirit world in terms of making their planet a gentle, kind, caring, nonjudgmental, compassionate, empathic, and loving place. This will be as the spirit world intended, and the experiences to achieve this will be the ones that will generate the pieces of knowledge the spirit world needs to restore balance. This discussion illustrates how evolution and the retracing of already existing evolutionary paths play an important role in enabling a planet to arrive at a stage at which the planet can fulfill its main purpose, that of helping the spirit world restore balance.

Living thing in such a planet might be able to develop ways to do space travel. The purpose will be for continued learning and not for invading or taking over other planets. After all, they already made their own planet a wonderful place to live. They will know that every planet is different and unique and that each will provide a different opportunity for learning. Therefore, they will know they must not ruin any of such opportunities by trying to change in any way the planet or the living things residing there. They will also be wise enough to know that if they try to change anything, they can cause incompatibilities with the way of life on that planet and thus cause problems that can be worse than any that might already exist there before.

OMG! This also sounds familiar. Why, because you think some humans have gone into other nations and tried to change things there and thus caused problems worse than any that might have already been there in the first place? Oh, now, why would any human want to do that? Yeah, I often wondered why.

In the case of our physical universe, every hospitable planet will be different and unique. The spirit world will logically design them to be different and unique so as to minimize overlap in possible experiences among the planets and thus maximize the potential to restore balance and to generate as many new pieces of knowledge as possible with a minimum number of hospitable planets. This implies that the most intelligent species residing in each hospitable planet will also be different and unique. In other words, don't expect to find living things exactly like us humans on other planets.

Incidentally, a planet with a moderate amount of life-supporting ingredients, such as how I think Earth is, need not make a mess or continue making a mess if a mess is already made. I think it is possible for such a planet to arrive at a stage at which living things there will continue to become more advanced over the remaining lifetime of our universe without exhausting the life-supporting ingredients of their planet.

The reason I think Earth is one that has at least a moderate amount of life-supporting ingredients, instead of an extremely low amount, is because the amount it has can satisfy its current population of living things, if we humans would apply our intelligence well enough. I think we humans have enough intelligence to form enough wisdom to do this. The main thing is for everyone to let go of "ego and the desire to enhance survivability" as our dominant basis for how we carry out our lives, and replace it with "empathy and compassion for one another." This is a tall order for our current situation, but not impossible, and it will take many generations and maybe many hundreds of years. However, we need to do it as quickly as possible before the amount of life-supporting ingredients dwindle down to where we don't have enough left to enable us to do it.

Incidentally, sometimes we hear people say about those who do horrible things to other humans as being "animals." I think we should not insult other animals that way. Other animals do not do such horrible things to their own species.

As an aside, in my mind we might have evidence that other hospitable planets exist and can be very different from Earth. Recent findings indicate some comets contain molecules that can make up living things. This means such comets might come from a planet that had living things residing on it, and that planet for some reason came apart. It might have collided with something very big, or it might have had a nuclear furnace inside of it that blew up. Such events can also explain why comets tend to contain a lot of water. Planets hospitable to living things are likely to have a lot of water. If such a planet were to blow up by itself, then it will have to be very different from Earth. As far as we know, the nuclear furnace inside of Earth is not likely to blow up.

We Are Responsible for How Our Species Is Evolving

One of the conclusions we can draw from the discussion in the preceding section is that highly intelligent living things that do essentially all their own thinking and have the freedom to chose will also have the responsibility for how their species is evolving. The notion that evolution and retracing of evolutionary paths are important parts of every universe means the intent is for highly intelligent living things to evolve to where they are advanced enough, spiritually and technically, to realize they have this responsibility and to understand their most important purpose is to help the spirit world restore balance. The highly intelligent living things are thus meant to eventually realize that it is to their benefit and the benefit of the spirit world if they would be sure their species is evolving in a manner that enables it to be increasingly spiritually advanced as well as increasingly technically advanced. This is so that their species will be increasingly more able to fulfill its most important purpose. At the same time the life their species will have in their universe is bound to become increasingly better as well. Thus, it is a mutually benefiting thing.

As with anything that grows it is possible for the highly intelligent living things to get caught in situations in which their spiritual growth essentially stops. A serious condition can strike and divert most or all of their energies into dealing with it. Examples are addictions, hang-ups, accidents, bad influences, bad environments, shortages of vital resources, diseases, etc. Such conditions could become chronic such that the living things could get mired in them for quite a while or even for the rest of the lifespan of their species' existence. The living things might not even realize this is happening to them. The chronic condition can also prevent them from realizing they have the mentioned responsibility. It is like how a human individual addicted to alcohol or drugs is mired in it and tends to not think about the responsibility he or she has for himself or herself and for how their children are growing up. Then something has to come along to help that individual understand what is happening, and then he or she might do something to get out of the condition. That individual would then need to do a lot of long-term long-range thinking to know where he or she is going into the future.

By analogy when highly intelligent living things residing in a universe get mired in a bad situation, something has to come along to make them to realize what is happening. An indication that they are mired in a bad situation is when their species is repeating the same bad behavior for thousands of years. And, any technical advancements they made would only enable them to repeat their bad behavior in more advanced ways. The sad part is that their technical advancements can make them think they are becoming more truly advanced. But in fact they made little or no spiritual advancement, and true advancement consists of both spiritual and technical advancements.

Since we humans on Earth are repeating our bad behaviors for thousands of years and are thus still mired in our mess, this is an indication we are caught in a bad chronic situation. On top of that, we are thinking we are becoming more advanced because of all the technical advancements we made, and thus the responsible that we have for how our species is evolving does not come to mind. It is because our technical advancements are satisfying our current dominant basis for how we are carrying out our lives, and it is "ego and the desire to enhance survivability." We study the evolution of other living things and how their evolution tends to be driven by forces beyond their own control, and I think we humans think this is more or less the same for how our evolution is being driven. The model indicates this is not meant to be the case. We are capable of determining how our species evolves and we should be mindfully doing so, whereas most of the other living things are not capable of mindfully determining how their species evolves. Some exceptions might be the very intelligent creatures such as dolphins, elephants, whales, etc. We need to make spiritual advancements along with our technical advancements in order for us to take up our responsibility for how our species is evolving. But first we need to have something to come along to help us better understand the bad chronic situation we got caught in.

Hey, do you suppose our book might be able to do this. Well, we hope, But actually each individual need to find his or her own personal spiritual model. It is that model that would help each individual, not necessarily someone else's personal spiritual model. And, this is where our book could perhaps help; i.e., by showing how we managed to find our personal spirit model by thinking unconventionally when conventional thinking did not work for us.

Can We Change Our Dominant Basis to "Empathy and Compassion for One Another?"

If we were to change our dominant basis for how we carry out our lives to "empathy and compassion for one another," we would have a much better chance of making Earth as much as possible like the spirit world in terms of being a gentle, kind, caring, nonjudgmental, compassionate, empathic, and loving place. According to the model, this is what we are here to do in the first place in order to help the spirit world restore balance. But the change in the dominant basis is likely to work only if essentially everyone on Earth makes the change, not necessarily suddenly, but gradually. It would take generations to change things such as perceptions, attitudes, values, etc. and to think longer-term longer-range than we do now.

"Ego and the desire to enhance survivability" has been the dominant basis for most of us humans for such a long time worldwide that most of us do not even think about other possibilities. We bring up our children with this basis generation after generation. We built much of our economy around this basis. Our educational system on all levels caters to this basis. This is partly why battles and wars erupt repeatedly, and why some rivalries rise to unreasonable levels. It has a role in widening the gap between the rich and poor and in individuals becoming corrupt or doing illegal things. It is partly why competition can have an ugly side. And so on.

While the current dominant basis could be perceived as having been very good for some, it has been very bad for some. For example, some have become super rich while some are dying of starvation. And, when wars erupt partly because of the dominant basis, it is bad for everyone. Such unevenness and unsteadiness are reasons to believe some other basis, such as "empathy and compassion for one another," could be a better dominant basis. It seems a change is worth a try. But we can expect problems during the changeover, because those who benefit from the old basis are bound to push back. So, how could we make the changeover as smooth as possible? Here are some ideas.

All of us would like always to be treated with empathy and compassion. We are intelligent enough to know this would happen only if each of us does our part to always treat all others with empathy and compassion. Since we know what we want and what we need to do to get it, there has to be a way to make it happen. This observation indicates the changeover could work smoothest if it began with each of us practicing it on an informal, person-to-person level.

Another observation is that conventional thinking has not done much. This indicates we might want to try some unconventional thinking. As a start, two examples of thinking that are at least somewhat unconventional are as follows.

Example (1): If every individual were able to easily, freely communicate with every other individual on Earth, this could promote mutual understanding, especially if we communicate with empathy and compassion. People basically want peace, safety, family, friends, food, shelter, etc. Communications among everyone could bring out what is needed to achieve this for everyone, beginning informally on a person-to-person level. This would then have a chance to trickle up to the government level. Our high-technology communication systems and high-technology devices could help make worldwide person-to-person communication easier and freer, especially if we develop some way to automatically translate one language to another.

Example (2): The spirit world is bound to have been issuing spiritual guidance to us all our lives beginning in our childhood. We only need to recognize the forms they come in and decipher the guidance messages. They are not likely to come in the form of a booming, commanding voice from outer space, but are more likely to be in the form of common things in our lives. Games are common things in our lives, for example and in my mind they are one of the forms spiritual guidance messages could come in. We have an endless variety of games covering childhood to adulthood. Games are almost always designed to have a win-lose outcome. But there is always a spiritual win-win outcome as well, when they are played among friends. This is more obvious in children's games, but it is also true for adult games. This is because no matter who wins and who loses relative to game rules, players who are friends have enjoyed sharing the experience with one another.

This indicates that games could provide spiritual guidance on how we humans could produce spiritual win-win outcomes as we interact with one another in general. The choice of attitude would have a lot to do with it, as would a prior cultivation of a good relationship between the parties involved. Both of these factors would influence the chances of our general day-to-day interactions successfully producing spiritual win-wins.

Being conscious that interactions can produce a spiritual win-win outcome or not, in addition to whatever else the interactions are set up to produce, is an example of being conscious that we are carrying out life in the spirit world as well as in our physical world.

Many decades ago, members of Congress cultivated good relationships with one another outside of formal sessions. They might have heated arguments during negotiations while in session, and some members might "win" the arguments and some might "lose." But they would have lunch or dinner together as friends afterwards. Congress got things done in those days. Good relationships are not being cultivated as much today outside of formal sessions, and a lot less gets done in Congress. Have we somehow become less advanced spiritually today?

Notice that the two examples are about getting things done by working through the spirit world as well as through our physical world, as opposed to working strictly through our physical world. Therefore, when we say let's try some unconventional thinking, that includes thinking that involves working through the spirit world as well as our physical world. It only makes sense that if we want to make Earth to be like the spirit world as much as possible, we would use the spirit world as a resource. Beside, we are carrying out our lives simultaneously in both worlds anyway. So why not use the resources of both worlds? It follows then that to help clean up the mess we made on Earth every world leader should cultivate a good relationship with every other world leader, setting aside ego on both sides while doing so. And, the people of every nation should support such efforts by their leaders.

Games are not the only common, everyday things that could embody spiritual guidance. People design games, but they do that by finding games in the spirit world that it's already created. So, what else do people design that might embody spiritual guidance? How about traffic rules, signal lights, stop signs, speed limit signs, painted stripes on roads, etc. They could all be perceived as being there to help us treat one another with "empathy and compassion for one another." Because motor vehicles move so much faster than humans can naturally move, the spirit world realized we need reminders to be empathic and compassionate since the act of driving occupies so much of our attention and decision-making. This suggests that we could use the time we are following traffic rules as opportunities to mindfully practice being empathic and compassionate of one another, and thus develop a habit for doing so.

High-technology systems and devices are amazing and could really leverage our abilities to make fantastic advancements in just about every field. They also tend to get us to think increasingly shorter-term shorter-range on a personal level. Each new generation of devices is faster, more capable and more enticing, and captures more of our time and attention even as they shorten the time it takes to perform various tasks, etc. This keeps decreasing the time we have left to think longer-term longer-range. We must not lose control of our future in this manner on a personal level. We need to balance long- and short-term thinking, and long- and short-range thinking. In today's high-technology environment, it takes more effort to achieve a good balance. If we do not do enough long-term long-range thinking, we will not even be aware that others are doing it for us, and they will determine our future for us.

For example, look at how we are being sucked into being "glued" to our smart phones by the makers of the devices and the inventors of social media so that they can profit from our being so "glued." So, are we determining our long-term long-range way of life or are they?

A Disconnection Between the Intended and the Actual

Situations such as the widening gap between the rich and poor, vanishing middle class, high homelessness, high unemployment or under-employment, one in seven nationally relying on food banks, low opinion of congress, infrastructures generally in poor repair, medical and other needs of veterans not handled well, etc. would not be expected in a nation that is supposed to be governed for and by the people. Such conditions are more like that of a nation governed for and by something else. The fact that such conditions exist in our nation indicates a disconnection exists between the intended and the actual.

The "intended" is a concept that exists in the spirit world. Our actions that bring about the "actual" are carried out in our physical world. We do our thinking in the spirit world, and we carry out our actions in our physical world in accordance with our thinking. A disconnect can occur when we are not aware enough of the part of our lives that exists in the spirit world, and thus we are not in touch enough with what is intended. Therefore, our thinking in the spirit world deviates from the intended and our actions in our physical world thus produce an actual that is different from the intended. Consequently, we have a disconnection between the intended and the actual. The "we" refers to us, the citizens, and to other living entities such as corporations, branches of government, various institutions, etc.

Our physical world on Earth is made of materials and energies that can be possessed and/or controlled. Combine that with our choice to make "ego and the desire to enhance survivability" the dominant basis for carrying out our lives, and we can become distracted from what was intended. This can happen, and apparently did happen, to everyone and every other entity referred to as "we."

For example, corporations were never intended to be a part of our government structure. However, we allowed them to develop such a strong influence on members of our government that, like it or not, they are now a very powerful part of our government structure behind the scenes. In fact, such corporate individuals are so numerous and hold so much power that collectively they are sometimes referred to as the "third house" of Congress. The members are not elected, are very well paid, and are often former members of Congress who thus know how to best influence current members of Congress. Something is wrong with this picture. For one thing, it can contribute to widening the income gap between the rich and poor, and this is not healthy for the nation in the long run.

Members of the "third house" working for corporations as lobbyists will naturally want to influence current members of Congress in a manner that benefits the corporations. In addition, corporations are experts at creating advertisements that influence the citizens. Consequently, they know how to present what their lobbyists are doing in a manner that can appear good for the citizens whether that is the case or not. Remember, there are no incorrect models, only incomplete models. Therefore, they are experts at formulating their models in a manner that emphasizes the correct part while hiding the incomplete part. This is why when we vote we need to be just as knowledgeable about the hidden, incomplete part as we are about the correct part, and not simply be sold by the correct part.

This is true for any issues and arguments we face in our everyday life. Every issue has a correct part and an incomplete part, as well as other opposing sides of the multidimensional tug-of-war that almost every issue is. Our knowledge on each issue needs to reasonably balanced in order for us to respond to it wisely. In terms of the discussion at hand, we are talking particularly about the "correct part" vs. the "incomplete part" as being among the more important opposing sides when it comes to how we respond to what members of our government are doing.

Some corporations, including a majority of the S&P 500, find ways to legally avoid paying their fair share of taxes. The nation needs tax money to cover essentials such as the cost of police and fire protection services, schools, infrastructure construction and maintenance, research, the military, etc. The citizens pay their fair share of taxes, but these corporations use such services without paying their fair share of taxes that pay for them. This is fundamentally wrong and is a part of the disconnection.

The wealthiest individuals make up one to ten percent of the population, depending how "being wealthy" is defined, and they pay something like 80 percent of tax dollars the government receives. This indicates they are the main supporters of what our government needs to pay for. Therefore, they can one way or another influence what our government does. This also indicates their incomes are amazingly higher than the incomes of the rest of the population, so much so that even as the rest are paying their fair share of taxes their incomes are so low by comparison that their tax dollars total to only about 20 percent of tax dollars our government receives. Therefore, even though the wealthiest pay a big majority of tax dollars, it does not mean they are all paying their fair share, as indicated by how a lot of them are hiding their income overseas to avoid paying taxes. Yet, some people use as reason for not increasing the taxes on the wealthiest the fact that they are already paying a large majority of total tax money. Then how about getting them to stop hiding their income overseas to avoid paying taxes. And how about decreasing the growing gap between their income and the income the rest of the population so that the 80 percent figure can be lowered? And, don't forget, the rest of the population includes the unemployed, underemployed, and homeless who have no or very low income, and some have to rely on food banks and other charitable organizations for food and other essentials just to survive. These folk are not able to contribute much, if any, to tax dollars, and it should not be implied that they are among the causes of the 80 percent figure. The cause is the large income gap.

Another thing that has been said is how our technological advancements are making our workers more productive. I.e., fewer workers are needed to produce more goods. Therefore, it is said that this helps make our nation richer. This is true for those with jobs that are enhanced by our technological advancements, and perhaps also true for the total dollars in our nation. But what about the productivity of the unemployed and under-employed? Their productivity becomes zero or is significantly decreased, and they became poorer. Our technological advancements are good. But how they are put into action (i.e., the spiritual advancements that need go along the our technological advancements) is lacking.

A better measure of productivity is the overall productivity of our nation's entire population, not just mainly the productivity of those with jobs enhanced by our technological advancements. For example, the average productivity per person that accounts for the productivity of every employable person in the nation, including those unemployed or underemployed, would be more meaningful and could provide better guidance for actions as needed for a better future. And a better measure of the nation's wealth would be based on the actually dollars in circulation, not the total dollars in our nation. The dollars in circulation determine the health and strength of our nation and are thus a better indicator of our nation's capacity to do things . Therefore, this too could provide better guidance for actions as needed for a better future.

Our nation is the wealthiest in the world, based on the total dollars, but a large portion of the wealth is held by relatively few and is not circulating and supporting the economy. Trickle-down economics does not work. Jobs are not created when the rest of the population does not have enough money to spend to support additional jobs. Therefore, big corporations do not create jobs; the common citizens do when they have enough money to spend. Notice how during the last recession (2008 to 2010), corporations have a lot of money in reserve and could hire and pay for more people, but they did not do so because business was too slow to justify adding more employees. After all, why hire more people and have some doing little or nothing even if the corporations have the money to pay for them.

Accordingly, based on the dollars actually circulating and working to keep our country healthy and strong, our country is not as wealthy, healthy and strong as we might think. How else can we explain the conditions mentioned in the first paragraph of this section. A nation that is truly healthy and strong should not be like this.

Almost all shortcomings in our nation's actions could be traced to a lack of funds to support what we should support and to the degree to which they should be supported. Looking from one side, we can say we should fund all that is necessary as if we were financially strong enough to do it all, and then when some areas run out of money some would say it is poor management. Looking from the another side, we can assess our finances and carefully allocate funds to what are most important and let the rest slide at least for a while. But what are most important is a matter of opinion. Thus, those with different opinions would say what is going on is poor management. Consequently, we regularly hear that poor management is a problem. But while this may to true, insufficient funds is more of a problem. After all, if it takes a certain amount of money to enable all necessary components of our nation to be functioning well, but the available money is less than that, then no management is going to be able to satisfy everybody. And, if the shortage of funds is severe enough, then most of the citizens could not be satisfied and would thus have a poor opinion about how our nation is run even if the problem may not be so much the management as it is a shortage of funds. We might want to ask, are we in that situation now? Instead of spending our time and energy blaming and fighting each other, we would be better off spending more time and energy on how to increase the funds.

In the past, both political parties had both liberal members and conservative member such that members of one party can reach across party lines to develop bipartisan solutions. Back then the government receives more tax dollars than it does now. We had a robust middle-class paying a lot of taxes and supporting a lot of businesses that then keep a lot of people employed and paying taxes. The tax rate for the wealthy was significantly higher than it is now. The capital gains tax rate was not held way down as it is now. Our natural resources were not as tapped out as they are now and they generated a lot of money. The net result seems to be that members of both political parties are more generous and more open-minded than they are now since there was enough funds to go around reasonably comfortably.

Today with a shortage of funds, the members seem to grab what they can and hold on tightly to what they have, and thus they become less generous and less open-minded. In general they seemed to have developed a hang-up to do with possessing and controlling whatever it is possible to possess and control, because today what is available to be possessed and controlled is scarce compared with what was available in the past. This behavior comes from our choosing "ego and the desire to enhance survivability" as the dominate basis for how we carry out our lives. Because of this, we humans in general tend to want to grab and hold on tightly anything that is vital and scarce. Therefore, it is not surprising that members of our government would behave this way when funds are scarce, and therefore the things that could be supported become scarce. Consequently, today, one party tends to be almost completely liberal and the other tends to be almost completely conservative. This could be a way for each party to cohesively try to possess and control as much as possible. This makes reaching across party lines to develop bipartisan solutions almost impossible.

We might ask; if this is the case, why aren't we recognizing it better and doing something about it? I am not sure if we really fully recognize it since, according to the model, it naturally develops from our choice of dominant basis for how we carry out our lives while living in a situation that has a shortage of funds. We humans are so used to behaving this way under similar conditions that I think most members of our governments probably see nothing wrong with the way they are behaving. Also, we have this powerful "third house" in Congress consisting of individuals and corporations that are "personally" benefiting by how things currently are. Therefore, they are more likely to influence members of our government to keep things as they are.

Another thing is our nation's collective ego is preventing us from saying out loud that our nation has this financial problem and therefore we are not as healthy and strong as we think we are, even though I think other nations are already aware of it. There are many obvious signs of it, such as those mentioned in the first paragraph of this section, for other nations to see and to figure it out. Also, some of them are having similar problems, so that if they point out our problems, then their problems would also be pointed out, and that would be bad for their egos too. Therefore, I think they know that they and we are not as healthy and strong as they and we think, and they being older nations than our nation is, they tend to be more realistic about most things that are happening in the world than we are. This is likely why our influence on them is lower than it used to be; i.e., they cannot rely on us as much as they can before.

The poor most likely make up most of our military personnel and are thus doing their part to keep our nation safe. This helps to enable big corporations to have the protection, freedom, and luxury to choose to behave unfairly if they chose to do so. For some, "ego and the desire to enhance survivability" seem to overtake good values. Yet, the Supreme Court consider them (corporations) as persons as far as how much they can contribute during elections. There is an unhealthy disconnection here.

Our nation's citizens can sense what is discussed just as other nations probably can, although our citizens might not want to say it out loud for other nations to hear. But it comes out in our frustrations and anger, and we have the right to be angry. Unfortunately, like any "itch" that we want to scratch at any opportunity to do so, our reactions to our anger are not always constructive and are sometimes irrational. Non-constructive irrational actions usually work against our best interests, as such actions often end up giving more power to those who use their power to manipulate us without our necessarily being aware. For example, they can steer our anger in a direction that benefits them at our expense. A well-intentioned, peaceful demonstration can be turned into a destructive riot by manipulators who are likely taking advantage of our having a bad itch and are getting us to scratch it at the wrong time, in the wrong situation, and in the wrong way. And scratching a bad itch is usually done irrationally, because if we were rational we would know scratching a bad itch only causes injury to ourselves. We need instead to do something to eliminate or decrease the itch in a constructive manner. To accomplish this in this case is not necessarily straight forward and will take a lot of creativity to make our actions effective.

For example, one thing we citizens can do is not limit our voting to elections but to exercise our voting power throughout the year, every year, through how we spend our money. This would help align the actual workings of our government and its powerful "third house" in Congress with what citizens actually support. We as voting citizens have not exercised the year-round part of our voting power very much, if at all. Because of that, we are unintentionally supporting what some of these corporations are doing behind the scenes in our government for their benefit and at our expense.

Issues Produced by the Spirit World While Caring About Every Living Thing It Creates

As new pieces of knowledge are generated and added to the spirit world, new issues are formed and may need balancing. Various previously balanced issues can become unbalanced and need re-balancing. Issues have multiple opposing sides, and are like multidimensional tug-of-wars. Knowledge on each side needs to be reasonably balanced with knowledge on every other side. Issues exist throughout the spirit world, and every one of them needs to be kept within reasonable balance at all times for the spirit world to be able to form wisdom at all times. Because the need for balancing and re-balancing is the result of new pieces of knowledge having been generated, the state of unbalance is different each time re-balancing is needed. Therefore, whenever a new universe is designed to help restore balance, it is addressing issues different from issues addressed by universes that came before it. Consequently, every new universe is naturally going to be different from every universe that came before.

The number of issues that can be formed is limitless, just as the number of pieces of knowledge that can be generated is limitless. Every issue is important to the spirit world regardless of how major or minor it might appear to us. Everything ranging from the enormous to the microscopic has a vital role in the spirit world. For example, as represented by the translation of spiritual entities into living things that exist on Earth, a typical living thing on Earth is alive and viable because of the microstructure of cells that make up its body, and the microstructure of its organs and bodily systems. The formation of the microstructures is in turn associated with the DNA molecule unique to each living thing. The DNA molecule is in turn made up of subatomic particles such as electrons, protons, and neutrons. Therefore, everything ranging from the whole living thing to the subatomic particles that the living thing is made of is important to the spirit world.

The spirit world cares about every living thing it creates. The issues any given universe is designed to address are bound to include some directly or indirectly associated with the spirit world caring for living things. When it takes designing a new universe to provide opportunities for the kinds of experiences needed to generate the kinds of new pieces of knowledge to restore balance, those kinds of experiences are obviously not possible to have in the spirit world. The spirit world is naturally a gentle, kind, caring, nonjudgmental, compassionate, empathic, and loving place. The world of any universe is purposely different from the spirit world and is brought into being by a spiritual entity that is smaller than the spirit world. Consequently, the world of any universe is less complete than is the spirit world and is thus less gentle, kind, caring, nonjudgmental, compassionate, empathic, and loving than is the spirit world. Therefore, the experiences needed to generate the kinds of new pieces of knowledge to restore balance are likely to be not as gentle, kind, caring, nonjudgmental, compassionate, empathic, and loving as experiences that can take place in the spirit world. This could explain why a lot of the experiences living things on Earth can go through are not always gentle, kind, caring, nonjudgmental, compassionate, empathic, and loving. For example, as discussed, living things on Earth need to eat other living, or formerly living, things to survive and be viable.

Every hospitable planet in our physical universe is likely different and thus each is designed to address a different set of issues. This supports the notion that most intelligent species are also different on each such planet. In general, the collections of living things in each planet are likely be different. The chemical basis for life could be different. Even on Earth while life is primarily oxygen supported, there is at least one other way to support life on Earth. As mentioned before, a species of clams are supported by hydrogen sulfide gas coming out of vents on the ocean floor where tectonic plates meet. This suggests that if the chemical makeup of each hospitable planet is different, even if only slightly, it might be enough to enable life to be supported in ways not found on Earth. After all, I suspect no body expected hydrogen sulfide is capable of supporting life until those clams were discovered.

Issues that hospitable planets would address would logically include some directly to do with the spirit world caring about every living thing it creates. Issues addressed by other very massive things making up our universe, such as stars, black holes, gas clouds, non-hospitable planets, white dwarfs, etc., would include those having to do indirectly with the spirit world caring about every living thing it creates. For example, they might produce some of the larger atomic elements necessary to make up living things.

On Earth, living things in general have to eat other living, or formerly living, things to survive and be viable. Exceptions include algae, mold, lichens, mosses, most plants, etc., but even some of these need the decomposed matter that came from once living things. It is unclear if this would be the case on other hospitable planets. It would not be the case if all living things on a planet were like some of our algae, mold, lichens, mosses, most plants, etc.

We might ask; how do living things needing to eat other living things to survive and be viable have anything to do with the spirit world caring about every living thing it creates? The answer is that "the spirit world caring about every living thing it creates" likely produces many issues that the spirit world needs to balance. In the spirit world, every larger spiritual entity is made up of smaller spiritual entities. Therefore, every larger spiritual entity needs the existence of smaller spiritual entities in order to exist. This could perceivably present issues for the spirit world. The issues would have something to do with concepts that exist in the spirit world but are not practices in the spirit world. Concepts need to be reasonably balanced in the same way practices do. Concepts are made of knowledge just as practices are in the spirit world, and issues associated with either or both need to stay reasonably balanced. To generate the kinds of new pieces of knowledge to achieve reasonable balance, concepts need to be translated into forms that can exist in a universe. It just so happens that the particular concepts that our physical universe is designed to address include ones that result in living things on Earth needing to eat other living, or formerly living, things to survive and be viable.

This could also explain why the spirit world designed our physical universe such that it is made of materials and energies that can be possessed and controlled by living things. The need for living things to eat other living, or formerly living, things to survive and be viable is a form of possessing and controlling the things they eat. This indicates we are likely here to evolve to the point we become able to handle the possession and control of substances and energies with the intention of sharing and caring for one another. Right now we tend to be self-absorbed, extravagant, and wasteful when we are able to possess and/or control a lot of materials and energies. The amount of food we waste is amazing, and food is just one of the forms of materials and energies we can possess and control, and waste.

Another kind of issues that Earth is likely designed to address are those perceivably brought on by larger spiritual entities sharing all their smaller spiritual entities with other larger spiritual entities. This could be the reason some of us humans have large egos and an excessive desire to enhance survivability. In the spirit world, the larger the spiritual entity, the greater the number of smaller spiritual entities it consists of. In concept, this sort of gives a larger spiritual entity possession of more things than a smaller one. But this is only in concept because all the smaller entities that comprise any larger spiritual entity are also making up other larger spiritual entities. Therefore, ego and enhancement of survivability are only concepts and have no real meaning in the spirit world. But, again, Earth apparently happens to be designed such that when such concepts are translated to exist on Earth they have physical meaning.

In both the "need to eat other living, or formerly living, things to survive and be viable" and "ego and the desire to enhance survivability" cases, the most tangible reasons these two concepts have meaning on Earth are the following. The materials and energies making up Earth can be possessed and controlled, and living things on Earth are physically separate entities. There are also intangible reasons, such as ones having to do with feelings.

This indicates that a possible intent is for us humans to evolve to the point "empathy and compassion for one another" becomes our dominant basis for how we carry out our lives such that we can handle these two concepts gracefully. It's obvious that an early stage of handling them could result in our making a mess and us being mired in the mess for a while. Intuitively, we can see how "empathy and compassion for one another" is a more advanced state for our dominant basis than the "ego and the desire to enhance survivability" state.

The discussion so far in this chapter indicates, in summary, that among the most important issues we humans are to address are ones associated with the following three obstacles designed into our universe.

> **Obstacle (1):** Our universe is made of materials and energies that can be posessed, controlled, and/or consumed.
>
> **Obstacle (2):** Highly intelligent living things such as us humans on Earth have egos and a desire to enhance survivability.
>
> **Obstacle (3):** Mobile intelligent living things (those that can walk, swim, and/or fly) need to eat other living things to survive.

These obstacles are first presented in Chapter Three and further discussed in Chapter Four. The current chapter provides plausible further explanations, according to the model, why the spirit world designed these obstacles into our physical universe, and particularly into Earth. In a sense, the model helps us figure out some of the stages of advancement we need to achieve that would lead to our fulfilling our purpose for being here on Earth. In other words, let's aim for eventually having "empathy and compassion for one another" as the dominant basis for how we would carry out our lives.

Broadening Our View of the Spirit World

Graciously receiving care and generously giving care is a part of making any partnership a mutually beneficial one. The model indicates each of us has a natural partnership with the spirit world. The intention is that we will do our part to make this partnership a mutually beneficial one. But if we are to give care to the spirit world as well as receive care from the spirit world, how can we do that when we cannot see, touch, feel, etc. the spirit world with our five major senses?

The answer is we can give care to representatives of the spirit world, and we can do it by using our spiritual senses as well as our five major senses. These representatives are other human individuals and other living things. Every living thing has a spirit that is a small portion of the spirit world. Therefore, our partnership with the spirit world includes our partnership with every living thing that exists in our universe, particularly on Earth. Thus, by our making our partnerships with other individuals and other living things as mutually beneficial as possible, we are making our partnership with the spirit world mutually beneficial as much as possible, a small portion at a time.

We might ask; how we could make our partnership with the living things we eat mutually beneficial? The answer is; we can't and still survive and be viable. This is likely one of the issues our universe is to address. One thing we can do is treat the living things we eat and their species with empathy, compassion, care, and respect by, for example, not consuming them to extinction, using humane hunting and farming methods, not hunt simply for sport, not removing a part and letting the rest of an animal die a terrible death, teaching our children where their food comes from and not waste food, etc.

A Native American princess I know described some of their beliefs and practices regarding food, and it is along the lines of what is mentioned. I found what she described spiritual and inspiring. She has a spiritual model that works for her. It is probably very ancient and has been followed by Native Americans for generations. It is so compatible with my model that it broadened my model and made it more complete.

What this indicates is that individuals who have found their personal spiritual models can be resources to help us broaden our own personal spiritual model, even if their models are different from ours. This would be particularly true if the individuals are from different countries and/or cultures, which may mean that parts of the spirit world their models are in touch with are less likely to already be a part of our own. It also supports the idea of, rather than looking for reasons to have conflicts with other religious models, as some individuals on Earth tend to do, we could instead look for ways other religious models could broaden one another and make each model more complete. This would be a spiritual win-win outcome.

The model in this book indicates we do not have incorrect models, only incomplete models. Thus, the combined effect of multiple models would be more complete than any one model. Therefore, we could all benefit by increasing the completeness of our own personal spiritual model by looking for ways to be inspired by the personal spiritual models of others.

Various other highly intelligent creatures such as dolphins, whales, elephants, etc. have senses, some of which are the same as ours and some of which are different. The same applies to their consciousness. It is not clear if they have personal spiritual models, but they have something that enables them to avoid the kinds of horrible things some humans do to one another. This indicates that they might be in touch with regions of the spirit world that we humans could benefit from also getting in touch with. Someday when we learn how to communicate telepathically, we might be able to find out from them the dominant basis for how they carry out their lives. It just may be a basis we human have not thought about because we do not have some of their senses or parts of their consciousness, even though we are perceived to be more intelligent.

Chapter Five described various configurations of spirits and souls, and how a human spirit is on the gradations among a variety of configurations. An individual can choose to be anywhere on the gradations and thus choose to be who he or she is, depending on the situation. This does not mean one location is better than another; our dominant basis for how we carry out our lives is the same regardless of the location on the gradation. Only the way we express our dominant basis differs.

One location is of particular interest to the current discussion, and it is the "colony configuration" location. This is where an individual acts as a member of a "colony," i.e., a group, organization, corporation, company, sports team, family, neighborhood, political party, etc. The "colony" has the main spirit which is made of the spirits of the members. The "colony" has a dominant basis for how it is carrying out its life and each individual who chooses to be a member contributes to it and supports it. Assuming the dominant basis of the "colony" is good, then being a member is an interesting opportunity to broaden that region of the spirit world we can be in touch with.

It is interesting because our interaction as a member of a "colony" with other members, to achieve something as a "colony," is different from our interactions as separate individuals. It provides a way to sense the spirit world differently from how we sense it in our common, everyday activities as separate individuals. When all the members of a "colony" are in sync and they really enjoy being with one another, magic seems to happen. A good marriage can happen, a close family can happen, and a team of "misfits" winning the World Series can happen. The 2010 San Francisco Giants were a team of "misfits" that enjoyed being together and helping one another. Magic happened when they won that year's World Series, and again in 2012, and again in 2014. In 2014, the historical statistics were not in their favor and yet they won. It was not simply the skills the team has in our physical world; the team also tapped into the powers of the spirit world.

We are Here for Two Purposes but are Doing Mostly the Less Important One

Recall, the spirit world has issues that are concepts but not practices in the spirit world. However, they can become practices when translated to be expressed or exist in a universe. That is one of the reasons these issues, along with every other issue in the spirit world, must be kept reasonably balanced so that their translations can be reasonably understood in a universe. The other reason is that every issue is a part of the total knowledge making up the spirit world, and therefore they must all be reasonably balanced in order for the spirit world to form wisdom.

A new universe is designed to address a certain set of issues, specifically those needing balancing or re-balancing at the time. Because the need to do balancing or re-balancing is a result of new pieces of knowledge constantly being generated and added to the spirit world, the set of issues needing attention constantly changes and is never identical to any in the past. Therefore, the set of issues any new universe is designed to address is different and unique, and that is why every new universe is different and unique.

Every new universe would likely needs to be designed to address some of the issues that are only concepts in the spirit world, along with various other issues. Our physical universe is obviously designed that way. For example, competition is a concept but not a practice in the spirit world, but when translated to be expressed or exist in our physical universe, in particular on Earth, competition is a practice. The reason competition is only a concept and not a practice in the spirit world is because every spiritual entity shares a part of itself directly or indirectly with every other spiritual entity. Therefore, if competition were a practice in the spirit world, which spiritual entity would compete with which other spiritual entity when they are directly or indirectly part of one another? Spiritual entities function together in partnership, not in competition, in the same way all the parts and limbs of our body function in partnership, not in competition. Competition can only be a practice when entities are separate things such as are the living and nonliving things on Earth.

As another example, since no spiritual entity can be killed or would kill another, killing a living thing is also an issue that is only a concept in the spirit world but can translate as a practice in a universe such as our physical universe, particularly on Earth. Since competition and killing are practices on Earth, they are obviously among issues Earth is designed to address. This means we are to help restore balance in these two issues, along with helping restore balance in various other issues. Evidence exists that indicates the issues of competition and killing need balancing or re-balancing includes the fact that competition in countless forms pervades our lives, perhaps far too much, and killing for bad reasons certainly happens far too often in our lives.

Both issues can be perceived as good, bad, or neutral depending on the situation. There has to be some reasonable state of balance such that bad reasons for competing and/or killing do not dominate to the extent that we make a mess on Earth. When competition becomes so pervasive and intense that it leads to constant high stress and all kinds of killings, battles, wars, etc., then we should realize both issues need balancing or re-balancing. The unbalanced condition as describe has existed on Earth for a long time and it does not seem to be improving. Thus, it is about time that we do something to restore balance in both issues. That is what we are supposed to do anyway, according to the model.

What we have been doing is not working. We need a new way of thinking, and one possible new way is to reassess the role and amount of competition in our lives. We have simply accepted competition in its current state as part of our lives. This could be a mistake. An improvement in the state of competition in our lives would likely also lead to an improvement in the state of bad killings in our lives. This is likely to have to begin with some significant movement away from "ego and the desire to enhance survivability" and toward "empathy and compassion for one another" as the dominant basis for how we carry out our lives.

A similar situation might also apply to other issues Earth is designed to address, including long-term long-range thinking versus short-term short-range thinking, seeking excitement versus seeking learning, available resources versus continued population growth, etc.

Notice how our physical universe is designed to be made of materials and energies that can be possessed and controlled. This tends to support the notion that the issues of competition and killing are among the issues our universe is designed to address. The model indicates every universe is different, which means every universe has a different set of issues to address. It seems reasonable that the issues making up a set are ones that need balancing or re-balancing because of some common factor that caused all those issues to become less balanced. This means each issue in the set must bear some relation with every other issue in the set. For example, if we look at all the issues we face on Earth, they all bear some relation with one another, and the center of this relation appears to be our choice of "ego and the desire to enhance survivability" as the dominant basis for how we carry out our lives. This could be why the spirit world combined these particular issues into a set for Earth to address. This also indicates we are to move away from "ego and the desire to enhance survivability" and toward "empathy and compassion for one another" as the dominate basis for how we carry out our lives so as to help the spirit world restore balance. So far we are not doing that.

The set of issues Earth is designed to address is a subset of the larger set of issues our physical universe is designed to address. Our physical universe happens to consist of an enormous number and variety of physical, separate things such as stars, planets, white dwarfs, black holes, gas clouds, galaxies, moons, etc. Some of them, especially some of the planets, are bound to be hospitable to living things. No two hospitable planets would be identical. Each would be different and unique and would be inhabited by a different and unique collection of living things. A likely reason the spirit world designed our universe to be this way is because the set of issues our universe is to address can be addressed better if addressed in subsets.

Each hospitable planet in our universe would thus be designed to address a different subset. Each subset would be a collection of issues that are interrelated, similar to how the issues Earth is to address are interrelated. The center of the interrelationship could be the same, similar, or different for each subset and therefore for each hospitable planet. If it happens to be the same for two or more hospitable planets, then each planet would be designed to address it from a different direction. This could happen since every hospitable planet is bound to have commonality. For example, each may be made of materials and energies that could be possessed and controlled, and in some cases this could override their differences.

On the other hand, the center of the interrelationship is likely to be different for most of the hospitable planets because countless ways exist for planets to be different. Therefore, the differences are more likely to override any commonality than the other way around. Some of the differences could result in the living things on other planets to choose "empathy and compassion for one another" as the dominant basis for how they carry out their lives. It is also possible that the living things would be intelligent enough to not waste natural resources by engaging in things like battles and wars, and instead apply their natural resources to develop ways to renew resources faster than they consume them.

Any given issue can be a part of more than one subset so that more than one hospitable planet can be addressing the same issue as part of their subsets of issues. After all, there are bound to be similarities among the various hospitable planets. For example, it is possible water is needed to sustain life in many of the hospitable planets. However, since there are likely to be life-sustaining mechanisms in our universe that we have yet to discover, it is possible some liquid other than water could be part of sustaining life.

If different life-sustaining mechanisms exist among hospitable planets, that would contribute to making the collection of living things on each hospitable planet different. Even on Earth, there are different life-sustaining mechanisms, as illustrated with the discovery of the creatures that survive by the vents in the seafloor pointed out previously.

This means additional yet unknown life-sustaining mechanisms could exist elsewhere in our universe. A different life-sustaining mechanism might result in living things having different values about the materials and energies making up our universe. For example, the living things might not need to possess and control materials or energies, and they might not need to eat other living things in order to remain alive and viable. Their spiritual and physical ways of life could be very different from ours.

What this means is that someday when we learn to do space travel or pseudo space travel that there is a lot we can learn from other hospitable planets, including a lot of spiritual knowledge as well as just physical knowledge. Right now, we tend to think there is mainly physical knowledge to be gained. Let's instead keep a more open mind about gaining spiritual knowledge as well.

In fact, we can gain some spiritual knowledge by looking at how some of the other highly intelligent living things on Earth are carrying out their lives. But we need to first lower our ego and start respecting them as possible sources of spiritual and physical knowledge and not as living things that have less knowledge of any kind than we have.

Another reason the spirit world would choose to address in subsets the set of issues our universe is designed to address is because certain combinations of issues could do more than the sum of what each issue could do individually. We could cite countless examples of this phenomenon on Earth. Certain drugs administered together as a cocktail are more effective than the sum of each drug administered individually. A team of individuals can do more than the sum of what each individual could do alone. A collection of materials assembled together can form a building, an airplane, a work of art, a can opener, etc., while the sum of each piece of material alone would not constitute anything more complex. Basically, it is similar to how a larger spiritual entity can do more than the sum of what each of its smaller spirit entities can do individually. These examples indicate the ways a combination of issues can be assembled together and can be more important than simply the sum of the individual issues alone.

Recall that planets, stars, black holes, white dwarfs, etc. that are not hospitable to living things are likely designed to address subsets of issues that deal only indirectly with living things, and some would be designed to form the larger atomic elements necessary for making up living things. Some, such as our Sun, would be designed to provide the energy some living things, such as those on Earth, need to stay alive. Some, such as the planet Jupiter, might be designed to help attract meteors away from hospitable planets such as Earth to help keep life going on those planets. And so on.

The philosophy of designing universes to address a set of issues in subsets is likely also why the spirit world choose specific elemental things such as electrons, protons, neutrons, etc. to make up our universe. These things can be assembled to make atoms, molecules, living and nonliving things, life sustaining mechanisms, energies, etc. It is also possible that not every universe would necessarily be designed with this philosophy in mind. Therefore, someday when we do inter-universe travel, or pseudo inter-universe travel, we should not expect to necessarily find separate things and separate things assembled into larger things etc. as on Earth.

As part of our being on Earth to address issues, we are here to fulfill two main purposes. The more important one is to help the spirit world restore balance. The other one is to help the spirit world continue to grow by our generating as many new pieces of knowledge as possible. In some ways, these two purposes are at odds with each other, creating the potential trap that would have us doing a lot more for the second purpose than for the first, which is the more important purpose. We apparently have gotten caught in that trap and thus made a mess on Earth.

To help restore balance involves getting interested in learning more about things, and that takes more long-term long-range thinking. On the other hand, to go through as many new experiences as possible to generate as many new pieces of knowledge as possible is more exciting, and short-term short-range thinking often suffices. We tend to find being excited about something more enticing than being interested in something.

Thus, we tend to go for excitement and consequently short-term short-range thinking. But, if we do not do enough long-term long-range thinking to determine our future, it will lack purposeful direction as it will go in the direction of whatever is exciting to do from moment to moment. This seems to be the trap we have got caught in. This naturally leads to a messy future, much like how a room can be messy if filled with things thrown into it in an unorganized manner.

Unfortunately, manipulators such as advertisers and campaign managers take advantage of our preference for excitement, and they use the lure of excitement to get us to "buy" what they are "selling" and thus profit from our responses. This tends to lead us to make a bigger mess as it further decreases the time we take to do long-term long-range thinking. For example, look at how we are increasing the time we spend using the exciting and amazing high-technology devices that are becoming an increasing part of our lives. Using them involves mostly short-term short-range thinking. Therefore, their taking up more of our time means less time for long-term long-range thinking.

Issues are neither good nor bad in the spirit world; they just need to be reasonably balanced. The various sides of an issue consist of pieces of knowledge. Pieces of knowledge form spiritual entities and they form thoughts. Consequently, some spiritual entities are thoughts, and all other spiritual entities are thought-like. Therefore, when a spiritual entity enables something to exist in a universe, it is essentially thinking it to exist. Accordingly, our universe and everything in it exists because spiritual entities in the spirit world are thinking all of it to exist.

This is analogous to how an author is thinking a story and all the things and events in the story to exist, as discussed earlier. As we read the story, thoughts in our minds enable those things and events to virtually exist, and we react as intensely as we would if they actually existed. This illustrates, in an analogous manner, that thoughts can be perceived as being more real than are things in our universe, because they exist, and are real, in the spirit world whereas things exist in our universe only because thoughts enable them to exist.

Recall, a researcher attempting to identify the smallest possible thing that could exist said that when we get down to that level of existence, the smallest possible thing appears to take on the qualities of a thought.

It would be interesting to find out how he or she came to that statement. The model in this book and his or her statement appear to arrive at the same or similar conclusion, at least for the moment until additional knowledge might bring forth a different conclusion. For example, the model now concludes that there is something more profound than pieces of knowledge, and it is intelligence. We all probably know of individuals who have not attended college but who are obviously more intelligent than some who have. Therefore, would the smallest possible thing then appear to embody some elemental form of intelligence as well as taking on the qualities of a thought?

Thoughts in general are neither good nor bad nor neutral in the spirit world. Thoughts when translated into forms that can be expressed or exist in a universe could be perceived as good, bad, or neutral depending on the universe and situation. Exceptions are thoughts that are intentions. An intention could be perceived as good, bad, or neutral in the spirit world depending on the situation. While this is true, intentions are only concepts and not practices in the spirit world. A spiritual entity cannot intend do something good, bad, or neutral to another spiritual entity because they are directly or indirectly a part of each other. However, when intentions are translated to be expressed or exist in a universe in which living things are separate entities, such as is the case for living things on Earth, intentions can become practices. And then the practices can be perceived as good, bad, or neutral, depending on the situation.

This is one of the ways universes provide opportunities for experiences not possible to have in the spirit world which thus can generate new pieces of knowledge that the spirit world cannot directly generate on its own.

We might ask; what about good intentions such as the intention to care for something? Couldn't that be a practice as well as a concept in the spirit world? The answer is that to care for something is naturally a part of the spirit world since everything is directly or indirectly a part of everything else. Therefore, while it is a concept in the spirit world, to have or not have the intention to care is irrelevant in the spirit world.

It is possible we were supposed to have the ability to communicate telepathically, and we might have had it but loss it because of our short attention span and our tendency to simply respond to what is easily seen on the surface. The best business people commonly have strong intuition and they tend to follow it. Such individuals must have developed a habit of responding to deeper things than what is easily seen on the surface, which requires a longer attention span to sense and decipher. Their habit of paying attention to their intuitions and following them strengthens their ability to sense their intuition and to maintain their long attention span. According to the model, the way intuition works is related to how telepathic communication works in that both abilities function in the spirit world.

Our short attention span contributes to our getting caught in the trap mentioned above, in that with it we are constantly looking for the next quick way to get excited. This makes us vulnerable to being manipulated by those whose long-term long-range thinking includes taking advantage of our preference for excitement, producing movies that tend to include increasingly exciting special effects such as massive explosions, spectacular collisions, huge buildings collapsing and other products discussed before. All such things are dulling our senses so that we are increasingly less able to sense the soft and gentle guidance signals from the spirit world.

The net result is we are doing a lot more to help the spirit world grow by generating as many new pieces of knowledge as possible and are helping the spirit world restore balance a lot less. Therefore, while we are here for two purposes, we are doing mostly the lesser important one.

Caring for Ourselves

"Caring for ourselves" refers to looking for and finding our empathic and compassionate selves. It is not that we are not already empathic and compassionate in varying degrees depending on the situation. It is that the model indicates being consistently empathic and compassionate of others is a good part of caring for ourselves. It is doing our part to make Earth as much as possible a gentle, kind, caring, nonjudgmental, compassionate, empathic, and loving place. It is being able to say in the last days of our lives that we have done our part to help Earth be a better place.

As mentioned earlier, a large number of individuals nearing death were asked what they wished they had done more of. The most common response was that they wished they had been nicer to others. In other words, they would have taken better care of themselves if they had had more empathy and compassion for others.

No one has said anything like they wish they had made more money or had lived more luxuriously. Thus, is seems as we age and come closer to the end of life we become more aware of the more important things about having a chance to be alive on Earth. For this reason, it would be great if old folks would think about this and convey their conclusions to the young. And it would be great if the young would seek such knowledge from the old.

However, not every old individual forms wisdom. I know an elderly individual who would repeatedly say something like "I have made all this money and now I cannot enjoy it the way I want to." The weird thing is that he used to always say "you can never make enough money." Oh, well. Therefore, the young would be wise to seek wisdom only from those who have wisdom to offer. The trick is, when we are young, how can we tell who has formed wisdom?

My suggestion is to start by finding those who are not self-centered to any degree and in any manner, and who have consistently shown a lot of empathy and compassion for others within and outside of their family. Be careful of those who are consistently kind to those outside their family but not necessarily to those within their immediate family. A young person outside the immediate family might be drawn to them, but whatever wisdom they have to offer would likely not be theirs but are likely based on common sayings, because chances are they do not have much.

1. Be Inspired Instead of Judgmental

Some individuals tend to be inspired when observing something. Such individuals tend to look for ways to improve themselves. Other individuals tend let their ego take control and look for reasons to judge what they see. Being too preoccupied with judging tends to block any wisdom from being formed. This suggests that individuals who are consistently judgmental and behave as if they know everything are likely to not have much wisdom to offer, even if their egos would have them give the impression that they do.

We might ask; why anyone would want to be like that? This question points out that such individuals might have chosen to be this way for the sake of survival and not as a preference. Therefore, such individuals need much love and support, even if that hang-up might prevent them from returning it in comparable magnitude. Sometimes at the end, they come to terms with themselves, and their love and support pour out in an overflowing manner. Then you know the love and support that has been pent up inside and hidden from view until now.

I know an individual who as a child was forced to take control in a situation she was far too young to control. Therefore, she became judgmental as a way of exerting control and as a way of keeping her ego up so as to be in control. She developed much anger beneath the surface the rest of her life. For various reasons, this situation she grew up in prevented her from being able to, or willing to, resolve the anger. I think it was because if she did resolve the anger, she feared she would lose control, and maintaining control was her way of surviving her childhood even though it was counterproductive as an adult. Unfortunately, that anger shortened her life considerably instead of helping her to continue surviving. The adults who did this to her never understood what they had done, and they never formed any wisdom from the experience.

My upbringing was rather conventional and it used to leave me thinking that living a conventional lifestyle was the only the way to become a "winner." But now I doubt it. What is perceived as a conventional lifestyle depends on the region, the nation, and mainly the people who reside there. What is perceived as "winning" depends on the people you hang around with, the culture, the situation, the fad, etc. The point is that there is no fixed conventional lifestyle or definition of a winner.

Conventional thinking and conventional lifestyles, whatever they are, have been practiced for generations, and they have not done much to clean up the mess we made on Earth. So it seems to be time to try what we might consider unconventional thinking and lifestyles to see if they can help us do better.

I am very close to an individual who lives a more or less unconventional lifestyle. I find a lot of what he is doing and has been able to accomplish inspiring. It takes courage and a strong sense of security to live an unconventional lifestyle. And it certainly has not prevented him from having a lot of empathy and compassion for others. Also, he is generally able to not let his ego get in the way. So his lifestyle is obviously good for him, and has enabled him to do certain things he enjoys. That certainly looks like success to me. This does not mean I am about to take up his lifestyle. I am sort of unconventional but not to the degree he is, and my "sort of unconventional" lifestyle fits me well, even if some of the things he has done I wish I could have done when I was young. Well, he said there are things he wishes he could do, but he can't because of his lifestyle. So, what the heck. Nothing is perfect, not even the spirit world. What he is doing has much to be admired, to learn from, and to be inspired by for an observer such as I.

In some ways, conventional thinking might have made the mess we made on Earth progressively worse. Consequently, I think unconventional lifestyles and thinking that are constructive and productive are inspiring, particularly in that they have the potential to embody something that could help clean up the mess. Being inspired would enable us to look for such a possibility, and being judgmental would not. If some unconventional ways of living could enable individuals to be more empathic and compassionate of others, that would be a big improvement over some conventional ways of living.

I was inspired by a recent article about what dyslexic individuals can accomplish, despite or because of being dyslexic. Such individuals commonly live an unconventional lifestyle out of necessity. Medical experts used to think dyslexia was a disability. But we now realize there are many very accomplished dyslexic individuals. Thus, the experts are thinking that dyslexia could be a gift instead of a disability. Dyslexic individuals tend to be very creative, intelligent, diligent, resourceful, empathic, and compassionate. I think it is possible their empathic and compassionate nature comes from their personal struggles with dyslexia. It makes them realize life in general has struggles as they sometimes depend on others to help them through difficult tasks. This enables them to see the struggles of others, struggles that individuals who are not dyslexic are less likely to understand.

The model indicates that dyslexic individuals commonly have to live an unconventional lifestyle that relies more than usual on feelings, intuition, instincts, and imagination, and creative uses of consciousness, intelligence, and memory. This has to be the case because they do their critical reasoning without putting it on paper. Thus, they tend to see the big picture, and this includes being able to do things such as solving complex mathematical problems in their mind without the help of writing the solution progression on paper. They develop an ability to remember things in detail because recording them on paper and looking up information in written texts don't work well for them. All these things, according to the model, are the results of their finding ways to bring their consciousness more than usual into the spirit world. In my mind, that also enables them to be more able than usual to find their empathic and compassionate selves, because that part of themselves can only be found in the spirit world and not in our physical world.

I find this especially fascinating and inspiring, because they are able to work with or around their dyslexia to achieve what most of the rest of us seem to want to achieve. And that is to be more consciously tuned to the spirit world.

If we allow ourselves to be more frequently inspired by others, this can promote mutual understanding of others. It is commonly said that most wars were fought over something having to do with religion. Therefore, if everyone were to be more frequently inspired by those of different races, religions, cultures, backgrounds, etc., instead of judging such differences, we could increase mutual understanding and decrease conflicts and wars. The trick is getting enough individuals on Earth to do this together. If enough national leaders with strong popular support were to do this together, we might be able to make a good start.

2. **Having Some Ups and Downs Could be More Fulfilling Than Not Having Any**

Some individuals seem blessed to have a comfortable time throughout their lives. Everything seems to go their way, and luck just seems to simply fall in place. Have you ever wished your life has been like that? I did a few times, when things got really bad. But now I've changed my mind. I am glad I had very bad downs and very good ups, now that I survived them all, and I like myself for what I learned. Therefore, I no longer think that being "blessed" as described is a blessing. We learn more by having ups and downs. My good and bad experiences have all been good learning experiences. They stimulated a lot of soul searching that I am glad I did.

What this suggests to anyone who is going through a very bad experience is that it is important to stay alive. Years later, when all the injuries have healed and you have a chance to pick up the pieces and to find them all useful in some way, just as how the spirit world finds all pieces of knowledge useful, you will be glad you have lived through it all. The key is to treasure all the knowledge you've gained even if from bad experiences, but not necessarily from just the bad experiences.

Be Ready to Give Care and to Receive Care

Among the spiritual messages from the spirit world is to generously give care when an opportunity arises, and to graciously accept care when it is given as needed. It is all part of the interactions that we have with the spirit world, even if it is all done via various representatives of the spirit world; i.e., the individuals we care for and the individuals who give us care.

We never know when someone will need help. Someone might need a door opened or an opening in traffic to enter a freeway; something might fall off a shelf in a store and need to be put back, etc. A neighbor might develop a bad back or knee and could use help getting the newspaper and mail. An elderly person might need to climb a ladder but is unsafe to do so at his age. We don't have to wait to be asked to help; we can simply provide help if we are available. It is always better to be able to give help than to be in a position to need help. Thus, giving help when we can and when needed is a way of expressing thanks that we are in good enough condition to be able to give it.

Life comes with surprises, good and bad. Our lives can suddenly change with a surprise, perhaps for the rest of our lives.

A man comes out of his medical examination and wonders how to tell his wife he was diagnosed with cancer. She suddenly becomes a caregiver. After three years and two surgeries his cancer seems under control.

Then he emerges from a consultation with her doctor following a surgery she had, and he wonders how he is going to tell her she has terminal cancer, without breaking down. He is suddenly a 24/7 caregiver, helplessly watching her slowly die over seven months. After she dies, his cancer is found to have recurred and is twice as bad as before due to the stress of being a caregiver. Now he is his own caregiver. How life has changed multiple times, each time with a surprise.

They have a piano that their daughter played, but she has her own family now. He never took lessons and just played by ear, usually kind of messing up the tunes he played. But his spouse enjoyed it, and he played mainly for her. After she died, he didn't think he could ever play again. He brought her ashes home in a beautiful cloisonné urn and placed it on the buffet across the room from the piano. It blended well with the Asian vases and other items there. Having her home again was comforting, for her warmth was felt with the urn's presence. It was also comforting to leave all her belongings in the house as they were when she was alive, for they too bring forth her warmth as a part of her remains still there in their presence. Gradually, he found he was able to play the piano once more, for her once more.

Chapter Ten
Possible Expectations Regarding Models

Creativity is One of the Most Important Things We can Instill in Children

Models have a technical part that captures a portion of the workings of our physical world and a spiritual part that captures a portion of the workings of the spirit world. Models in any field continue to expand to capture more of our physical world and/or more of the spirit world. Some examples of advances in technology are the following. Some diseases that used to be incurable are no longer so, because the mechanisms by which they work are determined and ways to disrupt the mechanisms have been developed. New automobiles are more fuel-efficient because they now have continuous variable transmissions, smaller turbo-charged engines, electrical propulsion and regenerating systems, lower rolling friction tires, slipperier motor oils, improved aerodynamics, variable valve timing, fuel injection directly into cylinders, lighter components, etc. Continuing innovations in the high-technology electronic and computer industries make doing lots of things quick and easy that were almost impossible to do before.

Spiritual advancements tend to be slower, are often not compatible with all cultures, and usually need periodic updating as times change. Some examples are the following. Acceptance of differences among people is improving but is spotty and very slow. What works in one culture might not work in another, and we often forget to account for that possibility. Parenting practices keep changing with changing times.

Parenting has changed a lot since I was a kid. Back then I would be outside all day with friends and do all kinds of things on our own in a diverse neighborhood made up of homes, stores, businesses, schools, churches, a variety of trees and plants, empty lots, etc. We could see and touch all kinds of grasshoppers, bugs, caterpillars, butterflies and the scales on their wings, dragonflies, grasses and weeds and their flowers and their pollens and seeds including dandelion and milkweed, etc. And we would wonder why these things of nature are the way they are and thus develop a habit of being deeply interested in things in general. A church had a mail slot near its front doors. I didn't know what it was for at the time, so being a mischievous kid I would gather a bunch of dried leaves and stuff them into the slot. We would climb the brick walls of a school not in session. We could hop on our beat-up bikes at any time while wearing regular street clothes and ride to places more than two miles away. Specific bike-riding gear did not exist, and bike riding did not require preparations, as it does today. The freedom kids had in those days gave me some of my most treasured experiences, and they contributed a lot to my imagination, creativity, and resourcefulness.

There was not the fear that parents today seem to have. Any kid was sort of like everyone's kid even if they do not know the kid. Adults tend to smile when they see a kid, and that makes the kid feel warm all over. Schools were among the safest places for kids. There seemed to be a lot more empathy and compassion for one another, especially for kids.

Competition was simply not a large part of a kid's life then so that kids would do things just for the fun of it. Thus, their imagination, creativity, and resourcefulness were freer to develop. By comparison, competition is explicitly or implicitly a large part of a kid's life today such that what they do today is more confined to being done a certain way in order to compete in accordance with certain rules and conventions. Such confinement suppresses imagination, creativity, and resourcefulness, in my opinion and according to my experiences as a kid in my days. I can't say the freedom we experienced existed in every neighborhood back then. Maybe it was just in my neighborhood.

There are no incorrect models, only incomplete ones, as explained in Chapter Three. The technical part of a model captures a certain portion of the workings of our physical world. We or someone else can formulate that part of the model and we can simply accept it and use it. The spiritual part of a model is a certain portion of our personal spiritual model. A person using the technical part will have a certain portion of his or her personal spiritual model as the spiritual part, and it will be different for each person. Therefore, while many individuals could use the same technical part of a model each individual will have his or her own variation in the spiritual part. The variations are normally small because the spiritual part for each individual is analogous to a specialized technical language used in that specific technical field. This enables interactions among the individuals involved in that field to be carried out more easily and with fewer words and/or actions.

Thus, the technical part enables us to understand how a certain portion of our physical world works, and the spiritual part determines how we interact with other individuals and other things regarding in that part of our physical world. The technical part tells us what to do to accomplish something. The spiritual part tells us how to go about interacting with other individuals and other things while we are doing it. Therefore, to execute the technical part our spirit needs to be tuned to our physical world, and to execute the spiritual part our spirit needs to be tuned to the spirit world. This is an example of how we are carrying out our lives simultaneously in our physical world and the spirit world. This is also why often we behave differently while doing different tasks or going through different experiences. Each task or experience involves a different model, and each model captures a different portion of the workings of our physical universe and of our personal spiritual model.

Therefore, life has a physical part and a spiritual part. The physical part is where we apply the technical and spiritual parts of our models. The spiritual part is where we formulate and/or acquire the technical part of a given model and where we decide the part of our personal spiritual model that goes along with the technical part. The spiritual part of life is where we decide what to do, and the physical part of life is where we put it into action. This is how our spirit pilots our body.

Synergism exists between the two parts of life. Everything we do is a new experience and new pieces of knowledge are generated and/or existing pieces of knowledge are gained. The pieces of knowledge added to our spirit can expand the technical part and/or the spiritual part of our models. Therefore, as times change, the technical part and/or the spiritual part of our models change. This is why, for example, parenting practices keep changing. This is also how the high-technology industry keeps coming up with new innovations. Executing the technical part of a model stimulates our imagination and creativity. Executing the spiritual part of a model can help us find ways to expand the technical part and/or to come up with new technology. It also in some cases expands and/or adjusts the spiritual part as necessary to fit an expanded technical part or a newly formulated technical part. Thus, "imagination and creativity" are what make expansions of models happen and form new models.

One conclusion then is that for our species to continue making progress and advancements we need to nurture our species' ability to use imagination and creativity. A well-known professor once said that creativity is one of the most important things we could instill in children. The model gives an explanation as to why this is the case.

We might say this is something we could intuitively figure out. Yes, but expressing it in a model provides a means to help explain other, perhaps more complex, attributes about how the physical and spiritual parts of life work and interact together. This enables us to better understand how our spirit pilots our body and thus learn how to pilot our body more proficiently.

Why Finding Our Personal Spiritual Model Could Make Us a Better Person

We all have a spiritual model, whether we know it or not, but it might not be the model we would try to find if we were to search for it. It might be the one our parents have, followed by the church we happen to go to, followed by friends, or one that we are trying out among many we are considering. Most of the general spiritual models, such as those of the various religions, say something about life after life, and most rely on faith for followers to accept what is said. It then follows that if a follower does not consistently behave in accordance with what is said, the follower may not be completely accepting what is said. The more the follower accepts it, the more consistently he or she would behave in accordance with it, and thus the closer the model would fit his or her personal spiritual model.

Individuals in general probably have not found to their satisfaction evidence indicating whether or not life exists after life, and thus I think most individuals do not put much effort into searching for their personal spiritual model. If an individual found extremely convincing evidence that life exists after life, I imagine he or she would be seriously searching for his or her personal spiritual model. The personal spiritual model would likely be such that it could explain how life relates to life after life. The individual would therefore want his or her behavior in life to mean something worthwhile in his or her life after life. This is why individuals upon finding their personal spiritual models become better people. In other words, it makes a difference whether individuals live their lives for life on Earth or for life after life.

Possible Ways to Sense Spiritual Signals Indicating Life Exists after Life

We might ask; if a serious search is motivated by evidence that indicates life exists after life how can we go about finding such evidence? My experience indicates evidence does exist indicating life exists after life. We need to be able to sense the spiritual signals and put them together to see if they form a cohesive picture that makes sense for the situation at hand.

Unlike physical signals from our physical world that tend to be loud and demanding and that our body is designed to sense, spiritual signals are soft and gentle and are thus easily drowned out by physical signals. Therefore, we need to handle spiritual signals differently. Sometimes this involves an unconventional approach and mindset. A conventional approach and mindset can prevent us from making sense of such messages. This is similar to the way we not only have to turn on the radio, but we also need to tune it to an unfamiliar setting to receive the messages from an unfamiliar station.

We all have deceased loved ones whose spirits are in the spirit world, and they are bound to want us to know life exists after life. Therefore, they are bound to issue messages to us to tell us this. However, they are not likely to be issuing such messages all the time. But in certain situations they are more likely to be doing so, and those are the times we could try sensing spiritual signals. Sometimes such messages are not meant for us but are meant for us to receive and then convey to someone else, particularly if we are more able to sense the spiritual signals than that other person could. Sometimes the spirit of a loved one does it this way on purpose to make his or her messages more clear. Chapter Two gives examples of this.

One example of situations in which spiritual signals are likely to be issued by the spirit of a deceased individual includes the period right after that individual died. Chapters Two and Eight give examples of the forms such signals can take. Signals described in Chapter Two came after my mom died, and signals described in Chapter Eight came after my wife died. In my wife's case, it seems pretty obvious to me that she is still issuing signals to me, now more than eight years after she died. She is unlikely to be doing it to continue convincing me life exist after life but to watch over me as I deal with my cancer, as she said she would do before she died.

To receive messages that indicate life exists after life, it helps to have relatives and friends who can participate in sensing the spiritual signals. Two or more sets of senses are better than one. Earlier it was mentioned that an unconventional approach and mindset might be needed to get more tuned into such messages, and that a conventional approach and mindset could prevent us from making sense of such messages. A conventional approach and mindset is likely to make us frightened by such spiritual signals and that would distract us from wanting to sense the signals and make sense of them. We need to, instead, embrace the signals and love them, and thus to sense them as fully as possible. Then we need to lovingly piece them together to see if they form a cohesive picture that makes sense for the situation at hand. Keep in mind that the signals are simply from our deceased loved ones. Therefore, embracing them and loving them is consistent with how they were issued to us in the first place.

The Physical Part of Life Eventually Degrades, But the Spiritual Part Does Not

Life on Earth has a physical part and a spiritual part. The physical part is where we put our models into actions in our physical world. The spiritual part is where we form or acquire our models and where our spirit uses its models as part of determining how to pilot our body. But our spirit has the freedom to choose. Therefore, it also has the freedom to make discoveries, improvements, alternatives, mistakes, inadvertent accidents, etc. In addition, no model is complete, and thus they can produce unintentional results. For example, a medical treatment for cancer can cause unintentional side effects that vary from individual to individual. Nothing is perfect, not even the spirit world.

If our body becomes disabled and cannot function in a normal manner, then the physical part of life can degrade. Our spirit would be unable to pilot our body in a completely normal manner, and thus some of its models could not be put into action in a completely normal manner. Usually, our spirit would then form new models that can compensate for the degradation. This would include altering our major senses as appropriate. This is further discussed later in this section.

If our brain becomes brain-dead while the rest of our body remains alive, the physical part of our life is almost completely degraded. Our spirit would not be able to put into action any of its models for piloting our body, because the part of our brain that translates spiritual signals into physical signals for doing so, and vice versa, no longer functions. However, the part of our brain our spirit uses to keep our body alive would still function. If this part of our brain dies, then our body could die regardless of the condition of the rest of our brain.

Our spirit has certain intelligence and consciousness it can put into action directly in our body without going through our brain. These give our body its body intelligence and body consciousness. This could explain why sometimes the body of a brain-dead individual physically moves or twitches when touched. How much this can happen depends on how often, and which, such intelligence and consciousness were put into action when the individual was healthy and active. For example, our body does not automatically have the body knowledge to keep a bicycle upright as we try to ride for the first time. Our body develops the body knowledge to do so as part of our becoming proficient at riding.

Other kinds of body intelligence and body consciousness are similar. I.e., our spirit has to generate and/or gain access to the appropriate pieces of knowledge in order to apply its body intelligence and body consciousness. Our spirit has to do likewise to apply its brain intelligence and brain consciousness. That is why we go to school and attend college etc. even though we already have our intelligence and consciousness.

In all the cases described, our spirit remains alive and well, because the spiritual part of our life does not degrade. I.e., a piece of knowledge once generated exists forever as a part of the spirit world, and our spirit is made of pieces of knowledge. This means, as mentioned earlier in the book, if we were able to communicate telepathically, we should be able to communicate with the spirit of a brain-dead individual.

We might ask; if this means we should then also be able to telepathically communicate with the spirits of dead people in general? Theoretically, we should be able to, but my guess is that we are not likely to be able to do so at will. The spirits of dead people are likely always doing other things and are usually not in a position to communicate with us when we want them to. As described throughout the book, the spirit world is a constantly busy place. And, when the spirit of a dead person finds time to return our call, we are likely busy and are not in a position to sense the soft and gentle spiritual signals.

If our body is severely disabled, but we can still interact with others to some degree, then it is still possible to continue carrying out a productive life. Individuals handicapped in certain ways seem to be able to compensate by becoming more able in other ways. As discussed before, a deaf person may develop other ways to sense music, and some deaf individuals can even compose music. The model suggests that such compensations could be due to the spirit getting more in touch with certain of its spiritual senses other than the five that give our body its five major senses. For example, music is simply made up of vibrations, and our body can sense vibrations in other ways besides with its ears. Therefore, if our spirit compensates in this particular manner for the loss of hearing, then it might essentially be having our body develop one or more major senses in addition to its usual major five senses. The very fact that some deaf individuals can sense and compose music could be confirmation that our spirit has spiritual senses in addition to the five that give our body its five major senses. This means if we lose one of our five major senses, we might gain one or more additional major senses that our spirit is able to enable us to have. The fact that other creatures have major senses we humans do not have also indicates spiritual senses exist in the spirit world other than the five that give our body its five major senses.

Our sense of hearing is likely the only one of our five major senses that can be lost and compensated for by our spirit developing one or more additional major senses for our body. This is because our sense of hearing is just one of many ways our body senses vibrations. But our body is not able to sense in alternative ways what our four other major senses pick up. More specifically, there are no other ways our body can sense light, touch, flavors, and odors other than with the major senses it already has to do so.

Every Model We Use in Our Physical World Is a Spiritual Model of Some Kind

Every model we use in our physical world is a spiritual model of some kind in that everything that exists and/or takes place in our physical world has its spiritual counterpart in the spirit world enabling it to exist and/or to take place in our physical world. Therefore, when we formulate a model to describe something in our physical world we are also indirectly describing the spiritual part of it in the spirit world. We say "indirectly" because we are describing the translation of the spiritual part into a form that can exist and/or take place in our physical world and not directly the spiritual part.

Remember that no model formulated by us humans is complete; therefore any model we formulate is only an approximation. This means that while we are approximating something in our physical world, we are also indirectly approximating the spiritual part of it in the spirit world.

The model itself exists in our physical world because it has its spiritual counterpart in the spirit world enabling it to do so. The spiritual part of the model is the spiritual entity that approximates the spiritual counterpart of it that the model approximates.

Consequently, when we formulate a model for something, we are capturing only a portion of it and only indirectly capturing only a portion of the spiritual counterpart of it. For a typical model, the portion captured would embody the essence of it as it exists and/or takes place in our physical world. By capturing only the essence, the model consequently had only a limited range of applicability; i.e., the model would not be complete enough to be universally applicable.

By analogy we can design hand-held drills to make holes. The size of the hole a drill can make depends on the size and power of the drill. A small, low-power drill is easy to handle and works well making small holes. A big and powerful drill is too big, heavy, and powerful and thus difficult to handle for making small holes, but it works well for making big holes. Thus, each size drill is like a separate model, each capturing only a portion of the ability to make holes. And, no single drill is universally applicable for all sizes of holes.

Thus, the portion that captures the essence of something would be the portion that matters most to us when we go through an experience involving it. The rest could be left out of our model as long as we apply our model within its range of applicability. If we were to go beyond that range, then some of what was left out of the model would matter. However, in most cases, including even a bit of the rest could make our model too complicated, inconvenient, and/or unreliable for practical use.

By analogy, I always prefer tools designed for a specific purpose, because each fulfills its specific purpose very well. Each tool thus has a limited range of use. A multipurpose tool designed for multiple purposes has a wider range of uses. But such a tool is usually more complicated and does not fulfill any purpose particularly well or reliably. Such a tool can be impractical in situations where precision is required and using it can seem like handling several tools all at once, which can be cumbersome and inconvenient.

Nothing is perfect, so that even if we stay within the range of applicability of a model, unexpected things can happen because what was modeled could have or could develop negative imperfections. Things may contain a flaw, wear out, corrode, fatigue, clog up, be assembled incorrectly, have been dropped, etc. To work with or around such imperfections, in some situations we may add safety factors or margins to ensure we stay well within the range of applicability. In other situations, we might do cross-checking if we have more than one model for the same thing, each model dealing with a different parameter. We can also build in redundancy or backup systems. These are examples of ways to work with or around possible imperfections.

The fact is that all models we formulate are approximations and therefore have limitations, but they're workable and therefore generally acceptable for our particular situations in our particular physical three-dimensional universe. The same approximations might not be workable or acceptable in another universe. Another universe might not be physical or three-dimensional. Even if it is physical and three-dimensional, its materials or types of dimensions may not be the same as ours.

Another consideration is that the spiritual part of anything in our physical world is only a portion of a larger spiritual entity in the spirit world. For example, the spirit of a living or nonliving thing on Earth is only a portion of the spiritual entity serving as the spirit for that living or nonliving thing.

This means, for example, in the case of a human, the same spiritual entity serving as its spirit can at some other time serve as the spirit for a living thing residing in another universe. The portion of the spiritual entity that would serve as the spirit for that living thing would be different from the portion serving as the spirit for the human on Earth. Since in both cases the same spiritual entity is doing the serving, we could say that the living thing residing in the other universe is spiritually sort of also a human. After all, as discussed earlier in the book, the spiritual entity can reincarnate to serve as the spirit for a different human, and the new spirit would be a different portion of the spiritual entity from the portions that were any of the past spirits. But, in every such case, each new human would be clearly a human. Therefore, the same spiritual entity serving as the spirit for a living thing in another universe could be perceived to be spiritually rather human as well. But, that living thing is bound to be very different from a human on Earth in all kinds of ways.

This could also mean when we humans on Earth are using our imagination and creativity to find things in the spirit world, our spirit is able to recognize only things that can be translated into forms that can be expressed or exist in our particular physical three-dimensional universe. That is because our consciousness is mainly tuned to our physical three-dimensional world. Everything else in the spirit world might be perceived as undefined background things, because it is not pertinent to our physical universe. However, such things as thoughts, concepts, intentions, feelings, emotions, intuition, instincts, etc. can be recognized by any living thing residing in any universe, because these are dimensionless and independent of what a universe is made of. Once our lifetime in our universe is over and our consciousness becomes fully tuned to the spirit world, we will be able to recognize everything. This has to be the case in order for our spiritual expression to function effectively thereafter forever as a part of the entire spirit world.

Regarding how our spirits can recognize only things in the spirit world that pertain to our particular physical universe, notice how we would have difficulty imagining a set of three dimensions different from our set of three dimensions. Anything we can imagine that we think might reside in a different set of dimensions is bound to instead embody something having to do with our set of three dimensions and therefore unlikely to apply to a different set of dimensions. Our imagination has difficulty going beyond our set of three dimensions, although we can go beyond it in abstract ways such as when dealing with certain mathematical concepts.

This makes me wonder if mathematics might in fact be different in a world dimensionality different from our world. After all, highly intelligent living things there would be dealing with a different set of dimensions than we deal with, and we cannot seem to envision their dimensions. Earlier in the book I mentioned that mathematics is a language that transcends different universes, and therefore might provide a means of communication. But, that might not be totally true, now that we have thought about it in this manner. Someday when we learn how to do inter-universe travel or pseudo inter-universe travel, it would be good to keep this in mind to help minimize confusion that is bound to happen because of the differences among universes.

The Level of Our Advancement Is Reflected in Our Models

In our everyday lives, in general we deal with living and nonliving things in both a physical manner and a spiritual manner. For example, while we are driving a car we are piloting it in a physical manner going from one place to another. At the same time, we are also piloting it in a spiritual manner in our interactions with other drivers and pedestrians, cyclists, roadway workers, etc.

In general, our models are personal and have a technical part and a spiritual part. This is because in general our models are about living things and nonliving things, and we shape our models to fit how we are. The model we use for driving a car is an example; i.e., each of us drives a car differently and in a personal way. The technical part of a model provides guidance on how to do a specific thing physically. The spiritual part provides guidance on how to do that thing spiritually.

It thus follows that when we as a species continue to advance, our advancements are reflected in the technical part and/or spiritual part of our models. However, depending on the situation, advancement in one part but not the other would not necessarily constitute true advancement. For example, if we develop weapons with greater killing capability and we actually use them to kill more people faster, this would not constitute true advancement. We made technical advancement but not spiritual advancement.

We might ask; what if we are fighting a war, and the development and use of such weapons could help bring the war to an end? Wouldn't that be a good thing? The answer is that would be a good thing, but it would not be true advancement. The fact that wars continue to erupt indicates true advancement is not happening in whatever we are doing that led to war.

We might ask; what if we simply do not use the technologically advanced weapons? Would that constitute spiritual advancement and therefore true advancement? The answer is; no. If we are never going to use the weapons, we should get rid of them or not development them in the first place. This means the development of weapons with greater killing capacity has no role in achieving true advancement. Continuing to develop weapons with increasingly greater killing capacity means we are stuck in a mindset that is holding us from achieving true advancement in this area.

However, the process of developing technologically advanced weapons could come up with technical advances that can be used to make advancements in other areas. In that case, while developing the weapons would not constitute true advancement, it could be perceived to be a part of achieving true advancements in other areas. This is a manifestation of how everything is directly or indirectly a part of everything else in the spirit world.

We might then further ask, is the development of technologically advanced weapons in general a good thing or a bad thing? The answer is it is neither good nor bad, but the use of such weapons could be perceived as good, bad, or neutral depending on the situation. In general, nothing is absolutely good or absolutely bad. And, being a good, bad, or neutral thing is separate from whether or not it enhances true advancement.

As already discussed, movies are being made with increasingly spectacular explosions, collisions, destruction, violence, killings, etc. perhaps to somehow reflect our continuing technological advancements. In my mind, this seems to promote a backward movement in spiritual advancement. If so, then it is an example of how our species is not always moving forward in its spiritual advancement, and therefore, true advancement. Another and fairly new example is how individuals who, while driving a car, talk on cellphones or text even though they know the danger to others and themselves this causes. Such individuals are applying technological advances in physically advanced but spiritually backward ways.

Many of our large corporations are doing things in spiritually backward ways as well, as mentioned earlier in the example of the seventy percent of S&P 500 largest corporations that were found to avoid paying much or all of their taxes.

The Spiritual Part of Models Might Help Explain Some Unexplained Things

Sometimes the technical part of our models cannot explain a phenomenon, while the spiritual part can provide plausible concepts that might be possible to explore technologically.

For example, we have yet to explain what causes gravity. The model in this book suggests that gravity could be a natural attribute of the particular kind of space our physical universe resides in. And, the mysterious dark matter and dark energy in outer space might be what our particular kind of space is made of. After all, if there was nothingness before our universe was brought into being, and our universe includes the space in which it resides, something has to make up the space in which our universe resides. Also, every physical thing in our physical universe requires some kind of matter and/or energy to make it up, and since space is something and not nothing, it is possible that it is made of the dark matter and dark energy.

The model further indicates that our particular kind of space might have been brought into being before any physical matter could be brought into being in it. Or, possibly space and physical matter were brought into being simultaneously. But, in order for the Big Bang to occur, space had to be brought into being first in order for the Big Bang to go "bang" into it. If physical matter and space were brought into being simultaneously, then the Big Bang would not have been a "bang" but more like a "Big Ooze."

Consequently, if the Big Bang really happened, it could only be if the physical material part of our universe were brought into being after the space part of our universe. This means, our entire universe was not brought into being with the Big Bang, but only the physical material part of it was, assuming the Big Bang really happened.

On the other hand, if all components of our universe were brought into being together and not one component at a time, then it is more likely that the process of bringing our universe into being is a gradual process and continuous and less likely it was a Big Bang. The plausibility of a gradual and continuous process was discussed earlier in the book. And if it is true, then the gradual process is likely to still be continuing, as also discussed earlier in the book.

Another unexplained phenomenon is how very heavy elements such as gold could be formed in the events observed in outer space such as supernovas, formation of black holes, occurrence of brown dwarfs, and collision of galaxies, etc. However, the model indicates that the spiritual entities that enable all possible kinds of atoms and stars, planets, galaxies, etc. that make up our universe have to already exist in the spirit world before the spirit world can design and build the mentioned things that make up our universe. This is like how we on Earth design things such as houses, automobiles, jetliners, high rises, cruise ships, can openers, etc. We always have a design plan and we always start with basic building materials such as steel, wood, glass, plastics, rivets, nails, nuts and bolts, glue, sticky tapes, etc. By analogy the spirit world needs to have all the basic materials available in order to design and build our universe. The basic materials for building our universe are all the kinds of subatomic particles necessary to form all the possible kinds of atoms, stars, planets, galaxies, etc. that make up our universe. The spirit world would also already have all the spiritual entities (design plans) that know how to assemble the subatomic particles into all the mentioned things that make up our universe.

To start building the mentioned things that make up our universe, the spirit world would begin by bringing into being all the kinds of subatomic particles necessary to form those things. Next, the spirit world would call upon all the appropriate spiritual entities to assemble the subatomic particles into all those things. And, because the spiritual entities are working with freely floating subatomic particles, they can directly assemble them into all possible kinds of atoms without going through fusion processes to form the heavier atoms out of lighter atoms. If space is made of dark energy and dark matter, as speculated earlier, they are likely to have played a role in the assembling process. For example, they might have been the energy and the "glue" the various spiritual entities used for assembling the subatomic particles into all the possible kinds of atoms, and they could also be the source of gravity to enable the atoms to coalesce into stars, planets, galaxies, etc. This means some amount of every possible kind of atoms are formed during the early moments of our universe, including gold atoms. Therefore, besides stars some amount of planets and galaxies can form soon afterwards without waiting for fusion processes that take place much later to make heavier atoms by fusing together lighter atoms.

A planet recently discovered and reported in early 2015 lends support to the discussion in the preceding paragraph. The planet was determined to be about 11 billion years old, almost as old as our universe which is believed to be about 13 billion years old. This puzzled the scientists because the heavy elements (heavy atoms) needed to make up that planet would have to be formed first, and our universe was thought to be too young at that time for the kinds of events, such as supernovas, formation of black holes, occurrence of brown dwarfs, and collision of galaxies, etc. to happen that could produce heavy elements by fusing together lighter atoms. However, as explained in the preceding paragraph, the model suggests that some amount of such heavy elements can form during the early moments of our universe. This can explain how planets such as the one recently discovered can be formed 11 billion years ago.

Ever since we humans emerged on Earth, we have not identified any region in outer space that is filled with nothing but all kinds of freely floating subatomic particles, and we have not produced such a region in a laboratory. Consequently, we don't know if what the model suggests can happen during early moments of our universe actually happened. If all possible kinds of atoms were formed in the manner the model suggests, then since hydrogen atoms are the simplest and the easiest to form, their number is bound to be orders of magnitude larger than that of any other kind of atoms.

If the process of bringing our universe into being is gradual and continuing, we could possibly find regions that are filled with nothing but freely floating subatomic particles. They would exist where our universe is continuing to be brought into being. The gas clouds seen at various locations in outer space could be where this is occurring.

There is a spiritual part to a lot of the phenomena or things for which we humans formulated models to approximate that we are yet to more fully understand. Therefore, the technical part of our models tends to be more complete than is the spiritual part. This could explain why some of our models are unable to explain certain things about some of the phenomena or things they are formulated to approximate. A more complete spiritual part might be needed to explain what the technical part cannot explain.

All this is only speculation, of course. We are not likely to know for sure if any of it is true probably until our consciousness returns to being completely tuned to the spirit world. On the other hand, as we become more spiritually advanced and our models are capturing more of what is in the spirit world, we might be able to see if any of such speculations are true while we are still alive on Earth. But to do this, we need to pursue advancements in the spiritual part of our models as well as in the technical part. We have yet to fully tap into the potential of what the spiritual part of our lives can tell us. Applying our imagination and creativity to spiritual matters, as opposed to physical matters, is a possible way to start. One of the purposes of this book is to promote such notions, in addition to promoting an approach very different from what we might have perceived spirituality to be based on what we experience, for example, in a church, during a wedding or funeral, etc.

Our Personal Spiritual Search Does Not Actually End

Because our models can always expand, particularly the spiritual part, and thus especially our personal spiritual model, our personal spiritual search never really ends. An individual might be satisfied with his or her personal spiritual model for the time being, and thus his or her search could slow considerably. What this says is that even once we find our model, it is reasonable for us to have some lingering questions that our model is yet to answer. But do not feel disappointed if this happens; no model formulated by a human is going to be totally complete or absolutely accurate. If an unanswered question becomes important enough, we automatically intensify our search again.

While writing this book, each time I reviewed the draft for typos, grammar, wording, and etc. new things would come forth, and I would end up rewriting a part of the draft. This happened over and over again and can't seem to stop. But I needed to take a break in the rewriting at some point and get the book out. Otherwise I could be finished before the book is. It is not surprising that new things would constantly come up. Spirituality is part of everything, and no model formulated by a human can capture the totality of spirituality. Therefore, our personal spiritual model is not a static thing. It is naturally a dynamic and growing thing, and its growth can be a fascinating journey if we put in the effort.

Sometimes I think the model is formulating me more than I am formulating it. That is what models often do. They can take the individual doing the formulation by the hand and guide him or her to new discoveries and wonders. This has always been a process by which we have achieved our technological advancements; i.e., by making new discoveries by virtue of existing models expanding to form more complete models or branching off to form new models. Therefore, if the process works for the physical part of our lives, it should also work for the spiritual part, if we invest the same degree of curiosity and exploration into it as we do the physical part of our lives.

**The Mess We Made on Earth Got Us Sort of Trapped.
But We Don't Have to Stay Trapped**

Going after win-win results is the only way issues are addressed in the spirit world, when the issues are of the kind that are practices as well as concepts in the spirit world. This has to be the case since every spiritual entity in the spirit world is directly or indirectly a part of every other spiritual entity in the spirit world. Thus, a win-lose result would be impossible, because then exactly which spiritual entities would be the losers and which would be the winners? And, of course, going after lose-lose results would be dumb since that would lead to the spirit world going nonviable such that it and everything it creates would then vanish.

Even we humans would not pursue lose-lose results, at least presumably not purposely anyway, although sometimes what we do locally or globally does turn out to produce lose-lose results. Someone may do something for personal gain or in response to a personal hang-up and cause lose-lose results for themselves and other people, or what might look like a win-win or win-lose in the short-term short-range, but has long-term long-range results that are lose-lose. Or we might support something without having enough knowledge about what it is, and it turns out to be a "lose-lose" situation. Such examples indicate we humans need to become more spiritually advanced to avoid such lose-lose results from being pursued unintentionally in the first place.

According to the model, the mess we have made on Earth and the way we are mired in it is a Catch-22 situation. Being mired in it is preventing us from spiritually advancing very fast or very far. Not being able to spiritually advance very well is causing us to not behave in ways that could clean up the mess. Given that the model has pointed this out, we might want to focus on how we can get out of this Catch-22 situation instead of living with it as if it is simply how life is, and will be forever, on Earth. The model indicates this does not have to be the case, and that the spirit world did not intend for such a mess to exist for as long as it has. I think the spirit world was thinking that if this were to happen, we would be intelligent enough to not get mired in it for this long a period.

We Are Capable of Being More in Touch with Our Spiritual Senses

If we could get more in touch with our spiritual senses, we would be more in touch with the spirit world. The model indicates this is the case because we use our spiritual senses to find things and our way in the spirit world. But, we could get more in touch only so far. After all, if we were "totally" in touch with our spiritual senses, then our consciousness would be tuned to the spirit world. Since we are designed to reside in our physical world, our consciousness must remain mainly tuned to our physical world as long as we are alive on Earth. This limits how much in touch we can be with our spiritual senses.

Various other living things on Earth are bound to have a higher limit than we have. For example, those living things that rely heavily on instincts to survive have the spirit world doing most or all of their thinking for them. This means their consciousness can be more tuned to the spirit world than ours. Their purpose on Earth is also bound to be different from ours, perhaps tied more to being part of making Earth's environment hospitable to highly intelligent living things such as various animals including us humans. The model indicates this might be the case since by the spirit world doing most or all their thinking for them, the spirit world is essentially taking an active role through them in shaping and maintaining Earth's environment. And, through our natural partnership with the spirit world, we should be working, as some of us are, to maintain Earth's environment instead of ruining it, as others are.

Personally, the notion that some living things are here to shape and maintain Earth's environment is interesting. The Reverend Tommy Smith, who is recognized in the Acknowledgements, once said that some individuals think most other living things on Earth are here for the benefit of humans. Shortly before that, I happened to mention that I think ego gets in the way of people behaving spiritually, and he agreed. I responded to his statement by saying "Boy, if that isn't an egotistical thought," and we both had a big laugh over that. But now, my model is indicating that such a thought might be at least partially true. However, a more accurate and less egotistical way to put it is that some of the other living things on Earth are here to enable humans to be viable so that humans can do what is necessary to help the spirit world restore balance and thus remain viable.

In other words, we need to see these living things as a part of our natural partnership with the spirit world and thus we must ensure they do not go extinct because of our actions. Some of these living things, such as rainforests, coral reefs, etc. are immobile and thus might not receive as much of our preservation efforts as mobile living things do. Actually, rainforests and coral reefs are among the most important living things in helping maintain Earth's environment, and they are among the ones most threatened with extinction. Rainforests are said to be one of the lungs of Earth in keeping our planet's atmosphere capable of sustaining life as we know it.

Evidence indicates we humans in general have not yet reached the limit of how in touch we can be with our spiritual senses. For example, some individuals have extrasensory abilities such as the ability to see auras, do telepathic communication, do remote viewing, etc. Such individuals are more in touch with various spiritual senses than the rest of us. And yet their consciousness remains tuned to our physical world. This indicates the rest of us could also be more in touch with our spiritual senses.

This is why I think we are capable of learning how to communicate telepathically. When we as a species learn how to do it, I think we will be much more able to clean up the mess we have made on Earth. I think part of the reason we made the mess in the first place was because our communications with one another were generally poor. An ability to communicate telepathically would significantly improve communications.

The model also says everything in the spirit world within our ability to find is meant for us to find and to explore as part of the experiences we can go through in our universe. What this implies is that we are meant to get more in touch with our spiritual senses so that we are more able to find things in the spirit world. Furthermore, getting more in touch with our spiritual senses might be the key to our eventually making "empathy and compassion for one another" the dominant basis for how we carry out our lives.

If this is true, then this means the spirit world has designed into our universe multiple possible pathways for us to use to help us do our part to help the spirit world restore balance. Addressing wisely the various issues we face in life is one such pathway. Recognizing we have a natural partnership with the spirit world and making it mutually benefiting is another. Another such pathway could be our first getting more in touch with our spiritual senses. This would enable us to find things in the spirit world we could not find before, enabling us to eventually realize we need to make "empathy and compassion for one another" our dominant basis for how we carry out our lives. This would thus help us find ways to clean up the mess we made on Earth and also realize we have to do more to help the spirit world restore balance, not just simply generate new pieces of knowledge to help the spirit world grow.

This is only a speculation. But there is at least some logic behind it. We made many technological discoveries in our physical world that began as speculations. It would seem a similar process could work for discoveries we could make in the spirit world. It is at least worth a try. After all, if we could find this particular speculative notion in the spirit world, then it is meant for us to explore as part of the experiences we can go through in our physical world.

Your Approach in Your Career Might be Best for Finding Your Personal Spiritual Model

There are bound to be notions and concepts in my personal spiritual model that some individuals disagree with or object to. But again, the purpose of this book is not to convince anyone to accept my model as his or her own. The purpose is to show by example how unconventional thinking can help individuals find their personal spiritual model if conventional thinking isn't working. Also, the unconventional notions and concepts presented in this book are not the only ones that would work. I am an engineer so that my approach, notions, and concepts are more along engineering lines. The best approach for any individual searching for his or her personal spiritual model is likely to be the approach he or she is use to using in his or her career. It is likely to be the most comfortable, the most proficient, and therefore the most natural approach. I would imagine that it could thus provide th best chance of working well for the individual than any other approach could.

A Possible Role of Religions in a Personal Spiritual Search

My personal spiritual model works well for me right now, but it will continue to evolve as my spiritual needs continue to change with time and my age. Conditions around me will change, loved ones and friends will change, and how I can continue to contribute to mankind will change. Changes will happen to all of us. We have to expect them and are prepared to make changes in our personal spiritual model to meet our changing spiritual needs. Also, keep in mind, our personal spiritual model could never be totally complete or absolutely accurate; therefore, making changes does not mean the model was less valid before or more valid with the changes. What is most valid at the time is what works best to enable an individual to become better.

A personal spiritual model capable of growing and evolving is a healthy model. If we have a personal spiritual model that has no capacity for change to meet our changing spiritual needs, then it is unlikely our personal spiritual model in the first place. It is more likely to be a model some other source imposed upon us, and now it is confining us instead of helping us. When this happens, it is an indication we need to begin, or reactivate, our personal spiritual search.

In my mind, a personal spiritual model is generally not the model of a religion. A religious model can provide a starting point for our search, but it does not have to be where our search ends. However, for some individuals, a religion alone can enable them to have "empathy and compassion for one another" as their dominant basis for carrying out their lives. I have seen it happen with some members of the church I attended as a child.

In a way, I see attending church regularly and listening to weekly sermons as opportunities for each attendee to expand the religious model of the church in a manner that can better meet their personal spiritual needs. What each attendee hears from a given sermon is different and unique since each attendee is different and unique. Therefore, each weekly sermon means something different and unique for each attendee. Eventually, while all attendees belong to the same church, each would be forming a different personal spiritual model. The church would thus be meeting a very valuable need for those individuals. The sermons are in a sense holding each attendee by the hand and guiding each through personal experiences that can help them find his or her personal spiritual model. It might seem strange that the same sermon can afford a different and personal spiritual experience for each attendee. But, isn't this the case for every shared experience in life? While a group of individuals might look as if all members are going through the same experience, in fact each member is going through a different and unique personal experience.

A lot of individuals are spiritual but not necessarily religious. I am one of them. Based on the discussion above, we could say that an individual is religious if he or she includes the weekly sermons given in a church as resources in his or her personal spiritual search. And we could say an individual is spiritual if he or she relies mostly on personal resources in his or her personal spiritual search. The former approach relies more on conventional thinking while the latter leaves open the possibility of including unconventional thinking. This does not mean one approach is better than is the other. Whichever works better for an individual is the better one for that individual.

Old People, Young People: Being Interested vs. Being Excited

As I age, I become more aware of the conditions of the old. Young people, not having been old, generally do not fully understand how it is. Conversely, the old generally do not fully understand the world of the young because they generally do not have the health, energy, and interest to fully participate in it. Consequently, unintentional miscommunications from insufficient understanding can frustrate both the old and the young. I converse regularly with two widowers in their late nineties. Both have mentioned such frustrations. At times I have difficulty fully understanding the situations of the young and getting some young people to fully understand my conditions. And I'm not sure how frustrated the young are with the old people's lack of understanding of them since it seems young people are so busy with everything else in their lives.

Our impressions of what others experience shape our models, in particular the spiritual part of our models. The accuracy of our models thus naturally depends on the accuracy of our impressions. Our impressions are likely to be more inaccurate when about experiences of individuals of a different culture. This includes differences in the cultures of the young and the old, even within the same family and circle of individuals.

The cultures of the young and old are bound to be different. A lot has changed over the lifetime of the old such that today's young people live differently from how old people lived when young. Age-related health and physical degradation also contributes to making the world of old people different from the world of young people. Thus, even while old people and young people are within a family or circle, they come from different cultures.

Technological advances create the most noticeable changes in the world, especially over the last few decades. The increased human population is another major factor. Increased congestion in traffic, housing, recreational areas, events, travel, and just about every other activity people do now requires more time and effort to deal with, and this makes everybody more stressed and less patient. We also have spreading industrialization, and increasing consumption of energy, clean water, and food, and this has led to dwindling easily accessible resources, degraded or destroyed ecosystems, and increased demand for rare earth and other raw materials of limited availability that tend to be concentrated in only certain regions on Earth. Such increased consumption, shortages, and limitations affect the powers of various nations and international relations such that no nation can be truly self-sufficient or self-contained in today's world. Therefore, all nations have to get along to some degree even when it seems almost impossible. This brings about all kinds of issues that people in the world try to handle through diplomatic and financial maneuvers, and sometimes through battles cold and hot, big and small.

In my opinion, the continued fast rate of change, particularly technological advancements, could leave some segments of the world's population feeling increasingly left behind and impoverished. Their circumstances tend to make this happen, not only for poor individuals in poorer nations but also for those in richer nations. Notice the high level of homelessness in our country and the statistics cited earlier regarding the high rate of reliance on food banks. In California alone, one out five people requires assistance with food, the same state where some of the most highly paid technology workers are employed, in Silicon Valley.

Feelings of being left behind and poor, if severe, can bring about increased lawlessness and, in some extreme cases, terrorism. The perceived blow to their "ego and the desire to enhance survivability" is bound to be part of what drives their behavior. Other factors besides feeling left behind or poor also bring about bad behavior and terrorism. Consequently, today's young people face a greater amount of lawlessness that cannot be dealt with in a straightforward manner than old people faced in their young days. When old people were young, they faced the Cold War and a nuclear threat, both more clearly defined and more straightforward, although no less scary.

Parallels exist between national problems and global problems when the gap between rich and poor becomes very wide, homelessness becomes a big problem, joblessness is extraordinarily high, etc. Various forms of unrest could emerge nationally or globally. Citizens of a nation can become more frustrated, angry, and lawless when they see no improvements in sight and they feel they have less and less to lose. Thus, we constantly see senseless shootings just about anywhere. People globally can also become more lawless, and in extreme situations terrorism can emerge when they see no improvement in sight and they have less and less or nothing to lose.

What this indicates is that when changes, particularly technological advancements, occur at a fast rate as has been the case the past few decades, the changes need to be accompanied with ways to bring everyone along such that no segment of the population in the world falls far behind. This is something we humans have not been doing enough of. It is as if the potential for problems that can accompany rapid changes is invisible to those who are at the moment benefiting from the changes. In my opinion, this is because, globally, we chose as our dominant basis for carrying out our lives "ego and the desire to enhance survivability" and not "empathy and compassion for one another." It thus follows that it probably has less to do with any form of government, but more to do with the need to pay more attention to the spiritual part of our lives.

On the other hand, we humans being how we have been for thousands of years, the idea of bringing everyone along such that no segment of the population in the world falls far behind is a great concept but not one necessarily practical, desirable, or even safe to do in the present, near future, or even ever. It is great to think long-term long-range, but we need to survive the short-term short-range situation first. Therefore, it depends on whether we humans can ever change the dominant basis for how we carry out our lives to "empathy and compassion for one another," i.e. to take much more into consideration the spiritual part of our lives.

A worldwide change in our dominant basis for how we carry out our lives from "ego and the desire to enhance survivability" to "empathy and compassion for one another" would take many generations and perhaps many centuries of concerted effort. Quick "fixes" such as "a war to end all wars" are unlikely to work in the long-term long-range. It has to be a gradual process in the same way that natural evolutionary change has to be gradual to enable a new species of living thing to successfully emerge from an existing species. The gradual process gives the emerging species sufficient time to develop long-term long-range compatibility with their environment and therefore achieve long-term long-range viability there. A change in our dominant basis needs to be a part of how we bring up our children, how teaching is carried out in schools, how our institutions are run, etc. While government and religion should be separate, government and spirituality should not be. For example, a government that is meant to be for the people and by the people should not, behind the scenes, be for powerful special interests and by powerful special interests. This is dishonest, fraudulent, and thus spiritually lacking.

Already discussed are some of the reasons why today's young people have cultures different from those of old people and how today's world is more complicated than the world in which the old people were young. This suggests today's young people might want to simplify their lives as much as possible. This would help keep them from being mired in too many activities that appear to call for immediate short-term short-range attention. Eliminating some of such activities would give young people more time to pay attention to what could happen on a long-term long-range basis and thus allow them to put more effort into shaping their future instead of allowing others to steal control of it. This might require some unconventional thinking and a somewhat unconventional lifestyle in that they might not be doing what "everyone else" is doing or what "others" are saying they should be doing. Conventional thinking so far has not come up with long-lasting long-ranging solutions for human-relationship and human-condition problems that have been in a mess for thousands of years. Conventional thinking and technological advancements have mainly made the problems more technologically advanced but essentially unchanged spiritually, and thus the problems are not being resolved.

In fact, it is possible that making technological advancements is so enticing and exciting that it is drawing essentially all of our attention away from finding ways to resolve human-relation and human-condition problems. This could explain why we have been able to make amazing technological advancements at a fast rate but they can only modify but not resolve human-relation and human-condition problems. Technological advancements cater to our "ego and the desire to enhance survivability," which is our choice of dominant basis for how we carry out our lives, and they do little to cater to our "empathy and compassion for one another." This suggests that to eventually clean up the mess, we need to consistently apply more of our imagination and creativity to making advancements that cater to our "empathy and compassion for one another." It seems that by the time we become old, we realize that this is the more important part of being alive. But, by that time we are too old and our health and energy are too degraded to enable us to do much about directly changing the course of human advancements. However, we who are old can still do something indirectly by conveying our conclusions to the young and encouraging the young to do something directly now before they become old.

This is one of the reasons I now see unconventional thinking and lifestyles differently from how I used to see them. However, unconventional thinking and lifestyles do not necessarily lead to our making advancements that cater to our "empathy and compassion for one another." But I now believe they are worth exploring if for no other reason than they are a step away from the conventional thinking and lifestyles that have not been effective for thousands of years in resolving human-relationship and human-condition problems.

So, what form of unconventional thinking should we consider that might do better? A good resource consists of old people who have gone through decades of experiences and are thus in a position to make sense of what they have observed. The trick might be to get them to think about their experiences and to distill some concise key points. Not every old person is inclined to do that, but I believe every old people can be motivated to do so if young people seek it from them. It would take imagination and creativity on both parts, but especially the young, to translate what comes from the past into something relevant and applicable to the present and the future. Therefore, the young need to keep this mind when tapping into the experiences of the old.

One way young people can find out what forms of unconventional thinking might be worth pursuing is to become more knowledgeable about the experiences of old people. Being successful in life is a personal thing, and it should not be defined by what others think it should be. Some highly successful old people could explain how this notion has worked for them and how they have eventually come to realize what success has really meant to them personally over the course of their entire lifetime. A young person's perception of success will repeatedly change as they continue to develop over their lifetime. By the time they are near the end of it, the totality of their experiences is likely to give them a perception of success that is different from what they had perceived throughout their lifetimes. This is illustrated in the previously discussed fact that when old people are asked what they wished they have done more of during their lifetimes, they most commonly say something like they wished they had been nicer with people. None say they wished they had made more money or had possessed more stuff.

This indicates that after individuals have gone through all the experiences of a lifetime, they generally conclude that the spiritual part of life is the most important. It would be good if every individual realized this while young such that he or she would have a lifetime to pay more attention to the spiritual part of life. It is possible to have this be the case if the young were to value more the conclusions of the old.

When a moment in a story and a movie brings tears to our eyes, it is usually about some unspoken connection, interaction, communication, etc. that takes place in the spirit world. By observing it, we are momentarily transported back to the spirit world. That is emotional because we are reminded of the permanent home where we came from and where we long to be again. Also, while momentarily in the spirit world, the empathy and compassion in the spirit world (and also in us) dominate and bring tears to our eyes.

Young people might be surprised to find many old people who consider themselves successful in a personal sense have led somewhat unconventional lives. But they might not talk about it much because they might not think their lives would be of interest to young people. After all, today's world seems so much different from the world of their young days. But it is the physical workings that have changed with time while the spiritual workings have stayed the same. Therefore, when young people and old people talk about each other's experiences, each might want to try capturing the spiritual part of the experiences instead of being caught up in only the physical.

There are bound to be experiences in old people's lives that today's young people can benefit from. History tends to repeat itself, usually in more technologically advanced forms as time passes such that we might not recognize what is being repeated. Thus, what transpired in old people's lives could indicate what might be in the future for today's young people, albeit in more technologically advanced forms. Tapping into this resource could give young people a leg up on preparing for their future. However, the trick is to translate the experiences of the past into forms that are relevant to the present and the future. This takes creativity and imagination because technologically advanced versions of past experiences are less likely to come to mind. It is more common to generally perceive past experiences as being obsolete and irrelevant to the present and the future. This could be part of why history tends to repeat itself. Our ego might also be getting in the way if we think the past is too "backwards" to apply to the present or the future. History classes in school simply describe what happened in the past, often in a biased manner, and the descriptions usually do not emphasize what "lessons might be learned" that could very useful to the present and the future. In retrospect, I think an emphasis on "lessons learned" should be what history class is mainly about, and it would make the classes much more interesting and stimulating besides.

In general, the young lives that old people once led are much less exciting than the lives of most young people today. Old people when young were more conditioned to look for things to get interested in and more likely to be motivated to do something because they got interested in it. Today's young people are more conditioned to look for things to get excited about and more likely to be motivated by the excitement. The lure of excitement has become a part of our teaching in schools, advertisements, recreational activities, social media interactions, special effects in movies, sports (and extreme sports in particular), ultra-loud rock concerts, workings of high-technology devices, overly flavored foods, etc. Therefore, the pursuit of excitement is simply a part of a typical young person's upbringing today.

But being excited about something is generally a shorter-term shorter-range thing, while being interested in something is generally a longer-term longer-range thing. Accordingly, then by "being interested" we are generally taking more control of our future than we are by "being excited." Therefore, instead of using the lure of excitement to get people's attention, we would do better in the long run if we used the lure of interest instead. However, this would require more planning, more creativity, and more work. But, anything that has longer lasting value generally requires more work and more thought.

Basic research is pursued because we are interested in finding out about things without necessarily knowing exactly what we will find out. The findings might not directly benefit the organization doing the basic research, but they can benefit the industry, the nation, and the world. Basic research was emphasized more in the past, but because it does not necessarily benefit the organization directly or produce new and exciting gadgets, interest in it is reduced. The actions of the Microsoft Corporation are an example. They used to do basic research because past managers were interested in the concept, but current managers decided to close down the basic research branch of Microsoft. This seems an unfortunate sign of the times since it is turning away from longer-term longer-range pursuits in exchange for shorter-term shorter-range pursuits, a turning away from being motivated by being interested in exchange for now being more motivated by being excited. However, it is clear that Microsoft is facing a lot more competition to stay viable than it did during its early days. Therefore, it is understandable that it would decide to go with the flow. Nevertheless, it is an example of some of the things young people can learn by becoming more knowledgeable about the experiences of old people.

Conversely, by young people seeking such knowledge from old people, old people would be encouraged to carry out the responsibility of making sense of their lifetime of experiences and by making what they find available to young people. This would also help keep old people feel more alive and more a part of a larger living entity and thus contributing to the life of that larger entity, much like how a living branch of a tree contributes to the life of the tree. Old people should not consider their life as over and that it is time to simply have fun if they can or to simply wait to die. There are always ways to contribute to the life of a larger living entity as long as we are alive. And there are always ways to acknowledge we are alive by contributing as much as we can, even if our contribution might seem small because that is all we can do.

Old People, Young People: Extrapolating the Past to the Present and Future

My observation is that most old people tend not to talk much about their past because they think today's young people would find it boring and unexciting, which is probably true when compared with the lives of today's young people. In some cases, old people might not want to talk about their past because they are embarrassed by, or angry about, what they did or what happened to them in the past. The existence of such feelings is important to be aware of and to think of ways to work around so that old people can feel okay talking about their past. For example, a young person might say "I understand you had to spend time in an uncomfortable holding facility before being allowed to set foot onto this country. What was the experience like and how did you manage to live through it?" This would show understanding, empathy, compassion, and interest, and would thus help an old person feel okay to talk about it.

It is beneficial for young people to know what was in the past that made the present and thus what should be considered in building the future. After all, while we make technological advancements, human nature remains the same. Thus, we should avoid building a future that includes things that are simply more technologically advanced versions of things that were bad in the past. For example, bad people are still killing people today as bad people did in the past, but by more technologically advanced methods. A future that is simply more technologically advanced would likely include such bad behavior. However, a truly more advanced future would be one that is also spiritually advanced as well and would thus not include such bad behavior.

So, how could we extrapolate the past to come up with information that would be relevant to the present and the future? One way would be for the old to layout as much as possible the conditions, environment, values, expectations, etc. of the past while describing their experiences. This would help the young immerse themselves in the past and thus be more able to capture the relevance of the experiences relative to the conditions, environment, values, expectations, etc. of the past. Then, by extrapolating such factors to present conditions, environment, values, expectations, etc., the young might have an easier time extrapolating the experiences to come up with information relevant to the present and the future.

This is similar to how Brent Waters, the host of KGO radio's program "God Talk," (unfortunately the program ended starting in 2015) helps listeners more accurately understand the writings made during the time of Jesus including what was eventually incorporated into the Bible. For example, he goes back to what various words meant and related to in those days compared with what such works mean and relate to today in order to come up with a more accurate meaning of the writings.

Other things to look for would be analogies. According to the model, oneness pervades the spirit world and thus oneness also connects the past, present, and future. After all, a piece of knowledge that existed in the past would continue to exist in the present and the future. Oneness can manifest as analogies. Thus, analogies could constitute one of the ways the past, present, and future can be interconnected.

For example, a living thing grows and changes, and thus its viability varies when it or its environment changes. On Earth, living things that usually come to mind are creatures, plants, algae, bacteria, etc. But they could also be corporations, lifestyles, ways of doing things, modes of transportation, equipment, concepts, designs, fads, etc. Various living things existed in the past and various other living things exist in the present and others still will exist in the future. And there are analogies connecting past, present and future livings. For example, they all play a role in enabling other living things to function regardless of whether in the past, present, or future. Thus, for example, piloting a horse is analogous to piloting a car, which in turn is analogous to piloting an airplane, which in turn is analogous to piloting a spacecraft, and all of these are analogous to our spirit piloting our body in the first place.

Old People, Young People: A Personal Sketch

One of the widowers, mentioned earlier, as a kid was stuck working daily on the family farm to help the family get on its feet, while also going to school. The other widower was stuck working daily in the family restaurant to get his family on its feet. As a kid, I was stuck working daily at the family store to help my family gets on its feet, while also going to high school and junior college. These examples are not at all exciting to listen to or for the old people to have lived through during their young days. But it created a sense of accomplishment, participation, and contribution to something bigger than themselves, analogous to being a living branch on a living tree and thus contributing to the life of the tree.

In my parents' family, I was the youngest of five kids and thus had a much easier time than the two oldest kids. My oldest sister Mabel and brother Walter set good examples on what it means to participate in helping the family get on its feet. They gave essentially all of their earnings from their jobs to our parents to help with family finances. Mabel stopped when she got married and needed her earnings to start her own family. Walter stopped when he started saving up to attend college. But even once married, Mabel remained our parents' main language translator, financial communicator, tax calculator, legal communicator, medical advocate, crisis responder, caregiver, etc.

Eventually the family was able to rent a store and start a grocery business. The entire family participated; some of us full time and some of us part time if we are still in school or had outside jobs. I was there every day after school and all day on weekends; no days off. In the beginning, I was not paid, and I did not expect to be paid. After two years, I got paid twenty-five dollars a month and got a half day off a week, essentially all of which was spent helping with chores around the house. The idea of any high school-aged young person getting stuck working daily to help his or her family get on its feet may be foreign to some young people today. My observations indicate some young people today tend to see their parents more as financial resources than as people needing their help.

Going back one more generation, our father was orphaned at age thirteen and was left completely on his own. On top of that, for the next thirteen years, he had to earn enough to pay back the debts he inherited from his parents. He had to also save enough money to then be able to marry the girl who would be our mother. Our mother worked in a cannery while bringing up five children, and she did it all without the convenience of appliances such as washing machines, clothes dryers, microwave ovens, dish washers, etc. Our father worked twelve-hour days. He left home before we kids woke up, and he returned home after we were in bed asleep. We would see him only on Sundays, the only day of the week he got off.

Such things as welfare, food stamps, food banks, soup kitchens, subsidized school lunches, etc. did not exist. If you decided to have kids, you were completely responsible for providing food for them.

On a couple of occasions, I would mention to my children how I was stuck working daily in the family store to help the family get on its feet while attending school, but I am not sure if it left any significant impression on them. Their lives were so different that my young days probably impressed them sort of like how a fictional story would. But who knows? They might, or might not have seen anything in my past that they could use in their lives.

The best part of my experiences could not be adequately conveyed within the short time available in my kids' busy lives to hear about my past. One of these days when I could, I would tell them that when all the members of a family struggle together to contribute to the well-being of the family, the members become spiritually very close with one another. A lot of empathy and compassion for one another developed. Each member understands the struggles of the others, and they all feel a sense of worthiness and self-respect having participated in the struggle and having contributed to something bigger than themselves. This idea of contributing to something bigger than themselves would hopefully tend to stick with them, and it would hopefully tend to be how they would carry out the rest of their lives. Earning a sense of self-respect is very valuable. It is much better than having self-esteem. Self-respect is more spiritual while self-esteem is more into ego (the dictionary relates self-esteem, in one sense, to self-conceit). Having earned self-respect is a wonderful feeling, and none of us in my parents' family have ever become selfish, for we know selfishness has no place in the mutual effort. It helps a lot that the oldest ones of us five children, Mabel and Walter, set such good examples.

I often wished there were something similar I could have had my children participate in. But having gone from being very poor to becoming middle class, my wife and I have become financial resources for our children instead of individuals who need our children's help to the family. Becoming middle class has resulted in something very spiritual and very valuable being more difficult for our own children to experience. We did our best to have them do regular house chores, but somehow that didn't work as well. Especially when they got paid for doing chores, the sense of participation in something bigger than them selves got diluted, and the main payoff became the money instead. I.e., their payoff became more physical and less spiritual.

As a kid, I was very happy and felt very much loved as a member of a struggling poor family. I understood the struggles and why we did not have a lot of things some other families have. But, we had love, empathy, and compassion for one another that were amplified by our mutual struggles. I am not sure if my children felt any happier or any more loved being members of a middle-class family. By this, I am talking about the spiritual part of life. Especially as I become elderly, I conclude the spiritual part of life is the more important part of life. The physical part begins and ends, but the spiritual part is everlasting, according to the model and also according to most other spiritual models.

Looking back, I am glad I had a chance to live a part of my life as a member of a struggling poor family, but I am also glad I am no longer there. But having been there enables me to emotionally feel some of the ways of life people in the world are going through. Observing it is not the same if we have never experienced it or anything close to it, in the same way we would not really know how a certain food would taste by simply observing it, hearing about it, or reading about it. In my mind, the more we are able to physically and spiritually, experience the range of life humans have lived through, the better we would be at making a meaningful contribution to mankind. Our decisions and choices are made in the spirit world while our actions corresponding with our decisions and choices are carried out in our physical world. Our experiences shape our decisions and choices, and this takes place in the spiritual part of our lives.

Here are a couple of examples of how certain common practices have changed over the lifetimes of the old, at least within my parents' family and circle of friends and relatives when I was young are. High school graduation was simply something we were expected to achieve. It was no big deal and there was no special celebration. After all, there were much more significant events to come in our lives. There were senior balls and stuff, and only one of the five kids in our family (not me) ever went to one. Today, graduation is often handled like a "once in a lifetime" event that if not celebrated to the limit would be a serious deprivation. Senior balls used to be just a one-evening event. Today, senior balls also include limousine transportation, an overnight stay in a hotel or cruise ship, and a following day of additional activities.

Likewise, weddings when I was young were usually performed in a church and receptions would be held immediately afterward in a room that was part of the church. We would all get a piece of the wedding cake and some ice cream, and that would be it. Today's weddings are usually much more elaborate. The cost of a wedding and banquet reception can add up to what could be a down payment for a house.

We might wonder whether such changes are a forward step or a backward step in the way we carry out our lives. It is likely to also depend on how it compares with conditions in the rest of the nation and the rest of the world.

Old people progress gradually through two situations as they continue to age. In the first situation, an old person can look perfectly fine, because their physical decline is not yet obvious. Consequently, most young folks think the old person is as capable as he or she ever was and treat the old person accordingly. On the other hand, the old person generally wants to remain independent and thus does not let his or her physical decline show. Therefore, the wrong impressions the young have of the old and the willingness of the old to promote the wrong impressions often result in miscommunications between the two.

For example, a recent finding indicates that in general old people prefer to avoid large gatherings, including large family gatherings. They instead prefer to interact with just one or a few individuals at a time. But they often attend large family gatherings anyway, if they are physically able to, mainly to keep the young people happy. Young people generally are not aware of this.

The second situation old people go through as they continue to age occurs when they can no long hide their physical decline. When that happens, young people tend to leave old people out of conversations and other activities. However, according to the model, an old person might be physically declining, but his or her spirit remains as healthy as ever. The brain may be in decline along with the rest of the body, and therefore the communication link between the spirit and the body has declined, but if we were able to communicate directly with their spirit telepathically, we would find the old person as mentally sharp as ever. It would be good if young people realized this and treated old people accordingly. In other words, even if old people are unable to physically interact with young people very proficiently, mentally and spiritually they are still very sharp and are trying their best to pilot their body as well as possible. Therefore, cut the old people some slack.

Twenty Seven Years

In case you feel discouraged because your personal spiritual search isn't making much progress or is very slow, my experience indicates this is natural. My search has been going on for more than twenty-seven years and is continuing. It moves slowly sometimes, goes quickly sometimes, and is dormant sometimes. Periodic dormancy is bound to happen. We have busy lives, business travel comes up, things require maintenance or repair, illness strikes, and other priorities would come and go. I had several long interruptions, and it was difficult to get back on track each time. Inconsistencies would crop up when starts and stops interrupted my chain of thought or changed the direction of my thoughts. They also made the wording in the book flow less smoothly. Such situations can result in the need to reformulate parts of my model and to rewrite various parts of the book. Thus, partial reformulating and rewriting commonly happen. The book I ended up writing turns out to be very different from the book I started out to write.

Since I ran into inconsistencies with my model, I imagine other individuals could also do so with their models. In retrospect, finding and resolving inconsistencies enabled me to make my model more complete. An inconsistency means something is missing. By resolving the inconsistency and adjusting the model accordingly means finding what was missing in the first place and thus making the model more complete. Therefore, if you run into inconsistencies, keep working to resolve them. The effort will be rewarding.

My experience indicates our ego can prevent us from finding our personal spiritual model. For example, we are likely to start out in life thinking that we are carrying out our lives only in our physical world, not partly in our physical world and partly in the spirit world. Therefore, we perceive our intelligence, consciousness, senses, thinking and reasoning ability, etc., must all reside in our body, and more specifically in our brain, in the way we have been led to believe. Consequently, if we were to hear notions that indicate our intelligence, consciousness, senses, thinking and reasoning ability, etc., do not reside in our brain but instead reside somewhere else not in our physical world, our ego is likely to reject such notions. In the case of my personal spiritual search, such rejections would have prevented me from finding my personal spiritual model. On other hand, a spiritual search is a personal thing; such rejections might not necessarily prevent other individuals from finding their personal spiritual models. In other words, conventional thinking might work very well for some individuals. But, in case conventional thinking has not enabled you to find your personal spiritual model, you might want to explore what unconventional thinking could do.

Preview/Index

The Preview/Index provides a preview and a summary of the book as well as the Index. Spirituality is revised in an unconventional manner that requires abstract thinking to follow. As a preview the Preview/Index prepares the reader for the presentation, and as a summary it recaps what is presented.

A

A person sketch and twenty seven years 472-8

Abstract thinking
   carrying out life simultaneously in the spirit
      world and our physical world 23
   examples of abstract thinking 395
   mathematics 450
   spiritual advancements takes place in the spirit
      world and has to do with the behavior and abilities of living things. In the case of living things on Earth, it is the increase ability to be more empathetic, compassionate, creative, imaginative, intuitive, instinctive, capable of abstract thinking, etc. 394-5
   the invention of languages might be associated
      with the initiated the ability to do abstract thinking 270-1

Acuity
   during sleep 302
   examples 261
   in general 138, 261, 264, 283, 202
   major senses differ for different species of
      living things 264
   senses of living things 138
   various human occupations 283
   why the acuity of our major senses is reduced
      during sleep 302

Adult, adulthood
   adults would smile at kids 440
   blind child gains eyesight as an adult 68
   children are better than adults with high-tech
      devices 84-5
   children are better than adults at sensing
      intuitive signals 237
   children becoming adults 43-4
   church groups 19
   confusion during upbringing could last a lifetime 254-5
   extrasensory ability during childhood 351-2

games with win-win outcomes 408
parental protection lasting into adulthood 333
unresolved anger 434

Advance, advancements
advanced living things likely first emerge on
  Earth as primitive living things 73, 396-8
advancements and increasing complexity in the
  spirit world 387-8
advancement does not necessarily mean
  improvement 282
advancements are fragile 81
advancements of living things other than humans
  389
advancements passed onto descendants are easier
  to access 82-4
advancements progress in spurts in our physical
  universe and most likely also in other universes. Humans advance in spurts from one generation to the next. Technical advancements progress in spurts from one generation of devices to the next. However, spiritual advancements (pertain to behavior of living things)
    progress gradually 90-3
antimatter living things 338-342

awareness or lack of awareness of other
  universes 100-1, 281
developed oneness would become inherited oneness for members of subsequent generations. Thus, each generation could be more advanced. It could also lead to the development of new species 198-200
dramatically new experiences will promote
  advancements 80-1
effects on evolution 181, 199-200, 220, 245,
  282, 287, 369, 393-4
extrasensory ability 353
high-tech devices 216, 410,
imagination and creativity 442
in general 100, 130, 202, 208, 220, 231, 265,
  282, 398-9, 421, 451
inherited oneness that was once developed
  oneness previous generations will lead to the development of more advanced generations and possibly to the development of new species 198-200
inter-universe travel, see **"Inter-universe**
  travel"
lack of fossils could mean retracing took place
  74-5

Index

migratory effects on advancement 80-1
new ways of thinking 270-1
our advancements of any kind whether technical
  or spiritual are greater when the experiences involved are more different from ones we've been through. The model explains how this is the case. We humans advance faster technically once we started advancing technically, because our advancements enable us to invent or create experiences very different from ones we've been through. This suggests we might be able to advance spiritually rather quickly by a similar process once we figure out how to get started, or how to free ourselves from what it is that is confining us from doing so 85-6
rate of advancement could depend on the state of advancement 79-81, 297
retracing an evolutionary path 396-8
role of reincarnation 109
role of religions 96
role of the amount of life-supporting ingredients
  on a planet 400-4
scientific pursuits will promote advancements
  85-6

specialization helps to preserve advancements
  81
spirit world's advancements 387-8, 396
spiritual advancements 148, 204, 208, 245,
  247, 394-5, 398-9, 409, 413, 439, 456-8
spiritual advancements takes place in the spirit
  world and has to do with the behavior and abilities of living things. In the case of living things on Earth, it is the increase ability to be more empathetic, compassionate, creative, imaginative, intuitive, instinctive, capable of abstract thinking, etc. 394-5
spiritual senses and consciousness 261-2
suppression hinders human advancements 94-5
technical advancements has to do with how
  nonliving things function and what they could do 180-1, 208, 328, 384-5, 395, 398-9, 439, 457
technical advancements effects on quality of life
  and formation of wisdom 144, 147, 245, 282, 338, 389, 413, 463-472
the level of our advancement is reflected in our

models 451-2
the more advanced the spirit world becomes the
    faster it becomes more advanced 86
the more advanced we are the faster we become
    more advanced 86
the use-it-or-lose-it phenomenon 81
three main obstacles for us humans to overcome 421
three possible ways evolutionary changes can
    happen. Only one of the ways produces advancements 79-87
true advancement is when spiritual advancement
    is achieved along with technical advancement 451-2, 471
we humans are responsible for our species'
    evolution 404-6
why humans are more advanced than other living
    things 26, 71, 86, 94, 245, 247, 336, 370

Allergies
    evolution does not begin and end over the
        lifetime of a universe such that it starts from scratch for each universe. Instead, it spans continuously over one universe to the next and the next, etc. Each universe puts its unique imprint on the evolutionary processes that pass through it. This could explain why we have incompatibilities such as allergies among some living things 70-7, 183-4, 347

Analogies appearing in the text: (the symbol " ~ " used here means "analogous to")
    a bad hang-up ~ bad itch 253
    a spiritual entity newly serving as a spirit begins
        with simple things ~ a new pilot begins with simple airplanes 397
    a person is a representative for the spirit world ~
        a person being a representative for an organization 190
    a spirit knows how to heal a body ~ an auto
        mechanic knows how to repair a car 310
    a spiritual entity serves as a different spirit on
        different times ~ a person takes on a different role in different situations 57
    an experience generates new pieces of
        knowledge ~ learning a new skill 335

Index

any model formulated by a human is incomplete
~ any piece of equipment designed by humans has limitations   448
energy is needed to produce matter and
~ antimatter ~ energy is needed to stretch a spring to produce opposing forces   330
each person is different ~ each language in each
technical field is different   411
evolution occurs in spurts with each generation ~
cars evolve in spurs with each redesign   93, 282
extrapolations forward and sideways ~ looking
into possible futures and possible analogies   152
if God issues a guidance you don't agree with,
you don't have to follow it ~ you don't have to follow a practice you don't agree with   279
indirect oneness occurs in the spirit world ~ a
friend of a friend is a friend   142
living things evolve to become more advance ~
technology evolves to become more advance   47
living things have instincts to help stay safe ~

modern cars have safety features to help stay safe   270
new pieces of knowledge will produce new
issues that will need balancing~ new information about something produces new perspectives that then calls for more information   258
new pieces of knowledge produce new issues ~
new information produces new perspectives   180, 258
oneness in the spirit world could manifest as
analogies in our physical world   472
our universe might have emerged gradually ~
how Brigadoon emerged gradually   62
pieces of knowledge acting together are more
capable than the total capability of each acting alone ~ components assembled are more capable than the total capability of each alone   269
pieces of knowledge ~ electron, protons, and
neutrons. Small spiritual entities ~ atoms   156
pieces of knowledge ~ words. A combination of
pieces of knowledge forms a spiritual entity ~ sentences. A combination of spiritual

entities forms a larger spiritual entity ~ paragraphs. A combination of larger spiritual entities forms an even larger spiritual entity ~ books and articles. The spirit world keeps just one copy of each piece of knowledge ~ a dictionary   48-9, 113, 115, 155, 171-2, 294, 326, 430

the ability to think abstractly ~ the ability to
    recognize analogies   271

the brain is the main computer control center for
    the body ~ computers are the main control center for a car   269

the spirit pilots the body ~ a human pilots an
    airplane   60

the spirit world is filled with pieces of
    knowledge for creating things ~ Earth is filled with materials for making things   76, 124, 454

the spirit world is vulnerable in its early life ~ a
    living thing on Earth is vulnerable in its early life   54

the spirit world knows the kind of new
    knowledge needed but doesn't know what knowledge will be generated ~ a person knows the kind of tools needed but doesn't know what tools will be available   132

the spirit world sends humans to Earth to
    generate certain kinds of new knowledge ~ humans send a rover to Mars to gather certain kinds of new information   158-9, 213

the spirit world's thoughts enable our physical
    world to exist ~ an author's thoughts enable the world of a story to exist   294

we can visit other planets and universes by going
    through the spirit world ~ ghosts can visit different places   289

we humans are addicted to wars ~ an addict is
    addicted to drugs   405

we shape our future with our decisions ~
    adjustments at launch determine where the missile will land   374

we tend to ignore the spirit world while focusing
    on our physical world ~ a person going to a store for a certain item tends to ignore everything else   353

when a living thing loses one of its major senses
    the spirit alters the brain to compensate ~ the spirit heals an injury   279

wisdom kept up to date and
relevant for the spirit
    world ~ maintaining mental
and physical health for
    humans 306

Ancient folks' practices and concepts often have
merit 292

Angels
angel of life, angel of death 292
angel statues 381-2
guardian angels 92, 109
highly intelligent living things (maybe even
    human or human-like beings)
made of antimatter 341

Anger, angry
an easy, often mindless response 195
dream images 318
regarding past events 470
response to political issues 416, 464
spiritual entities 114
unresolved anger could become a hang-up that is
    as distracting as a bad itch
253-4, 259, 434

Antibiotics
can only be extracted from plants and other
    living organisms 120
continuing research 378

having tug-of-wars with bacteria 327-8
overuse of antibiotics can cause super-bugs to
    develop. This could be explained in terms of natural tug-of-wars in the spirit world 327-8, 339

Antimatter
according to the model a plausible spiritual
    reason exists that can explain why the amount of antimatter in our universe could be less than the amount of matter 338
anti-energy might also exist 340
antimatter beings could exist 340-1
antimatter galaxies are difficult to find 340
antimatter naturally exists in our universe 330
highly intelligent living things (maybe even
    human or human-like beings)
made of antimatter 341
humans might see antimatter and anti-energy as
    energy sources for use and profit 339
its amount being less than the amount of matter
    could indicate our universe is still emerging into existence 340

relativistic quantum theory
predicted antimatter's
existence 345

Approximate, approximation
each human formulated model
approximates a
certain portion of the spirit
world 116-7, 385, 447-9,
455
human technology approximates
what the spirit
world creations 120-1
in general 64, 91, 144, 249, 286,
332

Assemble, assemblages
all living and nonliving things are
assemblages
of components 56, 57, 77-8
an assemblage of components is
more than the
sum of the individual
components 428-9
components can be assembled
imperfectly or
incorrectly even by the spirit
world. This is because the
spirit world is imperfect 448
dark matter and/or dark energy
might have
enabled subatomic particles to
assemble into electrons,
protons, neutrons, and atoms
454
everything in our universe is an
assemblage of
electrons, protons, neutrons,
and subatomic particles 120,
429, 454
how well a memory can be
recalled depends on
how well assembled are the
pieces of knowledge
associated with the memory
319-21
the assemblage of all pieces of
knowledge
existing at any point in time
forms the spirit world at that
point in time 65
the space station was assembled in
outer space
76
the spirit of anything is an
assemblage of
smaller spiritual entities 133
the spirit world assembles features
from its vast
collection of features to
construct living things 200
two or more pieces of knowledge
assembled
together form a spiritual entity
55

Artists
some individuals are artists or are
artists at heart
211, 256, 283
the spirit world creates artworks
and an artist
finds them in the spirit world
and translates them into forms
that can exist or be expressed

Index 487

in our physical world 68-9, 75, 116

Atom, atomic, subatomic
computers can be miniaturized down to the scale
of atoms 385
dark matter and/or dark energy might have
enabled subatomic particles to assemble into electrons, protons, neutrons, and atoms 454
electrons, protons, neutrons, subatomic particles,
and atoms are sometimes called "quantum particles" 122, 125
elemental things (electrons, protons, neutrons,
subatomic particles, and atoms) have elemental senses 46
heavy elements can form much sooner than
expected and could happen during the early moments as our universe is emerging 454
Higgs boson is sometimes called the "God
particle" 63, 121, see also **"Higgs boson"**
quantum particles are a source of oneness in our
physical world 141, 418, 429
quantum superposition and entanglement can be
explained by the spiritual model of this book 125-6, 128-9
subatomic particles are likely among the first to
emerge to form our universe 52, 120-1, 156
the formation of heavy atomic elements 419, 429
the smallest possible subatomic particle is said to
take on qualities of a thought 114
the spirit world ingeniously designed a small
number of elemental things that are capable of making our universe what it is 454-5
the spirits of electrons, protons, neutrons,
subatomic particles, atoms, and building material molecules such as DNA are different in that they could enable multiple copies of such things to exist 43, 141, 326
three isotopes of the hydrogen atom exist 123
we keep finding smaller and smaller subatomic
particles 218

Attitudes, see, **"Intentions and attitudes"**

Auras

a white aura could sometimes
appear   366-7
an uncommon white aura   32, 34,
36, 366-7
auras are produced by spiritual
energies
    traversing back and forth
    through the soul. However,
    white auras are produced
    differently, and they stay
    around only for a relatively
    short time; i.e., between a day
    and perhaps a year   365-7
auras are sensed with our spiritual
senses   459
examples of what could be
    revealed by auras   35
extrasensory abilities could be
taught or learned
    because they are likely to be
    natural human abilities   35-6,
    351
images of auras might be capable
of being
    captured on photographic
    development paper   227
the ability to see auras   24, 35,
170, 357
the ability to see auras takes place
in the spirit
    world   190, 351-2, 365-7,
    394

Authors
an author often day dreams about
a subject
    before putting it in writing
296

an author's thoughts enable things
to exist in the
    world of his or her writings
    like how the spirit world's
    thoughts enable things to exit
    in our physical world   115-6,
    294, 430
are among those who translate
things in the spirit
    world into forms that could
    exist or be expressed in our
    physical world   69, 116
Rupert Sheldrake gives examples
of telepathic
    communication in his book
    206

**Automobiles that can drive
themselves**
the people who design and build
such
    automobiles have done the
    thinking for the automobiles
    such that they could drive
    themselves. This is similar to
    how the Mar Rover and other
    vehicles we sent into outer
    space could drive themselves
    and conduct experiments on
    their own. This is analogous
    to how the spirit world does
    the thinking for living things
    that rely on the spirit world to
    do their thinking for them for
    their survival   269-70

Awake

awakening from a near-death experience 316
awakening from an out-of-body experience
    362, 364
being awake is a state of existence 129
ever wondered if we are awake or asleep?
    296-7
every experience we go through while awake
    will eventually be addressed during sleep 310
living entities in the spirit world, such as our
    spirit, are always awake and never need sleep 307, 309
our spirit is constantly trying to restore our body
    whether we are asleep or awake 300
our spirit is OK with our dreams being confusing
    and surrealistic, but is not OK if things are confusing while we are awake 104
sometimes we want to stay awake when our
    spirit says we need to sleep 304
we can be awaken while asleep but not so while
    in a coma 361
we sometimes could sense spiritual messages
    better while asleep than while awake 314-5

we sometimes find solutions while asleep that
    we could not find while awake 313-4
why the acuity of our major senses reduces while
    we are asleep? 302
why we need sleep after being awake long
    enough 202, 300

B

Bacterium, bacteria
    atoms have elemental senses and elemental
        consciousness enabling them to form molecules that could form bacteria 46
    bacteria are living things. Some are considered
        good on Earth and some are considered bad on Earth, but not necessarily so in other planets or universes 472
    bacteria employ ingenious ways to propel
        themselves. Thus, they have elemental
        intelligence 277
    bacteria have tug-of-wars with antibiotics and
        some could become super-bugs 327-8, 339
    bacteria likely do not need sleep 308

bacteria need to eat other living things to survive
    240
bacteria that cause diseases could indicate that
    evolution spans over multiple universes 72
hang-ups are like bacteria and viruses, they could
    infect us and they could spread 390
our spirit will recognize the bad bacteria as
    foreign and would work to eliminate it 240
some bacteria could invade some creatures
    without making them sick and will use them as carriers 343
the brain function of a bacterium resides in its
    outer membrane 45, 139, 277
the intelligence a bacterium has could be
    considered body intelligence 138
the spirit of a bad bacterium enables it to invade
    our body 229, 238, 240
the spirit world must have countless spirits to
    cover countless things such as bacteria on Earth and elsewhere 286

Bad behavior

a future that is more technically advanced but not
    more spiritually advanced is likely to enhance bad behavior 471
bad behavior could spread like a cancer 239
bad leaders, bad government can encourage bad
    behavior 392, 415
conventional thinking could confine us to make
    wars for thousands of more years as it has done for thousands of past years 27
hang-ups could cause bad behavior to continue
    generation after generation 254
humans are the worse among living things in
    terms of doing bad things to members of their own species 399
oneness could bring about bad behavior as well
    as good behavior 199
poor communication can lead to bad behavior
    393-4
self esteem can give some bad people the nerve
    to behave badly 240
some animals are capable of bad behavior
    272-3
some individuals who behave badly think their

personal God is promoting it 290
some large corporations got the government to
    care about them more than about the nation's people 416
the feeling of being left behind with nothing to
    lose could cause bad behavior 464
upholding ego is a major cause of bad behavior
    for thousands of years   272, 405, 415

Bad itch, see, **"Hang-ups"**

Balance
    ecosystems, bodily functions   24, 153-4, 228,
        309, 402
    issues, see **"Issues,** maintaining reasonable
        balance"
    knowledge, see **"Knowledge,** balanced
        knowledge, maintaining a reasonably balanced state of knowledge"
    one of the reasons we humans get into conflicts
        and battles is because when we generate pieces of knowledge we tend to not also generate opposing pieces of knowledge to achieve better balance in our total knowledge and thus achieve wisdom. We don't do this because our intelligence is limited. The spirit world could do it because its intelligence is unlimited, although not necessarily complete. Thus, it knows it needs to do something, such as design and bring into being new universes periodically, to help restore its state of knowledge to being reasonably balanced   334
thinking   410

Battles
    a win-lose mindset likely means we are not
        applying the wisdom available to us in the spirit world   196
    a win-win long-term, long-range outcome is
        always better, unless it is a life or death situation   194-5
    because the cancer stem cell acts as part of our
        spirit, the battle is in the spirit world as well as in our physical world   228
    hopefully we will eventually realize wars are a
        waste and are hindering our spiritual advancement   402
    if we stay with a win-lose mindset, we are more

likely to do battle whenever
we think we are losing   195
our current choice of dominant
basis for how we
carry out our lives could
occasionally lead us to battles
and wars as it has for
thousands of years   407
our usual mindset regarding
visitors from other
planets or universes is to do
battle or make war with them
192
visitors from other planets or
universes are likely
to have advanced to where
they use their resources for
further learning instead of for
making war   427
when we are constantly making
wars, we need to
balance the issues involved
such that wisdom could be
achieved to help us stop
making wars   425, 464

Behind the scenes
a government meant to be for the
people and by
the people should not be for
special interests and by
special interests behind the
scenes   465
large corporations have become a
powerful
unofficial unelected part of
our government behind the
scenes   411, 417

we need to use more our year-
round voting
power by how we spend our
money regarding corporations
that hold enormous power
over our government behind
the scenes   417

**Being interested about something vs.
being excited about something**
being interested is more a long-
term long-range
thing whereas being excited is
more a short-term short-range
thing   462-70

Big Bang theory
in general   53, 340, 453
the Big Bang might not have
occurred   61-3
according to the model, because
the spirit world
is continuously growing, and
thus evolution is continuously
progressing, some or all
universes might possibly be
brought into being gradually
and continuously as opposed
to suddenly as would be the
case if the Big Bang theory
applies. This could explain
why our universe is
expanding, and at an
accelerating rate at that. For
example, see **"Big Ooze
theory"**   181

Big Ooze theory

Index 493

the Big Ooze might have occurred
instead of the
    Big Bang 453
according to the model, because
the spirit world
    is continuously growing, and
thus evolution is continuously
progressing, some or all
universes might possibly be
brought into being gradually
and continuously as opposed
to suddenly as would be the
case if the Big Bang theory
applies. This could explain
why our universe is
expanding, and at an
accelerating rate at that 181

Black holes 61, 64, 75, 419, 426, 429, 453, 455

Body, brain-dead
    in general 275
    out-of-body experience 364
    telepathic communication 445-6

Body, drugs
    alcohol and some drugs could
degrade the
    brain's ability to
communicate with the spirit
and the rest of the body 137, 371, 405
    certain drugs taken with certain
other drugs are
    more effective than when
taken separately 428
    in general 249

Body intelligence and body consciousness
    in general 137-40, 170, 268, 313, 345,
    445-6
    instincts are likely a part of body
intelligence and
    body consciousness as well as
a part of brain intelligence
and brain consciousness
274-5

Body language 97-8, 270

Body: the range of things a body could do 45, 137-8, 272, 276

Body parts lost and regeneration 205, 299, 376

Brain activity
    in general 42, 277, 302, 352, 361
    contrary to common belief,
according to the
    model the entire brain is
active or ready for action
during sleep 309-13
    during sleep the frontal cortex
stays ready for
    action, but it usually gets no
calls for action during sleep.
Thus, it appears to shut down,
as commonly believed, when
in fact it is only inactive
309-13

Brain cells

a certain kind of brain cell is found to enable a
    living thing to have the capacity to be empathetic. Such cells are found in the brains of humans, elephants, dolphins, whales, and various other animals   277-8
there might be other kinds of brain cells for other
    kinds of mental states   278

Brain frontal cortex
    during sleep the frontal cortex stays ready for
        action, but it usually gets no calls for action during sleep. Thus, it appears to shut down, as commonly believed, when in fact it is only inactive   309-13

Brain function
    brain as a physical thing will decline with age
        and thus its function will decline as well   321
    declination with age can lead to poor short-term
        memory, as explained by the model   321
    in general   45

Brain, human
    in general   275-7
    the human brain is large because the human body
        is designed to do a multitude of different things   137-8

Brain, in unconventional configurations   45, 137-8, 277

Brain power   45

Brain size vs. body size
    everything else being equal, then the larger the
        body of a species the larger would be the brain to handle the work of keeping the body alive and healthy   274-6
    in general   45, 137-8, 202
    see also **"Brain, human"** and **"Size"**

**Brain size and its complexity vs. spirit size and its
complexity**
    in general   137-8, 202
    see also **"Brain, human"** and **"Size"**
    the larger and the more complex the spirit, i.e.,
        the knowledge base, for a given species of living thing the more intelligent and/or consciousness would be the species. The more dexterous and the more precise the ability of the body of the species to do things the larger and more complex would be the brain to handle the body's range of abilities. Thus, the

Index   495

size of the spirit and the size
    of the brain are not
    necessarily proportional with
    each other   45, 274-9
the wider the variety and range of
mental states
    possible for a living thing the
    larger would be its spirit and
    brain   278

Brain waves   277, 361

Brother   20, 30-1, 472

Building materials of our physical world   120,
    123-4, 454

Building materials of the spirit world   123-4

C

Cadillac automobile   29, 33-4, 36

Cancer
    cells   228, 240-1, 376
    spirit   240-1
    stem cell spirit   228-9
    stem cells   228-9, 328

Candidate
    a candidate will likely take on a
    different spirit
        type, and thus be a different
        person, once elected and is in
        office   248-9

because models are correct but
incomplete we
    can be easily manipulated by
    others such as candidates for
    office and advertisers   298
candidates for office   244

Care giving, caregivers   173-8, 437-8, 473

Caring for ourselves   432-8

Catch-22 situations   457-8

Cells
    body cells   226-8, 299, 343
    cancer, see **"Cancer,** cells"
    colonies of cells, see **"Colonies,** of cells"
    stem cells, see **"Stem cells"** and **"Cancer,**
        cancer stem cells"

Chemotherapy   173, 175-7, 311, 378, 381

Child, children, kids, see also **"Adult, adulthood"**
    a child could master certain skills
    more easily
        with the help of his or her
        inherited oneness   83-5
    a child could resemble a parent
    because of
        inherited oneness   82-3
    an adult is the same person as
    when he or she

was a child but the adult is
now a different individual   43
best friend, Joe, since childhood
113
children are likely to naturally
have extrasensory
abilities   352-3
cross-learning is likely to function
for humans,
especially children, as well as
for other living things   95,
111
give a kid lots of free time to
explore the world
around him or her just for the
fun of it and he or she will
develop imagination,
creativity, and resourcefulness
440
ideas keep changing on how best
to bring up
children   172
it is important for a child to
develop his or her
creativity and critical thinking
skills   380, 442
kids are likely more sensitive than
adults to
spiritual signals such as
instincts, intuition, cross
learning, inherited oneness
237-8
why kids can work high-tech
devices better than
their parents. Interestingly,
their parents' fear about early
high-tech devices "blowing
up" if they use them

incorrectly could be
contributing to why kids can
work high-tech devices better
than their parents can   237-8
why kids tend to be mischievous
and why being
mischievous could be a sign
of good intelligence and not
of bad behavior   238

Choice, choices
the spirit world gives highly
intelligent living
things, such as humans, a lot
of freedom to chose   133-4
the range of choices an individual
might make
depends on the role he or she
is in at the moment   248
the range of choices is more
limited for living
things with lower
consciousness and
intelligence   159, 224
the range of choices the Mars
rover has is
determined by humans   224
the spiritual expression of a
deceased person
could chose to appear as he or
she was at any point in time
of his or her past life   322
we make our choices in the spirit
world, and we
carry out the associated
actions in our physical world
193, 475

Index

we shape the spirit world positively or negatively
   through our intentions, choices, and actions   22, 50

Churches   19-20, 27, 440-2, 456, 461-2, 475-6

Citizens   193, 242, 411-7, 464

Clones
  a clone and the cloned individual would have the
   same inherited oneness but not the same developed oneness. This is because they have the same parents but different and separate spirits. In this sense they would be much the same as identical twins   213, 222

Cold war   327, 337-8, 464

Colonies of living things
  a member of an insect colony automatically
   knows its role and has the body configuration to match   203, 232-4
  a spirit of a living thing, especially of a human
   being, is a mixture of multiple spirit types   242
  an organization has a colony spirit type, but its
   spirit would be different from that of a colony of insects   423-4
  an organization requires a lot of spiritual
   considerations to work well, because humans think for themselves whereas a member of a colony of insects relies on the spirit world to think for it   423-4
  colonies of cells make up living things   232
  colonies of insects have a spirit type that is
   different from that of most other living things   169, 203, 232-4
  the colony itself has the main spirit. Each
   member has a sub-spirit that is a portion of the main spirit. All the members of a given type in a colony working together would function like a vital organ of the colony   233
  the sub-spirit of a member of an insect colony
   appears to reincarnate. The main spirit of the colony would then reincarnate piecemeal   349
  when a colony grows large enough, it divides to
   form two colonies   234
  while stem cells exist for living things whose

bodies consist of cells, no stem members exist for colonies of living things 232

Coma 42, 134, 300-2, 360-1, 376

Combinations
in general 79, 86, 193, 320, 340, 366
of attributes 77
of dimensions 88
of features of living things 77
of issues 428-9
of pieces of knowledge 48, 55, 67, 69
of senses 191
of signals 52, 69, 88, 127
of spirit types 242, 244

Commercials and advertisements
any model or statement reasonably formed
would be correct but also incomplete. The incompleteness cannot be avoided because we humans are imperfect. We are imperfect because the spirit world is imperfect. Therefore, we must not let ourselves be completely sold by the correctness, but rather we must always be aware of the incompleteness 95-9, 244, 411, 430

Commonalities
all planets in our universe hospitable to living things are bound to have commonalities 427
analogies have commonalities 271
evolution is likely to take place in every universe 183
genetics have commonalities among living things on Earth 197
growth is likely an attribute of every universe 182
mathematics is possibly a commonality among all universes 182, 184

Communication
a major problem is that our communication is generally correct but incomplete. This leads to misinterpretations, misunderstandings, and unintentional feelings that are often unresolved. We need to be more aware of the incompleteness and to find ways to communicate better. For example, face-to-face communication is better than any form of written communication 394
among living things across different universes

and across different planets 116, 315, 450
between the spirit and the brain, and between the
> brain and the rest of the body 41-3, 134-9, 185, 189-90, 205, 275, 279, 305, 321, 345, 353, 361, 371, 476

communicating through the oneness that
> pervades the spirit world would be one way for us to telepathically communicate among each other. We would be more able to avoid the conflicts and battles we tend to get into 212, 214-5, 393-4

encouraging, enhancing, and improving any
> extrasensory abilities is a good thing because they could provide additional channels of communications among individuals 353, 459

high-tech 257, 408
it seems likely that humans are meant to develop
> an ability to communicate telepathically 370

In general 158-9, 189
miscommunication 462, 476
takes place among all pieces of knowledge and
> thus among all spiritual entities 65, 165, 189, 391-8, 468

telepathic, see **"Telepathy, telepathic communications"**
when we learn something, our spirit grows, and
> it then has to make changes in our brain in order to be able to communicate with our brain regarding what it is we learned. This is why changes in our brain can be observed when we learn something. Therefore, changes in our brain when we learn something does not mean our brain did the learning. Instead, our spirit did the learning and then has to make necessary changes in our brain 41-3

Communication with deceased individuals, and other formerly living things
> examples are given in **Chapter Two**. See also **"Intuition", "Spiritual Messages"**, and **"Telepathy"**

we all have experienced some form of telepathic
> communication since we all have received instinctive and/or intuition messages. Instinctive messages are telepathically received from the spiritual entity serving as our spirit. Intuition messages are telepathically received

from other spiritual entities. Such communications work in the same way as telepathic communications among individuals would work   205-6, 215

Compassion
the spirit is where consciousness, intelligence,
senses, feelings, emotions, empathy, compassion, ego, reasoning ability, imagination, creativity, etc. reside. Different living things would have different such attributes and different strengths and/or acuities of their attributes   59-60, 133-5, 140, 227, 271, 295, 300-1
empathy and compassion   144-5, 435

Compatible, compatibility, incompatibility
a change in our dominant basis regarding how
we carry out our lives is needed. But it has to be gradual, because values, habits, customs, etc. change slowly. Our dominant basis needs to be compatible with prevailing values, habits, customs, etc. in order to be viable. Otherwise, the change is not likely to be successful   465

our technical accomplishments are formed in our
particular universe with its particular set of three dimensions such that they are not likely to be compatible with any other universe   395
various incompatibilities on Earth such as
allergies, bacteria and virus infections, food intolerances, cancers, etc. suggest evolution must have continued over the lifetime of one universe after another, and it will continue to progress in this manner   72, 183-4

Compensate
because models reasonably formulated by
humans are correct but incomplete, we need to include safety factors, safety margins, limits of applicability, etc. to compensate for their incompleteness   172
because the spirit world is imperfect, it forms
wisdom to compensate. Humans are imperfect, because the spirit world is imperfect, and need to compensate by applying the wisdom that is available to us in the spirit world   151

Index

if a person loses one of his or her five major
> senses, his or her spirit compensates by enhancing one or more of the other four major senses and modifying the brain accordingly. The spirit also compensates in a similar manner when the person gets disabled or handicapped   279, 371, 445-6

Competition
a win-lose mentality in most cases indicates we
> we are not applying the wisdom available to us in the spirit world   196

competition in various forms and degree is part
> of almost everything we do   194

competition is good if it is for self-improvement,
> pursuit of excellence, and/or produces a win-win outcome   149, 195, 426

competition is only a concept, not a practice, in
> the spirit world. Thus, one of the reasons our particular universe was created by the spirit world is to enable the spirit world to experience competition as a practice   149-50, 425-6

focusing too much on short-term short-range
> objectives tends to have us develop a win-lose mindset. This tends to create problems, because some body has to lose perhaps too often   195

friendly competition for promoting excellence
> and a win-win mindset   147, 149, 195, 426

good and bad sides of competitions   190-6

hostile competition for ego, control,
> enhancement of survivability   147, 196, 407

making competition too much a part of a very
> young child's life will stifle the development of imagination, creativity, and resourcefulness. It will instead enhance the development of persistent short-term short-range thinking and a persistent win-lose mentality   440

one of our purposes for being here is to find
> ways to work with and/or around the perception of opponent and competition without allowing them to have us develop a persistent win-lose mentality. This is a big challenge that very few seemed able to face and succeed, as evident by the

win-lose mentality that pervades mankind   150
spiritual oneness plus the physical separateness
   in our physical world tend to bring about
      competition and a win-lose mindset. This was purposely designed into our particular universe as a challenge for mankind on Earth to find ways to work with and/or work around, but not to which to give in   149, 199
   the spirit world might have grown beyond its
      vulnerable stage and is more able to maintain its own viability, or it might still be in its vulnerable stage. If the latter is true then the way we are handling competition could jeopardize the spirit world's viability as well as our own   53
win-win and win-lose outcomes   190-6

Complex, complexity
   advancements and increasing complexity in the
      spirit world   387-8
   evidence of the spirit world's genius is how it
      created a few simple things (electrons, protons, neutrons, etc.) that could form a countless variety of living and nonliving things, numerous forms of energy, and a wide variety of energy-associated physical phenomena   120
   quantum particles are tiny and simple and can
      have only a very limited variety of experiences. Larger, more complex things such as molecules can have a limitless variety of experiences   124, 129
   the amazing microscopic complexity of a vital
      organ, brain, body cell, inner ear, etc. indicate these things didn't simply happen by chance. They have to be purposefully designed and created   71, 344
   the larger and more complex the brain the greater
      the range and precision the tasks the body could do   274-6
   the more a living thing is intelligent and
      conscious the larger would be the number of pieces of knowledge making up its spirit enabling the living thing to exist. Thus the larger and more complex would be its spirit   58-9, 133, 138-9, 155-6, 201-2, 217, 225, 274-6
   the more a living thing is intelligent and

conscious the more likely it
will need sleep   308-9
the spirit world, and thus each new thing it
   creates, will be increasingly advanced, complex, and sophisticated. This could partly explain why the things humans are able to find in the spirit world and translate to exist or be expressed on Earth are increasingly advanced, complex, and sophisticated   47, 54, 155-6, 181, 262, 282, 345-6, 387-8
the spirit world starting from its beginning could
   quite quickly become able to create something as complex as our universe   49
thoughts in pure form (devoid of any spoken
   language) can be telepathically conveyed instantaneously regardless of the complexity of the though and regardless of the species of the sender and the species of the receiver   189

Computer, computer control center
   the brain as the computer control center for
      the body, but it is not where intelligence and consciousness reside   42, 136, 269, 275-7, 300, 321

Concepts of the model, examples include:
   a piece of knowledge would automatically form
      a connection of the first kind with every other existing piece of knowledge. This is the "force" that gives the spirit world its creative power and ability. See **"Connections"**
   any model that is reasonably formulated by man
      would be correct but still incomplete. See **"Correct but incomplete"**
   any statement that is reasonably composed by
      man would be correct but still incomplete. See **"Correct but incomplete"**
   anything we can find in the spirit world is meant
      for us to find and to explore   328
   learning takes place with the spirit in the spirit
      world and not with the brain in our physical world.   87-90, see also **"Spirit, spirits"**
   no two experiences are identical even if some are
      considered routine such as brushing our teeth everyday. Differences always exist, even if only very minor. Therefore, every experience will generate new pieces of

knowledge or enable us to
gain access to some already
existing pieces of knowledge
that is new to us. Notice how
we can continue to learn
something new even when
doing something considered
routine   84
the soul of a living or nonliving
thing consists of
   all the connections of the
second kind that connect the
spirit of a living or nonliving
thing to the living or
nonliving thing residing in a
universe. See **"Soul, souls"**
and **"Spirit-soul-body"**
the spirit world is the place, and
the only place,
   in which pieces of knowledge
reside. See **"Spirit world"**
concepts are neither positive or
negative in the
   spirit world, but in general
they have their positive side
and their negative sides when
translated to exist or be
expressed in a universe   291
perfection is only a concept and
could never be
   achieved 64-6, 119
the concept of a guardian angel
93
the concept of opponent   145

Congress, government, see
"Government, Congress"

Conjoined twins   234

Connections
connections of the first kind
connect every
   existing piece of knowledge
with every other existing
piece of knowledge   55, 59,
64-5, 82-3, 87-8, 90, 93, 105,
113, 131, 141, 146, 155, 165,
179, 198, 266-7, 307, 332,
345-6
connections of the second kind
connect every
   piece of knowledge making
up the spirit of a living or
nonliving thing with the living
or nonliving thing residing in
a universe   55-6, 59, 60, 105-
6, 116-7, 126-7, 136, 141,
222, 234, 274, 361

Conscious, consciousness
animal 46
body consciousness   268, 274-8,
313, 445-6
brain consciousness   268, 274-8,
446
consciousness level and
intelligence level do not
   necessarily go together   369
different living things have
different sets and
   acuity of major senses and
most likely also different sets
and acuity of spiritual senses.
Consciousness is associated
with the senses. Therefore

do much less, or no, horrible things to other living things other than for food. We humans with our consciousness tuned much less to the spirit world would do horrible things to living things; especially to other humans 398-9

the fact that a recipient of an organ in an organ
    transplant can sometimes take on attributes of the donor further indicate consciousness and intelligence reside in the spirit and not in the brain 140

the model indicates we have not reached the
    limit of how well we could be in touch with our spiritual senses. Thus, we could become more conscious than we are 459

the more conscious we are, the faster we can
    increase our consciousness 297

the more spiritual senses and the more acute the
    spiritual sense, the more consciousness a living thing has 261-7

the ratio of spiritual advancement vs. technical
    advancement is associated with the ratio of consciousness tuned to the spirit world vs. tuned to the world of the universe 398-9

the spirit is where consciousness, intelligence,
    senses, feelings, emotions, empathy, compassion, ego, reasoning ability, imagination, creativity, etc. reside. Different living things have different ones and degrees of such attributes 59-60, 133-5, 140, 227, 271, 295, 300-1

various nature of consciousness 263-5

we have the impression that our consciousness
    resides in our brain and not in our spirit. But the model indicates our consciousness resides in our spirit instead 301

Contribution, making a contribution to mankind
    Life exposes us to many conditions and
        situations over our lifetime. The more we go through, whether good and bad, the more we could understand about life, and the better we could be able to make meaningful and effective contributions to mankind 475

Conventional
    approach and mindset 443-4

do much less, or no, horrible things to other living things other than for food. We humans with our consciousness tuned much less to the spirit world would do horrible things to living things; especially to other humans   398-9

the fact that a recipient of an organ in an organ
   transplant can sometimes take on attributes of the donor further indicate consciousness and intelligence reside in the spirit and not in the brain   140

the model indicates we have not reached the
   limit of how well we could be in touch with our spiritual senses. Thus, we could become more conscious than we are   459

the more conscious we are, the faster we can
   increase our consciousness   297

the more spiritual senses and the more acute the
   spiritual sense, the more consciousness a living thing has   261-7

the ratio of spiritual advancement vs. technical
   advancement is associated with the ratio of consciousness tuned to the spirit world vs. tuned to the world of the universe   398-9

the spirit is where consciousness, intelligence,
   senses, feelings, emotions, empathy, compassion, ego, reasoning ability, imagination, creativity, etc. reside. Different living things have different ones and degrees of such attributes   59-60, 133-5, 140, 227, 271, 295, 300-1

various nature of consciousness   263-5

we have the impression that our consciousness
   resides in our brain and not in our spirit. But the model indicates our consciousness resides in our spirit instead   301

Contribution, making a contribution to mankind
Life exposes us to many conditions and
   situations over our lifetime. The more we go through, whether good and bad, the more we could understand about life, and the better we could be able to make meaningful and effective contributions to mankind   475

Conventional
   approach and mindset   443-4

lifestyle 434-5, 467
notions and concepts 21, 23-5,
  460-1
thinking and ways of doing things
  25, 112-3,
    135, 139, 151, 169, 256-7,
    272, 394, 406-8,
    434-5, 462, 467, 478

**Conventional vs. unconventional
  thinking**
conventional thinking and ways of
doing things,
    and our technical
    advancements, have not
    helped us clean up the mess
    we made on Earth for
    thousands of years. It is time
    to try some unconventional
    thinking and ways of doing
    things. Our spiritual
    advancements need to catch
    up with our technical
    advancements 466-7, 471

**Corporations (some big
corporations)**
  a disconnection between the
  intended and the
    actual 411
  are experts at creating
  advertisements that can
    influence us 298, 411
  are living things 472
  avoid paying their fair share of
  taxes 412, 416,
    452
  basic research 470

big corporations do not necessarily
create jobs
    413-4
lobbyists are often negatively
referred to as the
    third house of Congress 411
members of Congress could
personally benefit
    by how things are. Therefore,
    there is no incentive for
    Congress as a whole to made
    changes 415
members often become lobbyists
after leaving
    office 411
the Supreme Court considers
corporations as
    "persons" regarding their
    financial contributions during
    elections 416
we are supporting their actions and
influences by
    buying their products 417

Correct but incomplete
  any model or statement reasonably
  formulated
    would be correct but
    incomplete. The
    incompleteness cannot be
    avoided because we humans
    are imperfect. We are
    imperfect because the spirit
    world is imperfect.
    Therefore, we must not let
    ourselves be completely sold
    by the correctness, but rather
    we must always be aware of

the incompleteness 25, 64,
95-6, 117-8, 172-8, 243-4,
258, 327, 411-2, 423, 440
we humans need leaders because we are separate
    living things, and we do our own thinking instead of relying on the spirit world to think for us. This means we are vulnerable to being lead by bad leader if our leader happens to be bad. This is because statements made by anyone, including our leader, are correct but incomplete. We could get hooked by the correctness without being aware of the incompleteness. We have seen many cases of bad leaders gaining control of nations. We must be careful to not let this happen to our nation, because it could happen 391-2

Crazy quilt patchwork of models in our lives
    25, 121

Create, creation, sudden creation
    the spirit world creates everything 64-5, 88,
        116, 156
    everlasting desire to create 155-6
    creation of new features for living things 345-7
    humans might have emerged on Earth through retracing instead of through evolution. Thus, humans could be perceived as having been suddenly created 86-7
    in general 20-2, 25-6, 30-1, 40-1, 43, 47-51, 60-
        70, 131, 146, 151, 171, 179, 251, 262, 265, 267, 282, 285, 287, 289, 306, 311-2, 319, 325, 329, 331, 333, 355, 357, 409, 413, 429, 457, 463, 472
    missing links can be missing because retracing
        took place instead of evolution. Retracing could happen very rapidly such that sudden creation could be perceived. This could be the case for humans 73, 75, 86-7
    rapid evolution of some living things could be a
        form of retracing. Retracing is a process of rapid emergence of living things that has have already evolved on some past universe. Retracing is thus a rapid retracing of an evolutionary process that already taken place. Retracing could allow insufficient time to leave behind fossils behind, and thus, we would have missing links. This could apply to numerous living things besides us humans, in particular very intelligent living things such as

elephants, dolphins, whales, octopi, etc. 86-7
species with missing links are common and this
    could indicate retracing occurred instead of evolution for those species 74-7
sudden creation through retracing an
    evolutionary path (as opposed to gradual evolution on a new path) 72-3, 75, 86-7
the spirit world cares about everything it creates
    307-8, 326, 342, 376, 417-9

Creative, creativity
    an author's creativity 116
    applying creativity in the high-tech industry
        442
    creativity is one of the most important things we
        can instill in children 380, 439-42
    dyslexic individuals are very creative 435
    in general 48, 208, 216, 241, 246-7, 251, 327, 336-7, 417
    knowledge is the source of the spirit world's
        creative ability 47
    spiritual advancements take place in the spirit
        world. Any spiritual advancement that is relevant to the world of a universe would also take place in the world of that universe. In the case of our universe, spiritual advancements are achieved when, for example, we understand and accept each other better 394-5
the spirit is where consciousness, intelligence,
    senses, feelings, emotions, empathy, compassion, ego, reasoning ability, imagination, creativity, etc. reside. Different living things have different ones and degrees of such attributes 59-60, 133-5, 140, 227, 271, 295, 300-1
the spirit world's creative ability and power
    increase exponentially starting from scratch as pieces of knowledge are generated 49
we humans sometimes use our creativity in very
    negative ways 179
we humans expand our experiences through our
    creations and creativity 86, 449
we humans need to apply our creativity and
    imagination to the spiritual part of life as much as we do the physical or technical part of life 456, 466-9

Creator

a possible indicator of passage of time used by
    the creator   40, 50
in general   20-2
knowledge is the source of the creator's (spirit
    world's) creative ability   47
learns and grows   43
our creator has grown such that it is today much
    more advanced than how it was thousands of years ago. This could be why living things of today are more advanced than living things of thousands of years ago   51-2
the nature of the creator   40-1, 43
the spirit world (creator) must be a living thing
    (growing in some manner such as constantly learning) in order to create living things   41
what we do in terms of our thoughts, intentions,
    and actions will generate pieces of knowledge that get added to our creator. This will influence how our creator changes and evolves, and it could become better or worse. We nee to realize we have this responsibility   51

Creatures
    in general   46, 54, 58, 71, 75, 94, 103, 112, 133, 144, 160, 162, 170, 190-1, 197, 206, 224-5, 236, 261, 263, 270, 274, 276, 278, 311, 342-3, 347, 349, 369, 400, 406, 423, 428, 447, 472
    see also **"Living things that are mobile"**

Cross-learning
    appears to work particularly well for species that
        rely heavily on the spirit world to do their thinking for them   110-1
    business people who are well in touch with
        trends and with their intuition are possibly examples of how cross-learning can work with humans   110-1
    could be a form of telepathic communication   206
    could explain why some children could easily
        master the use of high-tech devices when there are other folks who have already done so   95
    could provide a lesser known way for evolution
        to take place   246, 263
    cross-learning is a proven phenomenon   110-1
    cross-learning works similar to how instincts and
        intuition work   211-2

defining what is cross-learning?
95, 211-2
examples of cross-learning among
cattle and
    among horses are presented in
    the book by Rupert Sheldrake
    211
examples of various animals and
birds following
    their instincts to leave shortly
    before an earthquake or storm
    strikes are given by Rupert
    Sheldrake in his book 206
how cross-learning works 110-1
instincts and intuition could be
among the
    manifestations of the
    mechanism that makes cross-
    learning possible 110-1
might be how the immune systems
of some
    individuals manage to
    develop ways to fight off the
    HIV virus without having
    prior exposure to the virus
    343-4
might be taking place with dogs
and other
    domesticated animals 237
some animals could learn certain
things through
    the experiences of other
    members of their species
    through cross-learning Two
    examples are given by Rupert
    Sheldrake 211
works among members of the
same species

110, 206, 211-2

Cultures
    a given spiritual entity translated
    to exist in our
        physical world for various
        cultures, traditions, customs,
        etc. will have various
        different meanings for the
        individuals involved 173,
        434, 439, 463
    rhythms are a commonality among
    all cultures
        and is one of the things that
        helps to bring various cultures
        together 283
    there are overlaps in the spirit
    world among all
        cultures such that each could
        be enriched by the others if
        we are wise enough let this
        happen 422, 436, 439, 463
    within a given group, family,
    nation, etc. the
        young and the old are often in
        different cultures. This is yet
        another factor that tends to
        divide us, even within a
        group, family, or nation 463,
        466

Cycles
    if evolution were to start from
    scratch with every
        new universe, it would not get
        very far, and highly intelligent
        living things would likely not
        exist 71

in general 284
in our universe, and likely also other universes,
    the building materials that make up living and nonliving things get repeatedly recycled 112, 160, 400
sleep involves numerous cycles, each cycle
    focusing on restoring a different part of our body in the order of priority. For example, the first cycle is likely to focus on restoring our brain, the next cycle is likely for our heart, etc. 305, 310
the process of life involves extremely fast cycles
    of communication between spirit and body, much like how a television image is kept moving by extremely fast cycles 269, 275, 284

D

Dark matter, dark energy
    dark matter and/or dark energy might be what
        make up the particular kind of space that is a part of our particular universe. They might also make up the particular kind of gravity that is apart of our particular universe 64, 453

    dark matter and/or dark energy might have
        enabled subatomic particles to assemble into electrons, protons, neutrons, and atoms 454
    if dark matter and/or dark energy is what space is
        made of for our particular universe, it must be balanced in some manner in order for both matter and antimatter to exist in space without one or the other being annihilated 430-1
    if dark matter and/or dark energy is what space is
        made of for our particular universe, then space is a physical thing just as everything else making up our universe is a physical thing 340
    zero-point energy might be the same as dark
        energy 64

Date, dating
    the person we date will likely become a different
        person as a spouse and then again likely a different person as a parent 249

Daughter 32-3, 178, 209, 303, 438

Decisions

the will and the decision to do
something are
    made in the spirit and not in
    the brain. The brain then
    translates the spiritual signals
    from the spirit into physical
    signals to send to the body to
    have the body act in
    accordance with the decision
    42, 60

Definitions
    what are spiritual senses? 69, 261
    what is a spiritual entity? 55
    what is cross-leaning? 95
    what is the soul of a living or
    nonliving thing?
        55-6
    what is the spirit of a living or
    nonliving thing?
        44-5, 48, 55-6
    what is the spirit world? 47
    what are handholds? 256

Denominations
    approximately 50,000
    denominations of
        Christianity exist world wide
    157
    of religions in general 385

Descendants
    differences in the descendants
    could be the
        start of a new species 199-200
    in general 94

    past advancements that faded in
    descendants
        could be resurrected easier
        than starting from scratch
        81-2
    some animals, such as lions and
    some primates,
        when becoming the dominant
        male of a group would kill the
        infants of the previous
        dominant male 272
    why descendants do not
    automatically know
        what their parents know or
        learned? 82-4

Develop, developed oneness,
    developed oneness 145-6, 149, 197-200
    developed oneness between pet
    and owner
        leading to the pets
        telepathically receiving the
        owner's thoughts 207-8, 210
    developed oneness can become
    inherited oneness
        and could possibly lead to the
        development of new species
        199-200
    developed oneness is more subject
    to the "use-it-
        or-lose-it" phenomenon than
        inherited oneness 198
    development of increasingly
    advanced weaponry
        could escalate global convict
        147

development of intuition regarding the use of
    high-tech devices   237
humans possibly had at one time a high level of
    developed oneness among each other and were able to telepathically communicate with each other   210, 370
identical twins have the highest level of inherited
    and developed oneness and thus many have some degree of telepathic ability between them   206, 212, 370
in general   148, 195-6, 337-9, 342-4, 346-7, 328
incompatibilities, such as allergies, that exist
    between humans and plants could mean the two did not evolve together but instead evolved separately on separate universes   184
it seems likely that humans are meant to develop
    an ability to communicate telepathically   370
organ transplant recipients can develop certain
    attributes of the donor   140
overuse of antibiotics can cause super-bugs to
    develop due to natural tug-of-wars in the spirit world   327-8, 339
possible existence of developed oneness also in
    other universes   149
surprisingly clones have neither inherited or
    developed oneness from one to the other   213
unfertilized eggs of honeybees develop into
    drones, and fertilized eggs develop into females   233
why a bad hang-up could cause multiple
    personalities to develop   254
why a pregnant woman talking and/or singing to
    the fetus is good for its development   221-2
why a tadpole developing into a frog loses some
    of its regenerative ability much like how a person also does with age   226
why an elderly person could develop bad short-
    term memory   320

Dimension, dimensionality
a living thing from a universe with a certain
    dimensionality could not fit into a universe with lesser dimensionality   280
a man blind all this life had his eyesight restored
    as an adult found that he was unable to make sense of the three-dimensional images he sees   68

Index

an x-ray microscope recently invent could
    provide three-dimensional image of the interior structure of a living cell 71
difference universes can have different number
    of dimensions, and those with the same number of dimension are likely to have a different set of dimensions each. Therefore, living things in one are not likely able to sense the existence of the other 49, 68, 262, 293
in general 102, 148, 182, 187, 216, 365, 395
issues and tug-of-wars in the spirit world are
    multidimensional 412, 417
mathematics is unlimited in dimensionality 188
models are only approximations of various
    portions of the spirit world. Approximations made for one universe are not likely to be applicable in another universe even if their dimensionalities are the same, because their specific sets of dimensions are likely to be different 449-50
our dreams could include images with more, or
    less, than three-dimensions and/or that are dimensionally different from the specific three we are use to. This could explain why our dreams tend to be surrealistic 317
our next level of technical advancement 385
pieces of knowledge all interconnected with
    connections of the first kind would resemble the microstructure within our brain 345
spiritual entities are unlimited in dimensionality
    49, 88
the evolutionary tree would have more than two
    dimensions but is usually shown in two dimensions 247
universes with different dimensionalities are
    likely to have different forms of energy. Thus, the forms of energy that exist in our particular universe are not the only forms that could exist 280
the higher the dimensionality the quicker the
    messages can be conveyed. For example, a three-dimensional rendition of something can more quickly reveal its configuration than a two-dimensional rendition can 49

Direct oneness, see **"Oneness"**

Disabilities, how the spirit compensates for them
dyslexia was considered a disability until we
realize many very accomplished individuals are dyslexic. Because they have difficulty writing things down, they can develop the ability to figure things out all in their head without writing it down. According to the model, this is an example of how the spirit compensates by strengthening other abilities when one of the regular abilities is not functioning 435
telepathy and brain disability: the spirit knows
how to compensate for any disabilities including brain disability. Thus, the model suggests that a person with brain disability might have a better chance at learning how to communicate by telepathy 371

Disconnect, disconnection
between the intended and the actual 410-7
during out-of-body experiences 363
stepping out of one body and into another 324-5
when living things die 57, 366
when living things that are designed to die
immediately after mating such as salmons, monarch butterflies, and cicadas 348

Diseases, illnesses
healing from diseases and illnesses 204
in general 20, 72, 183, 229, 240, 343, 395, 399, 405, 439
in other universes 239
mad-cow disease 46
stem cells 227
spiritual ways to counteract diseases 241, 376-80

Diversity
a possible reason Earth has such a diversity of
living things is the spirit world creates everything it could at any point in time with all the pieces of knowledge that exist at that point in time 21
an additional possible reason Earth has such a
diversity of living things is evolution spans over the lifetimes of multiple universes one after the other continuously 26, 70-1
diversity needs to be valued and embraced,

especially diversity in mankind. It offers us a better understanding of the spirit world and ourselves, and, according to the model, this would lead to countless spiritual treasures for mankind 66, 86

the diversity of living things in our universe
> might be to enable the spirit world to experience our universe in as many ways as possible 191

the 50,000 denominations of Christianity is an
> example of the diversity of mankind's spiritual needs 157

the Higgs boson is speculated to be the reason
> life and diversity came into being in our universe 63

DNA molecules

a collection of nonliving atoms followed spiritual
> instructions to form DNA molecules that then followed spiritual instructions to form living things 46

DNA molecules are building materials for living
> things; therefore their spirit could enable multiple copies of them to exist 124

DNA molecules are tuned into spiritual signals
> on how to heal and/or restore a worn out, injured, or diseased living thing 299

everything from subatomic particles to a
> complete living thing has a vital role in our universe for the spirit world 417-8

everything is on a gradation between being
> living and being nonliving. Where do DNA molecules fall on this gradation when they can reproduce but need spiritual instructions to form living things? 46

Doctors

a doctor sometimes induce a coma in a patient to
> promote healing 300, 313

doctors today in essence work through the spirit
> world as well as in our physical world when applying modern day treatments. For example, they often tap into the patient's own healing powers by relying on the placebo effect to help with their treatments 378

in general 321, 438

Dominant basis for how we carry out our lives

as an opening note: we have two possible

dominant bases for how we carry out our lives: 389-91
   1. ego and the desire to enhance
      survivability
   2. empathy and compassion for one another
We have essentially entirely chosen No. 1.
   as the dominant basis for thousands of years, and it has not worked very well globally 193-6, 389-91, 463-7
We need to choose No. 2. as the dominant
   basis instead 393
We could still switch from No. 1. to No. 2.
   as the dominant basis 401-4
changing the dominant basis for how we carry
   out our lives would give us a better chance at fulfilling our purpose for being here. The change must be gradual or it won't work 406-10, 420-1, 426-7, 460
most, or all, of our severe hang-ups come from
   our choosing "ego and the desire to enhance survivability" as our dominant bases for carrying out our lives 390

our technical advancements make us think we
   are meeting our responsibility for how our species is evolving, but in fact we are not. Our spiritual advancements lag far behind, and they count more in determining how our species is evolving We need to change the dominant basis for how we are carrying out our lives in order to have our spiritual advancements catch up with our technical advancements 405-6, 411
the human international problems and conflicts
   very likely have more to do with our global choice of dominant basis for how we carry out our lives **(No. 1. instead of No. 2.)** and less to do with the various forms of government 464-5
the role of religion regarding our choice of basis
   for carrying out our lives 461-2
we might be able to learn from other highly
   intelligent living things such as whales, dolphins, elephants as to what basis they chose to carry out their lives 423
we generally try to do good but often end up

doing bad without realizing it because we choose "ego and the desire to enhance survivability" as our dominant bases for carrying out our lives. This especially applies to many members of our government   390, 410-7

Donor and recipient of an organ transplant
    a transplant recipient borrows oneness from the
        donor and thus could receive telepathic message from the donor   213-5
    an experiment indicated that when tissue was
        removed from a person's body and taken to a different room it would still respond to signals from the person's spirit. This could explain why sometimes an organ transplant recipient could take on attributes of the organ donor   140, 214
    improvement in organ transplant procedures
        113
    instincts likely enable some transplant recipients
        to develop traits of the donor   213-5
    the cells of a donor's organ will all be gradually
        replaced by the recipient's cells   112, 213-4

the fact that a recipient of an organ in an organ
    transplant can sometimes take on attributes of the donor further indicates consciousness and intelligence reside in the spirit and not in the brain   140

Dormancy and hibernation
    extrasensory ability can go dormant if its use is
        discouraged   351-3
    some plants go dormant in the winter, and some
        animals hibernate. Neither condition restores as sleep does. E.g., some plants that go dormant in certain climates will not go dormant in others   308-9

Dreams, daydreams, dream images
    an author often daydreams a story several times
        before putting it in writing   296
    at life's ending, the life that was lived could feel
        like a big dream   251
    dreams are one of many kinds of experiences
        that can help us understand other universes and the spirit world better   298, 303, 315
    dreams can foretell events   209, 314-5

dreams during near-death experiences 316-9
    everything that happened in a universe could be
        perceived as a big daydream being made by the spirit world 296
    if what is happening in a story is dreamed up by
        the author and is then perceived by a reader to be real in the world of the story, then what is perceived by us to be real in our physical world could be considered to be a dream by the spirit world 296
    in general 24
    our dreams might include images with more than
        three-dimensions and/or dimensions different for the three we are use to and this could explain why our dreams tend to be surrealistic 317
    sleep, dreams, healing, etc. 298-322
    surrealistic quality of dreams 298-319
    why dreams tend to be surrealistic: 298-308
        1. the most common reason is likely to be
            that dreams will include signals from
                pieces of knowledge generated from other universes 104, 303, 315
        2. dreams include dimensions different our familiar three 298-319
        3. our spiritual expression interacting with
            spiritual expressions of formerly living things 107
        4. spiritual signals telepathically coming from other universes 185

Drowned out healing signals
    spiritual signals are gentle and soft and are easily
        drowned out by the loud and demanding signals of our physical world 201-4
    the signals of our physical world also drown out
        the restoring signals of the spirit world. Thus, during the day we get tired and need to sleep at night to get restored 300-4

Dyslexic individuals
    according to the model, they found ways to be
        more tuned to the spirit world than average 435-6
    dyslexia was considered a disability until we
        realize many very accomplished individuals are dyslexic. Because they have difficulty writing things

down, they can develop the
ability to figure things out all
in their head without writing
it down. According to the
model, this is an example of
how the spirit compensates by
strengthening other abilities
when one of the regular
abilities is not functioning
435
dyslexic individuals are very
intuitive,
    instinctive, creative,
imaginative, and in touch with
their feelings 435-6
dyslexic individuals rely more
than usual on
    feelings, intuition, instincts,
imagination, and creative use
of consciousness, intelligence,
and memory. This enables
them to develop amazing
abilities such that their
condition is often seen as a
gift 436

E

Earthquakes
    in general 20
    Napa Valley earthquake, August 17, 2014 358
    some creature could sense the precursors of
        earthquakes 191, 204, 206, 210, 315, 369

Educate, education
    education takes place in our spirit, not in our
        brain 268
    in general 328
    just about everything we do, including our
        education system, caters to our current dominant basis for carrying out our lives; i.e., "ego and the desire to enhance survivability". Unfortunately, this makes switching our dominant basis to "empathy and compassion for one another" more difficult 407

Einstein, Albert 25, 118, 125, 401

Ego
    animals cater to their ego probably because they
        lack the creativity to do better 272
    antimatter living things are more likely to have
        "empathy and compassion for one another" as their dominant basis for carrying out their lives since they tend to be the opposite of us in substance and probably in most other ways 341
    ego and excessive enhancement of personal
        survivability 186-7

ego exists in the spirit world only as a concept
    and not as a practice   291, 420
ego is designed into our universe because living
    things in it are separate beings and they need leaders to act cohesively, and leaders need some amount of ego to lead. Thus "ego and the desire to enhance survivability" is not necessarily a bad thing, but it shouldn't be dominant   392-3
ego tends to keep us from being more open-
    minded and thus we get stuck in our ways. This could get in the way of our finding our personal spiritual model   136, 272, 477
ego plays a role in starting wars, which in turn
    diverts our time, energy, and natural resource away from making spiritual advancements   96
government activities tend to be driven by ego
    143, 272, 415-6
having an ego is natural for the individually
    separate living things on Earth   178, 199, 221, 259, 265
the fact that we humans need leaders could
    explain why the spirit world designed us to have egos   391-2
humans would more likely cater to their egos
    when overly stimulated   273
in general   101, 133-6, 147, 162-4, 196,
    403, 411, 433-5, 459
leaders need egos in order to lead. But too much
    ego is bad. A good leader would have just the right amount; e.g., those who are not significantly driven by ego. Such leaders deserve our willingness to explore what spiritual advancements we can accomplish with that leader. An example is Nelson Mandela   392-4
letting go of ego and desire to enhance
    survivability would be helpful in finding ones personal spiritual model   26-7, 136
most or all of our severe hang-ups come from
    our choosing "ego and the desire to enhance survivability" as our dominant bases for carrying out our lives   390-1, 464-5
the economic effects of pursuing "ego and desire

to enhance survivability"
within each nation could be
undesirably uneven 143
the spirit is where consciousness,
intelligence,
   senses, feelings, emotions,
empathy, compassion, ego,
reasoning ability, imagination,
creativity, etc. reside.
Different living things have
different ones and degrees of
such attributes 59-60, 133-5,
140, 227, 271, 295, 300-1
we can lower our ego and consider
other highly
   intelligent living things such
as whales, dolphins,
elephants, etc. as possible
sources of knowledge that
could help us better able to
achieve spiritual
advancements 428
we have simply accepted
competition in all its
   forms as being a part of our
lives. This could be a mistake
because it strengthens "ego
and the desire to enhance
survivability" as our dominant
basis for carrying out our
lives 426

Elemental
   basic components making up
living and
      nonliving things 123-4, 141,
156, 255-6
   elemental atoms 121-3, 141

elemental conscious and
consciousness 46, 48,
266-8, 333
elemental energy 156
elemental intelligent and
intelligence 46, 48,
266-8, 333, 431
elemental life 59, 156, 266-8,
325

elemental molecules 128-9, 141
elemental senses are fundamental
to the
   workings of high-tech
systems in computers, cars,
smart phones, smart
refrigerators, airplanes,
medical equipment, etc. 255-6, 266-8
elemental spirits and souls 124
elemental spiritual entities, no
matter how small,
   must have some amount of
intelligence and
consciousness. That's
because every piece of
knowledge comes with its bit
of intelligence and
consciousness, and that is
why every piece of
knowledge forms a
connection of the first kind
with every other existing
piece of knowledge. A
spiritual entity no matter how
small is made of pieces of
knowledge and thus must
have some amount of
intelligence and

consciousness. This in turn
explains why elemental things
in our universe have some
amount of intelligence and
consciousness 333
elemental spiritual senses 48,
267-8
elemental things are sources of
basic direct
oneness among all things
142, 255-6
elemental things could each be in
a different
state. For example all
electrons share the same
spirit, but each can be a part
of a difference thing 126,
255-6
elemental things such as electrons,
protons,
neutrons, subatomic particles,
etc. 43, 121-3, 126, 128,
141, 151, 156, 217-8, 255-6,
326, 429
in general 218-9, 240, 251, 284,
331, 333, 359
some elemental things are subject
to quantum
superposition and
entanglement 125-30, 255-6
spirits and souls of elemental
things 122-5,
216

Embryos
early vulnerable state 54
gills can be seen in a human
embryo in its very
early stage of development
and disappear as development
continues 103, 347
the formation of two honeybee
colonies from a
single colony is similar to the
formation of identical twins
embryos from a single
embryo 234-5
the model explains how a mother
singing or
talking to the embryo would
have a beneficial influence on
the embryo's development
221-2

Emergence of a spirit world and universes
the nothingness beyond our
universe must be
some kind of spiritual
something that exists because
something enables it to exist.
That something might consist
of intelligence that could
figure out how to have
experiences that would then
generate new pieces of
knowledge that would start
the formation of various new
spirit worlds. This could then
lead to the formation of a
particular spirit world that is
able to create our particular
universe, as well as other
universes, and to bring it and
other universes into being
331

Emotions
in general 188, 254, 294-5, 298, 355, 361, 366,
390, 450, 468, 475
in war a solder might shoot someone considered
to be an enemy and thus both love and hate are triggered at the same time; i.e., he or she is supposed to hate an enemy, but he is also supposed to love a fellow human. Such events could change a person for the rest of his or her life 295
love is an emotion and emotions are a part of our
spirit. Thus, we cannot search for it in the spirit world, we can only trigger it, and we could trigger multiple emotions such as love and hate at the same time 295
some identical twins could feel the emotions of
the other twin 144
the spirit is where consciousness, intelligence,
senses, feelings, emotions, empathy, compassion, ego, reasoning ability, imagination, creativity, etc. reside. Different living things have different ones and degrees of such attributes 59-60, 133-5, 140, 227, 271, 295, 300-1

Empathy

a certain kind of brain cell is found to enable a
living thing to have the capacity to be empathetic. Such cells are found in the brains of humans, elephants, dolphins, whales, and various other animals 277-8
anti-matter living things 341
dominate basis for how we carry out our lives
390, 393, 402, 404, 406-9, 421, 426-7, 460-1, 465-7
excessive pursuit of ego and desire to enhance
survivability could lead to lack of empathy and compassion 26
having been poor, we would have more empathy
and compassion for those who are in such or worse conditions 30
in general 144-5, 311, 375-6, 433, 435,
440, 468, 471, 474-5
medical treatments 377-9
the oneness the pervades the spirit world fills the
spirit world with the feeling of love, empathy, and compassion 68, 97-8, 317-8, 323
the spirit is where consciousness, intelligence,
senses, feelings, emotions, empathy, compassion, ego, reasoning ability, imagination,

creativity, etc. reside.
Different living things have different ones and degrees of such attributes   59-60, 133-5, 140, 227, 271, 295, 300-1
there are likely to be living things elsewhere in
    our universe more spiritually advanced than we and thus are likely to have more empathy and compassion than we   101
three major obstacles   421-2
when the love, empathy, and compassion in the,
    spirit world are translated to exist in our physical world, they are less because only a portion of the spirit world is translated. This could explain why some humans are capable of doing terrible things to other humans   97

Energy
    a part of what things are made of   57
    anti-energy   340
    antimatter associated energy   330, 339-40, 342
    at the boundary of our universe separating our
        universe and the spiritual something beyond   62
    dark energy, dark matter, or zero-point energy

comprises about 80% of the matter of our universe   64, 340, 453-4
elemental energy   156
energy associated with restoration of the body
    302
energy and matter can be possessed and/or
    controlled   178
in general   35, 86, 94, 243, 256, 280, 321, 328,
    341, 354, 374, 401, 414, 429, 462-3, 466
personal   401-2
spiritual energy   88, 227, 365

Entanglement
quantum superposition and entanglement   125-
    30, 255

Environment
changing our dominant basis for how we carry
    out our lives must be done gradually. People change gradually. A quick change in dominant basis would not be compatible with the people involved (the environment involved) and would fail. It is like how evolution progresses gradually in order to be successful; i.e., a quick evolutionary change is more likely to produce a nonviable living thing   465, 472

changing environments leading to evolution and
    retracing 65, 72-5, 79-80, 86, 102, 245-6, 264, 465
earthly environments possible to find in the spirit
    world 221, 289
ecosystems 159, 231, 399-400, 458-9
environments appearing in dreams and near
    death experiences 317
environments in other universes 396
environments right next to human bodies stay
    virtually unchanged, and this could mean
    humans are not likely to physically evolve
    much 246-7
hospitable environments 52
human induced environmental changes 86, 140-1
humans could survive in almost any environment
    on Earth because they are able to make the environment right next to their bodies the same regardless of the environment they are in 246-7
in general 223, 328, 405, 471
pending environments 77
rhythms in the environment 283
the spirit piloting the body will keep tract of the
    environment surrounding the body 269, 279
today's high-tech environment 410
workplace environments 249

Events
    four strange events that indicate life exists after
    life 31-6

Everlasting
    desire to learn and to create 155-6, 285
    in general 40, 51
    the spirit of a living or nonliving thing is
    everlasting 475

Evidence
    in the form of four strange events 20
    that life exists after life 29

Evolution
    a possible reason Earth has such a diversity of
    living things is because evolution spans over the lifetimes of multiple universes 26, 70-1
    a spiritual entity that is serving as the spirit for
    a human could serve as the spirits for other living things at other times, and different portions of it would be active at those times. In a sense we

could say those other living
things are sort of human
and/or could contribute
indirectly to the evolution of
humans, and vice versa. This
might explain why dolphins,
elephants, etc. are so
intelligent; i.e., their
intelligence might be from the
same source as human
intelligence   449
according to the model, because
the spirit world
is continuously growing, and
thus evolution is a continuous
progress, every universe when
brought into being might be
done gradually and
continuously as opposed to
suddenly as would be the case
if the Big Bang theory
applies. This could explain
why our universe is
expanding, and at an
accelerating rate at that. For
example, see **"Big Ooze
theory"**   181
as the amount of inherited oneness
increases
from one generation to the
next, members of subsequent
generations become more
advanced than members of
previous generations. Thus,
this is one of the factors
driving the evolution of a
species, the branching off to
form new species, and

indirect evolutionary effects
on unrelated species   198-
200, 211-2
bacteria that cause diseases could
indicate that
evolution spans over multiple
universes   72
each generation of living thing has
a finite
lifetime possibly to enhance
the rate of achieving
advancements   93
effects of inherited oneness and
developed
oneness on evolution   199-
200
evolution does not begin and end
over the
lifetime of a universe such
that it starts from scratch for
each universe. Instead, it
spans continuously over one
universe to the next and the
next, etc. Each universe puts
its unique imprint on the
evolutionary processes that
pass through it. This could
explain why we have
incompatibilities such as
allergies among some living
things   70-7, 183-4, 347
evolution is a natural process that
takes place in
the spirit world, because the
spirit world keeps growing
and keeps becoming more
advanced. In the case of our
particular universe the process

manifests itself physically as well as non-physically 180-2
evolution is a part of universes to enable them to
> fulfill their purposes 394-404

different species could evolve over different
> paths and different universes, and this could cause incompatibilities such as allergies 72

three possible ways evolutionary changes can
> happen. Only one of the ways produces advancements 79-87

humans are said to evolve from apes. But there
> is some evidence this might not be totally true because ape intelligence appears to be very different from human intelligence.
> Because evolution is likely to span over the lifetimes of multiple universes, humans might have evolved from multiple species of living things. For example, we could evolve partly from dolphins in one past universe and we thus started becoming highly intelligent, partly from some undetermined living thing in another past universe and we thus started becoming very good at using our hands, and from apes in another past universe and that's how we got our bodily configuration, etc. This indicates evolution actually takes place in the spirit world and not within the world of any universe. Therefore, there is bound to be more to, for example, what humans have evolved to that we are unable to observe on Earth. We can observe only the part that could be translated to exist or be expressed in our particular physical world. A result of not being able to observe the process fully, some people would deny that evolution exists 246-8

in general 24, 26-7, 47, 51, 65, 76-81, 102-3,
> 109-10, 121, 180-4, 219-20, 244-8, 264, 279, 282, 287, 299, 303, 316-8, 346-7, 359, 369, 402-6. 465

inherited oneness that was once developed
> oneness previous generations will lead to the development of more advanced generations and possibly to the development of new species 198-200

our experiences enable the creator of our
> universe to be able to create things now that it had not

been able to create in the earlier times of our universe. This too could contribute to the evolution of living things on Earth 51
retracing an evolutionary path 396-8
some people do not believe in evolution because
    of the missing links for many of the living things on Earth, including humans. However, the model indicates that evolution could span over the lifetimes of multiple universes. Therefore, what are considered missing links might exist in various past universes. Therefore, if our view on evolution is basis only on what is found on Earth, it is possible to have doubts about the existence of evolution 248
sudden creation through retracing an
    evolutionary path (as opposed to gradual evolution on a new path) 72-3, 75, 86-7
the process of evolution is a process of
    generating and/or gaining pieces of knowledge and adding them to the spirit, and therefore also to the spiritual entity serving as the spirit, of the living thing. Thus, if a bird evolved from a dinosaur, it must take a larger spiritual entity serving as the spirit to enable the bird to exist than it does to enable the dinosaur to exist even thought the bird is much smaller physically. This also sets up the possibility for the spiritual entity to enable new species of living things to exist when conditions are appropriate for this to happen 57-8

Evolution, our awareness and responsibilities
humans are responsible for how our species is
    evolving. Humans can get caught in situations that sap their energy and thus their spirits stop advancing. The fact that humans keep repeating the same mistakes for thousands of years could mean humans are stuck in such situations without being aware of it. In addition, our ongoing technical advancements make us think we are advancing because they are satisfying our dominant basis for how we are carrying out our lives, which is "ego and the desire to enhance survivability", when in fact we are hardly spiritually advancing 404-6

our technical advancements make us think we
    are meeting our responsibility for how our species is evolving when in fact we are not. Our spiritual advancements lag far behind, and they count more in determining how our species is evolving We need to change the dominant basis for how we are carrying out our lives 405-6, 411
we can see how other living things on Earth are
    evolving in a manner driven by forces and experiences largely beyond their control. But our evolution is similarly driven when we chose "ego and the desire to enhance survivability" as our dominant basis for carrying out our lives. This basis creates forces and experiences that are largely beyond our control even though we think they are in our control. It is time we come to realize this has been the case for thousands of years and therefore chose a better dominant basis for carrying out our lives 406-10
we have the responsibility for the growth and
    health, and therefore the evolution, of the spirit world, and consequently for future of everything else 50

Evolution vs. Retracing vs. Sudden Creation
missing links can be a result of retracing.
    Retracing could happen very rapidly compared with usual evolution such that the perception of sudden creation could be perceived as being reasonable. Thus, for example, when humans are perceived as being suddenly created, such perception could be considered reasonable since it is likely that humans emerged rapidly by retracing 73, 75, 86-7
rapid evolution of some living things could be an
    indication of retracing, which is a process of rapid emergence of such living things. Rapid evolution could result in insufficient time to leave behind fossils along the way and thus the appearance of missing links. This could apply to living things besides us humans, in particular very intelligent living things such as elephants, dolphins, whales, octopi, etc. I.e., do these also have missing links? 86-7

Excitement vs. to be interested
    We are encouraged to seek excitement. But
        seeking excitement tends to be short-term, short-range whereas seeking to be interested tends to be long-term, long-range and is better in the long run   430

Experiences
    a descendant does not automatically possess
        advancements already made by those that came before. The advancements are in the spiritual entity serving as the spirit, but are not in the spirit. He or she has to go through the necessary experiences to gain them   82-90
    a living thing could make its own experiences
        while a nonliving thing has experiences happen to it   44, 59
    church   19-20
    designing and building our parents' house   31
    every experience is different, no two are exactly
        alike, even for routine activities. There are always differences even if only minor   84
    experiences could lead to evolution   80-1
    four strange events   31-7
    growing up   29-31, 472-6
    humans could form a significantly wider
        diversity of experiences for themselves than any other living thing on Earth can do for themselves. This is how humans became intellectually way ahead of other living things on Earth   245
    in general   69, 75, 92-5, 99-100, 102-5,
        110-1, etc. The topic of experiences is mentioned on almost every page of the book
    it takes more pieces of knowledge to enable a
        worn out pair of shoes to exist than it does when the shoes were new   44
    knowledge is generated or gained by experiences
        and only by experiences whether by a living thing or a nonliving thing   44
    our experiences enable the creator of our
        universe to be able to create things now that it had not been able to create in the earlier times of our universe. This too could contribute to the evolution of living things on Earth   51
    the knowledge base (the spirit) of a living or
        nonliving thing is what knows how to enable the thing to

exist at any point in time and
thus embodies a record of all
the experiences the thing has
gone through up to that point
in time   44-5
the range of experiences of
elemental things is
quite limited   122-3
the spirit and soul of a living or
nonliving thing
together embody a record of
every experience the thing as
gone through up to that point
in time   103
the spirit world needed to go
through the
experiences of learning how
to work with the materials and
energies of our universe
before it could create living
things that are viable in our
universe   76
the wider the range of experiences
possible for a
living thing the faster could
be the evolution of the living
thing   51, 85-7, 245

Expressions, see "Spiritual expressions"

Extrapolation
backwards from the past to the
present   260,
470-2
forward to the present and possible
futures   152-

4, 258, 260, 271, 336, 347,
372, 395, 470-2
sideways (also to make
interpolations)   152-3,
395

Extrasensory abilities
a person is more likely to have or
retain his or
her extrasensory ability if a
parent has extrasensory ability
351-3
encouraging, enhancing, and
improving any
extrasensory abilities is a
good thing because they could
provide additional channels of
communications among
individuals   353, 459
extrasensory abilities could be
taught or learned
probably because they are
likely natural human abilities
351
extrasensory images are sensed in
the spirit
world, and our mind
superimposes them onto our
physical world   351-3
extrasensory ability is a fragile
thing and could
easily be suppressed   352-3
examples   351-2, 354, 394, 459
our spiritual senses enable us to
have
extrasensory abilities   351-3,
459

extrasensory ability is likely a natural human
    ability because it is the workings of our spiritual senses and people are more likely to have it in ancient times   353

F

Family 24, 29, 31-3, 36, 51, 142, 144, 175, 195, 197-8, 257, 259, 287, 377, 381, 408, 423-4, 433, 438, 463, 472, 474-6

Father, dad 20, 29, 37, 179, 204, 257, 473

Feathers
    Feathers developing on some dinosaurs   78
    in general   77-8, 183, 200, 346

Features of living things
    creation of new features for living things   345-7
    features that are not used over a large number of
        generations will decline and can vanish. But, evidence they once existed will remain in the spirit of the living thing and also sometimes in some manner on the physical body of the living thing   347

    the pieces of knowledge for features that are not
        a part of a living thing are also not a part of the spirit of the living thing but are a part of the spiritual entity serving as the spirit   101-5

Feeling more alive with age
    as we age and age-related physical and medical
        problems increase, our consciousness and energy get increasingly taken up by such things. The world then seems increasingly unreal. We might start feeling less alive. However, one sure way to feel more alive is to be contributory to life for the benefit of mankind. By analogy, be a "living branch" contributing to the life of a "living tree" no matter how much or little and how we do it   217, 251-2

Feelings
    dyslexic individuals rely more than usual on
        feelings, intuition, instincts, imagination, and creative use of consciousness, intelligence, and memory. This enables them to develop amazing abilities such that their condition is often seen as a gift   436

feeling more alive 217, 251-2
identical twins could often feel the feelings of
    the other twin 212
in general 27, 34-5, 48, 69, 113, 128, 136-7,
    145, 166, 204, 210, 256, 289, 298, 302, 306, 311, 317-8, 324, 368, 420, 450, 464, 471, 474
the sharing of parts among all things in the spirit
    world creates a feeling of love, empathy, and compassion throughout the spirit world 68
the spirit is where consciousness, intelligence,
    senses, feelings, emotions, empathy, compassion, ego, reasoning ability, imagination, creativity, etc. reside. Different living things have different ones and degrees of such attributes 59-60, 133-5, 140, 227, 271, 295, 300-1
while feelings might be perceived the same way
    regardless of the universe, the response to the feelings might be different in each universe 188-9

Forever
    a piece of knowledge generated or gained by a
        spirit remains a part of that spirit forever 319

a soul once formed will exist forever 105-6
a soul will retain forever attributes of the world
    of the universe it was partially in 354
a spirit once formed will exist forever 105-6, 193
a spiritual entity once formed remains in the
    spirit world forever 325
a spiritual expression (combination of spirit and
    soul) will exist forever 107, 220, 347, 450
any alterations to a living (or nonliving) thing, in
    our physical world will be recorded in the thing's spiritual expression forever 205, 241
anything (spiritual entity) formed in the spirit
    world remains in the spirit world forever, and this could explain why certain attributes (e.g. some cancers) run in families 241
"forever" applies as long as the spirit world
    remains viable and continue to exist 47, 59
in general 103, 194, 258-9, 295, 322, 365, 458
once a connection of the first or second kind is

formed it exists forever 59, 105, 198
once a piece of knowledge is generated, provided
    it isn't a duplicate, it exists forever 47, 59, 82, 99, 105, 198, 325, 400-1, 446
nothing is assured of existing forever, not even
    the spirit world or life after life 59
some ghosts seem to stay around forever 360
the spirit world is forever growing and changing 22, 285
the spirit world is imperfect and will stay
    imperfect forever 66

Forgive, forgiveness
asking the Lord to forgive our sins 19-21
forgiveness in the spirit world, it's automatic 178-9
in general 259, 356
the spirit world accepts and forgives our going
    off course as we occasionally do. It's the risk the spirit world takes 132

Formation
of analogies 271
of black holes, supernovas, brown drafts,
    collision of galaxies, etc. 75, 453, 455
of hang-ups 254
of identical twins 234
of the microstructures of vital organs of living
    things 418
of new species 80, 200
of the spirit world's early stages 332

Formulation
a model could guide the person who is
    formulating the model 457
models in general could be more complete if
    spirituality were taken into consideration in their formulation 118, 121
the formulation of my model progressed in
    spurts 91
the start of the formulation of my model 25, 39-40, 44-8

Fossils
are some fossils evidences of retracing or
    evidences of evolution? 73-7
fossil evidence does not always indicate how
    some species evolved from some earlier species: i.e., such species have missing links 74-7
fossil evidence of evolution 71-2

humans might have emerged on
Earth through
    retracing instead of through
    evolution on Earth and thus
    could be perceived as having
    been suddenly created 86-7
living fossils 51, 245
missing links 72-4
some fossil evidences indicate
some living
    things never evolved into
    anything more advanced; i.e.,
    they just go extinct (or their
    evolution simply failed) 74
species with missing links are
common, and this
    could indicate they emerged
    on Earth through retracing
    instead of through evolution
    74-7
very few fossils show feathers on
dinosaurs.
    Therefore, the reason feathers
    emerged on some dinosaurs
    remains a speculation 78

Freedom
    having the freedom to choose also
    means having
        the responsibility for the
        evolutionary path of our
        species 404
    having the freedom to choose and
    also being
        separate individuals would
        naturally bring out attributes
        of ego and desire to enhance
        survivability 186

in general 165, 167, 178, 384,
416, 440
living things given the freedom to
choose means
    the natural partnership they
    have with the spirit world
    would not always function in
    a win-win manner 193
the freedom to choose also means
the freedom to
    make discoveries,
    improvements, alternatives,
    mistakes, inadvertent
    accidents, etc. 445
the freedom to choose and the
anti-matter living
    things in our universe 341
the spirit world gave us and other
living things
    the freedom to choose so that
    we and other living things
    could generate as many new
    pieces of knowledge as
    possible 143, 158-9, 163

Friend
    Best friend since childhood, Joe
    113

Fulfilling
    having some ups and downs could
    be more
        fulfilling than not having any
        436-8

Fulfilling our purpose for being here
    fulfilling our purpose 136, 159

obstacles to our fulfilling our
purpose 145
switching our dominant basis for
how we carry
    out our lives to "empathy and
    compassion for one another"
    would be a step toward
    fulfilling our purpose 421
The change in our dominant basis
for how we
    carry out our lives must be
    done gradually to assure how
    we behave would be
    compatible with values that
    are likely to change only
    gradually. Otherwise it
    wouldn't work 406-10, 420-
    1, 426-7, 460
three major obstacle to our
fulfilling our purpose
    421
we are here for two purposes
424-32
we might not be doing better than
other creatures
    162
we would generally be fulfilling
our purpose if
    the pieces of knowledge we
    generate help the spirit world
    restore balance 250

Fungi 133, 222

Future
    at any point in time, countless
    futures are

possible, and none are assured
of coming true, although one
will come true. According to
the model this condition is a
good thing because if any one
possible future is assured of
coming true, that would mean
we actually would not have a
future. This sounds strange
but the model gives a
plausible explanation 372
projections into possible futures
372-4

G

Galaxies and planets 49, 61, 64, 75, 154, 218, 284, 338-341, 427, 454-5

Garden 31-2, 173, 209, 249, 256-7, 381-2

Gas clouds in outer space 52, 61, 63-4, 75, 124-5, 181-2, 419, 455

Generations
    Baby Boom generation 30
    developed oneness would become
    inherited
        oneness for members of
        subsequent generations.
        Thus, each generation could
        be more advanced 198-200
    each generation of living thing has
    a finite

Index 539

lifetime, possibly to enhance the rate of achieving advancements 93
for living things that think for themselves,
    knowledge generated or gained by one generation will become instincts or intuition for subsequent generations and intuition for other species 235
in general 30, 75, 79, 81, 83, 98, 109, 145, 193,
    216, 223, 246, 254-5, 279, 284, 323, 327, 404, 406-7, 410, 434, 465, 473
instincts could grow or fade with subsequent
    generations of a species. Fading instincts are a concern in the case of, for example, laboratory born salmon. In the case of dogs, their instincts regarding their interactions with humans are likely to be growing. In the case of kids and the use of high-tech devices, their instincts are likely to be growing 236-8
new pieces of knowledge are being generated at
    an exponentially increasing rate 49
the process of evolution is a process of
    generating and adding new pieces of knowledge to the spirit and spiritual entity of the living thing. Thus, if a bird evolved from a dinosaur, it must take a larger spiritual entity serving as the spirit to enable the bird to exist than it does to enable the dinosaur to exist. This also sets up the possibility for the spiritual entity to enable new species of living things to exist when conditions are ready 57-8
the spirits of some living things, for example
    monarch butterflies, appear to continue on from one generation to the next 169, 229-232, 348-9

Genetic engineering
    is like how the spirit world would try out a new
        version of a feature for living things 77

Ghosts
    a ghost that is actually in our physical world is
        likely to have a strong reason to be there 356-7
    according to the model, it is possible for an
        individual to die and not realize he or she has died, and his or her ghost would go on doing what he or she normally did while alive 360

general anesthetics that puts an individual in a
    coma could cause the ghost of the
    individual to appear   363
ghosts are often depicted in stories and movies as
    being scary. According to the model, ghosts are naturally no scarier than you or I. However, they sometimes have reasons to behave in a scary manner, although not necessarily as scary as depicted in some stories and movies   360
ghosts could be sensed in the spirit world and are
    perceived to be in our physical world, or they could actually be in our physical world and are sensed there   356-7
ghosts from other planets in our universe or from
    other universes are not likely to be sensed by humans on Earth. Or, if they were sensed, they would be very different from anything on Earth and therefore would not be recognized as being ghosts. They are more likely to be perceived as undefined background things   359
how ghosts could make themselves present in
    our physical world   354-6

if only one person in a group could see a ghost
    while the others can't, then the ghost is sensed in the spirit world and not in our physical world   357
in general   37, 170, 354-62
individual not very in touch with their spiritual
    senses are not likely to be able to sense ghosts whether in the spirit world or in our physical world   359
it is possible to see the ghost of a brain dead
    individual   364
it is theoretically possible to see a ghost
    belonging to an individual in a coma, This supposedly has happen. It wouldn't happen with an individual who is asleep. The difference is a sleeping individual can be awaken at any time while a individual in a coma cannot. This means the soul of a sleeping individual never detaches from the body whereas the soul could detach in the case of an individual in a coma   361
nonliving things could also have ghosts since
    they too have spirits and souls. (For example, ghost ships have supposedly been seen)   362

possible configuration of a spirit of a living or
    nonliving thing 216
some ghosts are not real ghosts but are
    experiences of traumatic events that got imprinted onto the spirits of nonliving things that were nearby 361-2
the fact that ghosts have consciousness and
    intelligence supports the notion that consciousness and intelligence reside with the spirit and not with the brain 135, 361
the model indicates how ghosts could be sensed,
    and it would apply to other universes besides ours. Thus, we might be able to sense ghosts from other planets and universes, but we are not likely to recognize them. They are likely to be perceived as undefined background things. Also, ghosts from other than Earth would not likely want to be sensed by humans anyway since they are usually there to help members of their own species 358-9
we might be able to visit other planets and
    universes like how ghosts could visit Earth 289

why do some ghosts seem to stay around forever
    360

God
conventional concepts of God 20-1
each person has a different and unique concept
    of God; therefore, when we refer to God we are referring to our personal God 21, 23, 156
every personal God is as valid as any other
    personal God, according to the model. Therefore the model does not exclude any religion or percept of God 156-7
evidence supports the notion that God listens
    to our prayers 322
in general 21, 114, 292
no personal God could be the entire spirit world
    157
our personal God is essentially our personal
    perception of the spirit world 23
personal gods 21-2, 156-7, 290-2
radio station KGO's former Sunday show "God
    Talk" hosted by Brent Waters 471
the creator 20-2

those who perceives his or her personal God as
> favoring war, or any other negative activity, would be surprise when he or she returns to the spirit world to find his or her personal God holds such things only as concepts and not as practices 290-1

we have a natural partnership with the spirit
> world, or if we prefer, our personal God. It is met to be mutually beneficial for the spirit world and us 23

we need to give care to the spirit world (or our
> personal God) as well as receive care from it. It is a partnership 22-3

God particle, see "Higgs boson"

Goddesses 292

Gold
> According to the model, heavy elements such
> > as gold could form during the very early stages of formation of our universe, perhaps before stars were formed. This is because the spirit world bound to already have the spiritual entities (design plans) for knowing how to enable such heavy elements exist 453-6
>
> in general 29, 138, 257

Goldilocks zone 218

Government, Congress
> Congress 30, 272, 409-11, 415, 417
>
> we generally try to do good but often end up
> > doing bad without realizing it because we choose "ego and the desire to enhance survivability" as our dominant bases for carrying out our lives. This especially applies to too many members of our government 390, 410-7

Gradations
> a person can choose to be on any location of one
> > or more gradations and thus act differently in different situations. Actors and actresses are particularly good at this and that is why some are so successful 423
>
> every living thing is somewhere on a gradation
> > between relying completely on the spirit world to do the thinking for it and thinking completely for itself 201, 222, 235, 392
>
> every spirit is a mixture of types and therefore

is on a mixture gradations 242, 244
everything in the spirit world is on one or more
    gradations of various kinds 203, 219, 224
everything on Earth is somewhere on a gradation
    between being a living thing and a nonliving thing 46, 222
evolution corresponds to a spirit moving from
    one location on various gradations to another location and possibly also from one gradation to another 244-5
expanding our knowledge about the range of
    various gradations 218
gradations are commonplace in the spirit world
    219
gradations in the spirit world and our physical
    world are constantly expanding and increasing in number as new pieces of knowledge are constantly being generated 217-9
high-tech devices we humans build are
    increasingly conscious and able to think for themselves. Thus, they are on a gradation between being nonliving things and living things 216-7

multiple personalities occur when a person has
    somehow found multiple safe locations to escape to on one or more gradations when he or she feels threatened at the location he or she is at for a given situation 253-5
since living things are on multiple gradations,
    there are multiple ways for a living thing to be, and feel, more alive or less alive. It is easy to see how this is the case for us in real life 217
when a living thing gradually dies, its spirit
    moves along gradations away from being more alive toward being less alive 217

Gravity
could gravity simply be an attribute of the kind
    of space our universe has, and could the dark energy and/or dark matter in our space be making the gravity? 64, 453-4
many universes are possible and some might
    have gravity and some might not. And, what is gravity could be different for different universes 102, 182, 280, 284
in general 63-4
the kinds of structures and other things living

things in a universe build could indicate whether or not gravity exists in that universe 185

Groups
of human individuals, see **"Individual**, groups of"

Government
governmental actions driven by ego and desire to
enhance survivability would not improve international relations 143
in general government 30, 154, 193, 243,
295, 408-12
the mess we made on Earth for thousands of
years might have less to do with the various forms of government around the world and more to do with a lack of spiritual advancements among mankind 465
we generally try to do good but often end up
doing bad without realizing it because we choose "ego and the desire to enhance survivability" as our dominant bases for carrying out our lives. This especially applies to too many members in our government 390, 410-7

H

Handholds and mentors, see **"Mentors and handholds"**

Hang-ups
a bad hang-up could cause multiple personalities
to develop 254
a bad hang-up could infect a nation as well as an
individual 255
a bad hang-up could produce two personalities:
one is normal, the other is preoccupied with the hang-up 254, 355-6
a bad hang-up is like a bad itch that demands
scratching, and it colors everything we do 253-4, 259, 355-6
a persistent hang-up is likely to finally release its
grip when the person is about to die 354-6
catering to a bad hang-up at inappropriate times
and situations could confuse an observer 254-5, 355-6, 390, 416
catering to a bad hang-up will not resolve
anything and could be counterproductive 254, 416
hang-ups are like bacteria and viruses, they could

infect us and they could
spread 390
hang-ups can hinder our finding
ourselves if we
    let them, and we all have
    hang-ups 354-6
hang-ups could cause bad
behavior to continue
    generation after generation
    254-5
hang-ups could cause conflicts to
go on and on,
    even generation after
    generation, and even war after
    war, This indicates hang-ups
    need to be resolved as soon as
    possible if we are to achieve
    lasting world peace and to
    clean up the mess we made on
    Earth 255
if a child gets confused seeing
someone catering
    to a bad hang-up
    inappropriately, the confusion
    could last a life time 254-5
in general 258
most or all of our severe hang-ups
come from
    our choosing "ego and the
    desire to enhance
    survivability" as our dominant
    bases for carrying out our
    lives 390-1, 464-5
preoccupation with a hang-up can
distort one's
    reasoning, judgment, and
    wisdom 259, 283, 355-6,
    390, 416

we are often unaware we have
hang-ups or how
    much power they can have
    over our perceptions and
    behavior 355-6

Heal, restore
balance
getting more in touch with the
spirit world's
    restoring and healing powers
    376-80
healing and restoration by going
through the
    spirit world 376-80
healing and restoration during a
near-death
    experience 316-7
healing and restorations during
sleep or while
    unconscious 298-313
healing powers of statues and
other physical
    things 380-2
healing signals from the spirit to
the body 204-5
our spirit is constantly trying to
heal or restore
    our body whether we are
    asleep or awake 300
signals that heal or restore us are
the same
    signals that enable us to exist
    299, 376
sleep, dreams, healing, etc. 298-322
the fast advancing research in
genetics opens up

new ways of treating diseases
and illnesses. In my mind,
this is a start to bridge healing
by conventional methods and
healing by going through the
spirit world. This goes
beyond what's on pages 376-9
of the text.
the model plausibly explains why
prayers by a
    large group could improve
healing 322-3
the placebo effect and the work of
healers in
    India, referred to as medicine
men and medicine women,
could be perceived as healing
by going through the spirit
world. The work is done
directly through the spirit
world but indirectly in our
physical world. Such work
could be more powerful,
natural, and effective than
conventional medical
practices, and with fewer or
no side effects 376-9

Heaven and hell
    could have different perceptions in
different
    universes, and perceptions can
be found in the spirit world
289-90
    in general 20-1, 69, 167, 365

Heavy elements
    formation of heavy elements 124,
453-4
    possible alternative way heavy
elements are
    formed, soon after our
universe came into being
455

Hell, see "Heaven and hell"

**Hibernation and dormancy, see
"Dormancy and hibernation"**

Higgs boson
    sometimes called the "God
particle" 63
    the Higgs boson is speculated as
the reason life
    and diversity came into being
in our universe 63
    what scientists think it does 63,
121

High-tech devices
    advancements of high-tech devices
occur in
    spurts 91-3
    could promote person to person
communications
    around the world.
(Unfortunately it could also
spread fake news around as
well) 408
    children are able to master the use
of high-tech
    devices better than their
parents because of inherited

oneness and/or cross-learning
83-5, 237-8
cross-learning among children
regarding their
   ability to use high-tech
devices 95, 111
development of intuition regarding
the use of
   high-tech devices 237
high-tech devices and various
other things we
   design are increasingly living-
like with each iteration 216-7
high-tech devices do not always
improve the
   quality of life 147
in general 47, 192, 252, 266, 284, 367, 384, 469
some pros and cons regarding
high-tech devices
   147-8, 243-4, 410, 430
spirit types of high-tech devices
built by humans
   216

HIV
   Some individuals' immune
systems can
      develop resistance to the HIV
virus possibly through-cross
learning. Another possibility
is the spirit world uses its
increasing knowledge to
update the immune systems of
those individuals 343

Holes, black, see **"Black holes"**

Homeless, homelessness, see
"Unemployed, under-employed, homelessness"

Hospice care 175-6

Hospitable environments and planets
   evolution and/or retracing can be
driven
      by changes in environments
72-3, 75, 231, 397
   formation, and/or maintaining, of
hospitable
      environments 73-6, 159, 399, 458
   hospitable planets 191-2, 403, 418-9, 427-9
   life supporting natural resources
400
   our universe might be growing,
and thus the
      number of hospitable planets
could be increasing 286

House
   our parents' house the entire
family participated
      in designing and bringing into
reality 31-2
   the house my wife and I designed
and brought
      into reality 256-7

Human
   a plausible spiritual reason why
humans and

various other living things
have allergies   183-4
according to the model, some of our models
would be more complete if spirituality were taken more into consideration in their formulations   118
according to the model, the spirit world has two
stages of growth similar to how humans and various other living things on Earth do; i.e., an infancy stage and an adult stage. The model also suggests living things have these two stages because the spirit world has these two stages and would thus design living things to have these two stages   333
according to the model, theoretically, humans
could make miracles happen 324
acting to thoughts and acting to instincts   203
advancements are not random but are pursued
with purposes in mind   91
all the models that we reasonably formulate are
approximations; i.e., correct but not totally complete or absolutely accurate   121
almost everything humans design and build gets
increasingly complex and sophisticated with each redesign   282
any model or statement reasonably formulated
would be correct but incomplete. The incompleteness cannot be avoided because we humans are imperfect. We are imperfect because the spirit world is imperfect. Therefore, we must not let ourselves be completely sold by the correctness, but rather we must always be aware of the incompleteness   25, 64, 95-6, 117-8, 121, 155, 172-8, 243-4, 258, 327, 411-2, 423, 440, 447, 456
body, see also all **"Body – "** listings
body and bodily organs   60, 71
body knows how to heal   60
brain, see all **"Brain – "** listings
carrying out life simultaneously in the spirit
world and our physical world   96, 101
certain living things seem more able to sense
certain spiritual messages than humans can. For example some animals can sense an earthquake is about to happen, bird can sense a storm is about to arrive, etc.   315

children and high-tech devices 85
concept of opponent (or enemy) 145, 147
concepts that are not practices in the spirit world
    99, 145-6
could sense only a portion of the spirit world
    104
cross-learning 95, 110-1
cross-learning and instincts are forms of
    knowledge transfer. For humans these transfer mechanisms do not work very strongly because humans are designed to think for themselves 236
did the spirit world intend for us humans to do
    space travel to other planets and/or universe travel to other universes? If so, then is it possible what is spiritually holding us up is our tendency to do battle with others of our own race that are different from us? Could it be we need to first learn to get along with all others of our own race before we are able to develop the skills of space travel and/or universe travel? After all, we will need to be able to peacefully interact with intelligent living things on other planets and universes 375

different species of living things have different
    set of spiritual senses, and that's why different species could sense different things 204, 210
evolution continuing over the lifetimes of
    multiple universes. This could explain why we humans are the most intelligent living things on Earth; i.e., we evolved over more past universes than other living things on Earth did 26, 71, 369
expanding our knowledge about the range of
    various gradations 218
fulfilling our purpose 52, 162-5
figuring out what the spirit world is like 219
genetic engineering 77
getting along with other humans 78-9, 133, 143
highly intelligent living things in any universe,
    including humans in our universe, are likely to use mathematics 184
how many pieces of garbage is produced by a
    typical family of four in a year? 287
humans are not likely to be the only highly
    intelligent living things in our universe 192

humans are perhaps the only living thing on
    Earth that could individually specialize in what they could do to make a living 283
humans are responsible for how our species is
    evolving. Humans can get caught in situations that sap their energy and thus their spirits could stop advancing. The fact that humans keep repeating the same mistakes for thousands of years could mean humans are stuck in such situations without being aware of it. In addition, our ongoing technical advancements make us think we are advancing because they are satisfying our dominant basis for how we are carrying out our lives when in fact we are hardly spiritually advancing 404-6
humans are the primary physical means on Earth
    by which the spirit world applies its spiritual senses to learn about our universe and to learn how its inventions could be used in our particular universe 293
humans are unable to regenerate lost body parts
    for a plausible reason; i.e., the brain would have to be enormously big, and that would bring about conditions that preclude viability 299
humans build all kinds of things while other
    living things on Earth build only one or two kinds of things 124, 224
humans could be perceived to have been
    suddenly created 26, 72-3, 75, 87
humans could be easily manipulated because the
    information we receive is always correct but incomplete. We could be swayed by what is correct and not be aware it is incomplete 243
humans could create a significantly wider
    diversity of experiences for ourselves than any other living thing on Earth could for themselves. This is how humans became intellectually way ahead of other living things on Earth 245, 336
humans do not automatically know what our
    predecessors know 83, 90, 347
humans could induce changes in our
    environments and are thus able to get ahead of other living things on Earth 86

humans need leaders because we are separate
    living things, and we do almost all of our own thinking instead of relying on the spirit world to think for us. Thus, we are vulnerable to being lead by bad leaders, particularly since any statement by anybody is correct but incomplete. We could get hooked by the correctness without thinking much about the incompleteness. The fact that we need leaders could explain why the spirit world designed us to have egos 391-2

humans need to eat other living things to
    survive. Thus, humans could be perceived as being a disease for those other living things, much like how bad bacteria are perceived to be diseases for humans 239

humans were once sea dwelling creatures 103, 347

humans would not be the only highly intelligent
    things in the spirit world 26

in general 94, 109, 126, 128-9, 134, 144, 149, 156, 158, 160-2, 179, 221, 231

    instincts are a form of knowledge transfer from one generation to the next. For humans this transfer does not work very quickly because humans are designed to think for themselves 236

instincts and intuition 170, 211-2

living life for the spirit world vs. for our physical
    world. It makes a difference because the oneness that makes everything a part of everything else exists in the spirit world. In particular the spirit of every human is a part of spirit of every other human, whereas humans are physically separate individuals in our physical world 141, 385

migration 80

motivating ourselves to be more empathetic
    and compassionate of one another 273-4

near-death experience 221

no model formulated by humans can be totally
    complete or absolutely accurate 25, 53, 73

one of the reasons we humans get into conflicts
    and battles is because when we generate pieces of knowledge we generally do not generate opposing pieces of knowledge such that better balance in our total knowledge would be

achieved. Our intelligence is limited. Other living things on Earth are less intelligent than humans and they do a worse job of balancing the pieces of knowledge they generate. Similar conditions are likely to exit in other universes, and that is how the state of knowledge in the spirit world could go out of balance. The spirit world could do a much better job of generating pieces of knowledge that are balanced because its intelligence is unlimited, although likely still incomplete. This enables it to know that it has to constantly monitor its state of knowledge and to do something, such as design and bring into being new universes periodically, to help restore reasonable balance in its state of knowledge   334
our relationship with our creator   22
population   140-1, 144
world population is now approximately
   seven billion   144
recycling the materials making up our bodies
   112
reincarnation   109-10, 220
religions   96

responsibilities on Earth   132-3, 164-5
sense of humor   173
since humans are all a part of each other in the
   spirit world, it doesn't make sense to make war in our physical world   290, 385
sleep cycles might have evolved for humans
   because humans constantly do not get enough sleep to allow complete restoration of the body. An interesting question, do other living things have sleep cycles?   310
some animals take actions that cater to their egos
   probably because they lack the creativity to do better. Humans can act even worse even thought we have the creativity to come up with ways to do better. We can, and need, to learn to not let our egos have such a grip on us   272
some humans on Earth could communicate
   telepathically   185
something yucky to us humans in our universe
   might not be yucky to us if it and we were in another universe. It's like how a rotting carcass is yucky to us but not to a vulture   288

spirits and souls 59-60, 78, 219-22, 226
- spiritual entities serving as human spirits are
  - very large compared with those serving as spirits of other living things on Earth. Thus, our spiritual entities' signals that enable us to think are stronger and less likely drown out by signals from our physical world. This enables us to do essentially all of our thinking for ourselves, whereas other living things rely more than we do on the spirit world do their thinking for them 201-2
- spiritual expressions 109-10
- spiritual senses 96
- spectrum of spirit types, see **"Spirit types"**
- the concept of having humans become specialists
  - is developed as way to work around the "use it or lose it" phenomenon 81
- the human species is the only one on Earth
  - whose members could choose among a wide variety of careers for survival. This specialization also means we humans need to do a lot of learning in depth to perform well in our careers 208
- the human spirit does not reincarnate, but a
  - spiritual entity serving as a human spirit could reincarnate 220
- the mess we made on Earth 94, 96, 219
- the most likely trait humans would have in the
  - very early days of the human species 178, 186
- the purpose of us humans on Earth might
  - preclude our ability to do general and complete telepathic communications with one another 206
- the spirit configurations of the things we human
  - design and build, such as high-tech devices 216-7
- the spirit world 88, 96
- the things human design and build are not
  - going to be as complete as we are 149, 224
- the three most important obstacles that we need
  - to work with or around to fulfill our purpose for being here 164, 186, 421
- we do more horrible things to members of our
  - species than other living things do to members of their species. You would think that with our superior intelligence that we would do better than other living things. So, what is it that makes us to do

worse? Is it possible our purpose for being here on Earth is simply to generate as many new piece of knowledge as possible, and the purpose of helping the spirit world restore balance belongs to other living things on Earth instead of us as we had presumed?   389
we do not create thoughts; we find them in the
   spirit world   113
we formulate models to help us understand in an
   approximate manner how to do what the spirit world does   120
we humans long ago might have been able to
   communicate telepathically because we used to develop a lot of developed oneness and a high level of closeness . We might now be feeling the lose this oneness and closeness, and therefore this is yet another reason we are searching for our spirituality   210
we humans tend to think "winning" is a must
   194-6
what happens if we pass away after having done
   bad things?   179
what is embodied in the soul of our universe is
   what we are trying to capture with our countless models   117
whenever we look for something in the spirit
   world we need to also look for the wisdom that is associated with it   288
with just our sense of sight we enter the world of
   a story created by an author. This might be how we could enter the world of another universe; i.e., by using just the right one or more of our major and/or spiritual senses   115

Husband   32

Hydrogen sulfide gas sustaining life
   species of clams, crabs, etc. sustained by
      hydrogen sulfide coming out of hot gas vents on ocean floors   183, 360, 418-9

I

Identical twins   206, 212-3, 234
   Telepathic communications between identical
      twins   212-3

Ill, illnesses, see **"Diseases, illnesses"**

Imagine, imagination, imagined, imagining

the spirit is where consciousness, intelligence,
    senses, feelings, emotions, empathy, compassion, ego, reasoning ability, imagination, creativity, etc. reside. Different living things have different ones and degrees of such attributes 59-60, 133-5, 140, 227, 271, 295, 300-1

Immune systems
    immune systems, issues, intelligence, and
        knowledge 325-342
    in general 22, 228, 240-1, 305, 377, 381
    issues kept in balance is basically how our
        immune system works. I.e., if one or more of the issues involved with our immune system go out of balance, then our immune system would not work properly, and we could become ill 325-8, 342-5

Imperfect, imperfections
    any model or statement reasonably formulated
        would be correct but incomplete. The incompleteness cannot be avoided because we humans are imperfect. We are imperfect because the spirit world is imperfect. Therefore, we must not let ourselves be completely sold by the correctness, but rather we must always be aware of the incompleteness 25, 64, 95-6, 117-8, 121, 155, 172-8, 243-4, 258, 327, 411-2, 423, 440, 447, 456
    good thing everything is imperfect, and it is
        because the spirit world is imperfect 65-70

Impressions
    common impressions about our creator 40
    our impression of what other's think can shape
        the spiritual part of our models, and our models are less accurate when based on our impressions of others of a different culture 463
    some individuals' egos give the impression they
        know everything 434
    we have the impression that our consciousness
        resides in our brain and not in our spirit 301
    young people often have an inaccurate
        impression of old people 476

Improve, improvements
    advancement does not necessarily mean
        improvement 282

competition is good if it promotes self-
    improvement, is a pursuit of excellence, or produces a win-win outcome   149, 195, 426
encouraging, enhancing, and improving any
    extrasensory abilities is a good thing because they could provide additional channels of communications among individuals   353, 459
governmental actions driven by ego and desire to
    enhance survivability would not improve international relations   143
high-tech devices do not always improve the
    quality of life   147
improvement in organ transplant procedures
    113
improvements in automobiles 439
improving the jury system   253
our spirit has the freedom to choose and thus
    also to improve as well as to do other things   445
perceptions of improvements   282
the model plausibly explains why a good night's
    sleep improves memory   307-8
the model plausibly explains why prayers by a
    large group could improve healing   322-3
the wiser the spirit world is, the more able it
    would be to assure a better future   153

In between (this has two possible meanings)
    (Meaning 1.) living things that are in between
        being living and being nonliving such as viruses and prions
    (Meaning 2.) living things that are partly relying
        on the spirit world to think for it and partly able to think for itself, examples are mammals
instincts are a form of knowledge transfer from
    one generation to the next. Cross-learning is a form of knowledge transfer from one living thing to the next. For humans these transfer mechanisms do not work very quickly because humans are designed to think for themselves. They also do not work for living things that rely heavily on the spirit world to do their thinking for them, such as insects, because it takes thinking for oneself to have knowledge to transfer. However, these mechanisms work well for "in-between"

living things such as dogs and cats. This is because while they do much of their thinking for themselves, and thus have lots of knowledge available for transfer, they also rely to a good degree on the spirit world to do their thinking for them and therefore have strong instincts and good cross-learning ability. Thus, their knowledge transfer mechanisms work well, and this enables them to make wonderful pets for humans due to many generations and a multitude of members of their species interacting with humans   236-7

Incidental purposes
of living things. For example, the incidental
purposes of plants in general include serving as food for other living things, building materials for other living things, fuel for various purposes, builders of rich soils, components of gardens, etc.   160-2

Inclusive of all concepts of God and all religions
Chapter One might lead one to think the model
rejects concepts of God and is thus separate from religions. But as the model develops in Chapter Three, it becomes clear it is inclusive of all concepts of God and all religions   21, 156-7

Incomplete but correct, incompleteness
any model or statement reasonably formulated
would be correct but incomplete. The incompleteness cannot be avoided because we humans are imperfect. We are imperfect because the spirit world is imperfect. Therefore, we must not let ourselves be completely sold by the correctness, but rather we must always be aware of the incompleteness   25, 64, 95-6, 117-8, 121, 155, 172-8, 243-4, 258, 327, 411-2, 423, 440, 447, 456
humans need leaders. It is because we are
separate living things and we do almost all of our own thinking instead of relying on the spirit world to think for us. But this means we are also the most vulnerable to being lead by bad leaders, particularly when statements made by anyone, including leaders, are usually correct but incomplete. We get

hooked by the correctness without giving enough thought to the incompleteness. The fact that we humans need leaders could explain why the spirit world designed us to have egos   391-2

Independence
a spirit has a degree of autonomy and
independence from the spiritual entity of which it is a part   158-9

Individuals
disabled, see **"Disabilities"**
dyslexic, see **"Dyslexic individuals"**

Infrastructure
in general   76
the unemployed, under-employed, and/or
homeless part of the population includes many in the most potentially productive stage of their lives and they are willing but unable to contribute much to the strength and health of the country. This is an indication that the country is not as strong and healthy as we might think. The same can be said about the state of disrepair of our infrastructure   410, 412-3, 464

Ingredients
in general   22, 249, 267
life-supporting ingredients   400-4

Inherited oneness
as the amount of inherited oneness increases
from one generation to the next, members of subsequent generations become more advanced than members of previous generations. Thus, this is one of the factors driving the evolution of a species, the branching off to form new species, and indirect evolutionary effects on unrelated species   198-200, 211-2
inherited oneness of clones and transplant donors
and recipients   213
developed oneness can stand alone or be in
addition to inherited oneness   198
developed oneness will become part of inherited
oneness for the next generation   145-6
inherited oneness is less likely to fade than is
developed ones   198

Injure, injuries
a possible case of karma playing a role in injuries

383
one of my sisters knew, perhaps by some form of
    telepathy, one of her daughters was badly injured the moment it occurred even through she and her daughter were hundreds of miles apart 209
some animals could learn certain things through
    the experiences of members of their species through cross-learning. Two examples are given by Rupert Sheldrake 211
the model plausibly explains why prayers by a
    large group could improve healing 322-3
the spirit knows how to enable a living thing to
    exist in a universe. Therefore, if the living thing gets tired, injured, or ill, the same knowledge the spirit has to enable the living thing exist will also knows how to restore the living thing's health 204-5, 226-7, 279, 299-300, 316, 323, 376
when our body gets tired, injured, or ill, it
    communicates with our spirit through our soul, and our spirit issues signals to our body to help it heal. The signals would, for example, have us rest, go to bed, go to sleep, be in a coma if badly injured, etc. Our spirit never gets tired, injured, or ill. Our body does, and it has a limited lifespan 134-5, 226-7, 279, 299-300, 302, 312-3, 376

Inspire, inspiration
    be inspired instead of judgmental 433-6
    in general 19, 30, 69, 125, 187, 239, 353,
        379, 422-3

Instinct, instinctive
    according to the model a possible source of
        instincts is the interactions between
        one's spiritual expression with other spiritual expressions in the spirit world 105-9, 205-7
    cross-learning works similar to how instincts
        work 211-2
    for living things that think for themselves,
        knowledge generated or gained by one generation will become instincts or intuition for subsequent generations and intuition for other species 235
    human 170, 211-2
    in general 24, 60, 162

instincts and intuition are not parts of the spirit
    of a living thing but are signals coming from elsewhere and sensed by the spiritual senses or the spirit. Instincts come from the spiritual entity serving as the spirit, and intuition comes from parts of the spirit world beyond the spiritual entity serving as the spirit. Therefore, it becomes clearer why different species of living things has different kinds and levels of instincts and intuition. Examples are given on pages 203 and 204   134-6, 170, 201-4, 207

instincts and intuition messages come to the
    spirit of a living thing telepathically in the form of pure thoughts devoid of any spoken language. That is why living things besides humans have instincts and most likely also intuition   190, 205-6

instincts and intuition could be one of the
    manifestations of the mechanism that makes cross-learning possible   110-1

instincts could grow or fade with subsequent
    generations of a species. Fading instincts are a concern in the case of, for example, laboratory born salmon. In the case of dogs, their instincts regarding their interactions with humans are likely to be growing. In the case of kids and the use of high-tech devices, their instincts are likely to be growing   236-8

instincts do not reside in our spirit but reside in
    the spiritual entity serving as our spirit   133

instincts are a form of knowledge transfer from
    one generation to the next. For humans this transfer does not work very quickly because humans are designed to think for themselves. However, it works well for "in-between" living things such as dogs and cats   236-7

instincts are likely a part of body intelligence and
    body consciousness as well as a part of brain intelligence and brain consciousness   274

instincts likely enable some transplant recipients
    to develop traits of the donor   213-5

spiritual guidance messages include instincts and
    intuition   201-4

we all have experienced some form of telepathic

communication since we all have experienced instincts and/or intuition. Instincts are telepathically received from the spiritual entity serving as our spirit. Intuition is telepathically received from other spiritual entities, and this would be very much like telepathic communication with other individuals   205-6, 215

what is sometimes assumed to be instincts could,
    according to the model, actually be manifestations of the same life continuing from one generation to the next   169-70
1. An example is how monarch butterflies could find their way back to the same grove of trees returning from their annual migration covering thousands of miles and after passing through four generations such that the returning members are four generations removed from the members that began the migration.
2. Another example, similar but different from that of monarch butterflies, consists of insects surviving as members of colonies in which each member automatically knows its role in the colony and even have the body configuration to match its role

Institute for Quantum Computing   128

Intelligent, intelligence
    body intelligence   268, 274-8, 313, 445-6
    brain intelligence   268, 274-8, 446
    elemental, see **"Elemental, elemental intelligent, intelligence"**
    highly intelligent living things elsewhere in
        our universe   133
    human   160, 166, 281-3
    immune systems, issues, intelligence, and
        knowledge   325-342
    in general   46, 223-4, 227, 247, 297
    intelligence and consciousness don't necessarily
        go together   369
    kinds and levels of   159, 191, 197-202, 261-3
    living and nonliving things   41, 45, 48, 59-60, 265-6
    our state of intelligence can be malleable and
        fragile, and that could be positive or negative   297-8
    spirit   27, 60, 128, 133, 136-9, 268
    spirit world   120

the fact that a recipient of an organ transplant can
> sometimes take on attributes of the donor further indicate consciousness and intelligence reside in the spirit and not in the brain   140

the more intelligent we are the faster we can
> increase our intelligence   297

the spirit is where consciousness, intelligence,
> senses, feelings, emotions, empathy, compassion, ego, reasoning ability, imagination, creativity, etc. reside. Different living things have different ones and degrees of such attributes   59-60, 133-5, 140, 227, 271, 295, 300-1

Intentions and attitudes
a positive attitude enhances healing   377-80
an intention formed from an incomplete model
> could produce an unintended result   175, 416-7, 445, 457, 462

are among the most important things in the spirit
> world with which we need to stay in tune   271

are in the form of spiritual entities in the spirit
> world   134

attitude would play a major role in an attempt to
> change our dominant basis for carrying out life   407-8

correlation with brain activities   42
intentions are thoughts that when translated into
> forms that could be expressed in a universe would be perceived the same way in every universe   431, 450

our intentions do not always have us follow the
> spiritual guidance from the spirit world   149

our intention is part of the spiritual part of
> whatever it is we do   241, 353, 391, 394, 398

some identical twins could communicate
> telepathically, but it is unclear if they intentionally do so   212

the spirit world's intention is for us to make our
> natural partnership with it as mutually positive as possible   421-2

unlike most other spiritual entities, intentions
> and attitudes would take on the same forms in different universes   187-9

we all take part in shaping the spirit world by our
> intentions, choices, and actions   22

we are likely meant to evolve to
where we would
    take on intentions that could
lead us to fulfill our purpose
for being here   420
we are responsible for the health
and growth of
    the spirit world   50

Inter-universe travel and outer space travel
    pseudo   428-9, 450
    virtual   280-3, 342, 374
    with just our sense of sight we
enter the world
    of a story created by an
author. This might be how
we could enter the world of
another universe; i.e., by
using just the right one or
more of our major and/or
spiritual senses   115

Interact, interactions
    interactions among spirit, soul,
and body   133-40
    interactions between the spirit
world and our
    physical world. See Chapter
Seven starting on page 285

International relations
    in general   21, 24, 154, 463
    governmental actions driven by
ego and desire to
enhance survivability would
not improve international
relations   143

Intuition, intuitive
    according to the model a possible
source of
    instincts and intuition are
from the interactions between
one's spiritual expression
with other spiritual
expressions in the spirit world
107, 205-7
    for living things that think for
themselves,
    knowledge generated or
gained by one generation will
become instincts or intuition
for subsequent generations
and intuition for other species
235
    human   170
    instincts and intuition are not parts
of the spirit
    of a living thing but are
signals coming from
elsewhere and sensed by the
spiritual senses or the spirit.
Instincts come from the
spiritual entity serving as the
spirit, and intuition comes
from parts of the spirit world
beyond the spiritual entity
serving as the spirit.
Therefore, it becomes clearer
why different species of living
things has different kinds and
levels of instincts and

intuition. Examples are given on pages 203 and 204   134-6, 170, 201, 201-4, 207
instincts and intuition could be one of the
   manifestations of the mechanism that makes cross-learning possible   110-1
instincts and intuition messages come to the
   spirit of a living thing telepathically in the form of pure thoughts devoid of any spoken language. That is why living things besides humans have instincts and most likely also intuition.   190, 205-6
development of intuition regarding the use of
   high-tech devices   237
spiritual guidance messages include instincts and
   intuition   201-4
we all have experienced some form of telepathic
   communication since we all have experienced instincts and/or intuition   205-6

Invent, inventions
   in general   67, 69, 71, 81, 92, 94, 138, 156, 208, 216, 235, 246, 287, 293, 301, 329, 331, 339, 395, 399, 410
   the model explains in a spiritual sense why the
      number of things we can invent has no limit   333

Issues
   addressing a combination of issues together
      could be more productive than addressing each issues singularly   429
   an issue can be within a larger issue   342-3, 417-21, 426
   an issue could be complex enough to require
      multiple universes and/or multiple planets to address. For example, our particular physical universe or a specific planet might be able to address certain physical aspects while a nonphysical universe or another planet would be needed to address certain nonphysical or different physical aspects. Or, a different physical universe made up of substances different from what make up ours would be needed to address other certain physical aspects. Etc.   239-40, 417-21
   complex and increasingly complex immune
      systems, issues, intelligence, and knowledge   325-342
   examples of various issues or tug-of-wars that
      could be perceived as forms of immune systems   342-5

in general   60, 118, 143, 162, 186, 325
issues are essentially tug-of-wars in that they
 have multiple opposing sides   153, 180-5, 249-51, 325
issues created by the spirit world while caring for
 every living thing it creates   417-21
issues can be perceived as good, bad, or neutral
 depending on the universe into which they are translated to exist and on the situation   425, 430
issues regarding not knowing enough about
 something or someone but feeling we need to make a commitment about that something or someone. This can happen in a marriage, while serving on a jury, in a business deal, etc.   252-3
issues kept in balance is basically how our
 immune system works. I.e., if one or more of the issues involved with our immune system go out of balance, then our immune system would not work properly, and we could become ill   325, 342-5
issues that are practices (not just concepts) in the
 spirit world would be address there in a win-win manner. It is because everything is a part of everything else there   457
new issues are constantly being formed as new
 pieces of knowledge are being generated, and the new issues could need balancing. At the same time, old issues could go out of balance and need rebalancing   154, 157, 180-2, 239, 257-8, 306, 325, 417, 424
one of our tasks on Earth is keeping our issues
 reasonable balanced so that wisdom could be formed. And conversely we need wisdom to handle issues well. Thus, it is a balancing act; one that could become unstable if we do not do our part to keep it stable   151-5, 164
our dreams might include images with more than
 three-dimensions and/or dimensions different for the three we are use to. This is one of the reasons why our dreams tend to be surrealistic   317
produced by the spirit world because it cares
 about every living thing it creates   417-22
some issues might require multiple universes to

exist at the same time in order
to address the various parts of
such an issue. This would
mean multiple universes
could exist at the same time
even if living things residing
in one universe could not
sense the presence of the
other universes   359
the role of universes, and in
particularly some of
Earth's role, in addressing the
spirit world's issues   343,
359, 376, 394, 411-2, 417-22,
424-9, 460, 463-4
various forms of immune systems
keeping
"living things" alive besides
the immune systems keeping
our bodies healthy and alive
325-345

Itch, see, **"Hang-ups"**

J
Jesus   324, 471

Judge, judgmental, nonjudgmental
be inspired instead of judgmental
433-6
in general   23, 27, 40-1, 148-50,
163-6, 179,
197-8, 295, 324, 389, 402,
406, 418

Jury

issues regarding not knowing
enough about
something or someone but
feeling we need to make a
commitment about that
something or someone. This
can happen in a marriage,
while serving on a jury, in a
business deal, etc.   252-3

K
Karma
an actual possible case of karma
playing a role
in to events   382-4

Kids, see **"Child, children, kids"**

Kill, killing
in general   97, 101, 179, 272, 292,
425-6, 451-2,
471

Kinds of
elemental things; e.g., electrons,
protons,
neutrons, atoms, molecules,
grains of sand, etc.   122-7
issues and tug-of-wars in the spirit
world that
universes are created to help
restore to be within
reasonable balance   180
living things are likely to be
different on
different planets   418-20

past, present, future universes 61-2
physical nothingness to us could be spiritual
    something 329-32
physical, spiritual parts of models 118-20
possible multiple personalities that individuals
    could have 254-5
spiritual entities making up the spirit world
    132-4
unlimited new pieces of knowledge possible to
    generate 154-5
purposes living things are here to fulfill, and
    the three main obstacles we humans are to work with or around 162-6
spirits and souls of various kinds of single
    cells making up living things 226-8
spiritual advancements and physical
    advancements 395-7
spiritual expressions of living, nonliving, and
    formerly living things 288-9
things the spiritual part of models might help
    explain 453-5
thought-like signals issued by the spirit world
    294-8

Knowledge
a piece of knowledge is neither good nor bad
    171-2
a piece of knowledge is neither good nor bad, but
    when translated into a form that could exist or be expressed in a universe the translated form could be perceived as good, bad, or neutral depending on the universe and the situation 325-8
analogies between pieces of knowledge and
    words: 48-9, 113-6
1. A piece of knowledge is analogous to a word.
2. Multiple pieces of knowledge forming a spiritual entity analogous to multiple words forming a sentence.
3. It thus follows that spiritual entities are analogous to thoughts expressed by sentences.
4. Multiple spiritual entities together forming a larger spiritual entity analogous to multiple sentences together forming a paragraph.
5. Multiple spiritual entities of various sizes forming an even larger spiritual entity analogous to various paragraphs together forming a book.

6. The spirit world is like a dictionary, it keeps just one copy of each piece of knowledge analogous to how a dictionary keeps just one copy of each word.

immune systems, issues, intelligence, and
    knowledge 325-342
knowledge base 39, 41-8
knowledge is the source of the spirit world's
    creative ability 47
knowledge is what gives the spirit world its
    creative ability 47
knowledge that is generated or gained by
    learning something is different from knowledge that is generated or gained by copying or mimicking something even if the outward appearance in performance might look very much the same. The model explains how this is the case in spiritual terms 84-5
  one of the reasons we humans get in conflicts
    and battles is because when we generate pieces of knowledge we do not know how to generate opposing pieces of knowledge such that better balance in our total knowledge would be achieved. We can't do that because our intelligence is limited. Other living things on Earth are less intelligent than humans and they do an even worse job of balancing the pieces of knowledge they generate. Similar conditions are likely to exit in other universes and that is how the state of knowledge in the spirit world could go out of balance. The spirit world could do a much better job of generating pieces of knowledge that are balanced because its intelligence is unlimited, although not necessarily complete. This enables it to know it needs to constantly monitor its state of knowledge and to do something, such as design and bring into being new universes periodically, to help restore reasonable balance in its state of knowledge 334
once a piece of knowledge is generated it exists
    forever as part of the spirit world 325
the collection of all pieces of knowledge that
    exists at any given point in time makes up the spirit world at that point in time 47-8
the knowledge base of a living thing gets

redefined as being the spirit of
the living thing 48
the spirit world could never be
perfect because it
could never possess every
piece of knowledge that could
be generated. There is no
limit to the number of pieces
of knowledge that could be
generated. This means
nothing that is created by the
spirit world could ever be
perfect. Everything that
exists in the spirit world or in
any universe is created by the
spirit world; therefore,
nothing is ever perfect 49,
66, 119
what is a piece of knowledge and
what is a
spiritual entity? We can work
with both without knowing
exactly what they are just as
we can work with a "letter"
and a "word" without
knowing exactly what they
are 325-8

L

Languages
different languages would express
a given
thought somewhat differently.
This is one of the deficiencies
of languages 98, 369

in general 49, 84, 97-9, 172, 184-5, 187, 189-
-90, 270-1, 276, 284, 297,
335, 408, 441, 450, 473
languages are like filters in that
they distort
intended thoughts due to their
limitations and
incompleteness 369
the invention of languages might
be associated
with the initiated the ability to
do abstract thinking 270-1

Leaders
leaders do not exist in the spirit
world, but
humans on Earth need leaders
391-3
leaders need egos in order to lead.
But too
much ego is bad. A good
leader would have just the
right amount; e.g., those who
are not driven significantly by
ego. Such leaders deserve our
willingness to explore what
spiritual advancements we
can accomplish. An example
is Nelson Mandela 392-4
some living things that rely on the
spirit world
to do much of their thinking.
But their leaders are not likely
to be bad because they also
rely on the spirit world to do
much of their thinking 392

the fact that we humans need leaders could
> explain why the spirit world designed us to have egos 391-2

we humans need leaders because we are separate
> living things, and we do our own thinking instead of relying on the spirit world to think for us. This means we are vulnerable to being lead by bad leader if our leader happens to be bad. This is because statements made by anyone, including our leader, are correct but incomplete. We could get hooked by the correctness without being aware of the incompleteness. We have seen many cases of bad leaders gaining control of nations. We must be careful to not let this happen to our nation, because it could happen 391-2

Learn, learning
learning takes place in our spirit and not in our brain 268-74

Lichens 222, 419

Life
exists after life 29, 32, 34, 194, 214, 357, 443-4
continuation of life 231
early living things 74, 400
early vulnerable stage of life 53-4, 153, 236
elemental life 59, 156, 266, 325,
high-tech devices do not always improve the
> quality of life 147

possible ways to sense spiritual signals
> indicating life exists after life 443-4

spiritual part of life 98, 271, 441, 468, 475
the physical part of life eventually degrades but
> the spiritual part does not 445-7

what is sometimes assumed to be instincts could,
> according to the model, actually be manifestations of the same life continuing from one generation to the next 169-70

1. An example is how monarch butterflies could find their way back to the same grove of trees returning from their annual migration covering thousands of miles and after passing through four generations such that the returning members are four generations removed from the members that began the migration.
2. Another example, similar but different from that of monarch butterflies, consists of insects

surviving as members of colonies in which each member automatically knows its role in the colony and even have the body configuration to match its role

Life supporting ingredients
planets with a large amount of life supporting
    ingredients are likely to produce more advanced and more highly intelligent living things. Conversely, planets with a small amount of life supporting ingredients are likely to produce less advanced and less intelligent living things and are likely to have more unrest and conflicts as the ingredients continue to dwindle   400-4
the fact that humans on Earth have a lot of unrest
    and conflict but yet still have a fair amount of life supporting ingredients left indicates Earth probably has a moderate, not a large, amount of life supporting ingredients. This suggests we humans better 'wake up" right away and find ways to work around this pending crisis   400-4
the amount of life supporting ingredients on
    Earth is finite and is gradually being depleted as the human population continues to grow. Unrest and conflicts are bound to increase. This can be reflected even within our own government of the United States. The two major parties could have more conflicts and competition, and conflicts could even erupt between factions within a party. It basically comes down to each party and/or faction wanting to grab more control over dwindling life supporting ingredients   400-4, 410-17

Life-sustaining mechanisms   427-9

Lifestyles
    Conventional   434,
    Unconventional   434-6, 466,

Lifespan, lifetimes
    each generation of living thing has a finite
        lifetime possibly to enhance the rate of achieving advancements   93
    living things   57, 81, 89, 92-3, 103-4, 109, 191,
        193, 199, 205, 214, 219-22, 229-30, 232, 242, 347-8, 365-6, 383, 450, 463, 467-8, 470, 475
    spirit world's   400,
    universes'   26, 70-1, 74, 78, 106-7, 121-3, 125,

135, 182-4, 192, 247-8, 296, 303, 347, 369, 396, 400, 402-3,

Living life for the spirit world vs. for our physical world
    living life for the spirit world vs. for our physical
        world. It makes a difference because the oneness that makes everything a part of everything else exists in the spirit world. In particular the spirit of every human is a part of spirit of every other human, whereas humans are physically separate individuals in our physical world 141, 385
    since humans are all a part of each other in the
        spirit world, it doesn't make sense to make war in our physical world 290, 385

Living things
    a living thing's role in a universe 131-3
    according to the model, the spirit world has
        two stages of growth similar to how humans and various other living things on Earth has; i.e., a infancy stage and an adult stage. The model also suggests living things have these two stages because the spirit world has these two stages and would thus design living things to have these two stages. Page 333 explains how this works 333
    defining what is a living thing 55-60
    on Earth it is possible that living things other
        than humans are put on Earth to help prepare Earth to be hospitable to highly intelligent living things such as humans. This may seem somewhat egotistical, but it might be true 458-9
    the consciousness of living things in every
        universe is partly tuned to the world of their universe and partly tuned to the spirit world. Such division of consciousness is necessary in order to carry out life in any universe, according to the model. The more a living thing relies on the spirit world to do its thinking the more its consciousness is biased toward the spirit world. The consciousness of living things in a nonphysical universe is more biased toward the spirit world than the consciousness of living things in a physical world. That's because a nonphysical universe is more like the spirit world than is a

Index 573

physical universe. Notice how living things on Earth whose consciousness is more biased toward the spirit world would do much less, or no, horrible things to other living things other than for food. And we humans with our consciousness much less biased toward the spirit world would do horrible things to living things and especially to other humans 398-9

what happens to the spirit of a living thing and
    the spiritual entity serving as the spirit when the living thing dies? 103-5

Living things that are mobile
alligators 276
animals 46, 74, 84-5, 111, 142, 162, 170, 197,
    204, 206, 210-1, 217, 220, 224, 226, 231, 237, 263, 272-3, 277, 308, 315, 348, 398-09, 404, 422, 458
ants 145, 169, 203, 232
beaver 232
bees, honeybees 124, 159-60, 232-4
birds including chicken, vulture, etc. 45, 57-8,
    70, 78, 80, 135, 138, 144, 161, 191-2, 203-4, 235-7, 261, 275-6, 288, 308, 315, 334, 339, 343, 346
cats 210, 237, 263

cattle 211, 246
cicadas 229-231, 348
clams 76-7, 183, 359, 418-9
crabs 511
dinosaurs 57-8, 77-8, 80, 245, 346
dogs 191, 210, 237, 260-1, 263, 290
dolphins 87, 247, 276-8, 406, 423
eagles 261
elephants 87, 277, 406, 423
fishes 51, 77, 142-5, 160, 278, 308, 346
fresh-water polyp hydras 225
frogs 75, 226
geckos 120
giant sea turtles 203, 349
hawks 343
horses 211, 246, 362, 472
insects 74, 142-5, 162, 170, 201-2, 220, 232,
    236, 308, 342
jelly fishes 138, 232
lions 179, 272
lizards 74, 78, 225-6, 432-3
monarch butterflies 169-70, 229-32, 348, 399
mouse, mice 279
pigeons 144, 161, 191, 261, 339, 343
planarian flatworms 225
platypuses 191, 201
porpoises 278
primates 179, 272
salamanders 225-6
salmons 229-32, 236, 348
scorpions 21, 51, 288
sea squirts 225

sharks 191,
snakes, rattlesnakes 21, 75, 192, 261
starfishes 225
tadpoles 225-6
termites 124, 145, 232
whales 87, 276-8, 347, 406, 423
    one species of whales for centuries worked with fishermen to help each other capture fish 278
worms 74-5, 160, 225, 288, 308

Long-term thinking, long-range thinking
being interested is more of a long-term long-
    range thing, whereas being excited is more of a short-term short-range thing 462
in general 243-4, 410, 429-30, 465
the nation's economy is like a huge ship at sea;
    i.e., it takes a while to change directions after action is made to have it do so. Therefore, when the person who is the president of our nation is changed every four or eight years the wrong person often gets the credit for a good economy or the blame for a bad economy. This tends to contribute to the mess we are making in our nation if not in the entire world. Basically it is because we humans tend to think short-term short-range instead of lone-term long-range. We need to be more aware we tend to think this way and of the problems it causes 429-30
we need to think long-term long-range in order
    to have a better future but meanwhile we also need to think short-term short-range in order to survive the present and near future. This is an example of how establishing reasonable balance would mean forming good wisdom 465

Love and hate
an indication of a loved one's true love could
    include what paranormal things happen after the loved one dies 356
in war a solder might shoot someone considered
    to be an enemy and thus both love and hate are triggered at the same time; i.e., he or she is supposed to hate an enemy, but he is also supposed to love a fellow human. Such events could change a person for the rest of his or her life 295
love is an emotion and emotions are a part of our
    spirit. Thus, we cannot search for it in the spirit world, we

Index 575

can only trigger it, and we
could trigger multiple
emotions such as love and
hate at the same time   295

M

Major senses
different living things have different sets and
acuity of major senses and most likely also different sets and acuity of spiritual senses. Consciousness is associated with the senses. Therefore different living things have different kinds and levels of consciousness. That is also why various species could sense different things, some of which humans do not sense   204, 210, 261-4
examples of some species possibly knowing
what they sense in the spirit world is in the spirit world and what they sense in our physical world is in our physical world   263-4
the fact that other creatures have major senses
that we humans do not have also indicates that spiritual senses exist in the spirit world other than the ones that give us our major senses. This also indicates the spirit world exists   447
why the acuity of our major senses is reduced
during sleep   301-2
our major senses are certain spiritual senses
extended into our body   301

Mandela, Nelson   393-4

Mars Rover
Mars Rover   224
The people who designed and built self-driving
automobiles have done the thinking for the automobile such that it could drive itself. This is similar to how the Mars Rover and other vehicles we sent into outer space could drive themselves and conduct experiments on their own. This is analogous to how the spirit world does the thinking for living things that rely on the spirit world to do their thinking for them for their survival   269-70

Mathematics
highly intelligent living things in any universe,
including humans in our universe, are likely to use mathematics   184

Memory, memories

the model plausibly explains why a good night's
    sleep improves memory   307-8
why short-term memory declines with age but
    long-term memory can remain good   319-22

Mentors and handholds
    handholds are individuals who support you and
        give you the confidence and courage to push yourself to do something unconventional and/or difficult. A parent is more likely to be a handhold than a mentor   256-7
    mentors are experts at doing something, usually
        conventional, who are available to you as counselors and guides on how to do that certain something. A senior coworker is more likely to be a mentor than a handhold   256-7

Mess
    any model or statement reasonably formulated
        would be correct but also incomplete. The incompleteness cannot be avoided because we humans are imperfect. We are imperfect because the spirit world is imperfect. Therefore, we must not let ourselves be completely sold by the correctness, but rather we must always be aware of the incompleteness   25, 121, 155, 172, 447, 456
the mess we made on Earth   151, 164, 219, 457-8
the nation's economy is like a huge ship at sea;
    i.e., it takes a while to change directions after action is made to have it do so. Therefore, when the person who is the president of our nation is changed every four or eight years the wrong person often gets the credit for a good economy or the blame for a bad economy. This tends to contribute to the mess we are making in our nation if not in the entire world. Basically it is because we humans tend to think short-term short-range instead of lone-term long-range. We need to be more aware we tend to think this way and of the problems it causes   429-30

Messages
    intuitive, see **"Intuition, intuitive, messages"**
    instinctive, see **"Instinct, instinctive,** messages**"**

Microsoft 470

Middle class
a strong middle-class in our population is
> necessary for a strong economy. Today the middle-class is shrinking or disappearing all over our country. This is an indication our country is not as strong and healthy as we think   30, 410, 414

in general   475

Migration   86, 169, 229-32

Miracles
according to the model, theoretically humans
> can make miracles happen   324

Missing link
missing links can be missing because retracing
> took place instead of evolution. Retracing could happen very rapidly such that sudden creation could be perceived. This could be the case for humans   73, 75, 86-7

rapid evolution of some living things could be a
> form of retracing. Retracing is a process of rapid emergence of living things that has have already evolved on some past universe. Retracing is thus a rapid retracing of an evolutionary process that already taken place. Retracing could allow insufficient time to leave behind fossils behind, and thus, we would have missing links. This could apply to numerous living things besides us humans, in particular very intelligent living things such as elephants, dolphins, whales, octopi, etc.   86-7

some people do not believe in evolution because
> of the missing links for many of the living things on Earth, including humans. However, the model indicates that evolution could span over the lifetimes of multiple universes. Therefore, what are considered missing links might exist in various past universes. Therefore, if our view on evolution is basis only on what is found on Earth, it is possible to have doubts about the existence of evolution   248

species with missing links are common and this
> could indicate retracing occurred instead of evolution for those species   74-7

Models
    according to the model some of our models
        would be more complete if spirituality were taken more into consideration in their formulations. Our technical models tend to be lacking in this regard, and this could be why certain phenomena could not be completely explained by our technical models. Examples include what produces gravity, why quantum superposition and entanglement happen, what are the dark matter and dark energy, and what is beyond the edge of space, etc. 118-9, 455
    all the models are approximations; i.e., correct
        but not totally complete or absolutely accurate 25, 121, 155, 172, 447, 456
    all the models we have formulated when
        combined could be visualized as being like a crazy-quilt that covers spirituality well enough to enable us to carry out life as we do 25
    all models we have formulated are in various
        ways spiritual models 25, 447-50
    any model or statement reasonably formulated
        would be correct but incomplete. The incompleteness cannot be avoided because we humans are imperfect. We are imperfect because the spirit world is imperfect. Therefore, we must not let ourselves be completely sold by the correctness, but rather we must always be aware of the incompleteness 25, 64, 95-6, 117-8, 121, 155, 172-8, 243-4, 258, 327, 411-2, 423, 440, 447, 456
    Chapter One might lead one to think the model
        excludes all concepts of God and thus also excludes all religions. But as the model develops in Chapter Three, it becomes clear it is inclusive of all concepts of God and all religions 21, 156-7
    desired criteria for my personal spiritual
        model 40-1
    do we formulate models or do models formulate
        us, or is it both? 384-5
    effects of all models being not totally complete
        and not absolutely accurate 172-8
    spirituality is such an enormous subject, no
        model formulated by humans could cover it completely.

Therefore, countless reasonably formulated spiritual models, including personal spiritual models, will exist and all of them would be correct but none would be complete 385
the level of our advancement is reflected in our
models 451-2
the reason we understand a lot more about our
physical world than we do about the spirit world is because we formulated a lot of models that pertain to our physical world and relatively few that pertain to the spirit world. To understand the spirit world better, we need to formulate more models that pertain to the spirit world 385
the spiritual part of models could help explain
some unexplained things 452-6
we formulate models to help us understand in an
approximate manner how to do what the spirit world does 120, 447
why do some things fail, not function well, or
are disliked? The reason is the incompleteness (e.g., lacking in spirituality considerations) and/or

incompatibilities of the multiple models applied in their designs 118-9

Mother, mom 20, 29, 31, 33-7, 173, 204, 209, 222, 251, 257, 317-8, 357, 367, 378, 380, 383, 444, 473

Mother Nature, tinkering by Mother Nature 77, 102, 183, 246

Multiple personalities
a bad hang-up could cause multiple
personalities to develop and it could cause bad behavior to carry over from one generation to the next 253-5
according to the model, the human spirit
encompasses multiple spirit types. Consequently, every individual is capable of having multiple personalities. Therefore, multiple personalities could be perceived as natural, although usually undesirable 253-5
the process that causes multiple personalities in
people or bad behavior that carries over from generation to generation in people could apply similarly for nations. Thus, in this respect individual nations are like individual persons, and this could at least partly explain

why international conflicts often never get permanently resolved 255

Multiple universes 70, 72, 74, 78, 184, 248, 293, 369,

N

Nation, nation's economy
the nation's economy is like a huge ship at sea;
i.e., it takes a while to change directions after action is made to have it do so. Therefore, when the person who is the president of our nation is changed every four or eight years the wrong person often gets the credit for a good economy or the blame for a bad economy. This tends to contribute to the mess we are making in our nation if not in the entire world. Basically it is because we humans tend to think short-term short-range instead of lone-term long-range. We need to be more aware we tend to think this way and of the problems it causes 429-30

Native Americans
a Native American princess describes Native Americans' beliefs and practices regarding food 422

Natural resources 80, 390, 396, 400, 414, 427

Near-death experiences
dreams during a near-death experience 316-9
in general 68, 221, 316-9
neutral or unpleasant near-death experiences
are possible 316-9
what are near-death experiences? 316-9

Nonliving things
defining what is a nonliving thing. 55-60
nonliving things have spirits and souls just as
living things do 101-5, 112-3

Nonphysical things
for example, see **"Concepts - -", "Intentions and attitudes", "Notions - -", "Thought, thoughts"**, etc.
nonphysical universes and worlds 61, 69, 102,
182, 187, 239, 262, 280, 284, 307, 375, 395, 398,

Nothingness beyond the edge of our universe
the nothingness beyond the edge of our universe

must be something that exists
because spiritual entities in
the spirit world enable it to
exist. It might consist of
intelligence of a kind
unfamiliar to humans and that
could figure out how to have
experiences that then would
generate new pieces of
knowledge for the spirit
world. This could be how the
spirit world enable our
universe, as well as other
universes, to come into being;
i.e., though the intelligence
that exists in the nothingness
beyond the edge of our
universe   331

Notions in the Formulation of the Model
first notion: "something
somewhere somehow
knows how to enable our
universe and everything in it
to exist"   44
second notion: "new knowledge is
generated by
experiences and only by
experiences, and that living
and nonliving things gain
access to knowledge by going
through experiences and only
by going through
experiences"   44
third notion: "knowledge comes in
pieces." A

typical experience generates
many pieces of knowledge,
some are new and the rest are
duplicates of already existing
pieces. Multiple copies of a
piece immediately merge into
one. One of each piece of
knowledge is all that is
needed   47
fourth notion: "all existing pieces
of knowledge
reside in the same place, and
it is the only place in which
they reside." This is the place
we call the "spirit world"   47
fifth notion: "anything made of
two or more
existing pieces of knowledge
is defined as a spiritual entity"
48

O

Obstacles, the three major ones
the three most important obstacles
that we need
to work with or around to
fulfill our purpose for being
here   164, 186, 421

Old people
young people often have an
inaccurate
impression of old people   476

Oneness
clones and oneness   213

communicating through the oneness that
    pervades the spirit world. If we could tap into the oneness in the spirit world to communicate among each other telepathically we would have a better chance of developing the positive attributes of the spirit world 212, 214-5, 393-4
cross-learning and oneness 211-2
developed oneness 145-6, 149, 197-200
developed oneness between pet and owner
    leads to the pet being able to telepathically receive the owner's thoughts 207-8, 210
developed oneness would become inherited oneness for members of subsequent generations. Thus, each generation could be more advanced. It could also lead to the development of new species 198-200
developed oneness is more subject to the "use-it-
    or-lose-it" phenomenon than inherited oneness 198
direct oneness among all things 142, 255-6
effects of inherited oneness and developed
    oneness on evolution 199-200

humans possibly had a high level of developed
    oneness among each other and were able to telepathically communicate with each other 210
identical twins have the highest level of inherited
    and developed oneness and thus many have telepathic ability between them 212-3
in the spirit world 141
indirect 142
inherited 145-6, 149, 197-200
inherited oneness is less subject to the "use-it-
    or-lose-it" phenomenon than developed oneness 198
inherited oneness that was once developed
    oneness previous generations will lead to the development of more advanced generations and possibly to the development of new species 198-200
living life for the spirit world vs. for our physical
    world. It makes a difference because the oneness that makes everything a part of everything else exists in the spirit world. In particular the spirit of every human is a part of spirit of every other human, whereas humans are physically separate

individuals in our physical
world 141, 385
oneness between living and
formerly living
things 215
oneness in the spirit world comes
about in two
ways. One way is due the
spirit world keeping only one
copy of every existing piece
of knowledge. The other way
is that everything in the spirit
world is directly or indirectly
a part of every other thing in
the spirit world 197
oneness originates in the spirit
world and is
therefore a spiritual part of
every universe including our
physical universe 141-50
pervades the spirit world 197
rivalries, opponents, enemies, etc.
developed
from oneness 199
since humans are all a part of each
other in the
spirit world, it doesn't make
sense to make war in our
physical world 290, 385
surprisingly clones have neither
inherited or
developed oneness from one
to the other 213
tapping into the oneness that
pervades the spirit
world 393-4
telepathy and oneness 205-10

transplant recipients have
borrowed oneness
from the donor and thus
telepathic message from the
donor can be received by the
recipient 213-5

Opponent 145-7, 150

Opposing
pieces of knowledge 331-4

Organization 242, 271, 326, 412, 423, 469-70

Organs
vital organs 305, 311

Out of body experiences 170, 190, 362-5, 368, 374

P

Parasites 238-40

Parent, parents
grandparent of the creator 43
parents 29-34, 36-7, 57, 82-5, 95, 107, 111,
193, 195, 213, 237-8, 249,
343, 352, 354, 356-7, 367,
383-4, 442, 472-5
parent of the creator 43
parenting 440, 442

Particles

sub-atomic, see **"Sub-atomic particles"**

Partnership
    a natural partnership is automatically formed
        between the spirit world and every living thing it creates 22-3, 50, 62, 157-9, 163-4, 190, 193-4, 375, 421-2, 425, 458-60
    the natural partnership between the spirit world
        and each living thing can be perceived as having two parts. The first part functions in the spirit world and is between the spirit world and the spirit of the living thing. The second part functions in the world of the universe in which the living thing resides and is between the living thing and every other living thing in the universe 190

Past lifetimes
    Some individuals seem to remember bits and
        pieces of past life times. The mechanism for how it works is in the spirit world 347-8

Perceptions
    perceptions of advancements, improvements, and
        being gifted 282-3

Personal God 21-3, 156-7, 290-1

Personal spiritual models and personal spiritual search
    our personal spiritual search for our personal
        spiritual model never really ends. Our personal spiritual model will continuously evolve as situations change, as we age, and as our spiritual needs change with age and time 456-7
    spirituality is such an enormous subject, no
        model formulated by humans could cover it completely. Therefore, countless reasonably formulated spiritual models, including personal spiritual models, will exist, all of them would be correct but none would be complete 385
    why finding our personal spiritual model could
        make each of us a better person 422-3
    your approach in your career might be best for
        finding your personal spiritual model 460-1

Pets and domestication of some animals
    instincts are a form of knowledge transfer from

one generation to the next. For humans this transfer often does not work very well because humans are designed to think for themselves. However, it works better for "in-between" living things such as dogs and cats, because they rely a lot more than humans do on the spirit world to do their thinking for them. This and "cross-learning", which also works better for them, enable them to make wonderful pets for humans 236-7

Piloting or driving
airplanes 57, 60, 136, 398, 472
automobile or car 36, 91, 136, 216, 257, 269-
70, 273, 282, 316, 334-5, 384, 399, 409, 451-2, 472
horse 472
piloting the body demands more of our
consciousness as we age 320-1
spacecraft 472
the spirit pilots the body 60, 89, 100, 105, 136-
7, 202, 269, 274-5, 301-6, 309, 320-1, 324, 396-7, 441-2, 445, 451, 472, 476

Placebo 377-9

Planets

an issue could be complex enough to require
multiple universes and/or multiple planets to address. For example, our particular physical universe or a specific planet might be able to address certain physical aspects while a nonphysical universe or another planet would be needed to address certain nonphysical or different physical aspects. Or, a different physical universe made up of substances different from what make up ours would be needed to address other certain physical aspects. Etc. 239-40
each hospital planet in our universe is likely to
be designed to address a different set of issues associated with living things such that all such issues in need of attention intended for our universe to cover will be covered 426-9
other planets 190-6
planets, stars, galaxies, black holes, etc. 49, 61-
2, 70, 72, 75-6, 94-5, 124-5, 165-6, 181-2, 190-2, 200, 215, 218-0, 262, 281-2, 284-6, 289, 341-2, 347, 359-60, 370, 375, 401-4, 418-9, 426-9, 454-5, 459

Plants
    plants are examples of how consciousness and
        intelligence reside in the spirit and not in the brain 45
    why some plants can be propagated by cuttings 129

Politics, politicians
    any model or statement reasonably formulated
        would be correct but incomplete. The incompleteness cannot be avoided because we humans are imperfect. We are imperfect because the spirit world is imperfect. Therefore, we must not let ourselves be completely sold by the correctness, but rather we must always be aware of the incompleteness 25, 64, 95-6, 117-8, 121, 155, 172-8, 243-4, 258, 327, 411-2, 423, 440, 447, 456

Population increase and technical advancements without matching spiritual advancements
    increasing world population, now at seven
        billion, and technical advancements without matching spiritual advancements can worsen the mess we are making on Earth 463-6

Prayers and wishes
    effects of prayers and wishes 322-4
    the model plausibly explains why prayers by a
        large group could improve healing 322-4

Prions 46, 56, 217, 222

Productivity and rate of unemployment.
    Our nation's productivity is based on the
        productivity of those working. However, we have a lot of people unemployed or underemployed and a lot who are homeless. Our indicator of productivity should include all such folks, and then we will realize our productivity is much lower than we are led to believe. A similar accounting should apply to the rate of unemployment in that it should account for those unemployed who gave up trying to find jobs. And those who are holding part time jobs should not be counted as fully employed. Then we will find the rate of unemployment is worse than we are led to believe 413

Projections
projections into possible futures 372-4

Purpose
the more a living thing is able to think for itself
the more complex would be its purpose for being here. The more a living thing relies on the spirit world to think for it the simpler would be its purpose for being here. And if the spirit world does essentially all the thinking for a species, fulfilling the purpose would become essentially automatic 250-1
the purpose of any one species of living thing is
different from that of any other species of living things, even if the difference might be small 190
the purposes of other planets in our universe
239-40, 426-9
the purposes of other universes 239-40, 251
the purposes of our universe 429
the purposes of humans for being on Earth are,
1. to help the spirit world restore balance.
2. to generate as many new pieces of
knowledge as possible.
Purpose number 1. is more important, but we are doing much more for purpose number 2. 250, 424-32, 429
the purposes of living things in general on Earth
159-66
the purposes of non-human living things on
Earth 250-1
the purposes of us humans on Earth might
preclude our ability to do general and complete telepathic communications with one another 206
the spirit world ingeniously designed the
relatively few elemental things (e.g., electrons, protons, neutrons, etc.) making up our universe to be able to form the countless amazing things they form 454
the three most important obstacles that we need
to work with or around to fulfill our purpose for being here 164, 186, 421
we do more horrible things to members of our
species than other living things do to members of their species. You would think that with our superior intelligence that we would do better than other living things. So, what

is it that makes us to do worse? Is it possible our purpose for being here on Earth is simply to generate as many new piece of knowledge as possible, and the purpose of helping the spirit world restore balance belongs to other living things on Earth instead of us as we had presumed? 389

Q
Quantum particles
elemental things (electrons, protons, neutrons, subatomic particles, and atoms) are sometimes called "quantum particles" 122, 125-30
quantum particles and have a very limited variety of experiences, whereas larger more complex things such as molecules have essentially a limitless variety of experiences 124, 129

Quantum superposition and entanglement
quantum superposition and entanglement can occur with quantum particles, and here is how they can happen 125-30, 255-6

molecules, even elemental ones are not capable of quantum superstition or entanglement 129
the state of existence of, for example two electrons, will be difference when one of them is a part one thing and the other a part of another thing even though both electrons share the same spirit in the spirit world 126

R
Reasoning ability
the spirit is where consciousness, intelligence, senses, feelings, emotions, empathy, compassion, ego, reasoning ability, imagination, creativity, etc. reside. Different living things have different ones and degrees of such attributes 59-60, 133-5, 140, 227, 271, 295, 300-1

Recipient and donor of an organ transplant, see
"Donor and Recipient of an organ transplant"

Record of experiences of a living or nonliving thing
the knowledge base (the spirit) of a living or

nonliving thing is what knows how to enable the thing to exist at any point in time and thus embodies a record of all the experiences the thing has gone through up to that point in time   44-5

the spirit and soul of a living or nonliving thing
    together embody a record of every experience the thing as gone through up to that point in time   103

Regenerate, regenerative ability
    a tadpole developing into a frog loses some of its
        regenerative ability much like how a person also does with age   225-6

humans are unable to regenerate lost body parts
    for a plausible reason; i.e., the brain would
        have to be enormously big and that would bring about conditions that preclude viability   299, 376

human body parts   205, 225-6, 299, 376

human body tissues   24, 225-6, 299

regeneration of lost body parts of living things
    other than humans   225-6

Reincarnates, reincarnation

a spiritual entity that is serving as the spirit for
    a human could serve as the spirit for some other living thing at some other times, and a different portion of it would be active in serving as the spirit for that other living thing. In a sense we could say that other living thing is sort of human and could certainly contribute indirectly to the evolution of humans, and vice versa. That might explain why dolphins, elephants, etc. are so intelligent   449

the human spirit does not reincarnate, but a
    spiritual entity serving as a human spirit could reincarnate. This is likely to apply similarly for other, but not all, living things.   109-10, 220, 347-8

the spirits of some living things, for example
    monarch butterflies, appear to continue on from one generation to the next   169, 229-232, 348-9

Religions, religious models
    the model presented in this book is inclusive of
        all religions, although Chapter One might lead some readers to mistakenly think it is not

inclusive of any religions
157
the role of religion regarding our
choice of basis
for carrying out our lives
461-2

Remote viewing
In general 367-8
learning remote viewing could be
more difficult
than learning other
extrasensory abilities 352
spiritual senses and remote
viewing 459

Responsibility
we are responsible for how our
species is
evolving. Humans can get
caught in situations that sap
their energy and thus their
spirits could stop advancing.
The fact that humans keep
repeating the same mistakes
for thousands of years could
mean humans are stuck in
such a situation without being
aware of it. In addition, our
ongoing technical
advancements could make us
think we are advancing
because they are satisfying
our dominant basis for how
we are carrying out our lives
when in fact we are hardly
spiritually advancing 404-6

Restore, restoration, restoring, restored, see **"Heal, restore"** and **"Sleep"**
according the model sleep is for
restoration of
the body. However,
restoration could also take
place while awake by, for
example, being in a quiet
place and meditating etc.
310-1
getting more in touch with the
spirit world's
restoring and healing powers
376-80

Retracing evolutionary paths vs. Evolution
are some fossils evidences of
retracing or
evidences of evolution? 73-7
humans might have emerged on
Earth through
retracing instead of through
evolution. Thus, humans
could be perceived as having
been suddenly created 86-7
missing links can be missing
because retracing
took place instead of
evolution. Retracing could
happen very rapidly such that
sudden creation could be
perceived. This could be the
case for humans 73, 75, 86-7
retracing an evolutionary path
396-8

rapid evolution of some living things could be a
> form of retracing. Retracing is a process of rapid emergence of living things that has have already evolved on some past universe. Retracing is thus a rapid retracing of an evolutionary process that already taken place. Retracing could allow insufficient time to leave behind fossils behind, and thus, we would have missing links. This could apply to numerous living things besides us humans, in particular very intelligent living things such as elephants, dolphins, whales, octopi, etc. 86-7

species with missing links are common and this
> could indicate retracing occurred instead of evolution for those species 74-7

sudden creation through retracing an
> evolutionary path (as opposed to gradual evolution on a new path) 72-3, 75, 86-7

Roles
> the invention of languages might have partly
>> initiated the ability to do abstract thinking 270-1

> the roles of various living things on Earth are
>> different from their purposes for being here on Earth. Purposes are fixed while roles are usually multiple and can change with time as conditions change. For example, a major role of humans in the past was being the developer of agriculture. Now a major role is being the developer of high- technology (for better or for worse). Meanwhile the purpose of humans stays the same. A difference is humans can choose their roles while most other living things cannot or can do so only in a very limited way 264

> the various roles a person can take depending on
>> the situation and environment 248-9

Rover, Mars, see **"Mars,** Mars Rover"

Rhythms and beauty 283-4

S
Safety margin 26, 165, 186-7

Satellite 42, 395,

Science and spirituality
science and spirituality already go together
116-21

Scientist 25-6, 63-4, 69, 114, 121, 278, 283, 324, 455

Scratch, scratching
a bad itch 254, 283, 355, 416,
a hang-up 254-5, 259, 283, 354-5, 366, 390, 405, 415, 434, 457,

Self respect vs. self esteem
Self respect is better than self esteem. Self respect is earned whereas self esteem tends to be given. Criminals could have high self esteem, and that is why they have the nerve to do what they do. Sometimes people speak of having self esteem when what they really mean is self respect 240

Sense, sensing
Earth's magnetic field 76, 191, 210-1, 261,
earthquakes 20, 191, 204, 206, 210, 315, 358, 369,

Senses
different living things have different sets and acuity of major senses and most likely also different sets and acuity of spiritual senses. Consciousness is associated with the senses. Therefore different living things have different kinds and levels of consciousness. That is also why various species could sense different things, some of which humans do not sense 204, 210, 261-4, 267-8, 423
during sleep 301-2
elemental 48, 112, 266, 268,
examples of some species possibly knowing
what they sense in the spirit world is in the spirit world and what they sense in our physical world is in our physical world. This means we could learn more about the spirit world with the help of such species of living things, which includes dogs and cats 263-4
living things 265-8
major senses, see **"Major senses"**
nonliving things 265-8
spiritual, see **"Spiritual senses"**
the fact that other creatures have major senses
that we humans do not have also indicates that spiritual senses exist in the spirit world other than the ones that give us our major senses. This also indicates the spirit world exists 447
the spirit is where consciousness, intelligence,

senses, feelings, emotions, empathy, compassion, ego, reasoning ability, imagination, creativity, etc. reside. Different living things have different ones and degrees of such attributes 59-60, 133-5, 140, 227, 271, 295, 300-1

Sheldrake, Rupert 206, 209-11, 260, 368-9

Short-term thinking, short-range thinking
in general 243-4, 410, 429-30, 465
being interested is more of a long-term long-
range thing whereas being excited is more of a short-term short-range thing 462
the nation's economy is like a huge ship at sea;
i.e., it takes a while to change directions after action is made to have it do so. Therefore, when the person who is the president of our nation is changed every four or eight years the wrong person often gets the credit for a good economy or the blame for a bad economy. This tends to contribute to the mess we are making in our nation if not in the entire world. Basically it is because we humans tend to think short-term short-range instead of lone-term long-range. We need to be more aware we tend to think this way and of the problems it causes 429-30
we need to think long-term long-range in order
to have a better future but meanwhile we also need to think short-term short-range in order to survive the present and near future. This is an example of how establishing reasonable balance would mean forming good wisdom 465

Signal, signals
collection of 127
combination of 55, 88, 127
distorted spiritual 137,
electrical 60, 191, 261, 268, 275, 277, 301, 395,
    439
exchange of 55, 60, 303,
feedback 55, 60, 105, 136-7, 268-9, 275, 279,
    301-2, 304, 306, 312-3, 321, 360, 371,
instinctive 190, 203-8, 212, 215, 238, 274, 292,
    298, 370, 395
intuitive 66, 190, 192, 204-5, 207-8, 215, 236-
    8, 256, 292, 298, 311, 370, 395, 421, 442,
knowledge base's 42,
measurable brain's 361

new   279
physical   60, 136-7, 166, 185, 202, 268, 274,
   300-2, 310, 363-4, 443, 445
restoring, restoration   301, 303-4
specialized   227
spiritual, see **"Spiritual,** signals"
subconscious   107

Sister
   in general   20, 29-33, 107-8, 209, 472
   one of my sisters knew, perhaps by some form of
      telepathy, one of her daughters got badly injured the moment it occurred even through she and her daughter were hundreds of miles apart   209

Situation, situations
   bad   373, 405
   unfamiliar   271
   win-win   149, 190, 193-5, 260, 371. 408, 423,
      457
   win-lose   149, 190, 194-6, 199, 408, 457
   lose-lose   457

**Size of spirit, brain, features, universe, spiritual
entities, living things, etc.**
   a loose limit appears to exist as to how big or
      small plants can grow   223

finches can have long bills or short bills
   depending on their food supply, as observed by Darwin   79
models come in different sizes   121
spiritual entities come in all possible sizes   396
spoons come in various sizes   249
the larger the variety and range of mental states
   possible the larger would be the spirit and brain   278
the size and complexity of the brain depend on
   the range and precision of the activities the body is designed by the spirit world to be capable of doing and are not dependent on the intelligence of the living thing   275-9
the size and complexity of the spirit are directly
   associated with the level of intelligence and consciousness of the living thing   275-9
the size of a feature on a living thing increases
   or decreases depending on how much it is used or not used   346
the size of a spiritual entity serving as a spirit
   increases during its time of serving   345

the size of the spirit and the size of the brain are
    not proportional with each other   275-9
the spirit world's constant increasing size could
    be used by the spirit world as a measure of passage of time   50
the size of our universe might be increasing at an
    accelerating rate   181
the size of the tool needs to match the size of the
    task   448
the sizes of things in our dreams could be
    different from their actual sizes   303
the spirit of the brain of a bacterium is likely to
    be larger than might be suggested by the bacterium's physical makeup   277

Sleep
being asleep vs. being awake, see **"Awake"**
being unconscious is different from being asleep
    312-3
do all living things on Earth need sleep?   308-9
finding things in, and getting messages from, the
    spirit world during sleep   313-6
four non-REM stages of sleep plus one stage of
    REM sleep per cycle   310
healing and restoration during sleep or while
    unconscious   298-313
some things, particularly some with short life
    spans, appear to not need sleep   308-9
stages of sleep   305, 310
sleep cycles might have evolved for humans
    because humans constantly do not get enough sleep to allow complete restoration of the body. An interesting question, do other living things have sleep cycles?   310
sleep cycles, restoring the body one part at a time
    in the order of their priorities   309-13
sleep, dreams, healing, etc.   298-322
the common belief that sleep is for processing
    into memory what is learned while awake. However, the model instead indicates sleep is to restore the body and that processing into memory is only a byproduct   307, 311
the model plausibly explains why a good night's
    sleep improves memory   307-8

the more complex the living thing
intellectually,
  consciously, and structurally
  the more likely it is to need
  sleep 308-9
why our brain is active during
sleep, but our
  frontal cortex is not? 309-13
why we need sleep 298-313
why we sleep and dream, and why
dreams are
  surrealistic? 298-308

Smith, Rev. Tommy E. Jr. 324, 458

Son 32, 355

Soul, souls
  defining what is a soul 55-60
  souls of species of living things,
  see **"Spirits,**
    spirits and souls of species of
  living things"
  the soul of a living or nonliving
  thing consists of
    all the connections of the
    second kind that connect the
    spirit of a living or nonliving
    thing to the living or
    nonliving thing residing in a
    universe 55-60
  what is embodied in the soul of
  our universe is
    what we are trying to capture
    with our countless models
    117

Space station 76

Spaceship 62, 64, 339,

Space travel
  did the spirit world intended for us
  humans to do
    space travel to other planets
    and/or universe travel to other
    universes? If so, then is it
    possible what is spiritually
    holding us up is our tendency
    to do battle with others of our
    own race that are different
    from us? I.e., we need to first
    develop the skills of getting
    along with others of our own
    race who different from us
    here on Earth before we are
    able to develop the skills of
    space and/or universe travel
    where we will need to
    peacefully interact with
    intelligent living things not of
    our species 374-5
  unconventional ways to do space
  travel such as
    teleportation and doing it by
    going through the spirit world
    374
  when we do space and/or universe
  travel,
    intelligent living things we
    meet are bound to have
    abilities we do not have, and
    vice versa. Therefore, we
    might perceive them as being
    more advanced than we, and
    they might perceive us as

being more advanced than
they. This means it is best to
interact with them as equals
374-5

Specialized cells 227-8

Species
why there are such an enormous
number of
species of living things on
Earth 131

Spirit, spirits
a spirit has a degree of autonomy
and
independence from the
spiritual entity of which it is a
part 158-9
a spiritual entity that is serving as
the spirit for
a human could serve as the
spirit for other living things at
other times, and a different
portion of it would be active
during those times. In a sense
we could say that such other
living things are sort of
human and could certainly
contribute indirectly to the
evolution of humans, and vice
versa 449
defining what is a spirit 55-60
DNA molecules are building
materials for living
Things. Therefore, their spirit
could enable multiple copies
of them to exist 124

our spirit has the freedom to
choose and thus
also the freedom to improve
as well as to do other things
445
our spirit pilots our body mainly
by going
through our soul and brain
and in many situations by
communicating directly with
our body 60, 89, 100, 105,
136-7,
202, 269, 274-5, 301-6, 309,
320-1, 324, 396-7, 441-2,
445, 451, 472, 476
our spirit would recognize the bad
bacteria as
foreign and would work to
eliminate it 240
"supply and demand" and the
availability of
spirits for living and nonliving
things 285-7
the fact that the recipient of an
organ in an organ
transplant situation can
sometimes take on attributes
of the donor would further
indicate consciousness and
intelligence reside in the spirit
and not in the brain 140
the human spirit can be envisioned
as having
four kinds of pieces of
knowledge 128
the size of the spirit and the size of
the brain are

not proportional with each other   275-9
the spirit and soul of a living or nonliving thing
    together would embody a record of every experience the thing as gone through up to that point in time   103
the spirit is where consciousness, intelligence,
    senses, feelings, emotions, empathy, compassion, ego, reasoning ability, imagination, creativity, etc. reside. Different living things have different ones and degrees of such attributes   59-60, 133-5, 140, 227, 271, 295, 300-1
the spirit knows how to enable a living thing to
    exist in a universe. Therefore, if the living thing gets tired, injured, or ill, the same knowledge the spirit has to enable the living thing exist will also knows how to restore the living thing's health   204-5, 226-7, 279, 299-300, 316, 323, 376
the process of evolution is a process of
    generating and/or gaining pieces of knowledge and adding them to the spirit, and therefore also to the spiritual entity serving as the spirit, of the living thing. Thus, if a bird evolved from a dinosaur, it must take a larger spiritual entity serving as the spirit to enable the bird to exist than it does to enable the dinosaur to exist even thought the bird is much smaller physically. This also sets up the possibility for the spiritual entity to enable new species of living things to exist when conditions are appropriate for this to happen   57-8
when our body gets tired, injured, or ill, it
    communicates with our spirit through our soul, and our spirit issues signals to our body to help it heal. The signals would, for example, have us rest, go to bed, go to sleep, be in a coma if badly injured, etc. Our spirit never gets tired, injured, or ill. But, our body does, and it has a limited lifespan   134-5, 226-7, 279, 299-300, 302, 312-3, 376
why a newly born individual would not
    automatically know what the parents already know, but could have an easier time learning what the parents know   90
why does the spirit of a living thing needs a
    spiritual entity to serve as the spirit? It is because all the

advancements achieved by the predecessors are embodied in the spiritual entity and are not to be automatically a part of the spirit. The spirit needs to go through experiences to gain access to the pieces of knowledge that are the advancements. The spirit world purposely made things work this way as a way of enabling itself to grow and to maintain its own viability, It also enables the issues associated with the living thing and current times to be addressed and be brought up to date and relevant with the current times   87-90

with an ever increasing human population, can

    the spirit world ever run out human spirits to enable more humans to emerge?   285

Spirit size vs. brain size

    the larger and the more complex is the spirit

        (knowledge base) for a given species of living thing the more intelligent and/or consciousness would be the species. The more dexterous and the more precise in the ability of the body of the species to do things the larger and more complex would be the brain to handle the body's range of abilities. Thus, the size of the spirit and the size of the brain are not necessarily proportional with each other   45, 275-7

Spirit-soul-body

    interactions among spirit, soul, and body   133-41

    human spirit and soul   105-9, 222, 226

    of creatures other than humans   224

    of single cells that make up living things   226

    Spirit-soul-body communication process   300-1

Spirit types and configurations

    animals, birds, and retiles in general   219-20, 234-5

    colonies   232-4, 423

    colonies of cells making up the bodies of living

        things   226-9, 232

    colonies of cells are not the same as colonies of

        insects. Cells can have stem cells while insects cannot have stem members   226-9, 232

    colonies of insects   232-4

    creatures other than humans   23

    each living thing has a certain combination of the

various spirit types, and each spirit type is on a gradation ranging from strong to mild. A highly intelligent living thing will have a larger combination and a wider gradation for each spirit type, and the living thing could choose where on each gradation it wants to be depending on the situation it is in   250, 423-4
every spirit is a mixture of types   242-55
human   216, 219-22, 250
identical twins and conjoined twins   234-5
"in-between" things   222, 235-7
insects in general   219-20
living things that harm their hosts   229, 238-42
monarch butterflies, salmon, cicadas, etc.   219-32
nonliving things   55-6, 59, 101-5, 112-3, 265
plants, fungi, algae, molds, lichens, mosses,
   single cells   222-4
single cells that make up living things   226-9, 232
spirit types of high-tech devices built by
   humans   216, 234-5
stem cells   234
things that are between living and nonliving such as viruses and prions   46, 222-4
the spirit of a typical individual will encompass
   multiple spirit types. Which one(s) would dominate depends on the situation and the values and experiences of the individual. Examples are presented on pages   249-251
the various spirit types and configurations   215-41
tug-of-wars among the spirit types that a
   person's spirit can take will depend on the situation and environment   249-51

Spirit world
a disconnection between the intended and the
   actual   411
a natural partnership is automatically formed
   between the spirit world and every living thing it creates   157-9
a possible reason Earth has such a diversity of
   living things is the spirit world creates everything it could at any point in time with the knowledge it has at the time   21
according to the model, because the spirit world

Index 601

is continuously growing, and thus evolution is a continuous progress, every universe when brought into being might be done gradually and continuously as opposed to suddenly as would be the case if the Big Bang theory applies. This could explain why our universe is expanding, and at an accelerating rate at that. For example, see **"Big Ooze theory"** 181

according to the model, the spirit world has two
    stages of growth, similar to how humans and various other living things on Earth have; i.e., an infancy vulnerable stage and a self-sustaining stage. The model also suggests the reason living things have these two stages is because the spirit world has these two stages and would thus design living things to have these two stages. A difference is living things have a finite lifetime and thus have also a final geriatric stage that the spirit world could, but not necessarily, have. The spirit world would have a geriatric stage if it fails to keep its state of knowledge reasonably balanced and thus becomes unable to form wisdom. Page 333 explains how this works 151-5, 333

advancement and increasing complexity in the
    spirit world 387-8

any model or statement reasonably formulated
    would be correct but also incomplete. The incompleteness cannot be avoided because we humans are imperfect. We are imperfect because the spirit world is imperfect. Therefore, we must not let ourselves be completely sold by the correctness, but rather we must always be aware of the incompleteness 25, 121, 155, 172, 447, 456

broadening our view of the spirit world 421-4

Chapter One might lead one to think the model
    rejects the concepts of God and is thus separate from religions, but as the model develops in Chapter Three, it becomes clear it is inclusive of all concepts of God and all religions 21, 156-7

did the spirit world have a beginning? If so, how
    it might have begun? 53-5

everything from subatomic particles to a

complete living thing has a vital role for the spirit world 417-8
evolution is a natural process that takes place in
  the spirit world, because the spirit world keeps growing and keeps becoming more advanced. In the case of our particular universe the process manifests itself physically as well as non-physically 180-2
forgiveness in the spirit world, it's automatic
  178-9
getting more in touch with the spirit world's
  restoring and healing powers 376-80
how the spirit world came into being 328-37
implications of how the spirit world came into
  being 337-42
is it crowed in the spirit world with so many
  spirits and more are constantly being created? 288-90
issues created by the spirit world while caring for
  every living thing it creates 417-21
knowledge is the source of the spirit world's
  creative ability 47
living life for the spirit world vs. for our physical

world. It makes a difference because the oneness that makes everything a part of everything else exists in the spirit world. In particular the spirit of every human is a part of spirit of every other human, whereas humans are physically separate individuals in our physical world 141, 385
one of the reasons we humans get in conflicts
  and battles is because when we generate pieces of knowledge we do not know how to generate opposing pieces of knowledge such that better balance in our total knowledge would be achieved. We can't do that because our intelligence is limited. Other living things on Earth are less intelligent than humans and they do an even worse job of balancing the pieces of knowledge they generate. Similar conditions are likely to exit in other universes and that is how the state of knowledge in the spirit world could go out of balance. The spirit world could do a much better job of generating pieces of knowledge that are balanced because its intelligence is unlimited, although not

necessarily complete. This enables it to know it needs to constantly monitor its state of knowledge and to do something, such as design and bring into being new universes periodically, to help restore reasonable balance in its state of knowledge   334
possible beginning of the spirit world   52-4, 328-342,
since humans are all a part of each other in the
   spirit world, it doesn't make sense to make war in our physical world   290, 385
some creatures are more tuned to the spirit world
   than we are and thus we could learn something about the spirit world through them   265
tapping into the oneness that pervades the spirit
   world   393-4
the collection of all pieces of knowledge that
   exists at any given point in time makes up the spirit world at that point in time   47-8
the fact that other creatures have major senses
   that we humans do not have also indicates that spiritual senses exist in the spirit world other than the ones that give us our major senses. This also indicates the spirit world exists   447
the largest spiritual entity that exists at any given
   point in time is the spirit world at that point in time   47-8
the more a living thing is able to think for itself
   the more complex would be its purpose for being here. The more a living thing relies on the spirit world to think for it the simpler would be its purpose for being here. And if the spirit world does essentially all the thinking for a species, fulfilling the purpose would become essentially automatic   250-1
the spirit world brings into being new universes
   as necessary to help restore its state of knowledge into reasonable balance   157, 180
the spirit world could be nowhere in our physical
   world and yet be everywhere in our physical world   256
the spirit world could never be perfect because it
   could never possess every piece of knowledge that could be generated. There is no limit to the number of pieces of knowledge that could be generated. This means nothing that is created by the

spirit world could ever be perfect. Everything that exists in the spirit world or in any universe is created by the spirit world; therefore, nothing is ever perfect   49, 66, 119

the spirit world creates everything, and
   everything it creates is imperfect because the spirit world is imperfect   22, 64-70, 151, 156

the spirit world (creator) must be a living thing,
   (growing in some manner such as constantly learning) in order to create living things   41

the spirit world has an everlasting desire to learn
   (to generate new pieces of knowledge) and to create (to form spiritual entities with the pieces of knowledge that exist at any given moment)   155-6

the spirit world is constantly growing and
   changing as new pieces of knowledge are constantly generated. The nature of the growth and change depend on the nature of the experiences living and nonliving things go through. Thus, we humans could influence the nature of the growth and our relationship with the spirit world more than any other living thing on Earth. It is a responsibility we need to become more aware of   50

the spirit world is a forever growing and
   changing spiritual entity   22

the spirit world is likely to have vanished and
   emerged again multiple times, according to the model, and if we do not do our part to care for the spirit world it could vanish again along with everything it has created   54, 66, 135, 151, 153, 157, 258, 296, 330, 400, 457

the spirit world must keep its state of knowledge
   reasonably balanced to be able to form wisdom. Our most important purpose is to help keep the spirit world's state of knowledge reasonably balanced. If reasonable balanced is not maintained, the spirit world could vanish along with everything it created   151-5, 157, 258

the spirit world's creative ability and power
   increase exponentially starting from scratch as pieces of knowledge are generated   49

the spirit world's everlasting desire to learn and
   to create   155-6

the spirit world's restoring and healing powers 376

the reason we understand a lot more about our
   physical world than we do about the spirit world is because we formulated a lot of models that pertain to our physical world and relatively few that pertain to the spirit world. To understand the spirit world better, we need to formulate more models that pertain to the spirit world 385

thoughts from the spirit world 292-8

we do our thinking and decision making in the
   spirit world and we carry them out in our physical world 411

we formulate models to help us understand in an
   approximate manner how to do what the spirit world does 120

Spiritual
   a spiritual reason why living and nonliving
      things generally get more complex and advanced with each new generation or redesign 47
   elemental senses 267
   energies 88

guidance 27, 194, 201-3, 408-9

models 21, 23, 25-7, 39-41, 48, 74, 116, 136,
   167, 194, 219, 253, 272, 337, 385, 406, 422-3, 441-3, 447, 456, 460-2, 475, 477-8

personal spiritual search 20-1, 25, 27, 160, 456,
   461, 477-8

signals 60, 88, 136-7, 166, 185, 202, 227, 268,
   274-5, 277, 300-2, 307, 310, 312, 322, 345, 363-4, 366, 371, 395, 443-6

spiritual entities that reincarnates piecemeal
   110, 349

spiritual entities that could serve as spirits for
   living things 143, 156, 286,

messages 66, 167, 314-5, 437

the number of spiritual entities in the spirit world
   more than double with every new piece of knowledge generated 131

the spiritual part of models and of life 98, 236,
   271, 278, 395, 439, 441-2, 445-7, 449, 451-3, 455-7, 463, 465, 468, 475

Spiritual advancement
   conventional thinking and technical
      advancements have not help us clean up the mess we made on Earth for thousands of

years. It is time to try some
unconventional thinking plus
a large measure of spiritual
advancements   466-7, 471
if we find ourselves losing touch
with our
    feelings, intentions, attitudes,
emotions, intuitions, instincts,
creativity, imagination,
empathy, compassion, etc.
this could mean we are overly
immersed in the physical part
of life and not enough in the
spiritual part of life   271
increasing world population, now
at seven
    billion, and technical
advancements without
matching spiritual
advancements can worsen the
mess we are making on Earth
463-6
our advancements of any kind
whether technical
    or spiritual are greater when
the experiences involved are
more different from ones that
we have been through. The
model explains how this is the
case in spiritual terms. This
could explain how it is that
we humans can advance faster
technically once we started
advancing technically,
because our technical
advancements enable us to
invent or create experiences
very different from ones we
have been through before.
This suggests that we might
be able to advance spiritually
rather quickly by a similar
process once we figure out
how to get started, and even
more importantly how to free
ourselves from what it is that
is confining us from doing so
85-6
our spiritual advancement is
lagging far behind
    our technical (i.e., physical)
advancement. That is the
main reason we have so many
people-to-people conflicts of
all kinds   245, 471
spiritual advancements takes place
in the spirit
    world and has to do with the
behavior and abilities of
living things. In the case of
living things on Earth, it is the
increase ability to be more
empathetic, compassionate,
creative, imaginative,
intuitive, instinctive, capable
of abstract thinking, etc.
394-5
technical advancements progress
in spurts in our
    physical universe and most
likely also in other universes.
Humans advance in spurts
from one generation to the
next. Technical advancements
progress in spurts from one
generation of devices to the

next. Spiritual advancements
(pertaining to human
behavior) on the other hand
progress gradually   90-3
the mess we made on Earth for
thousands of
years might have less to do
with the various forms of
government around the world
and more to do with a lack of
spiritual advancements among
mankind   465

Spiritual attributes of living things
the spirit is where consciousness,
intelligence,
senses, feelings, emotions,
empathy, compassion, ego,
reasoning ability, imagination,
creativity, etc. reside.
Different living things have
different ones and degrees of
such attributes   59-60, 133-5,
140, 227, 271, 295, 300-1

Spiritual entities
a spiritual entity consists of two or
more pieces
of knowledge with each piece
having a connection of the
first kind with every other
piece of knowledge that is
part of the spiritual entity   48
a spiritual entity is neither good
nor bad, but
when translated into
something that could exist or
be expressed in a universe the
translated form could be
perceived as good, bad, or
neutral depending on the
universe and the situation
325-8
a spiritual entity that is serving as
the spirit for
a human could serve as the
spirit for other living things at
other times, and a different
portion of it would be active
during those times. In a sense
we could say that such other
living things are sort of
human and could certainly
contribute indirectly to the
evolution of humans, and vice
versa   449
anything that exists, or can be
expressed, in our
universe or in any other
universe has a spiritual
entities in the spirit world to
enable it to do so   292
defining what is a spiritual entity
55-60
elemental spiritual entities no
matter how small
must have some amount of
intelligence and
consciousness. That's
because every piece of
knowledge comes with its bit
of intelligence and
consciousness, and that is
why every existing piece of
knowledge forms a
connection of the first kind

with every other existing piece of knowledge. A spiritual entity no matter how small is made of pieces of knowledge and thus must have some amount of intelligence and consciousness. This in turn explains why elemental things in our universe have some amount of intelligence and consciousness 333

everything in the spirit world is in the form of a
- spiritual entity, even the spirit world itself is a spiritual entity; i.e., the largest one possible at any given point in time 47-8

once a spiritual entity is formed it exists forever
- as part of the spirit world 325

since every existing piece of knowledge is
- connected with every other existing piece of knowledge, how can one spiritual entity be distinguished from another? By analogy each spiritual entity is a unique combination of pieces of knowledge just as each sentence is a unique combination of words. Thus a spiritual entity could be recognized in a manner analogous to how a sentence is recognized 87-90

spiritual entities serving as human spirits are
- very large compared with those serving as spirits of other living things on Earth. Thus, their signals are strong and unlikely to be completely drown out by signals from our physical world. This enables us humans to do essentially all of our thinking for ourselves 201-2

the largest spiritual entity that exists at any given
- point in time is the spirit world at that point in time 47-8

the number of spiritual entities more than
- doubles with every new piece of knowledge generated and added to the spirit world. This means the creative power of the spirit world increases exponentially accordingly. Therefore, starting from scratch it would not take long for the spirit world to be able to create a universe 131

the process of evolution is a process of
- generating and/or gaining pieces of knowledge and adding them to the spirit, and therefore also to the spiritual entity serving as the spirit, of

the living thing. Thus, if a
bird evolved from a dinosaur,
it must take a larger spiritual
entity serving as the spirit to
enable the bird to exist than it
does to enable the dinosaur to
exist even thought the bird is
much smaller physically.
This also sets up the
possibility for the spiritual
entity to enable new species
of living things to exist when
conditions are appropriate for
this to happen 57-8
what is a piece of knowledge and
what is a
   spiritual entity? We can work
with both without knowing
exactly what they are just as
we can work with a "letter"
and a "word" without
knowing exactly what they
are 325-8
why does the spirit of a living
thing needs a
   spiritual entity to serve as the
spirit? It is because all the
advancements achieved by the
predecessors are embodied in
the spiritual entity and are not
to be automatically a part of
the spirit. The spirit needs to
go through experiences to
gain access to the pieces of
knowledge that are the
advancements. The spirit
world purposely made things
work this way as a way of
enabling itself to grow and to
maintain its own viability. It
also enables the issues
associated with the living
thing and current times to be
addressed and be brought up
to date and relevant with the
current times 87-90

Spiritual expressions
a spiritual expression of a formerly
living thing
   is everything the living thing
was, minus the part that used
to reside in a universe 105-9
according to the model a possible
source of
   instincts is the interactions
between
   one's spiritual expression
with other spiritual
expressions in the spirit world
105-9, 205-7
after a person dies his or her
spiritual expression
   would normally reside
completely in the spirit world,
but it doesn't have to. It could
remain for a while partly in
the world of the universe in
which the person resided 107
defining what is a spiritual
expression? 105-9
interactions among spiritual
expressions of still
   living persons with those of
deceased persons 107-8

spiritual expressions in general 134, 166,
    193-4, 205, 220-1, 231, 289-90, 319-22, 347, 351-2, 362-3, 365-6, 401, 450
the spiritual expression of a living person or
    deceased person   105-9, 352
spiritual entities capable of serving as spirits of
    living things would do so progressively starting first to serve as spirits of primitive living things and then working its way up to increasingly advanced living things to eventually be able to serve as spirits for highly intelligent living things such as humans. It is a matter of learning how to pilot the bodies of progressively advanced living things, analogous to a beginning pilot of airplanes starting out by piloting small airplanes and eventually becoming able to pilot giant airliners. Thus, the notion that humans and other living things originated from primitive living things is likely to be true according to the model   397-8
the spiritual expression of a deceased person can
    choose to appear as he or she was at any age during his or her life on Earth   321-2

Spiritual images
    spiritual images superimpose onto physical
        images   281

Spiritual messages, instructions, and signals
    a collection of nonliving atoms follows spiritual
        instructions to form DNA molecules that then follows spiritual instructions to form living things   46
    certain living things seem more able to sense
        certain spiritual messages than humans can. For example some animals can sense an earthquake is about to happen, bird can sense a storm is about to strike, etc.   315
    DNA molecules are tuned into spiritual signals
        on how to heal and/or restore a tired, injured, or diseased living thing   299
    everything is on a gradation between living and
        nonliving. Where do DNA molecules fall on this gradation when they can reproduce themselves as a living thing could do but yet they need spiritual instructions to form living things? Thus, they are not

absolutely living or absolutely
nonliving   46
spiritual guidance messages
include instincts and
intuition   201
we sometimes could sense
spiritual messages
better during sleep than while
awake   314-5

Spiritual model, see also **"Personal spiritual**
model"
every model we use in our
physical world is a
spiritual model of some kind
447-50
why finding our personal spiritual
model could
make us a better person   422-3

Spiritual search
our personal spiritual search for
our personal
spiritual model never really
ends. Our personal spiritual
model will continuously
evolve as situations change,
as we age, and as our spiritual
needs change with age and
time   456

Spiritual senses
animals seem to be more in touch
with their
spiritual senses than we
humans are with ours   210-1

certain spiritual senses are
extended into our
physical world to give us and
other living things our and
their major senses   261, 264, 268
different living things have
different sets and
acuity of major senses and
most likely also different sets
and acuity of spiritual senses.
Consciousness is associated
with the senses. Therefore
different living things have
different kinds and levels of
consciousness. That is also
why various species could
sense different things, some
of which humans do not sense
204, 210-1, 261-4
examples of some species possibly
knowing
what they sense in the spirit
world is in the spirit world
and what they sense in our
physical world is in our
physical world   263-4
examples of various animals and
birds following
their instincts to leave shortly
before an earthquake or storm
strikes are given by Rupert
Sheldrake in his book   112, 210
spiritual senses and consciousness
369-70
spiritual senses and major senses
261-6

spiritual senses are what we use to find or sense
    things in the spirit world such as thoughts, concepts, instincts, intuition, intentions, designs, wisdom, etc.   261-7
the model indicates we have not reached the
    limit of how well we could be in touch with our spiritual senses and thus how much more conscious we could be   459
the more spiritual senses and the more acute the
    spiritual sense, the more consciousness a living thing has   261-7
the fact that other creatures have major senses
    that we humans do not have also indicates that spiritual senses exist in the spirit world other than the ones that give us our major senses. This also indicates the spirit world exists   447
we are capable of being more in touch with our
    spiritual senses   458-60

Spiritual thoughts
    spiritual thought-like signals enable things to
        exist   292-9

Spirituality

according to the model some of our models
    would be more complete if spirituality were taken more into consideration in their formulations   118-9, 447
spirituality is such an enormous subject, no
    model formulated by humans could cover it completely. Therefore, countless reasonably formulated spiritual models, including personal spiritual models, will exist, all of them would be correct but none would be complete   385, 456
we humans long ago might have been able to
    communicate telepathically because we used to develop a lot of developed oneness and a high level of closeness. We might now be feeling the loss, and this is a reason we are searching for our spirituality   210
why do some things fail, not function well, or
    not liked? The reason is in the incompleteness (e.g., lacking in spirituality considerations) and/or incompatibilities of the models used in their design   118-9

Spirituality and science

science and spirituality already go together
    116-21
the spiritual part of models might help explain
    some unexplained things 452-6

Spoken language 49, 97-8, 185, 187, 189-90, 270, 368-9

Standard model of physics 63

Stars, planets, galaxies, black holes, etc. 49, 61-2, 70, 72, 75-6, 94-5, 124-5, 165-6, 181-2, 190-2, 200, 215, 218-0, 262, 281-2, 284-6, 289, 341-2, 347, 359-60, 370, 375, 401-4, 418-9, 426-9, 454-5, 459

Statue, statues
the spiritual powers of statues 382

Stem cell, stem cells
stem cells 227
stem cell spirit, cancer stem cell, and cancer
    stem cell spirit 228-9, 328

Stepping out of our body and into another body 324-5

Strange events Chapter Two

Subatomic particles, see "Atom, atomic, subatomic"

Sudden creation
sudden creation through retracing an
    evolutionary path (as opposed to gradual evolution on a new path) 72-3, 75, 86-7

Superman 70

Surrealistic
our dreams might include images with more than
    three-dimensions and/or dimensions different for the three we are use to and this could explain why our dreams tend to be surrealistic 317

Survivability 26, 96, 101, 143, 145, 163-4, 178, 186, 193, 196, 199, 221, 265, 273, 291, 341, 390-1, 393, 403, 406-7, 411, 415-6, 420-1, 426, 464-6

Symbiotic relationships between members of different species
possibly began with developed oneness that
    continued developing generation after generation, and all of it eventually turned into inherited oneness 198

T

Technical advancements
  advancements progress in spurts in our physical
    universe and most likely also in other universes. Humans advance in spurts from one generation to the next. Technical advancements progress in spurts from one generation of devices to the next. However, spiritual advancements (pertain to human behavior) progress gradually   90-3
  conventional thinking and technical
    advancements have not help us clean up the mess we made on Earth for thousands of years. It is time to try some unconventional thinking and certainly a large measure of spiritual advancements   466-7, 471
  increasing world population, now at seven
    billion, and technical advancements without matching spiritual advancements can worsen the mess we are making on Earth   463-6
  our advancements of any kind whether technical
    or spiritual are greater when the experiences involved are more different from ones that we have been through. The model explains how this is the case in spiritual terms. This could explain how it is that we humans can advance faster technically once we started advancing technically, because our technical advancements enable us to invent or create experiences very different from ones we have been through before. This suggests that we might be able to advance spiritually rather quickly by a similar process once we figure out how to get started, and even more importantly how to free ourselves from what it is that is confining us from doing so   85-6
  our technical advancements make us think we
    are meeting our responsibility for how our species is evolving when in fact we are not. Our spiritual advancements lag far behind, and they count more in determining how our species is evolving   We need to change the dominant basis for how we are carrying out our lives   405-6, 411

Telepathy
  a transplant recipient borrows oneness from the

Index 615

donor and thus could receive telepathic message from the donor 213-5
apparently we humans long ago had the ability to
    communicate telepathically, at least among members of close-knit groups 210, 368
author Rupert Sheldrake gives examples of
    telepathic communication in this book 206, 210, 368-9
certain groups of people currently have some
    level of telepathic communication ability. It is possible they were very wise to retain that ability if they had it from way back, or they are simply way ahead of the rest of us by being able to develop or regain the ability 185, 368-70
communicating through the oneness that
    pervades the spirit world. If we could tap into the oneness in the spirit world to communicate among each other telepathically we would have a better chance of developing the positive attributes of the spirit world 212, 214-5, 393-4
developed oneness between pet and owner
    leads to the pet being able to telepathically receive the owner's thoughts 207-8, 210
humans possibly had at one time a high level of
    developed oneness among each other and were able to telepathically communicate with each other 210, 370
identical twins have the highest level of inherited
    and developed oneness and thus many have some degree of telepathic ability between them 206, 212, 370
if other creatures on Earth are more able to
    communicate telepathically than humans could, the model provides a plausible reason why; i.e., they rely more on the spirit world to do their thinking for them than humans do 369-70
in general 24, 263, 315-6
instincts and intuition messages come to the
    spirit of a living thing telepathically in the form of pure thoughts devoid of any spoken language. That is why living things besides humans are able to have instincts and most likely also intuition 190, 205-6
it seems highly likely that humans are meant to

develop, or regain, an ability to communicate telepathically. In some cases and situations, certain individuals or groups of individual appear to have some degree of telepathic ability   185, 190, 209, 368-70
languages are filters in that they tend to distort
    thoughts when thoughts are express through a language   368-9
one of my sisters knew, perhaps by some form of
    telepathy, one of her daughters got badly injured the moment it occurred even through she and her daughter ere hundreds of miles apart   209
pure thoughts are not expressed in terms of any
    spoken language and could be immediately understood without any spoken language. Pure thought are transmitted by telepathy. This is how, for example, a pet could tune into its owner's thoughts   189-90
some creatures could communicate telepathically
    and thus we could learn something about such communications from them   265
some creatures could sense the precursors of
    earthquakes, floods, big storms, and other natural disasters perhaps by telepathy   206, 369
telepathy and brain disability: the spirit knows
    how to compensate for any disabilities including brain disability. Thus the model suggest a person with brain disability might have a better chance at learning how to communicate by telepathy   371
telepathy and oneness   205-10
telepathic communication works through the
    spirit world and are therefore independent of separating distances in our physical world   369
the model provides a plausible reason why we
    humans generally lost our ability to communicate telepathically as we evolved, and that we likely had the ability to do so before. It is also plausible that the spirit world's intends for us to regain the ability   206, 369-70
the purpose of us humans on Earth might be
    intentionally making the development or regaining of our ability to do telepathic communications difficult, and

that overcoming this difficulty
is one of the hurdles we must
learn to clear in order to fulfill
our purpose on Earth. Could
this be a reason why we
humans are constantly
seeking ways to enhance our
communications with each
other? Incidentally, we do
not always use our
enhancements in a positive
manner? Take for example
the way we use the Internet is
not always positive 206,
369-70
thoughts in pure form could be
transmitted
immediately by telepathy
regardless of their complexity
and are independent of spoken
language 189, 368-9
transplant recipients have
borrowed oneness
from the donor and thus
telepathic message from the
donor can be received by the
recipient 213-5
unintentional telepathic messages
from thoughts,
events, and situations 209
we all have experienced some
form of telepathic
communication since we all
have experienced instincts
and/or intuition. Instincts are
telepathically received from
the spiritual entity serving as
our spirit. Intuition is
telepathically received from
other spiritual entities, and
this would be very much like
telepathic communication
with other individuals 205-6,
215
we humans long ago might have
been able to
communicate telepathically
because we used to develop a
lot of developed oneness and
a high level of closeness. We
might now be feeling the lose
this oneness and closeness,
and therefore this is yet
another reason we are
searching for our spirituality
210
when I was a kid, one day my
mother and I were
working in the garden far
apart from each other, and it
was getting dark. I heard her
call me, so I went to her. She
was surprised and said she did
not call me but was thinking
she would like me to come to
her. That was a sweet
moment to recall decades later
209

The will to do something
the will and the decision to do
something
originate in the spirit and not
in the brain 42

Think, thinking

abstract   23, 270-1, 395, 450
long-term, long-range, see **"Long-term**
   thinking, long-range thinking"
short-term, short-range, see **Short-term**
   thinking, short-range thinking
we have many examples of how we tend to think
   short-term only to have long-term consequences in the future. The problem is that when we make decisions on a short enough time frame, everything can look OK when in fact things could be not OK in the long run   374

Thought, thoughts
   an author's thoughts enable things to exist in the
   world of his or her book. This is analogous to how the spirit world's thoughts enable things to exit in our physical world   113-6, 294, 430
our universe and everything in it exist because it
   is essentially the spirit world's thoughts that are enabling them to exist   113-6, 296
pure thoughts are not expressed in terms of any
   spoken language and could be immediately understood without any spoken language.

Pure thought are transmitted by telepathy. This is how, for example, a pet is able to tune into its owner's thoughts   189-90
spirit world's thoughts   113-6, 296
thoughts are among the most powerful spiritual
   entities   113-6
thoughts are pieces of knowledge connected
   together analogous to how sentences are words connected together   113-6
thoughts could be fragile and malleable, and that
   could be a positive or negative thing   297-8
thoughts from the spirit world   292-8
we do not create thoughts; we find them in the
   spirit world   113-6

Three major obstacles   145, 150, 163-4, 186-7, 199, 265, 421

Three dimensional
   our particular physical universe and vs. other
   universes   61-2, 68, 71, 88, 148, 182, 216, 280, 284, 293, 317, 345, 365, 385, 395, 449-50

Third house of Congress   411, 415, 417,

Time

how the passage of time could be monitored in
the spirit world 40, 50
how the passage of time is monitored on Earth
and why it is not the suitable for the spirit world 40

Time travel

projections into the future 372-4
time travel into the past 371-2

Tinkering by Mother Nature 77, 183, 246

Transplants

See **"Donor and recipient of an organ transplant"**
improvement in organ transplant procedures
113
instincts likely enable some transplant recipients
to develop traits of the donor 213-5

Traps

traps that could cause us to not fulfill our
purpose for being here 186-7, 199, 224,
429-30, 432, 457

Travel

mentally travel 337
time travel 371-2
travel into outer space 64, 95, 185, 192, 200,
262, 281-2, 341-2, 374, 403, 428
travel on Earth 246, 278, 306, 329, 463, 477
travel to other universes 115, 117, 133, 142,
148, 185, 280-1, 283, 315, 343, 374, 429, 450

Trees

grove of trees 169, 229-30, 232

Tug-of-wars

among spirit types 249-51
issues are essentially tug-of-wars in that they
have multiple opposing sides 153, 180-5, 249-51, 325
overuse of antibiotics can cause super-bugs to
develop due to the natural tug-of-wars in the spirit world 327-8, 339
some natural tug-of-wars humans participate in
have short-term and long-term effects that are at odds with each other. Part of it because the models we formulate are correct but incomplete and therefore do not account for all the factors involved 327
sometimes we want to stay awake when our

spirit says we need to sleep 304

Twins
identical twins have the highest level of inherited
and developed oneness and thus many have some degree of telepathic ability between them 206, 212, 370
some identical twins could feel the emotions of
the other twin 144

U

UFOs, unidentified flying objects
280-2, 338, 341-2, 375

Unconventional
approach and mindset to sense that life exist
after life 443-4
communications 393-4
forms of space travel and travel to other
universes 374-5
interpretation of brain waves 361
lifestyle 434-5, 466-8
necessarily unconventional lifestyles of
dyslexic individuals 435-6
notions and concepts 21, 23-5
thinking 25, 256-7, 272, 337, 406-9, 434-5,
460-2, 466-7, 478

spirits and souls of nonliving things 112

Unemployed, under-employed, homeless
the unemployed part of the spiritual entity
serving as a spirit of a living thing 102
the unemployed, under-employed, and/or
homeless part of the population includes many in the most potentially productive stage of their lives and they are willing but unable to contribute much to the strength and health of the country. This is an indication that the country is not as strong and healthy as we might think. The same can be said about the state of disrepair of our infrastructure 410, 412-3, 464

Universe
according to the model, every universe is
designed to have a finite lifetime 399-400
according to the model, because the spirit world
is continuously growing, and thus evolution is a continuous progress, every universe when brought into being might be done gradually and

continuously as opposed to suddenly as would be the case if the Big Bang theory applies. This could explain why our universe is expanding, and at an accelerating rate at that. For example, see **"Big Ooze theory"** 181

an issue could be complex enough to require
> multiple universes and/or multiple planets to address. For example, our particular physical universe or a specific planet might be able to address certain physical aspects while a nonphysical universe or another planet would be needed to address certain nonphysical or different physical aspects. Or, a different physical universe made up of substances different from what make up ours would be needed to address other certain physical aspects. Etc. 239-40

each universe is created for a different purpose
> depending on the needs of the spirit world at the time 60-1

every universe in the past, present, and future
> was, is, or will be different and unique. For example, some are physical, some are nonphysical, living things could be separate as in our universe or they could be part of each other, as in the spirit world. Some will have space as part of them such as our universe, and some would not have space. If space is needed, each such universe would have a different and unique kind of space 60-4

multiple universes can exist at the same time but
> living things in one might not be aware of the existence of the other universes. More than one universe could occupy the same location 99-101

our universe is possibly still being brought into
> being 124

some people do not believe in evolution because
> of the missing links for many of the living things on Earth, including humans. However, the model indicates that evolution could span over the lifetimes of multiple universes. Therefore, what are considered missing links might exist in various past universes. Therefore, if our view on evolution is basis only on what is found on Earth, it is possible to have doubts about the existence of evolution 248

speculations about our particular universe 61-4
the nothingness beyond the "edge" of our
    universe must be something that exists because spiritual entities in the spirit world enable it to exist. It might consist of intelligence of a kind unfamiliar to humans and that could figure out how to have experiences that then would generate new pieces of knowledge for the spirit world. This could be how the spirit world enable our universe, as well as other universes, to come into being; i.e., though the intelligence that exists in the nothingness beyond our universe 331
the spirit world brings into being new universes
    as necessary to help restore its state of knowledge into reasonable balance 157. 180
universes have limited lifetimes. Old universes
    have come and gone, and new universes will emerge in the future. Each universe is different and unique. Some are physical and some are nonphysical. Every universe is likely to have an infancy vulnerable stage where the spirit world learns how to work with the new universe, a self sustaining stage where the spirit world pretty much let the universe carry on life on its own, and a geriatric final stage where the spirit world does a final assessment of all the new knowledge the universe generated. 60-4
what is embodied in the soul of our universe is
    what we are trying to capture with our countless models 117
why are we unaware of other universes that
    might exist? However, we could eventually become aware 99-101
why might multiple universes exist at the same
    time? A possible reason is some issues might need more than one universe to address them at the same time in order to achieve reasonable balance. By analogy, we usually need teams of specialist to tackle complex projects such as to design and construct large buildings, conduct cutting edge research, address complex medical conditions, etc. 239-40
why were universes created by the spirit world?
    60-1

Universe travel

did the spirit world intended for us
humans to do
    space travel to other planets
and/or universe travel to other
universes? If so, then is it
possible what is spiritually
holding us up is our tendency
to do battle with others of our
own race that are different
from us? I.e., we need to first
develop the skills of getting
along with others of our own
race who different from us
here on Earth before we are
able to develop the skills of
space and/or universe travel
where we will need to
peacefully interact with
intelligent living things not of
our species   375
when we do space and/or universe
travel,
    intelligent living things we
meet are bound to have
abilities we do not have, and
vice versa. Therefore, we
might perceive them as being
more advanced than we, and
they might perceive us as
being more advanced than
they. This means it is best to
interact with them as equals
375

University   166, 208, 323

Unstable, instability   152-3, 258,

Use it or lose it phenomenon
    developed oneness is more subject
to the "use-it-
    or-lose-it" phenomenon than
inherited oneness   198
in general   81-3
the phenomenon functions in the
spirit world,
    and it is a natural part of the
inner workings of the spirit
world   141, 198, 345-7

V

Vantage point   117-8,

Viable, viability
    the spirit world might have grown
passed its
    vulnerable stage and could
now maintain its own
viability, or it is still in its
vulnerable stage   53

Vicious circle   49-50, 86, 152, 155, 258, 293, 379

Viruses   46, 56, 217, 222, 229, 238, 240, 309, 343, 390

Visitations   280

Vote, voting   243, 249, 374, 411, 417,

Vulnerable, vulnerability   22, 53-4, 153, 226, 243, 390, 392, 432

W

War
in general   25, 86, 96, 147, 150, 195, 199, 272,
    327, 337-8, 407, 425, 427, 436, 451, 464-5
since humans are all a part of each other in the
    spirit world, it doesn't make sense to make war in our physical world   290, 385
war is between the governments involved and
    not necessarily between the soldiers in the field   295

Water, water molecules   30, 44, 46, 51, 77, 80, 122-3, 128-9, 191, 209, 223, 225, 246, 261, 278, 284, 328, 374, 400, 404, 427, 463, 471

Waters, Brent   471

Weapons   147, 339, 451-2

Weddings   456, 475-6

Wife   19, 35, 107-8, 215, 256, 354-8, 381, 383, 437, 444, 474,

Win-win, win-lose, lose-lose
in general   147, 149, 190-6, 199, 260, 371, 408,
    423, 426, 457
we humans tend to think "winning" is a must

194-6

Wisdom, see also **"Spirit World"**
a human is designed to not automatically know
    what his or her predecessors know. This is to help the spirit world keep its ability to form wisdom up to date   347
an application of wisdom   190-6
a preoccupation with scratching a bad itch
    (catering to a bad hang-up) can distort one's reasoning, judgment, and wisdom   259, 283, 355, 390, 416
a win-lose mindset will likely mean we are not
    applying the wisdom that is available to us in the spirit world   196
how the spirit world forms wisdom and
    maintains its state of wisdom 151-5, 329
in general   143-4, 145, 164, 387
obsolete, out of date   259
old people are in good positions to form wisdom
    since they have gone through a lot of experiences and have generated and/or gained a lot of pieces of knowledge. But some old people do not update their wisdom and it thus goes obsolete or becomes irrelevant. Some never resolve their hang-ups and the

hang-ups hinder their ability
    to form wisdom 259
our ego and current choice of
dominant basis for
    how we are carrying out our
    lives are hindering our ability
    to form wisdom 265
the spirit world will, and must,
constantly update
    its wisdom. Thus, the
    wisdom we gain access to in
    the past can go obsolete or
    become irrelevant. Therefore,
    we too should frequently
    update the wisdom we gain
    access to 151-5
we need to think long-term long-
range in order
    to have a better future, but
    meanwhile we also need to
    think short-term short-range
    in order to survive the present
    and near future. This is an
    example of how establishing a
    reasonable balance would
    indicate good wisdom 465
we humans might be the most
advanced living
    things on Earth but we are not
    necessarily the wisest 144
when battles are constantly
happening on Earth,
    this means we need to balance
    the issues involved such that
    wisdom could be gained to
    stop the battles 425, 464
whenever we look for something
in the spirit
    world we need to also look for
    the wisdom that is associated
    with it 288
wisdom is a dynamic thing that
pertains to the
    future. Thus, it must be kept
    up to date to be relevant.
    Forming wisdom and keeping
    it up to date is one of the most
    important tasks of the spirit
    world. Spiritual guidance
    from the spirit world would
    indicate for us humans that
    we too need to gain wisdom
    and to keep it up to date 257-
    60, 329, 306
wisdom is formed by the spirit
world and it is
    available for us to gain access
    to it 329
wisdom to the spirit world is like
what health is
    to the body of a living thing.;
    i.e., a parallel exists between
    the quality of wisdom of the
    spirit world and the quality of
    health of a living thing's body
    306, 329

Words

defining what is a word? 326
words with multiple meanings and
therefore
    have multiple spiritual entities
    enabling them and their
    meanings to exist 326

Work

working the high-tech devices and other high
    tech topics   83-5, 91, 93, 95, 111, 192, 200, 216, 237-8, 243, 252, 257, 266, 269, 271, 273, 284, 287, 293, 368, 384, 393-5, 400, 408, 410, 430, 439, 442, 469

workings within the spirit world and in our
    physical world   93, 100-1, 130, 159-60, 190, 197, 238, 256, 266, 299, 306, 344, 401, 417, 439, 441, 468-9

X

Y

Young people
    young people often have an inaccurate
        impression of old people   476

Z

Zero-point energy
    zero-point energy might be the same as dark
        energy   64

About the Author

Looking back, Richard Gene must have wanted to find such a spiritual model all his life. At age nine he pestered the pastor of his church with mischievous questions like, "What if a person sins all his life but just before dying asks the Lord to forgive all his sins; would he go the heaven instead of hell?" The pastor answered "Yes" to this question, and Richard then wondered if he felt uncomfortable when asked such questions. At age 30, Richard's first oil painting was that of a tree with roots showing through the soil, called "The Other Part of Life." The roots signify the part of life not sensed by our five senses; i.e., the spiritual part of life. Richard likes figuring out how things work, and majored in structural mechanics. He earned a Ph.D. at the University of California, Berkeley, California, 1964, under his given name. (Richard Gene is his author name.) He enjoys using his creativity. He drew a lot of pictures as a child, designed futuristic cars and houses as a teen, and often takes unconventional approaches to resolve issues. He helped design his parents' house, and after marriage, he and his wife designed their house. When evidence came forth indicating life exists after physical death Richard was compelled to use his creativity to figure out a plausible way life and life after physical death are interrelated.

"The Other Part of Life"
Oil Painting by Richard Gene, Ph.D.

Richard painted his first oil painting at age thirty. Called "The Other Part of Life," the roots signify the part of life not sensed by our five senses—the spiritual part of life.

ABOOKS

ALIVE Book Publishing and ALIVE Publishing Group
are imprints of Advanced Publishing LLC,
3200 A Danville Blvd., Suite 204, Alamo, California 94507

Telephone: 925.837.7303 Fax: 925.837.6951
www.alivebookpublishing.com

www.ingramcontent.com/pod-product-compliance
Lightning Source LLC
Chambersburg PA
CBHW031246230426
43670CB00005B/68